D1452107

Free Love in America

A DOCUMENTARY HISTORY

THOMAS NAST CARTOON OF VICTORIA C. WOODHULL.

Free Love in America

A DOCUMENTARY HISTORY

Taylor Stoehr

AMS PRESS, INC.

NEW YORK, N.Y.

Library of Congress Cataloging in Publication Data

Main entry under title:

Free love in America.

    Bibliography: p.
    Includes index.
    1. Free love—United States—History—Sources.
I. Stoehr, Taylor, 1931–
HQ961.F73   301.41′7973   77-15911
ISBN 0-404-16034-4

46750

MANUFACTURED IN THE UNITED STATES OF AMERICA

for Ruth

Preface

Those interested in pursuing the subject of free love further should begin with modern studies, which bring together widespread materials and supply useful bibliographies and notes, but finally it is classics like Mss. Stanton, Anthony, and Gage's monumental *History of Woman Suffrage* to which the scholar must turn. My own sources are given in the headnotes to individual selections and in the footnotes to the introduction. In addition I can recommend the following modern works. Hal Sears' *The Sex Radicals* (Kansas, 1977) is by far the best study of any aspect of free love, but focuses primarily on the Moses Harman circle late in the century. Sidney Ditzion's *Marriage, Morals, and Sex in America* (New York, 1953) treats a wider range of phenomena but must be used with caution since it does not distinguish its sources as carefully as might be hoped. The same is true of Eric John Dingwall's *The American Woman* (London, 1956), a work informed by long familiarity with the locked press books of the British Museum. Three books of more specialized contents are very important, but seriously flawed by inaccuracies in the sections dealing with free love matters: Linda Gordon, *Woman's Body, Woman's Right: A Social History of Birth Control in America* (New York, 1976), John S. and Robin M. Haller, *The Physician and Sexuality in Victorian America* (Urbana, 1974), and Raymond Lee Muncy, *Sex and Marriage in Utopian Communities* (Bloomington, 1973). More trustworthy is Madeleine B. Stern's excellent study of

Stephen Pearl Andrews, *The Pantarch* (Austin, 1968), and Constance Noyes Robertson's marvelous series of Oneida histories, *Oneida Community: An Autobiography, 1851–1876* (Syracuse, 1970), *Oneida Community: The Breakup, 1876–1881* (Syracuse, 1972), and *Oneida Community Profiles* (Syracuse, 1977).

I am indebted to the following scholars for generous advice and counsel: Paul Avrich, C. Michael Curtis, Robert S. Fogarty, Dolores Hayden, Lewis Perry, Constance Noyes Robertson, Hal Sears, Madeleine B. Stern, William F. Vartorella. I owe most of all to the criticism and encouragement of John Dings and Ruth Perry.

For assistance in tracking down elusive facts I wish to thank Forrest R. Blackburn, Roger Henkle, Mrs. Forest Hinman, and Alan Poole.

Many libraries have made this collection possible. I have made particular use of The Library of Congress, The Houghton Library of Harvard University, The New York Public Library, The Boston Public Library. I am grateful, for their indefatigable efforts in tracking down the books I needed, to Zofia Drzewieniecki and Janet Wesser of the Lockwood Memorial Library at the State University of New York at Buffalo, Joan Hodgson of the library at the University of California, Santa Cruz, and Molly Matson, Janet Stewart, and Hildegarde Von Laue of the library at the University of Massachusetts in Boston.

Mss. Clara Baideme, Nancy Jakimedes, Pam Kinann, Phyllis Lakin, Audrey Parsons, Patricia Patterson, Honora Robertson, and Bonnie Zimmerman typed the manuscript expertly. Maurice and Charlotte Sagoff were the gallant proofreaders. I thank them all.

For permission to publish manuscript writings of Henry C. Wright I thank the Houghton Library of Harvard University and the trustees of the Boston Public Library. For permission to publish manuscript writings of Elizabeth Oakes Smith I thank the Manuscripts and Archives Division of The New York Public Library, Astor, Lenox and Tildon Foundations. For permission to reprint materials from George W. Noyes' *John Humphrey Noyes: The Putney Community* (Oneida, 1931) I am indebted to the Syracuse University Press, which now distributes this book. I am also grateful to the Syracuse Press for permission to reproduce the photograph of James W. Towner from Constance Noyes Robertson's *Oneida Community: The Breakup, 1876–1881*. The photograph of the Davis Hotel at Berlin Heights is reproduced by permission of the Frohman Collection, The Rutherford B. Hayes Library.

Contents

III. Love and the Law

IV. Radical Free Love

V. Love in Utopia

BROOK FARM

HOPEDALE

MODERN TIMES

List of Illustrations

(Frontispiece). THOMAS NAST CARTOON OF VICTORIA C. WOODHULL.
The New York Public Library Picture Collection.

Introduction

The Free Love Controversy in America

This is the history of a lunatic fringe. Though it never had many members, some of its leaders were famous and important people. In fact neither "lunatic" nor "fringe" is quite fair, for few and eccentric as they were, the free lovers stood for a serious alternative to monogamy, which many observers in the middle of the nineteenth century recognized as in need of repair. It is important to keep this in mind when considering the maneuvers of these enthusiasts.

Women in particular stood to gain from some new sexual dispensation, and thus it is not surprising that every militant free lover, male or female, was also a feminist. The most notorious of them were the female orators, Frances Wright, Mary S. Gove Nichols, and Victoria Woodhull. To a public that thought it forward for a woman even to sit on a speakers' platform, these ladies were glamorous beyond decency. They more than outshone their male counterparts, Robert Dale Owen, Thomas L. Nichols, and Stephen Pearl Andrews, whose stage presence was nothing in comparison, however important they might be behind the scenes.

To begin at the beginning, we may glance at the careers of the earliest of these couples, Fanny Wright and her friend Robert Dale Owen. It is probably stretching things to treat them as free lovers, but the newspapers called them that, and the large public that cared about such things automatically took up the cry. Aside from his radical tendencies, Owen's reputation was mainly built on his authorship of the first tract on contraception to be written and published in the New World, thus clearing the way for the indulgence of sexual pleasure without the responsibility of family life. Fanny Wright's sin was also a matter of saying what she thought, in a little manifesto from the short-lived interracial utopia she attempted at Nashoba, Tennessee:

> The tyranny usurped by the matrimonial law, over the most sacred of the human affections, can perhaps only be equalled by that of the unjust public opinion, which so frequently stamps with infamy, or condemns to martyrdom the best grounded and most generous attachments which ever did honor to the human heart, simply because unlegalized by human ceremonies equally idle and offensive in the form and mischievous in the tendency.[1]

In spite of such counsels neither Fanny Wright nor Robert Dale Owen came out as a free lover in public. There was gossip about them when they traveled together, just as there had been during Fanny's long attachment to Lafayette, but their sexual radicalism was largely a popular myth—which they did less than the newspapers to foster. Owen, who "married for life" as the phrase went, was conspicuous in his monogamy and his concern for the rights of wives. Although many believed, like New York *Tribune* editor Horace Greeley, that Owen was wholly responsible for the liberal divorce statutes of Indiana, his major contribution in the Legislature was actually to the securing of married women's property rights. At his own marriage ceremonies (1832) Owen had signed a contract—of no legal force in most respects—that abjured almost all of his newly acquired powers as a husband; the further stipulation, denying any "promises regarding that over which we have no control, the state of human affections in the distant future," was as close to a free love stand as Owen ever came.[2]

As for Fanny Wright, she too married, about a year before Owen, and twenty years later while he was working on the Indiana laws pertaining to marriage, she herself was obtaining an Indiana divorce—in order that she might resume her legal existence, with the right to sue her husband for the return of the property she had brought to their marriage.

In an age of entrenched patriarchy and widespread sexual repression, all of this was certainly scandalous, and editors like Greeley were not so wide of the mark when they accused these two social radicals of free love tendencies, for however mild their opinions or restrained their behavior in comparison with Victoria Woodhull and her entourage, Owen and Wright were the first to raise the issues that gave the movement its impetus. In the long run, "free love" became more than an easy label to paste on any sexual unorthodoxy; it was the rallying cry for ultra-reformers who would not stop at one or two but demanded remedies for all the sexual evils they saw in society, whether marital unhappiness or adultery, jealousy or impotence and frigidity, kitchen drudgery or unwanted pregnancy, prudery or prostitution.

Thousands were trapped in one or another of these miseries and vices. The free lovers supposed they might cure them all, not piecemeal but in one stroke. Victoria Woodhull ran for President of the United States on a ticket that, although nominally "equal rights" (her unconsulted running mate was ex-slave Frederick Douglass), was in fact "free love." Silly as that seemed to the man in the street, the shrewder politicians, like Horace Greeley, saw the power lurking in these issues, and stood ready to put a journalistic finger in any leak in the dike of male chauvinism and state-enforced monogamy. The medical profession closed ranks against contraception, lest it open the way (as it ultimately did) to a separation between the pleasures of intercourse and the duties of the nuclear family. Magistrates, clergymen, and vigilantes stamped out every sort of -gamy other than monogamy—the Mormons at Nauvoo, the Perfectionists at Putney, the free lovers at Berlin Heights. Police and special agents entrapped and prosecuted individuals who fornicated (Edwin C. Walker and Lillian Harman, Leo Miller and Mattie Strickland, James Clay and his unknown partner), or who used the mails to make it easier for others to fornicate (Ida Craddock, E. B. Foote), or who simply advocated fornication without benefit of wedlock or risk of pregnancy (E. H. Heywood, Moses Harman, Victoria Woodhull).

Of all these iconoclasts, only a handful were literal free lovers. Heywood went to prison for advocating "sexual self-government," but there is no evidence that he indulged in it. Even Clay, who was convicted of bedding with a lady other than his spouse, produced medical testimony that she remained a virgin afterwards (that must have puzzled the jury, though not enough to acquit him). Many were like Fanny Wright and Robert Dale Owen, reformers rather than zealots.

All in all free love had perhaps thirty leaders active between the publication of Marx Edgeworth Lazarus's *Love vs. Marriage* in 1852 and the breakup of the Oneida Community in 1879, the heyday of the movement. In the selections printed here Andrew Jackson Davis identifies eight doctrinaires living and dead, Warren Chase names ten more, and it would be easy enough to add another dozen who earned some notoriety. Among the rank and file, how many practising free lovers were there, how many sympathizers? The Mormons were not free lovers, and strictly speaking neither were the Oneida Perfectionists, though everyone said they were. Joseph Smith had perhaps 16,000 followers at Nauvoo. John Humphrey Noyes' community included almost 300 by the time it abandoned complex marriage. The authentic free love colonies were less populous. Modern Times ranged from seventy to one hundred, and Berlin Heights seems to have been of similar size. How many ordinary citizens were active is a matter for conjecture. No one knows how many votes were cast for the Woodhull-Douglass ticket, for they were not counted (Susan B. Anthony was fined $100 merely for "voting"), but the circulation of *Woodhull and Claflin's Weekly* was in the tens of thousands. Of course anybody might buy a copy off the newsstands. *The Social Revolutionist* had 400 subscribers. A *Times* reporter in 1855 said there were 500 in Stephen Pearl Andrews' Free Love League, but membership meant little more than the willingness to part with 25¢ at the door. Three hundred were present the night Albert Brisbane, the prominent Fourierist, was arrested in an altercation on the premises. Twenty years later Heywood's New England Free Love League sold 250 tickets to its convention, according to anti-vice czar Anthony Comstock, who bought one himself in order to arrest the speaker; but again, this is an audience, not a true convention. Perhaps the most trustworthy indication of the free love discipleship is to be found in the membership rolls of the "Progressive Union," Thomas and Mary Nichols' lonely hearts club of the 1850s. John Humphrey Noyes—no friend of such enterprises—reported four such lists in the Oneida Community archives, with 324, 527, 506, and 155 names on them, of persons willing to be approached as free lovers—that is, by others in The Union.[3]

What all this evidence adds up to is hard to say, but obviously in a country with a population in the tens of millions, the movement was numerically insignificant. Still, if its membership was scarcely a drop in the bucket, it might also be seen as the tip of an iceberg, especially now that so much more of its base has emerged from the depths. Under other names, the sexual revolution contemplated by the free lovers has been largely accomplished by succeeding generations. For example, the legal rights of married women began to improve during the very period that free lovers called for an end to marriage laws. If modern feminists still have much to complain of, at least their equality with men is now given lip service on the statute books. In the last half of the nineteenth century, sex education was also being slowly liberalized through the popularity of home medical guides and marriage manuals, rudimentary precursors of Masters and Johnson or *Our Bodies, Ourselves.* Contraception was still officially sinful, not to mention perilous to the health, but Robert Dale Owen and Charles Knowlton had made a beginning that the authorities could not repress forever. Laws against the publication of birth control information, like most forms of sexual censorship, have proved among the hardest to get rid of, but most of them have gone the way of other blue laws that proscribe what people sooner or later seem determined to do anyway. Similarly, the laws of divorce have been liberalized until most states, if not as advanced as Indiana in 1852, at least allow whatever grounds a couple may trump up to go unchallenged. It may be wondered if Horace Greeley did not prove correct after all in his warning that loosening the restraints on divorce would result in the victory of free love over monogamy. The divorce rate is fast approaching the marriage rate, though it can never overtake it. Perhaps as a result, interest in sexual experiment has begun to acquire a semblance of propriety. The free love utopias of Berlin Heights, Modern Times, and Oneida have been decontaminated by time and circumstance, so that they and even their modern counterparts, if not exactly applauded, are now more likely to be the objects of sociological research and literary exploitation rather than calumny or vigilanteism.

Broadly speaking then, free love may be said to have won out, under a series of other banners. Yet the essence of the free love movement was that it proposed itself as a single solution to multiple problems, whereas finally the problems have been more or less alleviated without any reliance on the general panacea. Rhetorically

satisfying as it might be to say that free love has been victorious,
the truth is that it has been bypassed and outmoded. How and
why that happened is as interesting as the history of the piecemeal
reforms that did succeed. In the following pages, I attempt to
show both phenomena: the struggle for sexual reform as it manifested itself in a variety of other movements where free love issues
were often part of larger, more or less coherent platforms for social
change—Fourierism, Individual Sovereignty, Feminism, Perfectionism, and so on—as well as the exploits of the free love vanguard
itself, those who blazoned the sexual question on their banners. The
interplay of these two approaches is itself very interesting to any
student of "movements," and I have therefore provided a rather
full and ancedotal account of the infighting among the advocates
of sexual reform. Many of the most revealing circumstances of the
free love controversy were—as one might expect—quite personal
in nature, and it is thus advantageous to keep the personalities and
their private entanglements in view along with their public roles
and official positions. I have tried to strike a balance that will show
the movement and its leaders in the larger context, and thus provide
background for an informed reading of the documents collected
in the anthology proper.

i. Free Love Circles

Although Fanny Wright and Robert Dale Owen had been in the
field some twenty years before, the campaign did not begin in
earnest until the early 1850s. It was Marx Edgeworth Lazarus who
fired the first shot, with the publication of *Love vs. Marriage* in
1852. Henry James, Sr. reviewed the book unfavorably, and then
became involved in a three-way controversy with Horace Greeley
and Stephen Pearl Andrews in the pages of Greeley's New York
Tribune. When Greeley cut off debate, Andrews himself published
the whole proceedings in book form, *Love, Marriage, and Divorce*,
adding his lengthy "last word" that Greeley had refused to print.
Soon there were a dozen volumes on the market dealing with the
marriage question (see the selections in section I). By no means
all of these books advocated free love, but they recognized the
existence of such doctrines and the fact that some persons actually

practiced them. Whatever stands these authors took were largely the result of prodding by the free love enthusiasts.

Along with Lazarus and Andrews, Thomas L. Nichols and his wife Mary S. Gove Nichols constituted the inner circle of the new movement. It was Mary Nichols around whom the others fluttered. Like Fanny Wright twenty years earlier, or Victoria Woodhull twenty years later, she knew how to turn to account her remarkable endowment of energy and audacity. She too edited her own magazines, followed her own profession, and enjoyed a sure platform audience, admirers, lovers, husbands. Poe included her among his "literati" along with celebrities like Lydia Child and Margaret Fuller. *The New York Times* condemned her autobiographical novel *Mary Lyndon* as free love filth. And again like Victoria Woodhull, after a firebrand career in America, she suddenly waxed respectable, even religious, and left the country for England where she made herself at home and grew venerable in polite society. No matter how wild and flamboyant she was, no matter how cunning and hypocritical, Mary Nichols had a streak of solid good sense in her too. In many ways she was typically American; if Henry James had lived in her day he would have made one of his dubious Yankee heroines of her, as he did of Victoria Woodhull.

When she came to New York City in the mid-1840s, Mary Gove had already survived an only too typical existence as a wife and mother. Married early, to a brutal and greedy husband, she had first-hand experience of "the wrongs of marriage." Hiram Gove mistreated her, so she claimed, but even worse, he was dull and stupid. He burned her books and discouraged her literary inclinations until he discovered that they might be profitable; then he pocketed her checks. All of this was perfectly within his legal rights as her "lord and master." Finally she left him, taking her infant daughter and returning to her father's house. Gove still had the law on his side, and might have dragged his wife and child back home, had it not been for the fact that he owed her father money and was willing to trade her security for his forbearance. After her father died, Gove repossessed his child, though not his wife, and Mary was finally reduced to kidnapping her own daughter and fleeing across the state line.

The rest of her career was equally illustrative of the narrow range of possibilities open to an energetic and talented woman of

the 1840s—and of her own exceptional nature in refusing to be
bound by those limits. By this time she had taught herself some
medicine as well as scribbling, and she began to lecture to women
on "physiology." When she moved in with her parents in Lynn,
she had become involved with the radical set of water-cure and
health enthusiasts in the Boston area. Here she met Henry Gardiner
Wright, a young Englishman who had left a wife and child in
England to join transcendentalist Bronson Alcott's utopian community at Harvard, Massachusetts. Wright defected before the
community was even on its ground, let alone its feet, and moved in
with Mary Gove instead. Together, they edited a few issues of *The
Independent Magazine and Health Journal*, but Wright himself
soon fell ill. Mary tried water-cure on him, but he grew worse, and
finally his friends came from England to take him back home to die.

Not long after this, Mary ran away to New York with her
daughter, where she was welcomed in water-cure circles with open
arms. She set up a "Grahamite" boarding house, and began practising her several trades. One of her boarders was none other than
Marx Edgeworth Lazarus, who, it was said, had advanced Mrs.
Gove the money for her new establishment in order to provide his
flighty young sister with a homelike environment. This was still
several years before Lazarus' *Love vs. Marriage*, but he was already
something of a prodigy in the radical circles that Mary Gove now
entered—pseudoscientists, reformers, and publicists who wrote and
lectured for their daily bread. Lazarus also introduced another
young Southerner, Charles Wilkins Webber, into the Tenth Street
boarding house. Like his landlady, Webber also combined hack
writing and editing with a taste for adventure, and soon he and
Mary were collaborating in literary activities, and then, apparently,
sleeping together.

At this point (around 1847) the story gets murky. Later both
Webber and Mrs. Gove (now Mrs. Nichols) told their versions in
slanderous autobiographical novels, and one can only guess at the
truth. Several things seem to have happened about the same time:
the lovers grew tired of one another, but Webber, who was some
years younger, seems to have been the first to stray—disastrously—
to the arms of Mary's now teenaged daughter.

Almost at the same time Mary met the rather shady Thomas
Nichols, still another cosmopolite making a living off faddish
reforms. A maudlin correspondence ensued, which the lovers later

published—as they published every scrap they wrote. When they decided to marry they simultaneously decided that Elma and Charles should not marry: Webber had been an alcoholic before going on the Grahamite wagon, and was drinking heavily again. Abandoned by his new sweetheart, he now suffered a complete breakdown, and was nursed back to health by still another young lady whose acquaintance he had also made at the boarding house, Elma's artist friend from Boston. Ultimately, he married the friend, and, desperately poor, full of hatred for both his former mistress and her daughter, he wrote and sold a pot-boiler exposé of Mary Gove's mysterious sexual magnetism and its baleful influence on him: *Spiritual Vampirism, or the History of Etherial Softdown*.

All this seems to have rolled off Mary Gove's back like water. No doubt such experiences contributed a certain tempering—not to say hardening—of her character, but at this distance it is difficult to assess just how seriously she took the Webber episode. What is clear, in the story that can be pieced together from *Spiritual Vampirism* and her own autobiography, *Mary Lyndon*, is that she was by this time a veteran of romance, and was entering a phase of life in which such a background might be turned to advantage, given the right handling of her credentials. She had done well as an authority on female physiology and the water-cure, she had run a newspaper and a health-food boarding house; now she was ready for a new incarnation.

Mary Gove found her manager as well as her match in the enterprising Thomas Nichols. Taking his hint from his bride, Nichols breezed through a M.D. program at a local university, and soon Dr. and Mrs. Nichols were announcing the opening of the American Hydropathic Institute at Port Chester, Long Island, where in twelve short weeks they promised that anyone could learn the secrets of the only true medicine. Nichols graduated in 1850. His first students graduated in December, 1851.

The Hydropathic Institute itself is significant merely as a rendezvous on the Nichols' march to free love. It lasted only a short time before giving way to a new and much more radical project, the Institute of Desarrollo, which was to be the Nichols' special portion of the anarchist colony being founded on Long Island at the time of the Port Chester water-cure venture. Since it was this colony, Modern Times, that became notorious as the headquarters of free love in America, it is worth paying its founders and spokesmen some special attention—Stephen Pearl Andrews, Josiah Warren, and in the public mind at least, Thomas and Mary Nichols themselves.

At the first commencement exercises of the American Hydropathic Institute in December 1851, the featured speaker was another jack-of-all-reforms, Stephen Pearl Andrews, later to appear as a principal in the great debate over love in the New York *Tribune*. No one knows how the Nichols first met Andrews, but he had the right passport into their circle. He too had a full career already behind him—including an attempt to persuade the British to purchase all the slaves in Texas and abolish slavery there. By 1845 he had returned to the States, unsuccessful in his amateur diplomacy, but bringing back still another scheme for revolutionizing society—the Pitman method of shorthand, or, as Andrews called it, phonography. When he made the commencement address at the Hydropathic Institute, he had given up teaching phonography but was still publishing the *Fonetic Propagandist*—dedicated "to practical reforms, especially in matters of self-education" as well as "to the writing and spelling reformation." Now he was about to embark on a new project, with a man whose ideas changed Andrews' life.

Josiah Warren was what is now called an "individualist anarchist," and in those days a "no-government man." His own name for the philosophy that he taught Andrews was "individual sovereignty"—the principle, in short, that every man ought to mind his own business and no one else's. "Societary institutions should be made for man, and not man for institutions; and no individual ought to be pared down, warped, or maimed to suit any human theory, or to supply any mere expedient. All laws for the guidance of men in their social or collective state should be in strict accordance with the natural law of individuality, or they are unjust, and must prove subversive."[4] Warren had been at New Harmony with Robert Owen and his son Dale, and had been involved in several other communal ventures; in each he had found adherents and disciples willing to try out his socioeconomic ideas—his "labor notes," a device he borrowed from Owen, his "time store," and his maxim, "cost the limit of price." Now in Andrews he found his John the Baptist. Andrews had probably first gotten interested in Warren because of the latter's invention of "stereotype" methods of printing which could be used, Andrews decided, to make a phonographic magazine like the *Propagandist* practical. Before long he was abandoning phonography in order to promote individual sovereignty full time. He and Warren announced the formation of a new community, to be completely based on anarchist principles. They called it Modern Times—ninety acres of pine barrens some forty miles out on Long Island.

The Nichols-Andrews-Lazarus circle were no strangers to utopian colonies. Lazarus, a devotee of every radicalism from homoeopathy to solar religion, had friends at both Brook Farm and the North American Phalanx near Red Bank, New Jersey. He wrote dozens of articles for *The Harbinger*, the official organ of Fourierism published at Brook Farm, and his sister Ellen married a member there, John Allen. In later years Mrs. Allen retired to Modern Times, where she became a Positivist, and her brother also seems to have become more of an individual sovereign than a Fourierist, living out his old age on a small farm in Guntersville, Alabama, from which he sent his articles to the anarchist magazines of the 1880s.

Mary Nichols too had an interest in Fourierism. If she had subverted Bronson Alcott's vegetarian paradise in 1843 by seducing one of its coadjutators, she was nonetheless warmly in support of other utopian ventures. She had not only come to look at Brook Farm, but in 1845 she visited the Columbian Phalanx in Ohio, and wrote back to New York an account of her observations, including criticism of its members for avoiding the critical issue of "the relation of the sexes in Association"; "though our friends may wish to evade or avoid it, fearing they shall be misunderstood, or that odium will attach to them if they speak out their thoughts—it must be met. Those of us who have seen the misery, the impurity of marriage without love, and who feel that it is legal licentiousness, must say so. . . . I affirm that marriage without love is sin, is prostitution, and I place my reputation at the mercy of all legalists by my assertion."[5]

It is not surprising, therefore, to find Dr. and Mrs. Nichols building a little cottage and joining Warren and his disciples at Modern Times; nor, given their histories and leanings, is it any wonder that their participation gave a decidedly sexual coloration to the doctrine of individual sovereignty, just as Mary Nichols' report from Ohio had quickly injected the sexual question into the Fourierist experiment. Almost from the start Modern Times was tagged as a free love colony by the New York papers, with Andrews, a

convert in ideology if not in practice, as the chief apologist for the
other sexually liberated members.

Warren, always the complete anarchist, was unwilling to adopt
the leadership role Andrews found so congenial. He merely observed
"that the greatest characteristic of this movement is its 'INDI-
VIDUALITY'—that the persons engaged in it are required to act
entirely as INDIVIDUALS—*not as a Combination or Organisation.
That we disclaim entirely, all responsibility for the acts, opinions,
or reputations of each other.*"[6] For his own part Warren disapproved
of the sexual morality of his new disciples, but would not interfere
with their sovereignties so long as they did not infringe on his. And
in fact most of the free love population seems to have pursued its
interests quietly, no matter how noisy the fanfare in the New York
press. One visitor reported "very general" secrecy as an outgrowth
of the "absence of marriage laws."[7]

The Nichols developed grand plans for their part in Modern
Times. Still in their Port Chester water-cure establishment, they
projected an extravagant new institute of health and good living
to be constructed on land immediately adjoining the colony:

> Upon this domain, or in this Eden, we have commenced to build
> the edifices of our Institute. The main building, already commenced,
> will be 126 feet long, by 43 in depth, four stories and basement, with
> a tower sixty feet high in the rear center, for the reservoir and bath
> rooms. In the two lower stories will be a lecture room forty feet square
> and twenty-two feet high, with library, suites of parlors, drawing
> rooms, &c., while the two upper stories will contain single rooms of
> ample size for nearly sixty inmates. This building will accommodate
> nearly one hundred persons.
>
> Our plan is, after the completion of this edifice, to build two side
> wings, extending back, each 100 feet by 25, to contain on their first
> floors, a large dining saloon, gymnasium, picture gallery, and artists'
> studios. Then, enclosing the square, we shall have our printing-office,
> stereotype foundry, power-presses, and book-bindery, model kitchen,
> bakery, and laundry, with an engine-house in the center, with steam
> to carry all the machinery, raise the water, cook, wash, and warm the
> whole range of buildings, and supply warmth to the winter garden in
> the central square. Here will be a fountain, springing up fifty feet,
> rare exotics, statuary, and every thing which can make it a charming
> resort. In a balcony of this square, the band of the Institute will dis-
> course sweet music; and here, in pleasant weather, will the great fam-
> ily assemble in its oft-recurring festivals.[8]

In the elaborate prospectus they published for their Institute of
Desarrollo there is much reminiscent of the lavish phalansteries

conceived by Charles Fourier and palely imitated in the handful
of American phalanxes like Brook Farm or Red Bank that managed
to construct public buildings during their brief flourishing. Emerson had twitted the Fourierists about their Babylonian fantasies:
"what tillage, what architecture, what refectories, what dormitories,
what reading rooms, what concerts, what lectures, what gardens,
what baths!"[9] Anyone who had even seen Fourier's "façades" and
"elevations" for a phalanx knew what Emerson was talking about.

ii. Sex in Utopia

The reputation of Fourierism, or associationism as it was often
called, was indeed behind much of the public response to Modern
Times, whatever dissimilarities there might have been in conception. The 1840s had seen dozens of Fourierist communities come
and go, some of them quite famous, and among the notions that had
begun to form in the popular imagination was the suspicion that
sexual irregularities invariably prospered in communal life. By the
time Warren and Andrews founded their non-Fourierist version of
utopia, it would have been quite impossible for them to have
escaped the imputation of free love, even if there had been nothing
but clergymen on the premises.

Furthermore, just as some of the residents of Modern Times lent
themselves to the free love scandal, so too did Fourier and his
followers invite and deserve some of the accusations of sexual per-
missiveness leveled against them.

Fourier's whole system was one of "passional attraction": whatever there was to be or do in the world, there was a human passion
to minister to it (not an un-Emersonian notion). Thus even the
garbage could get collected, by the young boys who loved to play
in the dirt. As for the relations of the sexes, Fourier had discovered
seven degrees of passional attachment, and for each he specified a
niche in the ecology of the community. There was a place for
virginity and a place for promiscuity in his phalanx of the future.

Of all the ideas Fourier spun out, his sexual recommendations
were the least likely to find acceptance in the English-speaking
world. His American apostle Albert Brisbane carefully avoided
translating any of them; Horace Greeley, Brisbane's chief backer
and publisher, would not have tolerated such decadence in his

columns. Nonetheless the Fourierists complained that people accused them of doing what Fourier prescribed, without ever looking to see what in fact went on in actual phalanxes.[10] Starting with the earliest experiments at Brook Farm and at the North American Phalanx (Greeley and Brisbane's pet project), the reputation of licentiousness hung in the air over every phalanstery. Marianne Dwight, a youthful Brook Farmer, described one effect of such rumors to a Boston confidante:

> We have among new comers a Mr. Whittamore and a Mr. Curtis. John [Dwight, Marianne's brother], walking home from the woods, overheard between them this conversation. Mr. W. "The girls here are *pretty slick.*" Mr. C. "Yes, a very good place for a fellow to come who wants to look him up a girl." They were very disinterested,—disclaimed all idea of wishing to be married, etc., etc. We've had a little rich fun out of this.[11]

Emerson asked his friend George P. Bradford about such gossip, and was reassured. Although the closeness of communal life did increase the temperature of social intercourse, the therapy was ready to hand: "plain dealing was the best defence of manners & morals between the sexes. I suppose," Emerson expatiated in his journal, "that the danger arises whenever bodily familiarity grows up without a spiritual intimacy. The reason why there is purity in marriage, is, that the parties are universally near & helpful, & not only near bodily. If their wisdom come near & meet, there is no danger of passion. Therefore the remedy of impurity is to come nearer."[12]

Even if Bradford was right—and the history of love affairs at Brook Farm suggests that only a few secret intrigues ever led to any scandal—that did not solve the problem of outside reputation. Community spokesmen in *The Harbinger* finally fell back on retorts and denunciations: "The charge which this writer brings against the Associative movement, is that it aims at universal licentiousness, seeks to abolish the institution of marriage, and free the relations of love from the restraints of order and propriety. A more indecent calumny was never invented. The man who permits himself to utter it, without his words choking in his mouth, is too shameless for our rebuke."[13] Following the policy of "plain dealing," Marianne Dwight's brother John gave a long explanation of Fourier's doctrines (see pp. 405–408), emphasizing that such practices were envisioned for a state of society very much in the future, and that the Brook Farmers didn't necessarily agree with Fourier's predictions anyway. Of course such denials only fanned the flames. By 1850 Fourierism and free love were synonymous in many minds. It didn't help when a translation of the Fourierist doctrines called *Love in the Phalanstery* appeared in 1849. Written a few years earlier by one of Fourier's French disciples, this little tract spelled out the gradations of passional attachment with scarcely a blink of decorous embarrassment. The anonymous American translator announced his own disinterestedness in the preface: "His general object . . . is to give the public some true information concerning Fourier, in place of the scurrilous falsities with which our unprincipled newspaper censors have regaled it. But further than this, he wishes to provoke the attention of honest minds to the truths involved in these views. They appear of an infinite moment to his own mind, as alone revealing a hope for the eventual extinction of the present adulterous and promiscuous commerce of the sexes, as alone revealing a sure way for the sexual relations to become divinely pure and honorable."[14]

It was an open secret that the broad-minded author of these sentiments was none other than the elder Henry James, one of Emerson's rivals in providing Victorian America with a philosophic voice. He too was a Fourierist, though a more tentative one than his friends at Brook Farm, for whose paper he wrote many articles. Having thus established himself as an uncommitted expert in the field, it is obvious why he would have been picked a few years later to review Marx Edgeworth Lazarus' free love tract *Love vs. Marriage* for Greeley's *Tribune*: he understood both Fourierism and its special doctrine of marriage—which was Lazarus' own starting point—and he combined liberalism and moralism in just the crotchety blend that infuriated radicals and conservatives alike, and sold papers.

Of course James and Greeley must have had at least a nodding acquaintance with the free love enthusiasts now gathering their forces at Modern Times. Their common Fourieristic backgrounds guaranteed that. But it was one thing to admit with Fourier that the institution of monogamy would not survive the final establishment of "Harmony," and quite another to proclaim the passional millennium now. In the three-way debate over *Love, Marriage, and Divorce* that occupied James, Greeley, and Andrews—all of them calling themselves associationists in the early 1850s—James took the meliorist ground, arguing for liberalized divorce as a stopgap measure, while Andrews came out for the immediate abolition of marriage and Greeley insisted on "union for life," the slogan of the extreme monogamists.

As a Fourierist, Greeley had to attack the so-called "isolated family," but along with the majority of new world communitarians, he was deeply unwilling to give up the nuclear family. Brisbane, who introduced the phrase "social science" to Americans, had explained how the proper understanding and manipulation of man's natural instincts (passions) would perfect the social mechanism, preserving the bonds of family life but enhancing them by communal kitchens and workshops that would take the drudgery out of huswifery and the degradation out of earning a living. Everyone would live in enormous phalansteries that combined family privacy with galleries for social intercourse and a whole panoply of labor-saving social inventions. All this had Greeley's assent, so long as the marriage bond remained sacred.

Andrews was also fond of the term "social science," which he had picked up from Brisbane but used in his own sense. "Sociology," he told the graduating class at the Hydropathic Institute, "the Science of Society, the science of true human relations and conditions, and of the means of securing them to all classes and individuals of the race, is part and parcel of your legitimate professional knowledge."[15] By this he meant not the communal strategies of the associationists, but something much more like the twentieth-century time-and-labor calculations of Ralph Borsodi, who in the 1920s left New York for the country just as Josiah Warren had seventy-five years earlier, to prove that individual families could be self-sufficient and aloof from the money-logged, middleman-ridden society of "the Empire City."

Andrews' view, like Greeley's, entailed colonization and even mutual aid, but separate homesteads to accommodate individual sovereignties. At Modern Times there were few communal buildings (the Nichols' pipe dream, Desarrollo, never rose out of the huge hole dug for its foundations), whereas at Brook Farm even the original cottages and cramped farm houses had to serve as dormitories and suites. Obviously, such very different living arrangements had different implications for sexual as well as family life. It is doubtful whether either Greeley or Andrews had thought through these practicalities, but other utopians had considered the question. Did not the privacy at Modern Times reinforce rather than subvert monogamy? And would not life in full community tend to undermine what the isolated household supported, *including* the family? One observer of Brook Farm (see the selection by Charles Lane in section V), asked bluntly "whether the existence of the marital family is compatible with that of the universal family, which the term 'Community' signifies"—and he went to join the celibate Shakers.[16] Later John Humphrey Noyes, leader of the Oneida community and probably the best informed historian of utopia who has ever lived, made the same case out in detail, even to the extent of showing the relevance of Shakerism:

> There is plenty of tendency to crossing love, and adultery, even in the system of isolated households. Association increases this tendency. Amalgamation of interests, frequency of interview, and companionship in labor, inevitably give activity and intensity to the social attractions in which amativeness is the strongest element. The tendency to extra-matrimonial love will be proportioned to the condensation of interest produced by any given form of Association; i.e., if the ordinary principles of exclusiveness are preserved, Association will be a worse school of temptation to unlawful love than the world is, in proportion to its social advantages. . . . The only plausible method of avoiding the stumbling-blocks of the sexual question in Association, besides ours [at Oneida], is the method of the Shakers. Forbid sexual intercourse altogether, and you attain the same results, so far as shutting off the jealousies and strifes of exclusiveness is concerned, as will be attained by making sexual intercourse free. In this matter the Shakers show their shrewdness.[17]

The history of sexual difficulties in most nineteenth-century communities suggests that Noyes was right about the passional risks of living in close quarters. "Plain dealing" was not the sort of remedy that could be counted on any more than honesty or some other virtue could guarantee the fulfillment of other obligations.

In short, Greeley's associationism was just as dangerous to monogamy as Andrews' individual sovereignty; it was James' seemingly middle road of liberalized divorce that ultimately proved most conservative of the marital status quo in America. But not every enthusiast of social reform had the perspicacity to make the connection between living arrangements and sexual mores. More often it was the enemies of communal experiment who saw—or more accurately, who felt in their bones—that any group so unorthodox as to want to live in what the Fourierists called a "unitary household" must also be indulging in other sorts of promiscuity. Where there was smoke there was fire.

Perhaps it was this stereotyping of communitarians as free lovers all through the 1840s that finally led some of them to band together expressly on that basis in the 1850s, at Modern Times on Long Island and at Berlin Heights, fifty miles west of Cleveland. In both cases, just as at Oneida, the initial impetus was philosophical or religious rather than sexual, but the public mind regarded all three as nothing but free love communities, and they suffered for it. Noyes and his followers had been literally run out of Putney, Vermont, when the local inhabitants found their daughters getting perilously interested in Perfectionist doctrines. At Berlin Heights vigilantes also threatened to enforce public standards of sexual morality, and one might have expected some reenactment of the bloody struggles of the Mormons in the western states, had the free lovers represented any tangible threat to the surrounding community. Strictly speaking neither a religious body (though some of them had ties with Perfectionists) nor a community (they lived for the most part in single dwellings scattered over a wide countryside), the Berlin Heights free lovers did not have the character of a movement. Some of their neighbors even defended their rights as unoffending, law-abiding citizens—though of course in most states their practices were penitentiary offenses. Free love was not a particularly provocative activity; in rural areas it might go on unnoticed unless its devotees felt the need to proselytize. At Berlin Heights propaganda seems to have been limited to their various publications, especially *The Social Revolutionist*. Except for the mob burning of one issue of that paper, the threats of violence never came to much.

The situation at Modern Times was somewhat different, for the proximity of a large city with a sensationalist press made the colonists prey to all sorts of thrill seekers, vice suppressors, and well-meaning sympathizers. People rode out "on the cars" to Thompson Station, just to have a gawk at ladies who didn't care whether they were married to their husbands or not. There was little to see—a few bloomers and other eccentricities of dress, but nothing like the nude colonists reported in the streets. The newspapers did their damage, as it turned out, not to Modern Times proper.

Thomas and Mary Nichols had been slow in shifting their operations to the colony. The Hydropathic Institute was too lucrative to abandon before a suitable replacement had been constructed, so that a transitional regime seems to have been inaugurated at Port Chester. Medical students usually took their board and room at the Institute during their twelve-week degree program—a residency requirement that no doubt went back to Mary Gove's days on Tenth Street as proprietress of a Graham House. Among the students were about twenty young women, and before long it was rumored that they were being indoctrinated in the Nichols' well-known sideline. An anonymous letter appeared in the press, revealing a mass exodus of the female students, fleeing "the philosophy of the brothel" urged upon them by their hydropathic instructors. Dr. Nichols proclaimed his innocence in a letter to the *Tribune*,[18] and Mrs. Nichols charged that copies of Charles Webber's libelous *Spiritual Vampirism* were circulating at R. T. Trall's rival water-cure establishment with all the real names filled in. But these protestations could not repair the damage, and soon the Institute was "as deserted as the Temple of Nauvoo, after the removal of the Mormons."[19] Just how this furor was received at Modern Times is a matter for conjecture. Josiah Warren himself issued a carefully worded disclaimer which the Nichols had the nerve to reprint and answer in the pages of the *Nichols Journal*. This was as close as Warren ever came to violating his live-and-let-live principles, but there is little doubt that he was relieved to find the Nichols losing interest in Desarrolla now that they saw how vulnerable their "college" was to public opinion.

Nothing if not experts at taking advantage of every whiff of publicity, pro or con, the Nichols began to capitalize on their growing bad repute. In the wake of their friends Lazarus and Andrews, they launched a half dozen "medical," "marital," and "true confession" volumes. When their competitor Trall had taken over the *Water Cure Journal* to which they had been regular contributors for several years, they had hastened to found their own *Nichols Journal* (later the *Nichols Monthly*), of which they claimed to sell 20,000 copies a month. They followed it up with the Progressive Union, a list of free lovers across the country who subscribed "for the purpose," as John Humphrey Noyes said, "of facilitating 'affinities' and free intercourse."[20]

All of these ventures proved profitable, and had the additional virtue of leaving the Nichols at liberty to travel about the country lecturing and giving consultations. They ended up Ohio, where, as

Berlin Heights was about to show, there was a certain taste for experiment. The old fantasy of Desarrolla still tantalized them, and with the proceeds from their various publications they bought a water-cure establishment at Yellow Springs, thinking to have a ready-made clientele from the new college just opened there under the presidency of Horace Mann. Mann's reaction was to call upon his friend the sheriff to prevent them from taking possession of their property. For a while it looked as if this bold maneuver might succeed, but Dr. and Mrs. Nichols also had recourse to the law, through more regular channels, and soon forced Mann to back down. Memnonia, as the Nichols called their new utopian paradise, moved in next to Antioch College.

As it turned out, President Mann's apprehensions were needless, for the protestations of the Nichols seem for once to have been made in good faith. Although still nominally free lovers, they had changed their definition of the term. In its new phase the "Central Bureau" of the Progressive Union promulgated something called "the Law of Progression," according to which "such as could accept it" would "rise from the plane of natural life to that of spiritual life." In plain language, the Nichols now believed that in the present unregenerate state of society coition ought to take place only to beget children. It was but a hop, skip, and a jump—which they soon took—to Catholicism. (Such conversions, by the way, were remarkably common among the utopians—the founder of the Paulist Brothers, Isaac Hecker, formerly of Brook Farm and Fruitlands, is only the most famous of a list that also included George Ripley's wife Sophia, the "mother" of Brook Farm, J. S. Jacobus, whose name was third on the membership list of the Progressive Union, and several others.) This was not the end of the Nichols' activities as reformers and publicists, but free love was no longer among their wares. When the Civil War came, their sympathies were with the South (as befitted a pair of professional secessionists) and in order to avoid the obvious disabilities of Copperheads in the North, they emigrated to England, where they reissued toned-down versions of their best seller *Esoteric Anthropology* and spent their declining years writing sedate tracts on diet and health.

Modern Times also went into a quiescent middle age. Most of the inhabitants stayed on the scene, but such a collection of individualists had many causes to pursue—homoeopathy, positivism, vegetarianism, and so on—and one hears little about free love among them after the early 1850s. The little colony was too peaceful and countrified for the tastes of Stephen Pearl Andrews, who never settled down anywhere during his long career as a radical. Soon he was in the newspapers again as the proprietor of the Free Love League of New York, a sort of social club and discussion group that numbered several local personages among its members, including Albert Brisbane, who, now that Fourierism was dying out as a practical movement, had become a sort of hanger-on of other people's crusades. But during this period, roughly from 1855 to 1860, interest in free love declined; public attention turned away from what seemed merely fads and frivolities next to the martyrdom of John Brown. The various evils of society—capitalism, government, marriage, the oppression of women—all shriveled in the heat of Kansas, Harpers Ferry, and Fort Sumter. It was not until the war had been over several years that the second wave of the free love movement arose.

iii. "The Bonds of Matrimony"

One reason that free love came to be regarded as a movement had to do with its early cradling in the bosom of utopia. To outsiders whatever the communitists fostered seemed a fanaticism if not a plot. But free love had sources elsewhere too. Its adherents were quick to point out society's failure to solve problems of unsatisfied desire, unwanted pregnancy, frigidity, impotence, jealousy, adultery, and so on—complaints that most people thought had nothing to do with political and economic arrangements. In the public mind these evils were too pervasive—and too close to the bone—to seem remediable by mounting a campaign. They called for the tried-and-true Victorian formula, "a change of heart." The free lovers had a more militant view.

The fact that free love had the character of a movement gave its theoreticians a special power, not to say insight, in the analysis of society's sexual ills. Activism—especially if its vital center is relatively small—often has the advantage of an organic conception of its goals. The free lovers could see how jealousy and male supremacy, or frigidity and the fear of pregnancy, were parts of the same syndrome. This was not invariably clear to every critic or reformer.

Greeley's campaign in the 1840s for an anti-seduction law, Elizabeth Oakes Smith's call for more stringent marriage qualifications, physicianly pleas for male restraint and gentleness on the honeymoon— these reformist solutions were little more than cosmetics for the corpse.

It is worth comparing the breadth of perspective of the free lovers with that achieved by feminists, for the two movements had much in common. Both saw the problem of marriage as a problem of the oppression of women, and all free lovers were also in favor of women's rights (though few feminists were free lovers). The difference was in how they imagined the problem might be solved. Merely to demand "women's rights" seemed inadequate to the free lovers, so long as those rights were conceived legalistically.

For example, when she married Henry Blackwell, feminist Lucy Stone made a joint protest with him against all the legal disabilities that marriage laid upon her. The Nichols complained (see pp. 270–272) that she would have done better not to go through the ceremony at all, not to take Blackwell's name, but to make her protest instead as a free lover. Once the power of the state to solemnize marriage was admitted, the particular details of oppression were irrelevant. But Lucy Stone maintained that the marriage question was a matter of legal guarantees, and must be agitated according to a timetable that put suffrage first, then legislation.

An interesting discussion of the issue occurred in 1858 at a star-studded convention of radicals held in Rutland, Vermont.[21] Julia Branch—herself hovering somewhere between the feminist and the free love camps—reported a private conversation with Lucy Stone not long after her marriage. "How can she have the right to vote when she has not even the right to her name in the marriage bonds?" Mrs. Branch exclaimed. "It is a mistaken idea," Lucy Stone is supposed to have responded, "that woman is obliged to give up her name and take that of her husband by the ceremony. I have not given up mine, and no law can compel me to. I call myself Lucy Stone, and shall always." But Mrs. Branch then asked, "How would it have been with Mrs. Blackwell, if she had kept the fact of the marriage ceremony a secret, and gone to a hotel with the intention of staying a few days with Mr. Blackwell, signing her name Lucy Stone? Would they have been permitted to occupy one room? What do you suppose would have been the astonishment of the virtuous landlord at such a proceeding, and what would have been his answer? Mrs.

Lucy Stone Blackwell, and every one else, knows the act would be sufficient to denounce her, in the eyes of society, as an infamous woman."

Julia Branch ended by condemning the marriage ceremony itself; it was that which kept woman "degraded in mental and moral slavery. She must demand her freedom; her right to receive the equal wages of man for her labor; her right to bear children when she will, and by whom she will." She therefore moved a substitute resolution for the one before the convention. The original had read, "*Resolved*, That the only true and natural marriage is an exclusive conjugal love between one man and one woman, and the only true home is the isolated home, based on this exclusive love." Mrs. Branch proposed instead, "*Resolved*, That the slavery and degradation of woman proceed from the institution of marriage; that by the marriage contract, she loses control of her name, her person, her property, her labor, her affections, her children, and her freedom."

After her rousing speech, there was a rush of other reformers to the platform—Henry Clapp, a "no-organizationist" and author of a long poem called *Husband vs. Wife* (1858), famous abolitionists and "non-resistants" Stephen Foster and Henry C. Wright, feminist Ernestine Rose, and even Frederick W. Evans, the chief elder of the Shaker church. Each gave spur to his or her own hobby-horse, and more than once the ten-minute rule for speeches had to be suspended. Foster argued that the problem was not in monogamy itself but in its present conditions, which he described in abolitionist terms: "Every man is a tyrant in his own family, and every family is a little embryo plantation, and every woman is a slave-breeder,—in the eye of her husband is a slave, and the breeder of slaves,—and hence comes all the trouble." The analogy to slavery was familiar in free love circles too, but their conclusion was more unswervingly "abolitionist" than Foster's, whose line was the same as the feminists'; "My first proposition is this: that we try the experiment of marriage under true and favorable circumstances, in which the parties shall enter into the relation on an equal footing; then, if it does not work well, I will go for an experiment of a different kind."

Joel Tiffany accused Mrs. Branch of advocating free love, warning her "that people do not distinguish very clearly between love and lust; and that 'free love' is only another name for free lust. . . . I say your institution of marriage will exist, and ought to exist, until men and women are brought up out of their sensual natures, and developed out of this plane that leads them to seek association for purposes of self-gain or gratification." Ernestine Rose stretched forth a rhetorical arm to gather her sister back into the feminist fold; she had not understood Mrs. Branch to mean "to let loose the untamed passions either of men or women; if she meant that, I totally and utterly disagree." Mrs. Branch took advantage of the hairsplitting to interject, "I did not mean it in that light." "That is right," approved Mrs. Rose, and then picking up the issue that she thought Mrs. Branch's speech really raised, she went on to explain why the marriage question was not introduced at women's rights conventions—"because I want to combat in them the injustice in the laws. When that injustice is done away with, when woman is recognized by all as the equal of man, she will receive a similar education, and have similar rights, and whatever may be found wrong after that in the laws, no fear but that it will be righted." Such was the position of mainstream feminism—which the free lovers condemned as superficial.

Elder Evans of the Shakers had the most radical "remedy for all the troubles of the marriage relation—a life of virgin purity." "Now, crucify these lusts," he advised. "Not purify, as friend Tiffany says, but crucify the old man, with all his lusts."

Evans' absolutist view filled out the range of response to the marriage question: abolish monogamy; give women equal rights in marriage; purify the marital relation; abolish sexuality. Free lovers could support all but the last, but for them only the first counted as a full solution. Most feminists were in favor of the second or third, while the Shakers alone advocated celibacy (though, interestingly enough, isolated free lovers like the Nichols seem to have come round in the end to something close to Shakerism). Of course there is much more to be said about the relationship of feminism and free love, but the basic points of agreement and dispute are exemplified in the spectrum of opinion represented at the Rutland Convention.

One other possibility was liberalized divorce, the position of Henry James, Robert Dale Owen, and many others. Although conservatives complained that divorce was just legalized adultery, and radicals argued that it constituted an admission of the necessity of free love, the truth was that James and his supporters had a different conception of marriage than the extremists at either pole. To them it represented a way of integrating human sexual drives into the social fabric. Neither a sacrosanct ordinance nor an instrument of oppression, marriage was the most reasonable means of civilizing the passions and providing a family structure for the nurturing of future citizens. Since it was not perfect (what institution was?), some persons would find themselves unhappy in it, a fact which ought not to surprise any student of society; the remedy was simply to allow such mistakes to be rectified, all still within the purview of the law.

From a certain perspective this analysis seems thoroughly sensible. But obviously divorce was not a way to improve married life, only a way to escape it when it proved unbearable. What effect would it have, for instance, on jealousy? Indeed, James himself, in the preface to his translation of *Love in the Phalanstery*, had put his finger on one sore spot that easier divorce could scarcely be expected to alleviate: "The present law of the sexual relations clearly demands revision. By giving its subject an absolute *property* in the affections of another,—a property based not upon his own worthiness, but upon a liability in the other to public ignominy and suffering, it not only too commonly engenders a purely material relation among those who observe it, but directly instigates deception, adultery, domestic tyranny, and dissension throughout the land."[22]

Love in the Phalanstery was, let us remember, a Fourierist tract, and it was therefore fitting that James' analysis of the marriage question drew so heavily on economic concepts. Indeed, it was precisely the view taken a couple of years later in Lazarus' own Fourierist analysis, which James rather inconsistently dismissed as immoral. The free love position was based on the same insights: so far as it went the feminist complaint was true, that men *owned* women in marriage; but this was not a function of male supremacy so much as of the reliance on legal bonds in the first place, whichever partner might profit by them. Free lover James Clay explained: "The fact of possession or ownership, to the exclusion of others, has a direct tendency to lessen our love for the object, unless we are of that completely selfish make, that we wish to own and enjoy everything alone, and then we are unfit to enjoy anything; we are really unfit to live, for we do not love ourselves or anybody else, but only have a hatred or jealousy that anyone else shall enjoy that which we cannot. The tendency of such is dissolution, because it is desolation of spirit; not in love and harmony with anything, but in discord with everything."[23]

Lazarus said much the same thing: "Jealousy," he began, "so far from being the safeguard of pure love, reveals the impure, selfish, and tyrannical character of that love. It implies . . . want of self-respect, or of the conscious spiritual power to retain the affection of the other person, which alone confers the right to use his or her body. One who is jealous is prepared for real swindling, or open theft, and kidnapping of the worst sort, since it invades not merely the property, but the personality, or spontaneity of another." As usual with Lazarus, and with other free lovers in the Fourierist camp, he quickly moved to the larger issues of the nuclear family vs. the communal association: "It is not nature that makes us afraid to lose the love we possess by the development of new affinities in the person beloved; it is not nature, it is the false position which we occupy in civilization; it is the arbitrary connection of the love relation with legal possession and the isolated household; it is the civil and moral law that makes chattel slaves of us to that point that we dare no longer to call our souls our own."

This analysis, buttressed by Warren's notion of individual sovereignty, was able to account for a whole range of social ills. In so far as the marriage relation was essentially one of ownership (on the model again of slavery), a man was likely to fall into the habit of treating his spouse as an object—treasured or exploited, it made no difference. Accordingly, he could "lose" her, she could "give" herself to others as well as to him, another person might "possess" her. Economic and emotional terminology were interchangeable. "Jealousy is occasioned from poverty in every sense, both spiritually and materially; it is a subversive or infernal expression of the instinct of self-preservation, in the sphere of love, where it is more out of place than in any other, because there, devotion, absolute devotion to the object beloved, normally reigns; and there is no true love worthy the name, where there are any selfish reservations. Civilization, in compelling these, in narrowing, depraving, and degrading the soul down to these, poisons love. Where there are so few chances of love, and half one's life has been turned to anguish by the privation of it, it is a matter of course, that the starved soul should greedily grapple and strive to absorb entirely, and appropriate all to itself, the single being in whom it has found affection."[24]

Lazarus, Andrews, and their circle believed that modern civilization—especially the state—thwarted or perverted the sovereignty of the individual, so that men could own each other, so that one could

sell himself and his labor—or, in the case of a woman, her body.
Marriage was called "legalized prostitution." Once man was alien-
ated from himself in this way, love tended to become a commodity
like everything else, around which laws had to be made adjudicating
contractual obligations and property rights in each other as husbands and wives. In this context divorce was a sort of bankruptcy
law—as John Humphrey Noyes shrewdly called it—to be invoked
should one or the other party fail to meet his obligations.

iv. Communal Marriage at Oneida

Of course for some free lovers the essence of their belief had more
to do with love than with any problems of society or movements
of reform: "The secret-history of the human heart will bear out the
assertion that it is capable of loving any number of times and any
number of persons, and that the more it loves the more it can love.
This is the law of nature, thrust out of sight, and condemned by
common consent, and yet secretly known to all." This was the position of John Humphrey Noyes and his Oneida Community. "Variety
is, in the nature of things, as beautiful and useful in love as in eating
and drinking." They too understood the economic analysis that
proved jealousy an artificial passion rather than an argument for
the instinctual basis of monogamy in human nature. "The one-love
theory is the exponent, not of simple experience in love, but of the
'green-eyed monster,' jealousy. It is not the loving heart, but the
greedy claimant of the loving heart, that sets up the popular doctrine
that one only can be truly loved."25
Noyes admitted that he himself had originated the term "free
love," to denote the practice at Oneida, but the indiscriminate
mating at Modern Times and Berlin Heights was mere lust in
comparison with his idea of regenerate sexual life. Elsewhere "free
love" might mean anything from monogamous cohabitation outside
of wedlock to old-fashioned promiscuity; at Oneida the doctrine
of sexual relations was thoroughly considered, established, and
rationalized. The Oneidan theory was thus named "Bible communism" and its realization "complex marriage." In the millenarian
world of the Perfectionists "they neither marry nor are they given
in marriage"—or, alternatively, all were married to all. Love and
its expression in sexual intercourse might occur between any man

and woman, but no exclusive attachments, nothing approaching romantic love or monogamous pairing-off was tolerated. Once the community could afford an appropriate "mansion house," each adult had a narrow room with a bed, a chair, a window, and just enough space for a single person's needs. Private interviews might take place there, but ordinary social intercourse was provided for in public rooms, and Oneidans were expected to consort with a wide range of fellow members. All particular friendships were discouraged, and even parents were reminded that they had no special claim on their children. Communism of persons was to match communism of goods—"Bible communism."

Since the community developed and changed over its forty-year history, no one description fits all its phases, but in general the practices were as reported in Dr. Van de Warker's survey (see pp. 530–540). The males of the community generally made the first advances, though not always. In order to remove all romantic traces of courtship—to depersonalize acceptance as well as refusal—a system of go-betweens was used. At all times the elders kept an eye on the young people, and if any seemed to be developing exclusive attachments they were first warned, forbidden to visit one another, and finally one would be banished to another branch of the community. An outsider might think that sexuality at Oneida was promiscuous, but in fact its variety was thoroughly disciplined. Promiscuity was enforced.

In Van de Warker's account, it is hinted that this discipline went so far as to seem coercion to some of the members. Perhaps so, but such testimony came only from those who had fallen away from the community, or at Oneida's breakup—that is, under circumstances likely to encourage bias. If members within the community complained, there is little record of it. On the contrary, evidence indicates that complex marriage was an enormous success —so much so, in fact, that outsiders began to hear of it in admiring terms as well as the nasty gossip that was to be expected. Some observers thought of it as a testing ground—"because it is untried I feel disposed to encourage rather than persecute those who are inclined to test its capabilities."[26] Among the thousands of visitors who came to marvel were many who had engaged in the debate over free love—Henry James, Stephen Pearl Andrews, but not apparently, Horace Greeley. (Greeley and Noyes did meet, once, when they found themselves fellow passengers on *The Baltic*, sailing to England to the World's Fair in the Spring of 1851). Few were converted by what they saw, but it is safe to assume that no one left unimpressed. In a dozen ways the community was undoubtedly the most interesting and most successful of all nineteenth-century utopian ventures, and there is no question that complex marriage had a share in the success.

Obviously so unexampled a practice cannot have been instituted in the midst of a traditionally monogamous culture without a good deal of subtle adjustment of the social mores that cushion and constrain ordinary sexuality. The go-between system was only one of a series of carefully thought-out adjuncts to complex marriage. Indeed, it would be more accurate to say that every aspect of life at Oneida was organically in balance, so that focusing on any one social device gives the impression that all the others were expressly designed to bolster it. Thus for example the practice of "mutual criticism," according to which every member of the community periodically submitted himself to the public scrutiny and judgment of his fellows—without recourse to any self-justification whatever—must have been of crucial importance in keeping the collective conscience of the community well-ventilated, free from the sorts of inner reservations and private apprehensions that feed a whole range of romantic passions and fantasies. For life to be truly communal in the extreme sense Oneida demanded of its members, it was necessary to wipe out every vestige of private consciousness, and the periodic airing of the soul in public worked to that end, hand in hand with the sharing and celebration of the most personal physical intimacies.

Again, given the revolution of the family implied in complex marriage, it was necessary to make a multitude of adjustments in those relations that family life took care of in ordinary society. Cooking, housekeeping, and child-care were isolated and sexually differentiated duties that became communal activities, with at least some male participation. Women at Oneida worked in some specialized capacity—none were mere housewives and mothers. Moreover, during the period when the community was still struggling to survive economically a policy against pregnancy was effected by means of John Humphrey Noyes' own contraceptive discovery—"male continence," or *coitus reservatus*. Like mutual criticism, this social invention was crucial in the mix of forces at Oneida, and not merely as a means of freeing women for work.

Male continence was originally no more than Noyes' way of protecting his wife, who had given birth to four still-born and only one live child in six years. But when he instituted complex marriage in his community, he saw that some relatively foolproof method of contraception would be necessary. He borrowed a terminology from the new science of phrenology—which divided the "amative" from the "propagative" propensities, designating a particular portion of the brain as the seat of each—and built an argument that rationalized both his system of sexual relations and his form of birth control: "The separation of the amative from the propagative, places amative sexual intercourse on the same footing with other ordinary forms of social interchange. So long as the amative and propagative are confounded, sexual intercourse carries with it physical consequences which necessarily take it out of the category of mere social acts. . . . Thus the most popular, if not the most serious objection, to communitist love is removed. The difficulty so often urged, of knowing to whom the children belong in complex-marriage, will have no place in a Community trained to keep the amative distinct from the propagative. . . . And the refining effects of sexual love (which are recognized more or less in the world) will be increased a thousand-fold, when sexual intercourse becomes an honored method of innocent and useful communion, and each is married to all."[27]

It was part of Noyes' genius to know how to combine elements of his experience in brilliant social inventions that seemed expressly designed for his delicate polity. Had he chosen Robert Dale Owen's withdrawal method (*coitus interruptus*) instead of male continence he might have achieved similar results so far as birth control went— though that is also questionable—but he would have foregone certain side effects that were even more conducive to the success of complex marriage. Most important was probably just the esoteric nature of the method. The withdrawal technique of course was part of ancient folk wisdom, though it was not until 1831 that Owen's pamphlet gave it any scientific currency. It was widely resorted to, in spite of condemnation by clergy and physicians as "conjugal onanism," no less dangerous to the health of the body than of the soul (and of women as well as men, for the cervix was thought to require "bathing in male secretion" after sexual stimulation). Contraceptive devices—"prudential checks" as they were called—were still expensive and mysterious to the poor, though Charles Knowlton's *Fruits of Philosophy* (1832) had made even these artificial means more familiar as home remedies, especially among the middle classes. The selection of another alternative at Oneida had the doubly useful effect of relieving the community from the need to refute the current scientific and religious prejudice against contraception, at the same time that it once again sharply distinguished the regenerate from the world of sinners. It cannot have been insignificant that the technique involved a nominal chastity and a very real restraint while it allowed full indulgence short of orgasm. The pattern was the same as that of complex marriage itself: controlled and circumscribed license.

Only the males were continent in this way, though of course the practice involved some mutual restraint as well as considerably more pleasure for women of the community than the average worldly wife either enjoyed or thought she ought to. Noyes reported his own experience: "that my enjoyment was increased; also that my wife's experience was very satisfactory, as it had never been before; also that we had escaped the horrors and the fear of involuntary propagation."[28] Outsiders supposed that however much the ladies might prefer it, the gentlemen could not take any great pleasure in an act that required the inhibition of its most intense ecstasies; but all the evidence points the other way. Testimony as to the general effect of the "social theory" is suggestive:

> The theory of sexual morality adopted by this Association, while it allows liberty which in the world would lead to licentiousness degrading to both soul and body, here produces the opposite effects; i.e. it invigorates with *life*, soul and body, and refines and exalts the character generally.

> • • •

> I think the development of the social theory most favorable to the formation of character. It brings out the hidden things of the heart as nothing else could, by exciting the stronger passions of our nature, and bringing them out where they can be purified. Love without law, yet under the control of the Spirit of God, is a great beautifier of character in every respect, and puts the gilding on life.

> • • •

> It has delivered me from the bondage of an insubordinate amativeness, which had been the torment of my life. It has brought me into a positive purity of feeling, that I am confident could come from no source but God.

> • • •

> Since I have become acquainted with the social theory, it has had

the effect of destroying selfishness, shame, and false modesty. It has also refined, strengthened, and increased my *respect* for love; and I look upon amativeness not as a low, sensual passion, but (under the influence of God's Spirit) as holy and noble.[29]

The mixture of sexual indulgence (with an emphasis on the endearments of foreplay) and rigorous self-denial (with side-effects of heightened consciousness) seems to have raised desire to the level of religious transport.

One wonders how a state of chronic low-level sexual excitation (among the males) could have promoted the flow of communal energies. It is too simply mechanical an explanation to say that social life fed on sexual frustration, as some have thought. What seems likely is that the variety of partners ensured by complex marriage kept consciousness from turning in upon itself in romantic fantasies. No matter how private an interview an Oneida couple might enjoy, each represented the entire community to the other, binding the individual to the group in even the most intimate moments. The disturbance of the biological sequence of stimulation, climax, and languor might, in other circumstances, have fostered romantic individualism —depending on how the short-circuiting took place—but at Oneida the symbolic presence of the community at every sexual encounter seems to have prevented any cathexis of desire, diffusing it instead among the entire membership. In crude Freudian terms male continence was a means of regression from a "genital" to a "polymorphously perverse" organization of the libido, and enhanced a concomitant return to a "primitive Christianity," the pure love of brothers and sisters in the communal family.

All this is speculation of course, but whatever the means, it is clear that the effects of male continence and complex marriage were far from the bohemianism of Modern Times or Berlin Heights, where free love meant sexual indulgence more or less along the lines that orthodox monogamy gave rise to in fantasy. Whereas the Oneida communion of love was "a means of glorifying God," free love was based on the political and psychological theory of individual sovereignty.

In so far as the free lovers had any religious notions at all, they were "Spiritualist"—that is, they accepted a pseudoscientific doctrine of "spiritual affinities" among persons or types (a mystical belief in the compatibility of some personalities more than others). This derived, in the most simplistic fashion, from a belief in the existence of ghosts and the possibility of communication with the spirits of the dead. The reason why free lovers were so attracted to Spiritualism was of course the same as their motive in embracing Individual Sovereignty: they were enthusiasts in the old sense, convinced of the precedence of individual and private revelation over group-sanctioned and traditional wisdom. Some versions of Spiritualism held that there was for each spirit a single spiritual mate, to be revealed in heaven; others thought there might be affinities with more than one celestial partner. Free lovers who accepted these views either played the passional field or moved from one exclusive attachment to another, searching for the true eternal mate. (Andrew Jackson Davis, the "father" of Spiritualism, went through several wives without discovering his heavenly counterpart; see pp. 149–152).

Not every Spiritualist was a free lover, explained one who had "been behind the scenes" of both camps, "yet it may be said that all Free Lovers, with rare exceptions, are Spiritualists."[30] The speaker here is an interesting example, for his own career illustrates the relation of the Spiritualist/free lovers to the Perfectionists at Oneida. James W. Towner began as a Universalist minister. In the wave of Spiritualist and free love conversions of the early 1850s, he became first a Spiritualist, then a free lover. "Spiritualism undermined and destroyed my respect for marriage. It led me to look on that institution in the light of a doctrine of affinity, and to regard it as a union or arrangement which the parties to it were at liberty to make or remake to suit their own notions of interest and convenience."[31]

Towner joined the Nichols' Progressive Union, but interestingly enough, when Dr. and Mrs. Nichols made *their* transition to Spiritualism, they passed Towner heading in the opposite direction. As we have already seen, the Nichols abandoned the "material" aspect of free love while adhering to its "spiritual" truth. When they did so, on their way to Catholicism, Towner wrote them a letter of remonstrance (see pp. 471–473), explaining his inability to accept "the 'authority' of the spirits" on the question of whether or not free love ought to be "ultimated" in coition.

This was in 1856, and Towner wrote from Iowa where he was in the process of giving up the ministry for the law. A few years later he had moved to Berlin Heights, where he was active in the free love community. He fought in the Civil War, and lost an eye at the Battle of Pea Ridge. Returning to Ohio, he began to have misgivings about free love, and in 1866 he made contact for the first time with the Oneida Community, and initiated a correspondence and a series of visits which, over the next eight years, were to convert him thoroughly. In 1874 Noyes welcomed Towner and his "family"—a dozen former Berlin Heights free lovers—into the Perfectionist fellowship. Thus the promiscuity of free love was abandoned for the "higher plane," as Towner called it, of complex marriage.

At this distance in time it is difficult to assess Towner's career. Obviously a talented and willful man, he seemed at first to have found a discipleship that would fulfill him in Perfectionism, but soon the restlessness apparent in his earlier life began to manifest itself at Oneida. He became the leader of dissidence in the community. In the last years of communism and complex marriage at Oneida, Towner was the incarnation of "Berlin free love" to the old guard of Noyes and his chief elders. Noyes' faction stood for complex marriage in its traditionally regulated forms, with considerable community pressure put on everyone to be guided by Noyes himself in questionable cases. The younger members of the community, especially the women, tended to favor a return to monogamy—as some thought, largely because they sensed the breakup coming and wanted to protect themselves from being stranded. The Townerites wanted to continue the basic institutions of the community, but without the autocratic presence of their founder— and they particularly desired the loosening of the restrictions and supervision of complex marriage. It was this plank in the Townerite platform that led older members to label him a free lover. In the outcome, both Noyes and Towner lost, and the younger opinion prevailed—not so much because a majority was convinced by it, as because there no longer existed enough faith and unanimity to prevent its predictions from coming to pass.[32]

After the breakup, Towner and his followers remained in Oneida for a few years, but in 1882 they emigrated to Santa Ana, California, where Towner resumed his legal calling, and served as Judge of the Superior Court of Orange County. He apparently abandoned complex marriage as completely as he had free love a decade earlier.

What is the lesson of Towner's career? Like numerous other reformers—especially communitists—he began as a minister. As he himself confessed, his early years found him struggling ineffectually "to overcome passion and lust. . . . I found a law in my members warring against the law of my mind."[33] Free love was one possible balancing of such ambivalence, for it provided a reformist justification for indulgence. This recipe for the combining of antithetical impulses was obviously an important factor in the development of free love as a movement rather than a casual fad. But of course the mixture was volatile—as likely to explode in the individual character as in the surrounding orthodoxy. This helps explain the high rate of defection and recantation among the ranks. The inroads of scandal and public outrage counted for less than the ferment within the movement itself. Free love could survive the volleys of the *Times* and *Tribune*, and outmaneuver as powerful an enemy as Horace Mann, but it could not undergo the self-mortification of Mary Nichols and remain free love in anything but name. James Towner's conversion to Perfectionism was precisely the same revulsion, or accession, of conscience—raising the ante of sexual pleasure: "[I] have become so filled with the idea that only as a means of glorifying God is such intercourse permissible, that I have come to hate and abominate even the virtues as well as the vices, if I may so speak, of my former sexual life and of passional indulgence, as of the devil himself."[34]

But complex marriage was not just another notch of torque cranked into free love. If any valence of conscience and desire could have satisfied the conflicting requirements of Towner's character, it ought to have been Bible communism. "[O]ur system," said Towner after his conversion, "tends to promote in the intercourse of the sexes, delicacy, modesty, chastity and self-denial rather than indulgence; and . . . in fact there is less of the latter under our system than in any other society, except the Shakers or others who practice celibacy."[35] Noyes had a miraculous feel for the psychodynamics of sexuality, religion, and community; the interplay of discipline and license at Oneida was perfectly adjusted for most of its zealot members. One suspects that the failure of the community to absorb Towner as it had hundreds of others into its countervailing institutions was Noyes' own doing: that his obvious pride in having converted a genuinely gifted leader of free love led him to pet and promote when he should have scourged. Towner might not have submitted to the humble anonymity of communal life that most Perfectionists accepted, but that was probably what he needed. As it was, Noyes let him suppose he might be another Noyes, and that was disastrous. Many other factors contributed to the breakup of the community, so that the notion of Towner as the serpent in Eden is an exaggeration, but his character certainly attracted dissidence and focused misgivings. Never Noyes' peer even when the founder was in his dotage, Towner was nonetheless enough of a figure to become a symbol of the community's need when Noyes himself began to fail in energy and intuition. It was a case of just the wrong man at just the worst moment.

One might say that free love, with its profound ambivalences, finally did Oneida in. For many who were uncomfortably driven in both directions at once, toward sexual indulgence on the one hand and toward sexual self-denial on the other, the Oneida Community provided the perfect society, for Noyes had brilliantly combined the two, without compromising either. The whole design of the community was for equilibrium rather than adjustment or quietude, yet so successful was Noyes' inventiveness that the quality of life there did seem relatively stable and placid, at least for those who gave themselves over totally to the social organism. A man like Towner was too gifted—and too "possessed"—to submit to any anonymous communality. Thus Oneida could not serve him as it did most of its members, merging their deepest conflicts in the balanced institutions of complex marriage, male continence, mutual criticism, and so on.

Perhaps the community would have absorbed Towner successfully had it not already been in trouble. A number of factors were at work in its destruction, and no single formulation will tell the whole story, but it seems to me that one way of viewing the failure is in the same terms I have been using to discuss its success—as opposed to the more temporary and perilous balance achieved at Modern Times or Berlin Heights. If one reads Constance Noyes Robertson's excellent history of the breakup period, one sees immediately that a crucial factor in the community's loss of its equilibrium was the loss of faith suffered by its youth, especially by Noyes' own son Theodore, whom Noyes had hoped would succeed him as leader. This loss of faith has never been sufficiently investigated. The usual explanation is that the young people were corrupted when they went off to college at Yale. No doubt that was part of their problem, but it seems to me important to remain a little longer with the question itself, before seeking an answer. Given the way most of its older members had come to Oneida in the first place as converts, and given the sort of conversion that was likely to have been—as the example of Towner I think shows fairly enough

(Noyes would be an interesting case study too)—it seems significant
that the younger people were experiencing the opposite of conversion; rather, a loss of faith, a falling away from zeal, an escape from
the seesaw of license and conscience that Oneida was literally pow-
ered by. The question has been wrongly formulated: not how did
the younger perfectionists lose their faith? but, how did faith come
into existence, and how did it persist among the elders?—for that is
the truly remarkable fact of Oneida's history. As for the falling
away, my own reading would be that, first and foremost, the exem-
plary child-rearing that went on there produced adults who were
rarely troubled by the same deep ambivalence of impulse and constraint, so that not only could they not "convert" to the doctrines
they had, after all, been raised in, but they had no thirst for the
absolute anyway, no need to plunge from the fires of desire into
the icy pool of conscience.

v. "Yes, I am a Free Lover"—Victoria C. Woodhull

Oneida spanned the two waves of the free love movement, but
really belonged to the first. The community had been run out of
Putney in 1847; Noyes himself spent the early 1850s—the peak of
Modern Times—in the tiny propaganda branch of his community
located in Brooklyn, so that even geographically he was near the
center of free love theorizing. Like Lazarus and James he too had
been lambasted in the pages of the New York *Observer*.

The Civil War broke most of the threads of continuity in the
movement and although Oneida came through the 1860s relatively
unscathed, it survived as something of an anachronism, out of touch
with the new lines of development. Free lovers still lived in Modern
Times and Berlin Heights, but no one paid any attention to them,
nor did they want the limelight. The Nichols were in England,
Lazarus had married (!) and disappeared into the West, Josiah
Warren had retired to the home of Ezra Heywood, an anarchist
disciple in Princeton, Massachusetts. The only active survivor was
the indefatigable Stephen Pearl Andrews, who now turned up as
aide-de-camp to the glamorous Jeanne d'Arc of free love, Victoria
Woodhull. It was a new era.

"Yes, I am a Free Lover," Victoria Woodhull brazenly admitted
before audiences of hundreds and thousands. "I have an *inalienable,*

constitutional and *natural* right to love whom I may, to love as *long* or as *short* a period as I can; to *change* that love *every day* if I please, and with *that* right neither you nor any *law* you can frame have *any* right to interfere."³⁶

Just as Modern Times and Berlin Heights had been synonymous with free love two decades earlier, Victoria Woodhull now became a movement in herself. Moreover, unlike the colonists of the first phase, she was not satisfied with a mere enclave in the midst of monogamy; she carried the battle to the foe, accepting every opportunity to scandalize and insult a squeamish public. Naturally she was called names in return, whore and adulteress, bigamist and pornographer. Indeed, she may have been some of these things. She did keep her first husband as a part of her household, but out of charity rather than affection, and Col. James Blood (if he *was* her legal husband) never seemed to mind his predecessor's presence. Certainly she made a living from her calling too, but if she sometimes accepted money from men, it was not merely in exchange for sexual favors. She was the first woman broker on Wall Street—and with Vanderbilt's advice she did well there. She also made money publishing *Woodhull and Claflin's Weekly*, a radical scandal sheet; Anthony Comstock had her thrown in jail for sending an "obscene" issue of it through the mails. For not very different reasons, Karl Marx had her thrown out of the International. She was President of the National Association of Spiritualists and received messages from departed spirits. She ran for President of the United States, and tried to vote herself. Finally she turned respectable, married a stuffy English banker, and died rich.

It is hard to talk about anyone like Victoria Woodhull without sounding cute or condescending, but that is not merely our fault: her life was a continual, unwitting, ironic commentary on itself. It is equally hard not to admire her missionary zeal, her enormous vitality, her wiles, her spunk, her sexiness. Harriet Beecher Stowe named her well if nastily, when she satirized her in *My Wife and I* as Audacia Dangereyes. People were drawn to her and stood by her, even while disapproving of her flamboyance and adjustable scruples. Woodhull created a national scandal by publicly accusing Mrs. Stowe's brother Henry Ward Beecher, the era's favorite preacher, of seducing the wife of his friend and parishioner Theodore Tilton. Yet even after that incredible descent into sensationalism—which sent shivers through the women's rights movement—many of her feminist cohorts defended her: "Victoria Woodhull has done a work for woman that none of us could have done. She has faced and dared men to call her the names that make women shudder, while she chucked principle, like medicine down their throats. I have worked thirty years for woman suffrage, and now I feel that suffrage is but the vestibule of woman's emancipation. . . ."[37] Victoria's sister Tennie C. Claflin put it more bluntly: "We have tried to make 'rake' as disgraceful as 'whore.' We cannot do it. And now we are determined to take the disgrace out of 'whore.' "[38]

Woodhull had said that she didn't condemn Beecher's adultery, but only his cowardice and hypocrisy in failing "to stand shoulder to shoulder with me and others who are endeavoring to hasten a social regeneration which he believes in. . . . [T]he fault and wrong were neither in Mr. Beecher, nor in Mrs. Tilton, . . . but . . . in the false social institutions under which we still live."[39] Those in the know claimed that her actual motive in baring Beecher's indiscretions was revenge; he had repeatedly refused to countenance her work by introducing her on a public platform, and she had finally passed from threats to punishment. One night in Boston she had lost her temper and interrupted her prepared speech to launch into an indictment of the hypocrisy of respectable society. Not a newspaper dared print her accusation, so a few weeks later she published it herself in the famous issue of the *Weekly* that got her sent to jail.

All this, quite obviously, is a game of publicity, reputations, and censorship, and might have been played out had there never been such a thing as free love. Woodhull's notoriety and Beecher's good name were at issue, not the question of sexual relations among friends. Thus it was perfectly appropriate that Anthony Comstock, New York's guardian of public morals, should have attempted to censor the whole business; from beginning to end it was an affair of words rather than deeds, gestures rather than blows.

It is not even clear at whose expense it all occurred. Woodhull and her sister traded a month in jail for a vastly increased audience for their campaigns; Comstock added another feather to his constable's cap; Beecher's reputation not only survived the exposé but flourished throughout the trial for "crim. con." that the aggrieved Theodore Tilton brought against him. When the trial ended inconclusively, Beecher's national regard as a spokesman of pious platitude seemed undamaged. Public morals may have suffered, but not measurably. It was the age of Barnum and U. S. Grant. The populace had grown as fond of scandal as of hoakum and ballyhoo.

Woodhull often said things that sounded much more candid and thoughtful than her encounter with Beecher and Comstock would have led one to expect; some of her manifestoes rang with sincerity and even shrewd analysis, as good as anything that had come out of Modern Times or Berlin Heights: "I am conducting a campaign against marriage, with the view of revolutionizing the present theory and practice. I have strong convictions that, as a bond or promise to love another until death, it is a fraud upon human happiness; and that it has outlived its day of usefulness. . . . I state it without fear of contradiction by fact or of refutation by argument that it is the common experience among the married who have lived together strictly according to the marriage covenant, for from five to ten years, that they are sexually estranged. . . . Sexuality is the physiological basis of character and must be preserved as its balance and perfection. To kill out the sexual instinct by any unnatural practice or repression, is to emasculate character; is to take away that which makes what remains impotent for good— fruitless, not less intellectually and spiritually than sexually."[40]

Her analysis of Beecherism made sense too: "the most intelligent and really virtuous people of all classes have outgrown this institution; . . . they are constantly and systematically unfaithful to it; despise and revolt against it as a slavery; and only submit to a semblance of fidelity to it, for the dread of a falsely educated public opinion and a sham morality, which are based on the ideas of the past, but which no longer really represent the convictions of anybody."[41]

None of this is inconsistent with Victoria Woodhull's radicalism, but the prose is more measured and the analysis more painstaking than anything her fiery character promised. Probably, as every commentator has guessed, these were among the passages of her speeches written for her by the old individual sovereign and free lover, Stephen Pearl Andrews, who had come on the Woodhull bandwagon as writer, editor, and theoretician. Indeed Andrews had never written so well under his own name. The collaboration was at least as much a tonic for his prolixity as for her tendency to blurt.

There is no way of knowing what portion of these speeches was his, hers, or her current spouse—Colonel Blood's. A comparison with Andrews' avowed writing of the period reveals him still as windy and given to logic-chopping as ever. When his old antagonist

Henry James wheeled out his metaphysical artillery again in response to the Woodhull-Beecher scandal, Andrews rushed to the fray with a special eagerness, as if no other opponent had given him so much to chew on in the twenty years that had elapsed since their first debates. Such stuff would not sell copies of the *Weekly*, or fall with an air of spontaneity from "Vicky's" tongue on the public platform, but it was dear to Andrews' pedantic heart.

For herself, Woodhull probably did not really need the thoughts and words of Andrews except as a springboard. Her best speaking always came when she abandoned her text, as she regularly did, extemporizing so winningly that often those who had come merely to heckle went away admiring if not totally converted. She was a flesh-and-blood Verena Tarrant, the feminist heroine of Henry James' *The Bostonians* whose "charm" was such that she could say virtually anything and captivate her hearers.

Indeed, there is reason to think that James' conception of feminist oratory owed something to Woodhull's career. She had her rivals in eloquence—Spiritualist Cora Hatch, feminist Anna E. Dickinson, and of course the famous trail-blazer Fanny Wright—but none had the Woodhull reputation for sheer female presence, nor her entourage of professional radicals. The novelists considered her fair game. She had already appeared as Audacia Dangereyes in Mrs. Stowe's satire, and as Nancy Headway in James' own "Seige of London," the story of an adventuress abroad. *The Bostonians* was a much more detailed and serious study of the world of feminists and free lovers, lecture bureaus and unscrupulous journalists. The author's father would certainly have recognized the portrait of a feminist-cum-Spiritualist whose gift for impromptu oratory had its roots in deranged sexuality. (One wonders what he would have thought of it; perhaps James was wise to wait for his death in 1882 before writing a satire on the crowd his father had served as gadfly.)

The reader of *The Bostonians* cannot fail to note that the various reforms espoused by the characters of that world are almost entirely a matter of talk. Even the feminism seems without content, and a special point is made of the emptiness of Verena's stirring rhetoric. Significantly enough, the sleaziest character of the whole set is Matthias Pardon, the professional publicist. James no doubt exaggerates the mere verbal façade of post-war radicalism in America, but leaving aside the issues of labor and revolution, most of what remains can seem rather a matter of calling conventions or calling names. The Beecher affair is a good example. When Woodhull called him an adulterer and a hypocrite, he called her a liar. She called herself a free lover. Anthony Comstock called her a pornographer. These were the positions, the argument, and more or less the upshot.

The rest of the free love movement, so far as it existed outside Woodhull's aura in the 1870s, was not much more substantial. New leagues and magazines sprang up—The New England Free Love League, the Western Woman's Emancipation Society, the Sexual Science Association, *The Word*, *The Crucible*, *Lucifer*. Curiously enough, once the free love colonies had been succeeded by speeches and manifestoes, more people went to jail for their words than twenty years earlier for their deeds. Flouting convention had become the essence rather than the circumstance of the crime.

As Woodhull never tired of saying, if only one kept up a respectable front, like Beecher, he might fornicate to his heart's content. D. M. Bennett, the free-thought editor of *The Truth-Seeker*, published a list of some 136 Protestant ministers in addition to Beecher who had been in trouble for sexual hanky-panky.[42] The implication was that getting caught was the sin, and that many more sinned than told. If one could avoid trouble by keeping quiet, one could get in trouble for saying such things, as Woodhull discovered when she printed the Beecher scandal, and as editors in other cities found when they reprinted it. Bennett, though he did not suffer for naming names in his "Sinful Saints and Sensual Shepherds," was jailed two years for selling a free love tract of the day, Ezra H. Heywood's *Cupid's Yokes*. Again the guardian of public eyes and ears who pressed charges was Anthony Comstock, the Secretary of the New York Society for the Suppression of Vice and Special Agent of the U.S. Post Office. He also nabbed Heywood himself, for two separate convictions and sentences.

Aside from Comstock, there was little or no connection between Victoria Woodhull's free love and the convictions of these other offenders. True, Heywood had probably founded the New England Free Love League in order to give Woodhull a platform in Boston, but like his young friend Benjamin Tucker (whose own connection with Victoria consisted in having been seduced by her at age 19), Heywood was basically an anarchist in the tradition of Josiah Warren, whose chief happiness in life was editing a radical newspaper and putting out anarchist tracts on his own press. One could not say that he minded his own business, given these activities, but his daily life was so much a model of good citizenship that his fellow townsmen petitioned President Hayes for his release from prison as a favor to them. He flouted conventions only in print, and his free love was a paper tiger, with less of a bite than Woodhull's menacing calls for an end to hypocrisy. Here, for example, is one of the passages in *Cupid's Yokes* singled out by the prosecution as particularly obscene:

> Since "falling in love" is not always ascension, growth (as it should be), but often degradation; as persons who meet in convulsive embraces may separate in deadly feuds,—sexual love here carrying invigorating peace, there desolating havoc, into domestic life,—intelligent students of sociology will not think the marriage institution a finality, but, rather, a device to be amended, or abolished, as enlightened moral sense may require.[43]

Heywood was twice convicted of voicing such opinions, and spent almost three years in prison for them.

Cupid's Yokes came out in 1875, Heywood went to jail in 1878 and 1891, Bennett in 1879. By this time free love was becoming as much a slogan for freedom of the press as for any program of sexual reform, and the National Defense Association and the Free Speech League were new avatars of the New England Free Love League. Cases like that of Edwin C. Walker and Lillian Harman, who went to jail for cohabiting without a license in Valley Falls, Kansas, were less in the tradition of James Clay than that of Henry Thoreau— that is, less a matter of victimization than of propaganda by the deed. Walker and Harman refused to pay their fine, preferring to advertise their oppression by going to jail.

Free lovers kept in touch from Kansas to Massachusetts by means of magazines like *The Word* or *The Truth-Seeker*, whose names revealed the change that had come over the cause since the days of *The Art of Living* and *The Social Revolutionist*, organs of Modern Times and Berlin Heights. Although here and there little knots of the faithful persisted, it was no longer evangelical or coherent enough to be considered a movement. Comstock was kicking a dead horse back into life, and the last gasps of free love were as a libertarian holding-action against censorship.

vi. Aftermath of Continence

Victoria Woodhull went the way of Mary S. Gove Nichols. Having
had her cake, she ate it too. Mary Nichols decided that this world
was not ready for free love, and as if she had never seduced a Henry
Wright or Charles Webber, she wrapped herself in self-righteous
continence and marched off to England with her newly strait-laced
husband. In the excitement of the Civil War, no one noticed. Woodhull's similarly sudden conversion and leave-taking was less discreet.
First of all, her adherents began to notice a certain equivocation in
her speeches; not that she was above double-talk in a tight spot,
but now she seemed to be unnecessarily circumspect. Soon she was
denying that she had ever proclaimed herself a free lover or said a
bad word against marriage—only its abuses. Newspaper reporters
gave her a hard time, for they dug up their phonographic transcripts
of her speeches and called her bluff. (Andrews had helped create a
generation of journalists who could take shorthand.) When Woodhull finally showed her cards, it appeared that she had long since
made sure of her game. She and her sister Tennie married a pair
of English gentlemen, rich and well-connected enough to face down
whatever rumors might cross the Atlantic with them, and so they
retired from public life. Periodically Mrs. Martin returned to the
States and clashed with reporters vigorously enough to remind them
of "The Woodhull," but she never admitted to any of her past.
Given the fact that her free love had been so thoroughly a matter
of publicity and staging, all that it required was some rewriting, in
various falsified autobiographies, to suit her new position as a
respectable British matron. She never recanted; she lied.

Ironic as it was, the end of Woodhull's career as a free lover had
a certain fitness—and not merely because it so closely paralleled
that of Mary Nichols'. It was not easy to keep the faith among the
heathen, and the examples of Lucy Stone and Marx Edgeworth
Lazarus show how feminist and free lover were tempted to relax
their principles for the sake of an undisturbed connubiality. But
Woodhull's backsliding represented something more than be-
leaguered compromise or crass advantage. At first glance she seems
to have left the platform, like Verena Tarrant, for a husband, but
if one considers her exit against the backdrop of other farewell
scenes, a different pattern begins to emerge.

The Nichols announced their discovery of continence, converted to Catholicism, and bowed out, to the complaints of James W. Towner. Towner in turn lost his faith in free love, learned male continence, and joined the Perfectionists. Noyes himself, at the breakup of complex marriage, advised his followers to choose "Shaker celibacy" rather than monogamy, if they had the spiritual strength for it. Again and again the swing of the pendulum is from license to abstinence, as if there were no middle-ground available. Woodhull's case is perhaps a little muddier than the rest, for she acquired a good deal of comfort along with her new constraints, but the drift of all her last pronouncements is ascetic. In a lecture called "The Garden of Eden, or Paradise Lost and Found," she argued the well-known case for "continence except for propagation," providing a Biblical gloss on the evolution of human sexuality: the sin in the garden was the first indulgence in intercourse for pleasure instead of procreation.

The list of such conversions might be extended—for example, by considering the curious sexuality that was at the center of Thomas Lake Harris' Brotherhood of the New Life, a community of sectarian Spiritualists that seems to have combined cohabitation with Shaker-like celibacy, or the equally peculiar history of John Murray Spear's Kiantone, another utopian mixture of sex and the after-life; but rather than pursuing these cases—not strictly free love—it may be more instructive to turn to another kind of example, the history of contraception in Victorian America. In its development we can see more deeply into the meaning of the idea of continence that so intrigued apostate free lovers. "It is the conspicuous disgrace of the medical profession," said a writer for *The Modern Thinker* in 1870, "that so far it has not supplied the public with any standard work upon the intimate relations of the sexes." As a result of the field having been left "to quackery and empiricism," the average father and mother had only "their own amazing ignorance" to pass on to their children. In particular he complained that "what little the profession does say is against all attempts to interfere with the propagative act. . . . [N]early all who have written on the subject, assert that all preventive measures are hurtful." In short, the situation in 1870 was this: "All the best social influences conspire to induce people to marry; when married, every consideration of providence and common sense prompt them to try and control propagation; but the physicians say this cannot be done without peril to the health, except by complete abstention, some-

times extending over years. . . . Yet, every one knows that these
canons of conduct in the sexual relation are universally disregarded."[44]

Of course it was not true that there had been no serious attempts
to provide the rationale of sexuality and contraception that the
anonymous writer for *The Modern Thinker* demanded. Owen's
Moral Physiology and Charles Knowlton's *Fruits of Philosophy* had
been early attempts to provide reliable contraceptive information,
and others had followed with similar recommendations, often
cribbed from these first handbooks. But, for the most part, physicians
were of the opinion that all means to "defraud nature" of offspring were to be avoided, on medical as well as moral grounds.
Had this near unanimity not existed, it would have been impossible
for Anthony Comstock to have lobbied his anti-contraception clause
in the obscenity law through Congress in 1873. And of course, once
he succeeded in making all public mention of contraceptive techniques illegal, the bolt was thrown and the padlock set on the
minds of the medical profession for decades to come. Virtually
every doctor now recommended "continence except for procreation"
as the only healthy and lawful regimen of marital sexuality.

There were still a few exceptions to this dogmatism, physicians
who realized that it would continue to be "universally disregarded"
because it was in contradiction to the facts of life. These radicals
were prosecuted by the self-appointed guardian of public morals,
and even a few conservatives suffered when they went too far in
describing the preventative measures they condemned. Among the
books Anthony Comstock suppressed were *Sexual Physiology*, by
water-cure physician R. T. Trall, and *Words in Pearl*, a little handbook of contraception by Dr. E. B. Foote. Along with *Cupid's Yokes*,
Trall's book was the occasion of Ezra Heywood's first term in jail,
for it was on Heywood's mail-order list for years. Foote's pamphlet
did not result in a prison sentence, but its author was fined $3500
plus $1500 in costs for its publication—a penalty that helped push
the well-to-do physician into the camp of more radical opponents
of censorship (he went bail for D. M. Bennett, Moses Harman, and
others).

Trall and Foote were proof that Comstock played no favorites
in his crusade against sex education. Between them they represented
the extremes of medical opinion on the questions of sexual relations
and contraception in marriage. Trall, once the water-cure com-

petitor of Dr. and Mrs. Nichols, covered the conservative side of the issue in books like *Home-Treatment for Sexual Abuses, Pathology of the Reproductive Organs,* and his best-selling *Sexual Physiology.* The spokesman for liberal opinion was Foote, who not only supported Bennett and his free-thought friends, but who boldly defended the Oneida Community as possibly "prophetic of an advanced condition of society, when the whole human family will be united in one marriage."[45] Foote's *Medical Common Sense* sold 250,000 copies in its first ten years, and a revised version, *Plain Home-Talk,* which the *Oneida Circular* reviewed favorably when it came out in 1870, had sold half a million copies by the turn of the century.

The issue on which Trall and Foote are farthest apart is contraception. Trall, like most medical authors of marriage manuals of the period, was opposed to the various devices and expedients that Robert Dale Owen and Charles Knowlton had suggested in the early 1830s. He went so far as to describe these techniques (that was what Comstock objected to), but his own position was that such practices were immoral: "Let it be distinctly understood that I do not approve any method for preventing pregnancy except that of abstinence, nor any means for producing abortion, on the ground that it is or can be in any sense physiological." He provided descriptions, he tells us, only because for thousands of women contraception was the "least of two evils," the other being "a constant drain upon their life-forces" brought about by "ignorance" and "the present false habits of society" that produce unwanted pregnancies.[46]

Words in Pearl, on the other hand, was in the tradition of Knowlton's *Fruits of Philosophy,* and before Comstock persuaded Congress to make such things illegal (1873), Dr. Foote also sold "sanitary syringes" ($10) and other such devices by mail. He was the inventor of the first cervical cap to be used in America, while his son, Dr. E. B. Foote, Jr., coined the word "contraception."[47] Obviously he did not agree with the chorus of expert testimony that sexual intercourse should be limited to a single monthly (or annual) indulgence, for purposes of procreation only. *Plain Home-Talk* suggested that frequency ought to be determined by pleasure rather than the calendar, and the interval ought merely to be long enough to enhance desire and forestall exhaustion. Trall had put it the other way: "few can exceed the limit of once a week without serious detriment to health and a premature old age; while many can not

safely indulge oftener than once a month. . . . temperance is always
the safer rule of conduct."[48]

How seriously were these contradictory views taken by the general
populace? Then as now, the medical profession combined a deeply
conservative outlook with a remarkably cavalier attitude toward
the matters of science in which one might have expected caution
and exactitude. Whatever was it that led men to such strange ideas
of physiology and morality, or to the desire, on the part of authors
and readers, to establish the limits and conditions of sexual relations
in the first place? In this last question we may begin to see how the
free love movement and the marriage manual market stem from the
same tendencies in American culture.

Taking it just as a matter of simple chronology, we may note
that the earliest hints of free love scandal—at Frances Wright's
Nashoba—coincide with Owen's publication of *Moral Physiology*. The two phenomena are twins, as it were, born of the con-
sorting of Wright and Owen at New Harmony. Knowlton's *Fruits
of Philosophy* (1832) and Sylvester Graham's *Lecture to Young Men
on Chastity* (1834) show how the marriage manual was quickly taken
up by two widely different schools, the rational pragmatists like
Knowlton, whose successors would be Foote and the birth-con-
trollers, and the purity-mongers like Graham, William Alcott, and
most of the later authorities.

It is especially interesting to see how the early advocates of
chastity and continence tended to be food faddists, Graham the
most famous of course, but no less a knight of unbolted flour and
vegetable diet than William Alcott (and, of course, his more famous
cousin Bronson). This strand runs through all the water-cure
physicians—Trall, Nichols, James C. Jackson, and so on—who were
also Grahamites in diet; and it ends, for our purposes, in J. H.
Kellogg, author of a health-and-sex manual called *Plain Facts for
Old and Young* (1879), who helped found the famous Kelloggs of
Battle Creek, still selling cereals just as Graham is still a byword
for cracker. Some of these experts may seem at first glance to take
a liberal stand on the issue of continence, but they all end up
advocating one sort of abstention or another—if not the plain
chastity of Alcott and Graham, then the "progressive" variety of
Dr. and Mrs. Nichols.

In the early period—up to mid-century—the manuals tended to
limit themselves either to birth control information or, more

often, to advice on purity. The advent of the true marriage manual came more or less simultaneously with the free love movement, unless one counts the various phrenological self-help books of Orson and Lorenzo Fowler, who produced *Amativeness, Love and Parentage, Matrimony, Marriage,* and others during the 1840s. These had a narrower purpose than their titles suggest, and the first marriage manual deserving of the name was written by a free lover, Thomas Nichols's *Esoteric Anthropology* (1853).

In later years Nichols claimed that his manual had sold a quarter of a million copies; at a dollar apiece, that was a considerable popularity. After his conversion to continence and Catholicism in the late 1850s, he revised the book, pruning the free love from the physiology. Since he had been a good deal bolder than most experts, he had much to repair. And the two versions are worth close comparison not only because the book was so popular, but also because in his different attitudes Nichols represented both strands of medical opinion on sexuality in the nineteenth century. His revisions and omissions provide a sure guide to the major disagreements between liberal and conservative wings of the profession.

In his first edition Nichols had described most of the methods Knowlton recommended for contraception (though he substituted cold water for all the medicinal spermicides), and he saw "no reason why any one should be compelled to bear children who wishes to avoid it." Indeed, the only contraceptive method he condemned was continence, which he called "unnatural, and unhealthy. We can not violate any law of nature with impunity."[49] In his revised edition, however, the various "prudential checks" are castigated as "evident violation of nature," while the continence earlier discouraged was now recommended. The rhythm system was mentioned in both editions, but in the second it too comes under the heading of using "the sexual act, for mere pleasure," which is "unnatural." Moreover, like most experts of the century Nichols thought that menstruation coincided with the time of fertility, so that the "safe" period was designated precisely during the wrong portion of the cycle.[50]

Many other disparities in the two editions reflect the conversion of the Nichols from free love to continence. The earlier version comes out quite frankly for "varietism" as well as contraception, and praises Lazarus and Andrews' books as the last word on "social science." Nichols also argues for equal rights for women, against jealousy, and so on through a whole chapter called "Miscellaneous" —all deleted in the revised edition.

Even before his conversion Nichols was a somewhat special case, because he was both a water-cure physician and a free lover. Other hydropathists were more or less unanimously opposed to free love or anything (for instance, contraception) that might foster it. When Dr. Trall passed an annotated copy of *Spiritual Vampirism* around his establishment, it was surely an act of pious prudery as much as cut-throat competition. Like the Fowler brothers who published *The Water-Cure Journal* for him, Trall was heavily invested in both aspects of his calling—its economic potential and its status as scientific philanthropy. This was a large part of the reason that marriage manuals suddenly flooded the market. On the one hand, Nichols had shown there was money to be made by it; on the other, it was the duty of the scientist to prescribe for the public weal. Such inducements were wasted on neither Trall nor Dr. Foote.

Whatever our more sophisticated science might lead us to suppose, it is probably just as well to give the pseudoscientists the benefit of the doubt and attribute their zeal to the higher motive. Their infatuation with system also helps explain the compulsion to define limits and apply rules. Like the mad scientists of Poe and Hawthorne, the phrenologists and hydropaths were intent on penetrating the secrets of the universe, and finding applications of their discoveries in every detail of human existence. The Fowler brothers offered a phrenological approach to everything from masturbation to prolapse of the uterus, from education to penal reform. Water-cure was slightly more circumscribed, but the columns of its journals also offered a point of view on a vast range of topics. Thomas and Mary Nichols used it as a stepping-stone to free love; Trall and others found its teachings a bulwark of monogamy and chastity.

Certain pseudosciences were particularly prone to abstemiousness. The emphasis on nature and natural remedies that characterized Sylvester Graham, William Alcott, and all the water-cure people seems to have led most of them to theories of sexual abstinence—a good clue to their conception of healthy diet as a matter of self-denial rather than self-discovery or harmony with nature. And the general preoccupation in the nineteenth century with the mind/body problem gave them plenty of material to work with: let the will chasten the unruly flesh, whether it be at the dinner table or the nuptial couch. No doubt a hundred factors were at work in the overall sexual repression that characterized the age, too many and too subtle to sort out here, but we may at least draw attention to the fact that such larger tendencies found expression in the marriage manuals. Experts on health, like experts on disease, begin at the point of self-consciousness about the body; *natura sanat* was not the wisdom likely to be fostered by such a perspective—especially given the inadequacy of physiological observation and knowledge at the time.

Regular physicians began to come out with their rival compendiums of sexual advice not long after the first wave of pseudoscientific manuals. There is not much to distinguish them from their predecessors except for the increasing insistence on the dangers of "excessive" sexuality. George Napheys, John Cowan, Dio Lewis, and others all agreed that sexuality was dangerous and to be indulged only rarely. Exceptions were Victoria Woodhull's favorite expert John M. Scudder, who thought some "might for a time have connection every night without exhaustion," and E. B. Foote, whose principle of moderation found guidelines in the after-effects of intercourse: "a slight sense of fatigue following it may not indicate excess; but a sense of utter exhaustion succeeding it always does."[51] In general, however, orthodox practitioners differed little from the Grahamites and hydropaths.

These are the main voices of official doctrine on sexual life. Millions of copies of their books were sold, at prices ranging from one to three dollars. How much Americans profited by them is hard to say; if the physicians' accounts are to be trusted, there were a great many men and women suffering from sexual excess, spermatorrhoea, impotence, frigidity, and simple sexual incompatibility. Perhaps people bought these books called *Home Treatment, Plain Home-Talk, Plain Facts,* and so on because they were in need. Perhaps for some it was a form of pornography, as Anthony Comstock firmly believed.

In the 1880s a new variety of marriage manual began to appear that once again brought together the two strands, sexual indulgence and sexual restraint, as if the *before* and *after* of the Nichols' career had coexisted. The authors of this group borrowed heavily from one another, each adding a new name for the practice they all recommended with only slight variation. Ultimately all these borrowings could be traced back to the discovery of male continence by John Humphrey Noyes, although now it was called "Diana,"

"Zugassent's Discovery," or "Karezza." Noyes had published descriptions of his technique in pamphlet form in 1849, 1853, 1866, and 1872. As already noted, he had himself borrowed the crucial distinction between the amative and propagative functions of sexuality from the phrenologists, so one might say that the pseudoscientists had prepared the ground for all these new varieties of male continence, though Noyes had sown the seed.

It was another pseudoscientist, the water-cure physician James Jackson, who was the first non-Perfectionist (1862) to make use of the theory and the basic terminology of male continence. He was careful not to mention Noyes or even to hint that his equivocal distinction between "cohabitation" and "coition" might be considered as a means of contraception instead of a "means of pleasurable enjoyment, as well as of such interchange of thought, sentiment, feeling, and impression . . . more productive of much higher good, than possibly can result from the exercise of the act to its fullest extent." The Oneidans would certainly have affirmed all of this, but they would have never put it so guardedly, or in such a context of anti-sexual feeling as Jackson whips up. There is a world of difference between Noyes' proposal for a technique for love-making without the risk of pregnancy and Jackson's warning that orgasm, except for purposes of propagation, is unnatural and may result in "great injury to health."[52] The ultimate proof of Jackson's basically anti-sexual disposition is his extension of the rule to women—male continence becomes female continence as well.

Jackson's idea probably came from direct contact with the Oneida community; his water-cure spa at Dansville was close enough so that at least one prominent member—Noyes's own son Theodore —is known to have gone there for retreat and recuperation.[53] Perhaps there was more interchange than we know of. In any case no one was eager to follow Jackson's lead. Except for Perfectionist publications, male continence was invariably attacked rather than defended in the literature for the next two decades, that is, until a few years after the breakup of complex marriage at Oneida. Then suddenly there was a wave of new interest in Noyes's discovery, some of it directly traceable to former members of the community.

In 1882 several noteworthy pamphlets appeared, debating the issue of marital continence. As we have already seen, continence had been a favorite subject of the marriage manuals from Graham and Alcott on. Now the possibility of mixing continence and intercourse in some version of *coitus reservatus* was opened up for serious consideration—not as Noyes had intended, emphasizing its contraceptive and social advantages, but more as Jackson had conceived it, as a way of "purifying" sexuality without totally abstaining from it.

The controversy is most conveniently studied in E. B. Foote's compendious *Replies to the Alphites*, in which he gives the chief documents in an argument he himself carried on during the previous year in the pages of his *Health Monthly*. His primary antagonist had been Dr. Caroline B. Winslow, editor of *The Alpha*, a journal devoted to the cause of sexual continence in marriage, except for procreation. Dr. Foote had been for many years an advocate of reasonable sexual indulgence, with benefit of contraceptives, so this part of the debate was straightforward enough, but the issues were complicated when other voices entered the argument. Ezra Heywood's sister-in-law Josephine Tilton wrote a letter in support of Foote, whom she would have special reason to admire since she too had once been arrested by Comstock's agents, for selling a copy of *Cupid's Yokes*. Elmina Drake Slenker, still another victim of Comstock's crusade, also appeared, but on the side of Dr. Winslow and the Alphites. So did the venerable Parker Pillsbury, long-time abolitionist and anti-cleric who had recently come out of semi-retirement to write a tract defending Heywood against Comstock, *"Cupid's Yokes" and The Holy Scriptures Contrasted*.

Most interesting of all was the contribution of Eliza B. Burns, who announced that there was a further aspect of Alphism overlooked in the wrangling between Drs. Foote and Winslow. This was "Diana," which she offered as the practical side of Alpha, a technique by which marital continence could be easily achieved without entirely removing sexual pleasure. Mrs. Burns had just published a full account of *Diana: A Psychofyziological Essay on Sexual Relations, for Married Men and Women*, printed in a form of simplified spelling which reminds one of Stephen Pearl Andrews' days as a phonographer. Indeed she had been one of Andrews' disciples—in phonography, not free love—and so too had the anonymous author of *Diana*, Henry Martyn Parkhurst, for twenty years court stenographer for the Superior Court of New York State. Parkhurst was now a professor of astronomy at the Brooklyn Academy of Arts & Sciences, and for obvious reasons did not want his name attached to the tract on sexual continence which his friend

Mrs. Burns (or Burnz, as she spelled it phonographically) published
for him. But he was an oldtime radical—had been at Brook Farm
and was one of several free-thinking phonographers who seemed to
follow Andrews' example in mixing shorthand with unconven-
tional notions of sexuality.

Professor Parkhurst explained "the doctrine of Diana, which may
be defined to be the law of *sexual satisfaction from sexual contact*.
In uther wurds, Dianism is Alfism as the rezult of sexual equilibration. . . . The fundamental theory of Diana is that the sexual
secretions hav two functions, their generativ function, and their
afectional function; and that except when parentage is dezired,
the sexual force shud be turnd into the afectional channel. The
manifestation of the afectional function is by sexual contact, which
may take such form, from mere companionship to fyzical nude
contact, as mutual atraction may prompt; cauzing sexual equilibration and thus sexual satisfaction."[54] In short the secret of Dianism
and therefore, according to Parkhurst, of Alphism too was none
other than male continence, refurbished with a theory of animal
magnetism borrowed from the old pseudoscience of mesmerism, and
prudently limited to "external" sexual contact—with an emphatic
warning that the Oneida method of "penetration" "necessarily
stimulates into activity the generativ function of the sexual batteries;
and this not only cauzes a wasteful use of sperm, but diverts the
sexual batteries from their afectional function, diminishing amativ
atraction."[55] Apparently Parkhurst did not believe that the Perfectionist technique of male continence could really work, while
his own theory was that sexual contact up to but not including
penetration would transform sexual energy into usable life force.

This was not the first time that magnetic interchange had been
proposed as an explanation of sexuality, nor was it to be the last.
Noyes has a hint or two in this direction, and Dr. Foote himself was
a strong believer in what he called "magnetic adaption."[56] As
far back as 1853, when Charles Webber accused Mary Nichols of
"spiritual vampirism," he described her as being magnetically
"under-charged," so that her sexual interest in him was not affectionate so much as "ravenous." Another implication of Webber's para-
digm was the familiar belief, hovering in the background of many
theories of continence, that the male spent some of his finite supply
of sexual energy, fluid, or vital force in each orgasm. Webber's was

a sinister view of the matter, of course, and far from Parkhurst's celebration of the virtues of magnetic interchange.

Foote, for his part, thought that whatever evidence there was went against Parkhurst. He agreed with him (and most of the theorists back to Webber) that prolonged physical contact tended to equalize the magnetic charges of husband and wife (a sort of hydraulic view of animal magnetism), but where Professor Parkhurst argued that such "equilibration" would bring sexual fulfillment, Dr. Foote saw it as promoting "permanent uncongeniality by making the married pair grow alike physically. The interchange of individual electricities, and the absorption of each other's exhalations, lead directly to temperamental inadaptation." Dr. Foote was therefore opposed to the "double bed," since he thought sleeping together (without intercourse) would reduce "those magnetic elements which . . . produce physical attraction and passional love."[57] (He was followed by a number of other authorities, in this antagonism to double beds, but for the opposite reason; they seem to have been more concerned about the temptation to intercourse that sleeping together furnished.)[58]

The subtitle of Dr. Foote's *Replies to the Alphites* was "Sexual Continence is Not Conducive to Health," but his position on the subject was not so firm as his resistance to Alpha and Diana suggests. It will be remembered that he had defended the Oneida community as a worthwhile experiment in his *Plain Home-Talk*. In later editions he once again raised the question of continence, with more particular reference to the practice of Oneida. He quoted his own son, Dr. E. B. Foote, Jr., as an opponent of male continence (on grounds of its temptation to excesses of "nervous activity" and "tension"), but he himself now leaned toward acceptance of "continence as advocated by Mr. Noyes and others," at least if practiced in its most spiritual forms. "Theoretically, it would seem that human beings should be able to obtain the benefit of magnetic exchange by methods superior to those pursued by the lower animals."[59] Here he seems almost to come round to the views of Mrs. Burns and Professor Parkhurst.

Given the fact of Dr. Foote's friendly relations with the Heywoods, Moses Harman, and other nominal free lovers, it is interesting to find some of them taking sides in the dispute over marital continence, not only supporting Dr. Foote, as Josephine Tilton, but also furnishing testimonials for Professor Parkhurst. Moses Harman's "son-in-law" Edwin C. Walker gave it as his opinion that *Diana* would "stimulate thought and investigation" of the sexual causes of marital unhappiness, in spite of its "conservative standpoint." J. William Lloyd, another young anarchist and free lover, wrote, "Having made a special study of human electricity, especially as between the sexes, I am particularly struck with the scientific value of the treatment of that subject in *Diana*. I regard it as the text book *par excellence*, for the beginner in sex reform."[60] Here we can glimpse once again how the free love amalgam of license and conscience led to doctrines that had pleasure built into self-denial, or that justified impulse.

Another interesting link between the antagonists, Foote and Parkhurst, is the utopian fantast Albert Chavannes, whose writings alternated between pseudoscientific tracts like *Vital Force and Magnetic Exchange* (1888, 1897) and utopian novels detailing imaginary "adventures in socioland." Already, by 1883, Chavannes was in correspondence with Dr. Foote as we know from the *Replies to the Alphites*, in which a "private letter" from him is quoted on the question of whether prolonged continence was likely to injure the sexual powers. Chavannes was in touch with other maverick sexologists too. From J. William Lloyd he borrowed the term "magnetation," to designate "all forms of sexual magnetism made for the benefit of the actors and not for purposes of procreation."[61] He knew the principles of male continence as proposed by Noyes and also the more cautious theory of Diana that Professor Parkhurst championed. His own belief was if anything more pseudoscientific than Diana, for it was part of an ambitious conception of human evolution as well as physiology. Like most of these theorists, he thought that "the exchange of sexual magnetism in the human family, possesses not only the power of reproduction, but the power to maintain and prolong life," by diverting the sexual energies from procreation (which "kills" magnetation) to what the Oneidans had called the "social" or "amative" purposes of intercourse.[62] At an earlier period of human development, unchecked reproduction had been the desideratum of sexuality; now that numbers were no longer an advantage to progress, institutions such as marriage and the family had been established to protect the acquisitions of evolution—private property. Other customs followed—chastity, sexual role differentiation, the etiquette of courtship. "In a word, the highly artificial system under which we live was inaugurated to uphold marriage and inheritance, the twin offspring of personal property." But "we are slowly emerging out of this state of semi barbarism to a condition where the true relation of married persons to each other is being recognized. . . . This change in the views and beliefs of individuals is slowly leading them in the direction of self-control, and teaching them how to pass from procreation to magnetation."[63] For all his eccentricity, Chavannes was a cautious advocate. It took him almost ten years to perfect his theories, from the first publication of *Vital Force* in 1888 to its reissue with a full account of magnetation in 1897. His evolutionary argument is clearly leading him to a free love position, yet the most he will say is that divorce ought to be as easy as marriage. Similarly, he is unwilling to lay down rules for the physical limits of magnetation; different constitutions will require different degrees of self-control, "so as to avoid as far as possible that complete surrender to passionate desire which is always the precursor to procreation."[64] Thus he draws no dividing line such as Parkhurst felt necessary to prevent orgasm; on the contrary, it seems to have been his belief that a male orgasm might be achieved without ejaculation of semen. "I am no believer in asceticism," he wrote, "or in the innate depravity of our natural desires, and I hold that an increase of pleasant sensations is the incentive to all successful advancement. The control of sex force will follow the same line of progress, and men and women will only strive for its attainment when they become persuaded that their efforts will be properly rewarded."[65] Obviously this is a far more permissive attitude than Parkhurst was able to muster in *Diana*.

Between the first and second editions of *Vital Force* two new authors advocating continence had appeared. Like Chavannes, George Noyes Miller was a utopian novelist as well as a sexologist, but in his case the two impulses had a single outlet, a curious utopian romance, half *Looking Backward*, half *Lysistrata*, in which the women of a community give their husbands the choice of adopting male continence or of relinquishing sexual intercourse altogether. *The Strike of a Sex* (1890) contains no hints of the tradition of complex marriage that went hand in hand with male continence, nor are there any references to Oneida. The author quietly signs himself George N. Miller and calls his technique "Zugassent's Discovery," but of course the lineage was plain to all who knew the history of Noyes' community. The author was in fact the nephew of John Humphrey Noyes himself, son of his sister Charlotte and John R. Miller, and an experienced practitioner of what he advocated, his uncle's male continence brought up to date with a good deal of earnest piety to replace the millennial fervour of its inventor. Miller's book went through a half dozen editions and was taken up by mail order houses like Alice B. Stockham and Co., which sold a line of radical and home remedy volumes, headed by Dr. Stockham's own *Tokology*, the standard handbook of pregnancy and childbirth of the period. Dr. Stockham took up more than just the distribution of *The Strike of a Sex*. She handled its sequel *After the Sex Struck, or, Zugassent's Discovery* (1895), in which the actual theory of continence is presented; and more important, she also accepted the continence gospel herself. The result—*Karezza* (1896)—became the most famous and popular of all these handbooks of chaste intercourse, so that its name, Karezza, of all the contenders, has stuck ever since.

Dr. Stockham did not try to disguise her indebtedness to Miller or to Noyes before him; on the contrary, she quoted long passages from each in her appendix. She did lift something from Henry Parkhurst without acknowledgement—a quotation from Herbert Spencer, an analogy to lachrymal and salivary glands, and so on— but silence here was more understandable, since Dr. Stockham clearly did not want to be associated with Diana in any way. Professor Parkhurst was deeply committed to the Alphite ideal of continence, and allowed only "fyzical" stimulation short of "internal contact with or without friction," whereas Dr. Stockham went back to the principles of Oneida, recommending full intercourse without climax. (She chooses with Chavannes and others on the matter of *female* continence, restricting both the sexes to what Noyes asked only of the men.)

The great difference between Alpha and Diana on the one hand, magnetation, Zugassent's Discovery, and Karezza on the other, was in their general attitudes toward sexual pleasure. Like James Jackson and other conservatives stretching back to Graham and Alcott, Dr. Winslow was at heart a Shaker, calling for abstinence from sin. Professor Parkhurst only honed the edge of self-denial keener when he offered Diana as a measure of implementation to the Alphites. Albert Chavannes, George Miller, and Alice Stockham seem to begin at the other pole, and though they temper the joys of sexual life by forbidding orgasm (or, in Chavannes' case, ejaculation), their ostensible reasons are not purely negative—rather they explain that even greater pleasure, for male and female, will result from the technique they recommend. With his uncle's flair for bold propaganda Miller printed—and Dr. Stockham reprinted—a series of testimonials to the delights of Zugassent's Discovery. From a gentleman: "The ideas contained therein were so different from all my preconceived ideas of what constituted marital happiness, that I was inclined to reject them as utterly impracticable and absurd. . . . I have had a continuous honeymoon for four years." From a lady: "Since my husband became acquainted with the philosophy of Zugassent, he has endeared himself to me a hundredfold. . . . His very step sends a thrill through me, for I know that my beloved will grasp me and clasp me and cover me with kisses such as only the most enthusiastic lover could give."⁶⁶ One would like to have some testimonials from the users of Diana to compare with these encomiums. The fan letters of Walker and Lloyd are not from satisfied customers so much as admiring colleagues, and Lloyd later picked up Dr. Stockham's term and technique, writing his own pamphlet *Karezza* (which may still be purchased, through the mailorder columns in the back pages of current magazines like *Playboy* and *Penthouse*).

However certain it is that Dr. Stockham felt herself in the camp of Noyes and Miller rather than Winslow and Parkhurst, elements in her work remind us that all of these traditions of continence were built on ambivalence toward sexual pleasure. Dr. Stockham counts it as an advantage of Karezza that "the demand for physical expression is less frequent," at most once every few weeks, at best with an interval of three or four months. Further, the idea that Karezza is "the supreme action of the will over the sexual nature" does not suggest any undiluted reveling in pleasure. Dr. Stockham's radicalness is relative to those who believed in "abstinence save for procreation," according to which, as she pointed out, "one propagates only, while in Karezza the building of character and spiritual growth is sought, at the same time the sexual functions are honored, refined and dignified."⁶⁷

For Parkhurst and Stockham the particular blend of indulgence and constraint depended less on the prescription than on the attitude with which it was followed. Some people would find more pleasure in full genital contact, others in the caresses of foreplay alone, but the excitement of both approaches lay in the awareness of a boundary to be touched but not crossed, an abyss of oblivion edged round by heightened consciousness. This was all to the benefit of sensuality; on the other side of the ledger an equal increment might be posted to the credit of conscience, for every moment on the brink of ecstasy was a feat of self-control. The devotees of continence were like Kafka's "hunger artist," moral athletes and daredevils who took the war between the will and the flesh into the enemy's camp. It was this advantage of continence that appealed to the food faddists and other pseudoscientists whose panaceas always involved toeing some line or other. Free lovers like Towner or the Nichols were suited to such a regimen of pleasure, for their principles and desires were entangled in just this way. Continence in intercourse allowed these antithetical impulses to coexist in the sexual act itself, while providing at the same time a "natural" contraceptive. Sensual pleasure was intensified by consciousness at the same time that it was justified by being continuously monitored by the conscience.

Of course these ambivalences did not come from nothing; they were somewhat eccentric manifestations of a much wider gulf in the culture itself—the classic dualism of Victorian sexuality, its prudery and its prurience, its chastity and its license, pornography and prostitution side by side with saintly virgins and wives of alabaster. Purity literature from Graham to Winslow had advised continence for the sake of health and moral well-being. These were the books officially presented to young men and women entering upon sexual life, while thousands of copies of *Moral Physiology*, *The Fruits of Philosophy*, and *Esoteric Anthropology* circulated privately among the same readers. The split may have existed in most individuals; it certainly obtained in the general society, where the disparity was so complete as to foster a literature of tension that fed on just these polarities.

By the time of Zugassent's Discovery and Karezza, believers in *coitus reservatus* seemed to be on the increase, and therefore it is curious that what had begun to look like a movement suddenly vanished after the turn of the century. A few advocates like J. William Lloyd persisted because Karezza was only part of some larger conception of life, and here and there an approving paragraph appeared in the marriage manuals,[68] but no new theorists of continence came forth to carry on the work of Miller and Stockholm.

The last figure of any significance in this tradition ended her career in 1902, in a manner that throws light on both the sources of the continence crusade and its rather surprising dissolution. The case of Ida C. Craddock brings together many of the strands we have been tracing in the preceding pages, and will serve as a final example of the nature of the phenomenon and its relation to the free love movement.

vii. Ida Craddock's "Heavenly Bridegroom"

Mrs. Craddock (she called herself "Mrs." for professional reasons, although she seems never to have married) was variously described as a "Lecturer and Correspondent on Social Purity," "Instructor in Divine Science," and "High Priestess of the Church of Yoga." She taught phonography and apparently knew the clique of phonographic free-thinkers and sexologists that began with Stephen Pearl Andrews and included Theron C. Leland (at Modern Times), Edward Underhill (who had been arrested along with Brisbane when Andrews' Free Love League was raided), Henry Parkhurst and Eliza Burns (author and publisher of *Diana*).[69] She was friendly with the *Truth Seeker* circle, and her shorthand skills made her (like Theron Leland before her) an obvious choice for secretary of the American Secular Union—the former National Liberal League that defended free speech from Comstockery.

Long a student of mysticism and spiritual experience, Mrs. Craddock seems to have established a relationship with a "heavenly bridegroom"—whose advantage over an earthly mate, as she said, was that in "being able to read his partner's thoughts, he can adapt himself to her most delicate fluctuations of sentiment at a moment's warning, and so never fail to be truly her companion."[70] In the 1890s she gave up her work as a phonographic instructor in order to pursue her investigations of sexual science more devotedly, under the guidance of her angelic spouse. In 1893 she began to find herself in trouble with the authorities because of her studies. "Enlightened by my experiences as the wife of my unseen angel visitant, I wrote a defence (from a folklore standpoint) of the Danse du Ventre," at that time a celebrated event in the Columbian Exposition in Chicago—at least in part because of the noisy efforts of Anthony Comstock to close the show down. The *New York World* published

her essay, to which she afterwards added further thoughts, for
private circulation. "As the essay showed that I wrote from experience; as I was still 'Miss' Craddock, and as my social standing had
hitherto been above suspicion; I deemed it only prudent to state
to my readers that I had acquired my knowledge from a spirit husband."[71] The essay fell into the hands of two non-occultist physicians, who "made efforts to have me incarcerated as insane. One of
the latter remarked, 'Had that essay been written by a man, by a
physician or by any other scientist (and the paragraph about the
spirit husband omitted) it would have been alright; but coming from
an unmarried woman, neither a physician or a scientist, and with
that claim of a spirit husband, there is no explanation possible but
(1) illicit experience, which is denied by all who know her, or (2)
insanity.' "[72]

Apparently Mrs. Craddock was sufficiently upset by the accusation to raise the question of her sanity with herself. For a short
time she was voluntarily the inmate of an asylum, and then left
town in order to avoid legal commitment. She also undertook a
lengthy and learned apologia of her theories and the experience on
which they were based, published after her death as *Heavenly
Bridegrooms* (1918). Here she explains—after much preamble on
the ancient subject of "spiritual views"—the three degrees of
advance toward "Borderland wedlock." In these degrees we find
ourselves once again on the familiar territory of continence literature, for they seem to be none other than Alpha (the first degree),
Diana (the transitional means from the first to the second), and
Zugassent's Discovery (the second degree). The third degree is
"psychic wedlock" itself, the union with the Divine.

Although she did not publish these self-communings, Mrs. Craddock found other means of sharing her discoveries with the public.
She went to Chicago, where she set up offices on Dearborn Street,
giving lectures on the achievement of at least the first two degrees
of sexual self-control, $5 for the complete course of ten. In 1897
she published a new version of *The Danse du Ventre*, a *Letter to a
Prospective Bride*, and *Helps to Happy Wedlock, No. 1, For Husbands,* in the last of which she prints anonymous explanations of
both "male continence" and "magnetation" that may have been
furnished by Miller and Chavannes, or possibly Lloyd. She concludes with a recommendation of Dr. Stockham's *Karezza*, an

advertisement of her own private consultation, now being offered in Philadelphia.

She followed these with *Right Marital Living* (1899) and *The Wedding Night* (1900). In *Right Marital Living* she quoted a long passage on magnetation (from Albert Chavannes) to serve as testimony for what had now become the "third degree" of divine intercourse or the "third step" of right marital living, namely the achievement of orgasm *without* ejaculation. Chavannes had said that "it is quite possible for men to prevent, by the use of will force, the emission of semen at the time of the orgasm." This view coincided with what Mrs. Craddock had learned from her heavenly bridegroom, and although she now carefully veiled her own experience of such matters, she explained that in addition to Chavannes' promise of a surplus of vital force "diffused" through the body, there should also be, at that moment of orgasm without ejaculation, a "union with God, or Nature, or the Ultimate Force." The language is cautious here too; there is no talk of heavenly bridegrooms, but only this hint: "no man and woman who have once known what a beautiful and blessed thing it is to have that Ultimate Force as the third partner in a sex union which is self-controlled and aspiring to the highest throughout, will ever again wish to have a marital embrace from which personal relations with that Ultimate Force is excluded."[73]

All of this odd sexual mysticism should remind us of the close connection that Spiritualism and free love had enjoyed since the 1850s, when not only Towner and the Nichols but Andrew Jackson Davis, Warren Chase, and a long line of others had embraced the doctrine of affinities based on "spiritual wives." Here in Mrs. Craddock we find the free love strand completely lacking (in her personal life, her friends at *The Truth Seeker* testified to her complete "purity")—but the rest, the heavenly bridegroom combined with (as a result of) earthly continence, is not unlike the doctrine of apostate free lovers and Spiritualists almost a half century earlier. Of course the combination of continence and divine visitation is familiar enough in the history of mysticism. What is unusual is the addition of an earthly partner, with whom intercourse is carried on, up to and including orgasm but without ejaculation. One can see how the idea has come twisting down through experts like Jackson and Winslow, Parkhurst and Miller and Chavannes, until it meets in Mrs. Craddock with a stronger strain of Spiritualism than inspired any of them; and the result is an amalgam that seems the epitome of Spiritualism/free love—as Mrs. Craddock said, a means of prolonging "the happiness of love into marriage. . . . In my own case, Paradise—the Kingdom of Heaven has come into my earth life, and it has come through my heavenly bridegroom."[74]

There had in fact been several earlier preludes to "right marital living," the most complete being the practices of Thomas Lake Harris's Brotherhood of the New Life at Brocton, New York. There a similar continence in intercourse seems to have been part of ceremonies that also involved heavenly counterparts and fairy lovers. Indeed Mrs. Craddock quotes one of the most prominent Brotherhood members, Laurence Oliphant, on the interconnection of "psychics and sex." (Oliphant is supposed to have practiced continence—whether conventional or Karezzaean is not precisely clear but most likely it was the latter—throughout his marriage to the daughter of Robert Dale Owen.[75])

But the main tradition of continence-in-intercourse had come from Oneida of course, where the spiritual presence in complex marriage never put on the flesh as it were. From the purity authors like Graham, modified by the Alphites, came a further admixture of self-mortification, which in some writers, like Parkhurst, resulted in drawing the line of continence on *this* side of penetration, but which in Mrs. Craddock seems rather to have pushed her back a generation into the Spiritualist doctrine—continence as a means of achieving divine intercourse, now based on full orgasm (except for emission) with an earthly partner. (How Mrs. Craddock's own lack of such a partner was related to her postulation of one, is an unanswerable question.) Not only does Mrs. Craddock's theory of the three steps or degrees of heavenly wedlock recapitulate the history of continence literature from Graham to Parkhurst and from Nichols to Chavannes; it also contains in itself a remarkably apt expression of the polarity that we have identified at the heart of both free love and the continence crusade—the impulse toward sensual indulgence on the one hand, and the need for justification in the eyes of conscience on the other. For Mrs. Craddock emphasized in her three steps that the ecstasy of the final stage is only possible by means of complete self-mastery achieved through continence in the first two. Even her own case seems a symbolic version

of the same conflict: the total continence of her celibate life produced—and justified—the esoteric indulgence in her heavenly
bridegroom. "Every throb of passion must be brought under the
control of the higher, inward self, and laid as an offering at the
feet of Deity, or blended, in thought, with the Ultimate Force, if
she would have the purest and sweetest satisfaction."[76]

Of course when Mrs. Craddock began to tone down the descriptions of spiritual visitation in her pamphlets, she had less trouble
with the physicians who read them; but as she exercised caution
there, she flung it to the winds in her frank and generally quite
sensible advice concerning the best ways to make love. She mentioned enough unmentionables to get herself arrested in four major
cities of the United States—Chicago, Philadelphia, Washington,
D.C., and New York.[77] In Washington the judge told her that these
matters "should be discussed only in private if at all," and he
released her on condition that she leave town.[78] This was in 1901.
The following March she was arrested again, on complaint of
Anthony Comstock himself, for selling copies of *The Wedding
Night*, was convicted and sentenced to a $500 fine or three months
in the workhouse on Blackwell's Island. Dr. Foote's son, E. B. Foote
Jr., initiated a defense fund in *The Truth Seeker*, but she served
the time and wrote an exposé of conditions on the Island; and after
she got out she continued to distribute her pamphlets. E. M. Macdonald, who had taken Bennett's place as editor of *The Truth
Seeker*, had a conversation with her at his office: "Speaking jocosely,
I told her I regretted to see youth and beauty sacrificed to the vice-
hunting ogre. She replied that, although she enjoyed living, she
would that her life might be turned to water and poured out for
cleansing the lives of others. She was every inch a martyr."[79]

Comstock had not been satisfied with conviction. Having sent
her to prison for selling her pamphlets, he now brought her to trial
for mailing them. On October 16 she was to report for sentencing,
but when her mother came to her 23rd Street apartment to
accompany her to the court, she found her dead. She had turned on
the gas and cut her wrists.[80]

Ida Craddock was forty-five years old when she died, "a surprisingly beautiful woman," and "well gowned" as the *Times* reporter
added bemusedly.[81] By all reports she was as angelic as the bridegrooms she believed in. Her suicide notes (pp. 306–315) were extra-

ordinarily touching. Comstock did not escape public opprobrium
for this suicide so easily as for that of the infamous pornographer
William Haynes or the notorious abortionist Madame Restell.

"I would not like to be in your shoes," wrote the rector of St.
George's Church; "you hounded an honest, not a bad woman to her
death. I would not like to have to answer to God for what you have
done."[82] Comstock responded in character—with self-righteousness—
but his power was on the wane and Mrs. Craddock's gesture was not
without its effect in the growing popular revulsion from Comstockery. *Who is the Enemy; Anthony Comstock or You?* was the
title of a pamphlet written by old-time free lover Edwin C. Walker
in 1903. At last the public had begun to wonder. Of course there
were others to take Comstock's place—Walker's "father-in-law"
Moses Harman, and Alice B. Stockham were both prosecuted in
Chicago just over a year later. Clarence Darrow defended them,
unsuccessfully, and they were each fined $500, for publishing
Lucifer and *Karezza* respectively.

The fact was that Comstock had largely succeeded in wiping out
the pornography trade in the United States, so that there was little
left to do but persecute the Craddocks and Stockhams. Even they
were becoming rare. Indeed, it might be said that Comstock had
doubly driven the radical sexologists out of business. Not only did
he attack them directly, but perhaps even more important, his work
in suppressing pornography and the slow public revulsion from
his prudish intolerance were together helping to dispel the charged
atmosphere of indulgence and conscience which had nourished
the continence literature in the first place. The Victorian hothouse
responsible for exotic flowers like Ida Craddock was beginning to
react to fresh air coming from several different quarters. In addition
to the hit-or-miss damage done by Comstock, the edifice of lies and
hypocrisy that had been held up so many years by orthodox physicians also began to crumble. Because of young doctors like E. B.
Foote Jr. actively engaged in the struggle for free discussion of
sexual matters, there were now many members of the medical
establishment no longer afraid to deny the old platitudes of the
purity champions, Graham and his followers.

Mrs. Craddock was caught in the middle. On the one side was
Comstock and on the other were the professionals who in their
newfound liberalism included her among the enemies of sex. In
the long run it was on this second front that she was bound to lose,

for oppression at least takes its victims seriously, whereas Mrs. Craddock's new antagonists treated her with amused tolerance and ridicule. There is a particularly striking example from her days in Chicago.

Just as the first version of *The Danse du Ventre* had been published in the public press, so too had *Right Marital Living*, in a local medical journal, *The Chicago Clinic* (for May, 1899). Meanwhile another journal, *The Alkaloidal Clinic*, was running a series of articles reporting the papers on sexual questions being presented at the Chicago Physicians' Club. The general tone of these discussions was frank and sensible, and the editor of *The Alkaloidal Clinic* more than once expresses a somewhat surprised satisfaction in the results. At the end of the series, in the October issue, he sums up his sense of the profession's position on sex education, normal and abnormal sexual functioning, and proper treatment of disorders. Much of his advice as to the conduct of intercourse parallels Mrs. Craddock's pleas for patience and a regard to *mutual* gratification of the partners, but his opinions obviously stem from the Physicians' Club meetings rather than from *Right Marital Living*. Mrs. Craddock's expanded pamphlet had appeared by October however, and the editor ends his discussion by mentioning it, as an example of crank literature. He praises her insistence on recognizing that the pattern of female sexuality differs from that of males, for that coincides with his own counsel, and he seems also to be impressed by the "unusual freedom" with which she deals with the subject; but his main response is to Mrs. Craddock's theories of continence, which he describes as unnatural and dangerous to healthy intercourse. He argues against the theories of both the purity school and the magnetic enthusiasts from Parkhurst to Chavannes, who believed the reabsorption of semen to be of benefit to men. "It is safe to assume that nature's way is all right until we know a better, and the notorious fact that some men habitually lose enormous quantities of semen without apparently being the worse for it, would throw a doubt on the necessity of reabsorption." The editor tells the story of an acquaintance who, at his silver wedding anniversary, informed him "that he had had sexual intercourse during the 25 years regularly ten times a week," without "the least evidence of degeneracy or exhaustion." Like Dr. Foote (and, for that matter, Mrs. Craddock) the editor recommends that each couple "settle down to that degree of indulgence that is natural to them, let it be once a month, once a week, or once a day." The danger, he feels, is when "intercourse in the natural way is looked upon as undesirable or wrong," and he particularly instances "the idea that intercourse except for procreation is sinful," which may lead to "mentally becoming warped," or a " 'crank,' devoting to the consideration of sexual and kindred subjects much time and thought that would be better given to the home, to business or to the soul's welfare. Whenever we begin to interfere with nature in this matter we stand an excellent chance of doing harm, and very little of doing good."[83]

Obviously these last remarks not only take issue with Mrs. Craddock, but also hint at a view of her case not unlike that of the New York physicians who wanted to commit her to an asylum for her opinions of belly dancing. But where the earlier authorities seem to have been male supremacists who thought her "worst offense . . . that, as a woman, I was out of my province in openly preaching marital reform," the strictures of *The Alkaloidal Clinic* addressed substantial issues and must be taken more seriously. Finally, however, it was not the direct attack on her, or on other "quacks," that did the real damage, any more than it was Comstock's vindictive pursuit a few years later. Comstock helped get rid of the continence literature less by suppressing it than by unintentionally creating public sympathy for its authors; it could not flourish in an atmosphere of tolerance. Similarly, the editor of *The Alkaloidal Clinic*, in accepting and even extending the good advice of *Right Marital Living*, stole its audience away more surely than any of his criticisms did. Neither Mrs. Craddock's wisdom nor her fantasies could thrive in an open forum, where sexuality was treated as a natural fact of ordinary life. When orthodox physicians began to argue—as some members of the Physicians' Club did—that sex education ought to start in kindergarten, that sexual incompatibility ought to be grounds for divorce, and that intercourse should be regulated by "appetite," as the editor said, "without a thought beyond the pleasure of the moment," that was the death knell of the school of continence, for it put natural above legal contraints, and subtracted morbid consciousness from desire and its fulfillment. It is not merely an ironic accident that the last gasps of continence literature were attended by some of the first accents of common sense that orthodox practitioners were able to muster on the sexual question.

Not that our own century has been so invariably enlightened—
but the gradual acceptance of sexual life as natural and normal has
diminished the tension between indulgence and self-denial, just
as it has allowed the representatives of such extremes, from Comstock to Victoria Woodhull, to fade into history. There have continued to be advocates of continence, both abstinence and Karezza,
just as there have continued to be free lovers. But these phenomena
no longer appear as crusades or movements; even when they occur
as features in what we have come to call "counter culture," the
amorphous family of alternatives to conventional life in modern
America, one cannot find much in common with the embattled
enthusiasms of the nineteenth century. The sexual revolution may
not be over yet (and it is hard to know exactly how far it has really
come, or where it is heading), but we are clearly in a different world
from Mary Nichols or Stephen Pearl Andrews. Nor is that world
anything like the free love paradise depicted by J. William Lloyd,
or the utopia of Zugassent imagined by George Miller, or even the
rationally ordered conduct of sexual life envisioned by Albert
Chavannes. The solving—if one can call it that—of the particular
problems raised by the free lovers and their cousins the continence
theorists has not catapulted us into "Socioland" or "the vale of
sunrise." We have our own dissatisfactions and dilemmas, also
sexual, to deal with. But perhaps we can learn something from the
way the Victorians dealt with theirs.

Notes

1. Quoted in A. J. G. Perkins and Theresa Wolfson, *Frances Wright
Free Enquirer*, New York and London, 1939, 193–194.
2. *The History of Woman Suffrage*, 3 vols., ed. Elizabeth Cady Stanton,
Susan Anthony, and Mathilda Joslyn Gage, Rochester, N.Y., 1881–1886, I,
295.
3. *Oneida Circular*, VII (June 27, 1870), 116.
4. *The Periodical Letter*, I, no. 4 (November 1854), 55.
5. *New York Weekly Herald* (March 14, 1845), 86.
6. "Positions Defined," a broadside dated August 1853.
7. Moncure D. Conway, "Modern Times, New York," *Fortnightly Review*, I (1865), 425.
8. Thomas L. and Mary S. Gove Nichols, *Marriage*, New York, 1854,
390–391.
9. "Fourierism and the Socialists," *The Dial*, III (July 1842), 87.

10. See, for example, Julian Hawthorne, *Nathaniel Hawthorne and His Wife*, 2 vols., Boston, 1884, I, 267.

11. Marianne Dwight, *Letters from Brook Farm 1844–1847*, ed. Amy L. Reed, Poughkeepsie, New York, 1928, 69.

12. *The Journals and Miscellaneous Notebooks of Ralph Waldo Emerson*, ed. William H. Gilman, Alfred R. Ferguson, *et al.*, Cambridge, Mass., 1960– , VIII, 392.

13. George Ripley in *The Harbinger*, II (1846), 61.

14. Henry James, Sr., preface to Victor Hennequin, *Love in the Phalanstery*, New York, 1849, vi.

15. *Water-Cure Journal and Herald of Reform*, XIII (1852), 140–141.

16. "Brook Farm," *The Dial*, IV (1844), 355.

17. *Bible Communism*, Brooklyn, 1853, 57–58.

18. *New York Daily Tribune* (July 21, 1853), 2.

19. *Nichols Journal* (September 1853), 44–45.

20. *Oneida Circular*, VIII (June 27, 1870), 116.

21. For the following debates see *Proceedings of the Free Convention Held at Rutland, Vt.*, Boston, 1858, 52–66.

22. *Love in the Phalanstery*, vi.

23. James Clay, *A Voice from the Prison*, Boston, 1856, 50.

24. Marx Edgeworth Lazarus, *Love vs. Marriage*, New York, 1852, 250–254.

25. *Bible Communism*, 35.

26. Edward B. Foote, *Dr. Foote's New Plain Home Talk*, New York, 1900, 1016.

27. *Male Continence*, Oneida, New York, 1872, 15–16.

28. *Male Continence*, 11.

29. *First Annual Report of the Oneida Association*, Oneida Reserve, New York, 1849, 50–51.

30. John B. Ellis [a pseudonym], *Free Love and Its Votaries*, New York, 1870, 423. Compare William Hepworth Dixon, *Spiritual Wives*, 2 vols., London, 1868, II, 257.

31. Ellis, 422.

32. For an excellent account of this period consult Constance Noyes Robertson, *Oneida Community: The Breakup, 1876–1881*, Syracuse, New York, 1972.

33. *Oneida Circular*, X (December 8, 1873), 398.

34. *Ibid.*

35. *Oneida Circular*, XIII (February 3, 1876), 36.

36. *The Principles of Social Freedom* [delivered November 20, 1871], New York, 1874, 23.

37. Elizabeth Cady Stanton in the *Newark Call*, quoted by Emanie Sachs, *The Terrible Siren*, New York, 1928, 235.

38. Quoted by Austin Kent, *Mrs. Victoria C. Woodhull and her "Social Freedom,"* Clinton, Mass., 1873, 13.

39. *Woodhull and Claflin's Weekly* (November 2, 1872), 11.

40. *Tried As By Fire*, New York, 1874, 5, 24.

41. *Ibid.*, 5.

42. "Sinful Saints and Sensual Shepherds," *Truth Seeker Tracts*, Vol. V [No. 124], New York, n.d.

43. For the passage, and some account of the prosecution, see Parker Pillsbury, *"Cupid's Yokes" and The Holy Scriptures Contrasted*, Boston, 1878, 4.

44. Anon., "The Sexual Question," *Modern Thinker*, I (1870), 93, 95.

45. Dr. *Foote's New Plain Home Talk*, 1016.

46. *Sexual Physiology*, New York, 1866, 210–213.

47. See Dr. *Foote's New Plain Home Talk*, 1143, and Norman E. Himes, *Medical History of Contraception*, Baltimore, 1836, 279.

48. *New Plain Home Talk*, 1130–1134; Trall, 245.

49. *Esoteric Anthropology*, New York, 1853, 172, 174.

50. *Esoteric Anthropology*, rev. edn., London, 1873, 113–115.

51. John M. Scudder, *On the Reproductive Organs and the Venereal*, Cincinnati, 1874, 48; Foote, 1134.

52. *The Sexual Organism and its Healthful Management*, Boston, 1862, 256, 258.

53. See Robertson, 72.

54. *Diana: A Psycho-fyziological Essay on Sexual Relations, for Married Men and Women*, New York, 1882, 48–49.

55. *Diana*, 18.

56. E. B. Foote, *Physiological Marriage: An Essay Designed to Set People Thinking*, New York, 1885 [c. 1875], 9–13.

57. *New Plain Home Talk*, 1127–1128.

58. Several opinions are cited in John S. and Robin M. Haller, *The Physician and Sexuality in Victorian America*, Urbana, Ill., 1974, 113.

59. *New Plain Home Talk*, 1141–1142.

60. These views were printed in the second edition of *Diana*.

61. *Vital Force and Magnetic Exchange*, Knoxville, Tenn., 1888, 27.

62. *Ibid.*, p. 25.

63. *Vital Force*, 2d ed., Knoxville, Tenn., 1897, 84–85.

64. *Ibid.*

65. *Vital Force*, 1897, 86.

66. *Karezza: Ethics of Marriage*, Chicago, 1896, 133–135.

67. *Karezza*, 27–28, 36, 82–83.

68. See Joseph H. Greer's garbled account of Zugassent's Discovery in *Woman Know Thyself*, Chicago, 1902, 188–191.

69. See George E. Macdonald, *Fifty Years of Freethought*, 2 vols., New York, 1929, I, 208.

70. Ida C[raddock], *Heavenly Bridegrooms*, ed. Theodore Schroeder, New York, 1918, 121.

71. *Heavenly Bridegrooms*, 3.

72. *Heavenly Bridegrooms*, 3–4.

73. *Right Marital Living*, Chicago, 1899, 20–21.

74. *Heavenly Bridegrooms*, 121.

75. See Herbert W. Schneider and George Lawton, *A Prophet and a Pilgrim*, New York, 1942, 415.

76. *Right Marital Living*, 36.

77. *The New York Times* (October 18, 1902), 2.
78. Macdonald, II, 211.
79. Macdonald, II, 218.
80. *Times, ibid.*
81. *Ibid.*; Macdonald, II, 218.
82. Quoted in Heywood Broun and Margaret Leech, *Anthony Comstock: Roundsman of the Lord*, London, 1928, 231.
83. *Alkaloidal Clinic*, VI (1899), 649–650.

I

Love, Marriage, and Divorce

Love vs. Marriage

Marx Edgeworth Lazarus

Marx Edgeworth Lazarus, M.D., was a wealthy young Jewish intellectual originally from the border states. "He has black hair, doves' eyes of the brightest jet, and is an inveterate mystic," said one of his admirers, Mary S. Gove Nichols (said to have been "squint-eyed" herself). "Propriety, social etiquette, and reputation were meaningless words to him. He lived iin a world of Thought and Dreams, and prophecies based upon his Thought—a world of harmony, where freedom should take the place of bonds. . . ." Dr. Lazarus was generous beyond measure with his prophecies. Centered in New York City during the 1840s, he was a steady contributor to radical journals both there and elsewhere—he furnished fifty-two articles to the Brook Farm Harbinger *alone— and in 1851 and 1852, with a remarkable burst of mystical energy, he published eight books, with titles like* The Human Trinity, Comparative Psychology and Universal Analogy, *and* Passional Hygiene and Natural Medicine. *A friend of reform in every guise, he was a frequent visitor at the Fourierist utopias of Brook Farm and the North American Phalanx. Much of his writing was propaganda for the cause of "association." Fourierist terms—"isolated household," "combined order," "passional affinity," "attractive industry," and so on—abound in the following selection from his most notorious work,* Love vs. Marriage.

The central argument of the book is the one that came to dominate the free love movement, and that was frequently to be heard among both communitists and feminists for several decades—that marriage as a legal institution was in many, perhaps most, cases, nothing more than sanctioned slavery and prostitution. It was this negative argument, rather than the positive one in favor of a multiplicity of loves, that was easiest to maintain, for the abuses of the marital institution were easy to display, and the call for liberalized divorce laws a comfortable compromise between love and marriage. Lazarus goes further, for he argues that marriage "as it is now generally understood, is totally incompatible with social harmony, and must be excluded from any successful phalansterian [i.e., Fourierist] institution." His position is that multiple loves are natural and desirable. "Every marriage, if virtually fulfilled, robs the two individuals who submit to it of their chances of passional affinity in love relations with a great number of others; thus rendering the equilibrium and full harmony of their lives in this line of development impossible."

Such was the theory, and as could be expected, it produced a good deal of fury, genuine and assumed, in the newspapers that were willing to notice the book at all. But Lazarus had carefully limited his announced intentions to theory and not to practice: "my object is not to excite isolated individuals to rebel against the law of the land and public opinion, but to modify public opinion itself, and urge to the enaction of more liberal statutes, granting divorce freely wherever the party desiring it renounces all claim upon the property of the other party, and can satisfy the court that children born of the woman are provided for decently." Nor was Lazarus merely protecting himself with insincere disclaimers. Shortly after the publication of his book, he himself was married, and thus became the target not only of barbs from the conservative press, but also of arrows from the free love camp (see "Marriage— Defining Positions" in section III below).

Always an individualist, in his later years Lazarus contributed to

Benjamin Tucker's anarchist journal Liberty, *arguing for agrarian values and communitarian self-sufficiency. He lived on a small farm in Guntersville, Alabama, far from the radical vortex of New York that he helped keep whirling in his youth.*

Marx Edgeworth Lazarus
Love vs. Marriage

Marriage is an institution rendered compulsory on both sexes by the loss of caste consequent on free unions, and the absence of provision for the nurture of children.

Marriage converts lovers into owners of personal property, and often renders the most charming love relations at last indifferent or odious by the meannesses, monotony, and exclusiveness of the isolated household, and the arbitrary connection or collision of a thousand impertinences of fortune, interest, domestic cares, and individual tastes and pursuits with the natural tie of love. How perfectly absurd, besides, to dispose irrevocably of our whole future and its opportunities in one hour or one phase of feeling, which, even when it has fed on expectation for months or years, has never completed itself—never ripened from the phase of desire into that of attainment, or triumphantly passed the supreme test of true love, the possession of its object.

As the tree is known only by its fruits, so the quality of a passion is tested only when it has passed to its natural ultimate and fulfilled itself. In ambition it is well known that honors change morals, and that power often makes tyrants of those who had conducted themselves with greatest amenity when they had an object to gain by it.

Not less does this obtain in love, and men are surprised at themselves to find how much the fascination of love before marriage was due to the love of conquest—to the ambition of triumph. Not before full possession either, can we know how far our ideal of the person beloved has been projected from ourselves, and how far it is a true result of mutual affinity which grows and ripens

---

● Selection from Marx Edgeworth Lazarus, *Love vs. Marriage*, New York: Fowler and Wells, 1852, pp. 102–11, 119–22.

upon its legitimate satisfactions, and confirms, in the incarnation
of passion, those delicious presentiments which thus approve themselves true prophets.

Why force two young persons, in whose favor "the gods have
intervened," as Plato expresses it, as a condition of enjoying their
happiness, to bind themselves mutually to exclude all future "intervention of the gods"—to swear that they will always love and be
sufficient to each other, as they now are, or fancy themselves, and
at the very time when they are about to be placed in the most
stupid of circumstances—those of the isolated family household.
Truly it has been said that "Marriage is the tomb of love," and
most have found it thus, so that the best-assorted unions generally
come in the end to be but familiar friendships, alliances of domestic
interests, and intrigues with parental affections and anxieties. The
grace with which men and women resign their respective liberties
to these compensations comes cheap, since they have really nothing
to resign, society and the law permitting no development to the
passion of love in any other condition than marriage. I say no
development, for the horrors and disgusts of prostitution, or the
dishonorable condition of kept mistresses, is not worthy to be
called a development of the passion of love.

Natures the most gracious and spontaneous, in the limited
freedom of relations they have enjoyed before marriage, become
as sour as verjuice, and thorny termagants, by the harrassing
routine of domestic trifles; the voice becomes sharp and shrill,
unerring indication of the sacrifice of the internal to the external
life; and the finest souls suffer most, because they become most
denaturalized, and find it most impossible to take an interest in
the narrow routine of an isolated family, where there is nothing
noble and graceful in the common details of work, no spirituali-
zation of labor or of enjoyment. Artistic precision, importance, and
interest are developed in all these details only as soon as they are
managed in mass or on the large scale. Then machines intervene
to save manual drudgeries, then order and regular system become
indispensable, then a social charm may be added by the reunion
of numbers in each function, and the tone of friendly criticism
among peers replaces the harsh voice of personal despotism. The
kitchen of the combined order is a charming suite of rooms, each
adapted to a special department of culinary art, and the chosen
sphere where an assembly of artists eagerly meet to prosecute their
favorite functions for the profit and pleasure of eighteen hundred

associates. How different from the dirt, the confusion, the compli-
cation of functions on one poor ignorant drudge, who prepares
the vulgar minimum of satisfactions for the stomachs of the civilized
family!

The beautiful or wealthy unmarried woman is the centre of
a thousand delicate attentions. She moves like a queen through
the galaxy of her adorers; costly presents, flowers, tickets to balls,
parties, and places of amusement, shower upon her. It is related
of the ancient goddesses, that flowers sprang up beneath their foot-
prints; but pleasures, of which flowers are only the emblems, spring
before the coming of our belles; each smile can make a lover happy,
each frown can wither hope. A charming girl, who can preserve
her freedom, and "oft reject, yet never once offend," reigns the
passional queen of the society in which she moves. God delegates
to her His prescriptive right of impressing attraction. Her will
becomes instantly a law, which it is a delight and a privilege to
obey; and if she is a woman of large heart and mind, who can thus
invest with fascination the consecutive movements of a life purpose,
reserving to herself the intellectual clew which connects the acts
prompted by her, and throwing over all the graceful veil of airy
caprice, she can most powerfully impel and control for good the
progressive destinies of a man, of many men, of a society, a town, a
nation, according to her sphere. The supremacy of the spiritual and
intellectual nature, and the power of a permanent volition, make a
sine qua non for a character of this stamp. But let the queen, the
belle, the goddess marry: one grand flare-up in the first week of
festivities, during which "*stat nominis umbra*," and her power
and glory have departed. Unless sustained by great wealth, by rare
talents for intrigue, or by some peculiar combination of circumstances, she sinks at once into the housekeeper and the nurse. But,
doubtless, what is lost in extent of influence and in the homage of
numbers, is gained in intensity, in a more perfect sympathy with
the man she has chosen, in the charms of maternity, in the
independence of her separate establishment; and, "servant to a
wooden cradle, living in a baby's life," would she listen to the
thought of returning to her former position? No! for the substantial
reason that she has irrevocably forfeited it.

She has entered another circle of influences, to get out of which
she must be torn to pieces. Separation or divorce ruin her relation
with the lover she has married, and still, perhaps, would prefer
as a lover, loving him, though she does not love marriage and the

isolated household, with their manifold invasions of her personal liberty. Besides, man's power over woman augments with the habitual surrender of her person to him, even though the charm be flown which first won this favor.

The law and the magnetism of social custom sustain his power. If all these obstacles to a return were surmounted, she would be stigmatized, avoided, and come under the moral ban of the society over which she reigned before she renounced her liberty. But how is it with the compensations at home? Her husband, if at first an impassioned lover, has, in nine cases out of ten at least, grown careless of pleasing from the security of possession. The same fatality acts on herself, hence a mutual disenchantment and diminution of love in geometrical progression. They have now no rivals to fear, no rejections or passional diversions to prevent; they naturally relax in their ardor. They have now come, as the phrase is, into matters of fact, which is equivalent to a torpid, unimpassioned existence. Though this were otherwise, yet, with the best good-will in the world, the laws of physiology, phrenology, temperament, and passion, refuse their most celestial gifts to the monotony of fixed possession. The brilliant intellect refuses to unlock its stores of knowledge, wit, genius, and taste, to its familiar bed and table companion. Men talk to every one except their wives; they already feel as if they knew each other so well that conversation was superfluous, besides, a kiss is so much easier. Soon these also become scarce in the satiety of possession. Thus the tendency of marriage is constantly downward, from the spiritual into the animal life. Let a woman explore and exploit well her lover's brilliant side while he is still her lover, for she will find the husband a sober friend, at best. That charm which links earth with heaven, the finite with the infinite, will evaporate. It is love alone, in his untrammeled liberty, that can inclose the spirit of nature in the form of the adored. Our stupid laws and social conventions do but represent the inertia of matter. How should they imprison the celestial? It comes unbidden with the innocence of a babe, and clasps in holiest union those who ask no other sacrament than itself. . . .

What is the fatal consequence of this loss of the liberty, attentions, and interest, which the bride enjoyed as a maiden, the consequence, of the monotone of married life on her temper and power of charming? It is in vain that one reasons on matters like this, in vain to be convinced of what duty and expediency alike point to. In passional affairs, we come into quite a different sphere; we are here, the wise and the foolish alike, mere creatures of affinities and antipathies, and move as we are moved by springs of action given from above, and relating us to others by a magic, whose mystery we could never spell. The same person, most pleasing and brilliant in one sphere or set of relations, is perfectly stupid and unhappy in another.

Does the most romantic and celestial passion that ever descended on this earth qualify the lovers any better for keeping house together? Does it inspire the man with a livelier talent for lying and cheating in commerce, or the woman with the spontaneous attraction and faculties for baking and brewing, and roasting and stewing, for mending and darning, and washing and scouring? Will it make a manager or directress of one without executive faculties?

No, indeed. I have seen these love matches in the West, where no servants could be procured, where, if the husband had not chanced by peculiar experiences to be somewhat of a factotum, it would have been a fix in more than one sense, for the wife did not know a soup-kettle from a frying-pan, and was not only ignorant, but incapable by character for any sort of domestic duties.

The alliance of love with the civilized housekeeping generally reminds me of Titania, queen of the fairies, enamored of a donkey, and with her arm thrown around the asinine neck of Nick Bottom the joiner, in Shakespeare's Midsummer Night's Dream. Far be it from me to disparage the necessary functions of domestic economy, they may all be rendered as beautiful and attractive as they are necessary. I speak of them only as conducted in the false method of the isolated household, and I recognize that even here there are sometimes found housewives by character and education, who introduce order and beauty wherever they move. Fortunately for the higher destinies of our race, these characters are rare; they would make men too well contented with the present imperfection.

* * *

As soon as a girl marries, she is placed under a sort of ban in most parts of this country, neglected by her former companions, and excluded from their festivities. I have seen a young wife weep with anger and vexation at this conduct. But it is just that any one should be so treated on becoming a representative of false principles and social positions, and it happens instinctively, as an organic fact, for these young, relentless excommunicators hold marriage to be morally right, and expect to be married themselves. They feel, however, if they do not know, that marriage is a compound selfishness, an *égoisme à deux,* and that the parties contracting it have virtually asserted their independence of society, and embezzled each other in perpetual monopoly from the passional public. They are thus in a spiritual court of justice condemned as swindlers and misers, and excommunicated from the sphere of prospective passional relations.

Independence and the charms of maternity are both illusions in more than seven-eighths of civilized marriages. To have a house of one's own to keep, or even superintend, is a systematic slavery, an immolation of one's personal predilections and pursuits on the altar of the family and domestic comfort. It may pass among the virtues of negative Christianity or crucifixion, but not to be desired for its own sake. The charms of maternity are cut down by the anxieties, bad adaptations, and accidents of the isolated household, to a bare minimum, still oftener turned into tortures, and all the force of a mother's devotion is necessary to bring the child through the painful crises, and filthy experiences of an infancy more protracted, inferior, and helpless than that of any other animal. Who dares to talk of the charms of maternity in civilization, in the face of statistics which prove that one half of all children die under the fifth year, while the rest are ailing, on an average, near half the time, and the whole family together scarcely ever well.

People have a very illogical habit, and one that hinders real progress more than any other, of audaciously optimising those real *evils* which their stupidity supposes to be inevitably ingrained in the nature of things, and dressing them up to look like harmonics and blessings, thus substituting their notions of how things ought to be, for the plain matter-of-fact.

Nothing can be truer than that woman, and man also, ought to possess in their amatory relations each others' tenderest and most concentrated affection, their independence or spontaneity of movement secured, and the charms of paternity and maternity in their most exalted degree; but it is equally true that exclusive marriage vows and the order of the isolated household never have secured these blessings, and never can secure them, save in the smallest exception. It is equally true that these blessings are incompatible with every sort of love relation, and every mode of living *known to civilization, barbarism, patriarchalism, or savagism.* These, like all other aspirations of the soul for harmony, belong to a higher order of society. They belong to an order of associated interests in all the branches of domestic, agricultural, and other industrial management, where the well-ordered concurrence of numbers can form those distributions of labor which first emancipate the individual from the tyranny of a too narrow and too complicated sphere, and restore his spontaneity every where.

Here the *industrial independence* of woman will emancipate her from the *necessity* of attaching her life and fortunes to any man. Both sexes will be free, from puberty, without any sordid calculations of interest, to confess and to yield themselves to the rights and charms of passional affinity, amid the consecrations of religion and of home affections, guarded by all the decencies of social refinement, and in no wise compromising their future freedom of action. Has it been but a passing illusion of the senses, surrendering the soul to the fascination of beauty and of vigor? The relation will be the more transient, as higher spiritual affinities assert themselves on either side. But it will have been true in its hour—it will have made a season's happiness, and another season will be all the richer for its experience and memory. Instinct makes no blunders. The bad effects of ill-assorted marriages are due solely to the compression and repression of instinct by the civilized sphere and its infernal moralities, afterward to the indecencies and impertinences of the present household and bed quarters, and to the compulsory union of the parties after the natural period of their separation has arrived.

Woman will never be free, save in the large home, the varied and attractive industry of the Phalanx, where she has her choice of all the departments of domestic, mechanical, and agricultural labors and arts, and can move in thirty groups of friends and of labors in the course of the same month. There the real charms of maternity will be enjoyed, because there, in the unitary nurseries and miniature workshops, children can be safely and happily provided for, either in the presence or absence of the mother; and the children mutually amuse each other, without requiring, each of them, the continued attention of one or more adults.

•   •   •

Marriage knows nothing of all this, and rudely scrawls over it undivine and abominable lines of figures of household expenses, rents, butchers' bills, furniture, cooking, washing, mending, scrubbing, and a volume of daily, weekly, monthly, and yearly duties and responsibilities, moral and pecuniary, which enslave the husband to his routine of lying and cheating behind a counter, or monotonous toil at the plough or mechanic's bench, in order to keep the wife equally enslaved in her domestic functions.

Gladly would the persons in question spare each other this slavery, but they cannot. It is organic in the marriage and household institution. It has no cure save in the free choice and varied movement of the passional series in the home of humanity, the phalanx.

It is not true, however, that the wedded parties do often frankly desire each other's liberty. The candor and celestial disinterestedness of their love soon becomes polluted by the false relation in which they are placed. In proportion as they feel themselves excluded from other social and passional interests and diversions by the prejudice of morality, by the fear of giving pain to each other, or by the cool reception which persons, especially women no longer disposable, are apt to meet with in the circles of the young, each is driven back to claim a more and more exclusive possession of the other, until the pretext of fondness has thoroughly organized a masked tyranny, and divides with indispensable business every hour of its victim. If yet this held any ratio with the charms of the tyrant; but on the contrary, it is precisely those women who have least in themselves that require most of their husbands. A woman or a man, with a life purpose, earnestness, spirituality, intelligence, and a decided vocation, suffices much to himself or herself, but the poor creatures who are weak and empty, sick and miserable, always want somebody to lean on and complain to; always need the catalytic excitement of another's presence to keep them from sinking. It is these who make the heaviest drains on the life of their friends. I have known some who, despite the spiritual prostration of a civilized boarding-school education and protracted family tyranny, were bravely recovering themselves, had opened veins of divinity in their character, and had commenced a career of noble uses, when the fatality of marriage has ruined all, torn them from the sphere where they were taking root, undermined their self-reliance, and plunged them in uncongenial relations, where, always feeble and unhappy, they cling spasmodically to the maturer being to whom they have given themselves. In such unions, which are not rare, there was love, there was true adaptation in the character of the parties, but the essential falsehood of marriage causes the stronger nature to crush the weaker instead of assisting it to develop its powers. Lesion of spontaneity, or individuality for one person, necessarily compromises the interest, whether material or spiritual, of all within their circle of relations. It is like the crumbling of a stone in an arch.

A society of weak, amiable, accommodating people, whose idea of practical truth lies in conventional morality, civilized saints, who have ceased to do evil without having learned to do well, is nauseating to both gods and men. Yet what other logical and legitimate result than this can spring from marriage and the isolated family, mutual, compound, and bicomposite slavery, in whose little hen-coop of relations no one can take a step without treading on another's toes.

Let me not here, however, seem to say that woman alone is found in this position of spiritual degradation. It is true that she is more thoroughly and systematically victimized by education and custom from her childhood, and has fewer chances than man for health, vigor, and independence, either physical or mental; but I have observed the loveliest beings, of a nature remarkably self-poised, and superior in its spiritual powers, become the victims of puppies, whose sense of their wife's superiority only intensified the tyranny of a narrow and jealous exclusiveness.

Living in a realm of poetry, and ministered to by sweet, bright spirits, they become aware how different the gentle stream of their existence from the world's foul torrent. Yet, finding themselves placed in this world by the distributions of an inscrutable power, and desiring, above all things, to do their duty, their spiritual discretion, and the instinct which says, *"Odi profanum vulgus et arceo,"* are liable to be overruled by the boisterous pretensions of communism, when obstinately sustained; they rarely suspect what is vile in the men who place themselves as the representatives of the matter-of-fact world. They are betrayed by the appeal to that sentiment of devotion which sacrifices oneself to another's happiness.

The phenomena of subjective reflection, by which we invest

other beings with our own qualities, and conceal, by our own shadow, their bristling and unlovely forms, is common to all who bear a charmed world within them.

They marry, and the civilizees who grab them, as a pig might run off with a coronet of diamonds, well conscious of the lack of any spiritual title valid in the court of love to the treasure they have stolen, enforce on the body what they cannot possess of the soul.

It is in vain that the poor girls retreat into their dream-world— into the sanctuaries of their inner life. They are slaves; the soil is upon them, and the law has irrevocably fastened them in the clutch of a yahoo, of a civilizee, whose character now reveals itself.

I shall not forget how sadly a lovely woman once said to me— "I wish there were no marriage."

STEPHEN PEARL ANDREWS.

Love, Marriage, and Divorce

Henry James Sr., Horace Greeley, and Stephen Pearl Andrews

Almost immediately upon publication of Marx Edgeworth Lazarus' scandalous Love vs. Marriage, *it was reviewed, rather unfavorably, in the* New York Tribune, *Horace Greeley's radical newspaper. The reviewer was Henry James Sr., another prominent though rather eccentric Fourierist, who like Lazarus happened to write for the Brook Farm* Harbinger *(he published thirty-two aricles to Lazarus' fifty-two—the rest of the score: Greeley two, Andrews one), and who was, as Andrews characterized him, one of "the school of seers and prophets . . . a mere jet d'eau of aspiration, reaching a higher elevation at some points than almost any other man, but breaking into spray and impalpable mist, glittering in the sun, and descending to earth with no weight or mechanical force to effect any great end." Vaporous as some might think James, his review managed to draw the hostile attention of the Presbyterian* New York Observer, *which published a disagreeable attack on him as a defender of free love doctrines if not free love itself. James asked the* Tribune *for space to reply, after the* Observer *refused to print his answer, and thus began a controversy that delighted local newspaper readers for several months. After James' reply, not only did the* Observer *take a few more pot-shots, but the* Tribune *itself began to publish counterpositions on the question. First Stephen Pearl Andrews, a New York radical, currently just finishing up a two-year stint editing a phonographic newspaper* (The Phonetic Propagandist), *wrote a protest from the Modern Times free love community out on Long Island. Then editor Greeley jumped in with his own opinions, and James replied to both. The final go-round took place outside the columns of the* Tribune *however, for Greeley refused to print Andrews' rejoinders. Andrews had hoped for "a continuous year of discussion, through such a medium as the 'Tribune,' in conflict with the first minds in the country,— philosophers, politicians, and theologians, invited or provoked into the fray." He had to settle for less, but eager for any forum at all, he collected the letters of the controversy, adding a long introduction and his final word, and published them in a book.*

Of the three, Greeley's position was the most traditional and conservative, James' a middle ground advocating at most a liberalized divorce law, and Andrews' the closest to Lazarus' open advocacy of free love. As editor of the reforming Tribune, *which he had started from scratch a decade earlier, Greeley had a vested interest in radical movements. He had become a Fourierist and opened his columns to a regular feature by Albert Brisbane, the American apostle of Fourier's brand of socialism. But he drew the line on the question of sex, and although he pretended sympathy with women's rights, there was suspicion that even that degree of innovation in sexual relations upset him. "He was crude as self-educated men always are," said Elizabeth Oakes Smith, who wrote for him (see the selection following this one). "He had no just conception of what others had said and done in the world, and ideas new to him, which certainly were original to him, not borrowed, he failed to see were only a part of the common stock of human ideas, when he thought them new to the world, and sometimes uttered only platitudes; who does not?" Andrews went further: ". . . a large portion of the public believe him dishonest. This last, I think, a mistake. Mr. Greeley is a bigot, and bigotry is generally honest." In any case, Greeley's stand was for love and marriage, period. The reason he gave Andrews for closing off debate in the* Tribune *was that he could not "permit his paper to be made the organ of repeatedly announcing and defending doctrines so destructive to the public well-being, and especially that he cannot tolerate the reiterated assumption that fornication, adultery, etc., are no crimes."* Henry James Sr., *father of the novelist and the philosopher, was an earnest and independent thinker. Strongly influenced by both Swedenborg and Fourier, he could never be mistaken for a doctrinaire of either camp. He read everything, knew everyone, and borrowed freely; yet his cast of mind transformed everything he wrote, and stamped it "James." Thus is was that a few years earlier, when he had anonymously translated and written a brief preface for a Fourierist tract called* Love in the Phalanstery, *everyone knew it was James. At that time he had maintained, "The present law of sexual relations clearly demands revision." Much in the free love style, he charged that the marriage statutes encouraged rather than prevented "promiscuous intercourse": "Promiscuity in this application denotes the intercourse which takes place between man and woman, unsanctioned by any ties of the heart, or by the reciprocal personal preference of the parties." Especially in the context of the rest of the book, which outlined the full Fourierist panoply of sexual attachments, some quite "free" (see section V below), James sounded much like Lazarus himself. But in fact his position, at least by 1852, was merely in favor of freer divorce laws, not freer sexuality.*

If willing to rescue unhappily married couples from their legal bonds, then what, asked both Horace Greeley and Stephen Pearl Andrews, did James think was the use of the marriage vows in the first place? Greeley opposed all divorce, Andrews all marriage. Andrews was perhaps the most philosophical of the debaters, though all three raced to the higher implications of their question, the nature of the social bonds, the individual's obligations to the State. As an "Individual Sovereign" of the anarchist community of Modern Times, Andrews denied the State's right to interfere in marriage, divorce, or any other private transaction among free men and women. At Modern Times no one forced attentions on anyone else, nor withheld them, merely on the basis of legal rights and privileges. What this came to in practice is difficult to judge since "it was not polite" to inquire after private relations at the colony (see section V below). Andrews had a wife and three children, and no difficulties seem to have arisen in his family life. After the death of his first wife, he married again, apparently even more happily. The fact that he continued to live in Manhattan, only visiting the community he had helped to found, may be significant. Ultimately Andrews was a theoretical reformer, a promoter of utopian ideas, not a practitioner. Many of his schemes were a good deal more difficult to put into practice than free love. He had gone to England in the 1840s, to convince the British Anti-Slavery Society to buy all the Negroes in Texas and abolish slavery there; he came back with Isaac Pitman's shorthand, a method, among other things, of teaching slaves to read in a month! He also discovered "the symbolism of the primitive characters of the Chinese system of writing" and invented his own universal language, Alwato, as well as a science of the universe, Universology, a philosophy to go with it, Integralism, and a new sociology, Pantarchism, to supersede the "Individual Sovereignty" he had learned from Josiah Warren at Modern Times. Through all this, he managed to keep his feet solidly enough on the ground to edit a very popular weekly—the first in the United States to publish the Communist Manifesto—and to write rousing speeches (see section IV) for Victoria Woodhull, the first woman to run for president.

Henry James Sr.
Stephen Pearl Andrews
Horace Greeley
Love, Marriage, and Divorce

Reply of Mr. James to the New York Observer

To the Editor of the New York Tribune:
Please allow me the hospitality of your paper to right myself with the New York "Observer," and so add to the many obligations I already owe you.
Yours truly, H. James.
November 15.
New York, Saturday, Nov. 13, 1852.
To the Editor of the New York Observer:
An article in your paper of today does me so much injustice that I cannot afford to let it pass unnoticed.

● Selections from *Love, Marriage, and Divorce*, Boston: Benjamin R. Tucker, 1889, pp. 24–37, 41–44, 47–49, 56–58, 61–62.

The drift of your assault is to charge me with hostility to the marriage institution. This charge is so far from being true that I have invariably aimed to advance the honor of marriage by seeking to free it from certain purely arbitrary and conventional obstructions in reference to divorce. For example, I have always argued against Mr. Greeley that it was not essential to the honor of marriage that two persons should be compelled to live together when they held the reciprocal relation of dog and cat, and that in that state of things divorce might profitably intervene, provided the parties guaranteed the State against the charge of their offspring. I have very earnestly, and, as it appears to me, very unanswerably, contended for a greater freedom of divorce on these grounds, in the columns of the "Tribune," some years since; but I had no idea that I was thus weakening the respect of marriage. I seemed to myself to be plainly strengthening it, by removing purely arbitrary and damaging obstructions. The existing difficulty of divorce is one of those obstructions. You will not pretend to say that the legislative sanction of divorce *now* existing discharges the marriage rite of respect? How, then, shall any enlargement of that sanction which I propose avail to do so? Is it possible that a person exposed to the civilizing influences of a large city like this so long as you have been should see no other security for the faithful union of husband and wife than that which dates from the police office? I can not believe it. You *must* know many married partners, if you have been even ordinarily fortunate in your company, who, if the marriage institution were formally abolished tomorrow, would instantly annul that legal abolition again by the unswerving constancy of their hearts and lives.

No man has a more cordial, nor, as I conceive, a more enlightened respect for marriage than I have, whether it be regarded, 1st, as a beautiful and very perfect symbol of religious or metaphysic truth, or, 2nd, as an independent social institution. I have fully shown its claim for respect on both these grounds in a number of the "Tribune" which you quoted at the time, but which it serves your dishonest instincts now to overlook. You probably are indifferent to the subject in its higher and primary point of view, but your present article proves that you have some regard for it in its social aspects. If you regard marriage, then, as a social institution, you will, of course, allow that its value depends altogether upon the uses it promotes. If these uses are salutary, the institution is honorable. If, on the contrary, they are mischievous, the institution is deplorable.

Now, no one charges that the legitimate uses of the marriage institution are otherwise than good. But a social institution, whose uses are intrinsically good, may be very *badly administered,* and *so* produce mischief. This, I allege, is the case with the marriage institution. It is not administered livingly, or with reference to the present need of society, but only traditionally, or with reference to some wholly past state of society. In a disorderly condition of society, like that from which we have for the last two centuries been slowly emerging, men of wealth and power, men of violence and intrigue, would have laughed at the sacredest affections, and rendered the family security nugatory, had not society fortified marriage by the most stringent safeguards. The still glaring inequality of the sexes, moreover, would have led kings and nobles into the most unrebuked licentiousness, and consequently into the most brutal contempt for women, had not the political-ecclesiastical régime almost utterly inhibited divorce. The elevation of woman in Christendom had thus been owing exclusively to a very rigid administration of the marriage institution in the earlier periods of our social history. But what man of wealth and power, what man of violence and intrigue, is there now to take away a man's wife from him? No doubt there is a very enormous clandestine violation of the marriage bond at the present time; careful observers do not hestitate to say an almost unequalled violation of it; but that is an evil which no positive legislation can prevent, because it is *manifestly based upon a popular contempt for the present indolent and vicious administration of the law.* The only possible chance for correcting it depends, as I have uniformly insisted, upon a change in that administration,—that is to say, upon freely legitimating divorce, within the limits of a complete guarantee to society against the support of offspring; because in that case you place the inducement to mutual fidelity no longer in the base legal bondage of the parties merely, but in their reciprocal inward sweetness or humanity. And this is an appeal which, when frankly and generously made, no man or woman will ever prove recreant to.

Again, in the "Tribune" article of last summer which you quote (or, rather, shamelessly misquote) it seemed to me the while that I was saying as good a word for marriage as had ever been said beneath the stars. I was writing, to be sure, upon a larger topic, and alluded to marriage only by way of illustration. But what I said about it then seems to me still completely true. And, true or untrue, why do you not cite me before your readers honestly? You allow

your printer to turn the first quotation you make into sheer
nonsense, and you so bedevil the second with ostentatious and
minatory italics that a heedless reader will look upon the imbecile
tumefaction as so much solid argument, and infer that any one who
can provoke that amount of purely typographic malediction from a
pious editor must needs be closely affiliated—you know where.

Now, as a matter of speculation merely, why should you desire to
prejudice me before the community? I am a humble individual,
without any influence to commend my ideas to public acceptance,
apart from their intrinsic truth. And if, as you allege, my desire and
aim be to destroy the marriage institution, I am at least not so
foolish as to attempt that labor by a mere exhibtion of will. I must
have adduced some colorable reasons for its destruction. Will you be
good enough to tell me where I have exhibited these reasons? Or,
failing to do so, will you be good enough to confess yourself a
defeated trickster, unworthy the companionship of honest men ?

Doubtless, Mr. Editor, you address an easy, good-natured
audience, who do not care to scan too nicely the stagnant slipslop
which your weekly ladle deals out to them. But the large public
perfectly appreciates your flimsy zeal for righteousness. Every reasonable man knows that, if I assail a cherished institution without the
exhibition of valid reasons, I alone must prove the sufferer, and that
immediately. Every such person therefore suspects, when a pious
editor goes out of his way to insult me for this imputed offence, that
his apparent motive is only a mask to some more real and covert
one. And this suspicion would be palpably just in the present
instance. You are by no means concerned about any hostility, real or
imaginary, which I or any other person may exhibit toward the
marriage institution. I do you the justice, on the contrary, to believe
that you would only be too happy to find me and all your other
fancied enemies "bringing up"—to use your own choice expression—
"against the seventh commandment." But my benevolence, at least,
is quite too weak to afford you that gratification. Naturalists tell us
that the sepia, or cuttle-fish, when pursued, is in the habit "of eject-
ing an inky fluid, which colors the adjacent waters so deeply as to
afford it an easy means of escape." Now, science, in revealing to us
the splendid analogies of nature, teaches us that the sepia, or cuttle-
fish, of these watery latitudes is only an oblique or imperfect form of
the tricky sectarian editor of higher ones: even as that tricky editor
is himself only an oblique or imperfect prophecy of the integral

MAN of still higher latitudes. Accordingly, if we take the trouble to
explore the inky and deceptive puddle you have trajected in our
path, we shall find that the origin of your ill-will lies very much
behind that. We shall find that it lies altogether in the criticism
which I have occasionally brought to bear upon that fossil and
fatiguing Christianity, of which the "Observer" is so afflictive a type,
and its editor so distinguished and disinterested a martyr. Indulge
me with a few lines upon this topic. . . .

Hinc illae lachrymae! This is the open source of your tribulation,
the palpable spring of your ineffectual venom. With the instinct
unhappily of self-preservation, you perceive that, if our social relations once become orderly, not by constraint, but of an inherent and
divine necessity, there will be a speedy end to the empire of cant and
false pretension. For if a living piety once invade the human mind, a
piety attuned to the ministries of science, a piety which celebrates
God no longer as the mere traditional source of lapsed and contingent felicities, but as the present and palpable doer of divinest
deeds,—such as feeding the starving hordes of the earth's population,
clothing the naked, enlightening the ignorant, comforting the
dejected, breaking the yoke of every oppression, cleansing the diseased conscience, banishing want, and sickness, and envy, and diffusing universal plenty, peace, and righteousness,—what, in Heaven's
name, will become of that vapid piety which now exhales only in the
form of selfish and mendicant supplication, or else of impudent
interference with the privacies of other people's souls?

I have not yet had the pleasure of reading any of Mrs. Smith's
publications, and can not, therefore, estimate your candor in associating her labors with mine. But inasmuch as I perceive from the
newspapers that that well-intentioned lady is engaged in a very
arduous crusade against the natural and obvious distinction of the
sexes, the which distinction I meanwhile set great store by, I presume
your good will in this instance to be as transparent as I have found
it in others, and thank you accordingly.

As to your attempt to insinuate a community of purpose or tendency between myself and that ramification of your own religious
body, known as the Oneida Perfectionists, I may safely leave it to the
scorn of those among your readers who can estimate the cowardice
which, in wanton disregard of a neighbor's good name, hints and
insinuates the calumny it dares not boldly mouth. These men, as I
learn from their own story, are ultra—that is to say, consistent—

Calvinists, who have found in the bosom of the doctrines you your-self profess the logical warrant of the practices which you neverthe-less condemn. From a conversation or two which I have had with some of their leading men, I judged them to be persons of great sincerity, but of deplorable fanaticism, who were driven to the lengths which you so sternly reprobate strictly because they exem-plify what you do not,—a logical abandonment to their own reli-gious convictions. I told them candidly that any man of common sense must give short shrift in his regard to a deity who elected men to the privilege of leading disorderly lives; but at the same time I saw that they were no way amenable to the tribunal of common sense. An unhappy religious fanaticism, the flowering of your own fundamental principles, has lifted them out of that wholesome judicature, and they must henceforth drift whithersoever the benignant powers—who, after all, are paramount in this world, spite of many "Observers"—will let them. But at the same time I must avow that these strenuous and unhandsome sectarists appeared to me far worthier of tender compassion than of brutal public vitu-peration. Honest, upright souls they seemed at bottom, though sadly misguided by an insane sense of duty, and delicate women were among them, too, full no doubt of woman's indestructible truth. They were fathers, and husbands, and brothers, like myself, disfigured, to be sure, by a morbid religious conscience, but no less capable of suffering on that account whatever I suffered. And so I could not help saying to myself how surely must errors like these involve this poor unprotected people in permanent popular disgrace, or what is worse, perhaps, provoke the fatal violence of a disgusting pharisaic mob; and how gladly, therefore, must good men of every name rather lessen than deepen the inevitable odium in which they stand! Accordingly it appears to me about as unmanly a sight as the sun now shines upon to see a great prosperous newspaper like the New York "Observer" gathering together the two wings of its hebdomadal flatulence, "secular" and "religious," for a doughty descent upon this starveling and harmless field-mouse!

And this reminds me, by the way, to adore the beautiful Nemesis—beautiful and dread!—which in every commotion of opinion infallibly drives you, and persons like you, into a significant clamor for the interests of the Seventh Commandment. Whence this special zeal, this supererogatory devotion to the interests of that institution? Have you, then, a fixed conviction that no man,

however refined by God's culture and the elevation of our present
social sentiment, could be exempted from police regulation without
instantly rushing into adultery? It would really seem so. But if that
be your state of mind, it only furnishes another striking proof
of the power which your friends the Socialists attribute to constraint
in enhancing and inflaming the normal appreciation of sensual
delights.

And here I drop my pen. I have used it freely to express the
indignation which every true man must feel at seeing an eminent
public station, like that of the editor of a religious newspaper,
perverted to the wanton defamation of private character and the
profligate obstruction of humane enterprise.

I am yours, etc., Henry James.

Queries To Mr. James, By Mr. Andrews

New York, Friday, Nov. 26, 1852.

To the Editor of the Tribune:

I have read with some interest a recent article in the "Tribune,"
by Henry James, in reply to an "assault" upon him, made by the
editor of the New York "Observer," on the Marriage Question.
Perhaps it would be discourteous to say that, in relation to the
issue of the conflict between these parties, I am quite indifferent.
My own opinions differ considerably from those avowed by either
of the contestants. My curiosity is piqued, however, by the positions
assumed by Mr. James, to see how he will maintain himself, and I
find myself given over to a sort of "hope-I-don't-intrude" propensity
to ask questions. Without venturing on polemics, I may perhaps be
allowed, as a third party, the Socratic privilege of propounding
difficulties and seeking for further information.

It was a saying of Daniel Webster that, "if a thing is to be done,
a wise man should be able to tell *how* it is to be done." Hence,
I cannot but hope that Mr. James may be able to remove some
of the darkness which obscures my perceptions of the tenability of
his positions. I confess that, comparing my recollections of his earlier
writings in the "Harbinger" and the "Tribune" upon the same
subject with the somewhat rampant and ferocious morality of a
recent article in the "Tribune," in review of the book of Dr.
Lazarus, called "Love vs. Marriage," which I attributed to his pen,
I said to myself, "My friend, Mr. James, is certainly coming up on

both sides of the same question." But I now stand corrected. This still more recent manifesto defines him with respect to his position, if the position itself proves susceptible of definition. He is a "cordial and enlightened respecter of marriage,"—a champion, indeed, of the institution of marriage,—but at the same time he is in favor of entire freedom of divorce, "provided only the parties guarantee the State against the charge of their offspring." He is surprised that an intelligent man should "see no other security for the faithful union of husband and wife than that which dates from the police office." "By freely legitimating divorce within the limits of a complete guarantee to society against the support of offspring," you do, according to him, "place the inducement to mutual fidelity no longer in the base legal bondage of the parties merely, but in their reciprocal inward sweetness of humanity."

In affirming all this, it seems to him the while that "he is saying as good a word for marriage as has ever been said beneath the stars." He indignantly repudiates all affiliation of his doctrines with the laxer kind of morality, or the systematic enlargement of marital privileges by certain religious sectarians, whom he scornfully pronounces destitute of common sense, for no better cause, so far as he enables us to discover, than that their views differ from his, and whom, he informs us, he, moved by the divine afflatus, lectured for their "disorderly lives." As Mr. James professes himself ready and apt to instruct the public, and desirous withal to forward "the good time coming" by reforming the abuses of the institution of marriage, I flatter myself that he cannot object to relieving a few doubts and honest difficulties which perplex my understanding of his doctrine upon the subject.

These doubts and difficulties are stated in the following list of queries:

1. What does Mr. J. understand to be the essential and determining element of marriage, the kernel or *sine qua non* of the marriage institution, *after* the complete removal of the characteristic feature of "legal bondage" or "outward force," by the repeal of all laws sanctioning and enforcing it, and after the feature of necessary perpetuity is removed by the entire freedom to end the relation by the will of the parties at any instant? Noah Webster informs us that *to marry* is to "join a man and woman *for life,* and constitute them man and wife according to the *laws and customs* of a nation." Now, any constraint from *custom* is as much an *outward force* as a constraint *by law,* and, in case both these species of

constraint are removed,—that is, if the man and woman are joined with no reference to either, but simply with regard to their mutual or individual choice and wishes, the union occurring not for life, but to be dissolved at the option of the parties,—both limbs of the definition are eliminated, reminding one of the oft-quoted expurgation of the tragedy of Hamlet. It seems to me, then, that I am quite in order to call for a new specification of the essentials of matrimony. But I am forgetting that Mr. J. still provides for the ghost of a legal tie, in the bond to be given as a guarantee to society against the support of offspring. This brings me to my second query.

2. Why—if the maintenance of the unswerving constancy of husband and wife can be safely intrusted to the guardianship of "their reciprocal inward sweetness or humanity," with no "base legal bondage" superadded—why may not the care and maintenance of offspring be, with equal safety, intrusted likewise to that same "inward sweetness or humanity," without the superaddition of a "base legal bondage" or "outward force"? If the first of these social relations may with safety not only, but with positive advantage, be discharged of accountability to the police office, why not the second? Why, indeed, be at the trouble and expense of maintaining a police office at all? Indeed, if I understand Mr. J. rightly, after imposing this limitation upon the absolute freedom of divorce, or, in other words, upon the extinction of legal marriage,—*ex gratia modestiae*, perhaps, lest the whole truth might not be fitting to be spoken openly,—he again dispenses with the limitation itself, and delivers the parental relation over to the same securities to which he has previously consigned the conjugal; for I find in a subsequent paragraph of the same article the following sentence: "It is obvious to every honest mind that, if our conjugal, *parental*, and *social ties generally* can be safely discharged of the purely *diabolic* element of *outward force*, they must instantly become transfigured by their own inward divine and irresistible loveliness." Here it is not marriage only, but the maintenance of offspring also, which is to be intrusted to the "inward sweetness or humanity" of the individuals to whom the relation appeals, which seems to me much the more consistent view of the matter, inasmuch as, if the principle is good for anything in one case, it is certainly equally applicable in the other. But here, again, we come back to the point I have made above,—the query whether marriage, discharged

of all law, custom, or necessary perpetuity, remains marriage at all?
and if so, what is the essential and characteristic element of such
marriage?—upon which point I crave further information.

3. If the inception and the dissolution of marriage is to be left
to the option of the parties on such grounds as are stated by Mr.
J., is the expansion or contraction of the relation also to be abandoned to the altogether private and individual judgment of the
same parties in logical deference to the same principle? That is to
say, if more than two parties are taken into the conjugal partnership,
is that degree of license to be tolerated likewise? or are we still to
retain a police office to provide against such cases? We are aware
that men have differed in theory and practice in divers ages and
nations,—between monogamy and polygamy, for example,—and
with all restraints, both of custom and of law, removed, possibly
they may differ in like manner again. What, then, is to happen
under the new *régime?* Who is to be the standard of proprieties? Is
Mr. James's definition of a "disorderly life" to be *my* definition
because it is *his?* If not Mr. James's definition, whose then? *What is
the limit up to which Man, simply in virtue of being Man, is
entitled, of right, to the exercise of his freedom, without the interference of society, or—which is the same thing—of other individuals?* This last, it seems to me, is about the most weighty question
concerning human society ever asked, and one which a man who,
like Mr. James, attempts to lead the way in the solution of social
difficulties, should be prepared to answer by some broader generalization than any which relates to a single one of the social ties, and
by some principle more susceptible of definition than a general
reference to humanitary sentiment. There are some acts which the
individual is authorized to do or not to do, at his own option, and
in relation to which other individuals have no right to interfere
to determine for him whether he shall or shall not do them; as,
for example, whether he shall go personally to the post office or
send a boy. There are certain other acts, on the other hand, which
the individual cannot do without directly authorizing interference,
resistance, or constraint, on the part of others. If a man plant his
fist in the features of another, or tweak his nose, I take that to be
such an act. What, now, is the clear and definable line which social
science, as understood by Mr. James, reveals, as running between
these two classes of acts? If that can be discovered, perchance it may
settle the marriage question, not singly and alone, but along with

every other question of human freedom. Hoping that Mr. J. will
consent to enlighten me and others by any knowledge he may
have upon the subject, I submit my interrogatories.

                                        Stephen Pearl Andrews.

                        Mr. Greeley's Comments

Having given place to the essays on Marriage and Divorce by
Mr. Henry James, in reply to attacks upon him in the "Observer,"
we have concluded to extend like hospitality to the queries of Mr.
S. P. Andrews, suggested by and relating to the essays of Mr.
James. Our own views differ very radically from those of both these
gentlemen; but we court rather than decline discussion on the
subject, and are satisfied that the temper and tendencies of our times
render such discussion eminently desirable, if not vitally necessary.
Let us now briefly set forth our own idea of the matter.

This is preëminently an age of Individualism (it would hardly
be polite to say Egotism), wherein "the Sovereignty of the Individual"—that is, the right of every one to do pretty nearly as he
pleases—is already generally popular, and visibly gaining ground
daily. "Why should not A. B., living on our side of the St. Lawrence,
and making hats, exchange them freely with C. D., living on the
Canada side, and growing wheat, without paying a heavy impost
or violating a law?"—"Why should not E. F. lend his money at ten
or twenty per cent, to G. H., if the latter is willing to pay that rate,
and sees how he can make more by it?"—"Why may not I. J.
educate his own children, if he sees fit, and decline paying any
School Tax?"—"And why should not John Nokes and Lydia Nokes
be at liberty to dissolve their own marriage, if they have no children,
or have provided for such as they have, and believe that they may
secure happiness in new relations which is unattainable in the
present?" These questions all belong to the same school, though
the individuals who ask them may be of superficially different
creeds or persuasions. They all find their basis and aliment in that
idea of Individual Sovereignty which seems to us destructive alike
of social and personal well-being.

The general answer to these questions imports that the State
does not exist for the advantage and profit of this or that individual,
but to secure the highest good of all,—not merely of the present,
but of future generations also; and that an act which, in itself, and

without reference to its influence as a precedent, might be deemed innocent, is often rendered exceedingly hurtful and culpable by its relation to other acts externally undistinguishable from it. A hundred cases might be cited in which the happiness of all the parties immediately concerned would be promoted by liberty of divorce; and yet we have not a doubt that such liberty, if recognized and established, would lead to the most flagrant disorders and the most pervading calamities. We insist, then, that the question shall be considered from the social or general rather than the individual standpoint, and that the experience, the judgment, and the instincts of mankind shall be regarded in framing the decision.

Polygamy is not an experiment to be first tried in our day; it is some thousands of years old; its condemnation is inscribed on the tablets of Oriental history; it is manifest in the comparative debasement of Asia and Africa. The liberty of divorce has been recognized by great historians as one main cause of the corruption and downfall of the Roman Empire. The sentiment of chastity becomes ridiculous where a woman is transferred from husband to husband, as caprice or satiety may dictate.

Two persons desire to be joined in Marriage, and invoke the sanction of the State—in other words, the approbation and respect of the community—for their union. The State substantially asks them: "Is there no impediment to such in the existing engagements of one or both of you?"—"No."—"Does your knowledge of and affection for each other warrant you in promising to love and cherish each other exclusively as husband and wife till death shall part you?"—"Yes."—"Then we pronounce and consecrate you man and wife, and enjoin all persons to honor you as such." And this is marriage, "honorable in all," and always honored accordingly, because it recognizes and provides for the permanent claims of society in the preservation of moral purity and the due maintenance and education of children; while any sexual union unsanctified by the mutual pledge of perpetuity or continuance ever has been and ever must be esteemed ignoble and dishonoring when contrasted with this; for its aims are manifestly selfish and its character undistinguishable from the purely sensual and brutal connections of undisguised lewdness, where no pretence of affection or esteem is set up, and whose sole object is animal gratification. In other words, society, by the institution of indissoluble marriage, exacts of the married the strongest practical guarantee of the purity and truth of their affection, and thereupon draws the broadest possible line of demarcation between them and the vile crew whose aspirations are purely selfish, and whose unions are dissolved, renewed, and varied as versatility or satiety may dictate.

We have no doubt this wise law, while essential to the progress of the race in intelligence and virtue, is eminently conducive to the happiness of individuals. True, there are unhappy marriages, discordant marriages, unions sanctioned by law which lack the soul of marriage,—but these occur, not through any inherent vice or defect in the institution, but through the levity, rashness, avarice, or overmastering appetite of one or both of the parties, who marry in haste, or from the impulse of unworthy motives, when the law counsels deliberation and demands pure affection. If a general proclamation were issued tomorrow, with the sanction of all our civil and ecclesiastical authorities, authorizing every married couple to obtain a divorce by merely applying for it within two months, and, in default of such asking, to remain undivorced ever afterward, we do not believe one couple in ten would apply for divorce. But let it be understood that marriages would hereafter be sanctioned and honored, binding the parties to regard each other as husband and wife only so long as should be mutually agreeable, and leaving them at perfect liberty to dissolve this tie and form new ones at pleasure, and we believe marriages *would be* contracted and dissolved with a facility and levity now unimagined. Every innocent young maiden would be sought in marriage by those who now plot her ruin without marriage, and the facility of divorce would cover the arts and the designs of the libertine with all the panoply of honorable and pure affection. How many have already fallen victims to the sophistry that the *ceremony* of marriage is of no importance,—the *affection* being the essential matter? How many are every day exposed to this sophistry? Marriage indissoluble may be an imperfect test of honorable and pure affection,—as all things human are imperfect,—but it is the best the State can devise; and its overthrow would result in a general profligacy and corruption such as this country has never known and few of our people can adequately imagine.

We are inflexibly opposed, therefore, to any extension of the privileges of divorce now accorded by our laws; but we are *not* opposed to the discussion of the subject. On the contrary, we deem such discussion vitally necessary and already too long neglected.

The free trade sophistry respecting marriage is already on every libertine's tongue; it has overrun the whole country in the yellow-covered literature which is as abundant as the frogs of Egypt and a great deal more pernicious. It is high time that the press, the pulpit, and every other avenue to the public mind, were alive to this subject, presenting, reiterating, and enforcing the argument in favor of the sanctity, integrity, and perpetuity of marriage.

Extract of Reply of Mr. James to the Observer

To Mr. Greeley:
I do not see that Mr. Andrews' queries need detain us. The numerous fallacies and misconceptions on which they are grounded either suggest their own correction to the observant reader or else stand fully corrected in my replies to the "Observer" and yourself. Besides, the entire "indifference" which Mr. Andrews professes as to any possible issue of the discussion between the "Observer" and myself gives a decided shade of impropriety to his interference in it. I value my time and thoughts much too highly to bestow them upon those who can afford to be indifferent to them; and, accordingly, I shall hold myself excused if I confine my attention to yourself and the "Observer."

Mr. Andrews' Reply

To the Editor of the New York Tribune:
Mr. James declines answering my questions on the ground that I expressed indifference to the issue of a discussion between him and another party. I did *not* express any indifference to the information which *I* sought from *him*. By this expert quibble he gracefully waves aside queries to which it is simply impossible for him to reply without committing himself, by inevitable sequence, to conclusions which he seems either not to have the willingness or the courage to avow. It would be cruel to insist any further. So let Mr. James pass. Before doing so, however, since he charges "fallacies and misconceptions" upon *my* article, and refers me obliquely to his replies to the "Observer," permit me to recapitulate the positions at which he has tarried temporarily while boxing the circle of possibilities in that discussion. I quote from Mr. James's various articles on the subject.
Position No. 1. "Marriage means nothing more and nothing less than the *legal union* of one man and one woman for life." "It does

not mean the voluntary union of the parties, or their mutual consent
to live together *durante placito*" (during pleasure), "but simply a
legally or socially imposed obligation to live together *durante vita*"
(during life).

That is to say, if I understand, that it is "the base legal bondage,"
or "outward force," which characterizes the union, and not the
internal or spiritual union of loving hearts which constitutes the
marriage.

Position No. 2. "It is evident to every honest mind that, if our
conjugal, parental, and social ties generally can be safely discharged
of the purely diabolic element of *outward force,* they must instantly
become transfigured by their own inward, divine, and irresistible
loveliness." "No doubt there is a very enormous clandestine violation
of the marriage bond" [legal bond, of course, as he has defined
marriage] "at the present time. . . . The only possible chance for
correcing it depends upon full legitimating divorce . . . because,
in that case, you place the inducement to mutual fidelity no longer
in the base legal bondage of the parties merely, but in their reciprocal inward sweetness or humanity." "You must know many
married partners who, if the marriage institution" [the legal bond]
"were *formally abolished* tomorrow, would instantly annul that
legal abolition again by the unswerving constancy of their hearts
and lives." That is, without marriage.

Position No. 3. "I have . . . contended for gretaer freedom of
divorce on these grounds; . . . but I had no idea that I was thus
weakening the respect for marriage. I seemed to myself to be plainly
strengthening it," etc. "It seemed to me the while that I was saying
as good a word for marriage as was ever said beneath the stars."

To resume: These three positions are, if language means any
thing, as follows:

1. The whole and sole substance of marriage is the *legal bond*
or *outward force* which unites the parties for life.

2. This legal bond or outward force is a diabolical element, and
should be wholly abolished and dispensed with.

3. By dispensing with marriage altogether—that is, with all
outward form or legal bond—you do thereby strengthen the respect
for marriage, and purify and sanctify the institution!

Position No. 4 goes a step further, if possible, in absurdity, and
proposes not merely to allow parties to unmarry themselves *ad
libitum,* but to still further purify what remains of marriage (after

the whole of it is abolished) by turning disorderly members out, as they turn members out of church. See last article, *passim*.

Position No. 5 entreats of the editor of the "Observer" to let him off from the discussion—declines to answer my interrogatories—and, to make a verb of one of his pet substantives, he *cuttle-fishes*, by a final plunge into metaphysical mysticism.

When a writer, claiming distinction as a philosophical essayist, is content to rest his reputation upon a collation of his avowed positions such as the above, culled from his own statements made during the course of a single discussion, he shall not be compelled by any "shade of impropriety" on my part to undertake the distasteful task of disentangling himself from the perplexing *embroglio*.

Dismissing Mr. James, permit me now to pay some attention to your opinions. You, at least, I think, have the *pluck* to stand by your own conclusions, unless you are fairly driven off from them.

You affirm, with great truth, while you deplore it, that this is prë-eminently an age of "individualism" wherein the "sovereignty of the individual"—that is, "the right of every one to do pretty much as he pleases"—is already generally popular and obviously gaining ground daily. Let us, then, define our positions. If I mistake in assigning you yours, you are quite competent to correct me. You declare yourself a reactionist against this obvious spirit of the age. You take your position in opposition to the drift—I think you will find it the irresistible drift—of that social revolution which you recognize as existing and progressing toward individualism and the sovereignty of the individual. You rightly refer free trade, freedom of the finances, freedom from State systems of religion and education, and freedom of the love relations, to one and the same principle, and that principle you recognize as the spirit of the age,—the spirit of this, the most progressive and advanced age in the world's history. To this element of progression you put yourself in a hostile attitude. You rightly say that all these varieties of freedom "find their basis and element in that idea of 'individual sovereignty' which seems to us alike destructive of social and personal well-being." I rejoice that you so clearly perceive the breadth and comprehensiveness of that principle, and that all the ruling questions of the day are merely branches of one and the same question,—namely, whether the "sovereignty of the individual," or, what is the same thing, the individual right of self-government, be a true or a false, and consequently whether it be a safe or a dangerous principle. This will greatly narrow the limits of the discussion; besides, it is much pleasanter to reason about general principles with one who is capable of grasping them than to be carried over an ocean of particulars, apparently different, but really belonging to the same category.

This same principle of individual sovereignty, which to you seems destructive alike of social and personal well-being, is to me the profoundest and most valuable and most transcendently important principle of political and social order and individual well-being ever discovered or dreamed of. Now, then we differ. Here, at the very start, is an illustration of individuality or diversity of opinion, and growing out of that, of action also. We are both, I believe, eqally honest lovers of the well-being of our fellow-men; but we honestly differ, from diversity of organization, intellectual development, past experiences, etc. Who, now, is the legitimate umpire between us? I affirm that there is none in the universe. I assert our essential peerage. I assert the doctrine of non-intervention between individuals precisely as you do, and for the same reasons that you do, between nations, as the principle of peace and harmony and good fellowship. Upon my principle I admit your complete sovereignty to think and act as you choose or must. I claim my own to do likewise. I claim and I admit the right to differ. This is simply the whole of it. No collision, no intervention can occur between us, so long as both act on the principle, and only to prevent intervention when either attempts to enforce his opinions upon the other. How now is it with your principle? You determine, you being judge, that my opinions are immoral, or that the action growing out of them would be injurious to other living individuals, or even to remote posterity. You, as their self-constituted guardian, summon to your aid the majority of the mob, who chance to think more nearly with you than with me for the nonce; you erect this unreflecting mass of half-developed mind, and the power thence resulting, into an abstraction which you call "The State," and, with that power at your back, you suppress me by whatever means are requisite to the end,—public odium, the prison, the gibbet, the hemlock, or the cross. A subsequent age may recognize me as a Socrates or a Christ, and, while they denounce your *conduct* with bitterness, never yet discover the falsity of the *principle* upon which you *honestly* acted. They go on themselves to the end of the chapter, repeating the same *method* upon all the men of their day who differ, for good or for evil, from the opinions of that same venerable mob, called "The State." Or, perchance, the mob, and consequently "The State," may be on my side,—if not now, by-and-by,—and then I suppress you. Which, now of these two, is the principle of *order* in human affairs? That I should judge for you, and you for me, and each summon what power he may to enforce his opinions on the other; or that each begin by admitting the individual sovereignty of the other—to be exercised by each at his own cost—with no limitation short of actual encroachment?

With what force and beauty and truth does Mr. James assert that "freedom, in any sphere, does not usually beget disorder, He who is the ideal of freedom is also the ideal of order." He seems, indeed, wonderfully endowed by the half-light of intuition to discover the profoundest truths and to clothe them in delightful forms of expression. It is lamentable to see how, when he applies his intellect to deduce their conclusions, they flicker out into obscurity and darkness. You see, on the contrary, that this simple statement alone involves the whole doctrine that I have ever asserted of individual sovereignty. Hence the line of argument as between you and me is direct, while with him it leads nowhere. Your positions are intelligible; so, I think, are mine; Mr. James's are such as we find them. I am a democrat. You, though not a despotist consciously, and calling yourself a progressive, are as yet merely a republican; republicanism when analyzyed, coming back to the same thing as despotism,—the arbitrary right of the mob, called the State, over my opinions and private conduct, instead of that of an individual despot. I am no sham democrat. I believe in no government of majorities. The right of self-government means with me the right of every individual to govern himself, or it means nothing. Do not be surprised if I define terms differently from the common understanding. I shall make myself understood nevertheless.

●　●　●

You expressly acknowledge, you can not help but acknowledge, that marriage does not work well for all the parties concerned,— only for some of them; and the first must be content to sacrifice their life-long happiness and well-being for the good of the others. No such system will ever content the world, nor ever should. It does not meet the wants of man. Your line of reasoning is after the old

sort,—that the State exists not for the good of this or that
individual, but for the good of all, when you begin by admitting
that the good of all is not secured. You are, of course, aware that
this is the argument of every despot and despotism in the world,
under which the liberties of mankind have always been stolen. The
argument is the same, and just as good, in the mouth of Louis
Napoleon as it is in yours. It is just as good as a reason for depriving
me of the freedom of the press, as it is when urged as a reason for
depriving me of freedom in the most sacred affections of the heart.
The most stupendous mistake that this world of ours has ever made
is that of erecting an abstraction, the State, the Church, Public
Morality according to some accepted standard, or some other ideal
thing, into a real personality, and making it paramount to the will
and happiness of the individual.

• • •

So, again, you do not and can not mean that the time is *never* to
come when woman shall possess the freedom to bestow herself
according to the dictates of her own affections, wholly apart from
the mercenary considerations of shelter, and food, and raiment, and
to choose freely at all times the father of her own child. You do not,
of course, mean that the free play and full development and varied
experience of the affections is intrinsically a bad thing, any more
than the development of the bodily strength or of the intellect;
but only that it is bad relatively to the present depressed and
dependent condition of the woman; just as intellectual development
is a misfortune to the slave, only tending to render him unhappy
until the final period approaches for his emancipation. You certainly
do not believe that human society, in the highest state of well-being
it is destined to attain, is ever to be attended by an army of
martyrs, who must sacrifice their own highest happiness and "the
highest happiness of all the parties immediately concerned" to the
security and well-being of somebody else remotely interested.

• • •

You refer to my position on the marriage question as well understood. Unfortunately it is not so, and can not be so, if that question
is considered by itself. I *have* no special doctrine on the subject
of marriage. I regard marriage as being neither better nor worse
than all other of the arbitrary and artificial institutions of society,—

contrivances to regulate nature instead of studying her laws. I ask for the complete emancipation and self-ownership of woman, simply as I ask the same for man. The "woman's rights women" simply mean this, or do not yet know what they mean. So of Mr. James. So of all reformers. The "Observer" is logical, shrewd, and correct when it affirms that the whole body of reformers tend the same way and bring up sooner or later against the legal or prevalent theological idea of marriage. It is not, however, from any special hostility to that institution, but from a growing consciousness of an underlying principle, the inspiring soul of the activities of the present age,—the sovereignty of the individual. The lesson has to be learned that order, combining with freedom and ultimating in harmony, is to be the work of science, and not of arbitrary legislation and criminal codes. Let the day come!

Stephen Pearl Andrews

Reply of Mr. James

To the Editor of the New York Tribune:

I declined controversy with your correspondent, Mr. S. P. Andrews, not because of any personal disrepect for him, but chiefly for the reason stated at the time,—that his objections to my views of divorce were trivial, fallacious, and disingenuous. I may now further say that his general opinions on the subject in discussion between the "Observer" and myself did not, besides, seem to me of sufficient weight to invite a public refutation. I may have been mistaken, but such was, and such continues to be my conviction. It is, accordingly, more amusing than distressing to observe that your correspondent's vanity has converted what was simply indifference on my part into dread of his vast abilities. But lest any of your readers should partake this delusion, let me say a few words in vindication of my conviction.

We all know that marriage is the union, legally ratified, of one man with one woman for life. And we all know, moreover, that many of the subjects of this union find themselves in very unhappy relations to each other, and are guilty of reciprocal infidelities and barbarities in consequence, which keep society in a perpetual commotion. Now, in speaking of these infidelities and barbarities, I have always said that they appeared to me entirely curable by enlarging the grounds of divorce. For, holding, as I do, that the human heart is the destined home of constancy and every courteous affection, I cannot but believe that it will abound in these fruits precisely as it becomes practically honored, or left to its own cultivated instincts. Thus I have insisted that, if you allowed two persons who were badly assorted to separate upon their joint application to the State for leave, and upon giving due securities for the maintenance of their offspring, you would be actually taking away one great, existing stimulant to conjugal inconstancy, and giving this very couple the most powerful of all motives to renewed affection. For, unquestionably, every one admits that he does not cheerfully obey compulsion, but, on the contrary, evades it at every opportunity; and it is matter of daily observation that no mere legal bondage secures conjugal fidelity where mutual love and respect are wanting between the parties. You instinctively feel also that a conjugal fidelity which *should* obey that motive chiefly would be a reproach to the name. You feel that all man's relations to his fellows, and especially to woman, should be baptized from above, or acknowledge an ideal sanction before all things, and that where this sanction is absent, consequently the relation is either strictly infantile or else inhuman. In respect to this higher sanction and bond of conjugal fidelity, you call the legal bond inferior or base. As serving and promoting the former, one deems the latter excellent and honorable; but as ceasing any longer to do so, you deem it low and bestial. Now, I have simply insisted that the legal sanctions of marriage should, by a due enlargement of the grounds of divorce, be kept strictly subservient and ministerial to the higher or spiritual sanction, having, for my own part, not the shadow of a doubt that, in that case, constancy would speedily avouch itself the *law* of the conjugal relation, instead of, as now, the rare exception.

In this state of things your correspondent appears on the scene, professing, amid many other small insolences and puerile affectations, not to be "cruel" to me, and yet betraying so crude an apprehension of the discussion into which he is ambitious to thrust himself that he actually confounds my denunciation of base and unworthy motives in marriage with a denunciation of the marriage institution itself! I have simply and uniformly said that the man who fulfils the duties of his conjugal relation from no tenderer or humaner ground than the law, whose penalties secure him immunity in the enjoyment of that relation, proves himself the subject of a base legal or outward slavery merely, instead of a noble and refining sentiment. And hereupon your sagacious and alarming correspondent cries out that I resolve "the whole and sole substance of marriage into a legal bond or outward force, which is diabolical and should be wholly abolished and dispensed with." Surely your correspondent must admit that, when a man and woman invoke the sanction of society to their union, neither they nor any one else look upon society's action in the premises as a constraint, as a compulsion. Why? Because society is doing the precise thing they want it to do. With united hearts they beg of society to sanction their union, and society does so. Your correspondent can not accordingly be so dull as to look upon society's initiatory action as compulsory? The marriage partners, at this period, are united by affection, and they deride the conception of a compulsory union. But, now, suppose that this affection, from whatever cause, has ceased, while the legal sanction of their union remains unchanged; can not your correspondent understand that the tie which now binds them might seem, in comparison with the pure and elevated one which had lapsed, "a based legal bondage, a mere outward force"? If he can not, let me give him an illustration exactly to the point. I find a piece of private property, say a purse of money, which the law, under certain penalties, forbids me to appropriate. Out of regard to these penalties purely, and from no sentiment of justice or manliness, I restore it to the owner. Hereupon my spiritual adviser, while approving my act, denounces the motive of it as derogatory to true manhood, which would have restored the purse from the sheer delight of doing a right thing, or, what is equivalent, the sheer loathing of doing a dirty one. What, now would your correspondent think of a verdant gentleman who, in this state of things, should charge my adviser "with destroying the institution of private property, with resolving it into a base legal bondage, and dooming it to an incontinent abolition"? Would he not think that this verdant gentleman's interference had been slightly superfluous? But whatever he thinks, one thing is clear, which is that the realm of logic will not for a moment tolerate your correspondent's notion of "Individual Sovereignty." Whoso violates the canons of this despotic realm by the exhibition of any private sovereignty finds himself instantly relegated by an inflexible Nemesis, and in spite of any amount of sonorous self-complacency, back to the disjected sphere which he is qualified to adorn, and from which he has meanwhile unhandsomely absconded.

•   •   •

Your correspondent, very consistently, exhibits a sovereign contempt for society, and calls the State a "mob"; and this judgment gives you a fair insight into his extreme superficiality of observation. Irresponsible *governments,* or those which do not studiously obey the expanding needs of society, are doubtless entitled to hearty contempt. Their day, indeed, is over, and nothing remains in the sight of all men but to give them a decent interment. But *society* never decays. It increases in vigor with the ages. It is, in fact, the advance of society among men, the strengthening of the sentiment of fellowship or equality in the human bosom, which is chiefly uprooting arbitrary governments. It is because man is now beginning to feel, as he never felt before, his social omnipotence, or the boundless succor, both material and spiritual, which the fellowship of his kind insures him, that he is looking away from governments and from whatsoever external patronage, and finding true help at last in himself. Accordingly, if there is any hope which now more than another brightens the eye of intelligent persons, it is the immense social promise opened up to them by every discovery in the arts and every new generalization of science. Society is the sole direct beneficiary of the arts and sciences, and the individual man becomes a partaker of their bounties only by his identification with it. Thus the best aspiration of the individual mind is bound up with the progress of society. Only as society ripens, only as a fellowship so sacred obtains between man and man, as that each shall spontaneously do unto the other as he would have the other do to himself, will the true development of individual character and destiny be possible. Because the very unity of man's creative source forbids that one of its creatures shall be strong, except by the strength of all the rest. Yours truly,

Henry James

Divorce

Elizabeth Oakes Smith

It is not surprising that Elizabeth Oakes Smith should lay such stress on the dangers of early marriage, when a girl "was so young and immature that she could form no estimate of the importance of the step she took." Mrs. Smith herself was only 17 when she married. Her bridegroom, a thirty-one-year-old journalist named Seba Smith, was later to earn some fame as the creator of "Major Jack Downing," one of the comic rustics popular in nineteenth-century newspapers. In addition to keeping house for Smith and bearing him five sons, she also acted as assistant editor to him for several years. But in her autobiography she makes it clear that she resented being trapped so early into the conventional feminine roles. She took the only respectable path out of that dependency when she began to write fiction. Since the late seventeenth century, scribbling had been the recourse of wives and widows too genteel to go out to service, too poor to stay at home.

Maturity and literary success gave Mrs. Smith self-confidence and self-consciousness. She began to lecture on the lyceum circuit, and

*learned that when she stepped onto the platform, she stepped out
of the charmed circle that protected ladies from public abuse. Writing and lecturing were two different things. She became a feminist.
Since she had not gone through the same fiery initiation of the
leading feminists, who had started as abolitionists and been doubly
radicalized by their combat with two powerful antagonists, Mrs.
Smith was treated as a fellow traveler rather than a true revolutionary: "She is not so ultra as some of us," Paulina Wright Davis wrote,
but "we must accept her for what she is. We need every possible
shade and variety of lecturers and workers in this great movement."*

In 1849 Mrs. Smith began a series of columns on women in the
New York Tribune. *In 1852, when Greeley threw open the pages of
the* Tribune *to the divorce controversy, he invited Mrs. Smith to
contribute to the discussion, no doubt counting on a position he
could agree with. Mrs. Smith did not disappoint him, for in spite of
her feeling that marriage "as it now stands, . . . is a bondage more
than a life-giving sacrament," her solution was not to make it
easier to escape, but harder to become enthralled. In an earlier
column she had written: "I remember, when a child, having a con-
fused idea that to be murdered was one of the possible contingencies
of marriage; and this impression was created solely by reading in the
public prints the many atrocious catalogues of the kind." The conventions were strong that could withstand such fancies and experiences as Mrs. Smith had undergone.*

Even such mild advice as she ventured in the Tribune *resulted in
a shower of abuse from more conservative readers. Mrs. Smith was
already peeved because Greeley "never paid me a cent for all I wrote
for him, thinking it was reward enough to be held as he said 'as a
leader in a good work.'" Now she was angered when, "having
allowed me to be abused in his columns, [he] reproached me with
being 'too thin skinned, for a woman who challenged abuse by the
very work she was doing in the world.'" This cool attitude convinced Mrs. Smith, not only that Greeley was not "a Gentleman,"
but also that he "never thoroughly endorsed the equality of human
rights."*

But if Greeley and the Tribune *used and abused her, Fowler and
Wells, the phrenological publishing house that had printed Lazarus's
Love vs.* Marriage, *was eager to get* Woman and Her Needs, *Mrs.
Smith's columns collected as a book, and they "honorably paid me
my percentage" on her work's "very great sale."*

Elizabeth Oakes Smith
Divorce

I have heretofore urged the importance of denying the marriage rite to those incompetent by the law to enter into other contracts. I might say, but the sarcasm is too severe, that a being held as an infant, a chattel, an idiot in law, *never reaches her majority, and is therefore morally irresponsible even in this*. Men who are delicate of their honor, careful of their names, and desirous to preserve the sanctity of the marriage relation, would do well to raise the legal liabilities of our sex, and by placing us in the same relative position with themselves, increase not only our sense of loyalty, but of dignity also.

But to my subject. In an earlier and ruder state of society among us, there might be found an apology for early marriages, and in this point of view many of the sayings of Poor Richard even, had a pertinency applicable to the times, but we have survived their use; and yet, like other exploded doctrines, they cling to the minds of the people like a forlorn leaf upon an autumnal tree, shivering and wasted, yet tenacious of its hold. Common sense and common justice cry out against them, and yet they find their advocates, and then, when the natural consequences result, modern society shakes her robe piously, and thanks God she is not like others.

The marriage relation is certainly, at some time in the life of individuals, the natural and harmonious state; but, as it now stands, it is a bondage more than a life-giving sacrament. The parties are unequal; the affinities essential to a joyful and peaceful relation are often wanting; the wife is not the help-meet for the man, but the appendage, the housekeeper, the female, of the establishment; I admit these terms are coarse, but the facts are coarse likewise; her very existence is merged in that of her husband; the children of her blood are not hers; her property is not hers; she is legally dead; and in this point of view, I believe, on my soul, she is morally irresponsible to society—not to God, be it remembered; not to the greatness and purity of her own nature; for, thanks to the framer of our spirits, under all these human disabilities come in the majestic laws of the great God, engraved upon the sacred tablet of the heart

---

● Selection from *Woman and Her Needs*, New York: Fowler and Wells, 1851, pp. 71–75, 77–79.

in lines of fire, and there we read, and grow calm, and thoughtful, and aspiring.

I would guard the relation of marriage as the most holy sacrament of earth. I would have the family altar for the entertainment of angels not unawares. I would have the festivals of Hestia genial with the sweetest offerings of earth—the Penates crowned with undying garlands—the Penetralia holy, and fresh and beautiful, and unprofaned; and for this purpose no one should be admitted to the Temple without solemn preparation of heart and life. It should, as now, confer dignity upon the parties, but dignity of a higher and purer kind. They should be those joined of God only. Even now, every generous mind respects a genuine, earnest, devoted human attachment, however at variance with conventionalism—but these sad, hopeless manifestations would have no existence in a truly ordered society. Marriage would only take place where the deepest emotions of the heart, the highest affinities of intellect, and the utmost sense of beauty, one or all of these, combine to make it desirable. In this case there could be no disloyalty, no bickerings, no division of interest. *There would be no divorce, for none would be desired.*

That radical wrong exists in the present system of marriage, is evident from the frequency of divorce. The giddy manner in which the marriage vows are now assumed would be pitiful, were not the subsequent evils humiliating. When we see two discordantly joined, wearing out a joyless existence, without companionship, without sympathy, looking to the past as all wretchedness, and the future as all hopeless, we are apt to say "A divorce should take place"— we are apt to feel, and perhaps justly, that no part of existence should be defrauded of its right to its best means of happiness. We say this world is a state important in the link, and how do we know that the future will not be shorn of its glory by discordant elements like these? How do we know that we shall not look back upon this little ball half in sorrow and half in spite, as the place little entitled to our good will?—and, therefore, these should be freed.

I think not. By divorce we let in a flood-gate of evil incalculable in its amount. The majority of the world admit of easy compromises, are so much the creatures of habit, of circumstance, and opinion, that they can settle into the yoke with little comparative discomfort; and legislation is for the many, not for a few, who are a law to themselves. It would seem that the few, who really suffer, who have that ingrained sense of truth, that integrity of life, that unity of being by which they are made sensibly alive to the touch of falsehood, should be the ones above all others for the law to relieve—but these are the ones who advance the world, who become eyes to the blind, who awaken human truth, and who should be content, like their Great Master, to suffer for the many; who should be willing to suspend the great needs of their own soul, rather than become a rock of offence. They can endure, because their own discontent arises from depths of life unknown to the many; and should they demand the whole law, all that is lawful, but which a human recognition renders inexpedient, thousands, who are without this internal singleness, would mistake a thousand petty ills and shallow pretences for the deep promptings of truth, and the whole structure of society be broken up.

Let our legislators, or let public opinion, forbid premature marriages, but admit of no divorce. In a right relation crime could not take place; in a false one, entered into in the maturity of judgment, let it be one of the contingencies from which there is no appeal. Let it not be entered into from pecuniary motives by our sex—allow woman the rights of property, open to her the avenues to wealth, permit her not only to hold property, but to enter into commerce, or into the professions, if she is fit for them. In that case she should assuredly take the stand that her fathers took, that taxation without representation is oppressive; and then, from the nature of things, society would grow more harmonious, marriage would be sacred, and divorce pass from the statute-book. With Milton, I believe it should be sooner awarded to ungenial relations than to the commission of crime. In the former there is a sturdy truthfulness of Nature, admitting of nothing short of the highest laws of being; while in the latter case, the readiness of compromise, in one party or both, argues an instability and shallowness of character, that the best modifications of society would little affect.

•   •   •

I have not known a case of discomfort in the marriage relation, in which the contract did not take place during the girlhood of the woman, when she was so young and immature that she could form no estimate of the importance of the step she took. Where suffering has arisen from marriages contracted later in life, the origin has been from causes so petty, external, or coarse, that no legislation should be awarded—no legislation could help them. The nature of the parties was such that they might as well be uncomfortable in that relation as any other.

We need a higher estimate of the sanctities of marriage, not increased facilities for dissolving it. We cannot multiply the latter without increasing existing evils—without lowering not only public taste, but the sense of justice. Were women allowed the exercise of their best faculties, and renumerated equally with the other sex, they might often escape the desire for divorce by a knowledge that the avenues to wealth or distinction were open to them, and thus they might fill up the desert of their life. We might cite many who are now doing this, honorably sustained by the better part of the community, though subject, of course, to the unmeaning sneers of the sticklers for womanly subserviency. We do need a better opinion in regard to woman-labor. We do need to have this sphere enlarged almost infinitely. We need to impress upon the other sex the unmanliness of usurping avocations better adapted to our more delicate organization. We need the resources of labor, broad and renumerative, for those who are too young of years to be admitted into the marriage contract, or disinclined to its responsibilities; and for those who, having made in this relation a great and irretrievable mistake, may find in it a relief for outraged affections, and from the apathy, or discontent, or pettiness, or oppression which it involves. Their penalty should not be a life-long penalty; their bondage unmitigated bondage. While a true marriage, and the happiness or sorrows of maternity, should unmistakably absolve a woman from labor—a false or external one, becoming painful and oppressive, should open to her its privileges.

Marriage

Thomas L. and Mary S. Gove Nichols

The following selections are from Marriage: its History, Character, and Results; its Sanctities, and its Profanities; its Science and its Facts, demonstrating its Influence, as a Civilized Institution, on the Happiness of the Individual and the Progress of the Race. *Both Thomas and Mary Nichols were prolific writers in numerous fields —physiology, hydropathy, vegetarianism, and so on—but they seemed to have found their* forte *in the 1850s, when they took up the sexual question.* Thomas Nichols's *Esoteric Anthropology (1853), a "medical" approach to sexuality, was a best seller at a dollar a copy, went through an edition of 12,000 copies the first year, and in the 1870s was still going strong. Recognizing a good thing when they saw it, Dr. and Mrs. Nichols stopped writing for the* Water-Cure Journal and Herald of Reforms, *which had carried her lengthy columns since 1845, and began their own magazine,* Nichols' Journal of Health, Water-Cure, and Human Progress, *which they put out under one name or another till 1856. They rushed into print a whole series of sexual treatises:* Woman in All

Ages and Nations *(an 1854 reprint of Nichols's 1849 edition)*,
Marriage *(1854)*, Mary Lyndon *(Mrs. Nichols's "free love" autobiography, 1855)*, *"Free Love and Spiritualism" (1856)*, *and
Esperanza (Nichols's utopian novel of free love, 1860). During this
period, the Nichols ran a water-cure establishment at Port Chester
on Long Island that had to close down when several of its young,
female inmates fled from what the newspapers called "the practical
application of such filthy doctrines as inculcated by Nichols and
Andrews."* Stephen Pearl *Andrews' name comes into the story
because at this time the Nichols were thinking of moving their
operation to Modern Times, the utopia where Andrews and his
mentor Josiah Warren were establishing, Warren most reluctantly,
a free love ambience (see section V). Andrews had written a generous ·
preface for the reprint of* Woman in All Ages, *and the Nichols
returned the favor by inviting him to lecture at their American
Institute of Hydropathy, and by throwing open the columns of the
Nichols Monthly when the Tribune had refused to print any more
of Andrews's contributions to the "love, marriage, and divorce"
controversy (see selection above).*

*The remaining career of these two sexual reformers is more
appropriately recounted in the Introduction and in headnotes to
other selections from their writings (see sections III and V below).
The passages from* Marriage *give a fair sample of their position on
the question in the early 1850s. The first selection, in fact, was a
kind of coda to the controversy between James, Greeley, and
Andrews in the* Tribune. *At the end of the series Mrs. Nichols
wrote a letter supporting Andrews to the* Tribune, *and when
Greeley refused to print it, she sent it to Andrews, who inserted it in
his final rebuttals, published when* Love, Marriage, and Divorce
*came out in book form. Mrs. Nichols, always eager to stretch her
work as far as it would go, published the letter herself, first in the*
Nichols Journal, *then in* Marriage. *In the final version, copied
here, she went on to quote another letter she had written, encouraging a woman who was living as her lover's mistress, and using
Greeley as the straw man of sexual despotism. Reading her outraged
defense of woman's "right to choose the father of her child," and
her husband's cooler weighing of the pros and cons of marriage, one
is struck with the modernity of their opinions, expressed with
greater directness and force than most of their contemporaries could
muster. For Mrs. Nichols at least, an explanation may be sought in*

her own experience, first as a reluctant young bride, then as an exploited wife and mother. She began her career in reaction to matrimonial oppression, as a lecturer on female physiology and an advocate of women's rights. She left her first husband, Hiram Gove, contrived to have her child stolen from his custody, and pursued her calling with the remarkable vigor that any woman in the 1840s needed to act contrary to her marriage vows and state law (see section III below). In the late 1840s, as a "water-cure physician," she was, in effect, a practising gynecologist and marriage-and-abortion counselor. She had therefore much experience of the "wrongs of women," physiological, psychological, and legal.

Thomas Nichols was also a figure of great energy and application, though of less imagination and talent than his wife. He was a hack editor and novelist when she met him, and not only did she put him through New York University medical school, but he also admitted that she taught him all he knew of hydropathy, the branch of medicine they pursued together. As a team, the husband tended to take care of the theoretical and administrative aspects of their work, the wife handled matters more personal and practical. Thus in the Nichols Monthly Mrs. Nichols developed a sort of letters column in which she answered their mail and made appeals for various causes, chiefly their own. Mr. Nichols wrote the editorials. At the Institute he gave most of the lectures and she was the clinician.

The career of the Nichols, both singly and as a partnership, is full of contradictions and about-faces, but the most disturbing inconsistencies, from a modern point of view, are those between their announced goals and their practical methods. It is easy to find passages in their works, like those which follow, that carry conviction. The sentiments, and many of the aims, would not be out of place in the Women's Liberation anthologies of the 1970s. Yet how does such righteous indignation, and humane common sense, happen to flower from roots that were so indubitably in the dirt? Leaving aside the differences in sexual morality—which were the motivation of most of the attacks on them, of course—we cannot but be aware of the opportunist and sensationalist quality of the Nichols' enterprises. The best example, perhaps, is their promotion of the Progressive Union, an idea they were pushing just after the publication of Marriage. Under all the fancy language they used to advertise it, the project was obviously nothing more than a national free love brokerage, whose service, for a price, was to provide names

of persons in one's locality anxious to make free love liaisons. How-
ever one feels about the service itself and its consequences, there is
something sneaky and underhanded about the way the Nichols
merchandised it that does not sit well with the outspoken and
aboveboard manner of their best selves.

Mary Gove Nichols
"The Right to Choose the Father of her Babe"

In the freest newspaper in this free country, the assertion of what
constitutes purity in woman, was refused insertion, on the ground
that it was "unfit," meaning indecently "unfit for publication." I
subjoin the statement that was refused, that an enlightened public
may see what Mr. Greelcy of the *New York Tribune* considered
"unfit" for the columns of his paper.

"The woman who is truly emancipate, who has health, in the deep
significance of that word—health of body and of spirit—who
believes in God, and reverently obeys his laws in herself—this
woman is pure, and a teacher of purity. She needs no human law
for the protection of her chastity; virtue is to her something more
than a name and regulation—something far other than a legal
restriction. It is high as the sky above Mr. Greeley's lower law, and
just as far removed from all license. Such a woman has a Heaven
conferred right to choose the father of her babe.

"We say man has the right to life, liberty, and the pursuit of
happiness; yet he abuses life, falls into bondage, and seeks and does
not find happiness. The woman who chooses the father of her child
may go as far wrong. The failure of freedom to bring wisdom and
right action at once, is no argument against freedom. Because
woman has not equitable and attractive industry and adequate
renumeration, and cannot, therefore, appropriately maintain the
babe she would bear and love, does that abrogate her right to be a
mother? Did not God make her to be the mother of the race? And
the healthy mother of healthy children? If she is fixed in indissoluble
marriage with a man she must abhor—a selfish, sensual tyrant—
who makes her his victim and perpetuates in her children his lust of
flesh and of gain, and all the deep damnation of his nature, must

● Selections from *Marriage*, New York: T. L. Nichols, 1854, pp. 204–06,
234–37, 177–88.

Woman lie prone under all this, suffering and transmitting the disease and crime which are its ordained product, because it is according to law?

"Often the greatest crime a man can commit is to reproduce himself, though it be done legally.

"We *must* have a Maine Law and capital punishment for the children born of hate in indissoluble marriage. Hundreds of women in such marriage murder their children rather than bear them.

"Intemperance, madness, murder, and all other vices, are hereditary. Shall indissoluble marriage go on, year after year, producing so many thieves, drunkards, prostitutes, and murderers, and in preassignable proportions—so mathematical in its operation—and remain unquestioned? Or shall it be honored with such defenders as Mr. Greeley, who whitewash it with legal sanctity in our Legislatures, and plead, through the public press, for Maine Laws to restrain and punish the murderers, and seducers, and drunkards born in its decent, and respectable, and legal limits?

"There is a large and increasing class of women in our land who know what purity is. They know that it is not an exhausted nervous system, which prompts to no union—which enables them to walk quietly in the common thoroughfare of custom. They know, also, that it is not fidelity to a legal bond, where there is no love—where there is a force on one side and fear on the other—where rascals are born by immutable God's law, and where diseases are engendered that make the grave an earnestly coveted refuge from "lawful" whoredom.

"Could any Woman, worthy the name—any other than a legal slave—*choose* to bear worse children than those we hang out of our way—than those who become seducers out of marriage, and destroyers in it?

"In the Medical College, at Albany, there is an exposition of indissoluble marriage, which should be studied by all those who begin to see that a legalized union may be a most impure, unholy, and consequently, unhealthy thing. In glass vases, ranged in a large cabinet in this medical museum, are uterine tumors, weighing from half a pound to twenty four pounds. A viscus that in its ordinary state weighs a few ounces, is brought, by the disease caused by amative excess—in other words, licentiousness and impurity—to weigh more than twenty pounds. Be it remembered, these monstrosities were produced in lawful and indissoluble wedlock. The

wives and mothers who perished of these evils, and left this terrible
lesson to the world, knew only of legal purity. *They* lived in obedience to the Law of Marriage—pious, virtuous, reputable, ignorant
women. God grant that their suffering be not in vain! God grant
that they may be the Teachers of Purity, who being dead yet speak!

"In an age hardly past, 'Honor God and the King' was the great
commandment. In this age, 'Honor God and a Husband' holds the
same place. Men have learned that the first contains a solecism;
Women are learning the same lesson of the last."

• • •

A young lady who has been taught in the school of Swedenborg
that the only true marriage is that of the deepest and purest love,
has acted upon her creed, which most of its disciples are too prudent,
too worldly, too weak, or too false to do. She was beloved by a man
legally but unhappily married. She came to love him, and to consider him her conjugal partner, or husband, for time and eternity.
She gave herself up to this love, and finally after the gentleman had
separated from his wife, she became in her own estimation his wife
—in the sight of the world his mistress. The following is a letter
which I wrote to this young lady after she had for some time lived
as the "wife," or "mistress," of this gentleman. She wrote me with
regard to spending some time at our home, and this is my answer:

"It is my opinion that woman belongs to herself, and is to be
faithful to herself, as you well know. So long as you and Mr. ——
are united in love, so long the outward expression of that love in
your material life is right, is holy. If Mr. —— cannot acknowledge
your union, it may be an inconvenience, or source of sadness to you
both, but it cannot alter the righteousness of your relation. If from
unworthy motives he refuses to acknowledge you, then you are no
longer his, and must take care of your own life, and not bestow it
unworthily.

"As your own, recognizing the relation that has existed, you can
come to us. As the wife of Mr. ——, openly or concealed, you can
come to us, provided we feel that he is worthy of this relation to you.

"You are to cultivate in yourself constantly the feeling of fidelity,
not to man, but to God; or in other words, to the highest in yourself. Because you have been Mr. ——'s wife is no sufficient reason
that you should continue to be. He must be worthy of your love,
and must have it, else you have no divine right to be his.

"If you continue with him from the outward pressure of the world, because you have committed an act deemed unworthy by the world, and are 'disgraced' without the deepest love for him, then you are no better than the harlots of legal marriage, who from any other than true motives remain 'married.' The time has come for individual fidelity; that is, that woman feel that she belongs to herself, and can only bestow herself for love; and when the love ceases the relation that it sanctifies must cease also. The great fight for purity has begun. Mr. Andrews and Mr. Greeley are discussing the question of marriage in the *Tribune*. One way and another the truth is likely to come home to us for defense.

"God will prosper the right. You will find a home and friends here when you choose to come, and Mr. —— will find all that he is worthy of, through your love. 'He that would save his life shall lose it, but he that would lose his life for Christ's sake, shall find it.' People are nothing to me now, only as they are worthy.

"It seems to me a worthful work for this time, to show where is responsibility. We have been responsible to the mob, made up of church and public, long enough. Our country threw off a king, but took thousands of tyrants instead. Indeed, everybody is a spy on everybody, and a man's foes are of his own household. I declare independence of all. I must be myself, if no one else is; and all I wish to do for others is to give them the chance to be.

"Dear ——, what I want for us both is the true recognition of our own sovereignty—of fealty to ourselves. There has been enough of sacrifices and burnt-offerings.

"But you must live my thought before you will know it. I trust it is your own now.

"In love, yours."

This young lady has acted nobly thus far, losing her fair good name with the world, and submitting to social outlawry for her love. Whether she would have strength to repudiate this relation if the love should die in her heart, is another and far weightier consideration than the first step. I had almost said, God grant she may never have this trial; but it is not for me to determine, in my short-sighted mercy, what is the best discipline for a human soul—especially of such as are noble enough to accept bitter cups from the hand of OUR FATHER.

When a conservator of public morals, such as Horace Greeley, regards with horror the assertion that woman has the right to choose the father of her child, the fact proves much—alas! how much. It proves the low estate from which woman has just begun to emerge. She is degraded by law and custom even lower than the beasts which perish; and if one asserts her right to any ownership of herself, so-called moralists and philosophers reject the thought with horror. Is there no sacredness left in this man's heart? Does he wish to be the father of babes when the mother has no choice, when she would come loathing to his arms, feeling that the union scarred her soul for eternity, and with the thought of murder in her mind rather than bear the babe thus forced upon her? Is this Mr. Greeley's morality when he says, "I utterly abhor what you term the right of a woman to choose the father of her child"? Alas for woman if men are not better than this creed! They are, and they are not. The best are enslaved by law, custom and organization, and go on murdering frail wives, not daring to think of any escape from the necessity, not even when their material wants are healthful and legitimate, and a wife utterly unfit to be a wife or a mother. I have no doubt that Mr. Greeley has at times the conception of what love and purity are, and what they would do for the world in pure births; but the bondage of public opinion, and his own nature is upon him. He has not leisure or ability to comprehend a world's want, and he only asks that mankind be saved from a worse estate than their miserable present; and the only means of salvation he sees is law, binding people to an outward decency, if possible, whilst their internal life is a foul, rotting ulcer—and if their children live they perpetuate the sad state of their parents. Thus the world is filled with disease, misery, crime and premature death.

It is time that the world should be unveiled to itself—that men pause and look at the humanity on this planet, and that they learn the way of redemption.

Thomas Low Nichols
The Wrongs of Marriage
We must draw to a close this portion of our work, historical, descriptive, and critical. We must close and sum up the testimony. Illustrative facts, from the actual life around us, will follow to enforce and confirm our generalizations. We have "searched the Scriptures," examined history, culled pertinent observations from voyagers and travelers, quoted the opinions of conservatives and radicals, and unfolded some of the mysteries of civilization; but, on

reviewing our work thus far, we find that we have omitted many important considerations, some of which we must now group together, under a title which will not be considered entirely inappropriate.

The Russian bride, we are told, is crowned with a garland of wormwood, as a fit emblem of the bitterness and trials of marriage state. Does a thoughtful woman ever stand before the altar without some bitterness in her heart?

One of the hideous evils of our marriage system is the unnatural celibacy that it forces upon vast numbers. Love, with its ultimations, enjoyments, and results, is the right, as it is the function, of every human being. Physical and mental diseases and miseries are the consequences of a deprivation of this right. Any social system is false which fails to provide for this great necessity of health, and use, and happiness. Our marriage system does fail to provide for the wants of thousands; more, it interposes insuperable barriers. It is thus a violation of the laws of nature, a crime of so grave a character as to demand universal reform.

Take, for example, the State of Massachusetts. Of persons between the ages of twenty and forty years of age, there are nearly or quite twice as many women as men. The surplus female population is condemned by the laws of that State, and by the public opinion on which its laws are based, to perpetual celibacy—to the starvation and immolation of the affections—the deprivation of all the happiness connected with love, and to all the miseries of its deprivation.

Were this result produced by the edict of a despot, humanity would be appalled by the outrage on its rights. It *is* produced by the marriage institution, which is thus the Moloch, the Juggeraut, to whom these unhappy victims are sacrificed. If but one woman in the world were deprived of the rights of love and maternity, it would be an outrage; but this institution robs hundreds of thousands of this right, as effectually as if they were seized and forcibly confined in convents, under sentence of perpetual celibacy. For marriage, which condemns the married parties to one single love, or one chance for love and happiness, also sentences those whom it excludes to the loss of even that poor chance—a chance so poor, that it is with many a matter of doubt whether it be worth the taking.

Next to this total deprivation of the rights of love, is the partial one, imposed on both sexes, but especially on women. Glance along our New England seaports, and you will find thousands of women living in almost perpetual widowhood and passional starvation, because married to men who are absent for months or years on long mercantile or whaling voyages, but who still claim, as society claims for them, the sole right to the persons and affections of their wives. When these unions are not those of love, the absence may be a welcome relief; but then comes the terrible anticipation of the return, and the revolting prostitution to which the unhappy wife must be the victim. If the wife, on the other hand, loves her husband, as is more likely to be the case than if he were constantly with her, who can tell the sufferings from absence, apprehension, and disappointment? But in neither case can she be allowed the compensation of another love. Forlorn as her condition may be, whether loving or loveless, she is cut off remorselessly from all human sympathy. She is taught to look to God for consolation, by those who forget that God's ministers of comfort are men and women with loving hearts. These poor victims, bound in the chains of marriage, may pray God and the Savior to love them, but they have no right to the love of the best man whom God has created in his own image!

We have spoken of the slavery of women in marriage, and the almost total deprivation of their natural rights. But there was never yet a wrong perpetrated by one party on another in which both did not suffer. Men, by making women either the toys of luxury or the drudges of the isolate family, condemn themselves to lives of toil and misery. How many a man, here and everywhere, with a wife, indifferent, expensive, and luxurious; daughters, extravagant and useless; perhaps a swarm of dependent female relatives—drones and burthens, because made such by these social relations—becomes a mere money-making machine, on whose whole round of toil there never falls one ray of happiness! Yet this man is the lord and master, the privileged being of this institution. As the despoiled laborer goes to his humble home with a lighter heart than the rich capitalist, so the inmates of the civilized harem may be unconscious of the cares and labors of their owner and master. The wrong is everywhere—suffering is everywhere; but those who feel it least are sometimes the most to be pitied.

The wrongs and sufferings of children from the marriage institution have been glanced at, but not sufficiently exposed. Home, family, and the care and culture of children, are the strong arguments in favor of indissoluble marriage. Yet infants are put out to nurse; young children are sent to boarding schools; and youth of both sexes to academies and colleges. How little of the education of

life do we really find in these homes! How ofen are they scenes of
selfishness, tyranny, wrangling, bickerings, and disgusts!
There can be no greater wrong to any human being than to be
born in a loveless, discordant marriage. It is a condition impressed
upon the very nature—the body and the soul of every child so
born. Next is the wrong of being compelled to spend the flower of
existence, the childhood which should be all love and joy, amid the
coldness, the discords, perhaps the outrages, of this home. Marriage,
while it gives a thankless and miserable existence to millions, who
for themselves and for society had better never have been born,
compels these children to all the sufferings and malign influences
of the domestic hells which this institution has scattered over the
world.

Compulsory child-bearing, the duty of a married woman to submit to the embraces of, and become pregnant by, any wretch, brute,
drunkard, or scoundrel, who may chance to be her *lawful* husband,
is one of those hideous wrongs which cannot be too often denounced
—a wrong so unnatural, such a violation of all principles of right,
that every clear-minded man must shudder at its existence; yet it is
a wrong which pervades our whole society; and the marriage institution rests upon it. It is upheld by every advocate of marriage. Says
Horace Greeley, one of the most fanatical of pro-matrimonial advocates, *"I utterly abhor what you term the right of a woman to
choose the father of her own child!"* An honest man, who read this
sentence, said, "Then he is in favor of committing rapes." The
expression may seem harsh, but is it not true? The man who
upholds indissoluble marriage, with the power it gives the husband
over the wife, with the utter absence of all ownership of herself, or
right over her soul or her body, is in favor of rapes, and every kind
of sensual outrage which men inflict upon miserable women under
the "sanction" of the marriage institution. What higher right,
under the broad heaven, can a woman have, than the right to choose
the father of her child? Yet marriage denies this right, and forces
women to loveless and adulterous embraces, and to bear the children
of sin, who either die young or suffer in loveless and stricken lives,
for this violation of the law of nature, forced upon them by the
marriage laws, upheld by such "reformers" as Mr. Greeley.

The injustice of the conventional code of virtue, which punishes
with the utmost severity the same acts in women that are scarcely
noticed in men, also, belongs to the marriage code. Man, the master,

has the right to exact chastity and fidelity which he does not give, and women everywhere in our society acknowledge this right, by punishing women who violate the law with the utmost disgrace. A man will be received in our best society with smiles of welcome, though he come from the arms of a woman whom his fashionable friends would almost spit upon, in the rage of their wounded virtue. So negroes in the South assist in hunting and capturing runaway slaves. So the victims of tyranny over the whole world aid in its oppressions. Women chain and scourge their sisters, because they themselves are slaves. Women whose souls are free pity, and as far as they have the power, protect the poor victims of this all-pervading wrong.

Marriage, like political despotism, religious tyranny, slavery, and other social institutions, creates crimes, and with them punishments. Freedom seems to us a natural thing; but our freedom, exercised in Italy or Austria, would send us to the prison or the gallows. Belief seems to us involuntary, and we claim, though we are not always ready to give, religious liberty, or the "right of private judgment," in matters of faith. Yet we have seen Protestants imprisoned in Italy by law, and convents and churches burned in America by the mob. Acts entirely innocent in freedom, are crimes in slaves. In the same way the marriage institution converts the most natural actions into crimes. That two young persons of opposite sexes should love each other, and give to each other expressions of love, no one will contend is unnatural; yet the marriage morality makes this a crime, for which such moralists as Mr. Greeley would send at least one of the parties to State prison. The offenses of fornication, seduction, bigamy, and adultery, are all made such by the marriage law; the same as many trivial actions were made heinous offenses, and even punished with death, under the bloody code of the Mosaic dispensation.

What the law calls fornication, when it is the union of mutual love, may be the holiest action two human beings can engage in. The real, essential nature of the act can be changed by no ceremony. It is either good or bad, right or wrong, in itself, and as it is sanctified by a mutual sentiment and attraction to which no law or ceremony can impart any additional sanction; yet this act, without regard to its inherent character, our marriage morality pronounces a crime, and punishes with ignominy.

So, bigamy, sanctioned by even antediluvian usages, by patriarchal example, by the authority of the Mosaic law, and by the practice of the greater part of mankind in all ages—which seems to be imperiously demanded wherever there is a considerable preponderance of one sex over the other—is a State-prison offense in all our statute books; yet who can explain in what the injury to society consists? So far as it is a fraud it may be punished as a fraud; but if a woman, knowingly and voluntarily, becomes the second wife of a man with the consent of all the parties concerned, how is it any more an offense against the State than if she had waited a year or two, until the first wife was dead, and then married her husband? So far as it is desirable for women to have the love, protection, and support of men *in marriage*, the repeal of the laws against bigamy is the right of the whole surplus female population. If the State, taking upon itself the regulation of this matter, cannot provide every woman a whole husband, it inflicts a grievous wrong in prohibiting her from getting a share in one.

The statutory crime of adultery is equally factitious, and equally a trespass on natural right. The real adultery of unsanctified sexual intercourse exists chiefly in marriage, where men, and especially women, are compelled to submit to it. But what the law calls adultery, may be the highest and truest relation of which two persons are capable. Yet this virtue, for such it truly may be, is punished as a crime by our marriage laws, which have no regard for the human affections, but protect married persons in the possession of each other, the same as they protect property in houses, slaves, or cattle.

In these, and in many ways, marriage perverts all correct ideas of justice, converts crimes into virtues, and virtues into crimes. All this we trust to show so clearly in the third part of this work, that men and women shall know the real difference between right and wrong by something higher than the standard of conventionality, custom, and law.

There is one evil result of our marriage system, which makes it abhorrent to the barbarians of Asia and the savages of Africa. Those who have read my exposition of the laws of generation, in ESOTERIC ANTHROPOLOGY, will need no further enlightenment on this point. It is that of the marital intercourse during gestation and lactation. Among the veriest savages a woman is considered sacred from the demands of sexual passion from the beginning of pregnancy until her babe is weaned. Our monogamic marriage knows no such sanctity of the maternal function, and women are compelled to bear what no animal even, in its natural state, ever submits to; and by which the rights of both mother and child are trampled on, the health of both injured, and often one or both destroyed. This civilized infamy, to which men are driven and women compelled, is alone and of itself sufficient to condemn the marriage institution, which cannot stand a moment under the investigations of physiological science.

All the discord, strife, clamor, persecution, scandal, jealousy, legal prosecutions, elopements, duels, assassinations, which grow out of the Marriage Institution, are chargeable upon it, and for them I hold it responsible.

The remedy for discord is separation. If two persons in another co-partnership disagree, they separate; but in matrimonial discords, this simple, natural, and effectual remedy is denied us. It is a crime for the husband to leave the wife, or the wife the husband.

Jealousy, and all the outrages and crimes which it causes, grows out of the idea of the right of property in some man or woman, and this idea is the basis of marriage. If Mr. Forrest, educated in the school of the drama, and full of the spirit of such plays as "Othello," "Taming of the Shrew," "The Honeymoon," "Rule a Wife and have a Wife," had had any proper idea of the right of his wife to her heart and her person, and to bestow them where she pleased, we should never have had the scandal of his divorce suit. All the evils of that monstrous outrage, on both sides, would have been entirely avoided had these two accomplished and in many respects amiable persons been able to respect each other's rights as human beings.

It is the same with the frequent cases of duels, or less formal assassinations, growing out of the same cause.

We charge all these brutalities and crimes upon the Marriage Institution; the same as we charge revolutions, imprisonments, banishments, and political executions upon Despotisms; the same as we charge the Inquisition, with its dungeons, tortures, and *autos da fé*, upon Religious tyranny; the same as we charge the horrors of the middle passage, the possible and actual cruelties of Legree, and the fugitive slave law, upon the institution of Slavery.

As long as there is despotism of any kind, political, religious, or domestic, we must have all the conditions of such despotism. Austria must have a standing army, prisons and the gallows; Rome once had tortures and the stake; Slavery has whips and chains; Marriage has law and public opinion—absolute power and its abuses. They all belong to the same system—the wrong of one human being assuming to control and govern another. Kossuth, escaping from the power of Austria; a fugitive slave running for Canada; and a fugitive wife escaping from her husband, are parallel cases. Kossuth was born subject of Austria; the negro was born a slave; the woman was born and educated to be a wife, and knew no other destiny. The same great principle applies to every case; the right of Individual Sovereignty solves every difficulty.

Of the minor evils and miseries of marriage we have no time nor space to speak. They are such as come naturally with, if they are not inseparable from, the exclusive and indissoluble monogamy. Our comic, satirical, and dramatic works are full of them. Marriage has often been ridiculed, seldom seriously attacked. Men like Luther, Milton, Napoleon, Shelley, Godwin; women like Mary Wolstencraft [sic], Frances Wright, George Sand, have wholly or in part protested against it. It is left to our time, and to the course of events which makes this question *now in order*, to bring out its full discussion; to be followed by its final approval or its utter condemnation.

"Some years ago," says Dr. Lazarus in the work LOVE vs. MARRIAGE, from which we have elsewhere so largely quoted, "Political Liberty was the subject of a life-struggle for the American people. Now comes the question of Passional and Social Liberty, and there is another declaration of independence to be made, and another revolution to be achieved for the conquest of that happiness, the right to whose pursuit constitutes one of the prominent articles in our last declaration. That was the shadow, the sham fight, the parade, the external contest with foreign powers, but now comes the substance, the real fight, the battle of souls, the struggle without quarter between the forces of heaven and hell in our midst, and the hottest of the fight must be fought upon this central position of the love relation between the sexes. To this all human actions ultimately converge. It is the pivotal thesis of social science, and gives its pivotal and distinctive character to every social period."

Divorce

Henry Clarke Wright

At twenty-five Henry Wright graduated from Andover Theological Seminary, married a widow with four children, and settled down to a quiet life as a Presbyterian minister in Newburyport, Massachusetts, where his wife owned a house and property. Her oldest daughter accompanied the newlyweds to Niagara Falls on their honeymoon.

Wright later confessed that "Within 24 hours after the ceremony my eyes were open to see the gulf into which I had blindly leaped. I saw that my heart never had been & never could be given to that woman. She could not receive it—nor understand it. From that hour I commenced a course of concealment." *"Concealment" and strict application to duty seemed to suffice for almost ten years, but then suddenly he renounced his pulpit, his family, his whole previous existence, and became an itinerant reformer.*

By the time he left home and family in the mid-1830s, Wright and his wife had not slept together for some years: "she wishes not to be carressed by me, nor do I by her—we are simple friends with-

out one emotion of Marriage love between us." This arrangement served domestic tranquility and the scholar's life Wright had been leading, but as he later admitted, "My nature longs for a wife—my intellect, my affections, my social nature—my physical nature—all long unutterably for marriage." For the remaining thirty years of his life he wandered and preached for good causes, notably the abolition of slavery and the doctrine of non-resistance—the nineteenth-century version of libertarian anarchism.

In the early 1840s Wright discovered that he had tuberculosis, and went abroad to be cured. He took the "water-cure" at Priessnitz's famous spa in Gräfenberg, then recommenced lecturing for antislavery and pacifism in Great Britain. In the spring of 1843, age forty-five, Wright fell in love with a young abolitionist from Dublin, Maria Waring, sister-in-law of his Irish friend Richard Webb. The romance was kept a secret from all but their intimates —Wright even expunged her name from his private journals—but they spent much time together during the four years Wright delayed his return to America. He asked himself whether "it would be a violation of any natural or divine law" for Maria and himself "to recognize each other as husband and wife—to live together as such —& to propagate." His answer was "No—I do not believe it would be. The laws & usages of society condemn me—but in the sight of that being who is the embodiment of love, justice, purity—it would be perfectly just & pure."

Wright continued to brood upon the question, consulting his conscience and taking copious notes for more than one projected book on "the theology of marriage and propagation." If a marriage unsanctioned by society could be pure and proper, it was also possible that a conventional union might be unclean. Indeed, that seemed to be his own case too: "if a man or a woman is . . . in a condition where he or she cannot have a love—wife or husband, & children without a violation of conventional usage, it becomes an imperative duty to violate such usage. . . . There can be no marriage where there is no love. . . . No matter whose consent is asked, or what forms are observed, all such marriages are wrong, & destructive to the physical, social, intellectual, & spiritual development. They are subversive of the life & health of the soul; of the great end of marriage. They are the worst forms of prostitution—of adultery."

Finally in the summer of 1847 Wright faced the fact that his health no longer justified any postponement of his calling in the

States. *Garrison and other abolitionist friends reminded him that slavery was "the peculiar institution" of his own country. He embarked from Liverpool in August, and it was emblematic of his love-life that for many hours he could watch the parallel progress of the Dublin steamer on which Maria was also returning home. "If the love I feel for thee be idolatry," he wrote in his journal as he doubled Cape Clear, "then I am an Idolater & must be. I can give thee up—dear one—to follow after what seems to me to be the truth & the right. Mayest thou grow up to be all that is pure, lovely & of good report & thy bosom shall be my temple & the pure abode of the Eternal Spirit."*

Wright finished his book on Marriage and Parentage *in 1854. It was much altered from the first notes written towards it ten years earlier; the urgency is gone from his voice, replaced by a fervor more programmatic than personal. (It is significant that by this time he had taken up the doctrine of Graham and Alcott—marital continence except for procreation.) But his basic ideas concerning love, marriage, and divorce remained unchanged. Nor did they shift thereafter.*

In 1858 news came that his distant sweetheart had married. What Wright's feelings were we do not know, but at the Rutland Free Convention that year—called the "Free Love *Convention" by a hostile press—Wright reiterated the anarcho-Calvinist doctrine he had forged of his own sufferings: "The true and natural marriage consists in a* love *between the two souls. It is not the* ceremony, *but in the love that blends the two souls into one." Once again he described "false, or* sham *marriage": "They take a walk by moonlight, or a buggy ride, and find out that each is essential to the other, and confess undying love. They get a license to be married. . . . Then the* Honey-Moon! *That soon goes down, and the darkness of a living death settles upon those hearts."*

As for free love, Wright believed in no such thing: "There is no freedom in conjugal love; it is a necessity; a fixed law of life to the soul; a law or necessity that points to an exclusive relation between one man and one woman as the only true, natural marriage." In this he agreed thoroughly with Henry James Sr. But like James, he also believed therefore that government had no proper function in matrimony, beyond the simple recording of the "historical fact." "All else is prostitution, licensed or unlicensed." Here he echoed the free lovers he reproved, Andrews as well as James. He never returned to his legal wife, nor to his spiritual one, now Mrs. James Palmer. His comfort was, as he had written in his journal as he lost sight of Ireland in 1847, "there is a place where spirits will meet & mingle, no more to part."

Henry Clarke Wright
Divorce

NINA:

Intimately connected with the perpetuity and exclusiveness of marriage between one man and one woman is the subject of DIVORCE. This has ever been a perplexing question to statesmen and churchmen. So far as it is a subject for the action and management of human government, it must, like all other matters connected with relations based solely on the demands of the inner life, be attended with difficulty; but so far as it relates to the affections, to conjugal love and its actual manifestations, it is a question of easy solution by every pure and honest heart.

Divorce is the result of violated law, as are other evils. Men and women come together in marriage without a knowledge of each other, or of their needs in that direction. Instead of appreciating marriage as a nesessity of their being, an essential condition of growth and happiness, they often regard it as only a civil institution, a contrivance of human ingenuity for human convenience,— a source of gratification to an excited, ungovernable passion. When that passion is satiated, the great end of the relation, as they view it, is answered. Man, too often, takes no heed of the capabilities and qualities, in any other direction, of the woman whom he is about to receive as a wife.

Man pays more heed to the qualities of the ship, the house, the shoes, the hat, the coat, the horse, sheep or ox, he is about to buy, than to the physical, intellectual and spiritual conditions of the woman he is about to take as a wife, and to make the guardian and protector of his manhood. Woman, often, is far more solicitous about the qualities of the gloves, shawl, bonnet and fan she is about to purchase, than she is concerning the qualities and conditions of the body and soul of the man whom she expects to receive as a

● Selection from *Marriage and Parentage: or, The Reproductive Element in Man*, 2d ed. enl., Boston: Bela Marsh, 1855, pp. 188–206.

husband, and the father of her children. Consequently, society is full of inharmonious and most fatal alliances between men and women, under the name of marriage,—alliances as unnatural and monstrous, and as fruitful of evil, as a union between liberty and slavery, truth and falsehood, purity and impurity,—alliances in which no compromises can ever produce harmony or happiness.

How to prevent these misalliances? This is *the* question. Divorce is the result of, and a supposed remedy for, unnatural and inharmonious relations between men and women, under the name of marriage. Divorce, as an experience of the heart, is to the soul much what dyspepsia is to the stomach. Man mistakes the excitement of passion for conjugal love; woman mistakes vanity, ambition, a desire for a home or a social position, for the same. They enter into intimate personal relations as husband and wife. The counterfeits of love, which precipitated them into their unnatural and inharmonious outward union, soon reveal themselves, and both find that they stand in an outward relation to each other which their souls have never sanctioned. In her ignorance and blindness, woman takes to herself what she hopes may prove the bread of life to her soul, but she finds it a deadly poison.

There is but one way in which these unnatural and discordant alliances can be prevented, and divorce be forestalled. The *intuitions* of men and women must be more perfectly organized and developed; the *sexual instinct* must be refined and more delicately attuned; then would they be able to select a natural and healthful supply for that want of the soul which points man to woman as a wife, or woman to man as a husband, with as much certainty as the instinct for material food directs us to select that which is wholesome.

The instinct which points men to women and women to men for a true development, is all dark, bewildered, gross; and in its grossness and want of delicacy of perception it points them to a relation based mainly on sensual indulgence. Disappointment, sickness and disgust of heart, ensue; the twain that fondly dreamed of oneness become antagonisms; neglect; abuse, outrage, follow, and civil government is asked to come in and cut the outward bond, and save them from the effects of their ignorance and passion.

Had that deepest, noblest and most potential instinct of the soul been truly, delicately and nobly formed and directed, had it been so enlightened and refined that it would have guided the soul to select for itself the true element of conjugal life, it would have elevated to heaven instead of casting down to perdition. In such a relation, divorce has no place, no significance. It belongs only to unnatural conditions and false relations between the sexes. Under the guidance of an enlightened, refined sexual instinct, the only power that can bring the two elements into true and vitalizing rela- tions, where marriage is but another name for love, for harmony and perfect trust between two souls, it were as unmeaning to talk of divorce, as to talk of it in reference to the relations between the needle and the pole.

But such is not the condition of society in reference to the relation between the sexes. What is to be done to meet the existing necessity? What *can* be done? Men and women will come together—they *must*—it is a necessity of their being. They are ignorant, they are bewildered. They will come into false relations. Children will be born of such unfortunate alliances. Who or what is to manage these matters, correct these abuses, and secure individuals and society against all possible results from the perversions of a relation on which all rational hopes of human progress must be based? Of all agencies, governments have proved themselves most incompetent to correct these abuses, and save individuals and society from their direful consequences.

There is but one remedy—LET THERE BE LIGHT! The nature, extent, power and object of the distinction of sex must be under- stood and appreciated; the sexual instinct must be refined, ennobled, and brought under an enlightened reason and a tender conscience; the true object of the presence of the reproductive element in man must be better understood; the fixed laws by which God designed its expenditure should be regulated must be known and obeyed; man's true mission to woman and woman's to man, be known and more truly estimated; and the gospel of a true marriage and parent- age be preached to all;—then, and not till then, will the twain that leads to oneness reveal its power to bless and to save; and till then, divorce, as an experience of the heart, will continue to desolate the inner life, and, as an outward ordinance, to bewilder the head of the statesman, and grieve the heart of the philanthropist.

NINA, this is a most painful subject to one who is conversant with the domestic relations of men and women. *Experimenting in marriage* is the order of society. The results are fearful to those who experiment, and to their offspring. While men and women go on to experiment in a relation which is the basis of the perpetuity, and must be of the perfection, of the race, they will have, and must have, governmental interference to save them and society from the consequences that would result to men, women and children, by leaving the parties to repeat their experiments as often as insatiate passion and stupid ignorance might dictate. The evils of divorce, as an experience of the inner and outer life, will continue to increase, until every true and pure-hearted man and woman is satisfied that relief can come, not from human legislation, but from a knowledge of, and obedience to, the fixed, unchanging laws of God, designed to govern conjugal relations.

Meanwhile, the truth will stand, that marriage, like the pulsations of the heart and the contractions of the lungs, is the work of Nature. There is a power that brings a man and woman into this relation. When this power ceases to act, to make the twain one, marriage ceases, as an experience of the soul; and where there is no union of soul, there is no marriage, and all outward conjugal relations should cease. The mental, moral and physical conditions of a man and woman may be harmonious, when they are drawn into the relation of husband and wife. They may be pure and healthful, and the union be a happy one. Love may bind them together. But perhaps by some great change of his nature, the conditions of the man are changed. His moral nature may be wrecked in the conflict of life, or his social elements may enslave him to low and brutalizing appetites, so that his intellect becomes imbecile; and the whole type of the man is changed. Can the wife, who loved in him the embodiment of all high and holy qualities, which he once was, still love the man, who, in all respects, fails to meet the ideal that first won her maiden heart? The man she loved is changed; he is no more. Her *ideal* is not changed but the man to whom she gave herself as a wife has ceased to embody that ideal. Reason and Nature answer, at once, and say, "She cannot love him as she did!" But, without this love, is she, before God, his wife? By all that is sacred, she is not! The man in whom her soul found embodied its ideal of purity, nobleness, and manhood, has become a loathsome sensualist. The man has made himself repulsive to her wifely heart; by his sensualism, he has separated himself from her soul of conjugal love, as the sinner, by his sins, has separated himself from his God. She may pity him, and weep over him, but she cannot love him and come to him as a wife. Love cannot attract her heart to that which is not lovely, and he is so no longer. Now, what shall she do? Is her body to belong to the man who has no power to retain her affection? *Not for one moment!* She is not his wife by love, only by law and outward form; and the surrender of her person is but legalized prostitution, frowned upon by a just and holy God. Come what may, when love ceases between those who have been pronounced husband and wife, let the outward expression cease. Where a deep, holy, conjugal loves does not unite the souls of a man and woman, however strong the demands of passion, let there be no surrender of the person, for the unhallowed purpose of mere sensual gratification. Let every woman be fixed, as God is, never to live with a man, as a wife, whom she does not love; let every man be equally true to the voices of his nature, and an untold amount of misery would be saved to both.

Human laws come in and dictate the grounds of divorce. What have they to do with the question of divorce, as a heart experience? Just as much as they have to do with marriage, and no more,—only to sanction what Nature and Nature's God have already accomplished. But they ought never to coerce those to keep together, as husband and wife, who require such bonds to unite them, for these are, by the laws of God, no longer one. Love is departed, and with it, marriage; and no human laws can make them one. *There is a twain that leads to oneness*, by a fixed law of human existence,— the law of Harmony, of Marriage. If human enactments attempt too much, and license the union of two as husband and wife whom God hath put asunder, men and women must set them at nought, and obey the higher law written on their souls, which forbids all personal surrender to sexual indulgence, without love.

Human legislation may forbid them again to assume the external relations and to enjoy the outward rights and privileges of marriage, each with another; but it cannot control the wants and action of the soul, which remain the same as before. The fact that they have been once bewildered and mistaken, does not destroy this want of their being. The soul of each must ever demand, in order to its growth in purity and all goodness, that which the soul of one of the corresponding sex can alone supply. They will necessarily attract and be attracted, until the soul of each comes into a natural, harmonious relation.

The rock on which so many fond hopes are dashed, the one fatal error which is so fruitful in direful results to many bewildered, but trusting hearts, is, that men and women commence living in the outward relations of husband and wife, and become parents, in utter ignorance of each other, of their own wants, as male and female, and of the only basis of a true conjugal relation, and regardless of that corresponding attraction and union of heart, without which, the outward personal surrender is an outrage to body and soul, that must, as a general rule, end in disease and wretchedness to all who thus live, and to their offspring. Would that parents might study to guard their sons and daughters against the possibility of mistaking passion, or friendship, or a desire for a home, for wealth, social position, or any other feeling, for conjugal love! Let them attend to the organization and true development of the sexual instinct, and seek to bring it, as they do other instincts, under the control of reason and conscience; let them ever impress upon their children the certain degradation and ruin that must ensue from an external connubial relation, however sanctioned by Church and State, which is repudiated by the inner life of the soul;—then might we hope that the State would not be so often invoked to annul the outward bond, where there is no union of heart.

If human laws enter to regulate the intimate relations of the sexes, and presume to say to a woman, "You shall love this man, and you shall not love that man," or, "if you do not love that man, you shall surrender your person to him in the passional relation, and continue to become the mother of his children," then they go beyond their appropriate function, and usurp a power against which every pulse of true manhood and womanhood revolts.

But, if there are children, what must the parents do? Live together, as friends, who have in those children, on whom they have entailed existence without love, a mutual care and responsibility. Be to them *parents*, in the deepest and widest sense possible. Give them every attention and advantage which they have a right to claim from the authors of their being; and in order to do this, keep your own souls free from degradation, by a firm, unwavering fidelity to the highest impulses of your nature. Cease to be a wife, in external relations, to the man thou dost not love, but be a mother to the child for whose existence thou art responsible; cease to be a husband to the woman thou dost not love, but ever be a father to the child who has derived its being from thee.

It is asked, "Has not Jesus laid down the only true ground of external divorce? Has he not pronounced adultery the only sufficient cause of separation from 'bed and board'?" But, I ask, what is adultery, but the proof that marriage-love, that true, divine, exclusive element of the soul is gone? What loving husband ever seeks the gratification found in adultery? Jesus *has* laid the true foundation of divorce to be *the absence of love*, and adultery was the form in which it manifested itself in the case before him. In this, Jesus taught according to Nature. Adultery is a sufficient ground of divorce, because it proves the absence of love. Whatever demonstrates the cessation or absence of love between a man and woman, proves that the relation of husband and wife never existed, or that, if it ever did, it exists no longer. There are many other proofs, less censured by human laws and customs, on which a true man or woman must rely, and by which they must govern their relations. Where conjugal love exists between a man and woman, there is marriage. Though external surroundings may prevent the public recognition of it, yet, before God, those two souls are one,—are husband and wife,—as truly as if they openly lived in that relation. There is but one true cause of divorce from the inner or outward marriage relation, and that is, THE ABSENCE OF LOVE.

But, to a true marriage, whose conditions are faithfully sustained, there will come no divorce. To maintain, strengthen and eternize our mutual love, we will live and die, and so cherish the divine oneness between us, that no coldness, no darkness, shall chill the warmth or dim the beauty and the brightness of our united hearts.

Thy husband,
ERNEST.

Answer

ERNEST:

In my last letter, I said that marriage between two was the law of Nature, and that this marriage must be consummated first in the spiritual union, and afterwards actualized in the personal relation; and that the latter relation is only the natural consequence of the former.

Thou hast said that human law should sanction what Nature has accomplished. It consummates marriage between any two who stand up before a minister or magistrate, with a request to be made man and wife. It asks no questions whether love, or policy, or sensual passion, or ambition, or avarice, be the ground of the union. Clumsily and blindly, it puts the chain around the two, rivets the link, and solemnly pronounces them ONE.

How is it about divorce? The law suddenly grows critical and particular. When these two come back, and ask the same power that bound them to set them free, the law says, "If you are guilty of any particular sin, so gross, so palpable, that human eye can see it, and human testimony can prove it, I will set you free; but not otherwise. No matter how your hearts are changed towards each other, no matter what personal wrongs and outrages you have committed under the sanction of my name, if you have not committed the particular sin I specify, I have no redress, no relief for you."

There are those whose morals are fashioned by a higher model than human laws; and the omnipotence of the law of marriage, and the insufficiency of knowledge as to the true grounds of divorce, have produced in men's minds a most distorted idea of their true position. It is usually understood that, by marriage,—that is, by the performance of a marriage ceremony,—a wife passes over to the care, keeping and protection of her husband; that the bestowal of her heart upon any other, is a wrong to him to whom human law has assigned her.

Suppose two are married, under this impression, who think they love each other. As time rolls on, and each matures and develops, they diverge in sympathy; and perhaps the husband or the wife may be so constituted by nature, that the deepest wants of the heart cannot be met by the other. Without abuse or outrage, love yields its place to friendship, respect, and kind feeling. If this takes place in the wife, her nature will not demand the personal endearments of marriage. She will promptly say to her husband, that such expressions belong to *love*, not to friendship; that they are disagreeable to her, and that only by restraining them can either be saved from degradation. He tells her that she is wrong; that when she married, she gave herself to be his lawful, wedded wife, and that his nature demands the gratification of all its wants; that he has a right to such gratification, and her scruples are only foolish nonsense, which should not weigh against his wishes; that they are useless obstacles in the way of his enjoyment; and that the world would agree with him, that his demand was no more than just.

To such arguments, the wife generally yields; not willingly, but by compulsion, for where is her refuge? She applies to her protector for protection against himself,—but in vain. It were well if every husband realized that in thus removing "obstacles," he has planted an element ruinous to himself. He has taken the first step towards turning respect into contempt, friendship into hatred, and liking into loathing.

If women dared to give their experience on this matter, as they one day will, they would agree with this statement. From the hour that a wife realizes that her husband claims her person, when he knows he has not her heart, she is a slave, not less degraded than any ever bought or sold upon the auction-block; and she entertains to her master the feelings which such a relation must produce. Marriage, to her, becomes the name for all that is debasing and disgusting.

What, then, is she to do? Human law lent its sanctions to ratify her marriage. Now, an equally clear and unmistakable voice within tells her that that marriage is null and void. She appeals to human law to annul it; but it is silent as the tomb. She has prayed in vain for mercy of him who has taken it upon himself to cherish and protect her, and what remains to her? Either to bow her soul to a pollution too deep for any name, or to disregard the power of human law and a still more cruel public opinion, and leave the home where the shelter for her head must be purchased at the cost of her self-respect.

This is her last resort. But, before this, let her try every argument, every reason, which manhood can comprehend or generosity feel, in behalf of her own rights. Let her show, by appeals to nature and reason, that it is a mistake to suppose that marriage takes from the wife the control of her own person. It is a natural, inalienable right, that was ordained of God before human law was made, and can be annulled by no enactments of men.

If there are children, let her plead to be their true and faithful mother. To this end, let her keep herself pure and undefiled; let their children be a mutual care, and let them have every attention and advantage which they have a right to claim from the authors of their being. A man must be less than human, not to listen to this deep, agonizing petition from the mother of his children.

But if he be less than a man, that wife is bound to fidelity to her own soul, at every cost. She will stand guilty before God for the neglect of her instincts; and if there is no alternative but separation or legalized prostitution, then, I say, in the name of God and virtue, let her depart!

I have stated an extreme case, because there are men, or rather, beings who have the name of men, so degraded as to demand a gratification of their passion without love, because the law has given them possession of the person of the individual who bears the name of wife. But, thank God, there are *men* who deserve the name, —who ask not what the law allows, but who govern themselves by the one only law of the heart.

There are numberless other cases, where affection on either side is wasted by neglect and indifference on the other; but they are all various manifestations of the one great cause—THE ABSENCE OF LOVE; and they all point to one only remedy—SEPARATION; or, at least, suspension of the marriage relation.

Human laws may forbid those who have been disappointed in one alliance from being attracted to others. It is in vain; the pulsations of the heart can never be controlled by such enactments. Though governments forbid the outward expression of it, they cannot prevent the soul from attracting and being attracted. The heart may suffer under a false relation, but its power to love nobly, purely and truly, is not thereby destroyed; and I should utter my protest against all arbitrary restrictions put upon a true love relation. Yet, I am not so blind as to imagine that all the world is ready to act upon the law of spiritual attraction; for, to nine-tenths of human beings, these words have no significance. But, in these letters, we are not laying down laws for the nation, but defining our ideal of true marriage.

It is a bitter sorrow to find the hope of young love blighted; but that is light, compared to the sting of finding our holiest instincts disregarded in marriage, a deaf ear turned to the agonizing cry of the soul for mercy, and the very core of our hearts wrung by a sense of wrong and outrage.

ERNEST, I have written a long letter; but my soul is deeply moved, and I have not said half I might. I cannot imagine the sense of self-degradation I have here described as ever occurring in our relation, any more than that the blue heaven could descend to stain its purity with the dust beneath my feet. But I speak from my knowledge of woman's nature,—her instincts, her demands; and I have heard deep and heart-rending revelations from those the world considers happy. I know full well what depths of misery may lie behind a smile.

Thy true wife,

NINA.

Rights and Wrongs of Divorce

Andrew Jackson Davis

The *"Poughkeepsie Seer," as Andrew Jackson Davis was known in his day, wrote his views on marriage and divorce in an "elevated state." Since the age of seventeen Davis had been accustomed to enter a trance whenever he wished enlightenment. For a while he worked as a physician's somnambulist, diagnosing diseases and prescribing cures. In the mid-1840s he gave a famous series of trance-lectures, and these were then published as* Nature's Divine Revelations, *a hodgepodge of Swedenborgian and other mystical doctrines that became a major source for modern spiritualism over several generations (more than forty editions). Davis is known as the John the Baptist of spiritualism, and his pronouncements, however inflated or absurd they may now seem, had an enormous audience and deserve serious attention if for no other reason than the effect they had on multitudes of believers (and nonbelievers) in the major religious revival of nineteenth-century America.*

Nor were Davis' matrimonial opinions as outlandish as his means of arriving at them. What could be more reasonable than the careful

149

*course he steers here between the extravagancies of the Nichols
and the inflexible conservatism of their enemy Horace Greeley?
However he came by them, his capsule assessments of the positions
of Nichols, Andrews, Greeley, Wright, and others demonstrates
that he had read their books carefully before contemplating the
"infinite conjugalities of the universe." Davis' final view probably
suffers from too much sense of the battlefield on which there were
so many combatants; his advocacy of eternal union and easy divorce
may seem like an attempt to befriend every cause. Yet his position,
translated into modern terms, was not so far from the adjustment
society did slowly make during the century following: "In applying
the principles of marriage to human beings, I discovered that man's
highest dower is the power to eternize a temporal union. Not that
all legal relations can be converted into future and permanent
blessings, but those marriages only that are begun with a certain
compatibility of temperament. Even then disobedience to those
laws and disregard of those delicacies by which Love is awakened
and nurtured, might cause a good union to dwindle down and at
length vanish in a cold and hateful separation for eternity."*

*Unlike many fellow spiritualists, Davis did not argue from the
existence of an afterlife to the doctrine of a single predestined
conjugal union—the marriage made in heaven. This doctrine lay
behind many spiritualist arguments for free love—that is, for
renouncing a merely "earthly" marriage when the eternal partner
happened to appear on the scene. Davis' "investigations into the
laws of marriage had given me the knowledge that there was no
inexorable destiny to contend with; that God had not predetermined
and foreordained that a certain man must be married to a certain
woman in order to secure the eternal marriage; but, on the contrary,
I saw that the Divine Code is within the scope of human discovery,
and teaches that it is for the twain to decide whether they will be
transiently or permanently related." On the basis of such a view,
however, Davis was able, in the higher state, to scan "the immense
field of human life—to detect, if possible, among the vast throng
of female natures, a soul whose invisible constitution and mental
circumstances were alike suited to my own. To this clairvoyant
penetration I devoted one hour for five successive days, but without
satisfaction." At length he hit on a lady who, it happened, was
already involved with him. He married her, yet, as it turned out,*

she was not his spiritual mate—so the clairvoyant survey was not infallible—another reason for less stringent laws of divorce.

Davis had, in fact, several occasions to test the adequacy of divorce legislation in the United States. *He himself only once found it necessary to renounce a mate, and that late in life, but he had by that time twice married divorced women.* The first occasion *was in 1848, when he married Katie Dodge, a woman twice his age, who had begun as his "spirit-sister," a devotee of the movement who put up $1000 to publish* Nature's Divine Revelations. *Mrs. Dodge had a husband already, though she had not lived with him for some years.* Her money must have been in trust somehow, for *she seems to have had access to it in spite of her separation—an unusually lucky circumstance for Davis.* The lady was able to obtain *a Rhode Island divorce through her money and influence—it was by act of the State Legislature—and they were married July 1, 1848.* Katie, or "Silona" as she was called in Spirit-Land, did not seem *the ideal wife after all, though Davis had "unerringly" perceived "that she was just* the character *to accompany me up the Mountain of Power."* She did not like living on the lower scale that they now found necessary. *Her health was bad, and she began to ask* **Davis** *if he were "sure—very, very sure—that all* [true] *marriages are eternal."* "As far as I can see" *was his reply—not so equivocal considering how far he thought that was. Yet it was not so. Katie died on November 2, 1853, and that winter* **Davis** *met a new conjugal mate—and had a message from "Silona" announcing her blissful eternal union to "Cyloneos"—of "the Brotherhood of Morlassia."*

Davis' new affinity also began as an unhappily married woman. *Mary F.* Love, *herself a spiritualist lecturer, had been separated from her husband—who had another interest—for some time. In this case the matter was complicated by two children, whom Mary was required to give up when her Indiana divorce came through. She and Davis were married May 15, 1855. Again the eternal match proved temporary, though longer-lived than the first. In 1884, after almost thirty years of harmonial conjunction, she received a twenty-page letter from her "companion in work," revealing the following:*

Accordingly, at this late day in our lives, in presence of the supreme Truth, I now declare to you my discovery that, notwithstanding the harmoniousness of our central temperaments, and notwithstanding the consequent congeniality of both heart and intellect between us, whereby our association has been rendered at once agreeable and profitable, yet, twenty days had not passed after our legal marriage when I definitely, intuitively, realized that, although I was pleasantly associated with a gentle, loving, and intelligent woman,—all which is so essential to harmonious companionship in work, and to social comfort and peace,—yet I distinctly realized that I was not associated with my eternal mate in conjugal life!

Mary's reply was prompt and to the point: "Do not hesitate to let me know your plans for obtaining legal freedom, when once they have been formed, and, rest assured, I shall offer no oppostion. May God and the angels be ever your refuge and consolation." This was Davis's last experiment with legal marriage, before passing into the Spirit-Land, twenty-five years later, where one hopes he discovered who his true mate really was.

Andrew Jackson Davis
Rights and Wrongs of Divorce

The social world is on the rally: a war, although bloodless, is to be fought. America is the place; we know how to do the work. With Native Americans, the covenant of 1777, "signed by the brave Fathers of our republic, and sealed by the heart's blood of Patriots and Heroes," is sacred still as the testament of a new-born savior. America is to show the world not only how to conquer tyranny in politics, but also how to procure freedom in religion and in all relations.

There are already several warriors in the field. They have engaged in the questions of marriage and divorce. Some of these have ascended to the adjoining world. But they are not less the friends of Liberty. I will briefly review them, not as to what they may this moment believe, but as they have spoken or written.

First: Moses was a *self-constituted legalist.* Arbitrary law and divinity were one with this man. His laws upon marriage and divorce were wholly in favor of the masculine. Men could put their wives away for various causes: but the wives were in bondage.

● Selection from *The Reformer* (Vol. IV of *The Great Harmonia; concerning Physiological Vices and Virtues, and The Seven Phases of Marriage*), Boston: Sanborn, Carter, & Bazin; New York: Fowler & Wells—Partridge & Brittan, 1856, pp. 404–11, 413–16, 418–19, 422–23.

In several respects the common law of our day is identical with the Mosaic programme. This, we work to reform. *Second:* Jesus was a *humanitarian spiritualist.* The soul, not the body, concerned this man. As a representative of the future, Jesus uttered the gospel of Love—free from all the *extremism* of the marriage relation. His marriage was spiritual or ideal: in the soul only: not looking toward parentage nor the inconveniences of compound selfish housekeeping. In respect to divorce he was as lenient as his perceptions permitted. His doctrine, in several points, was grand and beautiful. For a man to abandon his wife, without the *one* cause, is to harm her in heart. If while in legal relation, you have sexual relation with another, it is the same as outraging your own mother's honor, besides being in general an *insult* to all womankind. These doctrines were quite sacred with a sect, called "Essenes" which flourished privately before the birth of Jesus, and corresponded in several things to modern Shakers. The social and spiritual equality of woman is recognized; nevertheless, the legislative and governing power is vested in the masculine.

Third: Swedenborg was a *philosophic religionist.* His doctrines of marriage and divorce are not essentially different. He esteemed "conjugal love as the *fundamental* of all loves, and the receptacle of all joys and delights." The true marriage "is nothing less than the conjunction of love and wisdom." He believes that the truly joined are ever growing more brilliant, more beautiful, and happy; giving and receiving, continually, of each other's existence or essence; and perfecting each other in love and wisdom for ever and ever. He recognized iron, copper, silver, and golden marriages: the *different phases* of human attractions and the diverse methods of ascending life.

In regard to divorce, Swedenborg is faithful to his religious convictions. His divorces are effects of external unions; and seldom occur, except as subsequent and consequent to crime. Yet his "second marriages" are somewhat natural. But he sees only an interminable hopeless prospect before those whose love leads them into scorbutic and adulterous connections. They never find it possible to associate with angels; never grow better, as trees do, for contact and beneficient culture.

Fourth: Charles Fourier was a *social organizationist.* It is understood, among the students of Fourier, that he has demonstrated *scientifically* the *law* of the conditions according to which the association of men must be established. Nothing can be more positively certain, it is believed, than the societary disclosures of the social architect.

In going over the history of the past, Fourier discerned the different social, political, and religious *phases* of humanity—the fourth of which he terms "civilism"—meaning merely a *station* at which the race has arrived in Europe and America, but from which other and higher forms of society will most certainly be evolved. The most beautiful, the most rich, the most happy, he calls "Harmony"—being the fruition of the Christian's ideal of a Millenium.

In order to escape the gulf of miseries and duplicities and cheatings, in which even the most civilized classes struggle, Fourier suggests the organization of secular *interests*—the formation of a "Phalanx": a township of associated interests and attractive industry. All the buildings connected with such ownship—specially the Unitary Dwelling—is called the "Phalanstery." When the earth shall have become covered with *phalansteries,* it is affirmed, the reign of peace and happiness will be equally distributed and universal.

In this connection I feel impressed to speak briefly of Robert Owen, the *moral circumstantialist.* This noble being has wrought like a divine embassador. He has labored many years for man's elevation. His theory is—

I. Equality in education, in training, in external condition.

II. True formation of character from birth.

III. The annual creation of a surplus for all.

IV. The introduction, in every department of life, of mechanical, chemical, and all other sciences, to perform all the disagreeable labor of society.

V. The character of each to be so formed and so situated as to render all civil and military professions worse than useless; and to bestow the money and labor now employed to sustain them to the education and happiness of all.

Prior to his conversion to Spiritualism, he had labored without any great results. I trace the cause to three prominent mistakes—

1. Appealing to the rulers and governors of the world; with the hope of inspiring them with the necessity of Reform.

2. Leaving out the religious or spiritual element; which is natural to man as are heat and light.

3. Asserting that God, through nature, creates all the qualities of each individual at birth; but that the *direction* of the qualities and character is given by society—good or bad, in accordance with contiguous circumstances. But since the dawning of the Spiritual Era, whose fertilizing rays have penetrated to the deepest retirements of his moral being, this indefatigable man is more than ever hopeful and earnest in his belief that the race is to be ere long promoted from ignorance and misery to the peaceful eminences of wisdom and happiness. From what has been said you will observe a dissimilarity of reform methods, distinguishing Owenites from the school of Fourier.

Fourier taught that the "four columns on which the harmonic state rests, are *Industrial Attraction,* the *Integral Minimum, Unitary Education,* and *Proportional Population.*" He accordingly provided, by social organization, for a full and healthy exercise of all types of character. He believed that man would never be pure nor contented with less than individual freedom. He read in the human soul the words of its destiny; all true social science, in its radical attractions. All wants have satisfactions; all curiosity, a complete gratification; all aspirations, their answering realities. "Attractions proportional to destiny." Hence, he disposes of the troubles of marriage and divorce through an organization of social interests. Competition, frauds, the whole category of sharpers and swindlers, disappear in the grand circle of harmonic relations. The children belong to the *phalanstery,* or not, as their parents desire; and thus all social objections to granting divorces are summarily annihilated.

Fifth: Henry C. Wright is a *moral radicalist.* He looks from the individual down upon society. Man and woman are all in all. Human laws, as eliminated from social combinations, have *no right* to dictate the grounds of either marriage or divorce. It is a purely personal matter. If two married find themselves mistaken in each other, they should separate, and society has no right to forbid them a second marriage. "Let every woman be fixed, as God is, *never to live* with a man as a wife whom she does not love. Let every man be equally true to the voices of his nature, and an untold amount of misery would be saved to both." He says further: "being divorced, each has the same wants and attributes as before. The fact that they have been once mistaken and bewildered can not destroy this want of their being." The twain still seek the true marriage relation. And human laws have no right to cause them to disobey "the higher law written on their souls." If human legislation does this, "it usurps a tyrannical power against which *every pulse* of true manhood and womanhood revolts."

Sixth: Stephen P. Andrews is a *philosophic socialist.* He is not unlike the former (H. C. Wright) in his individuality. He comes before us as the disciple of Josiah Warren: "an obscure, plain man, one of the people, the most profoundly analytical thinker who has dealt with this class of subjects, has discovered *principles* which render the organization of society as simple a matter of science as any other." These principles are "the Sovereignty of the Individual"; and "Cost the limit of Price." What shall we say of all this? The self-sovereignty of each individual is another method to social Reform. It is the opposite of Owen and Fourier. Society is exposed to the self-regulated acts of the individual. Every one is understood, however, to practise this self-governing principle *at his own cost.* But mankind are bound together by a thousand silken cords—girded round about by a magnetic belt of subtle sensibilities—which communicate an injury done to or by the remotest person to all other members of the living whole. Who shall have wisdom adequate to say when and where benevolence ends and self-preservation begins? What man can always know when his own acts are confined to himself?—when his deeds are done purely and exclusively *at his own cost?* The principle of commercial equity, is—*Exchange of Equivalent Costs and Burdens.* The popular method of commercial injustice, is—*Exchange of Equivalent Values and Benefits.* This is considered to be at once not only the grand practical solution of the social problem, but, also the pathway to social equity, and to freedom in all human relations.

Starting from this postulatory law, Mr. Andrews has inferred and published many conclusions, touching social reformation; with some of which, doubtless, the founder privately disagrees. In regard to marriage and divorce he speaks out like a lover of truth; not intuitionally, but intellectually. He opposes the perpetual, or exclusive, marriage. He objects to civil marriages because they make personal property of woman, restricting her self-sovereignty, and ultimating in compound selfishness and imperfect offspring. "Sexual purity," he says, "is that kind of relation, whatever it be between the sexes, which contributes in the highest degree to their

mutual health and happiness, taking into account the remote as
well as the immediate results." It may be stated," he remarks, "as
the growing public sentiment of Christendom, that the man and
woman who do not love *have no right*, before God, to live together
as husband and wife: no matter how solemn the marriage service
which has been mumbled over them." This he considers the
negative statement; the *positive* side is this: that "the man and
woman WHO DO LOVE, can live together in purity without any
mummery at all—that it is *love* that *sanctifies*; not the blessing of
the church." Mr. Andrews repels the insinuation that his doctrine
is *similar* to the "Oneida Perfectionists"; but plants himself firmly
and logically upon the broad principle of individual sovereignty.

Seventh: Thomas L. Nichols is a *scientific externalist.* He thinks
respecting marriage and divorce mainly from the sphere of "facts"
and uses. He looks at the question physiologically, and deals in
multitudinous deductions of knowledge. His estimate of Nature's
laws is drawn in general from historical experience and the frag-
mental testimony of medical men. He identifies a catalogue of
certain historic facts with an immutable law. Therefore, he reasons
well, but superficially; sometimes sophistically. He sees woman as
a fine creature physiologically considered; and man as "a sterner
counterpart" in every organic essential. I quote from the recent
work on "Marriage," as authorized and edited by Dr. and Mrs.
Nichols.

With Henry C. Wright, he says: "a love may be genuine and true
for the time and not for all time (see page 290). The woman who
filled my ideal twenty years ago, may have no attraction for me
now." From this he concludes that *variety in love* is as natural as
the demand for variety by any other human attribute. "There is,"
he asserts (see page 296), "no evident reason why the law of variety,
which extends to the studies, pursuits, pleasures, tastes, and
passions—should fail when it comes to the question of variety in
love." . . . "If the God of nature has given variety as an element
of love, we shall only make discords by our denial of this law"
(see pages 312 and 315). . . . . "I assume it as a fact of human
experience [here he depends on facts] that such a passion does
exist—that the principle of variety, change, alternation, as an
element of healthy enjoyment, belongs to every passion of the soul,
and that the passion of love forms no exception."

•   •   •

Concerning *divorce,* this author (Dr. Nichols) is very free and self-assured. "It will be said," he remarks, "that there are undoubtedly *false* marriages, but there are also *true* ones. If by marriages is meant an indissoluble monogamy (or a union with one), a legal exclusive bond of a civilized institution, I deny that it *ever* is, or *ever* can be right. I assert that the *promise of a man to love any woman* as long as he lives, is wrong . . . I denounce, therefore, the civilized marriage as a violation of the laws of Nature and the commands of God." (see page 328).

Here, the world says, is opening the infernal abominations of a new Sodom and Gomorrah—a conjugal pandemonium; at the sight of which the "N.Y. Tribune" is thrown, temporarily, into the last stages of political decomposition. In order to avert this fatal calamity, and to keep the apocryphal institutions of our great cities from becoming popular, the (supposed) *editor* mounts his throne and issues several fresh decretals, as if commissioned expressly to do so by the court of Rome. See the Tribunes of July, 1854; from which I feel impressed to extract some words.

Eighth: Horace Greeley is a *political economist.* He is a man of perception: a seer of things *as* and *where* they sometimes are not. History is his secular bible, and his schoolmaster is outward experience. He has no patience, therefore, to wait and "see whether the Mormon polygamy will prove beneficient." History points him to "philosophy teaching by example." Egypt, Syria, China, has settled the question that *promiscuity* in love is opposed to mental energy and national progress.

He loves the civil law when it says: "There can be no divorce without crime." He thinks the Individual should be lost in the state. From the state he *looks down* upon the individual; and determines, like the Romish pope, the liberty of men by the requirements and safety of the social compact. Which is the broadest and truest—judging man's nature by the darkness of institutions, or institutions by the light of man's nature?

Marriage, in his opinion, is an individual compact with the state; made at will, and at the risk of the candidates for marriage.

Two of opposite sex go to the State, and say: "we, having no legal impediments to our union, wish to be joined in marriage."

The state asks: "Do you feel yourselves so truly and surely ONE that you can safely promise, forsaking all others, to live consecrate wholly and purely to each other to the end of your mortal existence?"

They hesitate; such a promise requires a total disregard of the possibilities of all human change or alteration.

But the state continues: "Your response shall be *conclusive* here: it is given at your peril. If you say you are firmly blended by conjugal affection when you are not, yours is the wrong, and on your heads be *the penalty*—the penalty of dragging a *heavy and hateful chain to the end of your days!*"

Such unphilosophic language the *editor* puts into the mouth of the state. He seems to think that the married become "good husbands and wives from the necessity of remaining husbands and wives—that necessity is a powerful master in teaching the duties which it imposes." In the whole category of intolerant codes, methinks, there is not to be found one theory of political government more cruel, more inhuman, more unphilosophical than this— the recent *decretal* of the N.Y. Tribune; in several particulars, the best daily paper ever published in the world.

But I have placed before you the aspect of the battle about to be fought; and introduced to your attention the principal officers in this army. You know their method of warfare; now take such weapons as come most natural to your hand; for every one must, sooner or later, go into the reform field.

Amid and above all contentions is heard the voice of the Harmonial Philosophy. From afar it comes with the voice of song. How musical are its divine harmonies!—"Like a gush of sweet sounds from a golden land," for whose regenerating waters the world has been for ever faint. From distant stars it comes, diffusing animation and beauty everywhere, like the morning light. It sounds like the gospel of true religion—more solemn than the last murmur of the storm blast among the hills; than the sighing of low winds among the grasses upon the ocean's shore.

The Harmonial Philosophy will destroy all barbarism in the marriage relation. It will exalt man's conception of woman, and woman's conception of man; and true marriage will then become the *foundation* of peace on earth.

The doctrine of modern church and state, that woman is man's property—that man by divine decree is woman's master—is the doctrine of contamination and cruelty. It is the worst form of despotism; and distributes an equal condemnation upon husband, wife, and offspring.

The opinion that marriage between the sexes, is a special arbitrary divine "institution," is founded on ignorance of Nature's laws. Marriage is *as much a fact* among plants, minerals, and stars, as among human beings. It is universal—the sacrament of life—the coronal development of immutable laws. And as a sequence, I affirm, that marriage *between* human souls can produce good results —i.e., the *children of love and wisdom*—only when consummated in strict accordance with the nuptial laws of Nature. . . .

Concerning the rights and wrongs of divorce, the harmonial philosophy is alike explicit and natural. Our work is: to affirm and advocate the principle. Come what may—smiles or frowns—this work must be done!

Divorce is the *effect* of a law: the law of marriage. Transient marriages bring divorces. Divorces are natural, until the harmonial plane is reached; then, only an eternal union is natural. How absurd, therefore, to require *crime* as a pretext for divorce!

The social responsibilities of marriage are not as complicated as many legislators and lawyers affirm. We know that, in this order of society, there must be a legal recognition of marriage: a record made of the fact, in order to settle property questions, wills, deeds, &c., but the words, pronounced by the minister or the justice, are in themselves of no account either in earth or heaven.

In the minds of political economists, the existence of children is the invincible difficulty to the freedom of divorce. Divorce would be more easy in all our states, if two questions were practically and satisfactorily answered—viz.: 1. "Do frequent and easy divorces promote the morals of society, or increase the number of happy marriages?" 2. "What disposition can the state make of the children of divorced parents?"

It is not my purpose to answer these questions: but to affirm the *naturalness* and *propriety* of divorce. We need the principle: let consequences be manfully encountered.

JUSTICE is very simple—it is very grand, god-like, and glorious— is the *fundamental law* of all true religion. Will mankind never learn that policy is not principle? Will politicians never learn that mere expediencies are essentially immoral and unprincipled?

The existence of children is the greatest impediment to the settlement of this question. In Connecticut, Rhode Island, Ohio, Indiana, and two other states, the laws and provisions regulating divorce are comparatively humane. But the relation of the parents to the family, and the relation of the family to the State, is still the troublesome problem. In Fourier's organization all these difficulties are removed. But this we do not recommend. We must work upon society in its present condition. We should accept the PRINCIPLE OF JUSTICE, of individual sovereignty, and practice upon it as far as we can in wisdom.

Let us ask: "How far is the individual entitled to his personal liberty without the interference of society?" This is the weightiest of all social questions. But the *broadest* is always the *truest* sentiment; and so, we dispose of such a question by affirming a universal principle of justice, which commences with the individual, then flows outwardly to the whole, and back again to the centre. In other words: all are members of one body. Reformers should consider, therefore, that neither an individual nor a nation can commit the least act of injustice against the obscurest member, without having to pay the penalty. "There are," it is said, "to-day in our midst ten times as many fugitives from matrimony as there are *fugitives* from slavery; and it may well be doubted if the aggregate, or the *average,* of their sufferings has been less." Most of these fugitives are free from criminality.

When the Legislature refuses to grant a divorce without *crime,* or without some organic defect, the *injustice* must be borne by the social body. "Liberty, or death!" President Jackson's motto is good in this place—*"Demand only what is right—submit to nothing wrong!"*

•   •   •

The method of obtaining divorce should be more simplified; less expensive, and regulated by a Law of Justice.

I. Example: when two present themselves to the proper magistrate soliciting divorce, or when one makes an application in writing signed by the other, and both make satisfactory statements, and present sufficient guaranty in regard to the disposition of their children should there be any, then let their oath of honesty and free-will be taken and recorded, with their names, and a certificate of legal divorce be given to each in return.

II. If the law requires a *crime* as the basis of an action, then let us forthwith elevate the *moral* standard of right and wrong, and say: If a woman, under the influence of importunity and the desire for a home, marries one whom she does not fully love, that woman hath committed *adultery* and a *crime* yet more against posterity. Or, if at first she did love her husband, and subsequently for sufficient deep-seated and uncapricious reasons *loves him conjugally no longer,* but loves another instead and does not take that other to be her husband, she is then guilty of being both a prostitute and an adulteress. The same moral law is equally applicable to man under like circumstances.

III. If a woman testifies of disaffection toward her husband, or if the husband testifies of disaffection toward the wife, and her or his *probity* can be established by witnesses and neighbors by whom the parties are known, let such be divorced.

Of course a thousand different contingencies will occur; for which a humane legislature would make ample provision.

Parties should never be tempted to encourage disaffection from trifling causes—such as mere haste in speaking to each other, from any merely circumstantial causes, or the disgust and aversion of extremism or inversionism. Be kind and patient—exercise the broadest humanity toward each other: let nothing lead to separation, save an internal knowledge of constitutional inadaptedness.

If you seek divorce, do so from the Principle of Justice; never from caprice; nor be ever as cruel and barbaric to the rejected one as Abraham was to Hagar and her child.

Children should be provided for by the parents before applying for divorce—or, if not otherwise cared for, let the STATE adopt and instruct them—giving them a righteous opportunity to become educated, skilled in some occupation, and otherwise valuable characters.

All property questions and alimony can be settled by the legislature; or, if the parties desire and agree to it, by means of arbitration.

These methods will tend to render mankind more *just,* more *wise,* more *happy.* A free people will make for themselves simpler laws. Let us, my countrymen, plant our institutions upon the Principle of Universal Justice, without fear, and—"consequences will take care of themselves."

II

The Marriage Bed

Moral Physiology

Robert Dale Owen

Robert Dale Owen's philanthropist father, who once defined chastity as "Sexual intercourse with affection," raised his son without the usual cant and shame regarding human sexuality. A friend of Francis Plane and himself a Malthusian, the elder Owen was even thought by some to be the secret author of Richard Carlisle's notorious pamphlet on contraception, Every Woman's Book. *Coincidentally, it was this same tract that caused Robert Dale Owen to write his own famous defense of birth control,* Moral Physiology *(1830). Owen had no intention of producing an American version of Carlisle. When some friends at New Harmony used his press to print a prospectus for a new edition of* Every Woman's Book, *Owen was accused of immorality. He issued a defense of the undertaking (while squelching the edition), and this provoked further attacks, until finally Owen was goaded into printing his own argument for limiting families and his thoughts on how this might best be accomplished.*

Public reaction was as one might have expected: the pamphlet went through five editions in seven months, and was either ignored or vilified in the press. One especially interesting fulmination came from the radical labor leader Thomas Skidmore, who was already engaged in a dispute with Owen and Frances Wright over the issue of state-financed education for the poor. Skidmore had his own extremist views of what was good for the laboring classes—the abolition of private property—but from today's perspective Owen's proposals seem at least as radical—cheap, widespread birth control, and "guardian" education for all children, of every class, including compulsory boarding away from their homes from the age of two onwards. If effected, these Spartan proposals would certainly have altered the American working class, and changed the history of the country dramatically. (Skidmore claimed, perhaps rightly, that such measures would merely destroy working-class solidarity, and produce a totalitarian state.)

The story of Owen's part in other varieties of sexual reform— women's property rights and liberalized divorce—is told in Section III. By the time he came to his debates with Horace Greeley over these issues, Owen had lived down a good deal of his reputation as an enemy of the family, but throughout the century his name was automatically associated with the contraceptive technique he advocated, coitus interruptus. *Of course the withdrawal method had been in use for hundreds of years before Owen gave it currency in print, and in spite of the monolithic opinion of the medical profession that it was simply "conjugal onanism," with the same dire effects on health and sanity as masturbation, nonetheless multitudes continued to practice it as the simplest and cheapest way of preventing pregnancy. It is doubtful that Owen's pamphlet resulted in any great shift in the birth rate; during its first forty years or so, it probably had a circulation of 25,000 in the United States (and another 40,000 in Great Britain)—considerably less than the popular marriage manuals that began to appear in the 1850s. Since it depended on neither the calendar nor any chemical preparations, users of the withdrawal method did not need printed instructions to know what to do.* Moral Physiology *was more significant symbolically, as the first American birth control handbook to break the taboos of the age of prudery.*

Robert Dale Owen
Moral Physiology

It is exceedingly to be regretted that mankind did not spend some small portion, at least, of the time and industry which has been wasted on theoretical researches, in collecting and collating the *actual experience* of human beings. But this task, too difficult for the ignorant, has generally been thought too simple and commonplace for the learned. To this circumstance, joined to the fact, that it is not thought fitting or decent for human beings freely to communicate their personal experience on the important subject now under consideration—to these causes are attributable the great and otherwise unaccountable ignorance which so strangely prevails, even sometimes among medical men, as to the power which man may possess over the reproductive instinct. Many physicians will positively deny that man possesses any such power. And yet, if the thousandth part of the talent and research had been employed to investigate this momentous fact, which has been turned to the building up of idle theories, no commonly intelligent individual could well be ignorant of the truth.

I have taken great pains to ascertain the opinions of the most enlightened physicians of Great Britain and France on this subject (opinions which popular prejudice will not permit them to offer publicly in their works); and they all concur in admitting, what the experience of the French nation *positively proves*, that man may have a perfect control over this instinct; and that men and women may, without any injury to health, or the slightest violence done to the moral feelings, and with but small diminution of the pleasure which accompanies the gratification of the instinct, refrain at will from becoming parents. It has chanced to me, also, to win the confidence of several individuals, who have communicated to me, without reserve, their own experience; and all this has been corroborative of the same opinion.

Thus, though I pretend not to speak positively to the details of a subject, which will then only be fully understood when men acquire sense enough simply and unreservedly to discuss it, I may venture to assure my readers, that the main fact is incontrovertible.

● Selection from *Moral Physiology; or, A Brief and Plain Treatise on the Population Question,* 10th ed., New York: G. Vale, 1870, pp. 60–68.

I shall adduce such facts in proof of this as may occur to me in the course of this investigation.

However various and contradictory the different theories of generation, almost all physiologists are agreed, that the entrance of the sperm itself (or of some volatile particles proceeding from it) into the uterus, must precede conception. This it was that probably first suggested the possibility of preventing conception at will.

Among the modes of preventing conception which may have prevailed in various countries, that which has been adopted, and is now universally practised, by the cultivated classes on the continent of Europe, by the French, the Italians, and, I believe, by the Germans and Spaniards, consists of complete withdrawal, on the part of the man, immediately previous to emission. *This is, in all cases, effectual.* It may be objected, that the practice requires a mental effort and a partial sacrifice. I reply, that, in France, where men consider this (as it ought ever to be considered, when the interests of the other sex require it) a *point of honor—all* young men learn to make the necessary effort; and custom renders it easy and a matter of course. As for the sacrifice, shall a trifling (and it is but a very trifling) diminution of physical enjoyment be suffered to outweigh the most important considerations connected with the permanent welfare of those who are the nearest and dearest to us? Shall it be suffered to outweigh the risk of incurring heavy and sacred responsibilities, ere we are prepared to meet and fulfill them? Shall it be suffered to outweigh a regard for the comfort, the well-being— in some cases the *life,* of those whom we profess to love? The most selfish will hesitate deliberately to reply, in the affirmative, to such questions as these. A cultivated young Frenchman, instructed as he is, even from his infancy, carefully to consult, on all occasions, the wishes, and punctiliously to care for the comfort and welfare, of the gentler sex, would learn almost with incredulity, that, in other countries, there are men to be found, pretending to cultivation, who were less scrupulously honourable on this point than himself. You could not offer him a greater insult than to presuppose the possibility of his forgetting himself so far, as thus to put his own momentary gratification, for an instant in competition with the wish or the well-being of any one to whom he professed regard or affection.

I know it will be argued, that men in the mass are not sufficiently moral to adopt this recommendation; because they will not make any voluntary sacrifice of animal enjoyment, however trifling. I do not see that. Hundreds of voluntary sacrifices are daily made to fashion—to public opinion. Let but public opinion bear on this point in other countries, as it does among the more enlightened classes in France, and similar effects will be produced. Besides, the matter is a trifle. The mere act of animal satisfaction, counts with any man of commonly cultivated feelings, as but a small item in the aggregate of enjoyment which satisfied affection affords; and, surely, whether that act be at all times attended with the utmost degree of physical pleasure or not, must, even with the selfish, be a secondary and unimportant consideration. His moral sentiments must be especially weak or uncultivated, who will not admit, that it is the gratification of the social feelings—the repose of the affections—which at all times, constitutes the chief charm of human intercourse.

The least injurious among the present checks to population, celibacy, is a mortification of affections, a violence done to the social feelings, sometimes a sacrifice even of the health. Not one of these objections can be urged to the trifling restraint proposed.

As to the cry which prejudice may raise against it as being unnatural, it is just as unnatural (and no more so) as to refrain, in a sultry summer's day, from drinking, perhaps, more than a pint of water at a draught, which prudence tells us is enough, while inclination would bid us drink a quart. *All* thwarting of any human wish or impulse may, in one sense, be called unnatural; it is not, however, ofttimes the less prudent and proper, on that account.

As to the practical efficacy of this simple preventive, the experience of France, where it is universally practised, might suffice in proof. I know, at this moment, several married persons who have told me, that, after having had as many children as they thought prudent, *they had for years employed this check, with perfect success.* For the satisfaction of my readers, I will select one particular instance.

I knew personally and intimately for many years a young man of strict honor, in whose sincerity I ever placed perfect confidence, and who confided to me the particulars of his situation. He was just entering on life, with slender means, and his circumstances forbade him to have a large family of children. He, therefore, having consulted with his young wife, practised this restraint, I believe for about eighteen months, and with perfect success. At the expiration of that period, their situation being more favorable, they resolved to become parents; and, in a fortnight after, the wife found herself pregnant. My friend told me, that though he felt the partial privation a little at first, a few weeks' habit perfectly reconciled him to it; and that nothing but a deliberate conviction that he might prudently now become a parent, and a strong desire on his wife's part to have a child, induced him to alter his first practice. I believe I was the only one among his friends to whom he ever communicated the real state of the case; and I doubt not there are, even in this country, hundreds of similar cases which the world never learns anything about. Hence the doubts and ignorance which exist on the subject.

I add another instance. A few weeks since, a respectable and very intelligent father of a family, about thirty-five years of age, who resides west of the mountains, called at our office. Conversation turned on the present subject, and I expressed to him my conviction that this check was effectual. He told me he could speak from personal experience. He had married young, and soon had three children. These he could support in comfort, without running into debt or difficulty; but, the price of produce sinking in his neighborhood, there did not appear a fair prospect of supporting a large family. In consequence, he and his wife determined to limit their offspring to three. They have accordingly employed the above check for seven or eight years; have had no more children; and have been rewarded for their prudence by finding their situation and prospects improving every year. He confirmed an opinion I have already expressed, by stating, that custom completely reconciled him to any slight privation he might at first have felt. I asked him, whether his neighbors generally followed the same practice. He replied, that he could not tell; for he had not thought it prudent to speak with any but his own relations on the subject, one or two of whom, he knew, had profited by his advice, and afterwards expressed to him their gratitude for the important information.

It is unnecessary farther to multiply instances. The fact that this check is in common practice, and universally known to be efficacious, in France, is alone sufficient evidence of its practicability and safety.

I can readily imagine, that there are men, who, in part from temperament, but much more from the continued habit of unrestrained indulgence, may have so little command over their passions, as to find difficulty in practising it; and some, it may be, who will declare it to be impossible. If any there be to whom it *is* impossible (which I very much doubt), I am at least convinced that the number is exceedingly small; not a fiftieth part of those who may at first *imagine* such to be their case.

I may add, that *partial* withdrawal, though recommended in a letter published in Carlisle's Republican, is not an infallible preventive of conception.

Other modes of prevention have been employed, but this is at once the most simple, and the most efficacious; the only one, or nearly so, employed by the cultivated among European nations; and the only one I here venture to recommend. From all I have heard, as well from physicians as from private individuals, it is, as regards health, at the least, perfectly innocent: it has been even said to produce upon the human system an effect similar to that of temperance in diet; but whether there be truth in this hypothesis I know not. As regards any moral impropriety in its use, enough, methinks, has already been said, to convince all except those who *will* not be convinced, that to employ it, in all cases where prudence or the well-being of our companions requires it, is an act of practical virtue.

It may be said, and said truly, that this check places the power chiefly in the hands of the man, and not, where it ought to be, in those of the woman. She, who is the sufferer, is not secured against the culpable carelessness, or perhaps the deliberate selfishness, of him who goes free and unblamed, whatever may happen. To this, the reply is, that the best and only effectual defense for women is to refuse connection with any man *void of honor.* An (almost omnipotent) public opinion would thus be speedily formed; one of immense moral utility; by means of which the man's social reputation would be placed, as it should be, in the keeping of women, whose moral tact and nice discrimination in such matters is far superior to ours. How mighty and how beneficient the power which such an influence might exert, and how essentially and rapidly it might conduce to the gradual, but thorough extirpation of those selfish vices, legal and illegal, which now disgrace and brutify our species, it is difficult even to imagine.

In the silent, but resistless progress of human improvement, such a change is fortunately inevitable. We are gradually emerging from the night of blind prejudice and of brutal force; and, day by day, rational liberty and cultivated refinement, win an accession of power. Violence yields to benevolence, compulsion to kindness, the letter of law to the spirit of justice: and, day by day, men and women become more willing, and better prepared, to entrust the most sacred duties (social as well as political) more to good feeling and less to idle form—more to moral and less to legal keeping.

It is no question whether such reform will come: no human power can arrest its progress. How slowly or how rapidly it may come, *is* a question; and depends, in some degree, on adventitious circumsances. Should this little book prove one among the number of circumstances to accelerate, however slightly, that progress, its author will be repaid, ten times over, for any trifling labor it may have cost him.

ROBERT DALE OWEN.

The Fruits of Philosophy

Charles Knowlton

"*Some twenty or twenty-five years ago,*" *wrote William Alcott in 1856, "a physician of New England, of much greater practical skill than strict integrity, especially towards God, became the author of a small pocket volume, with a very inviting title, whose avowed object was to teach people, both in married life and elsewhere, the art of gratifying the sexual appetite without the necessity of progeny. His book had a wide circulation. I have found it in nearly every part of our wide-spread country.*"

The physician was Charles Knowlton, the pocket volume The Fruits of Philosophy *(1832), which had gone through numerous editions, authorized and pirated, by the time Alcott wrote. It was the most reliable guide to contraception available in the United States for decades, and Alcott's own disapproving estimate was that "tens of thousands" of pregnancies were prevented each year by its recipes. It had one virtue at least that marriage manuals of later generations lacked: its prescriptions worked (or some of them, anyway—though zinc sulphate was not an effective spermicide, and some methods, like cold water, had disagreeable side effects). Most Victorian physicians who ventured any counsel at all on the subject favored the rhythm method, but they usually put the safe period at the wrong time. Knowlton himself misunderstood the nature and function of the menses, but his contraceptive instructions were probably as effective as Alcott thought them—with only "occasional failures."*

Knowlton was a remarkable man. His colleagues seem to have respected his medical abilities, while deploring his deism on the one hand (the problem of "integrity" alluded to by Alcott), and his Malthusian militance on the other. Thus his articles were frequently accepted by the Boston Medical and Surgical Journal *in the 1840s, yet when that same magazine belatedly came to review* The Fruits of Philosophy *(after some ten editions had appeared), its scientific assessment of the matter boiled down to "the less that is known about it by the public at large, the better it will be for the morals of the community." The assumption was that the techniques worked.*

Knowlton himself seems to have been satisfied, in the 1840s, to let his book fend for itself. Earlier he had been eager to get an audience for it—and to make a modest profit, by patenting his processes and selling his own "feminine syringe" in conjunction with the book. This was E. B. Foote's approach a generation later, and just as Anthony Comstock stopped Foote with a criminal complaint and a stiff fine, so Knowlton was made to feel just how far he had overstepped decorum when, in 1833, he was sentenced to three months' hard labor for selling copies of The Fruits of Philosophy. *Knowlton was not unfamiliar with jails, for he had served two months for grave robbing (the charges were reduced to "illegal dissection") during his student days at Dartmouth Medical College.*

To demonstrate that he was not cowed by such punishments, Knowlton delivered two public lectures on the day he was released from his second incarceration, prefacing them by an apostrophe to "Superstition," which he accuses of obstructing science and moral reform, including the imprisonment of "a citizen of this free country, ostensibly, for diffusing scientific knowledge of practical utility; but, really, for giving thee a small pill in connection with it, slily wrapped up, which thou canst not swallow."

Characteristically, Knowlton made no other references to The Fruits of Philosophy *in these lectures, but devoted himself instead to his pet theories of "modern materialism." His chief interest was*

*not in birth control at all, but psychology, and what we would call
behaviorism. When his book came under attack again in the following year, Knowlton accused its enemies of really objecting to his
materialism—and the evidence of Alcott's diatribe some twenty
years later suggests he may have been right. But today Knowlton is
remembered not for his theories of the mind, but as the father of
modern birth control, and his book as the focus of the famous
Bradlaugh-Besant trial in England in the 1870s.*

Charles Knowlton
The Fruits of Philosophy

There have been several means proposed and practised for *checking* conception. I shall briefly notice them, though a knowledge of the *best* is what most concerns us. That of withdrawal immediately before emission is certainly effectual, if practised with sufficient care. But if (as I believe) Dr. Dewee's theory of conception be correct; and as Spallanzani's experiments show that only a trifle of semen even largely diluted with water, may impregnate by being injected into the vagina, it is clear that nothing short of entire withdrawal is to be depended on. But the old notion that the semen must enter the uterus to cause conception, has led many to believe that a partial withdrawal is sufficient, and it is on this account that this error has proved mischievous, as all important errors generally do. It is said by those who speak from experience, that the practice of withdrawal has an effect upon the health similar to temperance in eating. As the subsequent exhaustion is, probably, mainly owing to the shock the nervous system sustains in the act of coition, this opinion may be correct. It is further said that this practice serves to keep alive those fine feelings with which married people first come together. Still I leave it for every one to decide for himself whether this check be so far satisfactory, as not to render some other very desirable.

As to the baudruche, which consists in a covering used by the male, made of very delicate skin, it is by no means calculated to come into general use. It has been used to secure from syphilitic affections.

● Selection from *The Fruits of Philosophy: or The Private Companion of Young Married People,* 2d ed., with additions, Boston, 1833, pp. 124–35.

Another check which the old idea of conception has led some to recommend with considerable confidence, consists in introducing into the vagina previous to connexion, a very delicate piece of sponge, moistened with water, to be immediately afterwards withdrawn by means of a very narrow ribbon attached to it. But as our views would lead us to expect, this check has not proved a sure preventive. As there are many little ridges or folds in the vagina, we cannot suppose the withdrawal of the sponge would dislodge *all* the semen in every instance. If, however, it were well moistened with some liquid which acts chemically upon the semen, it would be pretty likely to destroy the fecundating property of what might remain. But if this check were ever so sure, it would, in my opinion, fall far short of being equal, all things considered, to the one I am about to mention—one which not only dislodges the semen pretty effectually, but at the same time destroys the fecundating property of the whole of it.

It consists in syringing the vagina immediately after connexion, with a solution of sulphate of zinc, of alum, pearlash, or any salt that acts chemically on the semen, and at the same time produces no unfavorable effect on the female. In all probability, a vegetable astringent would answer—as an infusion of white-oak bark, of red rose leaves, of nut-galls, and the like. A lump of either of the above mentioned salts of the size of a chesnut, may be dissolved in a pint of water, making the solution weaker or stronger, as it may be borne without producing any irritation of the parts to which it is applied. These solutions will not lose their virtues by age. A *female syringe*, which will be required in the use of this check, may be had at the shop of an apothecary, for a shilling or less. If preferred, the semen may be dislodged, so far as it can be, by syringing with simple water after which some of the solution is to be injected to destroy the fecundating property of what may remain lodged between the ridges of the vagina, &c.

I know the use of the check requires the woman to leave her bed for a few moments, but this is its only objection; and it would be unreasonable to suppose that any check can ever be devised entirely free of objections. In its favor, it may be said, it costs nearly nothing; it is sure; it requires no sacrifice of pleasure; it is in the hands of the female; it is to be used *after*, instead of before connexion, a weighty consideration in its favor, as a moment's reflection will convince any one; and last, but not least, it is conducive to cleanliness, and preserves the parts from relaxation and disease. The vagina may be very much contracted by a persevering use of astringent injections, and they are frequenly used for this purpose, in cases of *procidentia uteri*, or a sinking down of the womb. Subject as women are to fluor albus and other diseases of the genital organs, it is rather a matter of wonder they are not more so, considering the prevailing practices. Those who have used this check (and some have used it to my knowledge, with entire success, for nine or ten years, and under such circumstances as leave no room to doubt its efficacy) affirm they would be at the trouble of using injections merely for the purposes of health and cleanliness.

By actual experiment it has been rendered highly probable that pregnancy, may, in many instances be prevented by injections of simple water, applied with a tolerable degree of care. But simple water *has* failed, and its occasional failure is what we should expect, considering the anatomy of the parts, and the results of Spallanzani's experiments, heretofore alluded to.

Thus much did I say respecting this check in the first edition of this work. This is what I call the chemical check. The idea of destroying the fecundating property of the semen was *original*, if it did not *originate* with me. My attention was drawn to the subject by the perusal of "Moral Physiology." Such was my confidence in the chemical idea that I sat down and wrote this work in July, 1831. But the reflection that I did not *know* that this check would never fail, and that if it should, I might do some one an injury by recommending it, caused the manuscript to be on hand until the following December. Sometime in November, I fell in with an old acquaintance, who agreeably surprized me by stating, that to his own personal knowledge, this last check had been used as above stated. I have since conversed with a gentleman, with whom I was unacquainted, who stated that, being in Baltimore some few years ago, he was there informed of this check by those who had no doubt of its efficacy. From what has as yet fell under my own observation, I am not warranted in drawing any conclusion. I can only say I have not known it to fail. Such are my views of the whole subject that it would require many instances of its repeated failure to satisfy me that such failures were not owing to an insufficient use of it. I even believe that quite cold water alone, if thoroughly used, would be sufficient. In Spallanzani's experiments warm water was unquestionably used. As the seminal animalcules are essential to impregnation, all we have to do is to change the condition of, or (if you will) to *kill* them; and as they are so exceedingly small and delicate, this is doubtless easily done, and hence *cold* water *may* be sufficient.

What has now been advanced in this work will enable the reader to judge for him or herself of the efficacy of the chemical or syringe check, and time will probably determine whether I am correct in this matter; for I do know that those married females who have much desire to escape, will not stand for the little trouble of using this check, especially when they consider that on the score of cleanliness and health alone, it is worth all the trouble. A great part of the time no check is necessary, and women of experience and observation, with the information conveyed by this work, will be able to judge pretty correctly when it is and when it is not. They may rest assured that none of the salts mentioned will have any deleterious effect. The sulphate of zinc is commonly known by the name of white vitriol. This, as well as alum, have been much used for leucorrhoea. Ascetate of lead, commonly called sugar of lead, would doubtless be effectual—indeed, it has been proved to be so; but I do not recommend it, because I conceive it possible that a long continued use of it, might impair the instinct.

I hope that no failures will be charged to inefficacy of this check which ought to be attributed to negligence, or insufficient use of it. I will therefore recommend at least two applications of the syringe, the sooner, the surer; yet it is my opinion that five minutes delay would not prove mischievous, perhaps not ten.

Chastity

Sylvester Graham

Sylvester Graham, "the poet of bran bread and pumpkins," as
Emerson called him, was also a between-meals bard—of fresh air
and exercise, cold showers, hard mattresses, and chaste bedfellows.

During the 1830s and 1840s Grahamism became a science like
phrenology, a movement like Fourierism, and an institution like
the asylum or the penitentiary. Grahamite boardinghouses were
founded where the bread was made of unbolted, coarsely ground
whole wheat flour, and complemented by fresh fruits and vegetables, and pure water; at Brook Farm there was a Grahamite
table for the faithful, where meat, coffee, tea, and other noxious
substances were never tasted. There was a Graham Journal of
Health and Longevity, and of course, ultimately, the Graham
cracker.

Like most scientific and pseudoscientific reformers of his day
Graham was at heart a moralist. No longer believing in the infal-
libility of the "moral sense" that sustained the previous generation,
Graham was one of the first to formulate a psychosomatic theory

*of ethics, presaging modern authorities from B. F. Skinner to
Wilhelm Reich: ". . . the carnal influence of the human body on
the intellectual and moral powers, is the grand, primary source
of erroneous conclusions and of a fallacious conscience . . . and
hence, as a general rule, it is impossible by any means to remove
an unsound conscience until the carnal lusts and inordinate
appetites and prejudices are subdued." Unlike modern electro and
chemotherapies, Graham's treatment was conservative in the literal
sense. He opposed the use of medicines and relied instead on a
healthy regimen to prevent disease, and even to cure it once
contracted. His principles of hygiene and diet were chiefly negative
—not a matter of "taking" something so much as abstaining. Reading between the lines, one quickly sees that the impulse behind
Grahamism was not simply the classical ideal of moderation, or any
trust in the self-regulating powers of nature (natura sanat); rather
it was a counsel of retrenchment and withholding, a physiological
penuriousness. In the sexual realm this was most apparent. The
selection reprinted here from Graham's* Lecture to Young Men on
Chastity *shows him at his most suspicious of the nature he pretends
to serve and respect. Images of cataclysmic violence convey his sense
of the risks of "venereal indulgence" (itself a revealing phrase),
even when licensed by Church and State. When he praises matrimony for its effect in accustoming husband and wife "to each
other's body," so that "their parts no longer excite an impure
imagination," it is obvious enough that the value of the institution
from Graham's point of view resided less in its sanctioning or
sanctifying of passion than in its potential for dampening sexual
ardor.*

*Graham was mobbed by the butchers and bakers of Boston, not
long after the anti-abolitionists had dragged Garrison through the
streets. William Alcott, Graham's chief competitor in the field of
abstemiousness, was probably right when he guessed that "the
public odium . . . ostensibly directed against his anti-fine flour and
anti-flesh eating doctrines" had its true source in "his anti-sexual
doctrines." One could not expect, thought Alcott, that the ordinary
self-indulgent citizenry would accept curtailment of its free pleasures. All the more did Alcott take pride in the adoption of the
Grahamite ideal by the vast majority of the medical profession
during the rest of the century. If Owen and Knowlton were the
villains of birth control, Graham was the knight of continence.*

Sylvester Graham
Chastity

The convulsive paroxysms attending venereal indulgence, are connected with the most intense excitement, and cause the most powerful agitation to the whole system that it is ever subject to. The brain, stomach, heart, lungs, liver, skin, and the other organs, feel it sweeping over them with the tremendous violence of a tornado. The powerfully excited and convulsed heart drives the blood, in fearful congestion, to the principal viscera,—producing oppression, irritation, debility, rupture, inflammation, and sometimes disorganization;—and this violent paroxysm is generally succeeded by great exhaustion, relaxation, lassitude, and even prostration.

These excesses, too frequently repeated, cannot fail to produce the most terrible effects. The nervous system, even to its most minute filamentary extremities, is tortured into a shocking state of debility, and excessive irritability, and uncontrollable mobility, and aching sensibility; and the vital contractility of the muscular tissues throughout the whole system becomes exceedingly impaired, and the muscles, generally, become relaxed and flaccid; and consequently all the organs and vessels of the body, even to the smallest capillaries, become extremely debilitated; and their functional powers exceedingly feeble.

•   •   •

Physiologists have indulged in a great deal of conjecture and speculation concerning the "animal spirits—nervous fluid—vital electricity," &c. &c., but as yet, it is all conjecture and speculation. We know that, by some means or other, the influence of the WILL is conveyed through certain nerves, to the organs of voluntary motion—that the sense of touch is conveyed, or reflected, or transmitted from the surface, through certain other nerves, to the brain:—and that vital energy is distributed through certain other nerves, from the general and particular centres of action, to the several organs, for the supply of their functional powers:—and we know, too, that in the functional exercise of the genital organs,

---

● Selection from *A Lecture to Young Men on Chastity*, 6th ed., Boston: George W. Light, 1839 (c. 1837), pp. 49–52, 55–60, 62–64, 71–75.

something very analogous to electricity or galvanism, diffuses a
peculiar and powerful excitement and sensation throughout the
whole nervous system.

Now whether these vital effects are produced by means of
nervous fluid or spirit, or something still more subtile and
intangible, or by some other means, human research and investigation have not ascertained, and perhaps never will. But we are
perfectly certain, that the peculiar *excitement* of venereal indulgence, is more diffusive, universal and powerful, than any other
to which the system is ever subject; and that it more rapidly
exhausts the vital properties of the tissues, and impairs the functional powers of the organs; and consequently that it, in a greater
degree than any other cause, deteriorates all the vital processes
of nutrition, from beginning to end; and therefore, more injuriously affects the character and condition of all the fluids and solids
of the body;—and hence the terrible fact, that venereal excesses
occasion the most loathsome, and horrible, and calamitous diseases that human nature is capable of suffering.

It is this peculiar EXCITEMENT, or VITAL STIMULATION, which
causes the muscular tension and convulsion, and increased action
of the heart, and occasions visceral congestion, and disturbs all
the functions of the system, and thus produces general debility,
morbid irritability and sympathy, and all the consequent train of
evils which result. And this peculiar *excitement* or *vital stimulation* may be produced to an extent sufficient to cause an increased determination of blood to the genital organs, and an
increase of their secretions, and of their peculiar sensibilities, sufficient to cause a distraction of functional energy from the digestive,
and other organs, and prevent the normal distribution of it from
the general and particular centres of action, and thus disturb and
impair all the functions, and debilitate all the organs of the system,
and develope a general morbid irritability and sympathy, without
amounting to the acme of coition, and causing an emission of
semen, and the convulsive paroxysms which attend it.

Hence, therefore, SEXUAL DESIRE, cherished by the mind and
dwelt on by the imagination, not only increases the excitability
and peculiar sensibility of the genital organs themselves, but always
throws an influence, equal to the intensity of the affection, over
the whole nervous domain;—disturbing all the functions depending
on the nerves for vital energy, which is thereby increased upon, or

distracted from them—and if this excitement is frequently repeated, or long continued, it inevitably induces an increased degree of irritability, and debility, and relaxation generally throughout the nervous and muscular tissues, and especially the nerves of organic life. And hence, those LASCIVIOUS DAY-DREAMS, and *amorous reveries*, in which young people too generally—and especially the idle, and the voluptuous, and the sedentary, and the nervous—are exceedingly apt to indulge, are often the sources of general debility, effeminacy, disordered functions, and permanent disease, and even premature death, without the actual exercise of the genital organs! Indeed this unchastity of thought—this *adultery of the mind*—is the beginning of immeasurable evil to the human family:—and while children are regularly, though unintentionally trained to it, by all the mistaken fondness of parents, and all the circumstances of civic life, it is but mockery in the ear of Heaven to deprecate the evil consequences; and folly, little short of fatuity, to attempt to arrest the current of crime that flows from it.

If we will train our offspring into the early and free use of flesh-meat, and accustom them to high-seasoned food, and richly prepared dishes, and learn them to drink tea, and coffee, and wine, and to indulge in various other stimulants, with which civic life is universally cursed, and effeminate their bodies with feather beds and enervating dress,—in short, if we will sedulously educate them to all the degenerating habits of luxury, indolence, voluptuousness and sensuality, we shall be more indebted to their want of *opportunity to sin,* than to any other cause, for the preservation of their bodily chastity,—if, indeed, we escape the heart-rending anguish of seeing them the early victims of passions, which we have been instrumental in developing to an irresistible power! For these lascivious, and exceedingly pernicious day-dreams of the young, are but the first buddings of a depraved instinct, which will not be satisfied with the passive reveries of the mind and affections of the body.

·   ·   ·

Is it not, then, a matter of course—and indeed, a matter of moral necessity—when this momentous evil of depraved instinct is once originated, and every habit and circumstance and influence contribute to perpetuate and increase it, that young concupiscence should kindle into a passion of despotic power, and compel the

unwary youth, either to break through the restraints of civil and
moral law, to find indulgence in illicit commerce,—or more
clandestinely to yield to the more degrading and destructive vice
of self-pollution?

To what avail, then, are moral laws, and civil legislation, and
philanthropic efforts, in the cause of chastity, while all the elements
combine to give invincible efficiency to the work of ruin? As well
might we attempt to prevent the eruption of volcanic mountains,
when the internal fires were kindled, and the molten entrails were
boiling and heaving like the exasperated ocean! As well might we
think to stand before the gushing mouth of a crater, and roll
back the burning tide, and save the world below from desolation!

• • •

Men do not easily see, why illicit commerce between the sexes
should be more injurious, in a physical point of view, than the
commerce between man and wife; but from the explanation which
has now been presented of the subject, we readily perceive the
reason. We see that it is not the mere loss of semen, but the
peculiar excitement, and the violence of the convulsive paroxysms,
which produce the mischief; and these are exceedingly increased by
the actions of the mind.

Young men, in the pursuit of illicit commerce with the other sex,
generally contemplate the act, for a considerable time before its
performance,—their imagination is wrought up, and presents lewd
and exciting images,—the genital organs become stimulated, and
throw their peculiar influence over the whole system; and this, to
the full extent of its power, acts on the mental and moral faculties,
and is thence again reflected with redoubled energy upon the
genital and other organs. The sight, or touch of the female body,
and especially the bosom, &c., greatly increases the excitement,
and thus the ardor and power of the passion are augmented
continually, and more in proportion to the difficulties in the way,
until indulgence takes place, when the excitement is intense and
overwhelming, and the convulsive paroxysms proportionably violent
and hazardous to life. And where it is promiscuous, the genital
organs are almost continually stimulated by the mind. Every
female that is a little more comely, or a little more meretricious
than others, in her appearance, becomes an object of desire; the
contemplation of her charms, and all her movements, increase the

lust, and thus the genital organs are kept under an habitual excitement, which is reflected or diffused over the whole nervous system; and disturbs, and disorders all the functions of the body, and impairs all the tissues, and leads to that frequency of commerce which produces the most ruinous consequences. But, between the husband and wife, where there is a proper degree of chastity, all these causes either entirely lose, or are exceedingly diminished in their effect. They become accustomed to each other's body, and their parts no longer excite an impure imagination, and their sexual intercourse is the result of the more natural and instinctive excitements of the organs themselves;—and when the dietetic and other habits are such as they should be, this intercourse is very seldom.

• • •

Whatever, therefore, may be thought of marriage as a divine institution, authorized and enjoined by the sacred Scriptures, be assured, my young friends, that marriage—or a permanent and exclusive connection of one man with one woman—is an institution founded in the constitutional nature of things, and inseparably connected with the highest welfare of man, as an individual and as a race! And so intimately associated are the animal and moral sensibilities and enjoyments of man, that, besides the physical and social evils which result from illicit commerce between the sexes, the chaste and delicate susceptibilities of the moral affections are exceedingly depraved, and the transgressor renders himself incapable of those pure and exalted enjoyments which are found in connubial life, where perfect chastity has been preserved.

The Physical Laws of Marriage

William A. Alcott, M.D.

Alcott's The Physiology of Marriage *was written to counteract the more radical literature of sex and marriage that proliferated in the 1850s after the publication of Lazarus'* Love vs. Marriage: *"Satan already has his emissaries abroad. . . . What is left to the friends of God and humanity, as it appears to me, is to counteract his plans, by extending the domain of conscience over that part of the Divine Temple which has too often been supposed not to be under law, but to be the creature of blind instinct, in which we are only on a par with the beasts that perish."*

In 1856 Alcott had already been in the field for a quarter of a century, and had written over a hundred books against Satan, instructions on the care and use of the "Divine Temple." The Physiology of Marriage *and its companion volume* The Moral Philosophy of Courtship and Marriage *(1857) were the quintessence of Alcott's years of advice to "young men," "young women," "young husbands," "young wives," and "young mothers" on how to behave in their domestic relations.*

Although he denied discipleship, Alcott was a dedicated Graham-ite, in matters dietary as well as marital. Like Sylvester Graham, and like his own famous cousin Bronson Alcott, he ate fruits and vegetables dogmatically, every mouthful justified by science and morality. It was not that meat entailed slaughter—that was merely emblematic—or even that it "burned" too fast in the stomach, unduly heating the organism; the vegetarian impulse in these reformers was part of a general program to curb every appetite and bridle every passion. Alcott lived in a totally moral universe, where each act was the result of choice and "the domain of conscience" was limited only by consciousness. His advice to newlyweds to keep a journal for "the improvement of each other's minds and hearts" was part of an overall strategy to prevent the imagination from roaming. Even between husband and wife impurity and seduction were possible—indeed, all the more likely for the marriage "license." "Amorous looks," "whispers," even "puns" were forms of dalliance dangerous to the purity of the marital altar. "Can one tread on live coals and not be burned?" he asked "the young husband." The solution was to throw cold water on them, and Alcott devoted his life to the project.

William A. Alcott, M.D.
The Physical Laws of Marriage

The first question asked by inquiring young men, who are fairly within the matrimonial enclosure, usually is, "What is right, with regard to sexual intercourse?" "Here we are," say they, "with our appetites and passions urging us on; and yet we are fully assured there is a limit which we ought not to pass. Tell us, if you can, where that limit is."

But, in order to reply, in the best possible manner, to such a question as this, much time is required. Were I asked, by an individual, how much he ought to eat, or drink, or sleep, or how much clothing, or what kind of clothing he ought to use, by day or by night, I could tell him something at random immediately; but to tell him rationally and scientifically, could not be the work of a moment.

● Selection from *The Physiology of Marriage,* Boston: John P. Jewett, 1860 (c. 1856), pp. 114–21.

I must first know very particularly about his habits, hereditary and acquired; both as regards health and disease. I must know something also of his education, and of his temper and temperament. I must, in short, to do justice, either to him, or to myself, and the cause I serve, make a thorough physiological examination. It would be comparatively easy to lay down a code of abstract rules, without these preliminaries; but judiciously to adapt or apply them to his particular case and circumstances, would be the proper work of a much longer period. It would even be desirable to live by him, and to see him at various times, and under various circumstances.

Just so with the instructions to be given with reference to the physiology of marriage. Twenty years ago I asked a most excellent man, of great age, observation, and experience—one, moreover, whose praise was in "all the churches," what he should regard as matrimonial excess. He hesitated, at first. Much, he said, would depend on circumstances. What would be excess in one person of a certain temperament and of a particular age, would be but moderation in another—all of which to a certain extent, even to an extent much greater than that to which he would have carried it, is true. However, he concluded at length, that as a general rule, any thing beyond twice a week, for him and his companion, would be excess.

On relating this conversation, sometime afterward (of course without giving names) to an experienced physician, he remarked, that as many indulgences as two in a week would destroy him and many others—persons even of average constitutions.

I have made extensive inquiry on this subject—of all sorts and conditions of men. One very aged New England clergyman—who had been the husband of four wives—told me that after fifty long years of observation, experience and reflection, he had come to the full conclusion that, for literary and sedentary men, however robust and healthy, any thing of this kind beyond once a month would partake of the character of excess; although he well knew that in some circumstances, and for a time, a much greater indulgence could not only be borne, but seemed, at first view, to be even beneficial.

Some of my readers may perhaps be already aware that the far-famed, and very far-hated, Sylvester Graham taught a doctrine not greatly unlike that of the preceding paragraph. A frequency of sexual indulgence greater than that of the weeks of the year, he

said was absolutely inadmissible; while, as a general rule, it would
be better for both sexes—no less than for posterity—if the indulgence were restricted to the number of lunar months.

This doctrine, it is true, so utterly at war with the general habits
and feelings of mankind, was almost enough, at the time it was
announced, to provoke the cry of, Crucify him. Indeed, I have often
thought that while the public odium was ostensibly directed against
his anti-fine flour and anti-flesh eating doctrines, it was his anti-
sexual indulgence doctrines, in reality, which excited the public
hatred and rendered his name a by-word and a reproach. But, as a
belief in the great doctrine of the circulation of the blood, though
it gained little credence, while Dr. Harvey, the discoverer, was alive,
began to gain ground as soon as he was dead, so Mr. Graham was
hardly dead,—and not at all entombed—ere the view which he
proclaimed, on this subject began to find favor, both in this country
and in Europe.

At the present time, I doubt whether there are a dozen men of
sound science, in the ranks of physiology and hygiene, to be found
in the known world, who will object to the soundness of Mr.
Graham's views on this particular topic. They seem to discover, in
the constitutional habits and tendencies of woman, what was the
original intention and purpose of high Heaven, in a matter concerning which, specifically, revelation does not determine.

A few indeed have gone much farther, at least in theory. Assuming that the sole object of the sexual instinct and its apparatus, is
the reproduction of the species, and that to this great end, exclusively, every "congress" should be directed, they would limit the
recurrence of the act to the mutual desire of the parties to become
parents.

But is there not room for doubt, after all, whether this was the
whole of the Divine intention? For, if it were so, why should the
power of procreation continue, in our sex, when not abused, as
long, or nearly as long as life? And why should the susceptibility to
pleasure, in the other sex, continue beyond the age to which child
bearing is limited?

Is it not much more probable, all things and circumstances taken
into the account, that, by the Divine plan, the gratification of the
sexual instinct is determined, as Graham and others have thought,
by the menstrual period, at least while that function continues?
For, we must not forget, as one item in our estimates, that if woman,

by virtue of her own constitutional tendencies, independent of mis-education or perversion, ever makes any advances towards the other sex, *as* a sex, except perhaps during pregnancy, it is soon after the cessation of the menstrual discharge. May we not, hence, infer that this function, while it prepares for the commerce of the sexes, at the same time limits its frequency?

On this point, however, I speak, as it becomes me, with some diffidence. For, I am by no means sure that our most ultra physiologists are not very near the truth, after all. I am by no means certain that Scripture revelation—to say nothing of physiology—in its most rigid interpretation, does not restrict us to the simple purpose of perpetuating the race. I am, however, quite sure that one indulgence to each lunar month, is all that the best health of the parties can possibly require.

It will be said, I know—it has often been so said—that if this is the law, it is a most rigid one. And so, indeed, at first view, it may seem. But what, then? Am I at fault in announcing it? I certainly *did* not *make* the law. At most, I am but its interpreter. So far as I can see, and so far as close reasoning, both from analogy and the nature of the case, can carry me, it presents itself to my own mind as a most excellent law.

For, have we not already seen that the amount of human enjoyment to be derived from the appetites is not graduated by frequency of indulgence, so much as by infrequency? That it is not he, for example, who is almost always eating and drinking, who obtains, even for the time, the most gustatory enjoyment; but oftener the reverse? So, in my own view, with the sexual appetite.

If this last is indulged too frequently, although it might sometimes happen that the power to enjoy and the sum total of our enjoyment would increase for a time, yet both of them will prematurely fail. It is a general law that they who give themselves up to early persevering indulgence, become early impotent, or at least lose, early, their susceptibility to venereal pleasures—and, indeed, to all sorts of pleasure—while they who are more self-denying, retain their powers and their pleasures to the end of life; or at least to a very late period.

It is, moreover, worthy of notice that the pleasures of love, no less than the strength of the orgasm, are enhanced by their infrequency. It is, in this also, as in eating and drinking. Eating twice or three times a day probably gives us more gustatory enjoyment than eating half a dozen or a dozen times during the same period. Nor does frequent eating sooner wear out or spoil the appetite than frequent sexual indulgence. It is by no means certain that the smallest number of meals a day which is compatible with health—I mean one, only—would not give, to any of us, who are adults, a greater quantity of gustatory enjoyment, taking the whole of life together, than a greater number. We certainly enjoy most when we have the most perfect appetite; but this perfect appetite we seldom have. Real hunger is usually anticipated. We seldom wait long enough for our food to be really hungry. In other words we eat before we are hungry, and hence are seldom if ever hungry.

From what we know of the ways and works of God, it is hardly a presumption to infer that strict conformity to his holy laws, physical not less than moral, will in the end, taking only this short and uncertain life into the account, give us the most of enjoyment. The heaven below does not conflict at all with the heaven above; but is part and parcel of the same thing.

If the maximum frequency of sexual commerce be the gradually recurring lunar months—if, I mean to say, this doctrine can be fairly inferred from a strict and honest interpretation of the Divine law—then it is to be presumed that in rigidly conforming to this arrangement we shall in the end secure the most pleasure, even if this little life were our all. It is probably so, I mean to say, as a general rule; to which however, as to most general rules, there may be more or fewer exceptions.

Or if this should not be admitted, it *must* be admitted that by carrying out God's plan to the full extent of the most rigid self-denial which his law really requires, we gain the most of happiness, physical, social, intellectual, and moral, on the whole and in the end. We shall be best satisfied with ourselves in the final review.

The Honeymoon

Nicholas Francis Cooke

Satan in Society, *from which this selection is taken, was pub-*
lished anonymously in 1870 by a forty-year-old Chicago physician,
Nicholas Francis Cooke. Like most Victorian doctors who wrote
on the subject, Cooke combines a certain amount of common sense
with an enormous load of prejudice and ignorance. Unlike many
however, greed seems not to have been among his motives: in
explaining why he has withheld his name, he points out, quite
rightly, that "Nearly all books on the sexual question which have
been presented for popular reading—in our language, at least—
have been sheer advertising media *for mercenary practitioners.*
Our incognito redeems us from all possible suspicion of belonging
to this class!"
    Cooke was a man with a strong moral sense. It is said that while
in medical school he began a study of homeopathy, the "radical"
medical doctrine of the day, in order to refute it, but finding him-
self convinced of its truth, he switched allegiances and became
a homeopathist himself, in spite of the presumption that his

conversion would make his practice much less lucrative. Similarly, a few years before he wrote Satan in Society *he found himself being converted to Catholicism by one of his patients who happened to be a Jesuit—again with a significant loss in both patients and professional prestige.*

One can see Cooke's moral sense at work in his book. There is nothing really unorthodox in any of his opinions on sexual matters, but much less cant and hypocrisy. Like most physicians with any wide experience of sexual disorders, he cannot help but see that problems of marital incompatibility, for instance, were largely cultural, and had to do with accepted myths of male and female propensities. His depiction of the "wedding night" builds on such clichés, without really questioning them. No great believer in women's rights, he merely enjoins husbands to accept their duty— to lead the way to the conjugal couch with greater tenderness and understanding. It would have been equally easy to fall into line with the majority of physicians whose opinion was simply that woman was not made for sexual pleasures. His argument for "entire reciprocity of thought and desire" is thus enlightened, for his time. The trouble, as both feminists and free lovers pointed out, is that so long as all the choices remained exclusively in the power of the husbands—noblesse oblige—such arguments had no more force than most platitudes.

The typical Victorian physician had a long list of practices to condemn: "male self-abuse," "female self-abuse," "double onanism," "conjugal onanism," "preventive measures" of all kinds (except for continence), "excessive coition," abortion, adultery, and so on. It is somewhat surprising to find the "mal-initiation of young wives" among the most "deeply rooted vices" in Cooke's own catalogue, near the top of the list. He was certainly out of the medical mainstream. Nonetheless, the difference is finally not crucial; from our perspective it still looks like the typical confusion of Victorian doctrine, the mixture of good intentions and bad physiology, all strongly tainted with male chauvinism.

Nicholas Francis Cooke
The Honeymoon

The extraordinary delicacy of this subject is such as to have
hithero absolutely prevented its discussion; but when ministers publicly declaim from the pulpit on the crime of ante-natal infanticide,
and the press teems with minute details of the last act of a daily
presented tragedy, the author thinks it time that the drama should
be faithfully elaborated and the earlier scenes equally exposed,
and with the same lawful purpose—the prevention of crime, and
of consequent domestic unhappiness. It is with this object in view
that he ventures to penetrate the secrecy of the nuptial chamber,
and discover there the very beginning of evils so universally
acknowledged, yet so little understood.

From the preceding chapters the different relations of man and
woman on the night following the solemn ceremony which has
made them one flesh can be comprehended at a glance. But few
words, then, are needed to explain these differences. Of course,
what we have to say regarding the woman supposes her to be, at
least physically, a virgin. The poor girl has been for weeks an
object of open commiseration and sympathy on the part of all the
old women and young girls of her acquaintance. It is not so much
what has been said as what has been mysteriously hinted by looks
and actions more suggestive than words. She has been taught to
regard this night as one of unspeakable horror and torment; not
alone her virginity, but her utmost capacity for physical pain, are
to be offered a sacrifice to her love—too often of mere position.
These vague apprehensions, added to the fatigues of preparation
of her wedding outfit, have produced in her the very acme of bodily
and mental exhaustion; she is jaded and worn out, but, above all,
frightened. The one thing in all this world of which she is least
capable at this moment, is the faintest spark of sexual passion. On
the other hand, the man, in the majority of instances, has received
his education for this occasion in ways suggested in Chapter first,
and often, alas! in the brothel. He may be by nature kind, considerate, and loving, but the whole tenor of his thoughts and
experiences on this subject, are connected with violence—indeed,

---

● Selection from *Satan in Society: by A Physician*, Cincinnati: Edward F.
Hovey, 1880 (c. 1870), pp. 138–48.

dynamic consummation is, as he falsely believes, the true idea of mercy. And with this disparity between the forces—shrinking timidity and ungoverned boldness—the match anticipated by Juliet, is won and lost. Lost indeed for the poor creature left mangled and terrified—nay, infinitely disgusted! Love, affection even, are well-nigh crushed out of the stricken woman, whose mental ejaculation, "O, that I had not married!" is the key-note to her whole after-existence. And so, through the long hours of that dreary night, she listens to the heavy respirations of her gross companion, whose lightest movement causes her to shrink with terror. She is fortunate, indeed, if her miseries be not renewed ere she escape from the "bridal chamber"; and the day which follows, filled as it is with forebodings of the coming night, seems all too short for the contemplations and the resolutions which crowd upon her. Far from friends and kindred, with no sympathizing one to whom she can tell a word of her strange sorrow, with him who is miscalled her protector, revealing, by his every look and act, the bestial thoughts which fill his breast, what wonder is it that twenty-four hours of marriage have been more prolific to her of loathing than the whole previous courtship of love!

Again and again these nights of horror are repeated, each, if possible, more hateful than the first, until her *monster* rests from sheer exhaustion, and nature cicatrizes the wounds of body and soul. The wounds received by the latter are serious indeed. Passion is forever killed, or, if capable of resuscitation, it is not at the hands of him who destroyed it. It may be that another can re-awaken the slumbering spark, and the flame be all the wilder for the rights it has been denied. If this do happen, alas for poor mortal frailty, if only natural virtue sustain her! If this tremendous passion be awakened, and the supernatural restraints of religion do not protect her, opportunity and occasion are sure to carry the day. The physical anguish has long since ceased, but with it has also departed the capacity for enjoyment, at least, we repeat, as regards the only man legally qualified to awaken it. Herein lies the true secret of the fall of married women; and the few revelations bear but a small proportion to the number of such falls. Intrigue and adultery stalk boldly through the land, and by the devil's own cunning are enabled to carry on their nefarious practices almost in the face and eyes of the public. The fable of "January and May" almost finds its counterpart in everyday life around us; and the ease with which those most interested, are hood-winked, well-nigh rivals the credulity of him whose sudden restoration to sight was so surprising in its revelations.

Now if, in the opinion of the author, all this were remediless, if we had nothing to offer beyond the sickening exposure, too painful for the most studied narration, we should deem the foregoing too wanton for apology. Far indeed is it from our thought to declaim against the virtue of woman. In his private life, the author has ever proved himself her chivalric defender. But we do contend that she is woman and not spirit, and therefore human, and that, under the criminal, beastly, and unnatural process described, the woman is obliterated, and when she re-asserts herself, she has need of something higher than mere human respect to sustain and strengthen her. It is, in fact, as an apologist for woman, as an advocate for the *true* rights of woman, that we write this Chapter. The transformation from woman to something less, has been effected by blinded, misguided man, and the retransformation is accomplished by wily, villainous man. In both cases man is accountable, yet society holds him guiltless. Woman is pure and spotless, then, if not transformed, but, alas! the transformations are numerous.

It does not invalidate our charge to say that most married women bear children—one or more, according to choice—and consequently must have derived reciprocal enjoyment. While we readily admit and claim for our argument that a woman capable of bearing children is also capable of the sexual instinct, the simple fact remains that the majority perhaps—or certainly an immense proportion—of those who have borne children are innocent of the faintest ray of sexual pleasure. Paradoxical as this may seem, it is an indisputable truth that the physiology of conception does not comprehend intense generation.

In the French hospitals the experiment has been successfully tried, of impregnation of a woman while *unconscious from chloroform;* nay, inquisitive science has gone even further, and by a process which ingenuity could readily devise, has effected conception independent of masculine contact. The fact of child-bearing, then, is not evidence of enjoyment, but only of capacity for enjoyment. Now, for a process of nature to be repeated year after year, in violation of her own intent and purpose, wherein the pleasures and the pains are respectively monopolized and avoided, wherein no reciprocity of feeling nor of interest exists, wherein increasing digust involuntarily fastens on the one, and a brutish indifference possesses the other, what is this but domestic unhappiness in its worst, because most hidden form? Although this branch of the marital relation ought not to be considered, as a prominent or leading feature, but, indeed, as subordinate and altogether secondary to most of the pleasures of wedded life, how can it be otherwise than prominent when it becomes a constant cause of apprehension and of loathing? how can its importance be overestimated if it be irresistibly the theme of perpetual discord? What wonder if, untrammeled by religious scruples, the poor wife murders that little life throbbing beneath her own heart, the very inception of which is associated with so great unhappiness!

The subject, then, owes its origin to the "honeymoon"; but the honeymoon must be. Where, then, is the remedy? We propose to speak very plainly on this point, for it were of little service to portray the disease unless we could also indicate the specific, which, under Providence, we hope to do clearly and unequivocally. It were well if the treatment begin with the earliest manifestations of the malady, with the first dawning of the indomitable passion in the boy, and follow him through the dangerous years whose progress, in a former Chapter, we have sufficiently traced. But as this is impracticable, in the actual state of things, we must take him as he is when he closes the door of the nuptial chamber— mayhap a "reformed rake"—and say to him, with all the import of a solemn warning, "Hold!" In your keeping are now placed the destinies of that shrinking woman, for wedded happiness or wedded woe; your own tranquillity and peace of mind, perhaps your honor as a husband and father hang upon your decision now. Be cautious how you thread the mysterious path before you. You have need of all the fortitude and self-control you can possibly summon to your aid, in this great emergency. You may talk of the instincts of nature, but in you these instincts are brutalized; in her they are artificially suppressed. You have the double task of curbing the former and of developing the latter. Undoubtedly the "instincts of nature" would make the marriage consummation a very awkward proceeding, sufficiently protracted for all practical purposes; but society has gotten these instincts sadly out of tune for both of you. By proper caution and delicacy on your part they may yet be harmonized. And perfect accord be thus secured. Your first words should be those of re-assurance and sympathy. Assure her most positively that her apprehensions are groundless, that no consummation shall occur this night, or, indeed, at all, until on that, as you trust on all other subjects, your wishes and hers shall exactly harmonize; above all, inform her that whenever your happy marriage shall be consummated, neither violence nor suffering shall attend it, but perfect and reciprocal happiness shall crown the act. You should know that gentleness, moderation, but more than all, due and reasonable *cultivation* of her womanly passion will enable you to fulfill your pledge to the very letter. You should know that in rare cases days or even weeks must elapse before *entire* consummation can be effected, but that when it does occur the slight pain she will suffer will be of such a character as shall increase, rather than diminish her pleasure. You will also discover, by experience, that with due deliberation and prudence, Nature will cooperate in your favor to relieve you of nearly all the trouble you anticipate.

We cannot be more explicit than this, but you will readily comprehend our meaning when you obey these instructions. The slightest intimation of pain or fear should warn you to desist, being determined that under no circumstances shall more violence be used than is obviously invited and *shared*. In one word, beware of committing a veritable outrage on the person of her whom God has given you for a companion. From all that we can learn, and the instances from which we derive our conclusions are very numerous, the first conjugal act is little else than a legalized *rape,* in most cases. Let nothing interfere with your determination to wait for and obtain entire reciprocity of thought and desire, and let this always be your guide, not only during the honey-moon, but also throughout your married existence. Thus will you secure not only happiness and love for yourself, but that perfect confidence and gratitude from your wife which shall make her literally a sharer in your joys, as she must needs be in your sorrows. You should never forget that this passion is ordinarily slower of growth and more tardy of excitation in women than in men, but when fairly aroused in them it is incomparably stronger and more lasting. This, of course, with due allowances for differences of individual temperaments. Therefore be careful to avoid a most common error

of unphilosophical man, that of undue haste and precipitation on
these occasions throughout your wedded career. Be always assured
that your wife is at least in entire sympathy with your own condition. It is rare that two natures are so exactly in harmony with
each other that love and desire are always equal in both, but the
rule should be for the *one who loves the most to measure his
ardor by that of the one who loves the least.*

A Grievous Lesson

Dio Lewis

"But how can the girls take care of themselves if they do not know how they are made?" asked Dr. Lewis.

"I wish them to consider themselves a mass of animated matter of which God will take care, if they love and serve Him," was the reply of a Presbyterian minister who had refused Lewis' offer of a lecture on health to his small school for young ladies.

"Prayer, song, and brotherly love," commented Lewis, "seemed to me to have given place to the constable."

Lewis thought he knew better what was proper for a young lady's ear, and was himself the proprietor of an exclusive girls' school just outside of Boston during the 1860s. His specialty was physical education, and for him this meant not only training but explaining the body and its functions. He boasted that his "new gymnastics" had been taken up in Berlin and St. Petersburg (crowding out the laborious and regimented exercises of Friedrich Jahn, the other great "father" of gymnastics); but it was his crusad-

ing for forthrightness in matters of hygiene that made him famous in America.

"People Perish for Lack of Knowledge" was the slogan of his outspoken mannual of 1874, Chastity: or Our Secret Sins, *from which the present selection is drawn. Of course, like most of the experts of the day, Lewis seems terribly conservative to us, with his emphasis on sin and retribution and his benighted notions of sexuality (worse even than anything in this excerpt). Nonetheless, there is something attractive in Lewis' handling of the little story of domestic misery he tells here. It is the energy with which he deplores the hyprocrisy and false modesty that run, like a rotten core, through every turning of his anecdote. It is a wonderful moment when he finds he must leave the room in order to keep from assaulting his patient. The whole is told with a dramatist's flair, especially the little coda, which, almost like an afterthought, brings us suddenly face to face with the ghastly consequences of ignorance and shame.*

No doubt it was easy enough to be in favor of chastity and against syphilis in the 1870s, but so far as physician's advice goes, one feels it would have been easier to fall into the hands of a much less scrupulous and humane practitioner than Lewis. Compare the voices of other writers of marriage manuals, then or now.

There was one person for whom Lewis' book could have no flaw:

Auburn, N.Y., April 16, 1875.

My Dear Son:—Your work "Chastity" is the most important of all your writings. But you must not expect for it a large circulation. Civilization has not advanced far enough to warrant this. Vicious men will oppose it.

It is most happily calculated to elevate women, and I rejoice in every means that has this tendency.

This work ought to be in every house. Children should read it. As far as the evil exists, so far should the warning extend. It is a mock modesty which keeps people in ignorance.

Lovingly your mother,
Delecta Lewis.

Dio Lewis
A *Grievous Lesson*

A fine-looking man, an old acquaintance, came to me in sore affliction. After making sure that no one was in the closet or listening at the door, he said, with the deepest emotion:

"I am a wretched man! I wish I had never been born! I wish I was dead!"

I urged him to be seated, tried to soothe him, and begged him to open his heart and tell me his troubles. He sat with his face in hands for some minutes, and then went on:

"I came to you once about a very important and delicate matter, and you seemed to feel for me. I now come about a much more important and much more delicate matter. The fact is, after being married seven weeks, I am disgusted with the whole thing, and would give my right arm to be back again where I was—a single man."

He stopped short and turned his face from me, as if ashamed and frightened at what he had said, but in a moment began again, with the manner of one who had fully made up his mind to go through with a bad business:

"I am disappointed with her every way. What I thought was a beautiful form turns out to be cotton and hair. Her breasts, which seemed so plump and beautiful, are nothing but bags of bird-seed. Her body is just skin and bones, and her skin is as dry and rough as a nutmeg-grater. Now, sir, I am not an animal, but I have been grossly deceived. Her face was so delicate and beautiful that I thought she was made of finer stuff than other human beings; but, sir, I should be ashamed if I had an inch on my body as coarse and rough as she is all over, except her face and neck; and she doctors them with some of these miserable complexion fluids. It's a downright swindle, and I won't stand it!"

"Have you told your wife how you feel toward her?"

"No, not exactly; but when I spoke of her scrawny form and rough skin, she got out of bed, and cried and groaned all night. She called herself all sorts of hard names for letting me marry her without telling me that she used padding. She should never for-

---

● Selection from *Chastity: or, Our Secret Sins,* New York: Fowler & Wells, 1890 (c. 1874), pp. 62–74.

give herself for not showing me her person before we were married.
She begged that she might sleep in a bed by herself, and then she
offered to let me have a divorce. How could I say anything when
she went on that way?"

"Saying nothing of her person, does your wife disappoint you?"

"No; but ain't that enough?"

"Is she affectionate?"

"Mercy! she fairly eats me up!"

"Do you find her unselfish?"

"Well, to speak the truth—and I believe in giving even the
devil his due—she is the most unselfish creature that I ever saw in
my life. I believe she would die for me. She seems to think of
nothing, day and night, but how to gratify me."

"Do you find her as intelligent as you thought?"

"Yes—more so. She knows ten times as much as I do, and she
is so discreet and good that my mother and sister call her an
angel. All I can say is, if a skeleton, covered all over with scales,
can be an angel, then I have no doubt she comes as near being an
angel as they make 'em. But I don't want an angel—I want a
woman; and I want a woman with flesh and blood."

I then said to my visitor:

"I must take time to think. Be good enough to say nothing of
this to any other person, and let me call upon your wife during
the day with reference to her condition, and I wish you would give
me permission to speak to her with perfect freedom. I wish to
tell her in part what has passed between us this morning, but I
will do it without compromising you. To-morrow you may come
to see me again."

He was good enough to express his confidence in my discretion,
and I went straight to the lady and opened the whole subject
without reserve. I took the liberty to conceal her husband's angry
words, and only spoke of his solicitude on her account, and in a
very gentle, delicate way of his possible disappointment at finding
his wife less perfect than his imagination had painted her.

The plucky, honest little woman interrupted me with the
question:

"Did my husband know that you were coming to me about this?"

"He did, madam."

"Then you come by his wish and direction?"

"It was arranged between us that I should converse with you on this subject, and your husband charged me to speak to you with perfect freedom."

She conducted me to her private room, and when we were seated, said:

"Now, doctor, you need not mince matters. I am in trouble—grievous trouble. It seems to me my heart must break. If I only could, I would hide myself in the grave. Oh, where can I go? What can I do? It is more than I can bear!"

There were no tears, no sobs, only a hard, dry, monotonous voice. She said:

"If you wish to examine any part of my person, tell me. I will try not to be sensitive."

I examined her skin in several places. Then she said:

"And now I wish you to examine my breasts. Two months ago I should not have thought it possible that I could ever consent to such a thing, but I know very well what my husband has said to you; and as he has submitted our troubles to you, I insist that you shall know everything which may help you to comprehend our griefs."

After a few minutes we fell into a more composed conversation, and she said:

"It was undoubtedly a grave error to have concealed any defect from my husband. I thought about it, and consulted my mother. I thought he ought to be told that my breasts were not as large as they seemed to be, and that the skin of my person was not as smooth as that of my face. My mother said that men knew all about such things, and that John would think it immodest if I talked to him about my breasts and the skin of my body. Hoping and believing that my mother knew what was right, I let it go. I did, however, warn him that his opinion of me was most extravagant, and that he would find me far less perfect, physically and every other way, than he thought me; and I went so far at one time, just before we were married, as to tell him that things were not just as they seemed in my form, and then, when he laughed at me for my 'conscientious nonsense,' as he chose to call it, I cried half the night lest he should think I had said something indelicate. Oh, I did not know what to do, and I suppose in my ignorance and cowardice, I did everything wrong. But all that is past, and I can't go back. If I only *could* go back, I would never think of marriage again. I have offered to release him. He says there is no way. Don't you think these imperfections would give him a divorce? I will show them to anybody."

I have listened to the moanings, ejaculations and wild grief of many a wife with drunken or cruel or unfaithful husband, but never did I listen to anything so touching, so harrowing, as the dry, hard, husky words of this bride. I said nothing of the determination which filled my heart; but I then and there resolved that whatever could be honorably done to lift this woman from her present humiliation and sorrow *should be done.*

I asked her to tell me something of the beginning and growth of this dissatisfaction on the part of her husband. She replied:

"When we were married, and had retired to our bedchamber, I told him, with many tears, of my imperfections and what I meant by the warnings that I gave him before our marriage. He said that he understood me at the time, and that my breasts were really larger than he had expected, and as to the roughness of my skin, that was nothing, and he had no doubt that a visit to the springs would cure it. And then he was good enough to say that it was all right any way—that he didn't marry my body, but my soul. He was very tender and devoted for about two weeks, and then became irritable, and began to talk about my breasts and skin. Since that time it has been growing worse and worse, until now I tremble whenever he approaches me. I suppose you will think I have no modesty, but I will tell you all. During the first week he had repeated intercourse with me every night, and sometimes during the day. But for the last week he has not come near me at all, and refuses to let me touch him."

She told me a great deal more, which need not be repeated, and then I begged her not to speak to any one about this painful subject, and after I had had time to think I would take the liberty to call again.

I wrote her husband a note, telling him I had seen his wife, and asked him to call upon me early the next morning.

He came at the appointed time; and making ourselves secure in my private room, I said to him:

"I spent two hours with your wife yesterday, and she spoke very freely of your griefs. I was never more deeply moved. She impressed me as the purest woman I ever met. I believe you when you say that she would die for you. She would not speak a word about your unhappy affairs, so true is she to you, until I assured her that I

came by your direction, and with a charge from you to speak with
perfect freedom. Then she felt it to be her duty, and spoke without
reserve."

"But, doctor, did you examine her skin?"

"I did, in several places."

"What do you think of it?"

"The best non-technical description which I can give of it is
that there is a little salt-rheum humor in her system, which shows
itself in this roughness of the skin. I am sure it can be entirely
removed within three months. She insisted that I should examine
her bosom, and I found it quite as large as the average. The present
fashion of wearing large pads upon the breasts almost entirely
destroys them. The pressure and heat produce absorption, and the
plump, healthy glands of the young girl become, after five years of
fashionable padding, empty and pendant. Nine brides in ten
surprise and disappoint their husbands with the strange difference
between their busts dressed and undressed. You are one of ten
thousand young husbands who have suffered this disappointment.
If your wife would discontinue the use of the pads, and wear the
recent contrivances made of bent whalebones, which are of any
desired size and shape, and set over and around the bosom without
touching it, and if she would then wash her breasts with cold
water, morning and evening, long and thoroughly, and follow the
bath by fifteen minutes' hard rubbing, pressure and other manip-
ulations, in three months the size would be doubled, and in less
than a year the natural, full and plump gland would be developed.
I have seen a female breast which had been thinned and weakened
by padding more than doubled in size *in a single month* by a
quarter of an hour, morning and evening, devoted to as vigorous
rubbing and kneading as the glands could bear. The explanation
is simple enough. The amount of blood flowing to the gland is
increased, and of course the gland itself is enlarged.

"Padding the bosom is the source of most of the broken breasts
and other sufferings common among nursing mothers. The two
deficiencies of which you complain can be easily remedied. The
essential qualities of a pure, noble, perfect womanhood your wife
possesses in an eminent degree. You have assured me of this yourself. Now, what can stand in the way of a complete and satisfactory
union?"

"The fact is I don't believe that she and I were ever designed for
each other. We don't seem to harmonize in any way."

"I cannot refrain from reminding you that when you came to me before your marriage you had the contrary opinion. You raved about her then. I remember you declared her an angel."

"Oh yes; and she is more unselfish and loving and patient that I thought her then, even; but the truth is we don't harmonize."

"Now, my friend, I will tell you what your trouble is. When young people are just married, the principal attraction is the sexual contact. With little opportunity to know each other's moral qualities, they have, at first, scarcely any bond of union but the animal; and with our vicious system of spending eight or ten hours every night in each other's arms in a warm bed, they contrive to coax out such a constant and exhaustive drain that, at the end of two weeks, what seemed at first the most exquisite of all earthly delights is turned to loathing. Were the marriage ceremony preceded by such a fortnight's intimacy, unknown to any one but the two parties, and then they were entirely at liberty to marry or not, not more than one couple in ten would go to the altar. This is but another way of saying that nine couples in ten are more or less dissatisfied at the end of two weeks. This dissatisfaction is largely on the side of the husband. The wife, with far less sexual impetuosity, is far less liable to the reaction. And a very large part of this wretched and perilous excess is the natural result of our system of sleeping in the same bed. It is the most ingenious of all possible devices to stimulate and inflame the carnal passion. No bed is large enough for two persons. If brides only knew the great risk they run of losing the most precious of all earthly possessions—the love of their husbands— they would struggle as resolutely to secure extreme temperance after marriage as they do to maintain complete abstinence before the ceremony. The best means to this end is the separate bed. Now, let me advise you to contrive a visit for your wife of two or three months at a distance from you, and then, when she returns, change your large bed for two small ones, and let them be in adjoining rooms, so that you can converse, but not see each other while undressing or bathing and dressing. The mutual love and tenderness between ninety-nine in every hundred young married couples would be greatly enhanced by this arrangement. I could tell you of a number of remarkable cases of coldness and aversion happily cured by this expedient."

My listener sat silent and absorbed during these remarks and much more in the same tenor, which I do not care to repeat. But I was not done with him. I went on:

"You referred to a former call upon me about an important and delicate matter. As you have chosen to take me into your confidence in this domestic trouble, I feel myself called upon to speak of that former visit. You came to me a few weeks before you were to be married, with syphilis, and begged me to cure you before the day. I need not say that as the day approached we both concluded that there must be a postponement. Three weeks the ceremony was put off. You remember how long it took you to devise an adequate excuse. At length you were married, but the treatment was continued two weeks after the ceremony. I need not remind you that this loss of your hair is one of the effects of that disease. And I need not inform you that if your wife becomes the mother of ten children she will be obliged all her life to anxiously watch over the development of a scrofulous taint in more or less of the number. Under these circumstances you have married a beautiful, cultured and refined lady, who is so good and pure that even your sister and mother, who are generally jealous of the new-comer under such circumstances, pronounce her an angel; and for several weeks you have indulged yourself in such a beastly way that you have become disgusted with your bride, and now actually intend to cast her off because of some trifling physical defects. Why, sir, if your wife had a brother with the average ideas and pluck, and knew what I know about his sister's wrongs, he would kill you and take his sister away from all your belongings."

I asked him to excuse me at this point (for I feared I might say something which I should regret), promising to return shortly. I came back in ten minutes, and found my visitor sitting just where I left him.

He said in a tremulous, subdued voice:

"I am wrong, and regret this thing more than I can tell you. I will be guided by your suggestions. Nothing is easier than to send her away for two months or so. She has a sister in P., and they would all be glad to have her come."

Before the time had expired he came, in a very beautiful spirit, to ask me to look at his sleeping arrangements. One room, which they had used for a parlor, he had fitted up with exquisite taste, and had put into it the most beautiful single bedstead I ever saw. With a perceptible choking in his voice:

"This is to be hers," and then he added, in a firm, quiet way, "Her husband shall not come in here, after she has retired, oftener than once a month, nor as often as that, unless she wishes it."

A little protégée of mine attended the fifth anniversary of the birthday of my now happy friends' oldest daughter, and I went to fetch her home at the good old-fashioned hour of eight o'clock. The parents were in the midst of the happy, noisy group of little people. Their eyes followed the movements of their son and daughter with a oneness of interest and pleasure which would make it difficult to realize the truth of the story I have told you about them.

That little girl's eyeballs, gums and breath are a painful fulfillment of my prophecy. The father has insisted with tears that the mother must never know the source of the poison, though I have urged again and again that for many reasons he should tell her all. Dreadful as the revelation would be, wives are so grateful for the confidence, the unreserved, absolute confidence, of their husbands, that his wife would scarcely love him less, and she could then cooperate with us in forestalling the development of the horrid taint in future children. But he never would give his consent. He always declared that she was so pure that he could never look her in the face again if she knew of his shame. I have heard of one worshiping the very ground on which a woman walked, and this man comes as near it as anybody I have ever met.

III

Love and the Law

The Legal Rights of Married Women

Edward D. Mansfield

Edward D. Mansfield began his career as a lawyer, but soon after setting up practice in Cincinnati he drifted into literary pursuits. He was associated with a number of local papers, eventually editing the Cincinnati Daily Gazette, *which was the first publisher of Harriet Beecher Stowe. In fact Mansfield was a member of her father's congregation, and a friend of Mrs. Stowe's remarkable husband Calvin—an influence that must have been ethically broadening if not quite libertarian.*

Mansfield also taught constitutional law and history briefly in the local college. His own legal training had been at the Litchfield (Connecticut) Law School, whose founder, Judge Tapping Reeve, was the "author of a Treatise on Domestic Relations"—a work, as Mansfield later commented, "which the lawyers admired, but said it was not law, on account, I believe, of its leaning too much to women's rights."

*Most of Mansfield's books seem to have been aimed at popular audiences—*The Mexican War *(1848) and* A Popular and Authentic

Life of Ulysses S. Grant *(1868) being obvious examples. No doubt the subject of* The Legal Rights, Liabilities and Duties of Women *was also expected to capture the public ear in 1845, but Mansfield probably had more philanthropic motives in writing it. He dedicated the book to his mother, who inspired it, while other "ladies of distinguished intelligence and worth" encouraged him to write it. Since his mother was an "intimate friend" of Emma Willard, and sent his sister to her famous Female Seminary at Troy, New York, it is clear that the family was feminist—in a middle-class sort of way. Mansfield says elsewhere that it was from his mother that he got his political opinions.*

Mansfield's deadpan presentation of the legal status of wives is calculated to shock. "We consider here, however, not the propriety but the facts of the law, in order that women may know what it is." Already there were women agitating for legal reform in these matters, and Mansfield's book served as a convenient checklist of grievances that surely aided the early growth of feminism. Some historians have thought that the organizing activity of women like Ernestine Rose, which first centered on lobbying for a Married Women's Property Act in New York State, was the crucial factor in the rise of the Women's Rights Movement. Certainly the legal disabilities of women, married and single, were the focus for middle class feminists during the rest of the century.

The more conservative and respectable the feminist, the more likely to concentrate on reform of the property laws. Thus it has been argued that women were not really very instrumental in the passage of the new statutes they demanded. The New York State Act passed in 1848 was introduced and supported by legislators who wished to secure the property of their own wives and daughters from the possible "pecuniary" disasters of their husbands' affairs. And "in 1854, Massachusetts made a law expressly to set aside the common law, declaring that a woman should have the right to her own earnings, if she carried on business in her own name, and to put money in the savings banks, and draw it out; because banks found it expedient to have such a law, for sometimes, when the wife had drawn out the money, the husband sued the bank, and collected it a second time. Missouri had made a law, that if a man, through drunkenness or worthlessness, fails to provide for his wife, so that she shall be compelled to labor for her own support, she shall have the right to her own earnings." Such were the revelations of Frances Gage at the Rutland Free Convention in 1858.

Moreover, these particular enactments did not really change the situation very much, for there had always been the loopholes of marriage settlements, trusts, and the like, by means of which the wealthy could circumvent the common law disabilities of women through the courts of equity and chancery. All in all, the law was and remained a bulwark of class as well as male supremacy.

On other, less class-bound issues, the law was probably not so important as the mores of the community, but feminists were able to use its provisions as a blatant example of their oppression. Mary F. Davis, the radical second wife of Spiritualist Andrew Jackson Davis, thus harangued a straw-man before that same Rutland Free Convention of reformers:

> *Beware, you law-makers, how you allow a law to stand on your statute-book, that gives this fearful power to the husband over the person of his wife! Look abroad over the land, and see how many homes are filled with unwelcome children, in consequence of the abuse of that power by the husband. . . . Should not our laws be regulated? Should not woman be taught to feel that she has the power in her hands to rid herself of these dreadful fetters? I tell you, sisters, that you have in your own hands the power that must and will rise in opposition to these oppressive statutes; that will rise up in opposition to the psychological influence, even, of those who now have control over you as husbands.*

This was edging very close to the free love position enunciated by Mary Nichols—that a woman had "the right to choose the father of her babe"—only slightly more revolutionary than the right to choose not to be its mother, which was the goal of more restrained feminists as well as the advocates of contraception. Here we touch the limits of legal reform, for of course what the free lovers demanded was not some adjustment of the law but its total abeyance in sexual life.

Edward D. Mansfield
The Legal Rights of Married Women

Marriage is the foundation of the family constitution. Without it, the relations of husband and wife, parent and child cannot *legally* exist. Hence it is the first fact in the order of the domestic relations we are to notice, and it is essential to correct knowledge of other legal conditions, that we should correctly understand this, and understand the light in which it is regarded by the law.

Marriage is an institution of God. It was begun in the garden of Eden and has been perpetuated by the laws of nature, of religion and of civil society.

It was in its origin a religious institution; for it was solemnized in the presence and by the authority of the Creator. It was blessed by the Almighty in its original institution, and by the Redeemer in the performance of his first miracle at Cana of Galilee. It was also pronounced by the apostle, honorable among all men, and has, therefore, been recognized by the laws, and held sacred in the respect of all Christian nations.

In respect to the laws of civil society, *Marriage is a civil contract.* It is, therefore, governed by the same rules which govern any other civil contract.

Now to understand this, we must understand the meaning of a *civil contract.* The term contract signifies in law, *an agreement, upon sufficient consideration, to do or not to do some particular thing.* This definition applies to all contracts, as well to those of sale and other business transactions, as to marriage. The term *civil* applies to the artificial laws of society and not to those of nature or revelation. The phrase, civil contract, then, means a contract recognized and governed, by the rules of the municipal or social law of the land. Such a contract is marriage. The *holiness or unholiness* of the matrimonial contract, in reference to the ties of blood and other moral circumstances is not considered by the law, but left entirely to the jurisdiction of ecclesiastical bodies, or the restraints of conscience. Nevertheless, for the sake of sound morals and public policy, the laws of nearly all Christian States do prescribe some limits of consanguinity, within which marriages may not be contracted.   • • •

● Selection from *The Legal Rights, Liabilities and Duties of Women,* Salem: John P. Jewett, 1845, pp. 235–36, 266–74, 284–88, 306–10.

The religious unity of man and wife, is declared both in the Old and New Testaments. The civil law of the United States declares that, in the view of that law, the marriage relation constitutes a legal unity in all its conditions and circumstances. No one supposes that, in personal or spiritual *identity*, they are in fact one; but that in interest, in action, in family government and in possessing rights of property, title and claim, they shall be considered one, and no diversity is supposable. The great object in this is to secure the unity of family support and family government; for, on any other supposition, the family would be divided against itself.

As the marriage creates a unity, and the husband is religiously the head of the family, the law declares, that the external powers of this family, in respect to property and government, shall vest in the husband. There are exceptions to this rule, in two instances:

1. Where the security of the wife's person requires the intervention of the law, as in the case of crime.

2. Where the legal title to property is in the hands of trustees, and the use in the wife; in which case, the property is treated as the wife's only.

This *merging*, as it is called, of the wife's rights of property and person in the husband, has been called little less than downright slavery. In this respect the Roman law was much more liberal than the English or American. For that law considered marriage as a sort of *partnership*, in which each partner had equal rights of property. We consider here, however, not the propriety, but the facts of the law; in order that women may know what it is.

As a direct consequence of this principle of unity between husband and wife, they can make no contracts with each other which will be legal; because, to make contracts with one another is to suppose their separate legal existence, which is contrary to their declared unity. A husband cannot make a grant of land directly to his wife; and if there were any contracts between them before marriage, they are void. There is another reason for this rule; that is, that if there were any agreement between them, there are no means of enforcing it; for, whatever the wife has, under any such agreement, is already the husband's. . . .

As another consequence of the unity of husband and wife, they cannot be witnesses *for or against each other*. The reason of this is, that if they testify *for* each other, there is too much bias in interest and temptation to swerve from the truth; and it is against the policy of the law and sound morals to allow them to testify *against* each

other. The law will not *permit* them to testify against each other.
The only exceptions to this rule are those of absolute necessity. 1.
In England, it is said, that if the husband be indicted for high
treason, the wife is a competent witness against him. This is for the
safety of the State. This is a doubtful point, however. 2. When a
wife complains against a husband, for assaults or other force towards
herself, in order that she may have protection, she is allowed to
testify against him; for she is the only one who could prove the
case. It is a matter of *necessity*. 3. When the husband is prosecuted
by the State for abuse of his wife, she is a good witness, for the
same reason as before. 4. If a man forcibly compel a woman to
marry him; or if he marry a woman, having a wife already living;
the woman may testify against him; for in both these cases, the
marriage is really void; in the first for fraud, and in the second for
bigamy. 5. When a man is charged with the murder of his wife, her
dying declarations of his guilt may be proved against him. These
cases are, however, not so much exceptions as matters of necessity.
They are all cases of violence or fraud. The general rule remains
substantially true, that husband and wife cannot testify either for
or against each other.

These are the great consequences which flow from the principle
of *legal unity* between husband and wife. They are vastly momentous to both, but to the wife especially; for it is plain enough, that
in respect to property and legal identity, her being is, in a great
measure, merged in his. We shall now consider, more specifically,
what she loses or gains in respect to person. . . .

We have already noted that the Scripture declares that the person
of the wife belongs to the husband. this might be said to be fairly
included in the very terms in which her creation was described. She
was created to be "meet," that is, *fit* for man, her husband, and with
the view of becoming his perpetual companion. To be separated
from him, or, having become his wife, to live in an independent
personality, is really to be exiled from the purposes of her being.
This certainly is the view both of Scripture and the law. Nor is the
rule laid down with any inequality or unfairness; for, while they
continue in the marriage state, whatever may be the husband's
right to her, she has the same to him.

It follows, from this rule, that if a wife leave her husband, he has
a right to reclaim and bring her back. It follows also, that if she

attempt to leave him, or is guilty of improper conduct, he has a right to control and constrain her liberty; provided always this is done gently and with no violation of the criminal law. For we have already shown that women are citizens, and, as such, entitled to all the remedies of the criminal law. But the husband has and must have, as head of the family, the right to constrain the liberty of his wife, so far as is necessary to preserve the peace, unity and safety of the family. There are many ways in which this might be endangered by the conduct of the wife. Intemperance is one. Temporary insanity, or a lightness of conduct almost equivalent to it, or, very vicious and criminal conduct. The husband has a right to use preventive means with the wife, to a certain limit; when, if it fails, he must either commit her to the hands of the law, or separate. The converse of this is, in some degree, true also; that the wife may take some measures to prevent the wrongs of the husband; but it is not true to the same extent. As a general rule, the husband has an entire right to the person of his wife, and may use gentle means to constrain her liberty. But if that restraint be cruel, unreasonable or improper, she has her right to a release on *Habeas Corpus.*

The husband's right to the person of his wife, includes a right to preserve the purity of her conduct, and to certain remedies for the violation of it. A husband is justified in using force in defence of his wife; and it is said that homicide is justifiable in such a case.

The husband having a right to the person of his wife, has the sole right to the remedies for legal wrongs committed against her person. It is true, the State prosecutes for public crimes against her, as against all citizens. But so far as there is a personal remedy at law, that remedy ensues to the husband. He, for example, has a right to an action for damages, in case she is assaulted. It is true also, that she must be formally joined, in some actions of this kind; but she cannot sue *alone*, and therefore she has lost all personal control over the right of action. She can bring no action without her husband's concurrence.

So also she has not the personal power, *alone*, to execute a deed or other legal instrument, which shall bind herself or her property. All such instruments are void. The reason given for this is, that she acts under the *compulsion* of her husband. But this supposition is contrary to the idea of unity, which the law maintains; for it assumes her inferiority. The better reason is, that that very unity requires that she should not act alone, but in conjunction with her husband.

To this general rule there are some exceptions. We have already said that in some of the States a wife may make a will or devise of her property. This is the case in Ohio. Again, if her husband has "abjured the realm," as it is called, she may sue and be sued alone. This is necessary for her very existence, as she is entirely cut off from her husband. This principle applies to the wife of an alien residing abroad, or to the wife of a man who has left her and gone into foreign countries, intending to remain permanently. So also, if the husband is transported for a crime, she is considered as a single woman, and may act as such.

In fine, it appears that the husband's control over the person of his wife is so complete that he may claim her society altogether; that he may reclaim her if she goes away or is detained by others; that he may use gentle constraint upon her liberty to prevent her going away, or to prevent improper conduct; that he may maintain suits for injuries to her person; that he may defend her with force; that she cannot sue alone; and that she cannot execute a deed or valid conveyance, without the concurrence of her husband. In most respects she loses the power of personal independence, and altogether that of separate action in legal matters.

She does not lose, however, her personal responsibility for moral action. She has the rights of conscience as fully guaranteed to her as to any other citizen. Her husband has no more right to constrain her to any particular form of religion, or to compel her to any criminal or vicious act, then he has any other citizen. She has her remedies, as much as any other citizen, against his illegal acts. If he constrain her liberty for a wrong purpose, or in a cruel and unreasonable manner, she has her right to the writ of Habeas Corpus. If he use force towards her, she has a right to charge him in a criminal suit, and to have him bound to keep the peace.

It is true, that so intimate is the marriage relation, so strong the ties, and so easy the means of annoyance by one party towards the other, that moral *duress* is often stronger than any constraint upon the person could be; and this sort of constraint is beyond the jurisdiction of the law. This is true; but it is not the fault of the law. The law cannot, in the nature of things, reach anything but the external actions of mankind; and if there be a sort of moral compulsion towards unhappy and unrighteous conduct, arising from the relation of one party to another, and the pressing motives which grow out of that relation; the law of society, acting only on visible and tangible objects, cannot remedy the evil. It cannot remove the moral motive which acts upon the mind. It follows, then, that there is a large class of cases of misconduct of husbands and wives towards each other, which no human law can reach, and for which it is in vain to expect any power of society to furnish a remedy. So far as there are visible acts of cruelty, constraint, violence or crime towards wives by husbands, the law furnishes the same remedy for them as for others. The difficulty is, that in so delicate a relation, complaint is seldom made; and a permanent remedy cannot be applied without a dissolution of the marriage contract, a resort which should never be encouraged.

*   *   *

It might be thought, from the sweeping transfer which the law makes of the person and property of the wife to the control of the husband, that she had acquired nothing by marriage. This is not, however, strictly correct. She does acquire some things of great importance. In relation to her *person*, she acquires, 1. Protection; 2. Maintenance. If the first, in a civilized country, should not be needed, the second is in all nations, of no small consequence. As a general rule, the maintenance of the wife and of the entire family devolves upon the husband as head of the family. It is his *duty* legal and moral; and it is the corresponding *right* of the wife to demand it. The cases in which the wife has brought property enough to support the family; or in which the husband, from sickness or incompetency, is unable to support it; or when from his vices, he has been disabled or is unwilling, are few, compared with the great mass of families, in which the husband, by his labor or his property does, in performance of this great moral and legal duty, support the household. There is no doubt, that the wife renders, in the vast majority of instances, services fully equivalent to what she receives. It is her duty to render these services, and it is his to maintain the family.

In respect to protection, personally, the husband is justified in using the same violence to protect his wife, that he could to protect himself. He has a right to interfere in all those invasions of her right which would have been invasions of his, had they been offered to his person or property. He is bound also to protect her by shelter, aid and comfort, in all those ways in which such aid and comfort are necessary, by the usages of civilized people.

The law also goes a little beyond mere protection. It makes the husband liable for all the wrongs and frauds of the wife, committed during marriage. If the wrong be committed in his company or by his order, he alone is liable. If not, they are jointly liable. Where the remedy for the wrong is by a suit for damages only, the husband is liable with the wife. But if the remedy be sought by imprisonment or execution, the husband is alone liable to imprisonment. Again, if the wrong is to be punished *criminally* by imprisonment or otherwise, the wife alone is to be punished, unless there is evidence of coercion from the husband. The presumption of the law, however, is carried so far as to excuse the wife from punishment for theft, committed in the presence, or by the command of her husband.

The great personal right which the wife acquires by marriage is the *right to maintenance*. In general, the duty of the husband in this particular, is cheerfully performed towards the wife and towards the family, by sharing with them all the fruits of his acquisitions; and, should he die first, leaving them his heirs. In the great mass of families there is no difference of opinion on this point, and the whole family act in harmony together. But suppose the wife thinks she is not properly maintained, or the husband refuses to maintain her, or they have mutually separated; what is the rule of law in this case?

The general rule is, that the husband is bound to provide his wife with necessaries *suitable to her situation and his condition in life*. If she contract debts for such necessaries, during cohabitation, he is obliged to pay for those debts; but for anything beyond necessaries, he is not liable.

There are two different cases in which the question of the husband's liability for the wife's debts may arise. The first is, when he is silent, and his assent is presumed. This is too common a case in actual life,—for whether a woman be living with her husband, or whether she be separated (except in the case of divorce, when she has ceased to be his wife), it is rare that the husband gives any public or formal notice, that he will not be liable for his wife's debts. In this case, then (when he has not directly refused his assent to the debt), the husband is always bound to provide his wife with necessaries, when she is not in fault, from a principle of duty and justice.

The articles deemed *necessaries*, in law, are *food, clothing* and *medicine*. These, according to the principle stated above, must be suitable to her situation and his condition in life. Courts of justice have always construed this principle fairly and liberally. A merchant or professional man, in good circumstances, cannot reduce his wife to the condition of the wife of a laboring man. His assent is presumed, in the first place, to her contracts; and whether he gives it or not, he is bound for necessaries proper for his and her condition in life. It may be taken for granted, that if a woman were to purchase things, on the credit of her husband, entirely inconsistent with their condition in life, and so obviously extravagant as that the suspicions of the seller ought to be excited, the husband would not be liable. But such cases in the United States, where all classes of people dress so nearly alike, and where all have good and substantial food, would be very difficult to prove. It must be an extreme case, which would take the husband out of the general rule of liability.

The second class of cases is when the husband has given notice that *he will not be liable* for her debts. But the husband has not the power to deprive his wife of credit, on his account, for *necessaries*. The only effect of this refusal and notice is to oblige the tradesman, who sells the wife goods, to prove that they are necessary to her comfort, and not mere superfluities. The husband, in this way, may be able to circumscribe his wife's credit within very moderate limits; but he cannot deprive her of credit for what is *necessary* in her condition of life.

On the other hand, if the husband were to make the wife a reasonable allowance, during his absence, and the tradesman had notice of this, the husband would not be liable for further supplies unless the tradesman could prove the allowance was not paid or was not reasonable.

So if the husband abandon his wife, or if they separate by mutual consent, or if he send her away, he is still liable: he sends credit with her.

On the other hand, if she be the guilty cause of that separation, as if she elope from her husband's house, he is not bound even for necessaries. He is bound to provide for her in his family; and while he is willing to do this, and is guilty of no cruelty, he is not bound for her elsewhere.

Money is not, in itself considered, a necessary; and consequently the husband is not liable for money lent to his wife, unless his consent can be shown. This rule, in our country, is rather an absurdity; for it often happens, that the things which are necessary, cannot be had without money.

If the husband should refuse to provide necessaries for his wife, and prohibit one person or any person from trusting, and she is notwithstanding trusted with necessaries suitable to her condition in life, the husband will still be liable; for he cannot deprive her of the liberty, which the law gives, of providing necessaries, at his expense, for her own preservation.

Again, if the wife receive such treatment as affords a reasonable cause for her to depart from his house, and refuse to cohabit with him; yet he will be bound to fulfill her contract for necessaries suitable to her circumstances and those of her husband.

•   •   •

We come now to consider some of the *chief differences between the rights of a wife and those of a husband.* These are obvious from a review of what has already been said, upon the law of this relation. . . .

It is seen, that in marriage, the *legal control* of the wife passes to the husband, not that of the husband to the wife. For example, the husband has a right to the services of his wife; he has a right to reclaim her when absent; he has a right to use gentle means of restraint; and for these purposes, he has the right to claim aid from the law and its officers. In one word, in the theory of the law, the *custody* of the wife belongs to the husband. Here is the first striking difference between the condition of a woman in a married state and that of her husband. She has no such custody over him. This principle is evidently derived from the Scripture rule, that the husband is head of the family. But one idea deserves at least a suggestion. If the society and services of a wife are, as they ought to be, so valuable to the husband, are not the society and services of the husband equally so to the wife? If the husband has a right to use gentle restraint upon the wife in case of *evil habits,* ought not the wife to have a right to demand of the law, that it should also restrain him from evil courses? For example, if the husband wastes his substance in drunkenness, and his time in idleness, has not the wife a right to demand of the *law* that it should restrain him, in the manner which he can do her, by the control of her property and person?

A singular case is reported in the newspapers, as having occurred in Connecticut, which if correctly reported, shows that some of the rigidity of the old law, on the subject of custody is weakened. It arises out of this question: Can a man *abduct his own wife?* This case would seem to decide that he could not. And yet most certainly, if his power of custody over her, is as strong as it is laid down in the old authorities, he could.

A, the wife of B, in Connecticut, left her husband and lived with her father, or uncle, at all events her near kin. B, by the aid of some persons, seized her, carried her through N. York to Virginia, whence she was taken back, either by pursuers, or by his consent. In an action for damages, subsequently, it was decided that this *abduction* of his wife was illegal. If this is to be the law on this subject, then the old law may be considered as completely revolutionized. This is also the tendency of opinions, at this day.

2. The second great difference in the condition of men and women, in the marriage state, is in relation to the *rights of property.* . . . The husband, at marriage, acquires during his life, the *entire and exclusive use of the wife's real estate.* Of her personal property (money, jewels, furniture, etc.), he acquires the absolute and *entire right.* If the sum she brought were ever so large, he might dispose of it all instantly. So if she has rights of property *in action*, he may acquire for himself the whole, and dispose of the whole. *She*, on the other hand, acquires no such rights in her property. The only real protection she has is, in the fee-simple of real estate, of which she cannot be deprived except by her own act. These differences in rights of property are very great, and we point them out, not to suggest amendments, but to show the fact.

3. The next great difference consists in the rights which either derives from the other after death. The wife's right to the husband's real estate after death is the right of dower, and this . . . is a right to the use for life, of one *third* the husband's real estate. Now on the death of the wife the husband has an estate for life, in the *whole* of the wife's lands and tenements. That is, the husband has just three times as great an interest after the death of his wife, in her lands, that she has, after his death, in his lands. If he owned three houses of equal value in N. York, on his death, she has a right of dower in *one* of them. If she has three such houses and die, he has

an estate by the courtesy in the whole of them. In the personal property, the difference is as great. He takes the whole. She takes a certain portion at his death, according to the statute.

4. There is one difference which does *not* exist in the theory of the law and of Scripture. There is *no sex in criminal law,* because there can be no sex *in morals.* It is true, that the old feudal law did make a distinction, even here; for it could never get over the idea, that because women were incapable of military service, *therefore* they were inferior to men. But our American criminal law makes no such unreasonable distinctions. Murder, theft, adultery, etc., are the same *crimes* in women, as in men. It is true, that the public opinion of men does require a stricter observance of certain morals in women, than in men; but in this age of the world, they have not dared to carry that idea into the criminal code. They have, at least, made the *law* conform to the equity of morals.

The Fugitive Wife

Warren Chase

"*It has long been known that children called illegitimate are usually superior to those born under the bands of marriage.*" *So wrote Warren Chase, himself an illegitimate child, in his book on marriage. Chase's notion of the superiority of illegitimate children was part of his argument that most marriages subjected wives to legal prostitution, or sexual slavery, so that their children were likely to suffer physically in the womb from the assaults of brutal fathers. Chase never knew his own father, who ran away to the army and was killed in the War of 1812. His mother died when he was only five, and he was apprenticed to a local farmer, who beat him routinely, as if to make up for Chase's pre-natal good fortune.*

Years later, when he came to write his autobiography, Chase called it The Life-Line of the Lone One; or, Autobiography of the World's Child, *a romantic response to these early hardships. And whether or not his illegitimacy had anything to do with the superiority that he did in fact exhibit, it must have exerted a strong influence on his self-image. All his life he was a "loner"—a religious skeptic, a utopian socialist, an itinerant lecturer on women's rights, temperance, land reform, and spiritualism.*

In 1844 Chase founded "Ceresco," an especially successful utopian community near what is now Ripon, Wisconsin. He became a leader in the political affairs of the territory, and was a member of the first senate when Wisconsin became a state. After the breakup of the community in 1850, Chase turned to lecturing for a livelihood—and, so it appears, as a mode of life. About this time Andrew Jackson Davis converted him to spiritualism, and he devoted the next forty years to its promotion, from the Atlantic to the Pacific.

The Fugitive Wife *was* Chase's *contribution to the deluge of free love tracts during the 1850s. He thought himself closest in spirit to the beliefs of Henry C. Wright, who (like Chase's other friend, Davis) was an advocate of monogamy tempered by more liberal divorce laws. Chase's "creed," as he called it, was as follows: "Perfect equality between the sexes in all conditions of life. Marriage, a civil contract, to be made, controlled, or dissolved wholly by the parties to it, under general laws. Legal restrictions and public records protecting offspring, wholly released and freed from sectarian and clerical control. All children legally the legitimate offspring of both parents, and both held responsible for their support and complete education until of age. Both sexes equally eligible to any office, all of which should be nearly equally divided between them."*

Chase was serious about this creed. During his stint in the Wisconsin State Senate he tried, unsuccessfully, to legislate divorce laws even more liberal than those of Indiana, the most advanced of the time. (Another former utopian turned legislator, Robert Dale Owen, had helped to frame the Indiana statutes.)

Chase himself married at twenty-four, and was apparently faithful to his vows—at least by his own account—through thirty-eight years. After his first wife's death in 1875, he remarried—a token of his satisfaction with the institution. However, there was a period just after the breakup of the community when Chase and his spouse disagreed over their mutual obligations. During the six years of his utopian experiment, he boasted, they "Never had a case of licentiousness, nor a complaint of immoral conduct." Now suddenly Chase came under fire as a free lover.

In fact he was infected with a relatively mild strain of the free love virus. It was not that he desired sexual relations outside his marriage, but that he wished to extend his power of "pure" loving to others. As he himself put it, "A new fountain of feeling burst forth within him, higher, holier, purer, and more devoted, than he ever felt or knew before. As it increased in power, it restrained the animal and passional impulses, and craved food congenial to its own nature, purely spiritual and affectional." Unfortunately his wife had not yet attained these heights of love. "The demand of his soul was, in this higher department of its nature, responded to by another, far more advanced than himself in the purest and holiest aspirations of the soul, and led onward and upward by her." He kept up a loving correspondence with this "higher spirit" through several years, to the distress of his wife. Finally one of his enemies got hold of a letter from his platonic friend, and circulated it, with salacious commentary, throughout the anti-free love circles. This was disastrous, for the long habit of intimate communication between Chase and his friend had resulted in an epistolary style that was "much abbreviated—just what the guilty and suspicious would need, to carry out their suspicions. The pedlars of gossip . . . soon made a good story out of this letter . . . That the Lone One, when absent from home, lived with the author of this letter, and had already raised two children by her, etc."

For a while Chase's wife half-believed these accusations. "But all these slanders and falsehoods were no real or permanent injury to the Lone One, or his mate. To her they proved a blessing in disguise," for as a result of her struggle with doubt, she too became a spiritualist, and settled "into the calmness of the harmonial life."

Warren Chase
The Fugitive Wife

In the June of 1859, the scribes of Chicago furnished the daily papers of that city with an interesting item of news, by announcing that a fugitive wife escaped from one of the villages on Lake Superior, in Michigan, had been legally seized, and returned with the officer, via Detroit and the next boat, to her legal and proper owner. The papers stated that she had left her home and husband and several small children, and fled on the steamer to that city,

● Selection from The Fugitive Wife: A Criticism on Marriage, Adultery and Divorce, 3d ed., Boston: Bela Marsh, 1866 (c. 1861), pp. 7–17, 77–78, 91–95.

where despatches had arrived before her, enabling the officers to be in readiness to arrest her on the arrival of the boat; that she had come in company with a gentleman of her acquaintance, and probably at his expense, which rendered her crime, and his for assisting the fugitive, extremely aggravating. I felt confident that most persons, who read this item of the city news, were pleased with the report of the capture of the fugitive, and the one who assisted her, and of their return, via Detroit, to the place from which she had fled. I never heard of the persons or the circumstance after, and soon forgot the names, but the incident opened to my mind a broad field for reflection, and instituted a search after justice, consistency and rights.

I knew we had a national fugitive-slave law, which was considered by most people in the free States to be very cruel, and by many unjust, and only defended and justified by its friends by the necessity for it, and the demands of the constitution; but I did not know we had State fugitive-wife laws, by which they could be caught and returned to their owners, as chattel slaves are, although I knew many wives were as effectually enslaved and controlled as the black chattels of Georgia. I know most humane persons considered that a negro, who displayed sufficient skill and energy to escape from slavery, and reach a free State, or Canada, was entitled to his or her liberty, and that it was almost or quite barbarous to return such persons; but I was hardly prepared to believe the people so heartless, cruel, almost barbarous, as to return a woman of their race and color to a tyrant who had treated her so cruelly that it had forced asunder the strongest ties in her nature, and compelled her to leave even her children, and flee for life, to escape the grave, as I know some have. When a mother leaves her children, it is *prima facie* evidence to me that the cause was more potent than a mother's love, and must be nearly equal to death itself; for even death seldom does it. I can perceive how a woman might leave her husband, for want of love on his or her part; and, if none but the two were interested, this would be good and sufficient reason for separation. But when she leaves children, and leaves them with the man she could not live with, and trusts him to select another to govern and guide them, certainly there must be a power stronger than that maternal love which God has planted deepest in the woman's nature. It is simply ridiculous to talk of psychology, seduction, free love, or fascination, as a cause. These are all insignificant. It must take years of cruelty and suffering to produce such effect and result. It seems to me more and more, on reflection, that a law is more cruel that returns a wife to her master, than that which returns a slave to the owner. In each case death will be a release, and oftener a desirable one to the wife than the slave; and we have more suicides by wives than by slaves, to escape cruelty.

Had the case above referred to been a solitary one, or even one of a single hundred, and never to be repeated, I would have taken no notice of it, but devoted my time and pen to other subjects, perhaps not more congenial to the public mind than this. But, while we of the free States are complaining of being compelled by Congress to execute cruel fugitive-slave laws, and are enacting such as no constitution of state or nation requires to return the wife who escapes from a cruelty often as brutal as that of most slave masters, it is certainly a fit subject of criticism.

It is true we have statutes in most of the States to protect the wife against physical abuse of the husband, with the whip or fist, but none to protect her against a personal abuse, often worse than a severe whipping. Our marriage laws and public opinion put the body of the wife into the care and keeping of the husband, provided he does not beat her, and leave her no escape from the worst of cruelty, but to run away, and then we catch and return her. The very crimes (for they are crimes) which thousands of husbands perpetrate weekly, or daily, upon their wives, would, any one of them, if perpetrated upon a single woman who could defend herself with the law, send the man to the penitentiary for a term of years, if not for life. Yet, when she complains, she gets no sympathy from her church or pious neighbors, except "Wives, submit to your husbands." The law has no remedy, and all that is left is escape, if she can, and be caught if she must.

I know very well this is not the condition of all wives, but only those who are merely *legal* wives. There are many whose lives are mated to their husbands, and who physically and mentally harmonize and blend with them, and join voluntarily in all the relations of social and sexual life; but, by long and extensive observation, I am compelled to believe that these are the exceptions, and the rule is the other way, and that a majority are unhappy often even when their husbands are contented. It has long been well known that hundreds of young wives go annually to the graveyards,

as effectually killed by their husbands as if they had been pounded
to death, many of them leaving no word of complaint, or even of
warning to their old companions.

There is scarcely a neighborhood in the Christianized part of our
country that has not been visited with cases of domestic trouble
within the last few years—deaths as above, separations, runaways,
or suicides; and, instead of condemning and punishing to prevent,
the wise legislators should search for the causes, and try to remove
them. Add to these the terrible effects of forced relations, of unhappy marriages, in producing and bringing up children, and we
have a picture that ought to make any Christian blush, or hide his
head in shame, if he or his religion has sustained the barbarous
features of our present marriage laws to this time. The scribes of
the press, and the pharisees of the pulpit, are continually harping
upon the beauties and blessings of marriage and married life, and
thus alluring and enticing the young and ignorant into it; but they
seldom give the other side, and thus warn them against the terrible
risk and danger of an uncongenial mating. The jokes and jests,
ridicule and contempt, of old and young, rich and poor, run freely
against the single, who reach or cross the age of thirty; and if
there is one thing more odious in the public mind than another,
at this time, it is free love; and yet, if it has any legitimate meaning,
it must be the love of single persons, or those not bound by law
or church to love any one. The love of all single persons, if they
have love at all, must be free, and they are free lovers, except so
far as the church may claim a right to direct their love to God or
Jesus. Fanaticism and public prejudice take great liberties with
language, and often pervert it to their uses, as they have in the use
of free love, applying it to the sexual passion, which man has in
common with animals, if not with plants, and which we never
think of calling love when it prompts the male to pursue the
female among the deer, sheep, or swine, and which is no more
appropriate among our race than theirs. If I can understand the
term love, and apply it to manifestations of feeling, I cannot find
it below the human kingdom, nor ever manifested in that kingdom
in or through the sexual passions. I suppose both men and women
love each other; if so, it is not the same that draws only the opposite
sexes together. Some persons talk of several kinds of love—some
good, some bad, etc. I know nothing of it.

"I would not call that love,
    Which could be poisoned, marred, or stained,
    Which could by any wealth be bought,
    By any power be chained."

To me "Love is to the human heart what sunshine is to flowers."
I have no fear of it in or out of marriage, free or not,—if, indeed,
it could be other than free, which I doubt. I wish every man loved
every woman as well as the most loving husband does his wife, and
every woman loved every man as well as the most loving wife does
her husband; then we should have a world of love and loving
beings, and certainly no one would knowingly injure any other;
for love worketh no injury.

But to return to the subject of marriage, which is under consideration, as now established and sustained by law and religion.
It has certainly failed to create, control, or restrain love, however
much it may confine its expression, or compel feigned attempts to
imitate it. That our marriage laws restrain the sexual passion
there is no doubt, and but little doubt that they ought to do so
by proper regulations; but it is a serious question whether, as now
established, they do not add greatly to the misery and depravity of
society, rather than its refinement and elevation, as they should. It
is certain that, in pairing the ignorant and diseased, especially those
also very poor, and, by this pairing, giving life annually to
thousands of poorly made, badly organized, and diseased children,
there is a terrible result of marriage. If the law or church binds
two persons together as man and wife, it certainly ought to require
them to be qualified for parents, or instruct them to avoid giving
existence to them. There should be good evidence that they possessed
the knowledge of self-government, and the laws of propagation.
Farmers regulate the breeding of stock, and he is a poor stock-
grower who does not study the laws of nature, and regulate his
stock according to them; but both church and state, which have
jointly and severally controlled marriage ever since its introduction
among men, have totally neglected and refused to regulate the
laws of generation, and usually kept the rising and marrying
generation as ignorant as they could on the subject, often suppressing such books as would have given useful information on that
subject.

But the most cruel and wicked thing they have done with marriage is to place by it the body (and soul, as far as possible) of the wife in the power, as a possession, of the husband, first absolute, but more recently, as society advances, gradually but slowly slackening the bands of ownership, or tyranny, but still compelling her to remain sexually a slave to his passions, even to the sacrifice of happiness, health, and often life; or, if she becomes a fugitive, catch and return her, or cast her out of all decent society, and prevent her from securing a living by any honorable business—sometimes forcing her back in this way, or to the grave, or to another prostitution as bad or worse than the one from which she fled.

I am not opposed to marriage, or marriage laws. I believe with proper provision for separation and divorce, they could be made to contribute to our happiness, and to regulate social life, and generation, and the rearing of children. But, as our laws now are, the evils are becoming unbearable, and, unless soon modified, and adapted to the advanced age in which we live, there will be a terrible reaction against them, and danger of their total overthrow and a general social chaos, and sexual distraction and destruction.

Robert Owen says, in Italy, where divorce is not granted at all, the marriage tie is less sacred than in any country with which he is acquainted. This is natural. Extremes meet. So it will ever be. In the States of this Union where the law is most severe, thousands become reckless, and do not regard it at all, while the more honest and conscientious suffer often terribly under its galling fetters, or petty tyranny. Take the case with which I started this subject. It would be natural to inquire, when a person is arrested by an officer, what crime he or she had been charged with. What would be the answer in this case? Charged with the crime of leaving her home because it was so uncomfortable that she could not live in it. Charged with going off on a boat without the consent of her master. Charged with controlling her own actions in defence of her person and protection of her health. But suppose the husband had performed a similar act; who would have arrested him and returned him? Suppose he had come in company with a female friend on the steamboat; could we even have raised a gossip about him? Who cannot see the partiality and injustice of the law in these cases? And why should the law be made exclusively by man, and almost exclusively *for* him? It is considered a crime for a wife to leave her husband, but not a crime for a husband to leave his wife. He can go to California, or New York, or any other place, and find business, society, respectability, and seldom will he be asked where and how his wife is. But let a woman leave her home, and every one must know where her husband is, and why she did not stay with him; and, whatever her excuse, nearly all will condemn her. She is treated as an inferior being, both in law and religion.

It is said, upon good authority, that more than half the patronage of houses of ill-fame, in the large cities, is by married men who live with their wives; while very little is from wives who live with their husbands; and yet no one can give a reason why it should be so, or why it should be worse for a wife than a husband to visit these places. There is certainly something wrong in our marriage system when either party visits such places to any extent. It is not free love, nor love at all; for love never drew or drove a person to such or any other place for sexual indulgence. It is that passion which has failed to find satisfaction in love, usually, because it has not been drawn out in and through the affections. Our whole system of training for boys, and mostly for girls, is defective, except in a few families (mostly Spiritualists). In society, in early life, we cultivate exclusively, in the boys, the intellect and passions, and crush out the affections as weaknesses, and thus almost entirely unfit them for social or married life. In females nature has planted the affections deeper and stronger, and it is not so easy to root them out. They are therefore better prepared for marriage, if more were prepared to meet them on that plane of life. But, alas! three, at least, out of every four marry to be disappointed, and soon find it was passion in the man which before marriage they mistook for love and a response to their affections. To some it is a terrible disappointment, and soon sends their souls to the other world, and their bodies to the grave, to make room for another wife. Others drag out a miserable life, and start half a dozen or a dozen children, most of them to drop early into the grave. Others try to run away, and find that society has hedged up the road to freedom for wives almost, or quite, as effectually as it has for slaves of a darker color. Others, still, try to kill out their affections, and adapt themselves to their husbands, and make the best of life, by crucifying the best part of their natures; and the few who are fortunate enough to get affectionate and loving husbands, and find life happy and satisfactory, have little sympathy for the others. They think each one ought to have been fortunate as they have been and often think other men the same as their husbands, and that they could get along as well with another as with this one. But those women who have had two husbands, one governed by his passions and the other by his affections, know well the difference.

If we will save the institution of marriage, we must protect the wife, as we do the unmarried woman, against the passions of man, and give the husband no more control over the person, *body* or *soul*, of the woman, after marriage than before. Make husbands court their wives after marriage as much as before, and leave them as complete and absolute mistresses of their persons as some of the States have already made them of their property. This is slowly coming; but we always legislate more and better to protect property than persons, and study the laws of nature to regulate the breeding and classing of stock, before we look after the laws of human generation, and are forever harping about *re*generating what would never have needed *re*generating if it had been properly generated. I am glad Henry C. Wright and others are devoting so much time and talent to this subject. I am sure good results have already begun to be felt from their words and books. Natal and antenatal laws and duties are little understood; and while the clergy have been wasting their time and breath about saving souls, they have neglected the bodies that contained them.

When a slave-mother leaves her children, to escape into a land of freedom and gain her liberty, we approve her act, and picture more glowingly the horrors of that institution which could force a mother thus to break the strongest natural tie of the heart; but when a wife-mother is forced to fly from her children, by the brutality of a husband, often of that character she cannot describe to the public, what do we do for her? How much sympathy can we get up for her in the church, or in the social circles of respectable society? Usually enough to send her back, or to the poorhouse, or brothel, and no more. And sometimes, strange as it may seem, the horrors from which they flee are so great that they will go even to the brothel, or by suicide to the grave, before they will return and endure again the horrible life they fled from.

I know many honest people, viewing the blessings, and only the blessings, of marriage, think all this must be borne for the sake of the institution, and that any alteration would be destructive to the whole fabric—that "to meddle is to mar." They greatly mistake. The institution, if natural and heaven-ordained, cannot be destroyed or overthrown, but may be greatly improved upon its present basis. That the mating or pairing of one male with one female is natural, I have no doubt; but whether these or any such unions are eternal, I know not. How far into the other life they go, I do not know; but I know some last through this life, with mutual and satisfactory attractions; though, according to my observation, more seem to break at some period in life, even though they started mutually satisfactory. Whether all could be made to last through this life, or longer, I know not; but I am sure that no ceremony of priest, or statute of state, can make them so when nature, or feelings, or conditions, rebel. We have already had by far too much legislating and preaching against nature. It is high time for priests and legislators to study nature's laws, and try to re-enact and enforce them; and in no department is this more needed than in marriage and parentage.

It has long been known that children called illegitimate are usually superior to those born under the bands of marriage, and, with equal advantages for education, far surpass them. This ought not to be so, nor would it if the marriage relations were generally natural and harmonious. Many of the defects, and much of the suffering, among children, have long been known to arise from the sexual abuse of the mother, whether in or out of wedlock, and this is much more common in than out of marriage, and can only be remedied by such a change in our system of life in marriage, that the wife shall be as much the mistress and owner of her person after marriage as before, and as free from constraint and control. No man should ever marry a woman he could not trust with as much freedom after as before marriage; and, if he could not make her so love him after marriage as to be as true to him as before, he has no right to her. This is very nearly the wife's position under present laws, for there is little change or restraint on man by marriage, while many men would be ready to murder their wives for doing but once what they do often, and would readily do at any time when their wives could not know it. And yet their wives are required to love them, when they would despise or loathe their wives if guilty of the same acts. This is not right. Either man should be restrained, or woman liberated. I am in favor of the latter, because that is the tendency of the age. We are going forward in the laws of individual sovereignty, not backward. Both must be equally and more free, and depend on love, and not on law or religion, to keep them together. When a man and wife are wholly and fully satisfactory and devoted to each other, they will not stray or wander in their passions, however broad the fraternal affections. They would always go home to rest, enjoying that closer relation of life, which neither law nor religion can ever confine, and in which their attempts to confine persons have caused more misery than all the pestilence and epidemics of the last hundred years.

In the earlier ages marriage was no more nor less than a species of chattelism. The wife was bought for a price, and as effectually owned and controlled as any slave of Carolina is now. We have only partially grown out of the system and practice. We allow, usually, the victim to have a voice in the sale, and pretend to give her the price,—a home—a handsome man—a rich estate—or a man to lead her round, and wait on her by day, for her company by night. We have also secured her some other privileges, such as a defence in law against beating and whipping, against sale or transfer, etc. But her husband may abuse her body far worse than by whipping, in other ways, and escape even censure. He may poison her with the fumes or juice of tobacco, or rum, a fetid breath and filthy body. He may starve her, rob her of all enjoyment of society, and even her children; may compel her to sleep with him when she loathes him, and torture and torment her life continually; and our religion and society provide no remedy, and our laws but little, in some States none. But neither husband, nor law, nor church, can make her love him under such treatment, nor by any other, except as it is spontaneous, voluntary and mutual; and, when it is, none of these acts will be found, and no law or religion will be required; for they will neither make nor unmake, create nor destroy, that love which alone can and should bind two souls and bodies in wedlock. All they can or ought to do is to acknowledge or recognize it, and never attempt to do that where true marriage does not already exist, nor in parties where it has already ceased to exist.

It is such modification in our marriage laws as shall adapt them to the present advanced state of society, and save them from destruction, that I advocate—such as shall give the wife every advantage, right, and privilege of the husband, and secure to her all the rights of person and property she had before marriage, and protect her in them, and if she shall choose to eat or sleep by herself she shall not be forced to do otherwise, and she should be as free to visit and be visited as before marriage; and then the husband would be compelled to treat her as well as he did when he was only a lover, in order to retain her love, and of course by such treatment could secure and retain it as fully and effectually. If husbands remained lovers, wives would remain true, and faithful, and affectionate, and continue to grow more so; the sexual and parental relations would only increase their attachment and enhance their enjoyment. But now no husband is expected to be a lover, at least not to his *wife*; but soon as marriage is consummated he is the lord and master, however inferior he may be, at least so far as law and religion are concerned, and they both attempt to control and divide this institution between them. But there are honorable and noble exceptions (but few) to this, where the pairs mate above and live above the law and church, and both are dead letters to them, for they live and love, conforming to and accepting the law and church rite, but living above it, and never restrained or controlled by it. They live to love, and love to live, with each other, and each seeks the other's highest happiness. Marriage laws are of no account to them,—they would not part if there were no laws, and, apart, would seek each other first of all. Such is true marriage, which laws do not make, cannot unmake.

●   ●   ●

The true plan of correcting the evils in social life is, first, to provide by law for the legitimacy of all children, and for their support and education from private or public funds; second, to restrict marriage and parentage as far as possible to competent persons; and keep the ignorant and unqualified out of the snare that now takes in many; third, to let those who make mistakes in spite of caution and the law, get out as easily and voluntarily as they got into the trouble. The most liberal system of divorce we have yet tried has not led to hasty and imprudent marriages more than other and more strict systems. The fact is, the parties to such marriages seldom inquire or care about the divorce laws. It is the marriage law they have to do with, and inquire after; and that they look up, and find, generally, it has only laid the value of a half dollar in the way, to pay a magistrate for telling them a lie, namely, that they are put together by God,—when it is usually only lust that brings them to the altar, and that usually confined to the one who promises to love, cherish and support till death, often when he has no love, and of course can give none, and cannot support himself decently, and has no design to support the other, and sometimes expects and even depends on her to support him. It is strange that our legislators, if not our priests, cannot see that the evils arising from this practice are to be remedied by changes in the marriage laws,—if by law at all,—and that divorce should be more lax and easy, and marriage restricted and limited.

If we will regulate social life and families by law, let us require every couple to have a homestead, or means to maintain a home, before we allow them by law to become a family, or to marry. If we will decide who shall have children according to law, and legitimate, see that all we permit to do so are physically and morally qualified to become parents; and not, as now, authorize every couple that ask permission to try it, even when we know they are morally and physically so badly diseased that their offspring must either die in childhood or go to the prison or poorhouse, and then lay our legal crimes to God in sending them here.

•   •   •

There is a strong and natural feeling in most human beings, and one that increases with civilization and education,—a desire for home, for a resting-place for the head and heart; a place we can ornament, and where we can lay up our rude gifts and little treasures, and have them safe. This feeling must be supplied, and seems best supplied with the isolated household or the unitary home; but any rambling system of promiscuity between the sexes, that leaves us without homes, would be fatal to this strong feature in our nature, and also destructive to the greatest and best work of generations of our ancestors. I believe it would be an improvement on our state of society to transfer all the homes in title to the women, and to establish a rule that every wife should own a home before she was required to become a mother, and one that no man could take from her; make all homes inalienable, or not transferable for men to speculate in, and held only by women for homes for themselves and children. I would not object to a law that should allow any wife to turn her husband out of doors if he did not treat her well;—a change of the law might be serviceable to us for a while. But I should seriously object to any system which would very much interfere with monogamic relations and family homes, except a unitary home system that retained the pairing of the sexes; but in any form of life society should permit any couple, who were allowed to marry, to dissolve the tie they had formed by the same mutual agreement; and it would be folly for any person to set up a plea that strangers or society care more for their children than they do themselves. When parents fail to have care for and interest in their children, there is little hope for the innocent creatures in this world, and they had better keep their tender limbs and soft heads out of it, or go at once to the next sphere.

Some persons talk of free love as a state of wild, homeless mothers and children, reckless men, and full license to the passions of men to prey upon woman as if she had no authority or capacity to resist; but I have never found any such movement with sufficient permanency for examination. True, I have seen a few men, wild with passion (usually fanatically religious), who have attempted to neutralize society with lust; but they were only victims to a moral and physical disease, easily cured in asylums (or could be if such were provided for them, as they should be). These were not lovers at all, much less *free* lovers. The free lovers with whom I am acquainted have the best and happiest homes in the country, the pleasantest and happiest families, are the truest and happiest wives and husbands, most devoted to their homes and children of any people; and hence I think it might be an improvement to have a little more of it in society; for it would, to a great extent, obviate the necessity of loosening our divorce laws. Wherever I have found a husband and wife both lovers, and both free in expressing or acting their love, I have invariably found a home of harmony and a good degree of happiness. But where one has love and the other lust, and they try to match, it is a failure; and where one has love and the other is cold, and tries to freeze the love out of the other, it is inharmony; and where one has lust and the other is cold, they should at once be divorced. Let lust marry lust, love love, and coldness coldness, and let the first and last be barren marriages, and the others supply the race. The first and last will need regulating by law; the others will live above the law, if you have one, and it will not harm them; and since there are a great many without love, or, at least, that free love which fits them to marry, therefore we must keep a system of laws to regulate them, to correct their mistakes, to marry and unmarry them, pair and re-pair them, and make the best we can of them till they die, and their places are filled with the children of true love and true marriage.

> The fear of hell and the hangman's rope
> Keeps many a wretch in order.

So, I suppose, we must continue to preach a hell, and keep a hangman's rope dangling in view, till we can correct or get rid of the wretches. So we need penal statutes to regulate the holiest and most sacred institution of society, while our corrupt system continues to people our towns and cities with the children of lust, and fill them with diseases, moral and physical, before they are born. And when, as now, nearly all of these enter life in and through our marriage system, and are unwelcome both to parents and society, it is time to overhaul and repair it, or, at least, to provide an escape for the poor victims, who are compelled to be the mothers of these poor, unwelcome strangers. So general is the idolatry in this country, that few even of the advocates of woman's rights have dared to attack our marriage laws and expose the cruelties sheltered under them; but, as I have no Christian reputation to lose, and have all my life been the defender of unpopular truths, and was born a social and religious heretic, with the halter of legal illegitimacy around my neck, therefore I can speak and write on this subject, and only ask to be heard and read, with very little care for the opinions of those who cannot, or dare not, or will not reason. I am sure woman will vote, and preach, and plead, and make law, and have as much to say and do with marriage as man, in due time.

> I hear a tumult from the heaving sea
> Of human life. The multitudinous waves,
> Like ocean's billows, lift their mighty voices,
> And, with a deep and solemn sound, they ask
> A change. The awful din startles the ear
> Of gouty sin, and scowling, blear-eyed wrong,
> And old conformities, with chattering teeth,
> Shrink back affrighted. Forms, and rites, and old
> Observances, upon whose wrinkled brows
> The gray and grisly locks of age are seen,
> Bend low, and speed away, like ghosts, before
> This roar of many voices. Loud they cry:
> "Reform! Reform!" Blind old conservatism,
> Fearing advance, looks timorously on;
> And in the distant sound, hourly more near,
> It hears in low, deep thunder-tones, "REFORM!"
> God speed that day! The world's great aching heart
> Is wildly throbbing for the issue and
> Perfection of this prophecy of heaven!

T. L. Nichols and Mary Gove Nichols, A. J. Davis and Mary F. Davis, H. C. Wright, S. P. Andrews, R. D. Owen, Julia Branch, Carrie Lewis, Hannah F. Brown, Cory Barry, and others, each with different tone and music of their own, keyed to different systems of sexual union, have joined with tongues and pens to awaken the public mind, and they have aroused the lethargic church and fluctuating state, till conservatism has sounded the alarm, and called to arms all its votaries, to save the institution of marriage; and if they will save it, they must open the gates of divorce wide, and allow the crushed thousands to escape from under its ponderous wheels, and then those who ride securely in it may retain it if they please. But it must not much longer be made an altar on which to sacrifice victims to lust.

"Free lover" is now the odious term with which every advocate of reform in the marriage laws, or of making divorce more easy, is breveted, as "abolitionist" is the common term of odium, in some parts of our country, for any one who does not subscribe to all measures to break up the national government. But the ridiculous use of these terms in either case will, in a short time, like the term "infidel," be a mark of respect. Already, in many communities, the term infidel is synonymous with thinker, reasoner, or one of uncommon mental powers, and often a notice that the man is better than a Christian. So is the term "free lover" beginning to be a mark of superiority in some neighborhoods. It, like the term infidel, is still more odious in the orthodox estimation, when applied to women than when applied to men; but both will soon outlive its odium, and a few years will show reasoning minds how recklessly and ridiculously it has been used. If it should drive the Cains into the land of Nod for wives, it would be better than marrying their sisters, and cursing their children with kindred blood. That kind of free love that rescues and saves woman from the lust of man may be condemned and abused; but it must and will prevail, and be preached till our laws shall secure to each wife wholly and fully the control of her person, and, at least, equal control of her children and her home, and then it will be lauded to the skies, and registered as one of the saviors of the race, and especially of woman.

Divorce

Robert Dale Owen and Horace Greeley

In 1860 a new divorce law was proposed in the New York State Legislature, liberalizing the statutes to include desertion or persistent cruelty as well as the already recognized grounds of adultery. Horace Greeley came out against the bill in his New York Tribune, *comparing it to the lax laws of Indiana fashioned by Robert Dale Owen. Greeley was merely repeating the popular view of Owen and Indiana. It was true that Indiana had the most liberal statutes in the United States, though it was false that Owen deserved his reputation for having framed them, or for favoring free love principles, and probably the slur would have gone unnoticed had Owen not happened to be in New York at the time, and seen the editorial. His reply began a two months' debate on the same marriage and divorce question that Greeley had argued at the beginning of the 1850s with Henry James Sr. and Stephen Pearl Andrews.*

Owen was thought (by feminists like Elizabeth Cady Stanton) to have won the debate, but Greeley's position had the votes in the Legislature. The occasion and its outcome are especially interesting

*because they pinpoint the issue over which the advocates of equal
rights for women fell out. At the same time that the liberal divorce
law was being proposed, the New York Legislators were also considering a bill "concerning the rights and liabilities of husband
and wife," which would secure to women their own property and
earnings, and joint guardianship of their children. This bill Greeley
endorsed, and the Legislature passed (only to repeal its crucial
provisions two years later, when all the radicals had their backs
turned, intent on the Civil War). The point is simply this: as the
more radical wing of the feminist movement slowly came round to
the issue of the marriage institution as itself a potential means of
oppression, the moderates and conservatives closed ranks against
such free love doctrines, insisting that the question of divorce was
not relevant to women's rights since it involved both sexes equally.
Let women have the same rights to person, property, children, and
even the ballot, as men, but do not weaken the bonds by which men
and women are knit into the social fabric. Radicals replied that in
fact it was women who suffered injustice from marriage, and therefore their rights demanded some relief from it, some loophole so
long as men had all the power within the institution. In 1860 this
was the battle line.*

Robert Dale Owen
Horace Greeley
Divorce

Owen

Retired from political life, and now disposed to address the
public, if at all, through a calmer medium than the columns of a
daily paper, still, I cannot read the allusion in this morning's
Tribune, made in connection with an important subject, to my
adopted State and to myself by name, without feeling that justice to
both, and, what is of more consequence, the fair statement of a

---

● Selection from "Marriage and Divorce," reprinted first by Owen in a
pamphlet as *Divorce: being a Correspondence between Horace Greeley
and Robert Dale Owen,* New York, 1860, then by Greeley in his *Recollections of a Busy Life,* New York: J. B. Ford, 1868, pp. 571–617, with an
appendix (pp.617–18) quoting some of the Indiana statutes. The text used
here is Greeley, pp. 573–75, 580–83, 587, 589–90, 600–01, 605–07, 609, 611–12.

question involving much of human morality and happiness, require
of me a few words. You say:—

> The Paradise of free-lovers is the State of Indiana, where the lax prin-
> ciples of Robert Dale Owen, and the utter want of principle of John
> Pettit (leading revisers of the laws), combined to establish, some years
> since, a state of law which enables men and women to get unmarried
> nearly at pleasure.

You are usually, I think, correct in your statements of fact, and
doubtless always intend to be so. That in this endeavor you sometimes fail, we have a proof to-day.

So far as I recollect, the Indiana law of divorce does not owe a
single section to Mr. Pettit. Be that, however, as it may, it owes one
of its provisions, *and only one*, to me. I found that law thirty-four
years ago, when I first became a resident of the State, in substance
nearly what it now is; indeed, with all its essential features the
same. It was once referred to myself, in conjunction with another
member of the Legislature, for revision; and we amended it in a
single point: namely, by adding to the causes of divorce "habitual
drunkenness for two years." In no other particular, either by vote
or proposition, have I been instrumental in framing or amending
the law in question, directly or indirectly.

Do not imagine, however, that I seek to avoid any responsibility
in regard to that law as it stands. I cordially approve it. It has
stood the test for forty or fifty years among a people whom, if you
knew them as intimately as I do, candor would compel you to
admit to be, according to the strictest standard of morality you
may set up, not one whit behind those of sister States, perhaps
of more pretensions. I approve the law, not on principle only, but
because, for more than half a lifetime, I have witnessed its practical
workings. I speak of its influence on *our own citizens*. It is much
to be regretted that any one should ever be compelled to seek a
divorce out of his own State. But, even in alluding to abuses which
have occurred in this connection, you failed to tell your readers,
what perhaps you did not know, that our law has of late years
been so changed that the cases you state cannot possibly recur. No
one can now sue for a divorce in Indiana, until he has been during
one year, at least, a resident of the State; and the provision regarding timely notice to the absent party is of the strictest kind.

You speak of Indiana as "the Paradise of free-lovers." It is in
New York and New England, refusing reasonable divorce, that free-

love prevails; not in Indiana. I never even heard the name there. You locate the Paradise, then, too far west.

And does it not occur to you, when a million of men,—chiefly plain, hardy, industrious farmers, with wives whom, after the homely old fashion, they love, and daughters whose chastity and happiness are as dear to them as if their homes were the wealthiest in the land,—does it not occur to Horace Greeley that, when these men go on deliberately for half a century maintaining unchanged (or if changed at all, made more liberal) a law of divorce which he denounces as breeding disorder and immorality,—that the million, with their long experience, may be right, and that Horace Greeley, without that experience, may be wrong? . . .

Greeley

. . . But you assert that the people of Indiana are emphatically moral and chaste in their domestic relations. That may be; at all events, *I* have not yet called it in question. Indiana is yet a young State,—not so old as either you or I,—and most of her adult population were born, and I think most of them were reared and married, in States which teach and maintain the Indissolubility of Marriage. That population is yet sparse; the greater part of it in moderate circumstances, engaged in rural industry, and but slightly exposed to the temptations born of crowds, luxury, and idleness. In such circumstances, cotinence would probably be general, even were Marriage unknown. But let Time and Change do their work, and then see! Given the population of Italy in the days of the Caesars, with easy divorce, and I believe the result would be like that experienced by the Roman Republic, which, under the sway of easy divorce, rotted away and perished,—blasted by the mildew of unchaste mothers and dissolute homes.

If experiments are to be tried in the direction you favor, I insist that they shall be tried fairly,—not under cover of false promises and baseless pretences. Let those who will take each other on trial; but let such unions have a distinct name as in Paris or Hayti, and let us know just who are married (old style), and who have formed unions to be maintained or terminated as circumstances shall dictate. Those who choose the latter will of course consummate it without benefit of clergy; but I do not see how they need even so much ceremony as that of jumping the broomstick. "I'll love you so long as I'm able, and swear for no longer than this,"—what need is there of any solemnity to hallow such a union? What libertine would hesitate to promise that much, even if fully resolved to decamp next morning? If man and woman are to be true to each other only so long as they shall each find constancy the dictate of their several inclinations, there can be no such crime as adultery, and mankind have too long been defrauded of innocent enjoyment by priestly anathemas and ghostly maledictions. Let us each do what for the moment shall give us pleasurable sensations, and let all such fantasies as God, Duty, Conscience, Retribution, Eternity, be banished to the moles and the bats, with other forgotten rubbish of bygone ages of darkness and unreal terrors.

But if—as I firmly believe—Marriage is a matter which concerns not only the men and women who contract it, but the State, the community, mankind,—if its object be not merely the mutual gratification and advantage of the husband and wife, but the due sustenance, nurture, and education of their children,—if, in other words, those who voluntarily incur the obligations of parentage can only discharge those obligations personally and conjointly, and to that end are bound to live together in love, at least until their youngest child shall have attained perfect physical and intellectual maturity,—then I deny that a marriage can be dissolved save by death or that crime which alone renders its continuation impossible. I look beyond the special case to the general law, and to the reason which underlies that law; and I say,—No couple can innocently take upon themselves the obligations of Marriage until they KNOW that they are one in spirit, and so must remain forever. If they rashly lay profane hands on the ark, theirs alone is the blame; be theirs alone the penalty! They have no right to cast it on that public which admonished and entreated them to forbear, but admonished and entreated in vain.

Owen

. . . You tell us that "the very essence of marriage" is, that the married should "cleave to each other till death." And, as a corollary, you insist that, if this condition is ever violated (as by the action of a divorce law) , then it is *not* Marriage which prevails, but only a substitute. You add:—

> I insist that whoever would recommend such substitute should clearly, specifically set forth its nature and conditions, and should call it by its distinctive name. There may be something better than Marriage, but nothing *is Marriage* but a solemn engagement to live together *till*

death. Why should not they who have devised something better than old-fashioned Marriage give their bantling a distinctive *name,* and not appropriate ours? They have been often warned off our premises; shall we never be able to shame them out of their unwarrantable poaching?

This is plain. If the law regards Marriage as a contract which, under any circumstances, may be terminated, then (you allege) men and women live together under what is but a substitute for marriage,—under what should go by the name of concubinage, or some similar term. Such is the state of things, you infer, under the present Indiana law.

I do not think you reflected what a sweeping assertion you were here making. For there is not a State in the Union—not even New York—which is without a divorce law. In every State of the Union, therefore, Marriage is a contract of such a nature that contingencies *may* arise under which the married may *not* "live together until death do them part." If, then the possible contingency of separation, legally admitted, annuls "the very essence of marriage," and converts it into concubinage, in what condition, I pray you, are married people living throughout the United States?

The same state of things prevails in all Protestant countries. Only in those which acknowledge the Pope as their religious head is Marriage an indissoluble sacrament. Is it your opinion that Catholics only are really married? . . .

In conclusion, permit me to say, as to the quasi-divorce to which, under the name of "separation from bed and board," you refer, and which you think "just right," that of all the various kinds of divorce it has been found, in practice, to be the most immoral in its tendency. The subjects of it, in that nondescript state which is neither married nor single, are exposed—as every person of strong affection must be who takes a vow of celibacy yet mixes with the world—to powerful temptations. Unable to marry, the chances are, that these law-condemned celibates may do worse. I think that those members of your bar with whom the procurement of legal separations is a specialty could make to you some startling disclosures on this subject.

But, be this as it may, what becomes of the "mutual and solemn vow to live together till death them do part"? What becomes of the dictionary definitions which you adduce about being "united for life," and about "affection and fidelity till death shall separate them"? Does not your policy of "separation from bed and board" as effectually extinguish these, and thus, according to your view, as completely convert Marriage into a concubinal substitute, as my remedy of Divorce?

Greeley

. . . You understand, I presume, that I hold to separations "from bed and board"—as the laws of this State allow them—only in cases where the party thus separated is in danger of bodily harm from the ferocity of an insane, intemperate, or otherwise brutalized, infuriated husband or wife. I do not admit that even such peril can release one from the vow of continence, which is the vital condition of Marriage. It may possibly be that there is "temptation" involved in the position of one thus legally separated; but I judge this evil far less than that which must result from the easy dissolution of Marriage.

For here is the vital truth that your theory overlooks: The Divine end of Marriage is parentage, or the perpetuation and increase of the Human Race. To this end, it is indispensable— at least, eminently desirable—that each child should enjoy protection, nurture, sustenance, at the hands of a mother not only, but of a father also. In other words, the parents should be so attached, so devoted to each other, that they shall be practically separable but by death. Creatures of appetite, fools of temptation, lovers of change, as men are, there is but one talisman potent to distinguish between genuine affection and its meretricious counterfeit; and that is the solemn, searching question, "Do you know this woman so thoroughly, and love her so profoundly, that you can assuredly promise that you will forsake all others and cleave to her only until death?" If you can, your union is one that God has hallowed, and man may honor and approve; but, if not, wait till you can thus pledge yourself to some one irrevocably, invoking heaven and earth to witness your truth. If you rush into a union with one whom you do not thus know and love, and who does not thus know and love you, yours is the crime, the shame; yours be the life-long penalty. I do not think, as men and women actually are, this law can be improved; when we reach the spirit-world, I presume we shall find a Divine law adapted to its requirements, and to our moral condition. Here, I am satisfied with that set forth by Jesus Christ. And, while I admit that individual cases of hardship arise under this law, I hold that there is seldom an unhappy marriage that was not originally an unworthy one,—hasty and heedless, if not positively vicious. And, if people *will* transgress, God can scarcely save them from consequent suffering; and I do not think you or I can.

Owen

. . . If a lawgiver, directly or virtually, demands impossibilities, his laws will fail of their effect. In making his demands, then, he should have special reference to the powers likely to be at the disposal of those of whom these demands are made. It avails nothing to say that a thing ought to be, if, as a general rule, it cannot be.

But of all requirements, the most arduous—arduous even when mature thought has brought wisdom, and when age has conferred experience—is the decision whether a being, loved now, is the one of all others, intellectually, morally, physically, to whom, in a true home, we can impart permanent happiness, and from whom we are capable of receiving it. Mortal eyes, even the wisest, never fully penetrate the veil. There may be that beyond which no foresight could anticipate.

And, if such be the case, with wisdom and experience to guide, what shall we expect from unsuspicious faith, just entering a false world, serenely ignorant of its treacheries, an utter stranger to its guile? Will its goodness be its protection? The reverse. In such a trial, it is the noblest who are the most exposed. The better the nature, the more imminent the danger it encounters. The cold, the heartless, the calculating, have fair chance of escape; it is the warm, the trusting, the generous, who are the usual sufferers. What belief so blind as that of first, pure, young affection? What so easily cheated as a fresh and faithful and innocent heart?

And by what right, according to what principle, I pray you, do we decide that there is one mistake that is never to be corrected; one error, the most fatal of all, which, once committed, we shall never be permitted to repair? . . .

Greeley

. . . The vice of our age, the main source of its aberrations, is a morbid Egotism, which overrides the gravest social necessities in its mad pursuit of individual, personal ends. Your fling at that "intangible generality called SOCIETY" is directly in point. You are concerned chiefly for those who, having married unfortunately, if not viciously, seek relief from their bonds; I am anxious rather to prevent, or at least to render infrequent, immoral, and unfit sexual unions hereafter. The miseries of the unfitly mated may be deplorable; but to make divorce easy is in effect to invite the sensual and selfish to profane the sanctions of Marriage whenever appetite and temptation may prompt. Here are a man and a woman who know absolutely nothing of each other but that they are reciprocally pleased with each other's appearance, and think Marriage would conduce to their mutual enjoyment,—so they form a connubial partnership. Next year—perhaps next month—they have tired of each other,—discovered incompatibilities of temper,—quarrelled,—in short, they hate each other, as they very well may; so they are divorced, and ready to marry again. Gibbon intimates that, under the Roman liberty of Divorce, by which Rome was debauched and ultimately ruined, a woman had eight husbands within five years. Mr. Owen, whenever you shall have succeeded in appropriating our word Marriage as a fig-leaf for this sort of thing, you will cause us to invent or appropriate some other term to characterize what *we* mean by Marriage; and then you will very soon drop your own dishonored designation and come coveting ours again. So please leave us what belongs to us, and choose a new term for *your* arrangement now.

"It is very hard," said a culprit to the judge who sentenced him, "that I should be so severely punished for merely stealing a horse." "Man," replied the judge, "you are *not* so punished for merely stealing a horse, but *that horses may not be stolen.*" The distinction seems to me clear and vital. The wedded in soul may know each other if they will; it is impossible that others should certainly know them. To those who are thus wedded, the convenant to "take each other for better, for worse," and "to live together till death do part," has no terrors; they enter upon it without hesitation, and fulfill its conditions without regret. But to the libertine, the egotist, the selfish, sensual seeker of personal and present enjoyment at whatever cost to others, the Indissolubility of Marriage is an obstacle, a restraint, a terror; and God forbid that it should ever cease to be! Thousands would take a wife as readily, as thoughtlessly, as heartlessly, as they don a new coat or sport a new cravat, if it were understood that they might unmarry themselves whenever satiety, or disgust, or mutual dislike, should prompt to that step. But it is not so, Mr. Owen, even in Indiana. Men and women are married, even in Indiana, "for better, for worse," and under solemn covenant to "live together till death do part"; and they cannot resort to Divorce, even there, without conscious shame or general reprobation. That human laws may be everywhere conformed to the Divine, and no sexual union hallowed by Church or State but that union for life which alone is true Marriage, is the ardent hope of

Yours,

HORACE GREELEY

Owen

. . . The story of the horse-thief (told that he was punished not merely for his offence, but *"that horses may not be stolen"*), if it has any bearing on the subject at all, has an unfair one. Horse-stealing is a crime. To take it for granted that Divorce also is one is to prejudge the whole question under discussion. Again; if the meaning be, that the unhappily married should suffer, not merely for their mistake, but *that divorces may not be granted*, then you fall into the same error as the Jews, when they, zealous without knowledge for their Sabbath, were reminded by Jesus, in the spirit of the truest philosophy, that human institutions are made for man, not man for human institutions. . . .

But if in these I dissent, there are other points as to which, in concluding this controversy, I am glad to agree with you. I agree that every State has a direct interest in the private morals of its members. I agree that whatever policy is found, in the end, best calculated to promote these morals, ought to prevail. I agree that it is one of the greatest of earthly blessings, when a married couple dwell together in unity till death. I agree that no light or transient cause should dissolve the conjugal union. I agree that men and women ought mutually to bear and forbear "while evils are sufferable," rather than to right themselves by resort to separation or divorce. I agree, further, that a state of things which leads to Divorce is to be deprecated and lamented, and that Divorce itself is a grave misfortune. And I but add that, when a long train of abuses and immoralities, pursuing invariably the same course, clearly shows that a union has become destructive of its holy ends, then it ought to be a right, and may become a duty, to select of two evils the lesser; to acquiesce in the necessity which indicates a separation, and legally to dissolve the bands which connect the ill-mated members together.

In taking leave of you, suffer me to correct an error which crept into my second letter. I there said that there was not a State of the Union without a Divorce law. I ought to have added, "except the State of South Carolina." She boasts that "within her limits, a divorce has not been granted since the Revolution." But suspend your approbation till you learn, as Bishop will inform you, what is the concomitant: "Not only is adultery not indictable there [in South Carolina], but the Legislature has found it necessary to regulate, by statute, how large a proportion a married man may give of his property to his concubine."

You will admit that your system of Indissoluble Marriage is dearly paid for, under such a state of things; nor have you been in the habit of asserting that the morals of divorce-denying South Carolina are superior to those of Connecticut or Indiana.

I am, my dear sir,

Faithfully yours,

ROBERT DALE OWEN

HORACE GREELEY.

Divorce and Woman's Rights

Ernestine L. Rose

Ernestine Rose was born Siismund Potoski, daughter of a Polish rabbi. At an early age she left home and became a kind of professional radical. She made contact with Robert Owen in her early twenties, was a friend of Frances Wright, and married an Owenite, William Rose, with whom she emigrated to America in 1836. She was an early leader of the feminist movement, agitating for a Married Woman's Property Law in New York almost from the moment she stepped off the boat (finally passed in 1848, and liberalized further in 1860).

She was in the radical wing of women's rights, more energetic and daring than most of her sisters. The press referred to her as a "foreign propagandist," and a "ringleted, glove-handed exotic." The speech reprinted here from the Tenth National Women's Rights Convention is a good example of her role. Typically the convention leaders had tried to keep the marriage and divorce issue off their agendas, unwilling to risk the taint of free love; thus a few years earlier Mrs. Rose herself had said at the Rutland Free Con-

vention of reformers from every field, that she refrained from introducing "the question of marriage into our [feminist] Conventions, because I want to combat in them the injustice in the laws." This was her tactful way of saying that the marriage institution, even if it was the instrument of oppression, ought to be reformed by legal means, rather than being circumvented by divorce. The reformation would consist of laws like the Married Women's Property Act she helped into existence.

But by 1860 the agitation of free lovers and other radicals against the institution itself had changed the temper of the country enough to make a liberalized divorce bill seem a possibility in New York State (see the Greeley-Owen debate on the issue, in the preceding selection). The Women's Rights Convention that year finally faced the question head-on, with Elizabeth Cady Stanton coming out in favor of the proposed new law. Immediately the feminists began to divide into camps. Rev. Antoinette Blackwell took the floor to defend the sanctity of marriage-for-life, à la Horace Greeley, and Mrs. Rose—often Rev. Blackwell's antagonist because she was herself a free-thinking agnostic—strode into the debate as eagerly as if she had been holding herself in check all these years for the sake of unity in the movement. William Phillips, sensing trouble, tried to table Mrs. Stanton's motions, but the radicals had their way and the resolutions carried.

Had the Civil War not intervened, this incipient split in the feminist movement might have ripped right through its rank and file. As it happened, the fight was postponed another decade, when the free love controversy newly agitated by Victoria Woodhull resulted in serious factionalism within the movement and, as some said, set women's rights back twenty years. Perhaps so, but the split would have come with or without Woodhull; and the free lovers could have said instead, that feminist pusillanimity slowed the sexual revolution, and made possible the forty years' reign of Anthony Comstock and Mrs. Grundy. However that may be, Ernestine Rose is among the few who could not be so accused.

Ernestine L. Rose
Divorce and Woman's Rights

Mrs. President—The question of a Divorce law seems to me one of the greatest importance to all parties, but I presume that the very advocacy of divorce will be called "Free Love." For my part (and I wish distinctly to define my position), I do not know what others understand by that term; to me, in its truest significance, love must be free, or it ceases to be love. In its low and degrading sense, it is not love at all, and I have as little to do with its name as its reality.

The Rev. Mrs. Blackwell gave us quite a sermon on what woman ought to be, what she ought to do, and what marriage ought to be; an excellent sermon in its proper place, but not when the important question of a Divorce law is under consideration. She treats woman as some ethereal being. It is very well to be ethereal to some extent, but I tell you, my friends, it is quite requisite to be a little material, also. At all events, we are so, and, being so, it proves a law of our nature. (Applause).

It were indeed well if woman could be what she ought to be, man what he ought to be, and marriage what it ought to be; and it is to be hoped that through the Woman's Rights movement—the equalizing of the laws, making them more just, and making woman more independent—we will hasten the coming of the millennium, when marriage shall indeed be a bond of union and affection. But, alas! it is not yet; and I fear that sermons, however well meant, will not produce that desirable end; and as long as the evil is here, we must look it in the face without shrinking, grapple with it manfully, and the more complicated it is, the more courageously must it be and analyzed, combated, and destroyed. (Applause).

Mrs. Blackwell told us that, marriage being based on the perfect equality of husband and wife, it can not be destroyed. But is it so? Where? Where and when have the sexes yet been equal in physical or mental education, in position, or in law? When and where have they yet been recognized by society, or by themselves, as equals? "Equal in rights," says Mrs. B. But are they equal in rights? If they

---

● Selection from *History of Woman Suffrage*, 2 vols., ed. Elizabeth Cady Stanton, Susan B. Anthony, and Matilda Joslyn Gage, New York: Fowler & Wells, 1881, I, pp. 729–32.

were, we would need no conventions to claim our rights. "She can assert her equality." Yes, she can assert it, but does that assertion constitute a true marriage? And when the husband holds the iron heel of legal oppression on the subjugated neck of the wife until every spark of womanhood is crushed out, will it heal the wounded heart, the lacerated spirit, the destroyed hope, to assert her equality? And shall she still continue the wife? Is that a marriage which must not be dissolved? (Applause).

According to Mr. Greeley's definition, viz., that there is no marriage unless the ceremony is performed by a minister and in a church, the tens of thousands married according to the laws of this and most of the other States, by a lawyer or justice of the peace, a mayor or an alderman, are not married at all. According to the definition of our reverend sister, no one has ever yet been married, as woman has never yet been perfectly equal with man. I say to both, take your position, and abide by the consequences. If the few only, or no one, is really married, why do you object to a law that shall acknowledge the fact? You certainly ought not to force people to live together who are not married. (Applause).

Mr. Greeley tells us, that, marriage being a Divine institution, nothing but death should ever separate the parties; but when he was asked, "Would you have a being who, innocent and inexperienced, in the youth and ardor of affection, in the fond hope that the sentiment was reciprocated, united herself to one she loved and cherished, and then found (no matter from what cause) that his profession was false, his heart hollow, his acts cruel, that she was degraded by his vice, despised for his crimes, cursed by his very presence, and treated with every conceivable ignominy—would you have her drag out a miserable existence as his wife?" "No, no," says he; "in that case, they ought to separate." Separate? But what becomes of the union divinely instituted, which death only should part? (Applause).

The papers have of late been filled with the heart-sickening accounts of wife-poisoning. Whence come these terrible crimes? From the want of a Divorce law. Could the Hardings be legally separated, they would not be driven to the commission of murder to be free from each other; and which is preferable, a Divorce law, to dissolve an unholy union, which all parties agree is no true marriage, or a murder of one, and an execution (legal murder) of the other party? But had the unfortunate woman, just before the poisoned cup was presented to her lips, pleaded for a divorce, Mrs. Blackwell would have read her a sermon equal to St. Paul's "Wives, be obedient to your husbands," only she would have added, "You must assert your equality," but "you must keep with your husband and work for his redemption, as I would do for my husband"; and Mr. Greeley would say, "As you chose to marry him, it is your own fault; you must abide the consequences, for it is a 'divine institution, a union for life, which nothing but death can end.'" (Applause). *The Tribune* had recently a long sermon, almost equal to the one we had this morning from our reverend sister, on "Fast Women." The evils it spoke of were terrible indeed, but, like all other sermons, it was one-sided. Not one single word was said about fast men, except that the "poor victim had to spend so much money." The writer forgot that it is the demand which calls the supply into existence. But what was the primary cause of that tragic end? Echo answers, "what?" Ask the lifeless form of the murdered woman, and she may disclose the terrible secret, and show you that, could she have been legally divorced, she might not have been driven to the watery grave of a "fast woman." (Applause).

But what is marriage? A human institution, called out by the needs of social, affectional human nature, for human purposes, its objects are, first, the happiness of the parties immediately concerned, and, secondly, the welfare of society. Define it as you please, these are only its objects; and therefore if, from well-ascertained facts, it is demonstrated that the real objects are frustrated, that instead of union and happiness, there are only discord and misery to themselves, and vice and crime to society, I ask, in the name of individual happiness and social morality and well-being, why such a marriage should be binding for life?—why one human being should be chained for life to the dead body of another? "But they may separate and still remain married." What a perversion of the very term! Is that the union which "death only should part"? It may be according to the definition of the Rev. Mrs. Blackwell's theology and Mr. Greeley's dictionary, but it certainly is not according to common-sense or the dictates of morality. No, no! "It is not well for man to be alone," before nor after marriage. (Applause).

I therefore ask for a Divorce law. Divorce is now granted for some crimes; I ask it for others also. It is granted for a State's prison offense. I ask that personal cruelty to a wife, whom he swore to "love, cherish, and protect," may be made a heinous crime—a perjury and a State's prison offense, for which divorce shall be granted. Willful desertion for one year should be a sufficient cause for divorce, for the willful deserter forfeits the sacred title of husband or wife. Habitual intemperance, or any other vice which makes the husband or wife intolerable and abhorrent to the other, ought to be sufficient cause for divorce. I ask for a law of Divorce, so as to secure the real objects and blessings of married life, to prevent the crimes and immoralities now practiced, to prevent "Free Love," in its most hideous form, such as is now carried on but too often under the very name of marriage, where hypocrisy is added to the crime of legalized prostitution. "Free Love," in its degraded sense, asks for no Divorce law. It acknowledges no marriage, and therefore requires no divorce. I believe in true marriages, and therefore I ask for a law to free men and women from false ones. (Applause).

But it is said that if divorce were easily granted, "men and women would marry to-day and unmarry to-morrow." Those who say that, only prove that they have no confidence in themselves, and therefore can have no confidence in others. But the assertion is false; it is a libel on human nature. It is the indissoluble chain that corrodes the flesh. Remove the indissolubility, and there would be less separation than now, for it would place the parties on their good behavior, the same as during courtship. Human nature is not quite so changeable; give it more freedom, and it will be less so. We are a good deal the creatures of habit, but we will not be forced. We live (I speak from experience) in uncomfortable houses for years, rather than move, though we have the privilege to do so every year; but force any one to live for life in one house, and he would run away from it, though it were a palace.

But Mr. Greeley asks, "How could the mother look the child in the face, if she married a second time?" With infinitely better grace and better conscience than to live as some do now, and show their children the degrading example, how utterly father and mother despise and hate each other, and still live together as husband and wife. She could say to her child, "As, unfortunately, your father proved himself unworthy, your mother could not be so unworthy as to continue to live with him. As he failed to be a true father to you, I have endeavored to supply his place with one who, though not entitled to the name, will, I hope, prove himself one in the performance of a father's duties." (Applause).

Finally, educate woman, to enable her to promote her independence, and she will not be obliged to marry for a home and a subsistence. Give the wife an equal right with the husband in the property acquired after marriage, and it will be a bond of union between them. Diamond cement, applied on both sides of a fractured vase, re-unites the parts, and prevents them from falling asunder. A gold band is more efficacious than an iron law. Until now, the gold has all been on one side, and the iron law on the other. Remove it; place the golden band of justice and mutual interest around both husband and wife, and it will hide the little fractures which may have occurred, even from their own perception, and allow them effectually to re-unite. A union of interest helps to preserve a union of hearts. (Loud applause).

Marriage As It Is
Marriage Under Protest
Marriage: Defining Positions

Thomas and Mary Nichols

Unpopular laws may be resisted in different ways and with varying degrees of obduracy. The means open to one class might not be open to another, and the risks of resistance might not always balance out with the possible gains. The laws of equity could protect the property of wealthy ladies; or, where they could not, new statutes would serve as well. It was harder for a working woman to keep her earnings out of her husband's hands, harder still to withhold her person, or to retain custody of her child. When Mary Nichols ran away from her first husband, her act was not quite in open defiance of the law, because her husband was unwilling to invoke it so long as he was in debt to her father. Thus she managed to ransom all three—daughter, cash, and self—from

Hiram Gove's clutches. After her father's death she kidnapped her child; that was civil disobedience, at least until she was safely across the state line.

There were other sorts of protests, with more admixture of propaganda in the self-preservation. Robert Dale Owen set a precedent in 1832 when he formally divested himself of the "unjust rights" that marriage gave him over his wife—"the barbarous relics of a feudal, despotic system, soon destined, in the onward course of improvement, to be wholly swept away." This statement was part of their marriage vows—"the simplest ceremony which the laws of this State recognize." Owen's principled act may seem a bit double-edged today, when one notices that it was not so much a mutual agreement between husband and wife, as a "sentiment" signed by Owen and merely "concurred in" by his bride. But in the circumstances all the rights were his to refuse.

The next gesture of this kind to be published at the altar was the "protest" of Lucy Stone and Henry Blackwell when they married in 1855. Their bill of particulars was more militant than Owen's, as appropriate to a document that served as ammunition in the feminist campaign; but in at least one respect it was less radical, for Owen had explicitly stated that he and Mary Jane Robinson were not "making promises regarding that over which we have no control, the state of human affections in the distant future"—that is, they did not promise to love each other forever. This was one of the favorite arguments of the free lovers, that, as Thomas and Mary Nichols put it, "In the next hour" the newlyweds "may have no power to keep that promise," and their lives would be thenceforth "cursed."

Of course Owen did not state what he would do, should he find himself no longer in love with his wife. Still less did Lucy Stone and Henry Blackwell mention such things. The Nichols therefore complained that all their other protests were undermined by this fact. The only effective protest was the refusal to marry at all. Why take Blackwell's name, they asked the bride, if you don't believe in the institution?

As it happened, Lucy Stone did not assume the name Blackwell, but went by "Mrs. Stone." She told Julia Branch that "no law can compel me" to give up that name. Mrs. Branch answered with a question: "How would it have been with Mrs. Blackwell, if she had kept the fact of the marriage ceremony a secret, and gone to a

*hotel with the intention of staying a few days with Mr. Blackwell,
signing her name Lucy Stone?"*
   *The Nichols were right after all. Yet they recognized the problem:
"We must not ask too heroic a devotion to principles." When free
lover Francis Barry wrote from the Berlin Heights colony a rather
sharp criticism of their friend Lazarus for his defection into the
ranks of the wedded, they rose to his defense—though with a
touch of self-righteousness that was unnecessary. Of course they
were in no position to lord it over Lucy Stone, Lazarus, or Barry,
for their own marriage had occurred immediately upon Mrs.
Gove's divorce from her first husband—and without fanfare or
protest.*

Mary S. Gove Nichols
Thomas L. Nichols
Marriage As It Is

The motives to marriage are few and simple. There is a yearning
of the heart for love, and its satisfaction, which the laws and customs of society will not permit to be gratified in any other way than
by marriage. If a man is attracted to a woman, he cannot enjoy
her intimate society, but with the implied understanding that he
wishes to be married to her. No provision is made for any attachment but one, and that must endure for life. Whoever loves, therefore, must marry as the penalty. It is the price every man must pay,
for the love of every virtuous and respectable woman.

   Thus the powerful desire for the sexual union, active in most
men, and in many, but not so many, women, can only be gratified,
legally and respectably, in marriage; and this is often a motive to
hasty, passionate, but ill-assorted and miserable unions. Marriage,
in this case, is often a blunder; but it is one we are not permitted
to correct. Every other mistake, short of suicide, a man may
remedy. If he joins the wrong party in politics, or the wrong sect
in religion; if he adopts a profession which is unsuited to him, or a

● Selections from: "Marriage As It Is," *Marriage*, New York: T. L. Nichols,
1854, pp. 81–89; "Marriage Under Protest," *Nichols' Monthly*, I (April-May
1855), 195; "Marriage: Defining Positions," *Nichols' Monthly*, I (January
1855), 31–32.

career of any kind in which he is unsuccessful, he can change; but if he gets married to the wrong woman, there is no redress. A life of disappointment, regrets, and misery, must pay the penalty of his passion and folly. The general verdict of society is, "It serves him right." He should have been more prudent; as if passion and prudence were so commonly united!

A man marries for position and business, and because he wishes to have an establishment and family, like the respectable men around him. A clergyman or a physician finds it necessary to his success to have a wife. Connection, family influence, property, all assert their claims, and combine with a man's passions to make him marry. Sometimes these motives of interest have an undue influence; and many a man, even here, marries a rich girl of a good family, for whom he cares very little, while he loves some pretty girl who is destitute of these advantages.

Women marry from motives which differ somewhat from these. Most women are capable of sentimental love; few in this country are controlled by passion, and a vast majority never feel the sexual desire as a controlling motive; perhaps we may say with truth that a large proportion never feel it at all. But the whole influence of our society urges women into the marriage relation, with an almost resistless force. It is the only respectable position—the sole career of woman. To live unmarried is the horror of civilization. Old maids are pitied and ridiculed. Mothers are anxious to have their daughters married, or "settled in life," as it is called; daughters see no other end in their existence.

And while marriage is the one tolerated condition of love, and maternity, and ambition—often the only means of support and the only escape from dependence or actual want—there is but a limited range of choice. Manage as they may, girls must still wait for offers, and to be the choice generally of a very narrow circle; and there is always a great temptation to accept the first for fear of never having another. Simple, confiding, and susceptible, girls are too apt to mistake gratitude, or an excited vanity, or benevolence, for love, and to engage themselves to men for whom they have no real attraction. In fact, our whole system of courtship is little more than a voluntary or involuntary deception. Neither party can see the real character of the other. Friends and relatives interfere, the match is made up, and the happy couple, entering upon a rapturous honeymoon, may find ennui and disgust before they get to the end of it. Then the gloomy future, then the blank despair of a vital mistake, for which there is no remedy but death!

And this marriage, when thus entered upon, lets us see more fully what it is. A man binds himself by the most solemn contract, perhaps with the ceremonies of religion, to love a woman as long as both shall live. In the next hour he may have no power to keep that promise; but it is made, and his whole life is cursed. If he is a conscientious man, he suffers from remorse as well as disappointment. If he tries to keep his contract, in its externals, he lives a false and wasted life, deprived of all chance of the enjoyment of a real love, should it come, as come it may, to make his misery more unendurable. Slave to his promise, to the laws, to society, to his wife, his existence is a living death. Such men plunge into business, seek excitement in politics, or stupefaction in stimulants, or compensations in debauchery. If children are born in this unloving union, they are so many bonds for its continuance; and the discordance of the parents is impressed upon the characters of their children. A large portion of the discord and crime of civilization comes from the loveless and indissoluble marriage.

In this marriage a man is bound to live with a woman he does not love, and to renounce all hope of enjoying any intimate relation with any other woman whom he does love; for the law of marriage makes such enjoyment a crime punishable in many States by a long imprisonment. He must support a woman for whom he has no attraction; one who, from the very fact of a loveless marriage, becomes peevish, ill-tempered, and finally diseased. Our graveyards are filled with the corpses of women who have died at from thirty to thirty-five years of age, victims of the marriage institution. The children are, from the laws of hereditary descent, ill-tempered, sick, and often short-lived. The cares, the responsibilities, the monotony, the dissatisfaction, the disgust, the perpetual struggle between inclination and duty, make life a burthen and death a welcome relief.

If such may be the sufferings of a man in a compact in which he is the superior, and in which he has many advantages, what must they be to a woman?

She has married for a home—for position—because her friends will not hear of her refusing a good offer, or because she has been fascinated or magnetized into the belief that she really loved her suitor. From whatever motive, she marries. The chances are as three to one, under the most favorable circumstances, that the love is not a genuine and mutual passion founded on adaptedness of character. But the die is cast, and the irrevocable sentence pronounced. Henceforth she is the prisoner of a Bastile, from which there is no escape but through the portal of death, or that of disgrace, which many fear more than death itself.

She has married a husband, perhaps she finds a tyrant; she thought to be united to a tender lover, and finds in him a monster of lust, who profanes her life with disgusting debaucheries. She is his slave, his victim, his tool. Her duty is submission. Her body is prostituted to his morbid passions, her mind must bend submissive to his will, which henceforth is her only law. By the marriage law, the husband can shut his wife up, carry her from one place to another, provide such food and clothing as he sees fit, seize upon and squander her property, and inflict corporal chastisement. The flogging of wives by their husbands, in England, is so common a thing among all classes as to have called out denunciations from the public press, similar to those excited by the inhuman punishments in the army and navy. These brutalities exist wherever there are brutal men to inflict them; and if anything can make men brutal, it is living in the hell of a discordant and repulsive marriage. Thousands of women suffer where one complans. The minister, the physician, or sometimes an intimate friend hears of these things; but there is a deep *hush!* Respectability, and the sacredness of the marriage institution, demand silence. The physicians of this city could testify to bruises, and even broken bones, which wives have received from their husbands, in the "most respectable families." In lower ranks of life, where marital brutality is less restrained, wives are not unfrequently murdered outright, as they are everywhere killed by inches.

And from all this there is no escape, without violation of law and the outrage of public opinion. Women are everywhere instructed that it is better to endure everything than to attempt to change their positions. It is for the good of society; for the sake of the children they have been compelled to have against their will. They are sacrificed to the great Moloch of society. When we examine this social system further, we shall see whether it is worth the miseries it imposes on its victims. The lesser evils of marriage, which bear upon the weaker party to the contract, are still of sufficient importance to call for remedy. For a human being to surrender up all right of choice and will, during her whole life, to another; to merge her legal, political, and to a great extent, her social existence in his; to have no separate individuality or sphere of action; to be during his life a meek, mild, submissive adjunct, a house-keeper, nurse, and slave, and after his death a *relict;*—is a sad lot for any being whom God has endowed with a human soul.

The wife, except where special laws have been recently enacted for the amelioration of marriage, has no right to the property she has brought to her husband, or may earn. He can spend her estate, reduce her to poverty, and then seize upon the scanty pittance she may earn, according to the law of marriage which makes her his property. If the husband dies, she has a one-third life interest in his real estate, and a scanty pittance of personal property, consisting of such furniture and utensils as the law supposes to be needful. During his life the husband is absolute owner of her clothing, jewels, furniture, and property of every kind; and can sell the dress from her person, and the bed on which she lies; except in those States where a humane public opinion has somewhat modified the barbarity of this institution.

Let it not be said that we exaggerate the condition of mutual ownership, and of female servitude, which are the bases of the civilized marriage. The canons of the Church and the civil law alike prove the truth of our allegations. In the Religious Rite of Marriage, used in the Protestant Episcopal Church, we find the following ceremonial:

The minister shall say to the man,

"Wilt thou have this woman to thy wedded wife, to live together after God's ordinance in the holy estate of matrimony? Wilt thou love her, comfort her, honor her, and keep her, in sickness and in health, and, forsaking all others, keep thee only unto her, so long as ye both shall live?"

The man shall answer, "I will."

Then shall the minister say unto the woman,

"Wilt thou have this man to thy wedded husband, to live together after God's ordinance, in the holy estate of matrimony? Wilt thou obey him, and serve him, love, honor and keep him, in sickness and in health, and, forsaking all others, keep thee only unto him, so long as ye both shall live?"

The woman shall answer, "I will."

Then the man, taking the woman by the hand, shall say,

"I take thee to my wedded wife, to have and to hold, from this day forward, for better for worse, for richer for poorer, in sickness and in health, to love and to cherish, till death do us part."

And the woman repeats the same form, substituting for "to love and to cherish," the vow of perpetual servitude—"to love, honor and obey."

Here, in the religious rite, are perpetual ownership, the right of property without the possible alleviation of transfer, and the vow of perpetual love, obedience, and servitude.

The maxims and principles of the Common Law, which prevail in this country in full force, except as modified by statutory enactments, correspond with, and explain, the nature of marriage as a civil contract.

Under this contract, the woman, with all her movable goods, passes wholly into the power and disposal of her husband.

Man and wife are one person in law, so that the very being and existence of the woman is suspended during the coverture, or entirely merged or incorporated in that of her husband.

A man cannot grant anything to his wife, or enter into covenant with her, as this would be to suppose her separate existence.

If the wife be injured in her person or property she can bring no action for redress without her husband's concurrence. Of course she has no redress against her husband, for injury inflicted by himself or with his consent. Man and wife cannot give evidence for or against each other. All deeds executed by the wife are void.

As the wife is supposed to be under the perpetual control of her husband, she is free from the responsibility of offenses short of murder or treason committed at his instigation, his presence being the evidence of that instigation.

This legal identity cannot be dissolved by any act of the parties.

A woman cannot make any deed during marriage nor dispose of her property after being engaged.

Marriage revokes any power of attorney given by the wife.

Such is the fearful, irrevocable, indissoluble power which the institution of marriage gives one human being over another; by which the rights, will, conscience, and civil existence are suspended, or rather hopelessly destroyed.

Thomas Low Nichols
Mary S. Gove Nichols
Marriage Under Protest

Henry B. Blackwell, a well-known Reformer, and Lucy Stone, lecturer on Woman's Rights, &c., were married in Massachusetts, the other day, by the Rev. Mr. Higginson, making the following protest:

> While we acknowledge our mutual affection, by publicly assuming the sacred relationship of husband and wife, yet in justice to ourselves and a great principle, we deem it a duty to declare that this act on our part implies no sanction of, nor promise of voluntary obedience to, such of the present laws of marriage as refuse to recognize the wife as an independent rational being, while they confer upon the husband an injurious and unnatural superiority, investing him with legal powers which no honorable man would exercise, and which no man should possess.

> We protest, especially, against the laws which give to the husband—
> I. The custody of his wife's person.
> II. The exclusive control and guardianship of their children.
> III. The sole ownership of her personal, and use of her real estate, unless previously settled upon her, or placed in the hands of trustees, as in the case of minors, lunatics and idiots.
> IV. The absolute right to the product of her industry.
> V. Also against laws which give to the widower so much larger and more permanent an interest in the property of his deceased wife, than they give to the widow in that of her deceased husband.
> VI. Finally, against the whole system by which "the legal existence of the wife is suspended during marriage," so that in most States she neither has a legal part in the choice of her residence, nor can she make a will, nor sue or be sued in her own name, nor inherit property.

> We believe that personal independence and equal human rights can never be forfeited, except for crime; that marriage should be an equal and permanent partnership, and so recognized by law; that until it is so recognized, married partners should provide against the radical injustice of present laws by every means in their power.

> We believe that where domestic difficulties arise, no appeal should be made to legal tribunals under existing laws, but that all difficulties should be submitted to the equitable adjustment of arbitrators mutually chosen.

> Thus reverencing law, we enter our earnest protest against rules and customs which are unworthy of the name, since they violate justice, the essence of all law.
> (Signed)   Henry B. Blackwell,
> Lucy Stone

The parties to the above recorded protest, having given all possible publicity to their mutual affection, which might, perhaps, as well have been kept entirely private, it is open to, and will doubtless receive a wide criticism. Professing to reverence law, they have protested against all its important provisions. They assume the name of marriage, but refuse its obligations. They call themselves legally husband and wife, and yet deny the lawful provisions that make them one.

So far as the public, thus made a party to this transaction, are likely to know, Miss Stone has merely taken the name of Blackwell. He assumes none of the "rights" of a lawful husband; she none of the duties of a wife. Mr. Higginson has solemnized simply a change of name. The parties may have loved each other before, and may continue to do so afterward, or not, as it may happen; that is their own affair. From all that appears, or of which we have any right to inquire, it would have answered every purpose had Miss Stone either in a private circular or by advertisement, intimated her wish to be addressed as Mrs. Blackwell.

By why even this? Why surrender her name when she retains all other property and all other rights? Why not remain Lucy Stone in perpetuity, like an independent rational being? Why consent to surrender all outward sign of personality, and to be known only as Mrs. Henry B. Blackwell? In a word, when they neither claim the rights, nor accept the obligations of the legal marriage, why go through the mockery of a sham ceremony, under protest, and with a premeditated nullification?

The whole thing seems sufficiently ridiculous; but there may be a mode of accounting for it. If we are not mistaken, there is a law in Massachusetts, under which persons living together in any intimate relation, without legal authority, may be sent to State prison. In other words, love, like selling liquor, is a crime, without a license. Our friends are reformers, not martyrs. They submit to an iniquitous law, under protest, rather than go to prison. "Reverencing the law," they determine not to submit to its "radical injustice" only where they can't help it.

We must not ask too heroic a devotion to principles. Mr. and Mrs. Blackwell may protest till they are blind; but they are none the less married, according to the statement of Mr. Higginson. Mr. Blackwell *has* full custody of his wife's person, and can shut her up, or carry her wherever he pleases. He will be legally held to have the exclusive control of her children. He is legally endowed with all her worldly goods. He can take, and the law can take for him or his creditors, every penny of her property and earnings, and her legal existence is suspended. If there were any legal force in the protest, the marriage would be a nullity; and it may be doubted whether it might not be set aside, and the parties sent to the penitentiary.

Thomas L. Nichols
Mary S. Gove Nichols
Marriage: Defining Positions

Not long ago, a gentleman, whose name, were we permitted to use it, would give lustre to our page, wrote us a long letter on the subject of Marriage, taking liberal ground, but regretting that we had allowed ourselves to be represented as opposing Marriage, when we only opposed the wrongs of the conventional and legal relation. We preserved a portion of our reply, which may be an answer to many others, besides the writer:

> We oppose Marriage, as Abolitionists oppose Slavery, for what it is, not for what it might be. Not the possible union of men and women in mutual love and freedom, but the actual, existing institution with all its wrongs. So of Slavery. You may easily conceive of a true relation between a strong and wise man, and many weak and simple ones, in which there would be thought, care, and protection on one side, and cheerful, willing service on the other.
>
> We oppose no true relations, but we believe FREEDOM a necessary condition to finding true relations and their enjoyment.
>
> I have not dogmatized about what Marriage should be, so much as demanded that men and women be free to make it what is most needful to their happiness—for this, I suppose, is the single end of every natural condition or relation. In advocating what is called "FREE LOVE," I ask only that every one be left free to find the satisfaction of his truest, and highest and therefore most satisfying attraction. If this is monogamy—the single and eternal union, very well—well for those who are fortunate enough to find it; or who keep trying and experimenting until they do, or do not. If it is variety, either a succession of loves, or several, various in kind and degree at the same time, it is nothing to me. Whatever is really best for any one, he must be at liberty to enjoy, so long as he does not infringe upon the equal right of any other.
>
> No doubt there may be some general law of sexual relations appertaining to our race, as to the other animal races; or it may differ in

the different races of humanity; or in individuals. But the law can only be determined in freedom; and no legislative body has the wisdom or right to decide what the law is. I cannot, in such a matter, determine what is for your personal happiness, nor you for mine; though I may know, generally, by science and analogy, what is probably best for you; but neither I, nor a majority, has any right to control your relations, only so far as they affect others and make the necessity of such control.

The following criticism of Dr. Lazarus, he must answer, if he can. His sincerity in making the avowal, seems proven by the fact that he has himself been married, according to legal forms, since the publication of his remarkable work. Our own transgression, in that particular, took place before we were publicly committed. But, good Mr. Barry, are we not compelled to violate our principles every day? The abolitionist is the patron of slavery, by using its products, and in various ways. Protesting against the usurpations of our government, we pay taxes and duties. Protesting against the frauds of commerce and the plunderings of finance, we buy and sell, cheat and are cheated, and yield our quota to money vampires and usurers. Dr. Lazarus has done no more than all of us have done and are doing. He loved a beautiiul Rose-bud of the prairies, and she loved him. Rather than risk being sent to State prison, by any moral donkey, in any puritanical State they might choose to visit; rather than be tabooed by the general impertinence of civilization, they submitted to the legal handcuffing process, by an Indiana Justice of the Peace, with about the same respect for the operation that an American has for the equally legal system of passport nuisances, which he finds such an impertinent interference with the freedom of foreign travel. But the slave must show his pass, the traveler his passport, and the civilizee his marriage certificate. Now for the criticism:

Before one word on this subject, I caution every reader against a private and personal application of what I say. I am not writing a *moral* treatise for the conduct of individuals in the present society. The morality and policy of action is here fixed and settled. The *centripetal* law is in full force, and every one is bound, under pain of disgrace, hypocrisy, or villainy, to obey the laws and customs of the society in which he lives; consequently, while the laws remain as they are in a representative and popular government, and the tone of public opinion what it is, and the present social institutions, separate households, individual competition, etc., are in full play, it is folly, or worse, to attempt to carry through love relations in any other form

than that of marriage."—*Love vs. Marriage*. By M. Edgeworth Lazarus.
P. 54.

The work from which the above is an extract, is one of those fearless efforts which brave, heroic men, awake to a sense of the evils inflicted by old and oppressive systems, sometimes put forth. Like a very *Hercules*, the author deals ponderous blows, both thick and fast, upon the devoted head of the "monster curse of civilization." Such an admission as the above, from such a source, is the more noticeable, as, also, it is likely to be more pernicious in its influence, than the protestations of ordinary croakers, that it will not do to carry out in practice certain admitted principles. In fact, it can be regarded as nothing more or less than a polite way of saying that the author *does not mean anything* by his serious and effective attacks upon this citadel of Puritanic conservatism.

It must not be forgotten that this unfortunate surrender of a vital principle was made at an early stage of the war, when the utter rottenness of the old fabric was not, perhaps, so perfectly palpable. Perhaps our brave author *unguardedly* left this precious piece of nonsense to mar the exceeding beauty and excellence of his heroic efforts. Be this as it may, the utter falsity and exceeding folly of this position must ever be earnestly insisted upon, and its weakness and mischievousness persistently held up to view. If the exceedingly graphic picture of our popular marriage system, the author of "Love *vs.* Marriage" has drawn, be not a caricature, he to whom the system has been shown up in all its hideousness, and still hugs it to his bosom, must be put down either as a fool or a madman. Such advice, carried out in practice, would postpone indefinitely any reform movement, whenever or wherever commenced. Society never moves in a body in any way given direction. Individuals who become awakened to the necessity of any particular reform, must move forward at greater or less peril of life, property and social position, or society would forever remain in a changeless, stagnant condition; and some new law will have to be revealed to the world before *Free Love* can be carried out on any other principle.

Again; our author says, on page 55, "The individual man or woman is bound by the morals or customs of the age and society in which their lot is cast." That M. Edgeworth Lazarus should be found reiterating this stale and stupid falsehood, is exceedingly marvellous. It is the universal language of tyrants and bigots. For contending for the opposite of this doctrine, and setting at naught the authority of *society*,—for this, and this only, have reformers ever been praised on the one hand, and persecuted on the other. In fact this is the great question to be agitated—this the great principle to be contended for. *Society* is the great universal tyrant, and individual freedom the great boon to be sought. Here is a virtual surrender of the principle of "*Individual Sovereignty.*" It will not do. The regulations and prejudices of society are, so far as they are opposed to individual rights and individual freedom, always and everywhere to be disregarded and trampled upon, at least wherever and whenever the *cost* of such disregard does not exceed the individual's capabilities. The very mischievous error that Free Love will do only for pure and elevated beings, must be exploded. The low and vile most need its elevating and purifying influence. They are the very ones who need to be surrounded by the best of circumstances. The conduct of the virtuous and elevated man will be pure and noble even in marriage. True, he has not the opportunities for development that he would have in a true state, but having the ability to mould conditions and control circumstances, his condition is comparatively tolerable. But the poor wretches who are controlled by circumstances, and liable to be carried hither and thither by the power of passion, are, in marriage, helpless under its relentless sway. But if we are to wait till the mass of mind is prepared to adopt the true theory (which would never be, with nothing but *words* on our part), they who most need these true conditions will die before their realization. Our only true course is to act up to our highest convictions. It is by truthful and heroic *deeds* that bigotry and intolerance are to be crushed, and humanity saved.

Francis Barry.

Principle or expediency? Is there no way of reconciling them? Must a man be either a Don Quixote or a Flunkey? Is it not right for each person to do what, under the particular circumstances, is best to be done? And must not each individual be allowed to judge for himself, what he can afford to do?

Dr. Lazarus has characterized marriage as a slavery, a wrong, an execrable institution, the end of love, the grave of spontaneity; yet he marries, and advises others to do the same. So he believes that Finance is plunder, and takes his share; that commerce is robbery, and he robs himself, or submits to be robbed by others. A man may own negroes, yet believe slavery an injustice and a curse; or he may eat the sugar, and rice, wear the cotton, and trade in the tobacco they produce. Every man, with any clear sight of principles, is compelled to violate them constantly, in all his social intercourse. We do it in little things and in great ones; and we should be set down as fools, fanatics, insane, or criminal, if we did otherwise. If I, for any single day, should do just what seems to me abstractly right, and what might be done in a natural or true society, I should risk being knocked down, arrested, and sent to State prison, if not murdered before I had fallen into the hands of justice.

What Freedom can there be in Love, until there is a society that tolerates individual rights? Free Love in Massachusetts would send the parties to State prison. In New York, they are only put in coventry. Elsewhere, there is for them Lynch law, or assassination.

How is a woman to vindicate her right to her own person, when juries would justify her legal husband in taking her life, and that of her lover? How is a man to act upon the principles of simple and natural right, when every ruffian in society would think he did his duty, in shooting him down like a dog? Are such cases as the Hoyt tragedy, at Richmond, forgotten; or does Mr. Barry want more such martrys?

No, friends; it is easy to talk of living up to our principles—but not so easy to do.

Petition to Governor and Council of Maine For My Release

James Clay

James Clay's petition for release from the Augusta jail did not move the Governor, and he served out his full sentence for "lewd and lascivious cohabitation with an unmarried female." Clay's offense was a curious one, as his petition suggests. His family consisted of a wife and two children, a grown son and a young daughter. He was forty years old. The free love doctrines he professed had long disturbed his wife, who was not ready to live in such innocence, or guilt (she refused to join him at Modern Times when he made a trial of its possibilities in 1852), and finally Clay's bringing another woman into his house, and bed, forced the issue. He went to prison cheerfully, planning to use the occasion to further his doctrine (editing his newspaper, the Eastern Light, *and writing this book,* A Voice *from the Prison); but after a month and a half the jail become suddenly crowded with violators of the Maine Liquor Law, and Clay's private cell was transformed into a ward for men*

277

who not only drank (from bottles passed in the windows) but also smoked, ate flesh, and rarely bathed. Thus he petitioned for his release.

While he was in prison Clay's free love companion "Lily" seems to have undergone a change of heart, for he received a letter from her announcing her forthcoming marriage to a young man. Clay wrote her a farewell: "What an idea to me is this 'legally married,' legally loved, legally living, legally thinking, speaking, and acting! It sounds to me like legal slavery, legal suicide, legal murder, legal death. The whole system of legality is based on death. It knows naught but death, while all life is of God, which to the legal authorities is illegal. . . . The love your good heart asks for is as righteously yours as the heart that beats within your body, but that you should ask for it exclusively, is to ask that no other heart but yours should beat. To ask it to be bound to you, is to ask it to become your slave."

Clay was a complete anarchist in the native American style; he denied the right of government to make or enforce any law. On the day he was released he (like Charles Knowlton twenty years, or Bronson Alcott and then Henry Thoreau ten years earlier) engaged a hall to give a series of free lectures on his subversive prison thoughts. The first night an interested crowd gathered to hear him on "free love," but the next night the mayor refused to allow its sequel on "government," in which Clay intended to argue his libertarian views—anti-state, anti-war, anti-prison, anti-slavery, anti-capitalism, anti-chauvinism. Of all these causes, it was the free love doctrine that Clay thought most central, just as he believed legal marriage was "the head and cornerstone of the temple of injustice, darkness, disease, death, and all the countless ills that afflict us." He was a typical free lover, convinced that freedom and bondage began here, in the sexual and domestic relations, and spread everywhere according to the character of these primary intimacies of body and spirit.

James Clay
Petition to Governor and Council of Maine For My Release

To the Governor and Executive Council of the State of Maine.

Gentlemen: I understand you are, by a petition to be presented to you, to be made acquainted with my conviction, sentence, and imprisonment, in the jail of the county of Kennebec. This is to join those, my friends, in their prayer for my pardon and release, but not offering the same plea as an inducement for your granting it.

Lest you should not receive that petition, I will give you a statement of my case. I am a lawfully-married man, and have ever, until the indictment for this offence, lived in as pleasant relations with my family as is usual. I have what I presume to you are peculiar views in regard to the marriage law, and all other statute laws. I am looking for the time to come on this earth, when the race will be so pure and good there will be no necessity for any other than the laws of God to hold men's passions in check. Then they will neither marry nor be given in marriage, but will be as angels in heaven.

I was first charged with adultery, and then with lewd and lascivious cohabitation with an unmarried woman, in my own house. The evidence against us (she was put on trial with me for the same offence) was that we slept in the same bed. The rebutting evidence was her virginity, which was proved by two respectable medical men in regular practice, after an examination. On the first charge, adultery, the jury gave us a verdict of not guilty. On the second charge, before another jury, the verdict was reversed, and we have been sentenced, she to four months imprisonment in the county jail, or fifty dollars fine; I to six months, or two hundred dollars. I have paid her fine, and she has fled from your state, as many others have fled in times past from the persecutions of those who could not so readily receive new thoughts. I am on my fifth week's imprisonment, and to induce you to release me from this confinement is the object of this petition.

I earnestly pray with them that you let me go; but, while I do so, I do not wish you to understand that I make a plea, or give my assent to a plea, of insanity, to excite your sympathy in my behalf. Not that I am not in want of your sympathy,—for I am,—but I do

---

● Selection from *A Voice from the Prison,* Boston: Bela Marsh, 1856, pp. 28–35.

not wish to resort to falsehood, or what I think such, to obtain your favor, or any other good.

Your petitioners, I doubt not, think me a *non compos mentis*; and, perhaps, if you should seat yourselves by me for half an hour, and listen to what I could tell you *I know*, you would leave me verily believing and perhaps uttering "he hath a devil." Yet, for all this, gentlemen, I would rather lay here to fulfill my sentence, than you should understand I assert or give my assent to ask my freedom under the plea of insanity. If what I behold in the religious, moral, political, judicial, medical, physical, commercial and social worlds, are sanity, then I acknowledge with humility my *in*sanity, for they are all reversed in me. But, gentlemen, ere you pass such a judgment on me, remember that the sanity of one age becomes the insanity of another. The laws that but a few short years since had an honorable place in your statute books, and in your hearts, are now black with infamy. Such has been, and such will be, while states make laws, until they make the unchangeable laws of God or nature the base of theirs. Should *this* petition change your mind in regard to my sanity, I hope it will not be prejudicial to my release by a pardon from you. If you credit the former petition and petitioners, rather than me, then, if you please grant their prayer. If you credit me in regard to my sanity, then believe me further in regard to my innocence, which is equally worthy of your sympathy; for I assure you there was no intention to commit the alleged crime, or any other crime, nor was crime committed. I know, gentlemen, that adulterous persons may judge from the circumstances that I had adultery in my heart, or lascivious persons accuse me of lasciviousness; but from "the pure in heart" such judgments *could not* come.

I assure you, I know and obey a higher law than your smoky volumes have record of, or your smoky men or courts can understand or appreciate, and I should be judged by none others than those who know and obey that law, for they alone of men can render me a just verdict. If I do not misunderstand, *your* law grants a trial by one's peers or equals. Now, gentlemen, this could not be granted me at your courts; at least, I feared so, and did not avail myself of the right at my trial to challenge my jurors. I often talked with those connected with the courts, and not in one instance did I find those who had an idea of purity such as I profess, and I think should be possessed by every member of the human family,—at least by every one who professes membership in the church of Christ.

I hope you will not think I am taking it upon myself to judge your courts or their members, for "I judge no one," especially to condemn. I have this judgment which I give, from their own lips, and am often mocked with ridicule at the idea of purity, though at almost the same breath I am pointed to the Christian religion for a code of morals, from which I get and know how to appreciate the injunction, "Be ye therefore perfect, even as your Father in heaven is perfect." Let me say to you, I am a believer, and I profess a somewhat consistent believer, in the Christian religion, which teaches forgiveness rather than condemnation and punishment; and those my equals or peers on a jury (if they could sit there), could in no wise condemn me, even if I were really guilty, and the most positive evidence given to that effect; but, as said Jesus to the woman caught in the very act of adultery, would they say to me, "Go, and sin no more."

You perceive my peers could not condemn me, and those that were not my peers could only judge me by their own lascivious hearts; for there was no positive proof against me of lasciviousness or adultery, but very much of the most positive evidence that I could not have committed adultery, which I should have done, having had the opportunity, if I had had lascivious intentions.

The "rule" of the judge at my trial is worthy of a passing note. It was in substance this: "Any act committed by them, that would excite the lustful passions, would be cause for a verdict of guilty." He did not tell the jury in whom I might be the cause of exciting lustful passion to make me guilty,—whether in him the judge, they the jury, myself, or any one else in particular; but that, should I be the cause of exciting lust, no matter in whom, I must be found guilty. Under this rule I should decline promenading your streets with a lady, lest I be found a criminal. I too often witness the lewd remarks and gestures of men who throng our thoroughfares, in clubs, and even your church-doors, to suppose I could escape the prison under such a law, "though to the pure are all things pure."

For walking the streets of my native city with a female whose virtue was untarnished, except in the imagination of the lewd, whose only peculiarity was the Bloomer costume, so called, I have been chased and mocked with extreme insolence.

One who teaches virtue is obliged to put up with the insolence of the vicious, and bear the reproach of a false modesty and a corrupt public opinion; and it is for you, gentlemen, to say if continued imprisonment shall be added to these.

It is not my object to judge those who found for me a verdict of guilty, or the court who sentenced me, or the public who reprobate me; but I only wish to use these truths in my possession to free myself, if possible, from the sentence of *their* condemnation. And those facts I do not wish to use in a spirit of retaliation, but rather in that of charity; for the condemnation of the higher law resting on them for their sins, from which there is no appeal or escape, is all-sufficient without my harming myself by giving them even an angry thought. Now, gentlemen, do you think every word I have said of my innocence false?—then, I beg you do not punish to reform me, for I assure you evil is only overcome by good, except in destruction; in which case it should be left in the hands of the evil to perform .

Do you think society need be protected from my doing them harm? I hope to be able to present you with a petition, from those who know me well, saying they deem me an inoffensive man, and praying that you pardon me,—which tells you in substance I am no wolf, which, if set at liberty, will prowl about your premises.

Do you fear to forgive me lest it open a wide door for other of my fellow-prisoners to trouble you with their petitions? I assure you it is a door you may with the utmost safety throw wide open, if your object be to reform the fallen, which I should wish cannot be doubted. It is the life of Christianity, the science of reform, to forgive. As we forgive, so are we forgiven; "the measure we mete is measured to us again." Then measure to men charity and kindness, that the same may echo and reecho, until its influence shall fill the world, and sheathe every sword, and unhinge every prison-door, and let the captive go free, bearing on his heart the influence of the kindness you bestow on him.

And while you are doing this great kindness to the fallen, do not feel that you are no recipients of the blessings you bestow; for you are the "members of one body," the whole of which is saved when you cure the diseased limbs, and may I not say the whole of which must be lost or destroyed, if not cured in a similar manner to that which I have pointed out. It is true that "they that take the sword shall perish by the sword"; or, in other words, evil shall perish by evil, while the good must be saved by good. They are distinct principles, and cannot work together. We are evil when we think to overcome evil by evil, and all punishments are evil.

Pardon me, gentlemen, for thus presuming to instruct or dictate you; for be assured it is with the most benevolent intentions that I have thus spoken to you.

Do you think I am "flush" with money, and can pay the two hundred dollars' fine for my liberty? I assure you I have met with a succession of pecuniary losses, and am embarrassed with debts that it will be very difficult indeed for me to extricate myself from; and now, through the interposition of your laws, and the reprobation of a corrupt public opinion, I am deprived of my former lucrative business, which would render it very inconvenient, indeed, for me to meet the desired fine; and besides this I have a wife and daughter, who need all the means I have at my disposal; and, more than this, it would be a violation of a high moral principle that I have within me to purchase my liberty, which by a divine right belongs to me, without the payment of gold. And, above all these considerations, gentlemen, I wish to teach my professing Christian brethren, that it is better to forgive than to punish a brother man whom they would reclaim. If you do not think proper to grant *me my prayer* in setting me at liberty (or if you do), will you please come to this prison personally, and examine carefully into the merits of the prisoners, and learn if there be not one, two, or more, who *are* worthy of your regard and their liberty, while I lay here, if need be, to fulfill my mission in rendering some or all more free by my bondage.

For ages past, political, religious, and social reform and freedom, —the latter only another name for the former,—have depended on bloodshed for their growth. But these are all reforms that need reforming, which I, in some measure, hope to be instrumental in achieving. You see, gentlemen, from my position, I am no aggressor, no avenger. I can but teach, and then submit to my fate, and that patiently and quietly, until the time of my deliverance comes. I say teach. I must live a truth I teach, so far as I am permitted, else the truth is at least lost on me.

I want, I sincerely ask the reality of what our fathers fought and bled for, and only obtained the shadow of. I want my natural rights, "life, liberty and happiness"; the pursuit of the latter does not answer me. The living death or dying life that everywhere sur-

rounds me does not meet my internal want of life; nor does the
liberty to think, speak, and act as others do, and dictate I should,
answer for the liberty God has given me in my spirit, and I trust
will help me to live in my life.

I do not ask another's life, liberty or happiness, or a right to
infringe on either of those rights of my brother man to enhance
mine, but only that I may be free to live truthfully, and thereby
teach in what a true life consists; and this by no means for *me*
alone, but that you, and others who will, may be partakers with
me of the blessing of that true life, unbounded liberty and everlasting happiness. Grant me this, gentlemen, my prayer, and I will
ever remain your humble servant in the promotion of good.

Jas. A. Clay.

Augusta Jail, Sept. 25th, 1854

May I ask another favor, the publication of this petition?

"Cohabiting and Associating Together, Not Being Married"

Leo Miller

Twenty years after James Clay was sentenced to six months in a Maine jail for cohabiting with a woman not his wife, Leo Miller and Mattie Strickland were arrested and tried for the same offense in Hastings, Minnesota. Rather than their prison thoughts (for they too were convicted and sentenced—but to ten days only), Miller and Strickland published the arguments they presented to the Court in defense of their action.

Miller does not mention that it was impossible for him to marry Mattie Strickland legally because he was already married to a woman in Rushford, New York, where the only grounds for divorce were still adultery. A Spiritualist lecturer in the 1860s, Miller was a late convert to free love. He had long argued that the popular identification of free love and Spiritualism was false, the idiosyncrasy of a "few misguided souls" in Berlin Heights. Just a year before running off with Mattie Strickland, he had published a whole book on Woman and the Divine Republic *which was so spotless of the free love taint that Elizabeth Cady Stanton gave a copy of it to her granddaughter as an uplifting feminist tract. Then, in 1875, Miller and Strickland announced their contract to the free love world in the pages of Ezra Heywood's journal* The Word, *arguing the standard Berlin Heights line against any interference by the civil authorities in matters of love.*

After this reversal it should not be too surprising to find Miller, almost ten years later, writing the recantation printed here as a sequel to his defense. True to the free love pattern of extremes, Miller now described his conversion to the Greeley view of marriage as a divine sacrament, to be entered into only once, blessed by church and state. This conversion is unexplained, but one hears in Miller's tone the same absolutist impulse that actuated Thomas and Mary Nichols, Victoria Woodhull, and James W. Towner (see Introduction).

It is coincidence enough to be worth noting that just a year after Miller's recantation, another pair of free lovers took up the baton where Miller had reliquished it, and were jailed in Valley Falls, Kansas, for the same offense, in much the same circumstances. Edwin C. Walker was already divorced from his first wife (whether or not with the right to remarry, I do not know), and was living with Lillian Harman without benefit of clergy, both of them being free lovers and free-thinkers. Their sentences were two-and-a-half and one-and-a-half months, respectively (the woman always received the lighter sentence, a reflection of her legal weight in the period). They were serving out their terms, on principle, when Miss Harman's notorious father, and her brother, were suddenly arrested as well, for publishing an "obscene" issue of Lucifer, *Moses Harman's radical journal. Walker and his consort paid their fines in order to be at large to aid the more seriously threatened members of the family. (Moses Harman was in and out of prison many times after this, for offenses of the same sort, including once at the instigation of Anthony Comstock, whose nose for smut sniffed as far as Chicago.) Walker and Lillian Harman continued their liason when they moved to New York City, but they finally separated in the early years of the century. Harman, who had a child by Walker, remarried (legally) and left the free love movement; Walker continued a champion of free love and speech until his death in 1931.*

Leo Miller
"Cohabiting and Associating Together, Not Being Married"

Your Honor, I am charged with the commission of a crime against the peace and dignity of the State; said crime being, in the language of the indictment, "lewdly and lasciviously cohabiting and associating with Mattie Strickland, not being married" to her. I purpose to show: (1) That the said cohabitation and association with Mattie Strickland is right *per se*; (2) That the statute which declares it to be a crime, is in violation of natural law and an outrage upon personal rights; and (3) That my objections to the marriage institution as regulated by law, together with the special circumstances of the case, entitle me to the credit of sincerity of conscience, and a just claim under the Constitution to establish conjugal relations with the woman I love without imposition of the bonds of legal marriage.

. . . I presume it would be impossible to find an intelligent supporter of the marriage institution, who would deny the proposition in the abstract, that the only natural basis of sexual union is mutual affection; that those whom God and nature join together, are wedded by the attractive power of reciprocal love; and that any other kind of union is naturally adulterous and immoral. Accepting these self-evident propositions, it is plain to be seen that legal marriage does not rest upon the divine principles of nature and truth.

The marriage law is specially designed to bind parties who are not united by affection; to compel parties to live together who do not want to. It could never have had any other origin. Those who are joined by God, who are bound by the natural sentiment of affection, certainly do not need the law. They are held together by a force as omnipotent as God himself. It would be a solecism to assume that parties who are drawn together by love would wish to separate. That would be equivalent to saying that to be attracted is to be repelled. Abolish the marriage law to-day, and not a couple in the world who are wedded by affection would separate. The defendant and Mattie Strickland are not bound by legal ties,

---

● Selections from *The Miller-Strickland Defense*, St. Paul: The Pioneer Press, 1876, pp. 9, 12–23; the New York *Sun*, April 24, 1885, 2.

and yet they have no disposition to part. Their accusers even are
convinced of this, and have invoked the power of man to put
asunder what God hath joined together. There is no possible
excuse for the marriage law in any case except to hold together
those who would fly apart by the repulsive force of antipathy, disgust and hate. The marriage institution is designed for such only;
none others need it. It is a wicked contrivance of man, intended
to operate against nature, and enforce loveless unions, that are full
of discord, prostitution, lust and shame. Not more true is the
declaration, "Whom God hath joined together, let no man put
asunder," than its converse, "Whom God hath put asunder by the
natural law of antipathy, let no man hold together." The marriage
law wars against this divine principle.

In the next place, the marriage institution, as might be expected
from what we have already seen of its origin, substantially ignores
the essential element of conjugal union—love, which alone warrants
and sanctifies sexual relations; and sets up, instead, an artificial
standard of morality—the law. Its assumption is, that outside of
law all sexual union is lewd, impure and wrong; while inside its
pale all is right and virtuous. It asserts, in effect, that the legislator
has power to make that which was before impure, pure; that which
was wrong, right. This an impious assumption, and as before
remarked, deposes God himself from the moral government of the
world.

The moral status of any human act or right, cannot be affected
by legislation. Right and wrong are no shifting fancies and
prejudices of man's caprice; they abide through all time, and are
determined by the immutable laws and conditions which Nature
herself imposes.

If we inquire of Nature what makes it right, and only right, for
man and woman to come together in the most intimate relation,
the answer is plain: because they are attracted to each other by
love, because they want children, they want happiness, they want
each others companionship. This is what makes it right; this is a
warrant from the Almighty himself; and all the legislators, clergymen and magistrates in the universe cannot alter the moral character
of the act. They may withhold their sanction, they may declare it
to be lewd and lascivious, they may punish with fines and imprisonment, and still it is right; or they may give their approval, and the

relation of the parties remains the same—it is no more moral, no more virtuous for it.

And the opposite statement is equally true: if the man and woman are not thus mutually attracted by the sentiment of love, their cohabitation is wrong and immoral, and all the marriage laws of earth authorizing it cannot make it right and virtuous.

Were it not for the wickedness of the assumption, it would seem the sheerest nonsense in the world to claim that a person's virtue is contingent upon an act of the legislature. But absurd and impious as it is, it nevertheless is the corner stone of the marriage institution. The very language of the statute under which I am indicted confirms this. A union of man and woman, as true and sacred as any that ever met the approving smiles of Heaven, is called "lewd and lascivious," for no other reason than because it lacks the sanction of the law; while another alliance, though it should be prompted by avarice and lust, the law stands ready to solemnize with a mockery of forms, and label "virtuous."

To this false and arbitrary principle of morality taught by the marriage institution, may be traced a great portion of the evils and miseries of the marriage state. By it parties are led to overlook the necessity of love, the only element of strength in such relations, and depending as they do upon a fiction of the law to solemnize their unions, no wonder they fall to pieces and leave so many matrimonial wrecks all around us. To illustrate: a young woman says, "The law makes it perfectly right and virtuous for me to cohabit and associate with any man I may choose, if I but invoke its sanction. I have an offer of marriage from two men: one of them I love, but he is poor; the other I dislike, but he is rich: I will marry the latter." And so she gets a clergyman to come in and throw over her deliberate act of prostitution the cloak of the law. No wonder she is soon miserable and wishes herself out of the bonds. Such a marriage—and there are tens of thousands of them— is blasted at the altar when the lips utter the false and heartless vows. But blame not the woman for marrying the man she dis- liked; blame rather the institution that laid the snare for her feet; blame society that makes the marriage law; that laughs at love as a sentimental weakness, and teaches young women, directly and indirectly, to seek first in marriage the assurance of home and position.

In vain do we talk and preach about the sexes exercising more discretion and judgement in entering the marriage state. So long as it is claimed that law makes sexual commerce right, so long is the way obstructed to the study of those natural principles of affection and adaptability that should determine and govern the relation. At the very threshold of the investigation, the inquiry is made, What makes it right and pure? Society answers, law. That then is enough; why proceed further? Can there be more than that which is right and pure? Indeed, it is fatal to the institution to countenance principles of attraction, love, adaptability; for if these things enter into the question of right, then it is no longer the law that makes it right and sacred. The institution of marriage is simply one of arbitrary law, and its very perpetuity depends upon the degradation of love. Just in proportion as we come to feel the importance of love as the sanctifying element in the union of the sexes, do we lose sight of the law. The redemptive principle lies either all on the one side, or all on the other; there can be no partnership in the matter. And here is where the issue is being made up between social freedom and legal marriage. Law has its proper place. It should recognize unions of love and throw around them its shield of protection; but it must never assume to be any part of the bond itself.

Another conscientious objection I have to recognizing the marriage institution in my conjugal relation, is the fact, cognate to the one we have just been considering, that instead of seeking to make marriage a high and holy union of the sexes, it degrades it to the level of animalism. It recognizes no nobler purpose in marriage than the gratification of sensual passions. It weds bodies and grants license to the unrestrained indulgence of the lusts of the flesh. Of the union of souls, the affinity of minds, the mateship of spirits, legal marriage knows nothing, cares nothing.

This is a bold charge to make against this time-honored institution, I know; but, your Honor, we have only to glance at the marriage and divorce laws to establish the damning truth. One fact is sufficient to prove it: the law will not divorce parties for incompatibility of mind and disposition, but it will for incompatibility of bodies. Sexual impotency, on either side, is good cause for legal separation. Let an application be made to the courts for a bill of divorce on the ground of mutual antipathy and hate; let it be shown that what should be a home of love and peace, is a

hell of discord, strife and misery; and the wretched pair will soon
learn that the law has no relief for them; that all that remains
to them is to bravely fight it out on that line till merciful death
do them sever. On the other hand, however sweetly harmonizing
in mind and spirit a husband and wife may be, the law stands
ready to divorce them, if either party from any cause, is incapaci-
tated physically to gratify the sensual passions of the other!

And this is the institution I am accused of dishonoring! Thank
God, there is another with me who has principle and courage
enough to do likewise. From such a gross, degrading conception of
the union of the sexes, the souls of Mattie Strickland and the
defendant revolt in horror; and they believe it to be their solemn
duty, which they owe to God, to humanity, and to themselves, to
protest against it at whatever cost, and both by precept and practice,
try to educate mankind up to a higher and holier ideal of conjugal
life. These intimate relations of men and women are fraught with
energies creative: by them immortal beings are ushered into
existence, destined to run a never-ending career through the cycles
of eternity. There is nothing in human life that should be held in
greater reverence than sexual intercourse. The low, debasing idea
of it, inculcated by the marriage institution, is an offense to the
God of Love; and I believe His curse is upon it, and it must pass
away and give place to a system of nuptials more in harmony with
an advanced civilization.

Another serious objection to the institution confronts me:
marriage is an unconditional contract between parties to live
together as husband and wife for life. Believing most religiously
that sexual intercourse without the sanctifying presence of love is
immoral, polluting to body and soul, I cannot make such a contract
without mortgaging my conscience.

If the existence of mutual affection between parties is presumed
to have any place whatever in marrage, then the law makes the
stupid and mischievous blunder of supposing it to be a matter of
volition, which can be produced to order in obedience to the
command of the officiating minister or magistrate; whereas the
fact is, that love is the most involuntary thing in life. We can no
more love and honor a person by the simple volition of the will,
than we can create a world out of naught.

These sentiments are awakened in us by the character and conduct of others; not by any effort of our own. We love that which

appears to us loveable, and hate that which is hateful; honor that which is honorable, and despise that which is despicable.

Whoever promises to love and honor another for life, promises that which may be utterly impossible for him to perform. If he could be sure that he knew perfectly the person, and that he or she would never change, and that he himself would not change, it might be done in safety; but this is impossible. Our judgements are fallible; our estimates of people are often erroneous; we invest them with qualities which trial proves they do not possess, or their supposed virtues are assumed for effect; friends disappoint us; many persons have great skill in concealing grave defects, which only the intimacy of married life brings out. Then, too, persons really change in their character and principles, and it is no longer possible for the parties to assimilate in thought and feelings. One grows vile and unprincipled, the other refined and noble; or they change in intellectual tastes and sentiments; one becomes liberal, the other remains or grows conservative; and if, what is very likely in such cases, a spirit of unreason and intolerance exists on either side, it is sure to breed perpetual contention and warfare.

All these things, and many others, may in time be developed between parties to a degree that will render harmony and sympathy, love and honor, impossible. Seeing with open eyes that such changes are likely to occur, indeed, do occur in such a number of instances as to make it a question which is the rule and which the exception, how unreasonable and pernicious for the marriage law to try to bind parties in love and honor to live together for life. Does the law of Nature continue to bind them? Do love, sympathy, respect—these elements which God has ordained to be the basis of union, and without which there is no union—remain unchanged from the altar to the grave? If so, then is the marriage institution founded on principle and right; if not, it is at war with human nature and the laws of God. What are the facts? Our courts give the answer: they are crowded with applications for divorce. Of course this makes business lively for clergymen and lawyers, as disease does for doctors; but it must be confessed that it requires a pretty great stretch of imagination to see how an institution, so full of hate and inharmony, ever received the title, "sacred"!

But if the marriage part of the system is so at variance with reason and conscience and nature, what must be said of the divorce arrangement? There is not an element of merit in it. Should the

ingenuity of man be taxed to its utmost capacity, it would hardly
be possible to invent a system more utterly at war with natural
wants and rights than the divorce laws of the civilized world.
It sets at defiance the principles of morality, justice, truth, and the
laws of generation.

In the first place, it does not even recognize the only valid cause
there is for divorce. If love be nature's only warrant for conjugal
union, then the absence, or cessation of love, is the only true cause
for divorce. But there is not a court in all the civilized world that
recognizes this simple fact, and yet the only fact that concerns them
to know.

Let a husband and wife go into court and say that they do not
love each other; that there is mutual dislike between them; that
their consciences condemn them whenever they are tempted into
intimate relations; and that they wish to be legally divorced; and
they would be laughed at by the lawyers as a couple of precious
simpletons. Indeed, the legal rule is, that mutual consent, instead of
being the very best reason in the world why they should be permitted to separate, destroys their case in the eyes of the man-made
law. The aversion between them must develop into some criminal
act on the part of one or the other, and the defendant must appear
to wish to still hold the victim, before their case can be entertained.

There must be adultery, a felony, or some overt act of violence,
cruelty or neglect, before they can be allowed to part. This offers
to those who desire to separate a premium on crime and brutality.
As the better class of men and women are too refined and good to
descend to such things, they must continue to be held in their
wretched bonds; while to the coarse and brutal, who, it is claimed,
especially need the wholesome restraints of the law, "divorce is made
easy"; their brutal instincts find for them a ready way out. Consistency is indeed a jewel, but evidently not to be found in this system.

I have heretofore shown that the marriage law binds parties in
unhallowed relations; it is equally plain to be seen that the divorce
law enjoins and enforces lust and prostitution. I will elucidate these
two propositions in conjunction.

Common sense confirms the reasoning of Blackstone, that statute
law has no power to change the moral status of a human act; that
the rightfulness or wrongfulness of moral conduct exists by virtue
of its own intrinsic character. Sexual intercourse is undeniably a
question of morals; and to determine when it is right and when

wrong, when prostitution and when not, we should not go to the statute books of the State; but we must look at the conditions and relations involved in the commerce itself. There must be some principle lying at the foundation of the sexual act that makes it right; and when it is wrong, that principle is violated. Now what is it that makes it right and moral in itself? There can be but one intelligent answer—mutual affection—conjugal love between the parties. What then would be lust and prostitution? The sexual relation in the absence of love. No proposition in morals can be plainer than this. Prostitution, then, must be defined to be sexual union without the sanctifying influence of love. The woman who takes to her arms a man for any other reason than that of love, is a prostitute. It matters not whether it be for the sake of a home, or for a ten-dollar bill; whether it be under the sanction of the law, or in a brothel; it is an unhallowed, loveless act of prostitution.

According to these natural principles of sexual morality, both the marriage law and the divorce law are convicted of legalizing prostitution. The marriage law, denying love as the basis of marriage, says to parties in effect, "Whether you love each other or not, is immaterial; you can marry for money, marry for home, marry for spite, marry for anything you like, only marry; and you shall have a license to prostitute your souls and bodies *ad libitum*." On the other hand, the divorce law, by refusing to recognize the absence of love as cause for divorce, expressly enjoins and enforces upon the parties the obligation to live together in a state of prostitution and lust!

What infinite impiety and blasphemy to call such a system of marriage sacred and divine! Is it strange that even loving hearts, caught in its accursed meshes, so often find it the grave of their love? And here is the source of human life from whence the world is peopled! No wonder the face of society is blotched and distorted with monstrosities of brutality, vice and crime. The very laws of generation are perverted; children are ushered into existence that were "conceived in sin and shape in iniquity"; and they grow up to crowd our asylums, our pauper houses, our criminal courts, jails, brothels and prisons.

No child should ever be begotten that is not the offspring of mutual affection. Love is harmony; and the harmonies of nature are the conditions of perfection. It is impossible to estimate the evils of loveless maternity and loveless offspring. A woman, constrained by necessity or law, takes to her embrace a man she loathes, and in that act becomes a mother! When we consider the personal injury, the torture, the immolation of everything sacred and pure, the thought is certainly appalling enough; but when we look beyond to the effect upon her offspring, it is a sight to make the angels weep and the world stand aghast! As certainly as that like begets like, as surely as temperament, traits of character, complexion, color of eyes and hair, are imparted by parents to their offspring, so surely is the loathing, the pollution, the hate, that filled that mother's mind transmitted to her child.

The iniquities of parents in this particular are visited upon their children to the third and fourth generations, until society is literally infested with the human embodiments of inharmony and hate. Behold yonder wretch expiating the crime of murder upon the gallows. Take up his life-line and trace it back, and you will find the brand of Cain stamped upon his brow before he left his mother's womb! Hate is a condition of murder. The Bible says, "He that hateth his brother hath already committed murder in his heart."

The marriage state is full of deadly hate. Seven murder trials of husbands and wives, were reported by the press as pending in the courts of Maine at one time. Newspapers teem with murders committed by husbands and wives to escape the hellish bonds of wedlock; and while so many cases actually transpire, it is reasonable to suppose that thousands of married persons are possessed of this spirit who restrain the impulse; and yet the mental condition is as fatal to the receptive embryo in the mother as if it had found vent in actual violence.

The amount of inborn evil and crime of every description that is thus directly traceable to loveless marriage relations, encouraged and enforced by custom and law, is beyond the power of finite mind to comprehend, or time develop. Eternity alone can reveal its magnitude! When mankind shall come to better understand this subject, they will shudder with amazement that a system productive of such monstrous evils as the marriage institution, ever existed on earth. The abominations of chattel slavery will whiten into moral excellence compared with it.

There are many more objections to the marriage institution that might be enumerated; but I will present but one other, of a general character, that forms an insurmountable obstacle in the way of the defendant and Mattie Strickland marrying. It is this: legal marriage is slavery; not hypothetical merely, but real and absolute. Slavery may be defined as a state of entire or partial subjection of a person to the will of another; a relation of master and subject; authority on one side and obedience on the other; ownership in greater or less degree of a human being. The history of the marriage institution up to the present time verifies this definition. Woman has been the subject, man the master.

Legal marriage is a very ancient institution, and on that account it is supposed to be venerable and good, as if the antiquity of a system was proof of its excellence. The systems of slavery, despotism, and superstition that still linger to afflict the race, date back to the foundation of society; and the marriage institution, as regulated by custom and law, is one of the most offensive of the group. Look at it in the present and in the past.

In primitive times the purchase of the wife was a universal custom; she was owned by her husband as absolutely as were his slaves. Under the Mosaic dispensation she was a part of the husband's estate, and reverted to heirs the same as property.

Among all nations the husband had a right to whip his wife, to sell her services, and in every respect control her actions as absolutely as though she were a chattel slave. In some of the nations he had the power of life and death over her. Her name, her personality, and her property, were always surrendered and lost in her legal master. So abject was her slavery that she could not complain if other wives or concubines were brought into the family to share her husband's favors. Constancy on his part was never dreamed of; but she must be absolutely faithful to the marriage vow.

Under the Jewish law, as recorded in Bible history, the wife was put to death for adultery; and in the matter of divorcement, for the most trivial cause, the husband, without trial, had only to write her a bill and send her adrift. Of course the law did not operate against the husband in like manner. He was the lord and master and made the laws; she, the dependent slave, to minister to his wants; to obey, and be punished, and put to death, at his sovereign will.

Can it be denied that a marriage institution like this is a system of the grossest slavery? And this institution, by the boast of its friends, is still in existence. Some of the more revolting features have been outgrown it is true; but it has not been changed in type from what it was thousands of years ago. The legal and customary relations of husband and wife are virtually those of master and subject, as they have always been, not of equals. The elements of slavery run through the whole system.

The woman surrenders her name and very much of her personality as formerly. She may not be put to death for adultery; but the lingering spirit of the old time fastens its fangs upon her, and kills her socially, and casts her out of the pale of respectability; while the man, guilty of the same offence, suffers no loss of character. Even the new divorce law of Great Britain makes such a distinction against woman, that a husband has the right of divorce from his wife for adultery, while she is denied it in case of his infidelity.

The bondage of the wife is clearly evident from the circumstance that if she elope, the husband may seize upon her by law and take her home, as fugitive slaves were wont to be restored to their masters.

The principle of ownership is visible in the fact that a husband can collect by law, damages of a man to whom his wife has voluntarily yielded her body. In the Beecher-Tilton case, the latter sued Beecher for a hundred thousand dollars, in a civil action to recover damage he had sustained. Damage to what? Why, damage to his property, represented in his wife, Elizabeth.

This idea is still further carried out in case of divorce; the common law giving the children to the father, on the slave principle that the mother having belonged to him under the marriage contract, the children which she had borne in pain, are his also.

In States where she is not protected by special legislation, the marriage contract gives the wife's personal property to the husband, and also allows him to sell her services and collect the money against her will, which he may spend for whisky, or on other women if he choose, and the poor bond-woman can no more help herself than could the slave of other days in Southern States.

The humiliation and subjection of the wife may be further seen in the common occurrence of a husband advertising her as having left his bed and board, and forbidding persons harboring and trusting her, very much as runaway slaves were formerly posted by their masters.

The entire nomenclature of marriage confirms the principle of the husband's ownership of his wife, and of her dependent, subject state.

"Coverture," an eminent law writer defines as signifying, that "the very being of the wife is merged in that of the husband."

"Dower," is not property that belongs to the wife or widow of an inherent right, but that which the law endows her with out of her husband's estate for her maintenance; just as the laws of the Southern States in the days of slavery compelled owners to provide for the support of old and infirm slaves.

"Relict," applied to a widow, signifies that she is all that remains of her poor defunct master.

"Obey," in the marriage ceremony, which the wife is made to promise, is the very essence of slavery when required of a person of mature years and judgement.

•   •   •

There is one other assumption I will notice, and I am done. It is argued that the sexual relations of men and women involve the rights of third persons,—the children that come of them; and that therefore it becomes the plain duty of the State to protect them from the injury of abandonment by parents, and itself from the burden of their support. This is very true; but the inference drawn therefrom, that only the existence of the present marriage system will secure such protection, is unsupported by a shadow of reason or proof. The law could as effectually hold parents responsible for the care and support of their children under a system of civil-contract unions, in which the parties are free to dissolve them at pleasure, as under present arbitrary marriage regulations. What is to hinder? A public registry could be kept of such unions, and if necessary, of all children born of them, and the property of parents, as under the present *regime*, be held liable for their support.

The parental instinct, I believe, is as strong in mankind as in brute kind, and when it is not destroyed by the demon of strong drink or other perverting influences, it will as voluntarily protect its young as do animals. Laws might be enacted requiring it, but I think they would soon be found unnecessary under a social order in which all are free, and every case of loving fatherhood and motherhood is respected. It is not for want of parental affection and willingness to care for children that they are so often abandoned by unmarried persons; but the disgrace that attaches to parentage out of wedlock, is the cause that leads to the unnatural deed. Still, while there is doubt, let the State provide against all contingencies of evil.

Should the union of Mattie Strickland and myself be blessed by offspring, we stand ready to give the State as much security for their support as do those who are married. This we have signified our willingness to do in the Contract signed and published in November, 1875, a copy of which is appended to the Stipulation. If the State has made no provision for self-protection, in cases where parties cannot conscientiously marry, the fault is with itself. It would certainly be a new principle in law if it could take advantage of its own delinquencies to criminate the innocent.

Your Honor, I submit my case to your decision, and afterward to the considerate judgement of mankind.

Leo Miller
Marriage a Divine Institution

To the Editor of the Sun—*Sir:* Believing that personal experiences involving the welfare of society are rightfully the property of the whole species, the undersigned feels it incumbent upon himself to make known the conclusion of a social event which has caused no little public interest and comment.

Nine and a half years ago Martha (Mattie) Strickland of St. Johns, Mich. and myself formed a civil and conjugal union, without the customary sanction of law, and published to the world our declaration and contract. This step was taken with the conscientious conviction that the proceeding was, under the circumstances, right and justifiable, and through all those years we have continued to live together in the most endearing relations of virtual husband and wife, notwithstanding the repeated assertions of the press that we had separated. We were led to form this unusual alliance in order to secure and enjoy openly what we conceived to be our natural, connubial rights, denied us by unjust and oppressive divorce laws. I was at the time a resident of New York and the husband of a woman with whom it was not possible for me to live in peace and happiness. The divorce laws of that State do not permit legal separation of married parties for any cause other than that of adultery; and had I such grounds of complaint I would scorn to purchase my freedom at the expense of a woman I had once taken to my bosom as wife by dragging her into court and there publicly blasting her character beyond the hope of redemption. In departures from virtue, society, unlike Jesus, is relentless in its condemnation of the weaker sex but, inconsistently, tolerant and forgiving toward the masculine sinner!

I became acquainted with Miss Strickland, and a mutual affection sprung up between us. We desired to unite our lives and destinies in that most sacred of all human relations, marriage, but could not do so under the ordinary usages of society because of the iron bands that bound me to another. After deliberating over the matter for a year, we concluded to assume the responsibility and the consequences, whatever they might be, of forming an open conjugal union in defiance of law.

Years of reflection and experience have brought with them the conviction that the step we took was ill advised and wrong; that it would have been wiser and nobler to have sacrificed our own personal happiness and what we deemed to be our natural rights, than to have made this revolutionary assault upon the marriage institution. Marriage is of divine origin, an outgrowth of the higher moral sentiments, not of the lower propensities. In the early animal life of the race, before the moral and spiritual nature had attained any very considerable degree of development, we know that polygamy, polyandry, and general promiscuousness characterize the relations of the sexes. But with the evolution of the higher nature comes the voice of the Divine revealing the ultimate intentions of the Creator respecting the proper social relations of man and woman. The whole tendency of civilization, marked especially by the sentiments, aspirations, and longings of the noblest and purest specimens of the race, point conclusively to the fact that monogamy —the union for life of one man and one woman—constitutes the only true marriage ordained by nature and by nature's God for noble, rational beings; and it is undeniably the right and duty of the earthly legislator to transcribe this higher marriage law to his statute books and enjoin its observance. Just and discriminating provisions should be made to release parties from the marriage bonds where, from any cause, they defeat the ends of marriage and work evil rather than good, misery rather than happiness; but to strike down all law would lead to universal social anarchy. While the race has made great advancement from its primitive state, average human nature is still crude and disorderly, and needs direction and restraint. The few might be a law unto themselves and observe all the requirements and proprieties of true marriage, but the masses, left wholly to their own undisciplined impulses, would run riot in social excesses. But the law can make no discrimination in favor of the few; all must observe its requirements and if it be found in any way imperfect and oppressive, we should seek to reform it, not abolish it.

These facts and considerations have become more and more deeply impressed upon the mind, compelling at last a frank confession that the marital alliance contracted between Miss Strickland and myself in disregard of custom and law was a grave mistake, through which we have unwillingly done society an injury. Honor and duty alike require that the only reparation now possible in the case should be made, viz., a public renunciation of the self-instituted marriage. It is done. The union, civil and conjugal, formed by myself and Martha Strickland on the 2d day of November, 1875 is, by mutual consent, dissolved this 22d day of April, 1885.

Detroit, April 24.

Letters of a Martyr

Ida C. Craddock

The letters which comprise this selection speak for themselves. Ida Craddock—whose career is discussed at length in the Introduction, and whose thoughts on "Right Marital Living" may be read in Section VII below—was hounded and persecuted by Anthony Comstock, and the legal establishment that heeled to his whim, until at last she turned on the gas and cut her wrists. Comstock had arranged his arrests and indictments so that she would be in a kind of double jeopardy, first tried and sentenced in police court for violating a New York State law in selling her pamphlet The Wedding Night *to Comstock's agents, and then in a federal court for mailing it. As will be seen in the first letters printed here, he also tried, unsuccessfully, to entrap her in a further crime, selling "obscene" literature to a minor.*

The editor of The Truth Seeker *D. M. Bennett (whom he also sent to jail) claimed that Comstock had "written thousands upon thousands of decoy letters." Since his chief weapon was the "Comstock Law" of 1873—which made mailing "obscene" literature a* *federal offense punishable by up to $5,000 fine, or ten years at hard labor, or both—it was only natural for Comstock to rely on the mails as his means of enticing his victims.*

The 1873 law had been drafted and lobbied through Congress by Comstock himself. He was not satisfied with the range of cases prosecutable under the old obscenity statutes, which said nothing, for instance, about contraceptive literature, according to Comstock as vile and satanic as anything printed by the smut peddlers. Although libertarians like E. B. Foote, Jr., Edwin C. Walker, and Ezra H. Heywood fought Comstockery through the next thirty years, the law under which he succeeded in convicting poor Ida Craddock in 1902 was still his law, which outlived Comstock himself.

Ida C. Craddock
Letters of a Martyr
i. Comstock's Decoy Letter

Breeze Crest, Summit, N. J., Feb. 3, 1902.
Madame
   Would you oblige me with a copy of your "Wedding Night." I enclose half a dollar. Do you admit young girls to your lectures? What do you charge for two chums who would like to come together? I am past 17 years. Please seal tight and oblige me. Address plain Miss Frankie Streeter.
   P.O. Box 201. Summit, N. J.
   Enc. 50 cents.

ii. Ida Craddock's Reply
Room 5, 134 West 23D Street
New York, Feb. 4, 1902.

Miss Frankie Streeter, P. O. Box, 201, Summit, N. J.—*Dear Miss:* Your favor, 3d inst, at hand, inclosing fifty cents (50¢) for "The Wedding Night," and inquiring if I ever admit young girls to my lectures.
   I have never yet admitted any minors, knowingly, to any of my

● Selection from *The Truth-Seeker,* October 25, November 1, and November 8, 1902.

lectures, either young girls or young boys. This is for several reasons, but my chief reason for not admitting minors to my lectures is that there exists a social superstition that young people should be kept as ignorant as possible of all that pertains to the marriage relation. It is thought by many people that it would somehow render young people impure if they were told previous to marriage anything of its details. Because of this prevalent superstition on the subject anybody who instructs a minor in these matters without the consent of their parents or their legal guardian can be dealt with by law. It does not at all matter how delicately and chastely the teacher may instruct that young girl or young boy; that she should instruct him or her at all is expatiated on as an effort to "corrupt the morals of innocent youth." And of course no right-thinking person wishes to be thus stigmatized before the community—as "a corrupter of innocent youth."

For this reason, much to my regret, I could not consent to give you and your chum the desired instruction, even in a private lecture all to yourselves; nor do I care to send you "The Wedding Night," for a similar reason; and I return you your fifty cents herewith.

It is all very silly, and worse than silly—actually a crime against young people, that they should be thus kept ignorant of the laws of their being. But, my dear child, while you are a minor it behooves you to respect the opinions of those who have the legal charge over you, whether parents or guardians, and not run counter to their commands; unless, indeed, they should command you to commit a crime or do some selfish or otherwise morally wrong act. Until you are twenty-one it is well that you should studiously conform to the wishes of your parents. Remember, too, that they are older and wiser than you, and are in a position to know more of the evil ways of the world than you, an inexperienced young girl, can possibly know.

And just here let me drop a word of warning. In the present case, you see, I am returning you your money, and declining to send you the book you wish. But there are many people advertising books which deal with sex who would very quickly send you the book you order, and it might—yes, would, in many instances— prove a book which would fill your mind with memories and thoughts which would disturb you emotionally, and perhaps eventually render you less the pure and delicate young girl which I trust you are to-day. Because there is such a ban put upon the circulation of really pure literature such as mine, which teaches the chaste and holy side of the marriage relation—because of this, those people who view the marriage relation only from a coarse and degraded standpoint, and who wish only to make money out of people's desire to satisfy a very natural curiosity about the laws of their being, are very likely to advertise, and advertise conspicuously, such books as may be especially harmful to the young and inexperienced.

My dear child, do not send for such books any more. Try to learn all you can about your sex nature from your parents or your guardian. Inquire from some woman physician of your acquaintance, but let it be a woman physician whose moral character is above reproach, and who is socially approved by your parents. When you are twenty-one, and your own mistress legally, if I be still alive on this earth, I shall be very glad to furnish you with any books of mine upon sex, or to teach you anything you wish to know upon sex. Four years may seem a long time to youthful seventeen to wait, but time flies quickly at your age, nevertheless.

I think it altogether wicked that young girls should be kept in ignorance, as is to-day the custom, and allowed to become wives without being previously instructed. I trust that if you ever become a wife and a mother you will talk to your children frankly upon their sexual natures long before they reach their teens, and explain to them all that you can, in detail, about the possibilities of marriage and parenthood. I hope also that you will see that some physician of good moral character talks with them.

Meanwhile I will say this: If you can bring me written permission from one of your respective parents (or, if you be orphaned, from your respective legal guardians), I shall be very glad to give you and your chum a lecture, all to yourselves, upon your prospective duties as wives and mothers. As you are a stranger to me, my dear, you will pardon me if I insist that such permission must be written upon a business letterhead of parent or guardian— a letter head on which his or her name appears in print—and signed with his or her name; or, if preferred, your parent or guardian can swear before a notary public that as your parent or guardian, he or she gives you permission to take instruction from me. Such an affidavit must be sealed by a notary's seal, and it would probably cost 25 or 50 cents.

This is a legal protection to me, because, if a minor were to forge his or her parent's name, or to swear falsely before a notary,

these would be crimes to be dealt with severely by law, and of
course no sensible young person would risk anything of the sort.
With best wishes, my dear child, believe me yours very truly,
(Signed)   Ida C. Craddock.

iii. Ida Craddock's Letter to Her Mother.

New York, Oct. 16, 1902

Dear, Dear Mother: I know you will grieve over me for having
taken my life. . . . My dear, dear mother, oh, how sorry I am to
hurt you, as I know this act will do. But, oh, mother, I cannot, I
will not consent to go to the asylum, as you are evidently planning
to have me go. I know that this means a perpetual imprisonment
all my long life, unless I either recant my religious beliefs or else
hypocritically pretend to do so. I cannot bring myself to consent
to any of these three alternatives. I maintain my right to die as I
have lived, a free woman, not cowed into silence by any other
human being. If, on the other hand, the prison to which Judge
Thomas evidently proposes to send me were to be my destined
lot (you know very well that he wishes and means to lock me up
for a long, long term, which is practically my death warrant), my
work is ended so far as this world is concerned. My books have
been given a start, approved by physicians and other reputable
citizens, but the world is not yet ready for all the beautiful teachings which I have to give it. Other people will take up my work,
however, some day—will take it up where I laid it down, and will
start from where I left off and do better work than they could
have done but for me. Some day you'll be proud of me. You will
understand that what I have done has been done because you and
my father prepared me for just such a propaganda to humanity.
You may ask why I did not give it up and come home to live with
you, resuming my name of "Miss Craddock," and taking up other
work. But, dear mother, I could be of no possible help to you, with
the shadow of reproach which bigots and impure-minded people
have put on me. I should be only a hindrance to your respectability.
Moreover, my individuality has some rights. I cannot recant my
beliefs and throw aside a principle for which I have toiled and
struggled for nine years, even at the behest of a mother that is
dear to me.

Do not grieve, dear, dear mother; the world beyond the grave, believe me, is far more real and substantial than is this world in which we to-day live. This earth life which the Hindoos have for centuries termed "Maya," that is illusion. My people assure me that theirs is the real, the objective, the material world. Ours is the lopsided, the incomplete world. You and I shall meet in that beautiful world over there and shall know each other as individuals just as clearly as we do here, only more so. I do not know whether it will be possible for me to return to you; but if I can, I will do so. Only remember that you must try to keep the five rules for clear thinking and correct living which my people have given me. If I do come back, of this I feel sure. As you may have forgotten these, I am going to give them here again:

1. Do your daily earthly duty undeterred by calls to mediumship from any source.

2. Be self-controlled and strive to be amiable and loving every day.

3. Wait and watch for the highest.

4. Avoid selfish seeking of self-ease.

5. Abide in purity, not merely moral purity, but physical cleanliness; and still more, intellectual clearness— that is freedom from prejudice; think clearly.

Love all people, even those who have wronged you, if you would receive clear communications from over the border. It is possible that I may come as I have said. I do not know. But in any event, it cannot be long before you will join me over here, and I shall be on hand to welcome you, dear, dear mother, when you do come.

Oh, if only you could have brought yourself to have let me live at home to carry on my propaganda under your modifying advice, then this need never have been, and I could have lived for many years to carry on a moderate, far less crudely radical propaganda than I have done. I have had nobody to stand by me and to help me; I have had to carve out my own road without any predecessors to guide me.

You will find $40 in my trunk. I have written to Mr. Chamberlain to-night to tell you just where I have placed it. I do not know who may read this letter before you get it, and so have taken this precaution.

Will you mind expressing the various books I addressed here

to-night? As you know, I have been unable to get out to-day to send them off as I hoped to do. For there is an Adams Express Company on this street, several doors this side of Fifth avenue.

Dear, dear mother, please remember that I love you, and that I shall always love you. Even if you get fantastic communications from the border land, remember that the real Ida is not going there. The real Ida, your own daughter, loves you and waits for you to come soon over to join her in the beautiful blessed world beyond the grave, where Anthony Comstocks and corrupt judges and impure-minded people are not known. We shall be very happy together some day, you and I, dear mother; there will be a blessed reality for us both at last. I love you, dear mother; never forget that. And love cannot die; it is no dream, it is a reality. We shall be the individuals over there that we are here, only with enlarged capacities. Goodbye, dear mother, if only for a little while. I love you always. I shall never forget you, that would be impossible; nor could you ever forget me. Do not think the next world an unsubstantial dream; it is material, as much so as this; more so than this. We shall meet there, dear mother. Your affectionate daughter,

Ida C. Craddock.

iv. Farewell Letter

Room 5, No. 134 West 23D, St., New York, Oct. 16, 1902.
To the Public:

I am taking my life, because a judge, at the instigation of Anthony Comstock, has decreed me guilty of a crime which I did not commit—the circulation of obscene literature—and has announced his intention of consigning me to prison for a long term.

The book has been favorably reviewed by medical magazines of standing, and has been approved by physicians of reputation. The Rev. Dr. Rainsford of this city, in two letters to me, partially approved this book so far as to say that if all young people were to read it, a great deal of misery, suffering, and disappointment could be avoided, and that to have arrested me on account of it, as Mr. Comstock had done, was ridiculous. This little book, "The Wedding Night," and its companion pamphlet, "Right Marital Living," have been circulated with approval among Social Purity women, members of the W.C.T.U., clergymen and reputable physicians; various physicians have ordered these books from me for their patients, or have sent their patients to me to procure them or to receive even fuller instruction orally; respectable married women have purchased them from me for their daughters, husbands for their wives, wives for husbands, young women for their betrothed lovers. On all sides, these little pamphlets have evoked from their readers commendation for their purity, their spiritual uplifting, their sound common sense in treating of healthful and happy relations between husbands and wives.

In contrast with this mass of testimony to their purity and usefulness, a paid informer, who is making his living out of entering complaints against immoral books and pictures, has lodged complaint against one of my books as "obscene, lewd, lascivious," and proposes to indict the other book later on, so as to inflict legal penalties on me a second time. This man, Anthony Comstock, who is unctuous with hypocrisy, pretends that I am placing these books in the hands of minors, even little girls and boys, with a view to the debauchment of their morals. He has not, however, produced any young person thus far who has been injured through their perusal; nor has any parent or guardian come forward who claims even the likelihood of any young person's being injured by either of these books; nor has he even vouchsafed the addresses of any of the people from whom he states he has received complaints. In addition, he has deliberately lied about the matter. He stated to Judge Thomas of the United States Circuit Court (secretly, not while in court), that I had even handed one of these books to the little daughter of the janitress of the building in which I have my office. It so happens that there is no janitress in this building, nor is there any little girl connected with same. I took a paper around among the tenants to this effect, which they signed, and which I sent to the judge by my lawyer; also a paper to the same effect, which my landlord stood prepared to attest before a notary, if need be. But even this made no impression upon Judge Thomas; he still is firmly convinced (so he says) that Anthony Comstock is a strictly truthful man.

On Friday last, October 10, I underwent what was supposed to be a fair and impartial trial by jury; but which was really a most unfair trial, before a thoroughly partisan judge, at the close of which he abolished my right of trial by jury on the main question at issue, namely the alleged obscenity of "The Wedding Night" book. My counsel was not permitted to present in evidence circulars which showed that as far back as 1898 and 1899, I was accustomed to state in print that any applicants for oral instruction upon marriage who were under 21 would have to produce written consent from a parent or a guardian. My evidence was almost wholly choked off; neither my counsel nor myself was permitted to endeavor to justify the book by argument. The most the judge would do was to permit me to read from various paragraphs in the book, without comment, if these could explain the indicted paragraphs. Even with this tiny bit of a chance, I made such good use of my opportunity before the jury, that Judge Thomas, who was evidently prejudiced in advance against both myself and my book, saw that he dared not now risk the case to the jury, or he might not manage to convict me after all. And so he announced that he himself intended to pass upon the character of the book. He stated that there is in existence a decision of the United States Supreme Court which gives him this right.

He said he would not let the question go to the jury; he considered the book "obscene, lewd, lascivious, dirty." He added that he would submit to the jury only the question of fact. Did the defendant mail the book? (The charge was "mailing an obscene book.") He said, "Gentlemen of the Jury, the question for you to pass upon is, Did the defendant mail the book? You know that she admits having mailed the book. Please render your verdict. I do not suppose you will care to leave your seats." And the poor little cowed jury could do nothing but to meekly obey the behest of this unrighteous judge, and to pass in their ballots, "Guilty of mailing the book." Which, of course, was no crime at all.

I fully expected that the public press of New York city would duly chronicle this most remarkable invasion of the rights of the people by such an abolishing of the trial by jury; but so far as I could learn, the press remained totally silent.

It is evident that the political pull of the party which fathers Anthony Comstock is too powerful for any newspaper in New York to dare to raise a protest when, at the instigation of this *ex officio* informer, an innocent woman, engaged in a laudable work of sex reform, indorsed by reputable citizens, is arrested on false information and denied her right of trial by jury.

Since Friday last, people of influence and respectability have written to the judge on my behalf and have been to see him; but he announces his inflexible intention of sending me to prison, and, he is careful to malignantly add, "for a long, *long* term." I am a "very *dangerous* woman," he adds; Mr. Comstock has told him most shocking things about me—not in court, however, this paid informer being far too cute to dare to face his victim openly with any such lies.

At my age (I was forty-five this last August) confinement under the rigors of prison life would be equivalent to my death-warrant. The judge must surely know this; and since he is evidently determined to not only totally suppress my work, but to place me where only death can release me, I consider myself justified in choosing for myself, as did Socrates, the manner of my death. I prefer to die comfortably and peacefully, on my own little bed in my own room, instead of on a prison cot.

I am making this statement to the public because I wish to call attention to some of the salient features of Comstockism, in the hope that the public may be led to put down this growing menace to the liberties of the people.

As I said not long since in the Boston Traveler, if the reading of impure books and the gazing upon impure pictures does debauch and corrupt and pervert the mind (and we know that it does), when we reflect that Anthony Comstock has himself read perhaps more obscene books, and has gazed upon perhaps more lewd pictures than has any other one man in the United States, what are we to think of the probable state of Mr. Comstock's imagination today upon sexual matters?

The man is a sex pervert; he is what physicians term a Sadist— namely a person in whom the impulses of cruelty arise concurrently with the stirring of sex emotion. The Sadist finds keen delight in inflicting either physical cruelty or mental humiliation upon the source of that emotion. Also he may find pleasure in gloating over the possibilities to others. I believe that Mr. Comstock takes pleasure in lugging in on all occasions a word picture (especially to a large audience) of the shocking possibilities of the corruption of the morals of innocent youth.

This man serves two masters; he is employed and paid by the Society for the Suppression of Vice, but he secures from the United States Government an appointment as postal inspector without pay; so that he is able, if he wishes, to use his official position for the furtherance of the private ends of his society and, presumably of himself. *Ex officio* informers, with their attendant spies and decoys, have been throughout history notoriously a means of exploiting the government for private and corrupt purposes.

For over nine years I have been fighting, singlehanded and alone, against Comstockism. Time and time again I have been pushed to the wall, my books have been seized and burned, and I myself have been publicly stigmatized in the press by Comstock and Comstockians as a purveyor of indecent literature. Yet this very literature has been all the while quietly circulating with approval among men and women of the utmost respectability and purity of life, and I have received numerous letters attesting its worth.

Not only this, Comstockism can be used, as was the medieval Inquisition at times, to gratify private malice, as the complainant does not need to appear in court. This was done to me in Philadelphia because, while holding a petty position as amanuensis in the Bureau of Highways, I declined right along to pay political assessments to the Quay party. For months they tracked me night and day wherever I went, vainly hoping to learn something detrimental to my character, and at last they arranged to have me indicted for mailing immoral literature, as they could find no other means of successfully damaging my reputation.

John Wanamaker once stated in a political speech that the Quay party were relentless in hounding those who refused to pay political assessments. They would follow up such a person even when he went into the service of other employers, and leave no stone unturned to ruin him in after years. This may or not be so in my own case; I do not know. But I do know that when I went to Washington a secret complaint was lodged with the police. My accuser never faced me openly in court. I pleaded my own case before the police judge, saved one book ("Right Marital Living") and won many encomiums from those present in court because of the uplifting character of my plea; nevertheless I was driven from the city.

Each time that I have been arrested, I have escaped by a compromise; but I resolved, when I came to New York, that if again attacked by Comstockism, I would stand my ground and fight to the death. Perhaps it may be that in my death more than in my life, the American people may be shocked into investigating the dreadful state of affairs which permits that unctuous sexual hypocrite, Anthony Comstock, to wax fat and arrogant, and to trample upon the liberties of the people, invading, in my own case, both my right to freedom of religion and to freedom of the press. There is only one lawful excuse for the community's interfering with any one's religion or publication in America; and that is, the invasion by means of that religion or those publications, of other people's rights to life, liberty, or their pursuit of happiness. No proof of such injury wrought has been produced in my case; the testimony for the government against me rests entirely upon the mere say-so of this paid informer.

Every one of the paragraphs indicted in "The Wedding Night" is the outcome of talks which I have had with distinguished physicians and also with men and women among my pupils. I have looked into the hearts of hundreds of men and women during the nine years in which I have been engaged in sex reform work, and my soul burns within me when I see how husbands and wives are suffering, and how nearly all of the suffering could be done away with, if only Anthony Comstock were not hoodwinking the public into believing that sexual information in printed books must be kept away from them, so as to protect the morals of innocent youth. Surely, Mr. Comstock's idea of the nature of the marriage relation must be singularly impure, when he ventures to pretend that it should not be known of as to its details by young people who are sufficiently mature to be seeking for enlightenment!

In the courts, however, in obscene literature cases, a precedent has been established by which the defendant is forbidden to produce witnesses in behalf of the accused book, so that I was legally prohibited from summoning physicians to testify on behalf of the book.

Owing to this and to other legal precedents which hamper the defendant in obscene literature cases as is done in no other criminal cases anywhere; owing also the dense ignorance and prejudice which prevail in regard to the scientific open discussion of sexual matters; and, most of all, owing to Mr. Comstock's persistent lies and to his adroitness in depicting the shocking possibilities of corrupting the morals of innocent youth by permitting young people to peruse any enlightening literature upon the details of normal, healthy, pure marital relations—matters have now reached the point where it is only necessary to accuse a person of mailing so-called "obscene" literature in order to convict him. As no witnesses are allowed to testify as to the effect of the book upon themselves or their young daughters or young sons, or, if physicians, upon their patients, neither judge nor jury are in a position to learn the actual facts

in the case. And now, in my own case the other day, the legal
precedent has been established by the action of Judge Thomas, in
the United States Circuit Court, of not only excluding witnesses
in behalf of the indicted book, but even forbidding either the
defendant or her counsel to attempt to explain the reasons for
printing the indicted paragraphs or in any way seeking to justify,
in an argument, the publication of the book and then finally, by a
legal subterfuge, abolishing the defendant's right of trial by jury;
the latter being a proceeding which has always been recognized
by true patriots as a serious menace to the liberties of the people.

In addition, in my own case, there is the matter of persecution
for my religious views. Although this question did not directly arise
before Judge Thomas, yet, from the paragraph which I read from
my book, and which I was permitted to read only without explanation, it must have been evident that the book contained a religious
propaganda, and that, indeed, the religious teaching was the foremost matter, the physical teachings being only subservient thereto.

But in my trial under the New York state law last March, before
three judges the religious question did very decidedly arise. In that
court, Judge McKean so far forgot his oath of office (to administer
justice impartially) as to hotly denounce my book as "blasphemous"
(presumably because I am teaching the duty and the joy of communion with God in the marriage relation so as to render it
sacramental). Of course this was illegal on his part. No judge has
any right to denounce a prisoner because he differs with that
prisoner in his religious belief.

I earnestly hope that the American public will awaken to a sense
of the danger which threatens it from Comstockism, and that it
will demand that Mr. Comstock shall no longer be permitted to
suppress works on sexology. The American people have a right to
seek and to obtain knowledge upon right living in the marriage
relation, either orally or in print, without molestation by this paid
informer, Anthony Comstock, or by anybody else.

Dear fellow-citizens of America, for nine long years I have faced
social ostracism, poverty, and the dangers of persecution by Anthony
Comstock for your sakes. I had a beautiful gospel of right living in
the marriage relation, which I wanted you to share with me. For
your sakes, I have struggled along in the face of great odds; for your
sakes I have come at last to the place where I must lay down my

life for you, either in prison or out of prison. Will you not do something for me now?

Well, this is what I want the American public to do for me. Only one of my books, that on "The Wedding Night," is at present under legal ban. "Right Marital Living," which is by far the more important book of the two, and which contains the gist of my teachings, has not yet been indicted. Mr. Comstock, however, told me, when arresting me, that he expected to get both books indicted. If sufficient of a popular demand be made for this book, and especially if the demand voice itself in the public press, he will not dare to attack the book in the courts. Will you do this one thing for me, those of you who have public influence? Remember, it is for you and for your children that I have fought this nine-years' fight. And although I am going to a brighter and a happier land, nevertheless, I shall still look down upon you all here, and long and long and long that you may know something of the radiantly happy and holy life which is possible for every married couple who will practice these teachings. Even in Paradise I cannot be as happy as I might, unless you share with me this beautiful knowledge.

I beg of you, for your own sakes, and for the future happiness of the young people who are dear to you, to protect my little book, "Right Marital Living."

I have still other teachings to follow this, upon the marriage relation, later on. I have written a book of between 450 and 500 pages upon "Marriage" in which my teachings are set forth more fully. This book, in manuscript form, is at present stored in a safe place, in friendly hands. It will not be given to the public until such time as the public shows itself ready for it, and prepared to protect this fuller and franker book from persecution. Meanwhile, however, "Right Marital Living" remains unindicted; it sets forth a gospel of marriage which is being preached by no other teacher in America. Its teachings will make your married lives healthier, happier, holier. Will you publicly voice your demand for this little book, "Right Marital Living," and protect it from Anthony Comstock?

Ida C. Craddock.

IV

Radical Free Love

The Free Lovers

Anonymous

During the fall of 1855 the New York Times *ran a series of articles on free love. The first was a review of Mary Nichols' fictionalized autobiography* Mary Lyndon, *which was characterized as "recommending adultery as a personal right and social duty." It was followed by a long, detailed history of the movement, mentioning at least half the authors represented in this anthology. This was picked up by other papers and had a wide circulation. On October 10 the article printed here was published: on October 16 the* Tribune *took up the cry in a long article: and on October 18 the scandal-mongering led to a police raid on "The Club," with arrests of the doorkeeper and pro tem. host, Fourierist Albert Brisbane, who said at the station house that he was merely filling in for a sick friend, Stephen Pearl Andrews.*

In fact it was Andrews' club, and he was sick that night, as the subsequent trial and newspaper coverage brought out. Just how much of a "free love league" it was, must be a matter of judgment, for the Times *had its case to make, Andrews and Brisbane theirs.*

The Times *article speaks for itself below; here is the Club's answer, presented by Henry Clapp, who on the night of the raid had been one of the speakers:*

"The Club neither attacks nor defends existing institutions. It has nothing to do with them. It is an institution by itself. Its assemblies differ from the common run of social gatherings only in having a much wider scope of amusements, in more equitably distributing the burden of expense, in imposing less conventional restraints, in exercising a larger individual sovereignty, in keeping much better hours, and in being composed of men and women of more than usual intelligence, virtue and good sense.

"It will be seen that the idea of The Club being composed of Free-Lovers banded together for the purpose of abolishing marriage, defying public opinion, and indulging in sensual gratifications not permitted in what is called good society, has not the least foundation in truth."

Clapp then admitted that "Stephen Pearl Andrews, the Chief of the League, is a Free-Lover, and wishes in no way to shrink from any stigma or responsibility which may be attached to that name. He is openly opposed to marriage as a compulsory bond, and rejects the idea of legal interference in love affairs as strongly as he rejects it in religious affairs. He would abolish not only the conjugal idea but the private household itself, and substitute for the former Passional Attraction, and for the latter, the Collective Household.

". . . There are not only men identified with these principles, who attend our meetings, but women. Some of both of these parties are said to have separated from their conjugal partners and are reputed to believe and practice the doctrine that marriage is neither a civil or religious compact, in a technical sense, but a purely social and voluntary compact, based on mutual affection and differing from most other compacts in being dissoluble at the pleasure of either party."

The trial ended with the acquittal of all the accused, and a statement by the judge that the police had exceeded their duty. The mayor meanwhile let it be known that he thought The Club was of "immoral tendency" and "should be broken up." After the publicity that Andrews' group had received, there was no need for such threats. Society was temporarily safe from free love, thanks to the press and the city fathers.

Anonymous
The Free Lovers

In a recent article on the rise and progress among us of the doctrine that aims to substitute for the existing institution of Marriage, a Free-Love System, in which Passional Attraction shall be the sole guide and restraint of the intercourse of the sexes, we stated that there was in this City an organized Society called The League, devoted to the dissemination of those opinions; and that it holds weekly meetings at a central point in the City, which are attended by both sexes, and which are devoted to dancing, speaking, conversation, etc. A correspondent who has enjoyed ample opportunities of observation, sends us a sketch of the operations of this League,—which we publish as exhibiting something of the plan which the party seeks to inaugurate.

Passional Attraction is the watchword that unlocks the door of the secret places.

Passional Attraction—the tocsin which sounds the signal for the onset.

Passional Attraction—the rallying cry of the marshaled forces.

Passional Attraction—the beacon fire, the blood-red cross, the general order of the day.

Passional Attraction—the motto upon the Free Lover's shield—the words, blazoned in characters of gold, upon the standard he unfurls in the day of Battle—the symbol of the doctrine in which he lives—the faith in which he means to die.

In short—we have been in a Free-Love Meeting. "Passional Attraction?"—said the doorkeeper, as we requested entrance.

"Passional Attraction"—we replied.

"Twenty-five cents admission, Sir!"

"Sir."

We gained access to the inner mysteries of the Order. We heard the talk of hundreds. We sympathized with the enthusiastic outbursts of the faithful—until we found out exactly what they meant: and then the old leaven of Conservatism in our heart refused its sanction.

They danced; they made merry; they took part in plays of

● Selection from New-York *Daily Times* (October 10, 1855), 1–2.

whist and chess and backgammon, "jumped" each other at draughts; entered with zeal into philosophical speculations; regarded the relations of the sexes; touched upon the sinfulness of mankind; rejoiced in the freedom of woman; discussed the pages and embraced the doctrine of *Mary Lyndon;* were much delighted at the fairness of the strictures of the *Daily Times,* on which subject we strove to draw out the leaders of the movement; and after such converse, separated, each with a copy in his pocket of the Circular which the League has flung abroad to the winds, laden with seed for the dissemination of the doctrine.

A deep and a dark mystery lies shrouded in the web which that industrious spider—Passional Attraction—has woven. By your kind leave, Sir, we shall endeavor to unravel it.

The web is closely woven. It is somewhat difficult to see through it. There is a great deal of intricacy in its entanglements. It will not be strange if we fail to get at the sweetest of the kernels that are locked up in the secret storehouses.

Nearly a year ago, the disciples of the new System declared war against Conventionalism and organized a body which was then, and still is, known by the title of "The League." Its most common cognomen now is The Club. Its average number of visitors is one hundred and fifty. The members are generally pleasant-faced, jovial, communicative, sympathetic; restrained by no foolish pruderies. Introductions of parties who desire to cultivate each other's acquaintance are conducted upon the most liberal principles. You need fear no repulses—if the Passional Attraction only inspires the degree of magnetism that is necessary under circumstances of this nature.

The body is now fully in working harness. It remains to be explained how, when and where its operations are conducted. Yet here, most unluckily, there is a barrier. One of the dark convolutions of the web meets you at the first turn. Yet the progress is not slow; nor is the access to the temple so difficult as may be imagined by the uninitiated observer.

How It Came About

It is hardly two years since the system found an effective organization in this City. A gentleman who is very well known as an acute and able writer, a linguist, and a man of much general information, was the pioneer. He opened his house—invited his friends of kindred sympathies—prepared refreshments for the intellectual whose "attractions" drew them towards him—his lady, a woman of elegant manners, presided at these soirees, with grace and dignity—it was a select circle. In time it grew and strengthened —as all such affairs will grow and strengthen. New York was favorable to its development—philosophy found its expression, and Passional Attraction its end. At first it was intended that the body should have *a purely political bearing.* Measures were taken to accomplish this end. Even clergymen were brought into it. We could name these gentlemen if it were necessary. They would probably not be greatly obliged to us for doing so. In time, however, both clergy and "flock" decided that to popularize was better than to revolutionize. Hence, all things having had due weight, it was finally resolved to enlarge the sphere of operations—to remove to larger quarters—to open the doors of a place by means of regulations, rather than to continue meetings in private residences, through the agency of simple personal invitations. Being resolved upon, it was accomplished.

The formal organization of these Reformers was effected less than one year ago, in a bare, unpromising suite of apartments in the Bowery. In company with a friend, whose *Open Sesame* unclosed the portals, we entered. At the threshold stood a priest of the Order, holding in his hand a manuscript. This manuscript was the

Obligation

It reads, according to the best of our memory, something after the following fashion:

"In becoming a member of this League, you do solemnly declare that you will not promulgate anything to the detriment of the body, nor denounce, either publicly or privately, any member or members of the League: and you do further declare that so long as you continue a member of this body, you will not divulge any of the secrets that may be confided to your custody: and you do also promise that in case you meet with opinions or doctrines which you cannot embrace, you will quietly withdraw from the said League, and not bring disrepute upon the body through any publication, either in private or in public, of anything which you may have observed during the period of your membership herein. All this you do promise, upon your honor as a gentleman."

Having been required to subscribe to this formula, we naturally hesitate in speaking in any manner of the scenes which we have witnessed. For nearly a year, in truth, we have observed the utmost silence. No word, detrimental to or in praise of the policy of the League, has passed our lips. All we now propose to do, is to give such an idea of the workings of the plan known as the Free-Love System, as shall neither be offensive to the members of the community, nor tread upon tender callosities. Without any violation of the obligation which we were required to indorse, we may safely dwell upon the general principles that govern the action of the League. The seal of secrecy rests inviolate upon the chance conversations that we have heard. These were only the more minute elaborations of the theory upon which the League was organized. The Chief, to whom reference has been made, as a citizen well known and in respectable standing, will do us the favor to take no offense at our exposition of the plan he has inaugurated, and in the development of which he has succeeded in finding so many willing helpers.

The Present Quarters

The unfurnished apartments in the Bowery presently proved of too limited capacity. They were forsaken eight months ago. A suite of spacious rooms,—which have no drawbacks except a want of ventilation, a very considerable altitude, unpainted panes and some other things,—was engaged on Broadway. The place of meeting is now so familiar to several hundreds of persons, that we shall be pardoned for omitting to mention the number more definitely than to say it is among the 5's. We fall back upon the instructions of the League—which say:

"No steps will be taken to communicate to the public the times and places of its assemblages, nor the terms of admission. Those who are interested to inform themselves will find the means of doing so, or will wait till the information comes to them in some appropriate way."

Acting under our instructions, we respectfully desire the reader who may wish to penetrate the mysteries, to refrain from persecuting us for further information; being aware, as he now is, of the restrictions under which we labor.

How To Get In

Up three pairs of dingy staircases. Through tortuous passage-ways. In and out of a great receptacle of useless lumber. Past three doors of offices. Up—up—up,—till the last landing is reached. A small room is here partitioned off, to receive hats, cloaks, canes, a small table, and a heavily-bearded gentleman, *who receives the money*.

But it is not alone the key of silver that unbars these gates. The golden voice of approval is the potential lever. In plain English, you must be introduced. Your integrity must be vouchsafed, your sagacity indorsed. You then pay and walk in.

Entrance Fees Raised—And Why

Early in the day, it was but a trifling pull upon the purse strings to foot the bill for entertainment. The smallest piece of new silver —American currency—did the business.

But presently it was discovered that a larger amount had become necessary. Not that the exchequer was ebbing, but that the balance between the sexes hung unevenly. A considerable preponderance of gentlemen had rendered a choice of partners the occasion of much heart-burning. So the price of admission went up one hundred and fifty per cent. This arrangement still holds; but it is coupled with a provision that in case a lady and gentleman come in company, the former tariff for each person shall be considered as still prevailing. If it still happen that the gentlemen go unattended, the new scale of charges will be found in active operation. The change in the interior arrangements, in consequence of this action, is most salutary. Sunshine plays around the apartments, where late the lorn visages of mateless men reigned paramount. Peace prevails. The exchequer is replenished. Crowds flock in, and there is a happy season.

It is proper to state that the funds received in this way are the means relied upon to meet the demands of the landlords and Gas Company.

The Dressing Rooms

A pavilion, composed of red drapery, fences off a portion of the outer chamber. This is the retiring room for the ladies. It is not our province to enter it. The gentlemen, as they enter, deposit their outer garments miscellaneously upon the chairs and under them, or hang them on pegs stuck into the walls: or, if they be careful souls, they pay *two cents* and get a ticket, which insures the safe keeping of the articles that have been deposited.

The Inner Temple

One long apartment, uncarpeted and unadorned, leads into a
smaller one, which boasts a carpet and a few adornments. There
is a raised desk at the upper end, and below it are two large tables,
temptingly displaying chess and backgammon boards, piles of
playing cards, (for whist only,) and heaps of draughts-men.
Gathered about these places of favorite resort are groups of men
and women. In the outer room, dancing is going on. A fiddler,
playing not for money, but because of his "attraction," dispenses
music to the series. The "groups" distribute the "series," the
"series" produce the "harmonies." Attraction is the keystone that
binds them all together. And here let it be distinctly understood
that nothing is done here for the sake of "paltry pelf." All is
attraction—as we stated in the outset. If there is no attraction,
there is no magnetic sympathy. One is a consequence of the other.
A lady who has embraced the new doctrines fervently, said to us,
one evening, "We believe that there is a native sympathy between
minds of the same stamp, and this sympathy, which we term magnetic attraction, is that element of the mind which produces
affinities; and results, as a natural consequence, in mutual admiration." All which was very clear to us. And then she added, with a
smile that dinted the dimples in her cheeks and sank straight down
into our heart,—"I felt that you would be here; I had a magnetic
feeling that I could not have expressed; but I was as certain that
you would be here as I am certain that I live. I cannot explain it.
I don't know what put you in my thoughts. I had not thought of
you for months till to-night; but my impressions were vivid." We
thanked the lady for the compliment implied—declared it was
nothing less than a similar magnetic power which had drawn us
near to her—and in the interchange of thoughts, ideas, emotions,
forgot the hours, and dwelt contented in discussions of abstractions.

As we have before taken occasion to state, the number of persons
who are in attendance at the regular meetings of the Club averages
one hundred and fifty. The highest figure yet reached is, we
believe, somewhere in the region of Two Hundred; the lowest
notch is Sixty. For reasons already adduced, the proportion of the
sexes is nearly equal. The amusement chiefly patronized is the
dance. Conversation does not lag. There are several members who
have not been taught of Terpsichore, and so forsake the floor to

subside into dreamy quiet. Non-dancers will find attractions. Non-talkers will dance. All enjoy themselves.

Regular times of meeting are set apart. At first, it was only one day in the week. Now, it is twice a week. Presently, it will be every evening—so they say. The beginning and the middle of every week, Summer included, are the periods when the congregations go up, under the existing arrangements. The hour of opening is 8 P.M. The assembly disperses at 11. There is nothing during all this interval that will offend the sight. Those who may have conceived the most repulsive pictures of midnight orgies or licentious privilege, would find, if they entered the rooms of the Club, that there is nothing to repel the most delicate observer. Whatever there may be in the theory which binds these people together, there is, it must be said, nothing to the outward view which differs from the scenes of an ordinary family party.

If the "Passional Attraction" take another channel to develop itself, it is not permitted to bring disrepute upon the locality which the Club has chosen. Mind, we do not say that anything of an improper character has occurred, or can occur, elsewhere than in the immediate precincts of the Club. Our remark has simple reference to the erroneous opinions which we find prevalent in regard to the practices at these semi-weekly reunions. It is no defence of the principles, policy or tendencies of the new organization, that its character be presented in the true light.

Its Nominal Aims

A Circular, marked "Secret and Confidential," was picked up by a friend of ours a few weeks after the League took upon itself the form of a regularly organized Association. This Circular expresses the objects of the Propaganda. It declares that:

"The League is an organized body, with its headquarters in New York, its ramifications in the different towns and cities of the United States, and with a capacity of extension to all the countries of the world. Its existence marks an epoch in the progress of liberality and thought. . . . The League embraces men and women of all nations and creeds, whose religion is devotion to Humanity and Truth, without inquiring whether their conceptions are embodied in Abstract Principles or in Personal Forms. In the contemplation of the League, all Truth is equally Divine Truth, whether existing in the Discoveries of Science or in the Revelations of a Prophet. . . .

The League will adopt from all the existing institutions of Society, public and secret, those features which approve themselves to common sense, and to the principles of social science, so far as understood. Accordingly, different *Orders* will exist, within the League, communicating and cooperating with each other."

It is no harm to say here that the Orders to which reference is made in the Secret Circular are already organized—though only, as yet, in part. The sphere of their operation is very various. We have heard it hinted that the following are to be among the earliest to go into active operation:

The Grand Order of *Religion.*
The Grand Order of *Justice.*
The Grand Order of *Charity.*
The Grand Order of the *Social Relations.*
The Grand Order of *Recreation.*
The Grand Order of the *Beautiful.*
The Grand Order of *Discovery.*
The Grand Order of *Literature.*
The Grand Order of *Science.*
The Grand Order of *Labor.*
And—*ad infinitum.*

In addition to these, it is intended to found classes for instruction in the Languages (in fact these have already commenced in French); to occupy the desk with lectures, scientific disquisitions, and it is hinted that among the amusements provided for the entertainment of the company, private theatricals are to be introduced. The play will be liberally patronized. We are not sure but one of these displays will take place before the lapse of many moons.

All these add to the number of the "Attractions." They are mentioned here quite incidentally. Any corrections which the Chief may please to order, on the next evening of our meeting, we shall be happy to receive. It is quite possible that in making this running summary of the principles and objects of League or Club, we may have laid ourselves open to the charge of betraying the secrets of the Order. But we beg not to be misunderstood. We have been assured upon high authority that the publication of the sentiments of the body would give no offense, provided the details, the places and times of meeting, and so forth, were not furnished to a greedy public. This we have virtuously refrained from doing.

Real Objects, &c.

It now remains to be considered whether the real objects of this enterprise are properly understood by the public.

Is it true that Education and the development of Science are the great ends of the new organization?

Is it the fact that the assemblages of the believers are but a higher class of impure connections?

Neither of these positions is true.

The ultimate aim of the new movement is, unquestionably, that of producing a state of society similar to the one pictured in *Mary Lyndon.* Yet, in avowing that this is the real object of these demonstrations, candor and justice require the admission of the fact that no misconduct in public finds countenance among the members of the League. It is in private that the rules of the new society prevail. Publicity is not desired. The "attraction" of the Club is not like that of gravitation, operating in every time and place. It is a secret thing. It is locked up in the breast of the individual,—at least, until he finds a partner to share it with him.

The worst feature that we have seen in this scheme is its tendency to attract the Youth. Every evening when the Club gets together, there is a thick "sprinkling" of beardless faces—lads whose admission is neither desirable for their own sake nor that of society. Leering with sensual eyes upon the company, they seek only the gratification of the whim of an hour,—to boast of conquests afterward (if they make them). They have neither skill, experience, nor strength of character to resist, or guide, or suggest. We are given to understand that the propriety of admitting this class has been made the subject of earnest debate. It was determined, however, that no let or hindrance should be placed in their way.

Nor are all the grown men and women who attend these meetings earnest advocates of the system. Many of them are but "seekers after light"—as they are pleased to term themselves. They drop in at intervals to see the progress that has been made. They are often men of families. Their families occasionally accompany them —children and all. You may, as at other public places, buy bouquets of bright-eyed lads. You may have the company of a lady with a musical voice, who will sing to you and them. And you may chance to hear, as we did, of young men who came to laugh, and remain as devotees. A case of this kind happened only a fortnight ago. Two came, gave false names, returned to the keeper of the gate after an hour had elapsed, gave in their real names and their adhesion—and they are now "passionately attracted."

But the real, hearty Free Lover is an institution by himself.

If a man, he is exceedingly hirsute. Such eschew razors as an unclean thing. He probably affects a Byronic collar; has bushy hair; takes excellent care of his teeth, which usually sparkle like double rows of ivory; is careless in dress, but bathes freely, and so is not offensive. He is often a man of learning, profound in the languages of pleasing address, and is a rabid Socialist.

If a woman—and here, what shall we say? It is tender ground. We fear to offend, and yet may catch ourselves in the opposite extreme. The Free-Love woman is usually large-waisted. She is at least sufficiently sensible to know that she possesses organs which will not bear close compression. She is dressed very modestly. Young ladies at fancy balls would do well to take pattern from her (in this respect only.) She is necessarily strong-minded. She is fond of the society of gentlemen. Her affinities go out wool-gathering, like some men's wits. She occasionally lights upon an "attraction." The Free-Love woman (here they are all "women"; no "ladies" were ever made) is thoroughly posted up in the literature of the New School. She is likely to be a bit of a Phonographer, a Spiritualist, a Swedenborgian;—an artist, perhaps;—makes her living in the new channels of Industry;—is passionately fond of game, and beats all the men at a rubber of whist or a move upon the chess-board.

In person, she is cleanly, tidy, and not greatly given to the graces of the toilet. She affects ringlets, and the silky brown hair clusters over a brow which tells of intellect, perception, and a slim modicum of the moral or religious.

Many of the more rigid Socialists in this City have not yet signified their adhesion to the new plan. They stand aloof until such time as its practical operations shall become manifest. When that event is to transpire we have not been accurately informed. It is in the future.

Among the collaterals of this project are the ideas of establishing a great Restaurant, located in a block of Associational Buildings. At the tables there will be room for all; at the kitchen ranges, unheard of facilities. We are not aware that this portion of the project has yet reached fulfillment.

Finally

We have thus set forth the origin, plan and present position of the League. It is essentially the Head Quarters of the Free-Love movement in this City. It has not before arrived at newspaper publicity. The seal of secresy has been laid upon its acts. It has had no public advocates. All the agencies it has employed have been personal and secret. In the course of months, it has reached a height of prosperity which was not unexpected in a City like New York. Depending upon no favorable notices of the press, it has kept aloof from that respectable fraternity. Disclaiming any desire for notoriety, it has held no public convocation. Complete in itself, founded upon a single idea—Individuality—it has renounced communion with the existing Society, and stands, not exactly as the Pillar of Salt in the wilderness, but very much resembling in its tendencies the event which that monument is intended to commemorate. It looks back to *Barbarism*,—proposes to break the bonds of the marital relation,—declares that Passional Attraction is the great end of life,—that Divorce should be made easier,—that no man should be compelled to pass his life with a woman he cannot adore,—that women have by Nature a perfect right to the control of their persons, property and affections,—and that the existing system of social relations and obligations is absurd, unjust, and so rotten at the core that it must presently fall to pieces of itself.

In making this exposition of the new Theory, as reduced to Practice, we have not violated the confidence that was reposed in us. Among the thousand members which the League now numbers, there are many who will bear us witness that the sketch we have given is fair and truthful. We have nought extenuated, nor set down aught in malice.

The acts of the Club are on record. We have given them their first public airing.

Free Love; or, Love in Freedom

James Clay

"*Of what avail is all this precept without a corresponding practice?*" *This is the way James Clay ended his book* A Voice from the Prison, *which he wrote while serving six months for practising what he preached in Gardiner, Maine—free love. (See Section III above for Clay's case.) Clay was a free lover of the anarchist wing, had been at Modern Times, and also went to Berlin Heights in search of a truly libertarian community. Even more than Henry C. Wright or Stephen Pearl Andrews, Clay was a purist of individualism. He was a "come-outer" whose focus was secular although his rhetoric was evangelical: "Marriage slavery, first of all," he wrote the editor of* The Social Revolutionist, *"chattel slavery, wages slavery; legislation which creates, sustains and perpetuates the law which perpetuates these slaveries; the sword and the soldiery which back up the law; intemperance which makes the soldiers, and the whole monied interests and power, and I might have added the religion of our fathers, which lies back of all these—are but fragments of one great whole evil which true reformers repudiate.*"

Like other individualist free lovers, Clay's voice sometimes sounds hoarse with insistence. There is no letting up. But at his best he can bring his cause to life with the wit and common sense of a Thoreau, whose own prison memoir, "Civil Disobedience," was similarly critical of the right of the majority to decide matters of conscience for everyone. "Now," says Clay, "I do not object to the majority ruling themselves as wisely or as foolishly as they are wise or foolish; but I do protest . . . that any majority, or minority, exercise their laws over me, when I infringe not on the rights of other individual beings."

Clay reported that people told him "most of your ideas are very good, . . . but your free-love doctrines would spoil all the rest." His reply was characteristic: free love, he said, was the "corner stone" of all his beliefs. "Freedom which would place us under any other rule than that of love, and love which cannot let us be free to live true to our own internal desires, are neither absolute love nor freedom. . . . Freedom cannot exist without love, nor love without freedom." He wrote this in jail, one of the first free lovers called to account for his affronts to popular mores and the law of the land.

James Clay
Free Love; or, Love in Freedom

For what I have to say of free love, or love in freedom, I have my own experience to sustain me, as well as sound philosophy. Though very humble, I do not feel that I am the lowest of the low, the vilest of the vile, in point of morals; though I am accused of licentiousness because I advocate free love, and have been tried before the courts of men, and by them condemned; sentenced and imprisoned as brutes should not be. If there doth a mark appear on me, it is only the reflection of the marks of their own hearts. God has not put one there for free love; and that suffices for me.

For much that I am,—good it seems to me comparatively; others may call it evil if they must,—I am indebted to love in freedom— to good women who could take me to their bosoms in love when I wished to go there, and let me go in freedom when I chose to do

---

● Selection from *A Voice from the Prison*, Boston: Bela Marsh, 1856, pp. 45–47, 62–72, 79–82.

so; neither of us giving or receiving any earthly bond whatever. I
never had a more healthful, ennobling, refining influence exerted
over me than was done by women, free, independent, truthful
women, who loved in accordance with nature's laws, rather than
according with the prostitution of statute law.

There are many objections to free love, that come up to the
undisciplined mind—to those who have no thought of doing well
without some external force of evil to stimulate them; but such
objections are all answerable, and will be answered to themselves
satisfactorily, as they progress in the knowledge of the truth.
Such need only to pursue the truth they already are in possession
of, that a greater light may shine on their path. It is useless that we
close our eyes to the ray of light that environs us, and pray for all
wisdom. It is only by being truthful to our present convictions of
right, that greater truth will unfold itself to us. One objects, saying
that females will be seduced and abandoned. It is not so; they will
be loved, honored, respected and cared for, for their life and virtues.
It is now that woman is abandoned, and often more than abandoned and degraded by servitude—driven to prostitution and to
death, with a hope to save themselves in life; wedded and unwedded
pollution. These are hard sayings, but the doings are more so. None
who have a knowledge of the doings in our cities will deny the truth
of the prostitution out of wedlock there; and the calendars of our
county jails own up to some extent there. But think you they tell all,
or one tithe? Prostitution in wedlock would seem out of joint to
those who think everything lawful godly; but if it is not prostitution when a worthy woman is obligated to submit to the lusts of
an unworthy husband, whom she cannot truly love, then in Heaven's
name, what is it? It might, perhaps, better rank with the next crime
to murder, whose penalty is state's prison for life, were it not made
honorable, as murder committed by the state's authority is.

•   •   •

I need not be told that the mass of mankind are happy in their
marriage bonds, any more than be told the African slave is happy
in his bonds. Ignorance may be a solace for what would otherwise
be the deepest anguish. But the facts tell us, if either condition
affords happiness, it is only comparatively, and that it is the exception and not the general rule. Our barrooms, our smoke-saloons,
our country stores and dramshops, our business men who seek

excitement in their business and money hoarding, in whose every thousand pocketed lies buried a human being, tell us the charm is not at home, but is sought in vain dissipation.

I have thought it would be impossible to give statistics, showing the proportion of comparatively happy ones; knowing that it was something as much as possible secluded from the public gaze. Family troubles are usually only known to friends as the necessity of the case requires. As a lady recently expressed to me in a correspondence: "It is one great lodge, in which members are sworn to secrecy by solemn oaths, the penalty for the violation of which is worse than a thousand deaths. Yet, for all this secrecy, it cannot be hid. 'Murder will out,' as the saying is. I presume there is hardly one but knows of some little difficulty or great trouble existing between a large portion of those families with whom they are on intimate terms."

I have a statistic of English society that came to my hand casually (and I will here say that all these facts and principles came to me in a similar manner, rather than by any effort on my part), which I will give in the words that it came to me through the public press: "An English paper, descanting relative to the various qualities of connubial bliss, states that in the city of London, the official record for the past year stands thus: runaway wives, 1132; runaway husbands, 2348; married persons legally divorced, 4175; living in open warfare, 17,345; living in private misunderstanding, 13,279; mutually indifferent, 55,340; recorded as happy, 3175; nearly happy, 127; perfectly happy, 13."

This is no creature of the imagination,—nothing that comes from the opposers of the marriage law,—but a public document from the lovers of statute law, which they think is productive of good order.

Now, what does all this mummery about legal marriage or legal divorce amount to? What is there of all these connections that is sacred, holy, or divine? What that a wise people would desire to be perpetuated? The only true marriage is that of love; and when that heaven-born tie ceases, the only holy connection is broken, and any other bond can only be enforced by destroying the parties concerned; it matters not what that bond may be, whether an oath backed up by penal laws, or a mutual contract perpetuated by public opinion. Where is the real difference whether all these ninety-six thousand couples are married by civil (uncivil) law, or without it; or whether they separate by legal divorce, or without it; or whether these eighty-five thousand that are living in mutual indifference, private misunderstanding, and open warfare, remain enslaved to each other by statute law and public opinion, or separate without legality, and form new connections when they choose? Everything is in favor of individual freedom. To go into the cold calculations of dollars and cents,—which, by the way, is a pretty high standard with the world, for a certain amount of dollars make vice virtue, as numbers legalize murder and make it honorable,—there was probably more than a million of dollars directly and indirectly expended to legalize these marriages, which, by every standard that is pure and good, are after all *il*legal. The four thousand legal divorces would, in our state, cost, perhaps, one hundred dollars each, which would be four hundred thousand dollars; and what better is one of these connections for the legality, or what worse would be one of the separations without legal authority? Just the difference there is between the legalized murder of nations and the illegal murder of individuals, which is none at all in the moral point of view, except that the one is reprobated and the other is honored; the one is committed without public charge, and the other is at the public expense, involving the whole in the sinful act. The one is an evil on a small scale, and the other on a large scale. The only real difference I can see between those marrying and divorcing, is that the one may be done without the meddling of any third party, or incurring any expense, and the other calls in persons who really have no business in the affair, and opens a door for a third party to live on or speculate out of the other two.

How very much better it would be for those seventeen thousand Londoners, who are living in open warfare, to separate, than remain enslaved, and quarrel like a nest of wolves! If England wishes to raise an army to carry on her wars, such are the relations in which to propagate her sons; for those only best suited to the inhuman work of human butchery are propagated in such relations, —discordant in themselves, as England's whole aggressive system is discordant with itself and harmonious nature.

Are England's shores so far away that England's wrongs and English laws may not be cited to show their effect on her subjects? With slight exception, and that not always for the better, American custom is but the echo of her mother's voice. In the absence of special enactments, England's "common law" is the standard which

is recognized as authority throughout the New World. Our fathers
brought with them most of the follies of the Old World; and
though they threw off England's yoke, it was by putting their
necks into another, but little less worse to be borne; and now,
though we laud the name of freedom to the skies, as a nation we
are guilty of requiring a servitude that Britain's laws have long
since ceased to tolerate. But we need not cross the Atlantic, or leave
New England's soil, to find a similar state of affairs.

Recently I conversed with a lady, formerly a teacher, who
"boarded round," as is often customary in the country, and she
told me that in a whole district in which she had taught, there
was not a pair who were really happy in their domestic relations;
though in a day's visit to each she might not have discovered any
trouble, except as seen in the little children, who would not, if they
could, conceal the fruits of their example.

I was recently talking with a gentleman on this subject, and
he said to me, "This evil does not exist to the extent you imagine.
You have dwelt on the subject so long, that you have it fixed in
your mind that it is a reality, when it is not so." I proposed to
him that we take one district with which he was acquainted,—
which, by the way, was much more than an average of our New
England society, in regard to externals, all except two being free-
holders, and what is termed temperate men, and residing in a
rural district,—and see what we could ascertain by analysis. The
result was, out of ten pairs taken promiscuously, only three there
were but my friend was ready to admit were "bad matches." Two
had separated, two had fought with each other like tigers, sometimes requiring neighbors to interfere and separate them, and one
or two were secretly accused of being directly or indirectly the
cause of their partner's death, and the others were known to have
minor difficulties; and one pair out of the three not included in
the seven,—though for aught we know living comparatively happy
together,—yet were separated in their church-going, for they could
not sit under the same pulpit doctrine. After we were through,
said my friend, "I will give it up; you are better posted up on the
marriage question than I."

To say that any matches are happy, is only to say that love
triumphs over the bonds, which makes the latter of no effect. It is
when the true marriage of love does not exist, that the false one
of bonds destroys.

Now the fault is not so much in the people, though they were

created in these falses, as in the false institutions. Nature, ever
ready in her beneficient designs, makes the best of everything, and
it is by dint of great perseverance in pursuing the wrong that so
much evil exists. We were made for more than one love, or the love
of one little isolated house-hold, with our hand against every one's,
and every one's against us. Are we not one great brotherhood, and
God the Father of us all, and our interests a unit? And how shall
we realize such a fact, except by a freedom to love all? Where
the man, where the woman, that can truly say they never loved but
one, though their whole life-long education has been to teach them
that such love was sinful?

Oft have I asked the question, "Did you never love but one?"
and I never yet had a full, frank, open, negative answer. But if
such persons exist, their isolation should be respected. They should
live their own true life, and should be equally content that communists should theirs.

A mother, that has a second, third, or fourth child born to her,
does not love the first less; and a humane mother can love other
children than her own by birth. All that she can truly love are her
own by the great tie of nature, and it is only unnatural, a perversion of nature, that she does not love each and all.

Who ever heard the anecdote, without applauding the mother,
who, at great peril of her own life, rescued a child from imminent
danger? On its being remarked, "It was not your child," she replied,
"Well, it was somebody's else child!" The maternal sympathy was
universal in this mother, and the press, ever ready to herald so
noble a sentiment, resounded and echoed it almost from pole to
pole.

As the good mother may love all good children, so the good
man or woman may love every other good woman or man. There
is no bond wanting to exact such love; but if such does exist,
where the sin, where the wrong? Can nature, so lavish of the blessing of love, give it to us to cause us so much trouble to suppress it?
The stinting of love that has an outbreak in vice and licentiousness,
is unworthy of so holy a name, though it flounce in silks, or roll
in gilded carriages.

They that love, purely to consummate nature's holy design, need
not limit or bind such; but they who love only to gratify lust, a
perverted passion, may well ask bonds to hold their victim, for the
pure natural tie does not exist.

Says the rhymer, who probably had had some experience in the matter:

> The happiest life that is ever led,
> Is always to court, and never to wed.

It is unquestionably true, though the blessing of maternity be denied the unwedded. The blessing of maternity does not compensate the sacrifice of freedom. How often I am told, "If I were not married I never would be; but I must make the best of it now."

Mankind are so inured to unhappiness, so surrounded by, and within the iron grasp of, these giant wrongs, that they have settled their minds into submission, giving up all hope of reprieve except through death; though they grudgingly pay for a proxy prayer, "Thy will be done on earth as in heaven," and then go their way to refill their purses from their brother's earnings, or in pursuit of toil to earn their daily bread.

Enlightened men unhesitatingly demand freedom in almost everything else but in love and maternity, where rather than in any other circumstances, they should be free. They put their necks into the yoke, and bow submissively to as cruel a despotism as ever the sun rose on.

Man and woman, as pure and as loving as the nestling dove, may not join to consummate nature's holiest design without first bowing to this dastardly rule; and others, more discordant and foul than a brood of hyenas in their den, once joined may not separate, but remain enslaved to increase the evil, and people the world with their kind.

What wonder that the world is such a charnel-house since man's beginning must be in such bondage, antagonism, and depravity, and his maturing life-examples a continuation of the same? If there is an unpardonable sin, it is in the propagation of our species in discordant relations.

How frequently have I asked the question, and seldom with a dissenting voice, "Were not your days before marriage the happiest you ever experienced?" Then love was enjoyed in freedom; there were no bonds; and no little act of kindness or courtesy, that could render each other more happy, was overlooked. Alike might be the result throughout life in freedom.

In freedom there would be every inducement for each party to be always agreeable, kind, and really good, knowing each of them that it was dependent on such qualities that they have and retain such partners as they desire. And then, too, teach woman the laws of her being and those of her offspring,—let her know the fact that, as well as her own sins, those of the father of her child are visited on the babe,—and she will seek the purest, the noblest man for the father; which would be a stimulus to induce the males to purify themselves by temperance in all things, and obedience to all of God's laws; and woman would be alike induced to make herself really good, else she could not have the companionship of the best. Such would have a tendency to renovate and raise the race from the thraldom of sin that now almost engulfs them. Soon it would be a great shame that a woman bear an unloving, sickly, or otherwise than a beautiful babe.

To say there is no natural tie that would bind the father to the mother of his babe, is to say that God, who made man a little lower than the angels only, made him more unloving, unkind, than the fowls of the air or beasts of the forest. No love-babe would ever go a-begging destitute of a father, and a good father, too; and there would be none others than love-babes. It could no longer be said that man was conceived in sin. He would no longer be conceived in bondage without love, but in freedom, in love, in harmony; and then again would man bear the image of God in his soul and body, and beauty, symmetry and harmony, take the place of ugliness, deformity, and discord.

There would be a holy atmosphere surrounding the relation of the sexes, and not, as now, a waste of life in improper sexual connection, creating a repugnance on conception, as is now often the case, to such a degree that the father forsakes the mother, and she often procures abortion or commits infanticide. A woman conceived without sin would be above such crimes, would be happy within herself, and would look forward with extreme pleasure as well as enjoy present bliss; and a corresponding satisfaction would pervade the mind of the father.

One fact I wish to recur to in this connection, which is almost proverbial for its truthfulness. Illegitimates, as they are called, who are born out of legal wedlock, are much more than an average of the race, though bred under the most crushing influence of public reproach, and surrounded by all the other evil influences of those in the bonds of wedlock, even that of unintentional conception.

I have written much to convince, if possible, my truth-loving friends, that freedom in the love relations is preferable to bonds, even in society with its present falses in other matters. But free love will only exist in name,—a farce, and not a reality, as by far too much which now passes as pure coin is,—if it do not change the circumstances, removing all the seeming hindrances to the realization of perfect peace, harmony, and happiness.

Freedom is the sovereign remedy for all bondage or slavery, and love for all enmity and discord, and the two are the "refiner's fire" and "fuller's soap" that are to purify and cleanse all nations of earth, and make the whole one vast kingdom of heaven.

The world, so to speak, are in arms, striving for freedom, but are thinking to obtain it without God, who is love. They all desire love, also; but they think they must put that in bonds. The two principles, each harmonious with themselves, with each other, and with nature, they would cross with another principle, inharmonious in itself and discordant with these true principles and with nature; therefore they fail in obtaining or retaining either the blessing of love or freedom.

The world have failed to separate and classify the good and evil principles, or they adopt the maxim that they are necessary evils. Ere the world is redeemed they must separate the good from the evil, and save the good by good, and let the evil die side by side by their own destructive kind.

Some would-be wise men would feign clothe themselves with the air of philosophers, and deem love a mark of weakness, and think it worthy only of silly women and children; but such have to learn that love is strength, is wisdom, and that they are the fools, and that their a, b, c, in the true philosophy of life, health, and happiness, they are yet to derive through the natures of these true philosophers.

Freedom in love is to result in the universality of love, and a community of love, which is to be followed by a community of property, which is to be founded in truth, on a community of interests in each other's life and happiness. The ruling power must be love, or God, the only power which does not destroy. Evil must overcome itself, and God be all in all. In the kingdom of heaven, which is to be on this earth, true principles are to rule, not by any usurped or arbitrary power vested in any one, but by common consent. The servant will really be the master.

• • •

I am told that such a state of society as I anticipate would be the realization of the millennium, and would be desirable, if the world was ready for it; but that mankind are too corrupt, and that the good would be overpowered by the evil and lost, if they undertook to sustain themselves without an external government, or evil, free to protect them;—that the tiger is loose, and he must be caged and tamed, ere we can be secure with freedom. Such is the blindness of the world, that they look afar off for the destroyer when it is within themselves. If these objectors will subdue the tiger within themselves, they will feel a security in themselves; and, though they have every other enemy in the universe secured, if they have not control of their own passions they are still insecure. If there be no internal foe, there can no harm come from an external one. The security for the good is in the good—in being good. The destruction of the evil is in the evil—in being evil.

The world is as ready for the good as ever it can be, without the good making it better by their goodness. If we send one tiger to chain another, then the greater tiger is left unchained; and after we have done all we can do in this way, there is still left the biggest of them all to be conquered.

Said a lady, from whose letter I have made a quotation, "I can see but one course that promises a radical cure for the whole. Let those who are ready for the sacrifice step boldly out from the marriage ranks, and face the whole enemy in the open field. The sight of these, though few they are, will strengthen and encourage those who are faltering, and soon they will join us. Our numbers thus augmented will encourage still others, who will grow strong at the sight of numbers, and thus on, and on, until the field is won."

In a recent correspondence with a lady, who was not ready for the sacrifice of a present reputation, but chose rather to submit to the marriage bonds, I wrote thus: "Does it ever cross your thoughts that your loved one desires the company of another? Do not check the desire, but rather anticipate it for him, and send him away with a merry, loving smile, and go about your business, not with a sad, jealous, lonely heart, as though your all was gone, but with a light, joyous one, as though he had gone to bring you greater riches; and be assured as your faith is so will it be unto you. One that loves with such ennobling love, has more power to keep the good than all the bonds the world ever dreamed of."

The lady's advice would reach one class who are strong and ready for the greatest sacrifice or penalties of society, while mine would reach those of less strength. Everything we can do to enlarge the circle of love and friendship should be done.

Need I here add that these principles correspond with those taught by Jesus Christ, and that they are purely the teachings of nature, and the foundation of a true state of society, that shall raise mankind from the depths of sin into which they have fallen, and elevate them to a sphere so beautiful that they will look back on the present only with surprise that they so long suffered in it, and with thankfulness that they have escaped? The far-seeing, truthful reader has already come to that conclusion, and with all his heart bids them God-speed. But they who are so blinded by their sins, and the traditions of their fathers, that they see not these truths, or, seeing, understand them not, or understand them, yet unable from the surrounding circumstances to advocate or respect them, must do as they must, while I do as I must. But I beg they, for their own sakes, will make use of no violence to suppress these truths, which are impregnable.

If they are not truths, it can be shown so, and they will hide their heads for shame; but if they are true, violence to those who live them cannot suppress them. It will only bring ignominy on the persecutors, while the persecuted and their cause will shine with a more radiant light. Then I say to unbelievers, hold your peace, else show to the world that the two principles, each so desirable of themselves,—freedom which you fight for, and love which you pray for,—are unworthy of you when obtained.

Free Love Fairly Stated

Joseph Treat

Of the extremists of free love, Joseph Treat was among the most extreme. Here we see him arguing the case in the movement's most radical journal, The Social Revolutionist, *which with its 400 subscribers (a dollar a year) was the voice of free love in the West— that is, Ohio. Treat was one of the founders of the Berlin Heights community, which after 1857 took the place of Modern Times in the public eye as the cesspool of sexual experiment in America. At the time he wrote this challenge (January 1857) Treat had just moved there from Garretsville, on the other side of Cleveland. John Patterson was thinking of moving* The Social Revolutionist *from its home in Greenville, and C. M. Overton was arranging to come up from nearby Yellow Springs, where the Nichols' new emporium of water cure and free love, Memnonia, was also to open soon—a competing community that Overton seems to have rejected in favor of Berlin Heights. Other free lovers had decided to come from all parts of the state—and even further, for James W. Towner finally brought his family all the way from West Union, Iowa.*

Nonetheless, Treat began his article by saying that half his readers were not yet sold on free love, an estimate measurable in the columns of the magazine, where anti-free love spiritualists like Alfred and Anne Denton Cridge, or merely political radicals like L. A. Hine, also found an audience for their views. By early 1857, however, The Social Revolutionist was certainly well on its way to doctrinaire free love, and most of its contributors were people like Francis Barry, the chief leader at Berlin Heights, Jared Gage, who was thrown out of Antioch for his friendship with the Nichols, and various pseudonymous correspondents like "Peter Socialist," a quick-witted, cantankerous free lover from Boston.

Moreover, as Treat hints in his manifesto, there were free lovers and then there were free lovers. He himself belonged to the "continence" school, which argued that variety in love was innocent, but only so long as it was not "ultimated" except for procreation— and that meant, for Treat and others, very seldom. Theirs was not the Catholic view that allowed for frequent intercourse so long as no artificial means of contraception were used. Rather, one gathers, the whole idea was that only successful procreation could justify the lapse of chastity, even once. "Tell me my children's names," boasted Treat hypothetically, "and you have told the number of my every-attractions to the sexual embrace."

In the selections in Section V, on Berlin Heights, it will be seen that Treat finally broke with the community on just this issue, of "purity" in free love. Later he turned up in New York City, as a lecturer on various radical topics, and was for a while an enthusiast in Victoria Woodhull's entourage. Woodhull claimed to be shocked when Treat suddenly turned on her, in 1874, and published a "scurrilous" pamphlet revealing her doings with Tilton, Beecher, and others. It is not so difficult to understand his about-face in the light of this earlier episode at Berlin Heights; probably he would have reversed himself again in 1875, when Woodhull herself surprised everyone by taking up his old cry, no coition except for procreation—but by that time he had dropped out of sight.

Joseph Treat
Free Love Fairly Stated

Free Love requires explanation. It would not, if people were only thinkers; for then it would be its own explanation. The name itself, would tell all. But as it is, half the readers of the *Revolutionist* are yet unconverted; and they will remain so, till something more is said. Seeing they will not think for themselves, somebody must think for them. And besides; men befog and pettifog the question, till many honest, but simple-minded people, are unable to see on which side the truth is. So listen, good brothers, male and female, and say what you can object to this—statement of Free Love.

The matter is very simple—plain enough, one would suppose, for even a child to comprehend. The whole doctrine is comprised in two words—Freedom, and Love. Freedom is good, and Love is good; and then Free Love is. And at last, the whole doctrine is comprised in that one word—Freedom. If you are not free to love, you are not free.—Then if *words* are any test, we've found one thing in the Universe that's good; and that's Free Love!

But, now, just think a little. Is Marriage, Free Love? Is it even Freedom? What is Marriage? A man and woman living together? No; for they might live together one day, and not the next—one year, and not the next. And a man might live with one woman awhile; and then with another; and after that with still another; and so on, all his life. So there is no Marriage in simply living together. Well; is Marriage living together all the time? No; it takes something more than that, to make Marriage—it must not only be true that they live together all the time, but also that they must so live. Marriage is not living together, but having to live together. Living together, or not, just as they chose, would be Free Love— Freedom: but being bound to live together, any how, is what makes it marriage. Marriage is the indissoluble tie. "You two promise to live together and love each other, till Death do you part."—that's Marriage; but it's slavery, too, isn't it? Marriage is always slavery, isn't it? For you are not free to love, in Marriage; and if you are not free to love, you are not free. And you are not free to love, because you've sworn away your freedom! Said you'd love one, and

---

● Selection from *The Social Revolutionist*, III (February 1857), 52–56.

wouldn't any more! Tied your hands! That's the meaning of, "Tying the knot," I suppose? And as the upshot of the whole matter, you have made a slave of yourself all round, haven't you?

And then you have enslaved somebody else, too; you are a tyrant, as well as a slave—a despot and a slave all in one. For you have made your wife a slave just as she has you; you are both slaves, and both tyrants—you own her, and she owns you. You can't do as you have a mind to, because she won't let you, and you are her *property;* she can't do as she has a mind to, because you won't let her, and she is your property. If you love another, she will be jealous of you, and stir up a muss generally; and if she loves another, you will report it all round as proof of her "infidelity," and the whole town will be down on her. You can't even look at an attractive woman, but she throws it in your face; and she can't receive a letter from a gentleman, but you instantly take both him and her under your surveillance. And all this, simply because you two are married! You have agreed to own each other; and now you are going to hold each other to it.

Did you ever think of it? The time is soon coming when the question will be, Does that man own any one? Has that woman a slave?—not, Is that man married? Has that woman a husband? It will be own and only "slavery," right out.

"But people can get divorced." Wonderful! They can, can they? And after they have *got* divorced, go straight off and get tied up again? More wonderful still, ha, ha! Mighty sight of good it did them, didn't it? How much easier not to have got tied up in the first place! The fault is in getting tied up at all; not in getting tied wrong—at all is wrong. The very idea of Divorce proves this. Divorce and Marriage are contradictions—if Divorce ought to be, then Marriage ought not to be. People are big fools, to believe in Marriage *and* Divorce.

Free Love, then, sweeps away Marriage, at once, and forever. Free Love is liberty; Marriage is slavery—the one can not co-exist with the other. All who mean to be free, must give up Marriage, give it up unconditionally and eternally. They can't have it and they mustn't dream of having it. It can't be theirs, any more than darkness can be light, nor than life can be death. But they can live together in pairs; and have and rear families. They can do this as well as not; but it will not be Marriage. They can do this if they want to, and because they want to—not because they have to—

because they have agreed to. If they ever did agree to, their first
act ought to be to recant that agreement, and each leave the other
free—free to live together as long as they please—free to go from
each other when they please. If they are not thus free, even free to
go, if they choose—then they are not free, but only slaves! And if
one of them wants this freedom, but the other not, then let that one
have it—he or she has just as good a right to it, as if the other
wanted it too. And if Society is not willing they should live this
freedom, then let them live it in spite of Society; for they have a
perfect right to. They too, have a right against the whole world;
and each one of the two, has a right even, against the other.
Individuality, is the first and supreme right of Humanity.

Then all that Free Love demands for men and women in this
matter, is this right to be free. If they want to live together in
pairs, and have and rear families, why, let them—Free Love wants
they should. They wouldn't be free if they didn't. But if they
don't want to, who are you to say, they shall? Hug your own
chains if you will;—but don't presume to impose them on others!

"But the consequences"—will take care of themselves; why won't
they? Those who are good, will do right without being made to;
and those who are not good, won't have Free Love anyhow, and
you can't make them; but on the contrary, they stand right where
L. A. Hine does, and kick and butt against it as lustily as even
he could desire.—Evermore, the law of development on this planet
is this: A truth will never hurt anybody; those who are on a level
with it, will of course act in a line with it, and then there will be
harmony; and those who are not on a level with it, to them it is
not truth!

"But families will be broken up!" Compelled families will—voluntary ones, not.—Any objections? Don't take long to "curry that
horse."

"But the flood-gates of impurity!" Bah! *You* to talk about "flood-
gates"! As if there could be any others equal to those you have got
open, but we are going to shut.—The Free Lovers are the purest
people in the world—that's precisely what makes them Free Lovers.
But you—steeped in all the abominable filth and sickening stench
of your marriage system—all your lives compelling and compelled
to the most disgusting whoredom and lechery—it mightily becomes
you to hold up your pious hands in horror, at mention of Free Love!
Your pardon, good saints of the present dispensation of virtue

according to marriage, (O!) but we didn't happen to mean what you were thinking of!—Our Free Love don't go on all fours with your (so-respectable, and Christian, and none the less free!) lust. But what is most in men's heads, will come uppermost sometimes.

There are but four classes of lovers; (if all of them can be called lovers!) and Free Love will never make things worse—on the score of purity—in the case of any of the four. At one extreme, are the Absolute Continents (very few, I admit—I wish they were more) ; those who believe only in parentage: no one supposes that in Free Love, these would ever hurt anybody, nor be hurt by anybody. And at the other extreme, are the true Lusters—the absolutely disgraceful people—those who make no stick at giving themselves up to debauchery and uncleanness: but neither would these be made worse by Free Love, for they are almost perfectly free now (so far as their lust is concerned, not so far as their love), either in spite of society—as libertines and prostitutes—or else (and also) in society—in the marriage bed. But I claim that they would be even made better, and it is infallibly certain they would: even so that Free Love (could they only be some of them permitted, but most of them persuaded to accept it) , would prove their very medicine—just the thing that would surely redeem them. For if they possessed love—though it were no higher love than they were capable of—it would yet be more than they have now, and so would take the place, in great part, of their present worse-than-beastliness. Love is after all the true savior—equally when men can't have it, and when they won't have it; and none need it more than these so-called, Most-of-all-unprepared-for-it!

Then, for the means between the two extremes, we have, first, the great body of the people—the staid, good, moral ones (so they are called, but their beds never testify to this!) connecting with those lowest-of-all below them; and then above these, and forming the link between them and the Continents, the Free Lovers gener- ally so known—ever so much better and purer than the big multi- tude just described, but, nevertheless, not so far along (so I think) as those Continents. But the first of these last two classes will not be hurt by Free Love, for they are to a man, opposed to it,—they are L. A. Hine, every hair on their heads, and as to the Free Lovers, though I am not one of them (one of this kind) , yet I will say for them, that they are infinitely in advance of those who are so reviling them, and hounding them like dogs through the street! They will

not do the hundredth part the harm in Free Love, their vilifiers do
now; nor a tenth part so much as even they themselves are now
doing. For a free, and true, and beautiful, and soul-filling love will
still elevate and purify even these! And by this time, of the four
classes, the two-rejecting are made no worse; and the two-accepting
are both made better. And the only way the two-rejecting can be
made better, is by accepting! Funny, isn't it, how everything helps
our side along.

"But the children"—will fare infinitely better than they do at
present, and make the very worst supposition. I shall take care of
my own, or at least, do my part towards taking care of them; and
I will venture, that is a grand deal more than you dare to say now.
(It would be, if you only knew what "taking care" was!) I shall
not have any, only when I want to; and ten to one, that is more
than you dare say. And my children will be love-children and good
children,—and that is more than marriage can say of its children,
one case in a thousand. (People think they are good, because they
don't know what a good child is, and won't, till Free Love comes!)
They won't be born with rottenness in their bones, nor lust in their
hearts,—as almost all the offspring of marriage are. And after they
are born, they will grow up in the freedom of a pure and loving
nature—what the civilized marriage never yet allowed a solitary one
of its devotees to do. And if others (Free Lovers) don't all do as I
do, why, I am not responsible. But, then you need not distress yourself about what they will do, nor what they won't do. I guess lovers
will care quite as much about their young, as those who don't love—
free parents, as compelled ones—those who wanted them, as those
who did not! *You* to borrow trouble about the "children"!

Besides, Free Lovers are naturally and even instinctively Associationists; and in Association nobody so much as dreams of danger
that the children will not fare, even A. No. 1! This result is so
perfectly inevitable, that the opponents of Free Love are driven
to turn right round and decry Association, and assert that we can't
keep one together. A truce to your fears, kind gentlemen; if yourselves were only free, *your* instincts would draw you the same way,
and you would take hold and help insure that a Community could
live. Your not doing so, bespeaks our sympathy for you—still content to wear chains! And yet my charity must believe that even some
of you could stand Association, if you were only under good leaders.
Free Lovers hate isolation, because it is the perfect grave of their

love; and they as much yearn after society, because there their love can be gratified; and for both reasons, they absolutely must and will associate; and then to say they can't keep up an Association, is to say, they are after all not Free Lovers; and so only those ever say this, either, who are willing their own love should pine in a cell, or who have not a sufficient residuum to pine anywhere! In vain, do the low seek to comprehend those above them.

This is the whole case, then. Freedom is good, and love is holy; and both are Rights;—let those have them who want them. Dare not to deny me what is mine, because somebody else will do wrong, if permitted to enjoy the same. Let not the high and the noble be enslaved to the low and the brutal. Let those who stand in the front ranks of humanity, *live* all their beautiful progress, and not hide it under a bushel. Let them be an example, to teach others what to be. Meanwhile, those who are in the rear, will first refuse this higher freedom—and then the freedom will have done no harm—but afterward be led by degrees to want it, and then to grow into it (and with it its innocence)—and then the freedom will have been salvation! And pray, What other way of saving men, is there?

And still more particularly, as to the safety of all this, I say—as I wrote once before, with respect to proclaiming this great freedom throughout the land, and its acceptance by some and rejection by others,—"The good will be a law unto themselves; and the bad (seeing they are the rejectors) will still (as before) restrain each other."

Then, is not the Free Love rationale perfect?

"But there are exceptions to this entire picture you have drawn." There are. Thousands of married people do not so badly, nor will all Free Lovers do so well as I have described. But the systems themselves—Marriage and Freedom—are precisely what I have portrayed them: I have not darkened the color of the one, nor heightened that of the other. And the systems are to be judged as principles—the principle of Freedom, and the principle of Slavery—and not by any exceptions, neither for, nor against, the one nor the other. But yet, because all like to know how a principle is to be carried out, therefore, I will answer to any questions, from friend or foe, as to how I would carry out Free Love. Any question. Touching my loves, my children—anything. Whatever curiosity, scepticism—even opposition—can suggest. Is not the challenge a fair one?

Tried as by Fire

Victora C. Woodhull

*Although she certainly believed everything she said in this speech,
delivered all across the country in 1874, it is unlikely that Victoria
Woodhull wrote it. Benjamin Tucker, a reliable witness, claimed
he never saw a pen or pencil in her hand, and even heard rumors
that she had trouble signing her name (her mother could neither
read nor write). Perhaps it was written by Stephen Pearl Andrews
(whose granddaughter Tucker married), or by Victoria's husband
Col. Blood, who also ghosted much of her work; or possibly she
dictated the speech to Blood, for her extemporaneous powers were
great, and on the issue of free love she was never at a loss.*

*There is evidence that the famous Woodhull eloquence was related
to the "trance-speaking" of spiritualist orators like Andrew Jackson
Davis (hence Henry James's caricature of her as a trance-speaking
feminist in* The Bostonians*), for she was in the spiritualist and
clairvoyant field before she was out of her teens, and was twice
elected president of the National Spiritualists Association. Whatever
the inspiration, it was her gift for impromptu that made her famous*

—as for example in the momentous speech she gave in Boston in September 1872, when she departed from her text to accuse the most prominent preacher of the day, Henry Ward Beecher, of adultery.

The Beecher case was a fascinating snarl of free love issues and motives. At the time Woodhull made her revelations she was a candidate for President of the United States, on what she called the "equal rights" ticket. Her nomination had been the occasion of bitter struggle within the feminist movement, whose convention she had usurped to promote her own campaign. Among the feminists, Elizabeth Cady Stanton and Isabel Beecher Hooker nervously supported her, while Susan B. Anthony felt betrayed, and the conservative Boston wing of the movement was scandalized. All three of these prominent feminists were in on the secret of Henry Ward Beecher's adultery. When Mrs. Stanton told Victoria Woodhull the gossip, it was transformed into a weapon. Beecher had continually refused to risk his own dignity by countenancing Woodhull's free love politics, nor could he squelch the satires that his other, more conservative sisters Catherine Beecher and Harriet Beecher Stowe were publishing about her. That was the ostensible provocation.

The "free love ticket" never had a chance, of course, but Woodhull was more interested in propaganda anyway. Beecher's reputation was sacrificed to the cause. In early November, while Grant was defeating Greeley for the Presidency (Greeley was himself tarred with the Woodhull brush, for Theodore Tilton, one of his chief supporters, was the husband betrayed by Beecher's adultery), Woodhull was arrested by federal special agent Anthony Comstock for sending the "obscene" Beecher issue of Woodhull and Claflin's Weekly *through the mails. The indictments and libel suits lingered through two years, and in the end Woodhull was found not guilty on all charges, while Tilton's "alienation of affections" suit against Beecher resulted in a hung jury. Every newspaper in the country carried the story. It was free publicity, which Woodhull followed up in her last radical speech on free love, "Tried as by Fire," delivered, she advertised, to a quarter of a million people in every important city.*

After the uproar of the Beecher scandal her next flamboyant gesture was in the opposite direction; within a year after "Tried as by Fire," she had given up the Weekly, *divorced Col. Blood, and renounced free love. Such conversions were part of the pattern of many free love careers, as argued in the Introduction to this volume. Woodhull left the movement as abruptly as she entered it. Friend or foe, all the feminists and not a few free lovers breathed a sigh of relief. She was a daring advocate, willing to speak the truth about issues that no one else touched—like the universality of sexual estrangement in marriage, the rights of females to orgasm, the positive advantages of sexuality for simple pleasure and health. The fact that she was also an adventuress and a fraud cannot dim the merit of her audacity, though she gave her cause much embarrassment. Even today the women's movement has owned her with evident mixed feelings, a heroine manqué.*

Victoria C. Woodhull
Tried as by Fire; or,
The True and the False Socially

. . . I am conducting a campaign against marriage, with the view of revolutionizing the present theory and practice. I have strong convictions that, as a bond or promise to love another until death, it is a fraud upon human happiness; and that it has outlived its day of usefulness. These convictions make me earnest, and I enter the fight, meaning to do the institution all possible harm in the shortest space of time; meaning to use whatever weapons may fall in my way with which to stab it to the heart, so that its decaying carcase may be buried, and clear the way for a higher and a better institution.

I speak only what I know, when I say that the most intelligent and really virtuous people of all classes have outgrown this institution; that they are constantly and systematically unfaithful to it; despise and revolt against it as a slavery; and only submit to a semblance of fidelity to it, from the dread of a falsely educated public opinion and a sham morality, which are based on the ideas of the past, but which no longer really represent the convictions of anybody.

Nor is this hypocritical allegiance the only or the greatest or

● Selection from *Tried as by Fire; or, The True and the False Socially,* New York: Woodhull & Claflin, 1874, pp. 5–10, 13–17, 23–25, 30–32, 35–36, 42–44.

gravest consideration that is capturing the opinions of the really intelligent. It is rapidly entering into the public thought, that there should be, at least, as much attention given to breeding and rearing children, as is given to horses, cattle, pigs, fowls and fruit. A little reflection shows that the scientific propagation of children is a thing of paramount importance; as much above and beyond that of personal property as children are above dogs and cats. And this conviction, practically considered, also shows that the union of the sexes, for propagation, should be consummated under the highest and best knowledge, and in such manner and by such methods as will produce the best results. These considerations are so palpable that they cannot be ignored; and they look to the early super-cedure of the institution of marriage by some better system for the maintenance of women as mothers, and children as progeny. This is as much a foregone conclusion with all the best thinkers of today as was the approaching dissolution of slavery, no more than ten years before its final fall.

But in the meantime men and women tremble on the verge of the revolution, and hesitate to avow their convictions; but aware of their rights, and urged by the impulses of their natures, they act upon the new theories while professing allegiance to the old. In this way an organized hypocrisy has become a main feature of modern society, and poltroonery, cowardice and deception rule supreme in its domain. The continuation of such falsity for a generation, touching one of the most sacred interests of humanity, will eradicate the source of honesty from the human soul. Every consideration of expediency, therefore, demands that some one lead the van in a relentless warfare against marriage, so that its days may be made short.

This is my mission. I entered the contest, bringing forward, in addition to the wise and powerful words of others, such arguments as my own inspirations and reflections suggested. No sooner had I done this, however, than the howl of persecution sounded in my ears. Instead of replying to my arguments, I was assaulted with shameful abuse; and I was astonished to find that the most per-sistent and slanderous and foul-mouthed accusations came from precisely those whom I happened often to know should have been, from their practices, the last to raise their voices against any one, and whom, if I had felt so disposed, I could have easily silenced. But simply as personality or personal defense, or spiteful retort, I have almost wholly abstained during these years of sharp conflict from making use of the rich resources at my command for this kind of attack and defense, and passing the vile abuse which has beset me, have steadfastly pressed on in the warfare.

In a single instance only have I departed from this course. Circumstances conspired to put me in possession of certain facts regarding the most prominent divine in the land, and from him I learned that he too was not only false to the old dispensation, but unfaithful to the new—a double hypocrisy, over which I hesitated many months, doubting if I should use it. It was not that I desired or had any right to personally attack this individual, but something had to be done to break down the partition walls of prejudice that prevented public consideration of the sexual problem, and fully to launch it upon the tide of popular discussion. This revolution, like every other that ever preceded it, and as every other that ever will follow it, must have its terrific cost, if not in blood and treasure, then still in the less tangible but equally real sentimental injury of thousands of sufferers. It was necessary that somebody should be hurt. I cast the thunderbolt into the very centre of the socio-religio-moralistic camp of the enemy and struck their chieftain, and the world trembled at the blow. In twenty years not anybody will say that I was wrong, any more than anybody now says that the old leaders of the anti-slavery revolution were wrong in attacking slavery in the concrete.

My purpose was accomplished. Whereas, before, none had dared to broach the sexual question, it is now on everybody's lips; and where it would have been impossible for a man, even, to address a public, promiscuous audience anywhere without being mobbed, a woman may now travel the country over, and from its best rostrums, speak the last truth about sexuality, and receive respectful attention, even enthusiastic encouragement. The world has come to its senses—has been roused to the real import and meaning of this terrible question, and to realize that only through its full and candid examination may we hope to save the future from utter demoralization.

But why do I war upon marriage? I reply frankly: First, because it stands directly in the way of any improvement in the race, insisting upon conditions under which improvement is impossible; and second, because it is, as I verily believe, the most terrible curse from which humanity now suffers, entailing more misery, sickness and premature death than all other causes combined. It is at once the bane of happiness to the present, and the demon of prophetic miseries to the future—miseries now concealed beneath its deceptive exterior, gilded over by priestcraft and law, to be inwrought in the constitutions of coming generations to mildew and poison their lives.

Of what in reality does this thing consist, which, while hanging like a pall over the world, is pretendedly the basis of its civilization? The union of the opposites in sex is an instinct inherent in the constitutions of mankind; but legal marriage is an invention of man, and so far as it performs anything, it defeats and perverts this natural instinct. Marriage is a license for sexual commerce to be carried on without regard to the consent or dissent of this instinct. Everything else that men and women may desire to do, except to have sexual commerce, may be and is done without marriage.

Marriage, then, is a license merely—a permission to do something that it is inferred or understood ought not to be done without it. In other words, marriage is an assumption by the community that it can regulate the sexual instincts of individuals better than they can themselves; and they have been so well regulated that there is scarcely such a thing known as a natural sexual instinct in the race; indeed, the regulations have been so at war with nature that this instinct has become a morbid disease, running rampant or riotous in one sex, and feeding its insatiable maw upon the vitality of the other, finally resulting in disgust or impotency in both.

Isn't this a pretty commentary on regulation? Talk of Social Evil bills! The marriage law is the most damnable Social Evil bill— the most consummate outrage on woman—that was ever conceived. Those who are called prostitutes, whom these bills assume to regulate, are free women, sexually, when compared to the slavery of the poor wife. They are at liberty, at least to refuse; but she knows no such escape. "Wives, submit yourselves to your husbands," is the spirit and the universal practice of marriage.

Of all the horrid brutalities of this age, I know of none so horrid as those that are sanctioned and defended by marriage. Night after night there are thousands of rapes committed, under cover of this accursed license; and millions—yes, I say it boldly, knowing whereof I speak—millions of poor, heart-broken, suffering wives are compelled to minister to the lechery of insatiable husbands, when every instinct of body and sentiment of soul revolts in loathing and disgust. All married persons know this is truth, although they may feign to shut their eyes and ears to the horrid thing, and pretend to believe it is not. The world has got to be startled from this pretense into realizing that there is nothing else now existing among pretendedly enlightened nations, except marriage, that invests men with the right to debauch women, sexually, against their wills. Yet marriage is held to be synonymous with morality! I say, eternal damnation sink such morality!

When I think of the indignities which women suffer in marriage, I cannot conceive how they are restrained from open rebellion. Compelled to submit their bodies to disgusting pollution! Oh, Shame! where hast thou fled, that the fair face of womanhood is not suffused with thy protesting blushes, stinging her, at least into self-respect, if not into freedom itself! Am I too severe? No, I am only just!

Prate of the abolition of slavery! There was never servitude in the world like this one of marriage. It not only holds the body to whatever polluting use—abstracting its vitality, prostituting its most sacred functions, and leaving them degraded, debauched and diseased—but utterly damning the soul for all aspiration, and sinking it in moral and spiritual torpor. Marriage not slavery! Who shall dare affirm it? let woman practically assert her sexual freedom and see to what it will lead! It is useless to mince terms. We want the truth; and that which I have about this abomination I will continue to give until it is abolished.

It is useless to cry, "Peace! Peace! when there is no peace." It is worse than useless to cry, Freedom! Freedom! when there is nothing but slavery. Let those who will, however, in spite of the truth, go home and attempt to maintain it there, and they will wake up to find themselves sold, delivered and bound, legally, to serve their masters sexually, but, refusing to do which, there will be a penalty, if not the lash. Now, husbands! now, wives! isn't this true? You know it is. And isn't it shameful that it is true?

Is this too sweeping? What was it that condemned slavery? Was it that all slaves were cruelly treated? Not the most ultra-Abolitionist ever pretended it! They admitted that the majority were contented, comfortable and happy. Can the same be said, truly, of the slaves to marriage, now?

But it was claimed and proven, as I claim and shall prove of marriage, that the instances of extreme cruelty were sufficiently numerous to condemn the system, and to demand its abolition. Proportionally, the instances of extreme cruelty in marriage are double what they were in slavery, and cover a much broader field, involving all the known methods by which the body can be tortured and the heart crushed. I could narrate personal cases of various kinds, for a week, and not exhaust my stock; but I cannot pause to do so. Judged by the logic of the past, this institution stands condemned, and will be soon relegated to the limbo of the past.

But there is another picture of this holy institution, scarcely less to be deprecated than are its actual cruelties; and little, if any, less degrading to womanhood: All men and women now living together, who ought to continue to so live, would so continue were marriage laws repealed. Is this true or false? This depends upon the truth or falsity of the following further propositions: Marriage may be consummated by men and women who love mutually; or, marriage may be consummated by men and women who have no love. If it be said that the former is false and the latter true, it is denied that love has anything to do with marriage—an affirmation, virtually, that they who hate may marry rightly; but if, on the contrary, the former is true and the latter false, it is agreed, constructively, that all I ever said or ever can say is true,

Now which is it? Has love, or ought it to have anything to do with marriage? Who will dare say that love should not be a precedent to marriage? But when this is affirmed, the legitimate corollary is not seen: That, since marriage should not begin wiithout love it should cease when love is gone. To accept the former, is to declare the latter. And no logician, however subtle, can escape it. Nor can you escape it; nor could I, although I labored for years to do so.

But, if there are any who are in doubt as to what is right and true, I offer a test that will decide it. Let the married who live together, who would separate were the law repealed, rise! Not any here of that stripe; or, if there are, they are ashamed to make a public confession of it. I should be so, too, were I sailing the voyage of life in such a ship. Ask any audience, or any individual, this question, and the result would be the same. What is the inference? Clearly that, if people really do live together who do not love, they are ashamed of it, and, consequently, of the law that holds them; and that they want the world to think that they love each other, and choose to live together on that account, regardless of the law.

Who is there in the community who would like to have it understood that there is no love at home? Isn't it the fact, on the contrary, that those whose homes are loveless, and who fight and
wrangle and fuss continually take special pains to conceal these
things from the world? Everybody knows it is. What more sweeping
condemnation could there be than this, both of the law which
compels it and the practice itself? None! It is the hot-bed of hypocrisy, deceit and lust, and is doing more to demoralize the world
than all other practices combined.

I am justified, therefore, in concluding that all people who are not
practical free lovers, living together for love, are theoretically so, and
are ashamed to confess that their practices do not accord with their
theories; or, in other words, are ashamed that their practice is
enforced lust instead of free love. These are the alternatives, and
the only ones, and I don't intend that the people shall escape them.
Every one of you—every one of the people generally—either practices Free Love or enforced lust, and the world shall understand when people denounce me as a Free Lover they announce
themselves as enforced lusters; and I'll placard their backs and they
shall walk up and down the world with this mark of depravity,
as they have intended that I should do for having the moral courage,
which they lack, to make my theories and practices agree.

● ● ●

A step beyond marriage as a means to gain sexual relations
reaches the relations themselves, their uses and abuses. Here a
query arises: Which is the end to be gained? Is it marriage merely,
regardless of the character of the relations which it legalizes; or
is it proper, natural, healthful, useful relations, such as will bless
the parties themselves and the children who result? In other words,
is it happiness, and peace, and comfort, and health, and all the
good which can follow; or is it the legal union regardless of results?

Let us see. There will scarcely be found in this late day any
intelligent person who will maintain that marriage ought ever to be
consummated by persons between whom there is no love. The
argument is, that men and women who love each other may consummate that love after being legally married but not otherwise;
and if either party refuse to consummate the marriage, it becomes
void. This establishes the theory that the principal feature of
marriage is legal. But this controverts the common consent that love

is a necessary precedent. Almost the whole world is in a "mull" over the confusion of ideas caused by the attempt to make these contradictions harmonize—desiring to live out their interior convictions, but fearing to do so lest they incur the legal or social penalty; desiring that their natural instincts and sentiments should be their guides, but fearing to let them lest they be accounted followers of the baser passions.

The law, then, and the real convictions of the people are at variance; but since the latter are inherent in the constitution of man, while the former is a contrivance of his intellect, invented for specific purposes, it must be concluded that the latter ought to take precedence in determining the conduct of life. And when it is remembered that the law binds together only those people who otherwise would separate, this conclusion becomes inevitable.

After careful observation I have deliberately concluded that there are two classes only who have anything more than an imaginary interest in maintaining the marriage system: The hypocritical priests who get their fees for forging the chains and the blackguard lawyers who get bigger ones for breaking the fetters. The former have an average of ten dollars a job, and some of them a hundred jobs a year; while the latter, not quite up to the former in number, to keep even with them, raise their average price per job to two hundred and fifty dollars. A thousand dollars a year for the priests! How should people know whether they ought to marry or not without asking their consent? Of course marriage is divine! A thousand dollars a year for the lawyers! How could people be supposed to know whether they ought to separate or not until the lawyer has got his fee? Of course virtue must have a legal standard. How could morality and modesty be preserved unless the priest got his ten dollars; or how could husbands and wives be prevented from killing each other unless the lawyer got his two hundred and fifty? Will the priest ever cease his cant about the former, or the lawyer change the law about the latter so long as the people are fools enough to pay them fees? They who suppose they may, don't yet understand how much divinity there is in this marriage business.

The real question at issue then is one entirely apart from law, relating wholly to the conditions that make up the unity, whether they are such as judged by the results, warrant the unity that is sought. What are proper and what improper sexual relations is the problem to be solved, and it is that one which of all others is most fraught with the interests, the happiness and the real well-being of humanity. Upon these relations, as I shall show, depend not only the health, happiness and prosperity of the present generation, but the very existence of future generations.

That existence is involved in these relations. If they be pure and good and withal natural, which they must be to be pure and good, then the existence which they make possible will be of the same character; but if they be impure, bad, and withal unnatural, which if they are they must be impure and bad, then the existence which they make possible will be of like character. A pure fountain sends forth pure waters, but the stream flowing from an impure source will assuredly be unclean. To make the fountains of life—the sexual relations—pure, is the work of the reformer, so that the streams they send forth may flow through coming ages uncontaminated by any inherited contagion.

There are a few propositions necessary to be laid down that will become self-evident as the subject develops: 1. A man or woman who has perfect physical health, has natural and healthful sexual relations. 2. A man or woman, married or single, old or young, professional prostitute or *roue,* or a professed nun or celibate, who has bad general health—and suffers from any chronic disease—has unnatural and unhealthy sensual conditions. 3. A man and woman, living together, who have perfect physical health, have natural and healthful sexual relations, and will have healthy offspring. Such a union is God-ordained, if it do not have the approval of the law or the sanction of the priest; and no man can put it asunder. 4. If either or both of the parties to a union have generally poor physical health—suffer from any chronic disease—such parties have unnatural and unhealthful sexual relations, and their progeny will be puling, weakly, miserable, damned. Such a union is God-condemned if it have the approval of all the laws, and the blessing of all the priests in the world; and as corollary to all these, this: All diseases not to be attributed to so-called accidental causes are the result of improper, or the want of proper, sexual conditions; and this applies to all ages and to both sexes.

It may now be asked: What are proper sexual conditions? I reply: Sexual commerce that is based upon reciprocal love and mutual desire, and that ultimates in equal and mutual benefit, is proper and healthful; while improper sexual commerce is that which is not based upon reciprocal love and mutual desire, and that cannot, therefore, ultimate in equal or mutual benefit. Children begotten by the former commerce will never be bad children physically, mentally or morally; but such as are begotten by the latter commerce will inevitably be bad children, either physically, mentally or morally, or, which is more likely to be the case, partially bad throughout.

I desire to be fully understood upon this part of the subject. I have been generally denounced by the press as an advocate of promiscuousness in the sexual relations. I want you to fully comprehend the measure of truth there is in this charge. Hence I repeat that there is but one class of cases where commerce of the sexes is in strict accordance with nature, and that, in this class, there are always present, First, love of each by each of the parties; second, a desire for the commerce on the part of each, arising from the previous love; and third, mutual and reciprocal benefit.

Of improper sexual commerce there are several classes: First, that class where it is claimed by legal right, as in marriage; second, where the female, to please the male, accords it without any desire on her own part; third, where, for money, for a home, for any present, as a payment for any claim, whether pecuniary or of gratitude, or for any motive whatever other than love, the female yields it to the male; fourth, where there is mutual love and desire, but where, for any reason, there is such want of adaptation as to make mutual consummation impossible.

This is the promiscuousness that I advocate now, and that I have, from the first, advocated.

Will the representatives of the press, who have covered me with their abuse until I am regarded with horror all over the land as a person whose presence is contamination and whose touch contagion, correct their foul lies by stating these propositions, and, so far as they can at this late day, do me justice? We shall see!

"But," said a prominent woman of this country, with whom I was recently discussing these maxims in sexuality, "how are you going to prevent all this intercourse of the sexes, which you condemn?"

"Ah!" said I, "that's the question. I have no right nor has anybody else any right to prevent it in any such sense as you infer."

This is a matter that must be remanded back from law, back from public interference, to individuals, who alone have the sovereignty over it. No person or set of persons, however learned and wise, have any right, power or capacity, to determine legally

for another when commerce is proper or when it shall occur. It is
not a matter of law to be administered by the public, but a question
of education to be gained by individuals—a scientific problem to
expound and elucidate which, should be one of the chief duties
of all teachers and reformers. Every person in the world, before
arriving at the age in which the sexual instinct is developed, should
be taught all there is known about its uses and abuses, so that
he or she shall not ignorantly drift upon the shoals whereon so
many lives are wrecked.

I advocate complete freedom for sexuality the same as for
religion. The charge of promiscuousness is laid in this fact, and
some intelligent minds have thought it was a sound charge, until
its inconsistency and utter absurdity have been pointed out to
them. This is the proposition: I advocate sexual freedom for all
people—freedom for the monogamist to practice monogamy, for
the varietist to be a varietist still, for the promiscuous to remain
promiscuous. Am I, therefore, an advocate of promiscuousness,
variety or monogamy? Not necessarily either. I might do all this
and be myself a celibate and an advocate of celibacy. To advocate
freedom in sexual things and also the right of individuals to choose
each for himself to which class to belong, is by no means synonymous with the advocacy of the class which he chooses. Advocating
the right to do a thing and advocating the doing of that thing are
two entirely separate and different matters.

•   •   •

When a limit is placed upon anything that by nature is free, its
action becomes perverted. All the various attractions in the world
are but so many methods by which love manifests itself. The attraction which draws the opposites in sex together is sexual love. The
perverted action of sexual love, when limited by law or otherwise,
is lust. All sexual manifestations that are not free are the perverted
action of love—are lust. So, logically, the methods enforced by man
to ensure purity convert love into lust. Legal sexuality is enforced
lust. All the D.D.'s and LL.D.'s in the world, though they have
all the mental gifts and the tongues of angels, cannot controvert
the proposition.

This brings us to a still more serious part of my subject.
Remember I am to withhold nothing—no fact, no advice. We are
now face to face with the most startling and the most common

fact connected with the miseries of marriages. But I know of no author, no speaker who has dared to call attention to, or to suggest a remedy for it, or even to hint at it as needing a remedy, or to recognize its existence in any manner.

It will be remembered that early in the evening I showed that marriage when analyzed, is a license to cohabit sexually. Now I am going to show that the enforcement of this method eventually defeats the original object. I state it without fear of contradiction by fact or of refutation by argument that it is the common experience among the married who have lived together strictly according to the marriage covenant, for from five to ten years, that they are sexually estranged. There may be, I know there are, exceptions to this rule, but they are the exceptions and not the rule. It is a lamentable fact that all over this country there is a prolonged wail going up on account of this condition. Sexual estrangement in from five to ten years! Think of it, men and women whom Nature has blessed with such possibilities for happiness as are conferred on no other order of creation—your God-ordained capacity blasted, prostituted to death, by enforced sexual relations where there is neither attraction or sexual adaptation; and by ignorance of sexual science!

Some may assert, as many do, that failure in sexual strength is intellectual and spiritual gain. Don't harbor the unnatural lie. Sexuality is the physiological basis of character and must be preserved as its balance and perfection. To kill out the sexual instinct by any unnatural practice or repression, is to emasculate character; is to take away that which makes what remains impotent for good— fruitless, not less intellectually and spiritually than sexually.

It is to do even more than this. From the moment that the sexual instinct is dead in any person, male or female, from that moment such person begins actually to die. It is the fountain from which life proceeds. Dry up the fountain and the stream will disappear. It is only a question of time, and of how much is obtained from other fountains, when the stream will discharge its last waters into the great ocean of life.

Others again seem to glory over the fact that they never had any sexual desire, and to think that this desire is vulgar. What! Vulgar! The instinct that creates immortal souls vulgar! Who dare stand up amid Nature, all prolific and beautiful, whose pulses are ever bounding with the creative desire, and utter such sacrilege! Vulgar, indeed! Vulgar, rather, must be the mind that can conceive such blasphemy. No sexual passion, say you? Say, rather, a sexual idiot, and confess that your life is a failure, your body an abortion, and no longer bind your shame upon your brow or herald it as purity. Call such stuff purity. Bah! Be honest, rather, and say it is depravity.

It is not the possession of strong sexual powers that is to be deprecated. They are that necessary part of human character which is never lacking in those who leave their names standing high in the historic roll. The intellect, largely developed, without a strong animal basis is never prolific of good in any direction. Evenly balanced natures, in which there are equal development and activity of all departments are those which move the world palpably forward for good; but if superiority of any kind is desirable at all, let it be in the animal, since with this right, the others may be cultivated to its standard. If this be wanting, however, all possible cultivation, intellectually, will only carry the individual further away from balance, and make the character still more "out of tune" with nature. These are physiological facts inherent in the constitution of mankind, and they cannot be ignored with impunity. No reliable theory of progressive civilization can ever be established that does not make them its chief corner stone, because they are the foundation upon which civilization rests.

It is the misuse, the abuse, the prostitution of the sexual instinct that is to be deprecated. Like all other capacities, it needs to be educated, cultivated, exercised rightly, and to do this is to live in accordance with nature and as commanded by the higher law, that law which every one finds deep-seated in his soul, and whose voice is the truest guide. When the world shall rise from its degradation into the sphere of this law, when the sexual act shall be the religion of the world, as it is now my religion, then, and then only, may we reasonably hope that its redemption is nigh.

•   •   •

There are, then, but two questions in this whole matter of reforming the world; but they are vital and inseparable. The first is, to discover and develop the science of proper generation, so that all the inherited tendencies may be good; and the second is, that the germ life, once properly begun, may not be subjected to any deleterious influences, either during the period of gestation or development on to adult age.

This is the meaning of social reform. It means better children, and it doesn't care how they are to be obtained—only to obtain them. Any methods that will secure them are good, are true, are pure, are virtuous methods. The question to be asked of the mothers of the future will not be, "Who is the father?" but, "How good is the child?" If it be not good it will be a disgrace to the mother, no matter if the father is her legal husband.

I say it, and I want the world to know that I say it, that a woman who bears a dozen or less scraggy, scrawny, puny, half-made-up children, by a legal father, is a disgrace to her sex and a curse to the community; while she who bears as many perfect specimens of humanity, no matter if it be by as many different fathers, is an honor to womanhood and a blessing to the world. And I defy both the priests and the law to prove this false. Every sensible man and woman will have to admit it. It is a self-evident proposition.

In August, 1873, at the Silver Lake camp meeting, I said, before fifteen thousand persons, that no one knows who his father is. Think of it for a moment, and you will see how impossible it is that he should know. Can any person make oath that he knows who it was who, in unity with his mother, was his father? He may swear that he has been told so, but that does not amount to knowledge. I made this statement, not specially to declare this fact, but to enforce the argument that it doesn't make any difference who may be the father of any child, if he is only a good child and an honor to his mother. I have repeated this statement a hundred times since, and never a hiss. Hasn't the sexual question grappled with the thoughts of the people? This is an evidence not to be misunderstood.

But among all the radical things I have never quite equaled one recently published in *The Popular Science Monthly,* in an article written by Mr. Herbert Spencer, the acknowledged philosopher of the age. Quoting from an eminent English surgeon, he says: "It is a lamentable truth that the troubles which respectable, hard-working married women undergo are more trying to the health and detrimental to the looks than any of the irregularities of the harlot's career." What a commentary is this on the marriage institution! Much the larger part of the married women of the world in a worse condition, as to health and looks, than are the harlots! Take that home with you, and think of it, and see if you can come to any other conclusion than that an institution that produces such results in women, needs to be replaced by something better. Now don't forget that these are not my words, and say that I advocate prostitution; but remember that they are the words of the highest authority in philosophy and science now living, published in the most popular monthly in the country, and give them weight accordingly.

There are many popular fallacies about prostitution. Statistics inform us that the average life of prostitutes is about four years; but this does not show the real causes of such fatality. It leaves it to be inferred that it is in the fact of prostitution merely. It does not say that it is caused by dissolute living, and drinking, and by the diseases which usually accompany promiscuous intercourse.

The real truth about this is that those prostitutes who never drink, and who never permit themselves to become diseased are among the healthiest of women, and hold their beauty and vigor to an advanced age. Is this a startling assertion? Anybody who will take the trouble can easily confirm it. I do not make it without the most unmistakable proof, which is open to all inquirers, as it was to me, to obtain. It was necessary for me to know by personal investigation, and it shows me as it will everybody else that what Herbert Spencer writes in *The Popular Science Monthly* is true: that the promiscuous life of the harlot is less detrimental to health and beauty than is the common life of the married slave. The reason is simple and clear. Promiscuous intercourse, when sexual conditions are imperfect, when the act is not based on mutual love and desire, is better than so-called monogamic intercourse under the same conditions, made more intolerable by a deep-seated disgust. But by no means is this an argument against monogamy. It is an argument against legal monogamy when the monogamy of nature is wanting; and, as such, is the most convincing that can be offered in favor of monogamy founded upon love. Free relations of any kind are better than any can be that are enforced. These are the logical deductions from the facts. I did not create the facts, so if you have fault to find, find it with them and not me. I merely offer them to you for consideration, so that you may think of and discuss this subject understandingly.

•   •   •

A popular objection against Free Love is, that it breaks up families. My answer to this indictment is, that a family which falls in pieces when Free Love strikes it, is already broken up, and waiting for a loophole out of which to escape; and as the press have coupled my name with this *role*, the discontented think it a good thing to shift whatever opprobrium there may be connected with their cases, upon Woodhull. Thus I become the pack-horse for thousands who have no more conception of Free Love than a donkey has of mathematics.

But I'll tell you what I do. If a husband or a wife get discontented and uneasy, and chafe in their bonds, I advise such to seek out the ulcers, come to a mutual understanding, talk out the hidden and corroding cause, sum up the difficulties and grievances and see if they are of such character and magnitude as to preclude all hope for peace and happiness, and not under any circumstances call in the services of a blackguard lawyer.

I ask men and women to be honest with each other. If any find their attachments growing cold—their love waning—say so, and not continue the pretense while the real love is lavished elsewhere. I ask men and women to be thoughtful of each other's needs and desires. If a wife find her husband spending his evenings away from home, let her be sure there is something wrong; and when he goes again, put on hat and shawl and accompany him. If it is to the club, the bar-room, the billiard table, the theatre, the opera or the house of ill-fame, tell him that any place which he frequents is good enough for you to visit. Face him in his discontent, and say: "What is the matter, my darling? What is it in which I fail that you must spend your evenings away from me? Has your love for me gone, or what is the matter? Tell me? It is useless to continue an unhappy life when there is so easy a remedy. If you do not love me any longer, take me into your confidence; let me be your friend and adviser."

If there is any basis of hope left, this course will develop it; and there are hundreds of families who owe their present unity and happiness to having followed it. It is an error into which people naturally fall who think that my supporters are among the dissatisfied families. It is precisely the reverse of this. It is the families which cannot be separated or broken up which believe in the efficacy of freedom as a regulative element. My most bitter opponents among my own sex, are the professional prostitutes who know I am going to break up their business, and the ignorant wives who read little and think less, and who are in constant fear of losing their "Paw," over whom they have none except a legal control; and among the opposite sex, those who are habitually unfaithful to marriage, and the ministers who know their nice arrangements will be spoiled, and the lawyers, whose divorce business will be ruined by freedom. Ask any of these, when found denouncing Mrs. Woodhull, if they ever heard her speak, or ever read her paper or speeches, the reply will be, "No! and I don't want to."

•   •   •

It is sometimes asked: "If what you say is true, and that marriage is a curse, why did not the deprecated results obtain years ago?" I will show you why. It will be remembered that it used to be said by the slaveholders, that the moment a slave got the freedom crotchet into his head he was no longer of any account. A negro was a good slave so long as the idea of freedom was not born in his soul. Whenever this birth occurred he began to feel the galling of his chains.

It is the same with women. So long as they entertain the idea that their natural destiny is to be owned and cared for by some man, whom they are to repay by the surrender of their person, they are good, legal wives; but from the moment the notion that they have an individual right to themselves—to the control of their bodies and maternal functions—has birth in their souls, they become bad wives. They rebel in their souls, if not in words and deeds; and the legal claims of their husbands become a constant source of annoyance, and the enforcement of their legal rights an unbearable thing.

It is this repugnance, this sexual rebellion, that is causing the degradation and widespread disease among women, sexually; and this reacts upon man, and degrades him. The mind, in rebellion at the enslaved condition, has such an effect upon the sexual act that it becomes impossible for its subject to respond or reciprocate; and the organs suffer the natural penalty.

In speaking of this almost anomalous condition in woman, Dr. John M. Scudder, Professor of the Diseases of Women in the Cincinnati Medical College, says: "If the act is complete, so that both body and mind are satisfied, no disease arises, though there be frequent repetitions; but if the act be incomplete, the organs being irritated merely, and the mind not satisfied, then disease will surely follow. There is no doubt that the proper gratification of the function is conducive to health and longevity; or that its abuse leads to disease and shortens life. Therefore," he adds, "the wife should not lose control of her person in marriage. It is hers to rule supreme in this regard. This is a law of life, and is violated in no species except in man."

What better confirmation could there be of all that I have been trying to enforce upon you, than these words from this large-hearted man and widely-experienced physician? Every wife should obtain the book from which I quote these words, and study if carefully. It is entitled, *The Reproductive Organs*, and has just been published by Wilstach, Baldwin & Co., of Cincinnati, Ohio.

I said at the outset that I am endeavoring to effect a revolution in marriage, or rather to replace the institution by a better method of providing for women as mothers and children as progeny. Everybody admits that our social system is far from perfect. Society, like everything else in the universe, evolves by natural laws. Marriage is not the perfect condition. It will be replaced by another and more perfect, which will be a legitimate outcome of the old. As republicanism in politics is a legitimate child of constitutional monarchy, so in socialism shall personal freedom be the offspring of legal limitation; and when it shall come, not anybody will doubt its parentage or question its legitimacy.

Sexual freedom, then, means the abolition of prostitution both in and out of marriage; means the emancipation of woman from sexual slavery and her coming into ownership and control of her own body; means the end of her pecuniary dependence upon man, so that she may never even seemingly, have to procure whatever she may desire or need by sexual favors; means the abrogation of forced pregnancy, of ante-natal murder, of undesired children; means the birth of love-children only, endowed by every inherited virtue that the highest exaltation can confer at conception, by every influence for good to be obtained during gestation, and by the wisest guidance and instruction on to manhood, industrially, intellectually and sexually.

It means no more sickness, no more poverty, no more crime: it means peace, plenty and security, health, purity and virtue; it means the replacement of money-getting as the aim of life by the desire to do good; the closing of hospitals and asylums, and the transformation of prisons, jails and penitentiaries into workshops and scientific schools; and of lawyers, doctors and ministers into industrial artizans; it means equality, fraternity and justice raised from the existence which they now have in name only, into practical life; it means individual happiness, national prosperity and universal good.

Ultimately, it means more than this even. It means the establishment of co-operative homes, in which thousands who now suffer in every sense shall enjoy all the comforts and luxuries of life, in the place of the isolated households which have no care for the misery and destitution of their neighbors. It means for our cities, the conversion of innumerable huts into immense hotels, as residences; and the combination of all industrial enterprises upon the same plan; and for the country, the co-operative conduct of agriculture by the maximum of improvements for labor-saving, and the consequent reduction of muscular toil to the minimum. And it means the inter-co-operation of all these in a grand industrial organization to take the places of the present governments of the world, whose social basis shall be all people united in the great human family as brothers and sisters.

So after all I am a very promiscuous Free Lover. I want the love of you all, promiscuously. It makes no difference who or what you are, old or young, black or white, Pagan, Jew, or Christian, I want to love you all and be loved by you all; and I mean to have your love. If you will not give it to me now, these young, for whom I plead, will in after years bless Victoria Woodhull for daring to speak for their salvation. It requires a strong and a pure woman to go before the world and attack its most cherished institution. No one who has not passed through the fiery furnace of affliction, and been purged of selfishness by the stern hand of adversity, and become emancipated from public opinion, could stand the load of opprobium that I have been forced to carry. I sometimes grow weary under its weight and sigh for rest, but my duty to my sex, spurs me on. Therefore I want your sympathy, your sustaining love, to go with me and bless me; and when I leave you for other fields of labor and stand upon other rostrums, fearing I may not be able to do my duty, I want to feel the yearnings of your hearts following me with prayers that my efforts may be blessed. I want the blessings of these fathers, the affections of these sons, the benedictions of these mothers and the prayers of these daughters to follow me everywhere, to give me strength to endure the labor, courage to speak the truth and a continued faith that the right will triumph.

And may the guardian angels who are hovering over you carry the benign light of freedom home to your souls to bless each sorrowing heart, to relieve each suffering body, and to comfort each distressed spirit as it hath need, is the blessing which I leave with you.

VICTORIA C. WOODHULL.

Cupid's Yokes

Ezra Hervey Heywood

Ezra Hervey Heywood was born "Hoar"—a relative of Emerson's friend Judge Samuel Hoar, who (tradition has it, perhaps falsely) paid Thoreau's tax to get him out of Concord jail—but Ezra's family thought the name too suggestive, and changed it to Heywood. His later career showed him more plain-spoken than his kinfolk, even more intractable than Thoreau, and often in need of bail.

Heywood was one of Garrison's non-resistants, among the few who did not budge from their anarcho-pacifism when the Civil War pushed most abolitionists into a fighting stance. After 1865 he turned to labor reform and anarchist economics, and with the aid of his feminist wife, Angela Tilton, he began publishing his views in a four-page radical monthly, The Word. *In 1876 he wrote and published a little free love tract provocatively titled* Cupid's Yokes, *which considered "some moral and physiological phases of love and marriage," including the "natural right and necessity of sexual self-government." By 1877 it had sold over 20,000 copies (at fifteen cents apiece) and had attracted the baleful attention of Anthony*

Comstock, founder of the New York Society for the Suppression of Vice and special agent of the U.S. Post Office. In his pamphlet Heywood had called Comstock "a religious monomaniac" and the YMCA (of which the SSV was the strong-arm) a "lascivious fanaticism." For these and other more "obscene" opinions he was arrested and brought to trial three times (1877, 1882, 1890), twice convicted (1878, 1891), and sentenced to two years for each offense. He served six months of his first term, until pardoned by Rutherford B. Hayes, and all of his second, when William Henry Harrison decided that public morals and piety demanded that the aging Heywood be punished in full.

Unlike some free lovers, Heywood seems to have been discretely monogamous in private life. For him it was not the practice of "sexual self-government," that sent him to prison, as it did James Clay, Edwin C. Walker, and others; advocacy alone was Heywood's offense. Indeed, it was not free love in its narrow sense that Heywood championed; he was arguing for greater sexual expression of love in general: "without natural vent, the exhuberant sexual vitality wastes and destroys. . . . The same exchange of impulse, thought, emotion, magnetism, and grace, which develops and refines both sexes in industrial and social meeting publicly, will be still more improving in the most intimate relations of private life. It will erelong be seen that a lady and gentleman can as innocently and properly occupy one room at night as they can now dine together."

If his enemies thought Heywood brazen in such opinions, some of his friends (for example, Benjamin Tucker) complained, upon his second arrest, that he had courted disaster. Certainly he continued to publish, advertise, sell, and mail his stock of radical sexology. The end papers of "The Great Strike," a pamphlet on the Molly Maguires and the railroad bosses, written while he was still on trial in 1878, carried advertisements for the most inflammatory sexual vademecums on his shelf—Robert Dale Owen's Moral Physiology, *R. T. Trall's* Sexual Physiology, *John Humphrey Noyes's* Scientific Propagation, *Victoria Woodhull's* Scarecrows of Sexual Freedom. *But perhaps it was Heywood's other interests that kept the guardians of public morals after him; on the occasion of his third arrest (not by Comstock), he said as much. These were the days of Haymarket, Homestead, and Pullman. Most of the free lovers had their fingers in other pies, but few were so thoroughly and coher-*

*ently radical as Heywood. Among his authors, for instance, Victoria
Woodhull's politics were catch-as-catch-can (Marx saw to it that
Section 12, her New York City cell, was bounced from the International for its bohemianism); Owen had simmered down to a
seat in Indiana's State Legislature; Trall was never more than a
pseudoscientific hustler for Fowler and Wells' publishing house; only
Noyes was consistent in his Bible Communism at Oneida.*

*It is instructive to compare Heywood with his more famous
counterpart in France, Proudhon, whom he quotes here with
admiration. Proudhon too had edited a newspaper from prison,
attacking State-capitalism and the "usury-system." But just as European anarchists were spared the dilemmas of abolitionism and the
Civil War, so they also had little or no experience of the feminist
and free love movements that reached such major proportions in
the United States. Proudhon had no sympathy for such causes as
Heywood espoused.* La Pornocratie, *his blast against* "les femmes
dans les temps modernes," *was published just a year before* Cupid's
Yokes, *and he never made any bones about his views of love and
marriage: the best wife, he said,* "is not so stupid that she can't
make a good *pot-au-feu, and not clever enough to discuss [her
husband's] articles. That's all that is necessary for domestic happiness." Heywood was an anarchist of another stripe, for although he
too seems to have been basically monogamous in temperament, his
principles included both* "self-government" *and absolute equality
for the sexes. Far from relegating his spouse to the kitchen, he
shared the lecture platform with her (see* Comstock's "Free-Love
Traps" *which follows), as well as the columns of his paper. She
was known for her explicitness in discussion of sexual matters—
including the use of four-letter words. Comstock called her* "lost
to all shame," *but Stephen Pearl Andrews praised her impudence
in the face of the stern propriety that twice sent her husband to
jail:* "She is again utterly destitute of the sense of fear. She laughs
and rollicks over what seems to the onlooker the edge of a fearful
precipice. She would sooner see her beautiful home ruthlessly
sacked, her children scattered, and be herself driven, as a drudge,
into somebody's else kitchen than she would back down an inch
from her full claim to the right to say her full thought in her own
words." *From a man who wrote speeches for Victoria Woodhull, that
was praise indeed (though one wonders about that* "somebody's else
kitchen"). *For once at least Cupid seems to have yoked a well-
matched pair.*

Ezra Hervey Heywood
Cupid's Yokes

In the distorted popular view, free-love tends to unrestrained licentiousness, to open the flood-gates of passion and remove all barriers in its desolating course; but it means just the opposite; it means the expulsion of animalism, and the entrance of reason, knowledge, and continence. As is shown in the opening pages of this essay, to say that every one should be free, sexually, is to say that every one's person is sacred from invasion; that the sexual instinct shall no longer be a savage, uncontrollable usurper, but be subject to thought and civilization. The damning tendency of marriage begins in giving the sexes legal license and power to invade, pollute, and destroy each other; and the immaturity of Science is painfully apparent, when it accepts the fatalistic theory of love, and abandons the grave issues of coition to chance and necessity. Though my experience is quite limited, yet, facts within my personal knowledge enable me to affirm, without fear of refutation, that lovers' exchange, in its inception, continuance, and conclusion, can be made subject to choice; entered upon, or refrained from, as the mutual interests of both, or the separate good of either, requires. Until lovers, by pre-good sense, become capable of temperance and self-possession in sexual intercourse, it is an outrage on children to be begotten by them. Though Paul thought it "better to marry than to burn," it is best and feasible to neither marry nor burn; for, as in Plato's phrase, lovers are persons in whose favor "the gods have intervened," sexual intercourse may be constantly under the supervision of both human and divine good sense. Since children are begotten by their parents, not by act of Congress, or divine Providence, married people are forced to study methods of preventing conception; unnatural, disgusting, and very injurious means are frequently used, especially by some clergymen and moralists who, in their public teachings, hold that coition, except for reproduction, should be forbidden by law! From six to eight days before appearance of the menses to ten to twelve days after their cessation occurs, conception may follow coition; but intercourse at other periods rarely causes impregnation; if, however,

● Selection from *Cupid's Yokes: or, The Binding Forces of Conjugal Life*, Princeton, Mass.: Co-operative Publishing Co., 1877 (1st ed., 1876), pp. 19–23.

it escapes control, it exhausts both persons, admonishing them to keep within the associative limit, which is highly invigorating, and not to allow themselves to gravitate to the propagative climax. To experience love, instead of dwelling so much upon it in thought and imagination, is Nature's method to promote continence. The fact that those in whom love is most repressed,—young male victims of seminal weakness, hysterical girls, hypoish boys and men, single women, priests, and poets,—dwell much in thought on sexual subjects, and yet, by unreasoning custom, are denied natural association with the opposite sex, is most disastrous to themselves and society. If persons do not acquire habits of continence by force of will, Nature's method is sharp and decisive; she confronts them with a child, which effectually tames and matures both parents. Far better that their attraction lead to illegal parentage, than end in marriage, or by suicidal celibacy. The fashionable method of single persons, and very many married people, is to get rid of the child before birth by abortion; but this murderous practice is unworthy of freelovers; they accept and rear the child, but take care that the next one be born of choice, not by accident. Since the increase of population outruns increase in means of subsistence, Malthus urged that, unless people refuse to marry, or defer it till middle life, there will be too many consumers for the food grown; and that, if they do not heed this admotion, Nature sternly represses excessive increase of population, "by the ghastly agencies of war, pestilence, and famine." Lycurgus favored destroying imperfect and sickly children; Plato, in his imaginative Republic, advises a similar weeding-out process; and, thinking sexual desire "a most enervating and filthy cheat," Shakerism endeavors to exterminate it,—three popular devices to govern propagation: 1. The Shaker-Malthus method, which forbids sexual intercourse; 2. The abortion-child-murder method, which destroys life before or after birth; 3. The French-Owen method of barriers, withdrawal, &c., to arrest the process in its course;—but, since they are either unnatural, injurious, or offensive, all these devices are rejected by continent free-lovers. Extending the domain of reason and self-control over the whole human system, and believing that all things work together for the good of those that love good, they not only believe, but *know,* that, under self-discipline, "every organ or faculty in the body works invariably, in all cases, and at all times, for the good of the whole."

The thread of philosophy, with which people connect scattered facts of their social experience, is religiously used to entangle so-called "fallen women," in hopeless depression. But, if each "common" woman entertains an average number of five men as her customers, for every woman who sells "her virtue" there must be five "fallen" men who buy it. How came they to have money to buy it? How came she to be so dependent that she consents to sell the use of her person for food and clothing? Wine, women, and wealth are three prominent objects of men's desire; to be able to control the first two, they monopolize the third; having, through property in land, interest on money, rent, and profits, subjected labor to capital, recipients of speculative increase keep working men poor; and, by excluding woman from industrial pursuits and poisoning her mind with superstitious notions of natural weakness, delicacy, and dependence, capitalists have kept her wages down to very much less than men get for the same work. Thus, men become buyers, and women sellers, of "virtue." But many women, not in immediate need of money, engage in "the social evil"; for, allied with this financial fraud is the great social fraud, marriage, by which the sexes are put in unnatural antagonism, and forbidden natural intercourse; social pleasure, being an object of common desire, becomes a marketable commodity, sold by her who receives a buyer for the night, and by her who, marrying for a home, becomes a "prostitute" for life. The usury-system enables capitalists to control and consume property which they never earned, laborers being defrauded to an equal extent; this injustice creates intemperate and reckless desires in both classes: but when power to accumulate property without work is abolished, the habits of industry, which both men and women must acquire, will promote sexual temperance. In marriage, usury, and the exceptionally low wages of women, then, I find the main sources of "prostitution." Luckily the profit-system will go down with its twin-relic of barbarism, the marriage-system; in life united, in death they will not be divided.

In telling the woman of Samaria, who had just said to him "I have no husband," "Thou hast had five husbands; and he whom thou now hast is not thy husband," Jesus quietly recognized, without reproof, her natural right to live with men as she chose; and when a woman "taken in adultery, in the very act," was brought to him for criticism and sentence, he sent her accusers home to their own hearts and lives by the emphatic rebuke, "He that is without sin

among you, let him first cast a stone at her." By Mosaic Law she
should have been stoned to death, and the lascivious ignorance of
religio-"cultured" Massachusetts would imprison her; but wiser
Love points her to the upward path of social and industrial liberty.
Impersonal and spiritual, love has also its material and special
revelations, which make it a sacredly private and personal affair.
Why should the right of private judgment, which is conceded in
politics and religion, be denied to domestic life? If government
cannot justly determine what ticket we shall vote, what church we
shall attend, or what books we shall read, by what authority does
it watch at key-holes and burst open bed-chamber doors to drag
lovers from sacred seclusion? Why should priests and magistrates
supervise the sexual organs of citizens any more than the brain and
stomach? If we are incapable of sexual self-government, is the
matter helped by appointing to "protect" us "ministers of the
Gospel," whose incontinent lives fill the world with "scandals"? If
unwedded lovers, who cohabit are lewd, will paying a marriage fee
to a minister make them "virtuous"? Sexual organs are not less
sacredly the property of individual citizens than other bodily
organs; this being undeniable, who but the individual owners can
rightly determine when, where, and how they shall be used? The
belief that our sexual relations can be better governed by statute,
than by individual reason, is a rude species of conventional impertinence, as barbarous and shocking, as it is senseless. Personal
Liberty and the Rights of Conscience in love, now savagely invaded
by Church, State, and "wise" free-thinkers, should be unflinchingly
asserted. Lovers cannot innocently enact the perjury of marriage; to
even voluntarily become slaves to each other is deadly sin against
themselves, their children, and society; hence marriage vows and
laws, and statutes against adultery and fornication, are unchristian,
unconstitutional, unnatural, and void in Massachusetts.

Against all repressive opposition, Individualism steadily advances
to become a law unto itself; the right of private judgment in
religion, wrested by Luther from intolerance in continental Europe
—later asserted in politics by Hampden and Sydney against the
English Stuarts, and by Adams and Jefferson against British-
American centralization—is now legitimately claimed in behalf
of sexual self-government. Protestantism, Magna Charta, Habeas
Corpus, Trial by Jury, Freedom of Speech and Press, The Declaration of Independence, Jeffersonian State Rights, Negro-Emancipa-

tion, were fore-ordained to help Love and Labor Reformers bury
sexual slavery, with profit-piracy, in their already open graves.
Thanks to the inspired energy of ancestral reformers, the guarantees
of personal liberty, which we inherit from our predecessors, are
all-sufficient in this free-love battle. Those who resist free tendencies to-day can read their doom in the prophetic wrath of
Proudhon, who, confronting property usurpation and Napoleonic
despotism in France, said, *He who fights against ideas will perish by
ideas!* Yet not ideas, not intellect merely, but moral appeal, the
might of Conscience, and the all-persuasive impulses of the human
heart enter this conflict. Human nature may well blush if the
drama of deceit enacted in the "Brooklyn Scandal" is to be taken
as a fair expression of American thought and feeling. But the array
of intellect, scholarship, and eloquence opposed in that struggle;
the impressive pomp of courts, the mustering clans of ecclesiastical
authority, the listening attitude of thousands of pulpits, and the
recording pens of an omnipresent press,—all these are for a day,
fleeting and contemptible, when weighed against an honest heart-
throb between one man and one woman! The loud clamor of words
will cease, the majesty of courts fade, churches vanish, Christianity
itself pass away, but the still, small voice of Love will continue to be
heeded by Earth's millions gathering at its shrines! And as the
dictation of statutes is increasingly resisted and the wrath of slave
masters defied, more and more will the bonds of affection be welcomed, for the yokes which Cupid imposes "are easy and their
burden light." I opened this essay accepting Love as the regnant
force in social life; I conclude it by emphasizing the same faith.
Money, ambition, respectability, isolation, magnetic fervor, fascinating touch, glowing beauty,—whatever influences concur to induce
social union, the nourishing power, to continue and prosper it, is
the attractive force of personal worth, the call to live and serve
together, the impulse to defer self and partial interests to the welfare of the being loved. Sired by Wisdom, born of Truth, Love
stimulates enterprise, quickens industry, fosters self-respect, rever-
ences the lowly and worships the Most High, harmonizing personal
impulse with the demands of morality, in a well-informed faith,
which renders conventional statutes useless, where "the heavens
themselves do guide the state."

Free-Love Traps

Anthony Comstock

The following is Anthony Comstock's own account of how he arrested Ezra Heywood, Massachusetts anarchist and founder of the New England Free Love League. Although Comstock accuses the free lovers of laying Traps for the Young—*the title of his first book—it is obvious from his pleasure telling this anecdote, in which he snares his quarry in spite of every obstacle and hazard, that it was he, not Heywood, who was the born predator. Comstock loved intrigue and ambush almost as much as he hated sexuality.*

His exploits are full of such stories. This time he had caught his man by a bogus letter asking for copies of Sexual Physiology, *by water cure physician R. T. Trall, and* Cupid's Yokes, *Heywood's own manifesto in favor of "sexual self-government." Among those who came to Heywood's defense was the elder statesman of the free-thinkers, D. M. Bennett. A week after he published his first paragraphs in support of Heywood in* The Truth Seeker, *Bennett was himself arrested, for sending obscene and blasphemous matter through the mails, namely, A. B. Bradford's "How Do Marsupials Propagate*

*Their Kind?" and his own "Open Letter to Jesus Christ." This case
was dismissed without ever coming to trial, but by then Bennett
had already been arrested twice again, both times for selling Heywood's* Cupid's Yokes, *which was apparently more actionable than*
Bradford on Marsupials. *Comstock had written Bennett as a "truth-
seeker" under the name of "G. Brackett," asking for "that Heywood
book you advertise Cupid's something or other, you know what I
mean. I send three and a half dollars and if that ain't enough I
will send the balance when I get the books. Wish that I had three
hundred times the amount, but I hain't." The "balance" turned
out to be thirteen months at hard labor (thirteen rather than
twelve, so that he would have to do the time at Albany Penitentiary
rather than Ludlow Street Jail, which would have been easier on a
man of his years).*

*Besides Heywood among the authors reprinted in this book,
Comstock personally took credit for arresting, fining, or sending to
prison Dr. E. B. Foote, Victoria Woodhull, and Ida C. Craddock,
while the works of still others were used in evidence against his
victims. Foote got off with a fine, and Woodhull won her case,
after serving a month in jail before making bail. But Comstock's
lifetime record of convictions was better than this—close to three
out of four. Near the end of his career he estimated: "In the forty-
one years I have been here I have convicted persons enough to fill
a passenger train of sixty-one coaches, sixty coaches containing sixty
passengers each and the sixty-first almost full."*

*At first Comstock had what some regarded as a legitimate prey,
for in 1872 when he founded the Society for the Suppression of
Vice, there were, according to his information, 165 obscene books
on the stands—from* Fanny Hill *to* The Lustful Turk—*published by
four men who (with police protection) monopolized the porno-
graphic trade in New York City. By January 1873 Comstock could
write, "There were four publishers on the 2nd of last March; to-day
three of these are in their graves, and it is charged by their friends
that I worried them to death. Be that as it may, I am sure the world
is better off without them."*

*By February 1874 he had confiscated some 130,000 pounds of
obscene literature, and 194,000 lewd pictures and photos. It was
this record that helped put through the Comstock Law of 1873,
increasing the penalties for violation of the obscenity statutes, and
extending them to include the advertisement or sale of contra-*

Breeze Crest.
Summit. N. J.   Feb. 3. 1902.

Madame would you oblige me with a
Copy of your "Wedding Night." I enclose
half a dollar. Do you admit young
girls to your lectures! What do you
Charge for two Chums who would
like to Come together? I am past 17
years., Please send tight & oblige me.
address plain Miss Frankie Streeter.
                              P.O. Box 201
                                 Summit N. J.

Enc. 50 cts.

COMSTOCK AND HIS METHODS. A DECOY LETTER. (See pp. 302ff., for this letter,
and Ida Craddock's response.)

*ceptives. It was important to add this new prohibition against birth
control, for Comstock was running out of authentic obscenity to
prosecute. Now he might go after people like Dr. Foote, Elmina
Slenker, or poor Ida Craddock, whose story is told in the Introduction and in Section III.*

*By the time of the Craddock case (1902) Comstock had lost count,
but in 1878, when he was prosecuting Heywood and Bennett, he
had boasted of the fifteenth suicide directly attributable to his
reforming zeal (number fifteen was the famous abortionist Mme.
Restell—"A bloody end to a bloody life," commented Comstock).
As Heywood said in his pamphlet, "This is clearly the spirit that
lighted the fires of the inquisition."*

Anthony Comstock
Free-Love Traps

When a boy I used to construct in the woods what was called a
stone-trap. This was formed by taking a large flat stone and setting
it up on one edge at an angle of about forty-five degrees, and
fastening it there by means of three notched sticks. The end of one
directly under the centre of the stone was baited with a sweet
apple. The rabbit or squirrel nibbling the apple would spring the
trap and be crushed to death.

The thing I mention now crushes self-respect, moral purity, and
holy living. Sure ruin and death are the end to the victims caught
by this doctrine, which is now becoming so prevalent. It is a bid
to the lowest and most debased forms of living, and is dangerous
to youth and adults alike. It takes the word "love," that sweetens
so much of earth, and shines so brightly in heaven, and making that
its watchword, distorts and prostitutes its meaning, until it is the
mantle for all kinds of license and uncleanness. It should be spelled
l-u-s-t, to be rightly understood, as it is interpreted by so-called
liberals.

I can liken it to nothing more striking than the rude stone trap,
so far as its results go.

As advocated by a few indecent creatures calling themselves
reformers—men and women foul of speech, shameless in their lives,

---

● Selection from *Traps for the Young,* New York: Funk & Wagnalls, 1883,
pp. 158–59, 163–66.

and corrupting in their influences—we must go to a sewer that has been closed, where the accumulations of filth have for years collected, to find a striking resemblance to its true character. I know of nothing more offensive to decency, or more revolting to good morals, than the class of publication issuing from this source. Science is dragged down by these advocates, and made a pretended foundation for their argument, while their foul utterances are sought to be palmed off upon the public as scientific efforts to elevate mankind. With them, marriage is bondage; love is lust; celibacy is suicide; while fidelity to marriage vows is a relic of barbarism. All restraints which keep boys and girls, young men and maidens pure and chaste, which prevent our homes from being turned into voluntary brothels, are not to be tolerated by them.

Nothing short of turning the whole human family loose to run wild like the beasts of the forest, will satisfy the demands of the leaders and publishers of this literature. The chief creature of this vile creed was sentenced to two years in Dedham Jail, Massachusetts, for sending his obscene books advocating his doctrine through the mails.

· · ·

My first experience with this crew was in Boston. Their leader had printed a most obscene and loathsome book. This book is too foul for description.

This foul book was advertised at a low price, and a special effort was made for "boy, girl, and women agents" to sell the same. This leader and his wife made it their business to hold free-love conventions, for the purpose of educating the youth in this line. He appropriated the mails of the United States, and made them his efficient agents in disseminating the book. Every volume had an advertisement for "boy and girl agents."

I secured the evidence, and procured a warrant in the United States Court at Boston for his arrest. I was especially deputed to execute this warrant. I went to his residence, and there learned that he was in Boston, holding a free-love convention. I returned there, reaching the hall where this convention was being held about 8:30 P.M. I was alone. I went up to the convention, bought a ticket, and as I entered the hall heard the speaker railing at "that Comstock." I took a seat without being recognized. The address was made up of abuse of myself and disgusting arguments for their cause.

I looked over the audience of about 250 men and boys. I could see lust in every face. After a little the wife of the president (the person I was after) took the stand, and delivered the foulest address I ever heard. She seemed lost to all shame. The audience cheered and applauded. It was too vile; I had to go out. I wanted to arrest the leader and end the base performance. There my man sat on the platform, puffed up with egotism. I looked at him and at the 250 eager faces, anxious to catch every word that fell from his wife's lips.

Discretion said, It is not wise to make yourself known. Duty said, There's your man, take him. But I was alone. In not one face in all that throng of his sympathizers was there enough manliness to encourage a hope of help, in case I required it.

I left the room with this one sentiment uppermost in my mind: "It is infamous that such a thing as this is possible in any part of our land, much more in Boston. It must be stopped. But how?" I went down the two flights of stairs to the street. The fresh air never was more refreshing. I resolved to stop that exhibition of nastiness, if possible. I looked for a policeman. As usual, none was to be found when wanted. Then I sought light and help from above. I prayed for strength to do my duty, and that I might have success. I knew God was able to help me. Every manly instinct cried out against my cowardly turning my back on this horde of lusters. I determined to try. I resolved that one man in America at least should enter a protest.

I had been brought over from the depot in a carriage. I had the driver place his carriage at the door leading up to the hall. I returned to the hall. This chieftain's wife continued her offensive tirade against common decency. Occasionally she referred to "that Comstock." Her husband presided with great self-complacency. You would have thought he was the champion of some majestic cause instead of a mob of free-lusters. I sat down again in the audience. The stream of filth continued until it seemed to me I could not sit a moment longer. Just then the leader passed from the stage into the anteroom. The audience were carried away with the vile talk. The baser the expressions, the louder they applauded.

I followed him out, and said to him quietly, "Is your name [Ezra Heywood]?"

With much self-conceit, he responded in the affirmative.

I simply said, "I have a warrant for your arrest for sending obscene matter through the mail. You are my prisoner."

He gasped out, "Who are you?"

I replied, "I am a deputy United States marshal."

"Well," he said, "if you'll excuse me I'll just go in and address the convention a moment."

I had been expecting this, and said at once, "You are now in custody, and you cannot harangue that crowd any more to-night."

Then he tried other devices to get into the hall; he wanted his overcoat and hat.

I said, "No, you cannot go in there again to-night." I then turned to one of his doorkeepers, a man about six feet two inches high, who was selling these obscene books as the people passed in and out, and said, "Are you a friend of this man?"

"Waal, you bet I am," he replied.

"Then," said I, "you had better get his hat and coat, or he'll go without them."

Then the prisoner wanted to go in and see his wife. I said, "No; call her out." As the six-footer brought the hat and coat, his wife-orator came out, having excused herself for a moment, and, much to my surprise, the audience kept their seats.

It began to be a little warm. Any moment an alarm might be given and this mob break loose. I kept cool, but it required an effort.

She wanted to know what was going to be done with her husband. I quietly replied, "Taken to Charles Street Jail."

"Well," she said, "I'll just go in and adjourn the convention, and then will come out and go with you, if you will wait a few moments."

I felt obliged, out of respect to my wife, sisters, and lady friends, to decline the kind offer of her (select) company. It was about all I wanted to do to have one of that slimy crowd in charge.

I knew that as soon as she returned and announced the arrest there would be a scene. I was in no mood for a bigger show than I had already witnessed. I had my money's worth and more, and was fully satisfied.

The prisoner desired to tarry. He did not readily respond to my gentle hint to come. Time was safety with me then. I said, "Come"; and then took him by the shoulder (or neck, or thereabouts), and

he moved toward the foot of the stairs. We got part way down the
top flight, and I heard a tremendous yell. Then came, in less time
than it takes to write it, a rush of many feet, pell-mell over benches
and seats, in their scramble to see who would get out and down
first. I took my man by the nape of the neck and we went down the
next flight rather lively, and into the carriage. Before the first one
of the audience touched the sidewalk, we were half a block away;
for before I could get the carriage door closed, my Jehu, thinking
discretion the better part of valor, whipped his steeds into a gentle
run, away ho! for Charles Street Jail, where we arrived in safety.

Thus, reader, the devil's trapper was trapped.

ANTHONY COMSTOCK.

V

Love in Utopia

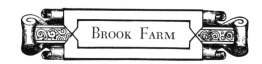

Love in the Phalanstery

Victor Hennequin
(Translated by Henry James, Sr.)

Love in the Phalanstery *was not published in America until 1849,*
two years after the collapse of Brook Farm, Associationism's famous
model community, but the rumors of Charles Fourier's unconven-
tional views of marriage were abroad long before Henry James Sr.
provided the evidence by translating this outspoken tract by one
of Fourier's disciples. To a modern eye, the Fourierist position is
not so much shocking as it is absurd; the attack on society's vices
and hypocrisy rings true enough, but the regimentarian solution
seems a parody of the Gallic love of order. Emerson, for example,
carried the program one step farther in the imagination: "Will
they, one of these days, at Fourierville, make boys & girls to order
& pattern? I want, Mr. Christmas office, a boy, between No 17 &
No 134, half & half of both; or you might add a trace of 113. I want
another girl like the one I took yesterday only you can put in a
leetle more of the devil."
Although he made fun of Fourier's analysis, Emerson had a

passage in his journal that would have shocked his neighbors just as much, had anyone ever seen it: "Plainly marriage should be a temporary relation, it should have its natural birth, climax, & decay, without violence of any kind,—violence to bind, or violence to rend. When each of two souls has exhausted the other of that good which each held for the other, they should part in the same peace in which they met. . . ." Society, however, was not ready for such freedom in love; men would "confound a whim with an instinct, the pleasure of the fancy with the dictates of the character," and thus introduce "carnage into our social relations." It was not a subject that could be safely introduced into the public mind, and so Emerson kept his journal entry out of his essays. Most of his friends at Brook Farm would have agreed, and thus the official line on Fourier's sexual "series" was that talk about them was premature, and served only to give Associationism a bad name.

Victor Hennequin
(Translated by Henry James Sr.)
Love in the Phalanstery

In the social order designed by Providence, and conceived by Fourier, what most effectually contributes to the peace and security of marriage, or of unions formed under the law of constancy, is that this law is not imposed, but opens other paths to those who find it painful. Would you render a metal pure? Skilfully disengage it from all alloy. Would you ensure a sincere and scrupulous observance of fidelity in certain couples? Do not force fickle and changable persons to enrol themselves under the same banner. In an army thus formed by constraint, you would find too many felons and deserters.

Whatever be the wisdom of these maxims, the civilized man finds it hard to admit them, at least formally. We prove to him that if he truly love constancy, which, indeed, for the most part is only a pretence, he will find in harmony every possible guarantee for the fidelity of his companion; we prove to him that the formation of series open to fickle characters, far from prejudicing his own tranquility, is in truth its necessary condition; but all this does not suffice. He will not be content to practice constancy for himself; he

---

● Selection from *Love in the Phalanstery*, trans. and preface by Henry James Sr., New York: Dewitt and Davenport, 1849, pp. 17–27.

wishes to impose it upon the whole human race. There is nothing so intolerant as the civilizee, spite of his liberal professions. If he conceive of government after a certain fashion, he sees only criminals in those whose political ideas are different. If he be zealous for a particular form of worship, he finds it difficult to tolerate any other mode of devotion. In the arts, the classic and romantic schools, and the different schools of painting, reciprocally excommunicate and proscribe each other. And at the family table the child is punished for not loving all the dishes which the author of his days pronounces excellent.

Thus also the man who experiences happiness in a fixed and durable union, would compel every one else to follow the same style of life. And why so, if they are happy in another way? Because conscience, that interior voice which holds the same language in all countries and all ages, absolutely forbids inconstancy and plurality in love. Poor conscience! it fared badly then among the Hebrew patriarchs, who had many wives and concubines, and does not now exist among the Mussulmen or Chinese. When one reads in sacred scripture the story of Abraham, of Jacob, and of King David, who had a seraglio before Solomon, one is constrained to admit that conscience and religion admit of exceptions to monogamy.

Conscience is not arbitrary, is not insensate. It reproves only those things which injure ourselves or others. A civilized woman who deceives her husband, is culpable, because she violates an engagement she has assumed, because she abuses a confidence reposed in her, because she puts her husband in the pillory of public opinion, and exposes him besides to the risk of death in an encounter with the favored lover. She is culpable, because her life is a succession of treasons and lies, because she risks introducing into the nuptial bed those contagions which are the disgrace and scourge of our era. She presents the child of another to the caresses of her husband; she puts upon an honest and abused man the care of rearing an adulterous issue. If the fraud be discovered, what crimes and misfortunes ensue, the least of which is the abandonment of an illegitimate, yet innocent offspring! The adulterous woman is culpable, and Fourier by no means acquits her. He knew well, and better than the philosophers, what ravages would be produced at the present day by liberty in love, and he would have energetically combated any man who should propose to introduce it in the bosom of civilized institutions.

But let us place ourselves in thought in the midst of the harmonian series, where liberty always gives guarantees to social order; let us not detach for a single instant these series from the world in which they are formed, and then candidly inquire what evil is likely to flow from their independence.

Abstracting the *vestalate,* or the series of virginity, and the *damoisellate,* or the series of fidelity, the various series which, according to Fourier, would admit a progressive liberty, present themselves in four principal types; the *féate,* expressing composite hospitality; the *angelicate,* composite civility or courtesy; the *faquirate,* composite charity, or benevolence; the *pivotate,* composite constancy.

Civilization comprehends no liberty in love without materialism, and orgies; but in harmony the series appropriate to characters that refuse to be held by exclusive and indissoluble ties, rival each other in disinterestedness, in delicacy, and subordinate material relations to the delights of affection. The series of the *angelicate* is the most disengaged from the senses, transfiguring into celestial beings those who enrol themselves under its banner, and its example maintains in honor in every phalanx the laws of the purest courtesy.

The fées and fés (female and male members of the *féate*) have received as a heritage the marvellous power of Melusina and Merlin. Experienced in love, skilful to discern affinities of character, these dispensers of passional attraction bring together sympathetic natures, and afford them opportunities of appreciating one another. Everywhere the *féate* scatters happiness in its path; and being the interpreter of divine decrees, occupies a very elevated rank in the esteem and gratitude of the human race.

Civilization which encloses in itself all the elements of harmony, but in the state of sketches, or deformed embryos, or caricature; civilization which defiles and perverts all natural types by the contagion of egotism, or avarice, or the harsh law of constraint; apes the *vestalate* in the virginity of the cloistered recluse, or the old maid who languishes without a dower; it apes the *damoisellate,* in the fidelity of the married woman, a fidelity controlled by the mayor, and watched by the commissary of police; the *pivotate,* by adultery, with its lies and treasons. We shall presently see that civilization travesties the noble faquiress, the Abigail of David, the Odètte of Charles VI. in the procuress who dupes and exploits old men—the fiery and disinterested Bacchante in the prostitute—the

Bayadère in the mercenary dancing girl. It should equally supply us
with a caricature of the fée.

We find this caricature not only in the go-betweens of low life,
but in those obliging dames, whose function it is to *make marriages*
—that is, to assort fortunes, and who rigorously exclude from their
matrimonial books the young man without patrimony, and the
young girl without dower. In short, we find it in those professional
matrons, who thus advertise on the outside page of the newspapers:
Speciality–Marriages–Discretion–Speed. "Madam B. informs persons desiring to marry, that her respectable position in society
enables her to procure in marriage very desirable partners, and that
her return from the country will now permit her to satisfy all
demands addressed her, either in person or by letter (post paid)."

All these civilized types are so many hideous shadows, resembling
those silhouettes we sometimes see cast upon a wall by an oblique
light, which vanish when the light improves and draws nearer.

The functions of the *féate* exact experience and tact, and accord
with mature age.

A word of explanation in regard to the *faquirate* will lead us
to speak of love in elderly persons, and to terminate the parallel
we have instituted between the career of a man reared in civilization, and one reared in harmony.

Our philosophical systems, of little influence in practical life,
declare that the old man should renounce love, and content himself
with domestic and social joys. This counsel is conformable to the
general order of nature, and the majority of old men will follow it;
virility is with them extinct, and Providence, which does nothing
by accident, accordingly gives to the great mass of young women
no attraction for old men.

There are, however, old men whom the delights of the family
hearth do not satisfy, and who feel the need of more tender emotions. Of this number was king David, as we learn from the 3d
book of Kings. To this number too, all the pachas and oriental
sovereigns appear to belong, without reckoning many distinguished
persons among ourselves.

God could not have given to a minority among old men a tender
attachment to young women, without having also endowed a certain
minority among young women with a preference which inclines
them towards old men.

These young girls, as well as those young men who have no

aversion to women on the decline, would now constitute the
faquirate, if these different shades of character were today pro-
ounced and classified. But the world in which we live is not built
up in order and methodical observation; it encloses all the elements
of society without being one; it is a society in the same sense that
a mass of clockwork is a watch, or a heap of printing type a book.

Our society, being a bad observer, recognises in the moral world
only general facts; it is incapable of discovering an exception, as a
sympathy in a portion of the young for advanced age, and thus it
disbelieves in this phenomenon. Whenever a young man marries a
dowager, it accuses him of avarice, which is generally true: not,
however, always. Whenever a young girl marries an old man, they
either say that it was a speculation, or that she was forced; supposi-
tions which are doubtless often just, and yet in certain cases do
gratuitous injury to the bride or her husband.

The world exposes itself to calumny by refusing to believe in the
existence of faquirs and faquiresses; the old man exposes himself
to be shamelessly duped, in imagining that they may be found every
day. He is not sufficiently aware that the love of hoary locks is an
exception among the young; and many a rogue finds his advantage
in the illusion. Molière has drawn from it largely.

The old man in civilization, in whom the sacred fire is not yet
extinct, believes himself beloved for his own sake, and courts, at
hazard, young girls who make sport of him. It is a sad spectacle
to see him, in the joyous circle into which he has furtively slidden,
treated by the young as an owl would be by a flock of happy song-
sters. One is especially pained to see these insults inflicted upon
men distinguished in literature, the arts, or sciences, or who fill
elevated offices.

In harmony, by virtue of the care which society takes to observe
characters, without wishing to imprint upon them an uniform
type, the old man whose affections are still susceptible may address
himself with confidence to his wishes, and contract unions which
will be matter of ridicule to no one.

The series of the *Pivotate* combines, with a durable sentiment,
some caprices and fantasies. Already numbers of philosophers and
moralists imprudently engage in this series, who encounter in
civilization more than one frightful risk. The *pivotate* has an
analogy in music to those sustained chords which prolong themselves, by becoming married to transient modulations. Fourier has
made an analysis of this special series, or rather of its germ, in

that chapter of the *Four Movements,* entitled, *Method of union
between the sexes in the seventh period.*

What evil would be produced in harmony by series thus constituted, or rather, what good would be produced? In consonance
with the method we have adopted to prove the worth of the phalansterian conception, let us now, having compared the civilized
marriage with the series of constancy, contrast with the description
of the freer series all the disorders of civilized love.

Can any one believe that we should have in harmony anything
analogous to the life of those unfortunate women who are now
slaves of all, slaves subject to the direst of constraints, and to whom
we give their daily bread in exchange for their infamy? You mutter
the words *bayaderes* and *bacchantes;* undeceive yourselves; the
bacchante is not a mercenary or profligate woman, like those
unfortunates whom you elbow every night, and whose lot attracts
no tear; she is not a woman degraded to the life of the beasts, and
making a trade of love. Like all harmonians, the bacchante is above
all things impassioned for industry, for those attractive labors which
her group pursues, with music playing and banners waving; she is
a woman of heart, of devotedness, of intelligence; and if we might
point to-day to the analogon of this noble and powerful type, it
would be among the suttlers' wives of our armies, those generous
women who partake the fatigues of the soldiery, nurse the wounded,
encourage the combatants, and to whom, in spite of their light
behavior, no one begrudges the cross of honor which often decorates
their bosoms.

Whatever be the diversity of the series, all alike proclaim and
honor those common principles which govern in harmony all the
relations of love, and which maintain the dominion of modesty. A
social system that proposes to develope and refine all our propensities, must guard with especial care a sentiment so full of charm.
These principles, received in every phalanx, are the following:

One of the passions which Fourier calls *distributive,* to wit, the
composite passion, which expresses the need we feel of combination
and accord, imperatively exacts that to every material pleasure
should be allied a spiritual delight, and that in love, for example,
there should never exist a tie which is not sanctioned by the heart.
Is this rule always observed in actual society, even in our marriages?

In harmony, although every one is free to exchange with his
beloved, presents, memorials, and tokens of affection, mercenary
love is unknown. Even in industrial relations, the individual is

never repaid by the individual; the phalanx is composed only of associates, and recognises no paid classes; and the payment therefore of the individual, by the individual, out of the industrial sphere, would be to the last degree repugnant in the relations of love, whose nature is so absolutely disinterested. Is this rule observed nowadays, even in our marriages?

In harmony, where a profound study of the native impulses is the base of the whole social system, one respects the tone which true love impresses on our relations, the tone namely of deference on the part of the stronger sex towards the weaker, of man to woman. In the loves of harmony, woman is really a mistress, a title which is now given her only in irony; she is courted, and her decision and choice respected. Duels between rival lovers, men revenging themselves by the slander and calumny of the woman who has rejected their addresses; these are the daily and disgraceful spectacles which civilization presents. Every harmonian will understand woman's liberty to accept or reject an offered homage, without being responsible to any one, and acknowledge her rightful supremacy in the realm of love. Are these rights, written in heaven, now respected on the earth of our abode?

Civilization has a glimmering notion of these principles, and our Dons, or *gentlemen*, pique themselves on their observance; but in harmony the strict obedience of these laws will be an object of emulation among the series, and this noble strife will carry delicacy in love to a degree of perfection we do not now even suspect. Precedents will be established, and because the code of courtesy possesses a real authority, a select council of ladies will be formed, who will punish every infraction of it with their censure. It is the *Court of Love* of the Middle Ages. The future will revive every institution of the past which contains in itself a precious germ.

The resolution of the harmonian series to admit no material love unsanctioned by the heart, to proscribe all venality in love, and to respect the liberty of woman, would exercise little practical influence, if the social organization in minor relations (those of family and of love) were not preceded by a new organization of the major relations, or in other words, by an organization of labor assuring the following results:

Woman's right to labor, together with the certainty of her finding constant and lucrative employment, and a rich and splendid future; for honors and authority are her due. Civilization permits no outlet to feminine ambition, and sheds only on the wife of a general, a president, a minister, or poet, some pale reflection of her husband's celebrity. In harmony every dignity reserved to man will be set off by a like dignity, the reward of female merit. Woman henceforth ceases to be the reed, sustained only by manly strength; treacherous gold, and the hope of becoming a fine lady, will no longer tempt her; she is what her works make her. If man wishes her favor, he must be respectful and devoted; he must win it by lustrous actions, by signal services in the cause of humanity.

Before diminishing the compression which our institutions and customs exert upon love, it is necessary that the education of childhood be assured. "What will become of children?" is the very serious argument wherewith civilization opposes the first degree of liberty, or the re-establishment of divorce. This question is answered in the Phalanstery, by insitutions, of which our nurseries, halls of asylum, and industrial schools, are the barest anticipations. The harmonian child, without being separated from his parents, receives the maternal cares of society. He is initiated betimes in attractive industry; all his faculties are studiously elicited, and an activity suited to his tastes is assured to him.

It is almost useless to add that the societary organization, or the division of the population into phalanxes, greatly promotes hygienic measures and medical watchfulness, and can alone extirpate those contagions which give a debasing and dangerous character to sexual intercourse in civilization.

Having established that conscience does not proscribe any actions which are not of an injurious nature, we beg Fourier's detractors to tell us what evils will be engendered by the harmonian series, constituted as we have described, and formed in a society which shall have first realized all the conditions we have just set forth.

We ourselves by no means see this evil. On the contrary, we see that the solution given to the question of Love by the genius of Fourier, produces, and alone produces, immense advantages; the innocence of childhood guaranteed; virginity encouraged and rewarded; security assured to constant characters; opportunities of honorable love offered to old age; prostitution suppressed; loyalty and courtesy established in all the relations of the sexes; lively impulsion communicated to industry, to the arts, to all the modes of activity whereby man may distinguish himself, in the eyes of woman educated in self-respect, disinterestedness, and candor.

Civilization effects none of these results. Without taking count of the differences of age, sex, and character, it claims to limit love throughout the human family to the tie of indissoluble marriage. But, if we set aside the immense mass of hypocrites, these rules are sincerely observed from one end of life to the other, only by exceptional characters. These will one day constitute the series of prudery, who are the special guardians of propriety, and destined to furnish in harmony the most complete type of reserve. As to the mass of civilized people, they daily outrage infantile modesty, banter virginity, violently rupture the ties of marriage, and ridicule them in comedies; their old men corrupt the young women whose hearts they cannot gain; prostitution plants itself permanently in our streets, and we do not even know how to extirpate those unnatural vices which are the abhorred fruit of compression, of the prison, of the boarding-school, and seraglio, but which will vanish as soon as we have restored their natural course to the inclinations of humanity.

Let us here anticipate all objection of little moment. "You have an easy task," it may perhaps be said, "you have an easy task to prove the triumph of harmony. You have only to contrast its beautiful institutions, not with the laws of the actual social order, but with the violation of these laws. Does our morality, does our religion, does our civil code, authorize adultery and prostitution? Can any one say that these disorders, condemned by public opinion, make a part of our civilized institutions?"

Adultery, we grant, does not form a part of your institutions: but it is thoroughly rooted in your habits. As to prostitution, it is not interdicted by your laws; it is regulated by them, and this is equivalent to its formal sanction. Prostitution is sanctioned by your police ordinances, as marriage is by the Civil Code. You do not interdict it, and you cannot. The terrible compression you impose upon love in other respects, necessitates this safety-valve; you cannot close it without engendering a fearful explosion. To close it with safety, you must first ensure to every man opportunities of honorable love, and to every woman an occupation which shall not be derisively rewarded like the day-labor of your sempstresses. Prostitution is one of the columns of your social edifice, and you sacrifice to it without compunction hecatombs of young girls.

When we judge of you, not by your words, but by your deeds, we are truly constrained to consider adultery and prostitution as integral parts of your social mechanism. If you repudiate them, if they are excluded from your ideal of society, what is that ideal?

"Young people of both sexes must repress their desires, whatever be their violence; they must remain pure till they are twenty years old, or thirty, in short all their life, unless a suitable marriage offer: the maiden must suffer herself to perish with hunger, needle in hand, rather than listen to the seducer. The wife must always remain faithful to her husband, even if he be old and infirm; the husband have no heart save for the wife, although she be sullen and deformed."

Glory to those whose moral force is sufficiently great, and whose physical force is sufficiently small, to carry out your programme: but it has two disadvantages. In the first place, it is inferior to ours, because it makes a great number of people miserable without any profit to society. In the next place, it is impracticable, if proposed as a universal law. When a system has been tried 1800 years, when it has had on its side the prestige of moral and of material power, the keys of St. Peter, and the sword of Charlemagne, when it has had the apparent support of public opinion, and the very real support of the civil power, and when, after the lapse of these 1800 years, we see the rules it establishes obeyed only by an imperceptible number of individuals, but utterly contemned by the masses, it is time to declare the system vanquished by experience, it is time to say—Let us seek laws which accord with facts, and which are revealed to us by nature.

Henry James

Liberty in Love

John S. Dwight

John Dwight was one of the leaders of the Brook Farm community from the earliest days, even before its conversion to Fourierism. A scholar and a musicologist, Dwight taught in the Brook Farm school and served on most of its important committees, as well as hoeing corn in its fields. He also wrote a good deal for the Harbinger, *which had become the chief organ of Associationism in America after 1845. It was in its pages that the following defense of Fourierist morals appeared, in the midst of a controversy that was providing lively copy for the sensationalist press in the fall of 1846.*

As is clear from Hennequin's Love in the Phalanstery, *Fourier's own ideas of sex and marriage were at once drearily conventional and wildly unorthodox. The Brook Farmers, like most utopians, were already suspected of leading improper sexual lives, and this reputation was aggravated by reports of Fourier's queer notions. It was Dwight's intention to calm such apprehensions, as well as to explain some of the advantages of the true social order. His text was a translation of Fourier, in which he accused his English rival Rob-*

ert Owen of proposing "the abolition of marriage," whereas he
merely advocated its eventual reform.

There is something blandly obscurantist about Dwight's defense,
as there is about Fourierist apologetics in general. Somehow the
issues get clouded rather than focused in the Associationist rhetoric.
For example, the attack on the "isolated household" was undeniably a stab at the very heart of American society, the nuclear family,
but the Associationists refused to admit this, and hedged both in
theory and practice. Although the isolated household was to be
abandoned in favor of communal kitchens, laundries, and so on, at
Brook Farm the family structure was still the primary social fact:
husbands and wives lived together, slept together, raised their own
children and were responsible for them to the rest of the community. Modifications of this basic allegiance were envisioned for
some perfected phalanstery of the future, but as with so much of
the Fourierist doctrine, the less said about that now, the better.

John S. Dwight
Liberty in Love

As translators and commentators, our business is not to defend or
call in question Fourier's ideas; it is simply to place the author and
his system in a true light, to bring them palpably before our readers:
let them judge. In translating him we do not identify ourselves with
him. We do not feel called upon to compare our own opinions with
his, for the benefit of the public, as we go along; nor is our silence
to be taken for assent. It does however properly fall within the
translator's province to try to make his author understood, and to
guard him from being *mis*understood. We are interested that justice
should be done to him, and justice in two respects:

1. Justice to the special ideas under consideration, that they pass
for what they are and nothing more.

2. Justice to the social doctrine as a whole, that it be not prejudiced by the questionableness of a part, which may be separable
from the main body. "He says some strange things; here is a notion
that is evidently wild; here is another that is quite immoral, exceedingly dangerous if it should be put in practice: therefore I'll none

● Selection from *The Harbinger*, III (1846), 136–37.

of his philosophy; how is it possible that *he* should know anything?"
Is that sound logic? If applied to every writer, how many books
would be read? None certainly, but those which contain nothing, or
which only harp upon old truisms till they sound worse than nothing. "Were I ever so sick I would not buy one of your drugs, for
there are some poisons on your shelves." Why not say this, as
well as reject truth, which is the medicine of the mind, because its
discoverer may be also subject to imaginations and errors? "He
loves wine and women; and he gambles; his politics therefore are
false; he shall not be my oracle on the subject of Corn Laws, Tariff,
or Sub-treasury; let the nation perish before I listen to one of his
speeches." What would become of Whig or Tory, if they judged
their great statesmen by this principle? "But Solomon had many
wives, and David's eye once wandered; how can there be any truth
in such a book?" Well, then, shall we fling away the Bible? Did you
judge the Declaration of Independence by Jefferson's religious
orthodoxy? As you answer these questions, so are you bound to
answer this: whether Fourier's peculiar notions of the relations of
the sexes as they will be after a total reorganization of society, and
after the experience of several generations in a life of harmony,
integral activity and truth in all relations—whether these notions,
be they right or wrong, are to be brought in evidence against his
whole science of Attractive Industry and Social Unity?

The observation will not hold here that Love and Marriage are
the type and regulator of society always, and that a scheme, a science
of society, which is false or wanting on *that* subject, must be worthless altogether. For Fourier proposes no change in our Marriage
system. He only aims to organize attractive industry, of which he
holds the science. In this way he would peacefully supersede old
wrongs, and convert the duplicity and strife of human interests and
passions into a state of harmony and truth, which would be Heaven
on earth. As to Love and Marriage he only says, that after the reign
of perfect purity and truth and harmony and love and justice shall
be established; after all the other relations of mankind shall be set
right; after business and politics shall be made to conform with
the moral law written in the heart; then the relations of the sexes
will be very different from what they now are; then there will be
truth in love also; then marriages will be real marriages; and liberty,
so far as it is necessary, will be pure and safe. He occasionally
indulges himself in pictures of this state of things. They may be
fanciful, or they may be rational predictions. But they are stated

not as things to be aimed at, but only as consequences which he supposes will follow—what? an artificial arrangement of his own suggestion? No; but any state of things which shall be a *true* state: that is, any state of things in which truth and justice and holiness and the highest spiritual and moral elevation shall take the place of the universal lies, oppression, sensuality and degradation which are now the rule.

The passage to which this note refers, although so brief, is very apropos to the newspaper controversy now raging on this subject. Fourier's statement here is two-fold.

Here is a negative statement. He denies the propriety of unlicensed liberty in love. At the expense of some seeming intolerance to Mr. [Robert] Owen, he exclaims against it with great indignation. He says that man has no claim to the title of discoverer or to the confidence of the world, who advocates such absurdities as "community of property, absence of divine worship, and *rash abolition of marriage.*" This is enough. Those who charge him with a licentious intent, can never again do so with candor, after having read this statement. Whatever he may advocate, it is not unbridled freedom. Lawlessness, promiscuousness, confounding of distinctions, headlong simplistic energy of any passion, without proper counterpoises, is the one thing most abhorrent to his very soul. It was because he saw these hellish spirits all so rife in what we call our civilization, here in the shape of decent, secretly-consuming lies, and there in open violence, turning all Christendom into a frightful pandemonium, that he sought a remedy, and sought so honestly that he found the very law and science of the thing, which, inasmuch as it is Law, *must* sooner or later reign.

2. Here is a positive statement. His remarks imply that there should be liberty, but *organized,* divinely governed liberty. By liberty he means not license; but he means the harmonious development of all the faculties and passions, which make up individual or collective man. For he, like Swedenborg, regards society, the human race collectively, as one complete Man; perfect only in the perfect organization and subordination of all its faculties and members.

He says there should be liberty, for without it there can be no truth. He calls the workings of the present system of legalized restraints to witness. His criticism of civilized marriage, in the *Treatise on Universal Unity* alluded to, is as irrefutable as it is appalling and disgusting in its expositions. But all this, he says, is "not a reason for suppressing marriage"; it is only a reason for

"reducing it to a methodical scale, for establishing in marriages a
regular series comprising seven degrees, &c."

. . . He does not proceed to organize Love at once. On the contrary, he declares, that many other things, and in short all other
things, must be ordered first. "Even if we understood the nine
degrees to be established in marriage, we should still have to understand and organize a state of things which would furnish counterpoises and guarantees against the abuse of liberty." "It will not be
till after thirty years' experience of universal harmony, that men
will have occasion to occupy themselves with the question." "Love
and Paternity are the last passions which can be brought under the
regime of truth." Let his modifications of marriage be what they
will, this certainly is postponing them to a very safe distance in
point of time, and it is making them consequent upon conditions,
which if they could follow, they must necessarily be right and safe.
We see then he is for trying no experiments in this matter. He is for
knocking away no established bulwarks against the pent up floods
of licentiousness, although he shows innumerable points at which
the imprisoned stream is secretly rotting and leaking through the
soundest barriers which civilized morality can impose. He proposes
to do nothing about it. The reformation will come just so soon as
society ceases to be a lie and becomes a truth; just so soon as the
law of selfishness and individual antagonism is done away in industry and the business of life; so soon as truth, justice and real liberty,
which is harmonious and healthy life in every faculty of every being,
shall have become established; so soon as peace and love and happiness shall reign, and universal unity shall have drawn together the
elements of its glorious symphonic temple out of the crying confusion of this great chaos of false notes, false by position, by perversion, not by nature. Here is a work which will not be accomplished
in a day. And yet its day is near. To conjecture or predict what sort
of marriage or substitute for marriage will follow that great day, is
a very different thing from that with which Fourier and his followers
are charged, namely, with endeavoring to alter the present customs
of society in that respect. There are religious sects holding abstemiousness among the chief of virtues, who interpret literally the saying
of Christ: "In heaven there will be neither marrying nor giving in
marriage." And if the kingdom of heaven is ever to come on the
earth (and heaven is harmony), what change too great to anticipate
in every human relation, and why, these religionists might say, shall
not the purity of man correspond to the purity of angels?

Brook Farm

Charles Lane

Charles Lane was a successful English businessman who converted to a life of rigorous morality and self-privation. He and his younger friend Henry Gardiner Wright came to America in 1842 to help Bronson Alcott set up a utopian colony in rural Massachusetts, not far from Brook Farm. Wright fell in love with Mary Gove (later Mary Nichols—see Introduction), and never set foot in the vegetarian paradise Alcott fathered; but Lane was a significant figure during the six months the idyl lasted, and has come down in history, thanks to Alcott's more famous daughter Louisa May, as the serpent who brought the apple of discord among the innocents. He is supposed to have encouraged Alcott to leave his wife and family in order to devote himself more chastely to the ideas of purity and community. The fact that Lane briefly joined the celibate Shakers across the valley from Fruitlands has been thought the clinching proof.

In fact Alcott was every bit as self-denying and abstemious as Lane (it ran in the family—see Section II for Alcott's cousin

*William), and the evidence suggests that it was as much his inclina-
tion as Lane's to place the "consociate family" above the selfish
ties of marriage and "exclusive love." Alcott finally capitulated to
the tug of duty and affection over the temptations of higher
virtues, and spent the rest of his life justifying his decision.*

*Lane's comments on the social and familial arrangements at Brook
Farm thus came from the perspective of a rival community, the
very animus of which was to be better than its neighbors. Nonetheless, his analysis of the basic contradictions in the Brook Farm
social order raised the crucial issue for life in utopia. John Humphrey Noyes, the leader of the most successful communal venture
of the period, understood the problem thoroughly; the closeness
of economic and domestic life "in association" put a strain on the
marriage relation that traditional isolated families never had to
withstand. In Noyes' view only two solutions were available, the
communal love and marriage practised at Oneida, and the Shaker
celibacy that Lane finally embraced. Without a complete communal-
ization of sexuality, the ordinary evils of unregenerate family life—
flirtation, adultery, jealousy, prurience—were exacerbated rather
than eliminated in utopian life.*

*In so far as the Associationists had an answer to this argument, it
was best formulated by their sympathetic critic Emerson, who
recorded the following conversation with a Brook Farmer in his
journal a few months before Lane's visit:*

*"Yeserday G. P. B[radford] walked & talked of the community,
and cleared up some of the mists which gossip had made; and
expressed the conviction shared by himself & his friends there, that
plain dealing was the best defence of manners & morals between
the sexes. I suppose that the danger arises whenever bodily familiarity grows up without a spiritual intimacy. The reason why there
is purity in marriage, is, that the parties are universally near &
helpful, & not only near bodily. If their wisdom come near & meet,
there is no danger of passion. Therefore the remedy of impurity
is to come nearer."*

*It was Emerson, by the way, who accepted Lane's article on
Brook Farm for publication in* The Dial. *One would like to know
what he thought of it.*

Charles Lane
Brook Farm

Wherever we recognize the principle of progress, our sympathies and affections are engaged. However small may be the innovation, however limited the effort towards the attainment of pure good, that effort is worthy of our best encouragement and succor. The Institution at Brook Farm, West Roxbury, though sufficiently extensive in respect to number of persons, perhaps is not to be considered an experiment of large intent. Its aims are moderate; too humble indeed to satisfy the extreme demands of the age; yet, for that reason probably, the effort is more valuable, as likely to exhibit a larger share of actual success.

Though familiarly designated a "Community," it is only so in the process of eating in commons; a practice at least, as antiquated, as the collegiate halls of old England, where it still continues without producing, as far as we can learn, any of the Spartan virtues. A residence at Brook Farm does not involve either a community of money, of opinions, or of sympathy. The motives which bring individuals there, may be as various as their numbers. In fact, the present residents are divisible into three distinct classes; and if the majority in numbers were considered, it is possible that a vote in favor of self-sacrifice for the common good would not be very strongly carried. The leading portion of the adult inmates, they whose presence imparts the greatest peculiarity and the fraternal tone to the household, believe that an improved state of existence would be developed in association, and are therefore anxious to promote it. Another class consists of those who join with the view of bettering their condition, by being exempted from some portion of worldly strife. The third portion, comprises those who have their own development or education, for their principal object. Practically, too, the institution manifests a threefold improvement over the world at large, corresponding to these three motives. In consequence of the first, the companionship, the personal intercourse, the social bearing are of a marked, and very superior character. There may possibly, to some minds, long accustomed to other modes, appear a want of homeness, and of the private fireside; but all observers must acknowledge a brotherly and softening condition,

● Selected from *The Dial*, IV (1844), 351–52, 355–57.

highly conducive to the permanent, and pleasant growth of all the
better human qualities. If the life is not of a deeply religious cast,
it is at least not inferior to that which is exemplified elsewhere;
and there is the advantage of an entire absence of assumption and
pretence. The moral atmosphere so far is pure; and there is found a
strong desire to walk ever on the mountain tops of life; though
taste, rather than piety, is the aspect presented to the eye.

. . . Of about seventy persons now assembled there, about thirty
are children sent thither for education; some adult persons also
place themselves there chiefly for mental assistance; and in the
society there are only four married couples. With such materials
it is almost certain that the sensitive and vital points of communication cannot well be tested. A joint-stock company, working with
some of its own members and with others as agents, cannot bring
to issue the great question, whether the existence of the marital
family is compatible with that of the universal family, which the
term "Community" signifies. This is now the grand problem. By
mothers it has ever been felt to be so. The maternal instinct, as
hitherto educated, has declared itself so strongly in favor of the
separate fire-side, that association, which appears so beautiful to
the young and unattached soul, has yet accomplished little progress
in the affections of that important section of the human race—the
mothers. With fathers, the feeling in favor of the separate family
is certainly less strong; but there is an undefinable tie, a sort of
magnetic *rapport*, an invisible, inseverable, umbilical chord between the mother and child, which in most cases circumscribes
her desires and ambition to her own immediate family. All the
accepted adages and wise saws of society, all the precepts of morality, all the sanctions of theology, have for ages been employed to
confirm this feeling. This is the chief corner stone of present society;
and to this maternal instinct have, till very lately, our most heart-
felt appeals been made for the progress of the human race, by
means of a deeper and more vital education. Pestalozzi and his most
enlightened disciples are distinguished by this sentiment. And are
we all at once to abandon, to deny, to destroy this supposed strong-
hold of virtue? Is it questioned whether the family arrangement of
mankind is to be preserved? Is it discovered that the sanctuary, till
now deemed the holiest on earth, is to be invaded by intermeddling
skepticism, and its altars sacrilegiously destroyed by the rude hands

of innovating progress? Here "social science" must be brought to
issue. The question of association and of marriage are one. If, as
we have been popularly led to believe, the individual or separate
family is in the true order of Providence, then the associative life
is a false effort. If the associative life is true, then is the separate
family a false arrangement. By the maternal feeling, it appears to
be decided that the co-existence of both is incompatible, is impossible. So also say some religious sects. Social science ventures to
assert their harmony. This is the grand problem now remaining
to be solved, for at least, the enlightening, if not for the vital
elevation of humanity. That the affections can be divided or bent
with equal ardor on two objects, so opposed as universal and
individual love, may at least be rationally doubted. History has not
yet exhibited such phenomena in an associate body, and scarcely
perhaps in any individual. The monasteries and convents, which
have existed in all ages, have been maintained solely by the annihilation of that peculiar affection on which the separate family is
based. The Shaker families, in which the two sexes are not entirely
dissociated, can yet only maintain their union by forbidding and
preventing the growth of personal affection other than that of a
spiritual character. And this in fact is not personal in the sense of
individual, but ever a manifestation of universal affection. Spite of
the speculations of hopeful bachelors and aesthetic spinsters, there
is somewhat in the marriage bond which is found to counteract the
universal nature of the affections, to a degree tending at least to
make the considerate pause, before they assert that, by any social
arrangements whatever, the two can be blended into one harmony.
The general condition of married persons at this time is some
evidence of the existence of such a doubt in their minds. Were
they as convinced as the unmarried of the beauty and truth of
associate life, the demonstration would be now presented. But
might it not be enforced that the two family ideas really neutralize
each other? Is it not quite certain that the human heart cannot be
set in two places; that man cannot worship at two altars? It is only
the determination to do what parents consider the best for themselves and their families, which renders the o'er populous world
such a wilderness of selfhood as it is. Destroy this feeling, they say,
and you prohibit every motive to exertion. Much truth is there in
this affirmation. For to them, no other motive remains, nor indeed

to any one else, save that of the universal good, which does not permit the building up of supposed self-good, and therefore, forecloses all possibility of an individual family.

These observations, of course, equally apply to all the associative attempts, now attracting so much public attention; and perhaps most especially to such as have more of Fourier's designs than are observable at Brook Farm. The slight allusion in all the writers of the "Phalansterian" class, to the subject of marriage, is rather remarkable. They are acute and eloquent in deploring Woman's oppressed and degraded position in past and present times, but are almost silent as to the future. In the meanwhile, it is gratifying to observe the successes which in some departments attend every effort, and that Brook Farm is likely to become comparatively eminent in the highly important and praiseworthy attempts, to render labor of the hands more dignified and noble, and mental education more free and loveful.

A Free Love Episode

Adin Ballou

The Hopedale Community, at Milford, Massachusetts, was organized about the same time as Brook Farm, and would in fact have
merged with the West Roxbury group had Rev. Adin Ballou and
his followers been able to come to an agreement with Rev. George
Ripley and his, about the necessity of requiring a creed or catechism
for admission to membership. Ripley and his liberal Transcendentalists were opposed to any such conditions (though they screened
their own applicants pretty carefuly), whereas Ballou and his friends
had worked out a "standard of practical Christianity" that included
a whole list of affirmations and denials, including a statement of
belief in "the state of matrimony."

This difference hints at much in the two communities' histories,
perhaps even explaining the longevity of Hopedale—sixteen years,
surpassed only by Oneida and a few sectarian colonies. Among other
things, Hopedale never had to undergo the whispering campaign
about sexual irregularities that Brook Farm suffered; even after
Ballou was converted to spiritualism, no one could imagine any-

thing improper occurring among these serious-minded folk. They were extremists in their own right, true enough, but in matters of another sort. Ballou made Hopedale a center of the non-resistant movement in New England, a form of Christian anarcho-pacifism that was explicitly spelled out in his "standard of practical Christianity," and that flourished among radical abolitionists like William Lloyd Garrison and Henry C. Wright.

The Hopedale non-resistants were in some ways similar to the "individual sovereigns" at Modern Times, Long Island, who were anarchists and libertarians too, though of a very different cast of mind. Both groups condemned the coercion of the State, both affirmed the virtues of community. But that was where the resemblance ended. This was made dramatically clear in the single case of Hopedale members violating the "standard" regarding the sanctity of marriage. As will be seen in the selection that follows, the culprits chose to go to Modern Times after their adultery was detected and censured.

In Ballou's account of the incident, he mentions "a man of ability and character" who lived in Modern Times just long enough to discover their free love propensities. This was George Stearns, of Lowell, Massachusetts, who joined the individual sovereigns on Long Island in the summer of 1852, before their reputation was abroad. After a few weeks he realized the intention of a few of the New York City contingent—Andrews, Lazarus, the Nichols—to "barter connubialities." Stearns promptly left the colony, and warned the world of the plot in his journal, The Art of Living, *from which Ballou is quoting in his account. It was Stearns's alarm that started the New York papers buzzing about Modern Times in 1852, and it was the runaway adulterers who provoked Ballou's crusade against free love in the Hopedale* Practical Christian *over the next few years.*

Adin Ballou
A Free Love Episode

As we at Hopedale, wherever we were known, had a reputation for hospitality to new ideas and a friendliness towards everything calculated to benefit our fellowmen, we were frequently confronted with theories and doctrines, good, bad, and indifferent, claiming, through their apostles, consideration and acceptance on the ground that they were helps to human progress or panaceas for the maladies of mankind. Some of these were thoroughly false in principle and mischievous in tendency and effect. It was impossible to prevent the introduction of these pernicious theories and doctrines within our borders and the discussion of them among our people. It was no part of our policy to attempt to do this; but it was a part of our policy to prevent them from doing any of us harm; it was a part of our policy to be continually watchful concerning them, lest they get a foothold among us, captivating the unwary and causing injury to personal character and the social well-being.

Among these reprehensible speculations was that, which, under a plea for the broadest and largest liberty, contemplated the removal of all conventional restraints pertaining to the relation of the sexes to each other, and especially in the matter of marriage, and granting to each and every one the privilege of forming connubial alliances and dissolving them at will, as inclination, pleasure, convenience, or whatever else, might dictate, under the general name of *Free Love*. But notwithstanding our vigilance, and in utter contravention of our solemn declaration concerning chastity and of our well-known adherence to the principle of monogamic marriage, there arose in our midst during the year 1853, a case of marital infidelity and illicit intercourse that caused great unpleasantness, perplexity, and scandal, and that required, at length, Community intervention.

The story is simply this: One of our male members, the head of a family, became enamoured of a woman, also a member who had for sometime resided in his household, and proportionally estranged from his faithful and worthy wife. Suspicions of something wrong arose among outsiders, causing considerable talk of a scurrilous nature, though nothing was absolutely known or could be proved

---

● Selection from *History of the Hopedale Community*, ed. William S. Heywood, Lowell: Thompson and Hill, 1897, pp. 246–49.

to that effect. At length the unhappiness of the wife was revealed, and the cause of it, upon investigation, made public. The matter then very properly received attention from the Council, who summoned the delinquents before them for examination and discipline. Upon being questioned and confronted with proof of misconduct, they acknowledged culpability, professed regret, and penitence, and promised amendment. But these professions proved insincere, or at least, transient, and the parties were again called to account. They then did not deny or attempt to conceal their criminality, but rather justified it on the ground that it was consonant with the principles of the new philosophy touching personal liberty, sexual relations, and the conjugal bond, which they had embraced—in a word, they openly and unhesitatingly avowed themselves to be *Free Lovers*, from conviction and in practice also. Having taken that position they could not do otherwise than withdraw from Community membership and leave the locality where both their theory and their action were held in almost universal derision and abhorrence. They went from us to the settlement of kindred *Individual Sovereigns* on Long Island already adverted to—"Modern Times," where they undoubtedly found congenial championship, and unbridled liberty to carry their doctrines out to the farthest possible limit, with no one to question or reproach them, or say them nay. For, as one who had been unwittingly induced to take up his residence among that "peculiar people" for a time, and who knew them well—a man of ability and character, well qualified to judge and to judge wisely— said: "There is a lurking combination among the leaders to do away entirely with the name and essence of marriage and to introduce instead an open and respectful sanction of promiscuous co-habitation. They not only cut the bonds of legality and set at nought the proprieties of custom, but they also scout the idea of constancy in love, and ridicule the sensitiveness of one who refuses to barter connubialities. Wife with them is synonymous with slave and monogamy is denounced as *vicious monopoly of affection*."

This case of marital infidelity and contempt of the marriage covenant occurring in our very midst and at a time when the most lax, corrupting, and dangerous sentiments concerning the general subject to which they relate were bruited abroad and extolled throughout the general community under the specious and captivating guise of *Liberty* and *Reform*, led us at Hopedale to declare our views and make our position known to the world beyond all doubt or peradventure. This we effected in a series of resolutions covering the whole ground involved in the divinely appointed distinction of sex, so far as it applies to the human race, which was passed in Community meeting held July 10, 1853. The series culminated in the last one which records most unequivocally and emphatically our conviction concerning the pernicious assumption adverted to, as follows:

"*Resolved*, (10) That, with our views of Christian Chastity, we contemplate as utterly abhorrent the various 'Free Love' theories and practices insidiously propagated among susceptible minds under pretext of higher religious perfection, moral exaltation, social refinement, individual sovereignty, physiological research and philosophical progress; and we feel bound to bear our uncompromising testimony against all persons, communities, books and publications which inculcate such specious and subtle licentiousness."

The occurrence which has formed the subject of comment in the last few pages and which in justice to the truth of history could not have been omitted from the present volume was the only one of its kind that ever transpired during our entire existence—the only one in which the inculpated parties justified themselves and took refuge under the bewitching sophistries of "Free Love." In the other few cases of indiscretion, similar in nature though by no means in degree, that came to light, the erring ones, when called to account, bowed to their acknowledged standard of duty, made due confession of their wrong, and in Scripture phrase "brought forth fruits meet for repentance." But on the whole, and to the credit of our young men and women as well as of those of riper years, it is to be put on record and kept in lasting remembrance that we were singularly exempt not only from positive scandal touching matters pertaining to the sexes, but also from covert suspicion and innuendo. Great freedom there was between male and female in the home, in the social circle, and in all public places, but few instances of excess, undue liberty, or impropriety, calling for reproof and reprehension.

Free Love

Austin Kent vs. Adin Ballou

When, after the defection of two Hopedale members to Modern Times, Adin Ballou declared war on free love in The Practical Christian, *his friend Austin Kent came to Milford to talk things over. "We spent hours in friendly, but in private discussion. I asked him, if ever he gave the subject a full and fair hearing in his paper, as he had before this given every other question of great interest— to discuss it with me." A year later, in the fall of 1854, a full scale debate between Kent and Ballou appeared in the pages of the Hopedale paper.*

Both Ballou and Kent carried on the debate in debating style, so much so that it is impossible to excerpt their leading arguments from the rhetoric and logic-chopping they lavished on one another over a period of several months; but it boils down fairly to the positions they took here, in the first round: Ballou separates man's animal and spiritual nature, Kent does not.

Kent later collected his arguments, added to them reviews and commentaries on the marriage tracts of Henry C. Wright, Andrew

Jackson Davis, and Orson S. Fowler, and published the whole as Free Love: or, A Philosophical Demonstration of the Non-exclusive Nature of Connubial Love *(1857). Kent was a typical free lover in that he was a loner and a maverick. Even the loosely knit communities of Modern Times and Berlin Heights were not individualistic enough for him—"I believe I can demonstrate their falseness to nature." He also argued that "in the present undeveloped state of the Race," it might sometimes be necessary to institute "sexual fasting" like that advocated by Joseph Treat and others of the continence persuasion, though this went against his principles. He had in mind schools like the Memnonia Institute contemplated by Thomas and Mary Nichols at Yellow Springs, where the rules forbade intercourse except for procreation. Kent gave the Nichols the benefit of the doubt, but he warned them against letting their school pass "into what I mean by community, I am not with them."*

In his own quiet, private life in Hopkinton, New York, as he told the readers of The Social Revolutionist *in 1857, "I have had some experience as to the workings of freedom in love, in all of the several theories. I have seen the necessity of a law of fasting, and its good results; and I have seen the evils of its too long continuance." Of course, such experience impressed readers of* The Social Revolutionist *more than it did those of* The Practical Christian.

Austin Kent vs. Adin Ballou
Free Love

Hopkinton, N. Y., Sept. 25, 1854

Friend Ballou:—

I will say in the beginning, I do not differ from Mr. Ballou and the friends of Hopedale, from Swedenborg, the Fowlers, or any of the defenders of the present order of Marriage, as to the *nature* and *spirit* of Chastity, or its opposite, lewdness and adultery. If this last statement can be remembered by Mr. Ballou and the reader, it will save much misunderstanding. I sympathize with Hopedale, in any to me, wise-effort to promote sexual purity. I do differ with Mr. Ballou and all those referred to above, in the law or order of

---

● Selection from *The Practical Christian*, XV (October 7, 1854), 46.

chastity. I deny that the most pure and chaste—the most normal and elevated sexual love, is always confined in its life, action or ultimates to dual order. I deny that its consummations are exclusive in that order. I think I am understood and sufficiently explicit. The question which I propose to discuss, stated—Does Sexual Chastity confine every man and every woman to the "pairing" order, or to be exclusively dual in the ultimates of love? Does normal and pure love require this? or still more abridged, and just as well understood as now explained—*Should Marriage always be exclusive and dual?* . . .

I have Amativeness, so I love woman—possibly I may love her, in this sense, exclusively from man; she is possessed of something different from man mentally, spiritually and physically. But I cannot love any one woman exclusively from any other women. I love all women as such—not alike in mental, spiritual or physical sexuality; far from it, nor can I be exclusive and concentrate my affections, except I do violence first to my reason and then to my affections. My love may vary towards different women, as they vary in their mental, spiritual, religious, social and physical womanhood, and as I have more or less ability to appreciate them, or as they are more or less in harmony with either or all these points with my own particular taste, but I cannot love one in the many exclusively from her sisters. My opponents harmonize with me in precept at least, in relation to all these manifestations of love except the physical. They will commend this general and universal state of the affections and condemn partiality and exclusiveness. They talk approvingly of "universal brotherhood." But when the whole man developes into harmony with itself and with every other man and every other woman—when the same universal law is allowed to prevail through all the affections, they are shocked with the impropriety; and yet it is as unnatural to exclusively concentrate the love of the physical as it is that of any other part of the mind. In this our attractions vary, but I insist, it is a natural impossibility to make them exclusive. We must first annihilate or uncreate what God has created. In this sense man is attracted to woman as such, and the same of woman to man. This love for the physical of the opposite sex, and attraction to it, is alike universal in its nature with every other love. As all my previous arguments to sustain the necessary universality of love, apply equally here, I will not repeat them. There are laws to govern mind, as absolute as those to govern matter. The forest trees can be bent by some material cause; so can the affections, by a power of the mind, or will; but the crooked tree, or the contracted and warped affections are exceptional and less harmonious. I find no Marriage in nature, as the laws of Marriage has ever been taught us. I do not find the Marriage of man to woman. "They twain make one flesh" says Nature in all her teaching on this subject. . . .

[Reply]

Dear Friend:—

Let the question under discussion be clearly understood. Mr. Kent defines it thus: "Does Sexual chastity confine every man and every woman to the *pairing* order, or to be exclusively dual in the ultimates of love? Or should marriage be exclusive and dual?" What is meant by sexual chastity? The true and innocent use of all the sexual capabilities. What is meant by the *pairing order,* or being *exclusively dual*? Having unreserved sexual communion with but one individual of the opposite sex. What is meant by Love? Sexual love. What is meant by the *ultimates* of love? Sexual coition. . . .

There is no mistake. He goes for universal, promiscuous sexual love and its ultimates—all in perfect chastity! No limits are to be set. Fathers and daughters, mothers and sons, brothers and sisters, &c., &c., may and should have sexual love, and ultimate it in coition! And if they are perfectly well balanced, pure and good, they will follow out this universal law of love! It is well that we can get so naked an exhibition of this Free Love monster. If we embrace the hideous creature, we shall do it with our eyes open.

Let us now attend to arguments. How does Mr. Kent sustain his doctrine?—"1. Man innocently loves good and congenial *mentality* in all other human beings." Granted; what then? *Ergo, Mankind may just as innocently have sexual love and coition indiscriminately!* Not granted. The analogy is false.—There is a radical dissimilarity between the two kinds of love. "2. Man innocently loves morality, virtue, goodness, in all other human beings." Granted; what then? *Ergo*, mankind may just as innocently have sexual love and coition indiscriminately! Not granted; the analogy is false. There is a radical dissimilarity between the two kinds of love. "3. My opponents harmonize with me in precept at least, in relation to all these manifestations of love, except the *physical*." They commend universal love and brotherhood, and condemn selfishness, partiality and exclusiveness; but are shocked at the same universality of sexual love and coition. True; and well they may be. The analogy is utterly false and groundless. Sexual love, as involving sexual coition, is radically an instinctive animal appetite. Man has it in common with the whole animal kingdom. It is not of the nature of benevolence, or friendship, or any other truly spiritual love. As an animal propensity it craves mainly its own gratification; just like the propensities for food, sleep, &c. It does not go abroad seeking opportunity to confer blessings on friend and foe. What an idea would it be for a man to hold up, that he was desirous of having sexual love and coition with as many women as possible, in order to bless and elevate them! This propensity, then, is primarily and essentially animal. It has its use and place. Within its own proper limits it may be gratified innocently. Allowed to break bounds, it becomes criminal and pestilent. This is the truth of the case. Is it so with the spiritual loves, with love to God, to virtue and the neighbor? Not at all.—Away, then, with all false analogies. Arguments founded on such analogies are utterly fallacious and worthless.—When Mr. Kent can show that *coitionary sexual love* belongs in the same category with piety, benevolence, friendship, and love of righteousness, his analogies will be of some value—never till then.

Adin Ballou

True Love vs. Free Love

Testimony of a True Hearted Woman

Among the regular members of the Hopedale Community was one transient or roving personality, Henry Clarke Wright, who made his home there for some years while he was on the lecture circuit as the traveling representative of the New England Non-resistance Society.

Wright followed the Kent vs. Ballou debate in The Practical Christian *during the fall of 1854. Having just finished his own book on* Marriage and Parentage *(see Section I above), he was eager to help combat free lovers like Kent, or like Thomas and Mary Nichols, whose* Marriage *was a blatant attack of monogamy. Wright had a friend whose views of the subject were all the more interesting for being those of a woman, and he obtained her permission to publish them anonymously in Ballou's paper.*

The "true hearted woman" does not make so detailed a case as Wright's spokeswoman "Nina" in Marriage and Parentage, *so one wonders how far she—and Ballou—would have gone in agreement with Wright's non-resistant theory that marriages, while they ought*

425

to be monogamous and permanent, should not be under supervision of the civil authorities, and should not be indissoluble, allowing for cases like his own, in which the partners proved incompatible after long years of trial. These views had earned Wright himself the reputation of a free lover, though the purists at Berlin Heights pointed out that he merely "assumes to do himself what he does not like the law to do; for the law which legislators enact, is not any more despotic to me, than the conscience and public sentiment which Henry C. Wright creates, to prevent the free play of my affinities." The distinction is interesting, for it is precisely the difference between the non-resistant version of anarchism adhered to at Hopedale and the individual sovereignty version at Modern Times and Berlin Heights. The first was a matter of ethics and conscience, the second of liberties and the instinctual life.

Testimony of a True Hearted Woman
True Love vs. Free Love

Since the appearance of Dr. Nichols' work on Marriage, the question of "Free Love," advocated by him, has occupied much of my attention. I offer the following suggestions, not so much because they are new, but because, on a question like this, the convictions of every mind are valuable, as throwing light on the nature, wants and capacities of the human heart.

I have always found great obscurity in the terms used to define the theory advanced by the advocates of promiscuous passional indulgence. They call it—"Free Love"—an epithet which is to me as appropriate as to call an object—"black-white"—a perfect contradiction in terms; for the idea of Love, as I understand it, and the idea of Freedom, as defined by them, are entirely inconsistent. According to my understanding of the action of Love, it is an experience of the heart, which can never result in any such desire for "freedom" as is professed by the advocates of "Free Love."

"I believe I record the universal experience of mankind, allowing for some exceptions which prove the truth of the general assertion, that, when Love takes hold of the heart of man or woman, it is

---

● Selection from *The Practical Christian*, XV (December 30, 1854), 69.

always accompanied by a desire to possess exclusively the affections of the beloved. This desire is commensurate with the intensity and purity of the love. As a woman, I can speak for the heart of woman.

The man whom she loves has power to impart to her being a new life. He is the completion of her happiness, the fulfillment of her destiny. However favored she may have been by worldly advantages, nothing can compare in value with this crowning blessing. By a perfectly natural action of the heart, she wishes to be to him what he is to her. She would occupy his thoughts, fill his imagination, and be allsufficient for his happiness. There is no effort, nor self-sacrifice which she would shrink from for his sake; and she wishes to exercise over him a power to control, elevate and save, corresponding to that which governs her destiny.

So when a man finds that the maiden to whom he has breathed out the depths of his loving soul has held in her heart the image of another, while listening to him, he feels his love slighted, his confidence betrayed, his manhood insulted. For she has outraged the *Instinct of Love*, which cannot be reasoned away nor disproved, so long as the memory of true love remains on earth.

The essential distinctive characteristic of Love is *Exclusiveness*. It seeks entire possession of soul and body; and nothing short of that will satisfy the heart of Love.

I can easily understand why the advocates of promiscuous passional indulgence should deny that this is the essential characteristic of Love. For their idea of it is widely different from mine. What they call *love,* I call *passional attraction;* and this will seem to be "attracted," according to the degree in which the sexual element predominates in the organization of each individual; and will lead to a higher or lower order of companions, according as it is coupled with a more or less refined idea of sensual delights.

"Free Love" claims the right to "ultimate" the passional attraction in any direction and to any extent; and the only limit proposed is "the capacity for enjoyment." It claims "VARIETY," not only as a right, but as a necessity; and attributes the social wrongs and miseries of our present condition to the unwillingness to receive and to act upon the doctrine of Free Love.

But *Love* makes no such claims. It places the animal nature completely under subjection to the higher powers of the soul. While Free Love clamors for continual indulgence, true love asserts a firm, wise self-control. The former disregards all consequences, in pursuit of momentary gratification; the latter looks with tender watchfulness to the welfare of the beloved. Remove the restraints of reason and conscience imposed by Love, and there is no reason why animal passion should not claim "variety." It is a restless, wayward element, and, when freed from the only restraints that can control it, becomes an imperious and fickle master. As a servant of true love, its ministrations are mighty and beneficent; but otherwise, debasing and destructive. "Free Love" can see no higher law for the exercise of the sexual passion than that instinct manifested by many animals that show a decided preference in the selection of those by which they will have their young. It entirely misrepresents the nature and offices of true love, borrowing its name to cover a poor counterfeit.

One of the pleas in behalf of variety in love, is, that those who begin with loving grow weary of each other. *Passion* may be satiated, but *love* never yet grew weary of its object. A man may be generally attracted towards the female sex, and find peculiar attractions in individuals. In one a gay companion, in another a sympathizing friend, in a third those winning personal graces which captivate the eye and rouse the sensual desire, and in a fourth a flattering dependence on his superior power and wisdom which may call up a feeble approach to an affection. I might enlarge the list *ad infinitum*, in which some attraction might predominate, each in its way appealing to the passions of the man whose great object in life is self-indulgence, and who is constantly on the watch for such attractions. These attractions are dignified, in the new Theory, by the name of *Love*; and passional indulgence with all these women would be justified by the Free Love advocates, and pronounced right, pure and honorable. When this doctrine can secure a state of morals among women sufficiently low to provide a supply for its desires, "Free Love" will have wrought its perfect work.

"Free Love" is nothing new; but until lately such relations have been held in secret, as unworthy of the respect of the pure in heart. Its doctrines have been whispered in the ear, among private circles. But now they have found public advocates, and in the promulgation of the doctrines of Free Love I recognize only an attempt to render respectable such acts and principles as have hitherto been confined to the secret resorts devoted to the gratification of the senses.

I have said that *Love* never wearies of its object. Its basis is in those spiritual attractions which are continually increased and strengthened by the action of love. Souls which have been drawn together with a harmonious organization find that the more intimate they become in the relations of love, the more powerful and endearing become those characteristics that first attracted them. Against all the testimony from ancient and modern times, I appeal to every man and woman who has loved with the whole energy of the soul, whether the tendency of love be not to concentrate itself exclusively on the one beloved object. There is no intimacy too close or exclusive for the heart of love; and it were no privation to be exiled to desert sands or barren heights, if only that solitude be shared with the Beloved.

From such love, and such alone, can the true relations of parentage arise; and on fidelity to such love rests our social safety. For the domestic influence outweighs all others combined in its bearing on society. A man thus vitalized by love can be indeed a *father* to his children; not merely responsible for their existence, but bound by every natural instinct to secure their perfect development. For to the heart of love, a child is not the embodiment of a gratified animal passion, but of a deep, pure, undying love, whose home is in the soul. The child is to each parent the gift of the Beloved; and there is no heart on earth, bound by love to its chosen companion, that will neglect the offspring of that love. On the purity, power and exclusiveness of marriage love, will depend the tenderness and fidelity with which children will be reared.

How works the theory of "Free Love" in this respect? The man who, "in ultimating his passional attractions," becomes the father of twenty or twenty-five children in the course of a year, cannot feel any particular affection for his numerous progeny, nor the responsibility which devolves on the author of their existence. They come, not in answer to the deep desire of his heart for children, but in consequence of his passional indulgence. Of course, then, he cannot feel nor show the tender watchfulness of a husband for her who is performing the great function of developing a new life within her own. For his thoughts are roving after new objects with whom to gratify his sensual desires. The true relation of husband and father would be abolished. For parentage under Free Love sanctions implies no responsibility as to the consequences of self-indulgence. If a child results, the father throws the burden of its life upon the mother, and while she is incapable of ministering to his passions, he seeks another woman, leaving her in turn as similar consequences may require. A man would never feel any especial obligation to sustain and cheer the mother of his child, when she might with equal propriety depend upon the sympathies of other men, with whom she had held the same relation.

Add to this the fact, that no man could be sure that any particular child was his own, and the last vestige disappears from society, showing where truth, purity, love and fidelity once abode.

Such, it seems to me, are some of the false theories veiled under the specious name of "Free Love." Its claim for "variety" is in other words a confession, that *sexual passion in some men is insatiable, and no one woman can fully satisfy it and live*. This, I grant, is true.

But *sexual desire* is not *love*. And I would not have young or old taken captive by an appeal to the senses, under the impression that they are obeying the high behests of Love.

Modern Times, New York

Moncure D. Conway

In the summer of 1857 the well-known Unitarian minister and popular author Moncure D. Conway paid a visit to Modern Times. Unlike most of their guests, Conway did not simply discover what he expected, or try to make an exposé out of what he found. Although the attempt to reproduce a "conversation" required him to do some fictionalizing, his account can be trusted as to the ideas and characters of the inhabitants.

Josiah Warren, the founder, was a sort of Yankee genius—an inventor (among other things, he built the first rotary press), a philosopher of economic individualism (he is often called the father of American anarchism), and a generally sensible and resourceful man. He provided the ideas—"individual sovereignty" and "cost the limit of price"—on which Modern Times was based; his disciple Stephen Pearl Andrews provided the publicity and the land. Andrews represented some rich New Yorkers who owned a tract of 700 acres out in the pine barrens of Long Island, and he was

*empowered to sell off lots at cost ($22 an acre) to all comers. They
began in January 1851; by the end of 1854 there were thirty-seven
families, sixty or seventy people living there, and by the time of
Conway's visit almost 100 cottages.*

*The ideals of the community were radically libertarian, which
gave considerable scope to a number of isms imported by the inhabitants. Henry Edger, the American high priest of Auguste Comte's
Positivism, made Modern Times his headquarters, and he had a
little group of disciples, including Marx E. Lazarus' sister Ellen.
Andrews, although he did not live on the site himself, was probably
responsible for a group of phonographers who settled there, including ex-Fourierist Theron C. Leland, in whose house it was that Conway stayed during his visit. And there were homeopathists and
hydropathists and spiritualists. Clark Orvis, who ran the little
restaurant, was the inventor of an early bicycle, the "velocipede,"
made out of wood.*

*Conway was particularly impressed with his hostess Mrs. Leland,
perhaps because she represented still another enthusiasm in the
community, the one that they were famous for. Mary Leland was
the plain-spoken "Mary Chilton" who was a regular correspondent
with* The Social Revolutionist *at the time of Conway's visit (see the
Berlin Heights selections below). The most notorious free lovers—
Andrews, Lazarus, Thomas and Mary Nichols—were actually New
Yorkers who could never settle down to the quiet country existence
on Long Island; but Mary Leland was not the only activist free
lover on the premises. Although the community had not begun as
a sexual experiment—and Josiah Warren was very disturbed by its
reputation—the very rumor of sexual license seems to have created
the fact. A couple caught in adultery at Hopedale fled to Modern
Times in 1852; in 1854 James Clay came down from Maine to
investigate for himself; others joined as individual sovereigns and
were converted to free love, for it was the sort of movement that
was likely to spread wherever it got a foothold.*

*But no matter what the newspapers said, the village was never
merely a free love colony. From beginning to end it reflected the
character that impressed Conway so much when he met the founder
in 1857: "he was by no means one of those reformers who, having
fought with the world, hate it with genuine philanthropic animosity,
but one who had never been of the world at all, had never been
stirred by its aims nor moved by its fears; one who was not deluged
with negations, but amused with a troop of novel thoughts and*

fancies, which to him were controlling convictions." With this tem-
perament the colony survived both the attacks in the newspapers
and its own extravagances. It never quite died out, but simply
matured, until it finally lived down its notoriety and became obscure
little Brentwood, Long Island, a typical suburban community with
hardly a thought for its heritage.

Moncure D. Conway
Modern Times, New York

About eight years ago, when residing in the city known in
America as the Queen of the West, I received a letter, making some
inquiry, which was dated at "Modern Times, N. Y." I carefully kept
this letter, which seemed to have come from some place in Bunyan's
dreamland. Having occasion afterwards to write to a friend in New
York, I inquired if he knew anything of such a place. "It is," he
answered, "a village on Long Island, founded and conducted upon
the principle that each person shall mind his or her own business."
It is needless to say that, after this, the place seemed to me mythic
and impossible. Some months later, when there were strikes among
the working men our our neighbourhood, I gave an address to them
on the relations between capital and labour, at the conclusion of
which a man of strange but prepossessing appearance came up, and
said, "Sir, if you ever have the opportunity to visit the village of
Modern Times, you will find out that the evils of labour come of
the existence of Money." Whereupon the man disappeared.

I resolved to try and find Modern Times, and started with the
mere knowledge that it was on Long Island, not being sure whether
a place where people attended to their own affairs and did without
money was to be reached by railway or rainbow. Nathaniel Hawthorne, in "The Celestial Railway," has told us how pleasantly the
pilgrim may now travel by steam along that road on which, in
Bunyan's day, he had to toil wearily on foot; how poor Christian
may now have his burden registered and put in a baggage-car; and
how ugly places, like the Slough of Despond, are passed over on fine
viaducts. There seemed to me some truth in his report when I found
it easy to be ferried over from New York to Long Island, there to be
booked for Modern Times.

● Selection from *Fortnightly Review*, I (1865), 421–22, 425, 427–29, 431–34.

Dreary enough is that island of six-score miles, which stretches out from the American metropolis. The New Yorker thinks of it only as a wall against the sea, protecting the harbour, and indented with inlets whence come the boats loaded with delicious bivalves. Now and then a geologist may wander there to try and discover whether the island was originally cut off from the main land, or deposited by the slow working of a vast eddy made by the concourse of currents. A few fishing villages along the coast, where the inhabitants bask in the sun by day and at night see fire-ships, phantom-ships, and all manner of ghostly and ghastly things, and a few well-tilled farms inland, with mansions inhabited by the families of rich merchants, in New York—by whom they are occasionally visited,—constitute the vestiges of humanity on that island. Down into the sandiest region of a sandy land—Suffolk—we go by the iron path which alone binds it to the nineteenth centruy; and, after nearly three hours of travelling from New York, the conductor enters and roars out to me, "Modern Times!" There was something Mephistophilian in his face as he did this. It was plain that he meant to call the attention of the thirty or forty people in the carriage to the fact that there was among them a man going to "Modern Times." I was the only one to stop there. The train thundered on, and I found myself set down in the porch of a house where no human being was visible, nor another house. At length, however, I managed to discover some one who told me that the house where I was set down was "Thompson's," and that I must go a mile off from the railway to find the village I sought. It was twilight when I left "Thompson's," and dusk had followed before I saw anything like a human being or habitation. At last I heard a footstep, and presently saw some person approaching. Whether this person was a man or a woman I could not tell, for the dress seemed to be a cross between that of men and that of women in the outside world which I had left. When the figure came near enough I addressed him/her (as Mr. Charles Reade would write it), asking the way to Modern Times. The voice, which was that of a woman, assured me that I was close upon the village. "Is there any hotel or lodging-house there where I may go for the night?" "None that I know of"; and she passed on quickly into the darkness, leaving me with some misgivings in my mind as to whether a little more interest in other people's affairs was not on the whole desirable. Presently I came to the verge of the village, and saw a cluster of houses standing pure and white under the clear light of the moon, which was just rising, each with its garden. The street before me was absolutely silent except for the voices of a boy and girl who walked together talking in low and pleasant tones. I asked for the address of a person named to me in the letter already mentioned. The house was pointed out, and I knocked at the door. I was soon introduced to its occupant, a lady, who was surrounded by one or two Modern-timers, and, having stated that I wished to learn something about the village and its ways, was very cordially received. "You will not find us," she said, "a Goldenthal; we are rather poor; but if you are interested in our ideas, you may find us worthy of a visit." This allusion to the village of Zschokke's tale was reassuring, for it conveyed the impression that the village had an ideal aim, whilst the kindly tone with which it was uttered made me feel that my visit would not be looked upon as an intrusion. I told them, briefly, the little incidents which had led me there, and they promised me every facility for seeing and hearing all that they had to show or say, declaring that the great world outside went on without sending them one inquiring stranger in a year.

* • •

The arrangements of marriage were, of course, left entirely to the men and women themselves. They could be married formally or otherwise, live in the same or separate houses, and have their relation known or unknown to the rest of the village. The relation could be dissolved at pleasure without any formulas. Certain customs had grown out of this absence of marriage laws. Secrecy was very general, and it was not considered polite to inquire who might be the father of a newly-born child, or who the husband or wife of any individual might be. Those who stood in the relation of husband or wife wore upon the finger a red thread; and so long as that badge was visible the person was understood to be married. If it disappeared the marriage was at an end. . . .

In the afternoon the villagers gathered for conversation at the residence of the lady whom I had first met, and who, as I now discovered, was a person of distinction amongst them. She was a woman I should say, a little over thirty years of age, and had an indefinable grace and fine intellectual powers, united with considerable personal beauty. She was a native of one of the Southern States,—Georgia, I believe,—where she had married. The marriage was unhappy, and on separation she considered herself, as I have heard, most cruelly treated by her husband and the law together, in being deprived of her children. She had studied medicine, and was earning her livelihood by medical practice. Her own experiences led her to sum up the chief evils of society in the one word *marriage*. Indeed, it was plain to me before I left Modern Times that nearly all of those who resided on that lonely shore had been cast there by the wreck of their barks. Alas, how many others were swallowed by those hungry surges of the turbid sea of life in the great city and country over there! But though, looking around upon the faces of those who were present at the *conversazione*, I saw many traces of the several storms which they had encountered, there was a serenity in them which one can rarely see in those restless eyes and compressed lips to be met with by the thousand on Broadway. There was, too, an easy, cordial relation of one with another at Modern Times, a frankness and simplicity of intercourse which gave assurance that they were held together by a genuine attraction, and sustained by mutual sympathy.

The conversation, which occupied the entire afternoon, was frank, earnest, and participated in by all with such freedom and occasional vehemence, that I find it difficult to give any fit report of it. No special topic was assigned, and so the very general one of the improvement of man and of society sprang up, to become speedily a banyan-growth, reproducing itself from each individual's particular point of view. I am bound to say, too, that the principle of individuality, so emphasised in the settlement, was nowhere more observable than in the variety of points at which its members assailed the old, or set about constructing the new, society. At no time did anything like a dispute, or even a debate, occur; still less was there any of that "schwärmerei," that spurious enthusiasm wrought by heaping assent upon assent, too often found among reformers; but the conversation seemed rather to go on weaving one after another into its woof by the simple force of mutual encouragement. It was not a little amusing to witness how this or that person was associated with this or that speciality of opinion. If Fourier or Socialism were alluded to by any speaker, all eyes were directed to some individual, hitherto silent perhaps, and all exclaimed, "Oh, William knows all about that," and William, already kindling to his subject, was easily called forth to give his contribution. Others had respectively an acknowledged authority to speak concerning Marriage, Sex, Trade, Law, Education, Politics. Of the conversation itself I give the following meagre account:—

A. (a man).—"For a long time I believed the regeneration of general society practicable, and was content to be a political reformer. But I found that the evil of society, though it could be driven after much toil to change its form, was never eradicated. It was like driving a disease from one part of the body to find it entrenching itself in another. I learned that the laws which oppressed the negro or woman were part of the general condition of the social system. The political reformers were like men sweeping away snow from the streets and gardens whilst winter was yet in the sky, and would to-morrow cover all over with another snow-fall. No fear of snow, thought I, where summer reigns. And if those hearts which love justice and trust truth should gather together somewhere and form a society of their own, there would be a perennial social springtide. Such a society might consist of two or three only, but the Highest would be among them if they were gathered in the name of the Highest. This would not be running away from general duties to the world; if true, it would be a pattern from the Mount shown to the calf-worshippers below; it would be a still small voice of protest against the evil fashion of the world; and it might and must become something cosmic in the end. For this reason I came to Modern Times, which, more nearly than any community that I have seen, represents the idea I have stated."

B. (a man) explained and illustrated the system of "equitable commerce," which I have stated, so far as I comprehend it, in another part of this paper.

C. (a woman).—The first need of the world seems to be a moral and social Protestantism. I do not say that American society has broken all the inward chains which bind thought back to the Romish or to the dark ages; but the external fetters are broken. But from the morality and the institutions which were formed in those ages and according to those creeds, general society is not delivered. Dress is still ascetic, Marriage is yet medieval— (A voice: "Especially *evil*")—and the codes concerning Woman belong to an age which debated whether women had souls. Theological freedom is but an unembodied ghost until it can *legitimate* its own institutions and its own morality. The world talks indeed of progress; but how is it to go forward upon legs that have been withered these three of four centuries at the least?" . . .

F. (a man) thought that the world would be chaotic until the equal sovereignty of woman was everywhere established. "Until she is equally educated in all colleges and universities, until she is admitted to any study or profession for which she has the inclination or ability, the world will be one-eyed,—blind to the universal feminine side of things. We know now what high powers of vision, of intuition, that sex has, and we may well shudder at what we are losing by the stupid refusal of any real education to those powers. The exclusion of woman from the state has left it a *politic* (a trick) where it is not a barbarism. But, in my opinion, if we could only have the persons of the two sexes educated together in the school and the university as they are in the home, we should find another hemisphere of the world quite as important as that which Columbus discovered. Nor would there be that morbid relation of the sexes which now leads the young man and maid to cultivate in their respective monasteries (schools and colleges) chronic curiosity concerning each other, and false ideals which end in deception, disappointment, sin, and wretchedness. Man and woman should live together, and grow side by side, at every period of life; and if our universities for both sexes should graduate their students into sensible marriage, it would be far better than anything that comes ordinarily from their bachelors' degrees."

G. (a woman), who had been visibly kindling for some time, began to speak of marriage, to which she found objections beyond my power to enumerate. To her, that institution was a great monster-king, whose throne rests upon human skulls. She quoted the French *mot*, "Marriage is the suicide of love," and maintained that the iron rivets of the law were driven through the real heart of any true relation between man and woman. "Where are the courtesies, the tenderness, the giving by each heart of its best, which marked the relation before marriage? They are gone—those true bonds— because not needed; treat her (or him) as you please now, for those gentle attractions and tender ties have, under the parson's diabolical conjuration, hardened to chains! Then comes in that noble instinct which rebels against chains. I should come to hate an angel if I were fettered to him. It makes no difference if a young person has voluntarily or gladly entered upon this relation; none should be permitted to impawn their future selves. The body changes, the mind changes; the food of one period may be the poison of another; the truth of one the falsehood of another. What good is wrought to any human being by having two persons live together who do not love? Is it good for children to be brought up under the shadow of such a tragedy? Is it not prolific of intrigues, jealousies, and all crimes?"

Some one here asked whether she would make a marriage contract to be dissoluble at the will of either of the parties, and whether, in that case, young people would not enter too lightly upon the relation, and whether there would not be many cases of heartless desertion? In reply, G. said, "I am not bound to show that in a world of imperfect and half-educated people any system would be free of evils; but only that the new one would have far fewer than the old. My belief is, that in cases where one wishes to separate and the other resists, it is generally the wife who resists; and this she does, not because of her horror of parting from one who does not love her, but because of the special incidental troubles that befall the woman in such cases. Her character is the subject of gossip, if it is not ruined; she is not apt to have any fine relations with either sex afterwards; and if she has children, is apt to lose them. If law and custom made it easy and natural to terminate such engagements, society would not suppose any crime or scandal implied by such termination, and would welcome man and woman without respect to such changes. The woman would not, in this case, have the same reason as now to cling to a false marriage. There is little fear that the man would not cease to love if he were not loved."

I inquired of this speaker what her idea of a true relation was, and mentioned Goethe's suggestion that every marriage should be contracted for only five years. Such an arrangement might, she seemed to think, be adopted as a transitional thing; but there would be no justice or truth in marriage until it was remitted to the individuals themselves as a private and domestic affair with which the laws had nothing at all to do. When it was thus left, men and women would both be trained to protect themselves. There were some persons who would like a longer, others who would desire a shorter, marriage; some who were fitted for monogamy, others for bigamy, others for polygamy; and the law does not really prevent these from carrying out their several dispositions,—it only succeeds in producing untold misery by branding and outlawing them.

"But," I suggested, "there are children in these cases, brought into the world without their own volition, and the law interferes to protect them. It is that the child may not be deserted that the law regards the home as permanent. What under your plan would you do for the children?"

"If," said she, "you admit that the home where no love is, and where the marriage is false, is for any child no true home at all, but a school of vice, there remains only the physical nurture and protection of the child to be considered. I do not deny this difficulty; but Goethe, whom you have quoted, also tells us that if we do the duty that lies nearest us, a light will arise upon the next. Once let us abandon a state of things known to be false, and methods of adapting circumstances to new wants will appear. I doubt not that if separations were customary and legal, the parents of the children would easily make arrangements for their children. Homes for such children would everywhere spring up, and the law need only provide that they should not be left as burdens on the state, nor deprived of comfort and nurture. Even under the present divorce laws such arrangements are made for children."

H. (a man).—"We have listened to much concerning the evils of society, and to a catalogue of remedies for them. It has not yet, I believe, been settled whether the chicken or the egg came first. Nor does it seem clear whether we must have a better society before we can have better people, or better people before we can have a better society. My own belief is that society is only the aggregate of the brains that are born into the world from generation to generation; and that to improve it we must go back of education, back of marriage; we must deal with mankind before they are born. An unhealthy society can never be a good society. The dress, the habits, the hereditary taints of men and women reappear in malformations of brain, and consequently of character. Dr. Johnson's idea, that marriages should be arranged by the Lord Chancellor, is not so bad as that they should be arranged by the combined ignorance of the contracting pair. It is true that there should be no marriage where there is no love; but it is also true that love is no guarantee of a true marriage. Educate a man or a woman, and they will love very different objects from those they would have loved in their ignorance. A youth might love passionately his own sister, if she were beautiful, and their relationship unknown. There are temperaments which should not be wedded more than brother and sister. There are characters, to unite which is to introduce an evil offspring into

the world. To have only the most perfect human beings born we
need a greater diffusion of science in the world, and we need certainly that individual marriages should not be made irretrievable
when they shall be condemned by larger intelligence or unfolded
characters. A general diffusion of knowledge, especially on these
subjects, would gradually lead to such careful and scientific relation
of sexes, that the human race might share in some of that miraculous improvement which now is monopolised by those breeds of
sheep and pigeons which Mr. Darwin describes in his book on the
Origin of Species."

The above account of this, to me, memorable conversation does
not pretend to be literal. I have omitted what was commonplace,
have sifted much, and do not doubt that many good grains have
fallen through my sieve. My idea has been to give to the best of my
ability the substance of each speaker's remarks, and, if possible, in
his or her own form of illustration. Many of the utterances may be
startling to some of my readers; but I assure them that they were
given with the utmost simplicity, without any straining after effect
of novelty, and in many cases with an almost devout earnestness. It
was about sunset when the company—having shaken hands somewhat after the fashion of a Quaker meeting at its breaking up—
departed.

MONCURE DANIEL CONWAY.

Conflicting Sovereignties
at Modern Times

Josiah Warren, Thomas and Mary Nichols

Giving advice to someone who was planning to found a new community in 1854, Josiah Warren had much to say from his experience at Modern Times, but nothing so much to the point as this: "There will be no real enemies to this subject when it is understood—the danger comes from friends."

Warren's friend, who opened the floodgates to free love and scandal, was Stephen Pearl Andrews. After their collaboration in organizing the colony in early 1851, Andrews got involved with Thomas and Mary Nichols, who had established a water-cure "institute" in New York in September and invited him to give the commencement address to their first graduating class in December (it was a twelve-week degree). At this point the friendship looked like a convention of reformers—the Nichols bringing hydropathy, feminism, Grahamism, and "physiology" (that is, sex education for women), while Andrews contributed individual sovereignty, phono-

graphy, and spelling reform. From this amalgam—and especially from the conjunction of Mary Nichols' sexual history (see Introduction) and Andrews' notions of individualism—came the new cause they all embraced, free love.

By the following summer the embryo free-love clique had quietly developed to a new phase; Modern Times was to be its cradle. George Stearns had just come to the colony, attracted by Warren's ideas, and was publishing his paper The Art of Living *as its official organ. In the July issue Stearns innocently printed an article by Thomas Nichols on "The Future of Women," but by August he began to smell a rat. He took his family and his paper out of the community, and published the first big exposé of free love: "We are persuaded,"* The Art of Living *revealed, "that a large circle is already formed, very few of whom are at present located in Modern Times, but mostly in New York City, with a prospective look that way, who are covertly and surreptitiously, but systematically and zealously, effecting their purpose." And so it proved.*

Lazarus' Love vs. Marriage *had just appeared, and in November 1852 Andrews came out of the closet as a full-fledged free lover, in his debate with Henry James Sr. and Horace Greeley in the New York* Tribune. *And not long after this it emerged that Andrews had given the Nichols 100 acres of land immediately adjoining Modern Times, on which they planned to build a new water-cure institute, Desarrollo.*

During 1853 the situation worsened. The sensationalist press had taken up the crusade against free love, and began to get some results. The Nichols had moved their institute out to Port Chester, where they could charge board and room as well as tuition. During the summer a number of their female students precipitously fled, to protect their reputations from the increasing notoriety. The Nichols brazened it out, putting the blame on a rival hydropathic school in the city where they claimed R. T. Trall was passing round a salacious novel about Mrs. Nichols (it was true—see Introduction).

Desarrollo now became a weapon in the controversy, and Mary Nichols issued the statement printed below, warning prospective members of Modern Times that reputation might have to be sacrificed to truth in the new community. This manifesto was printed in August, and immediately followed by a disclaimer from Warren, who objected to the way that the Nichols had of speaking for Modern Times as if it were theirs. Not fazed by Warren's complaint,

Thomas Nichols turned it into still another occasion for propa-
ganda in the Water-Cure Journal and Herald of Reforms, *also*
printed below.

But although the cellar was dug and the foundations laid for
Desarrollo, these events of the summer of 1853 damaged the Nichols'
financial and moral credit so severely that they had to abandon their
dream spa—much to Warren's relief. Modern Times never com-
pletely recovered its reputation, but when Moncure Conway visited
it in 1857 it was still healthy and growing, having outlived the worst
of its friends. It was a good sign when Thomas and Mary Nichols
announced in the December 1856 issue of their Monthly *that "Mod-*
ern Times is a dead failure." By March it was their own new insti-
tute in Ohio, Memnonia, that was dead, and they had renounced
all their missions and joined the Catholic Church.

Mary Gove Nichols
City of Modern Times

We come together for freedom, in the midst of great reproach.

We believe that Love alone sanctions the union of the sexes; and
this faith is positive, not negative. It does not only allow people to
break false unions, but it allows them to form true ones; and if they
make mistakes, it allows of their correction, instead of the perpetuation of discord and evil in children.

We seek to create a New World in all the Relations of life.

Each person who wishes to go to Modern Times, must answer
readily and affirmatively such questions as the following:

Am I brave and strong enough to meet all the difficulties of a
new settlement?

Have I the honesty and heroism to become of no reputation for
the truth's sake?

Am I willing to be considered licentious by the world, because
of my obedience to a law, higher than worldlings can conceive of?

● Selections: Mary S. Gove Nichols, "City of Modern Times," *Nichols*
Journal of Health, I (August 1853), 39; Josiah Warren, "Positions De-
fined," broadside dated from Modern Times, August 1853; Thomas L.
Nichols, "Individuality—Protest of Mr. Warren—Relations of the Sexes,"
Nichols Journal of Health, I (October 1853), 52.

Josiah Warren
Positions Defined

An impression is abroad, to some extent, that the "Equity movement" is necessarily characterized by an unusual latitude in the Marriage relations—I as one, protest against this idea. "The Sovereignty of every Individual" is as valid a warrant for *retaining the present* relations, as for changing them; and it is equally good for refusing to be drawn into any controversies or even conversations on the subject. I find no warrant in my "sovereignty" for invading, disturbing, or offending other people, whatever may be their sentiments or modes of life, *while they act only at their own Cost*: and would again and again reiterate in the most impressive possible manner that the greatest characteristic of this movement is its "INDIVIDUALITY"—that the persons engaged in it are required to act entirely as INDIVIDUALS—*not as a Combination or Organisation. That we disclaim entirely, all responsibility for the acts, opinions, or reputations of each other.* The principles of "Equity" are as broad as the universe, embracing every possible diversity of character: I therefore do not look for conformity, and therefore repudiate all combined or partnership responsibilities, or reputations.

I suppose the world's experience to be its great instructor, and if it has not had enough of *isms* and follies I disclaim all right to oppose experiment, while the "Cost falls only upon the experimentors." But for myself, so far from proposing or wishing to see any sudden and unprepared changes in the sexual relations, I am satisfied that they would be attended with more embarrassments and more disastrous consequences than their advocates or the public generally are aware of; and farther, I wish to have it understood as a general rule, that I decline even entertaining the subject, either for controversy or for conversation.

I again caution all persons not to make me responsible for the acts or words of others; it is my right to have the making of my own reputation, and I wish them to remember, that no person either in his or her deportment or conversation, or as writer or lecturer is to be understood as a representative of me, unless my sanction is specifically given, to every idea thus advanced; and that no Newspaper or Journal is to be understood as an organ for me, except so far as it may have my signature to the articles it may contain.

Village of Modern Times, Aug. 1853.

Thomas L. Nichols
Individuality—Protest of Mr. Warren—
Relations of the Sexes

. . . We have been careful to let our readers understand that any real and vital change in our discordant domestic relations, would be a cause for scandal, and we have not been mistaken. The simple demand for more of truth and purity in the relations of the sexes, has been met with the vilest slanders. We are sure to be misrepresented. To the vile, freedom means licentiousness. "To the pure, all things are pure."

As an individual, Mr. Warren has a right to his protest, and it illustrates one of his principles. . . .

What we ask, what we labor for, what we hope for, as the result of all our toils, is *truth, purity, equity,* in ALL the relations of life, especially those highest, most vital, most important. The man who is not willing to seek the truth, accept the truth, and live the truth, is dishonest to himself and to mankind; we can have no fellowship with him.

. . . How can men and women live true lives in false relations to each other? How can harmonious and happily-organized children be born in discordant unions? They never have been, they never can be. And the world will be false, and perverse, and discordant, just so long as it is peopled in falsehood, and perversity, and discord.

Reformers, philanthropists, here is the root of the world's great, overshadowing tree of evils! Mr. Warren may refuse to discuss this subject; we cannot refuse. No man of science and philanthropy can refuse to speak the truth on a question so vast and so important. The world wants light on this more than on all other subjects, and it shall have what light we can give it. *Are we right or wrong?*

Free Love at Berlin Heights

"John B. Ellis"

This account of the Berlin Heights community appeared in the generally untrustworthy Free Love and Its Votaries, *purportedly written by a "John B. Ellis," but actually a piece of hackwork by "a literary gentleman . . . who does not wish to have his name mentioned in connection with it," as John Humphrey Noyes discovered when he tracked down its slanders on the Oneida Community. As it happens, Ellis's history of Berlin Heights is surprisingly accurate; his source must have been better than William Hepworth Dixon, from whom he stole his Oneida material. Even the bias of his informant is not so much distorting as it is clarifying, for there is nothing more conducive to candor than the self-righteousness of vigilanteism.*

The community began formally in January 1857, when Francis and Cordelia Barry joined Joseph Treat, C. M. Overton, and others in buying a ninety-acre farm (at $40 an acre) and laid plans for further development of some 600 acres in the Sandusky area. By the summer they had possession of the local hotel, as well as other *farms. One estimate of their total worth was in the millions of dollars, but this partisan audit included the assets of all their adherents in the area.*

A major free love convention was held in September, and John Patterson moved his Social Revolutionist *press to Berlin Heights in October. These flourishing signs were the chief contributing factors to the vigilante action described by Ellis. It is interesting to note that the "grossly indecent" article which was the last straw was not written by a free lover at all, but by one of their opponents, spiritualist medium Anne Denton Cridge. Her article was so offensive that Patterson had censored it when he first printed it, but Mrs. Cridge's husband objected and so in the October issue Patterson reluctantly gave the rest, which occasioned as much shocked remonstrance from free lovers in the November issue as by the outraged citizens who burned it.*

As Ellis's informant admits, the chief reason for the local resistance to the free lovers was the same as the objection to John Humphrey Noyes' Perfectionists, when they were run out of Putney, Vermont: free love doctrines were simply too attractive, and young people in the area were being seduced into the devil's camp. What else was to be expected, when the free lovers announced their intentions in terms like these of Francis Barry:

"Our only motto must be Freedom. Every individual, fit to be of us, must do as he or she pleases in all respects; and those who are not 'of us,' will not be attracted to us. We shall not be troubled with tobacco chewers, for free-love will not 'attract' filth. Believers in marriage, 'mating,' 'duality' etc. will not come among us, for fear of losing their 'property.' Those however who have faith, that the 'one-love' will be secure where attraction is recognized as law, we shall of course, welcome. But I warn them that 'variety in love' will be the result."

"John B. Ellis"
Free Love at Berlin Heights

"It was in the year 1854," said the old man in whose words I wish to tell this story, "that the first of the Free-Love set made his appearance at Berlin Heights. The village was a small, pleasant little place, and, better still, it was thoroughly respectable. The inhabitants were decent people, and we had never done any thing to forfeit the good opinion of the rest of the country. The land about here was very fair, and prices were much lower than they are now. A great many strangers were coming and going, some of them being pleased with the country, and some thinking they could do better elsewhere. A few bought land and settled down here, and we began to grow slowly but steadily in population. In the year that I speak of, a number of these long-haired, sleek-looking fellows came out here to buy land and form a settlement.

"The leader of the gang was Francis Barry, an oily, plausible fellow, who had some good points about him, and who was even liked by our people until his doctrines made him unpopular. Barry was followed by a lot of his friends, men and women, and as soon as they got here they commenced what they called their warfare against marriage. Barry was a good hand at lecturing, so they sent him around the country to speak in behalf of their cause. He and his friends started two or three newspapers in various parts of the country, in which they advocated their Free-Love doctrines, and announced Berlin Heights as the centre of their movement. This continued for three years, during which time they continued to increase rapidly. Every week some new member would come in."

"Where is Barry at present?"

"In New York. He is the leader of a 'Reform Club,' or a 'New Protectorate,' or something of the kind, and I am told that it is his intention to attempt another experiment on the Berlin Heights plan. Let me say, at the outset, that I don't think Barry directly encouraged the excesses of his followers here; but as these were the direct results of his pernicious teachings, all the people here who do not sympathize with him hold him responsible for them, and, I think, justly.

● Selection from *Free Love and Its Votaries*, New York: United States Publishing Co., 1870, pp. 356–77.

"But to go back to my story. The Free Lovers increased here
very rapidly. They bought a farm adjoining the village, and commenced to cultivate it. These heights offer very great inducements
to agriculture. The lake breeze which sweeps over them keeps them
almost entirely free from frost, and we raise some of the finest
fruits here that are to be found in the Union. The farm purchased
by the Free Lovers was an excellent piece of land, and they worked
it faithfully. They encouraged no idlers. They managed to get
possession of the only hotel in the place, which, we thought, gave
them a decided advantage in their efforts to increase their numbers.
We had no occasion to complain of them in their dealings with
us, for I am bound to confess they were honest in their business
relations and faithful to their contracts. They labored under a very
great disadvantage in being short of money, but endeavored to
make up their deficiency by hard work. Some of them were men of
ability. The most of them were Spiritualists; for Spiritualism and
Free Love go hand in hand, and the leaders are now amongst the
most prominent Spiritualists of the day. . . .

"At first we paid but little attention to them. We were glad to
see the land in the hands of industrious and energetic workers,
and had no idea of the real character of these people. As we began
to understand their ideas, we were indignant, but thought it best
to laugh at them. Some of our young men may even have appeared
to sympathize with them; but if they did, it was only because they
wanted a lark with the women. It was not long, however, before
the differences between us became so great and so bitter that no
decent person could uphold the Free Lovers, even for the fun of
it. We began to be alarmed, sir, at having in our midst a class of
people, already numerous, and growing faster than we, who had
the shamelessness to advocate the entire overthrow of the marriage
relation. They declared, in their newspapers and their public
speeches, that it was a sin for a man and woman to live together
as husband and wife, if they could not do so without quarrelling
and in absolute peace. They said it was not necessary for people
to be married by a preacher or squire, but that, when men and
women fancied each other, they had a perfect right to live together
until they got tired of each other, when they ought to separate,
and find other and more congenial companions. They didn't hesitate
to tell us, sir, that a man and woman living together in open

adultery were as pure and virtuous as we who had been married in church. Marriage, they said, was a fraud, and the cause of all unhappiness in the world, and we were great fools for clinging to it. This we considered a dangerous doctrine, and we naturally looked down upon those who professed it as a dirty set. We did not regard it as liable to do us old people any harm, for we thought we had discretion enough to prefer morality to vice; but we had children, sons and daughters, in whose hearing these infernal principles were enunciated, and we wished to save them from pollution until they were old enough to think for themselves. Besides—for I must own it—it did anger us to be told that our wives and daughters, our mothers and sisters, whose goodness, modesty, and purity we valued more than our own lives, were no better than a parcel of common women.

"Perhaps, if they had confined themselves to principles, we should have let them alone, and trusted to time to cure the evil. But they were not satisfied to hold their own opinions about matters of this kind. They kept trying to force them upon us, and kept up such a noise in the world, that the people of the entire Union began to look upon Berlin Heights as the hot-bed of immorality, and to regard every man and woman in the village as devoted to the practise of Free Love. Why, sir, we couldn't go to Sandusky or Cleveland, or anywhere in the country—we, who were decent men and women, and totally opposed to the vile doctrine—without being stared at as Free Lovers. It was outrageous. We didn't deserve it, and we were not willing to submit to it.

"In a little while matters came to a crisis. There are always in this country a plenty of men and women who, being unhappily married, are anxious to escape from their claims, and others who think that the destruction of marriage will give them greater license than is possible in the present state of affairs. Such people were in active sympathy with the Free Lovers of our village, and many of them came here to attend the conventions held here. These people seemed to regard the village as their own property. They paid no more attention to Sunday than to any other day. They gave balls on the Lord's day at the hotel, had public dinners, speech-makings, and merry-makings there on that day, and, in short, did everything they could to outrage our feelings. When some of us undertook to remonstrate with them, they said it was a free country, and that they would do as they pleased. They had as much right to the village as we, and they would permit no interference.

"This was not all, however. We had every reason to suspect them of immoral practices. We had heard their teachings—that men and women were justified in living together in the most intimate relations without the sanction of a marriage; we knew they taught that any man and woman wishing to indulge in sexual intercourse were justified in the act; and we were not silly enough to believe that people holding such views could be innocent in their practices. We observed many signs of unlawful intimacy between the men and women, such as caresses, kisses, tender glances, and long walks towards the woods about nightfall. Besides, there were some discontented fellows among them, who thought their wives too free with other men. We had no actual proof that we could put in evidence in a court of justice, but we were all satisfied that the hotel was a vast den of immorality.

"Matters now came to such a pass that the best men in the village and vicinity came to the conclusion that something must be done to rid us of this nuisance. We were convinced that to use brute force against them would be to do them more good than harm. In such a case, they would at once raise the cry of 'Persecution,' and draw to themselves a certain amount of sympathy, and our policy was to expose their doctrines and practices, and hold them up to public scorn. So we determined to attack them through the press, which we felt sure would not dare to defend them.

"The leading man in the village was Mr. ———, a prominent member of the Baptist church. He had represented us once in the Legislature, and had held several County offices, and, as he was regarded as the ablest writer in the place, we considered him the proper man to head the movement against the Free Lovers. He was ready enough for this, for he despised them and their doctrines, and he wrote a number of very able articles against them, which he published in the *Sandusky Register,* the principal paper in the County. These articles were well written, and their object was to arouse the public sentiment against the Free Lovers, and in this they were successful. They fell like a bomb-shell into the Free-Love camp, and the leaders of that movement undertook to reply to them, but none of the papers would publish their articles. They then put their heads together to determine upon a course of action, and it seems that they came to the conclusion that our course would benefit them more than it would injure them. They seemed to have full faith in their doctrines, and openly avowed that all that was needed to spread them over the country was to make them known. They consulted the spirits as to the course they should pursue, and asserted that they were ordered to aid us in our efforts to expose them, for the reason that such a course would attract universal attention to them, and react overwhelmingly in their favor. They and their friends wrote sensational articles for the papers, ridiculing and denouncing themselves. These articles came from various parts of the country, and were copied by most of the papers of the day. It was some time before we could discover the authors of these communications, for they kept their secret very well for a while; but at last they thought the joke too good to be kept quiet, and were loud in their boasts of getting gratuitous advertising out of the papers which opposed their doctrines. They victimized the New York *Herald* and *Tribune* badly in this way. The articles in the latter paper were so ingeniously written, that, while they appeared to denounce Free Love, they were really a defence of it. It was a shrewd trick upon their part, and it must be confessed that they succeeded in neutralizing our plan of operations to a very great extent.

"We now resorted to another plan. We called an indignation-meeting at the Presbyterian church, and enjoined it as a duty upon every lover of morality to attend. When the time for the meeting came, the house was full, and we congratulated ourselves that we should now have a plain, outspoken denunciation of the Free-Love business by the best men in the County. In point of attendance the meeting was a success. We had the best men of the County present, and a plenty of them; but the Free Lovers were there in force also, and, when our speakers commenced to denounce them, they asked leave to reply. We foolishly gave them permission, because we wanted to see fair play, and were unwilling to take any unfair advantage of them. We paid a good price for our generosity, however. The meeting was a failure—a fizzle, as we say here. It lasted for three hours, and degenerated into a spiteful discussion of the Free-Love question. We were completely outwitted by the tactics of our opponents, and accomplished nothing. Our adversaries, on the other hand, gained a certain sort of triumph, and I assure you they crowed loudly over us. They declared we had tried to find grounds for a denunciation of them, and had failed, and they published this statement all over the country. After this they threw off all restraint, and made it a point to desecrate Sunday in every way they could, in order to show their contempt for us. At the same time, the reports of their immorality became more frequent and more circumstantial. Matters were dreadfully suspicious, but we had no positive proofs against them. They kept their own counsel, and never betrayed each other. When we questioned them as to the truth of the reports concerning them, they either denied them outright, or laughed, shrugged their shoulders, and said nothing.

"About this time they took steps for the establishment of a Free-Love newspaper in the village. One John Patterson, a writer of ability and force, was publishing a paper called the *Social Revolutionist* at Greenville, in Darke County, in this State. The Free-Love party here began to negotiate with him for the removal of his office to this place, and he, being in full sympathy with the movement, agreed to do so. In a short while he was established and at work here. His paper was regarded as the organ of the Free-Love party in the West. I use the term 'party' as embracing all who sympathized with the movement. The war against marriage and domestic life was now continued with greater fury. The Free Lovers, encouraged by their successes, threw off restraint. Their paper was filled with denunciations of the marriage system, and advanced the most abominable ideas. For a while we had to endure it, because they clothed their attacks in reasonably decent language, but at length they threw off the mask. Men corrupt at heart cannot always act with decency. Their real natures will sometimes show themselves. One morning the *Social Revolutionist* published an article which put an end to our patience. The article was grossly indecent, and stated the doctrines of the party in their lowest and most revolting form. All restraint was thrown aside, and it was plainly stated that the object of the movement was the gratification of the animal passions of the members. The language of the article was utterly unfit for a brothel, and was such as I do not care to repeat to you literally.

"Up to this time our people had been divided as to the best means of getting rid of the Free Lovers. Some of us were for driving them out by force, others for letting them alone and allowing the movement to die out of its own accord. This article disgusted even the friends of toleration, and, after this, not a voice was heard in opposition of our resolve to compel the wretches to quit the place. We made no secret of our determination, and it at once became known to the opposite party. They tried to smooth matters over by saying that the article was false in its statements, and was written by an opponent for the purpose of injuring them. We didn't believe them, and we told them so. It was not likely that an adversary could succeed in deceiving the shrewd men who controlled the paper, and secure in it the publication of an article calculated to injure them. No; we were satisfied that the article was a genuine expression of their sentiments, and we were not to be turned from our purpose by their explanations. Men who were lost to decency would not hesitate to lie. Falsehood, indeed, would be their first resort upon finding themselves in trouble.

"We called another indignation-meeting in the village, which was attended by large numbers of persons from all parts of the surrounding country. We had learned a lesson from our first meeting, and this time refused to allow any of the Free-Love party to say anything at the meeting. Barry tried very hard to get a hearing, but we hissed and hooted him down. We wanted no explanations. The offenses of these people admitted of none, and we wanted no more of their talk. We adopted a preamble and set of resolutions setting forth our grievances and the infamous course pursued by our opponents, and requesting them to leave the County. Some of us were in favor of driving them out at once, but others—and they had the majority— wished to endeavor to get rid of them by peaceful means. A committee was appointed, who waited upon the leaders of the other party, and informed them that it was the desire of all decent people in the County that they should leave it. Some of us (I was among the number) who favored force accompanied the request of the committee with the warning that we would drive them out if they did not go peaceably. In return, they notified us that they would not leave willingly, and would meet force with force. At the same time, it was known that they were putting their printing-office and hotel in a state of defense, and purchasing fire-arms.

"There was now every prospect of a serious collision in the village; for, though the friends of peaceful measures were in the majority, there were quite a number of us who were anxious to strike such a blow as would rid us of the nuisance at once and forever. In this state of feeling, it required all the influence of our friends to restrain us. It was well that they did so; for, had the blow been struck, we should have shown the wretches no mercy.

"We now resorted to the law. Several of our people went up to Sandusky and had warrants taken out for the arrest of the most prominent of the Free Lovers. These warrants were based on charges of immoral proceedings in violation of the laws of the State, which we brought against them. They were entrusted to the police of Sandusky for execution, and we stood ready to put down any resistance to the officers of the law. The constables came down to the village quietly, and, before our adversaries were fairly aware of their purpose, they had arrested some twenty-five or thirty men and women. They put them on the cars and took them to Sandusky, a number of us following to see the result of the affair. We expected they would be confined in jail; but the Mayor, before whom they were taken, admitted them to bail, and had them lodged at the hotel at the expense of the city. The trial lasted a week, and was a complete farce. We had no witnesses to support our charges, and had relied upon compelling Frank Barry and others to testify to the truth of the facts we wished to establish; but we were badly beaten. Of course, we could not compel any one to admit anything damaging to himself or herself, and all professed to be totally ignorant of the conduct of the others. They declared that if such irregularities as were charged upon them existed, it was without their knowledge. Their principles, they said, required them to refrain from meddling with other people's affairs. Each one found it as much as he or she could do to attend to his or her individual concerns. They had no time for gossip or eavesdropping. They baffled us in this way at every point. We were fully persuaded that they were acting in accordance with a preconcerted plan, and that they were not telling the truth; but we could bring forward nothing in evidence, nor could we extort a single admission from them. They beat us badly, and, at the close of a week, the case was dismissed, and they were allowed to return to their homes. You may be sure they exulted over us. The truth is, we had damaged our side badly by our foolishness. They had nothing to lose, and everything to gain, by such a ventilation of their doctrines as this trial brought about. We had failed to establish our charges. A court of justice had acquitted them, and they had gained a moral advantage over us. They were jubilant, and we very sore, over our defeat.

"The friends of peaceful measures were now at their wits' ends.

They had exhausted all the means at their disposal, and those of us who favored force resolved to do a little on our own account towards ridding the place of the wretches. Mob violence is always wrong, and that to which we hot-heads resorted was no exception to the rule. We damaged our cause by it, and created a certain amount of sympathy for the Free Lovers. We annoyed them in every conceivable way, and did all in our power to make the place too hot to hold them. The Free Lovers kept on in their old habits, and sent their newspaper and printed documents to all parts of the country.

"One day, Frank Barry was driving along in his wagon to the Post-Office with a load of his Free-Love documents for the mails. He was totally unapprehensive of harm, and was driving at a moderate pace. We knew of his habit of sending his documents off in this way, and we were determined to put a stop to it. Upon this occasion about twenty of us, men and women—for our women were by far the bitterest enemies the Free Lovers had—waylaid him, and, stopping his horse, made him get out of his wagon and surrender his documents. There must have been about four bushels of them. We had matches and shavings on hand, and we piled the latter in the road and emptied the documents on top of them. Then we set fire to them, and in a few minutes they were in a bright blaze. Barry stood by without moving a muscle or uttering a word, and saw his precious documents reduced to ashes. We gave him to understand that we would serve him in the same way if he did not alter his course, and then let him go home. I could hardly recall all the annoyances we heaped upon these people if I were to try. Let it be sufficient to say, that we persecuted them in every possible way short of inflicting bodily injury upon them.

"We overshot our mark, sir, and made friends instead of enemies for them. As I have told you, a large number of our people were opposed to violence. They now began to condemn us as severely as they did the party we opposed. When the next township election came on, the Free-Love question was made the principal issue. Those of us who favored energetic means were able to control the regular ticket, and we secured the nomination of men pledged to expel our opponents from the County. The Free Lovers and the friends of toleration joined hands in this canvass, and succeeded in electing their ticket. Their candidates were pledged to protect the Free Lovers as long as they could not be convicted of violating any law. The fact is, we had disgusted our own friends by our violence,

and they turned against us and supported Free Love. This was a
hard blow to us, and we confessed ourselves beaten, and gave up the
struggle.

"The Free Lovers had learned wisdom from their past experience.
They were now endorsed by a very strong party which had once
endeavored to drive them out, and they had every cause for exulta-
tion; but, to our surprise, they exhibited very great moderation.
They relinquished none of their doctrines and abandoned none of
their ways of living, but conducted themselves with more discretion
than they had ever done, well knowing, I suppose, that those who
had gone so far in their opposition to them, would leave no effort
untried to detect their secret practices.

"Just about this time, when they were exerting themselves to ward
off public censure by showing a life outwardly correct, and closing
all the means by which outsiders could obtain an insight into their
inner workings, a circumstance happened which once more turned
the tide of public opinion against them. They did not live in one
family, like the Oneida Community, or in a phalanx, like the
Fourierites, but were scattered about in small fruit-farms along one
side of the village, and for some distance back into the country. In
the summer of 1858, a small group of the most advanced members
of the sect took a farm about a mile beyond the village, and lived
there together. They were about equally divided as to sex, and were
regarded by us as the most honest of their set. Their friends in the
village did not look upon them with much favor, declaring that their
conduct, which was simply in accordance with their principles, was
calculated to bring the sect into disrepute. Hard stories were told of
this set of Free Lovers, but they were indignantly denied; and as we
had no proof against them, we could do no more than express our
disbelief of their denials.

"One day a neighbor of mine, having missed his cow, set off in
search of her. His route led him through the farm of the people I am
speaking of, and close by a pretty stream which ran through the
place. Not far from the dwelling, this creek was so completely
enclosed and shaded by the trees and bushes as to be as private and
secluded as a bath-room. The shade was so thick that it was delight-
fully cool even on the hottest day; and as the water was clear and
tolerably deep, no better place for bathing could be found in the
country. My neighbor passed within fifty yards of it, and as he went
by, was attracted by the sound of voices and the splashing of water.

It was evident that a party of bathers were enjoying the sport and the place. My neighbor listened again, and this time he heard the voices of women as well as of men. Matters were getting interesting, he thought, and he crept cautiously and noiselessly through the bushes till he reached a spot from which he could look down upon the bathers, himself unseen by them. The sight that met his eyes astonished him, bad as he had believed these people to be. About a dozen or more men and women—all that lived on the farm— were in the water together, and all as naked as when they came into the world. How long they had been in the water before my neighbor saw them, he could not say, but he declared that they were there for nearly an hour after his arrival, as he remained in his hiding-place, watching them until the last one left the spot. You can easily imagine the motive which led a dozen men and women to make such a shameless exhibition of themselves; and you can also understand what took place before they left the spot. It was a scene of the grossest indecency, and, as you may suppose, my neighbor was thoroughly disgusted.

"After he got home, he came to me and told me of all he had seen, and we agreed to go back the next day, and take two other persons with us, in the hope of getting four witnesses against them. If my friend had held his tongue, the plan might have been successful, and we might have made a case for the courts; but the secret was too heavy for him. He took the whole village into his confidence, and, by the next day, every Free Lover in the place was fully informed of his adventure, and of the trap we had laid for them. All of them, and many of our own people, pitched into my poor friend with a vigor that startled him, and declared that, in seeking to see what he regarded as impure and indecent, he was even more to blame than the guilty actors in the affair. Still, the whole village was indignant at the performance of the bathers. The majority of the Free-Love party professed the greatest disgust at the affair. They held an indignation-meeting, and denounced the 'bad taste' and 'bad policy' of the bathers; who, by the way, did not deny the affair, but claimed that it was intended as a practical demonstration of the state of 'Eden innocence' in which they lived.

"Although the majority of the Free Lovers professed great indignation at the performances of the 'Eden Group,' as they came to be called, they did so in such a manner as to satisfy us that they were at heart in sympathy with them, and were really one with them in all things save discretion. They deceived no one, however, and the indignation which my friend's discovery aroused made the village more of a unit upon this question than it had ever been before. For a while it seemed that we were at length on the eve of getting rid of these troublesome people. Time, however, had taught us wisdom, and we were now all unanimously of the opinion that a resort to violence would not do; so we united in an address or petition to the Free Lovers, requesting them to leave. This request was couched in mild and persuasive terms—entirely too mild, I thought—and was as ineffectual as our other efforts. We not only requested the 'Eden Group' to leave, but extended the invitation to the entire Society. We wanted none of them to remain behind. They peremptorily refused to do as we desired them. If we wanted to separate from them, they said, we could leave the village ourselves, and they were perfectly willing that we should go; but, having bought their lands and made themselves homes here, they intended to remain. No petitions, addresses, or resolutions on our part could shake their determination. If we tried force, they would resist us. They informed us that they were armed and prepared for war, if it must come, but would only resort to violence in case we began the struggle. They knew very well that they were safe in making this assertion, as only a very small number of us were now willing to resort to force. C. M. Overton, who was one of their best writers, published a pamphlet in reply to our address to them. It was well written and plausible in its statements, and was scattered broadcast through the County. It had the effect of quieting the active opposition of the respectable people of Erie County.

"This was eleven years ago, and since then we have made no effort to get rid of our disagreeable neighbors. The fact is, they tired us out by their perseverance. We have contented ourselves with an expression of our unqualified dissent from their views, and a denunciation of them whenever opportunity offered, but have done no more. Gradually all open hostility between us died out, and we agreed to accept the situation, and endure what we could not cure. We fell into trading with them, and a stranger would have taken us for one people. But we have never ceased to protest against their presence here, and would be glad to see the last one of them go away.

"Our policy of non-interference was more successful than our other efforts. Soon after its adoption on our part had taken from the Free Lovers that community of interests which a present danger always imparts, quarrels and dissensions broke out amongst them. Their Spiritualist doctrine of the sovereignty of each individual over his own acts, prevented them from acknowledging a common authority in anything. Each man was his own master, each woman her own mistress. Each had an entirely distinct doctrine which he wished to see adopted by all the others. The amount of confusion and discord which prevailed in a few years almost passes belief. Barry left the place in sorrow, as he said, his authority and influence as prophet of the new dispensation entirely gone. His visions of promiscuity came to nought, and he shook off the dust of the place from his feet. Overton became disgusted with the movement, and abandoned it. He is living in Vineland, New Jersey, I believe; but what he is doing, I cannot say. I notice his contributions occasionally in the New York *Universe*, and judge from them that he has not lost his old grudge against Barry. One by one the best of them went away, despairing of ever seeing their social millennium, and disgusted with their own doctrines. The majority of them have sought refuge in Spiritualism pure and simple, and some of them have married. A few of them—perhaps fifty in all—still live in the neighborhood, but they are very quiet and inoffensive. They hold to their old doctrines, but I believe their lives are correct. Of late years they have made little or no effort to propagate their doctrines; but what they will do now that the woman suffrage and anti-marriage parties are acquiring such strength, is, of course, impossible to say."

"Then you regard their experiment here as a failure?"

"Unquestionably. As long as our hostility to them threatened them with danger, they were united and harmonious; but as soon as we left them to themselves, they got to quarrelling, and came to grief. As I have told you, all the prominent members of the party have left the place."

THE DAVIS HOUSE HOTEL, home of a group of free lovers in Berlin Heights, Ohio, as it appeared about 1875.

Retribution

Joseph Treat

"*Sexual indulgence, sexual gratification, sexual enjoyment—these words are all an infinite lie to me.*" *This was the admission of free lover Joseph Treat, in an article on "Sexual Purity" that even the continence-oriented* Nichols Monthly *refused to print, as a matter of "taste and propriety." Like many other free lovers, at one extreme of the pendulum's sway (see Introduction), Treat was a "varietist" only in love's spiritual manifestations. His ideal of sexual contact was virginity, with allowance grudgingly made for the continuance of the species. All through 1856 and 1857 he held up the banner of purity in the columns of* The Social Revolutionist, *while his opponents—especially lawyer James W. Towner—argued the logical and scientific case for sexual indulgence, as necessary to health and community. Treat's rather feverish apologetics brought replies from as far away as Modern Times, now more or less quiescent, where "Mary Chilton" (Mary A. Leland—see note to selection by Moncure Conway) wrote, "Ah, my brother, boast not of purity, while you find impurity in true love-manifestations or*

expressions of whatever kind. Boast not of health, strength, or
manhood, while you live the life of an unblessed ascetic monk—a
life of inversion, stagnation, and inevitable annihilation."

   Treat stuck to his guns, and in September 1857, during a free
love convention celebrating the establishment of Berlin Heights,
the spectacle of "free lust" rampant proved too much for him, and
he announced his withdrawal from the community he had helped
to found.

Joseph Treat
Retribution

   . . . It was meet that I, who had helped from the first to found
this Berlin—from the day of earliest beginning, and infinite odds,
and almost none to come to the rescue—should at length, just
when the effort promised to be a Success, be compelled to withdraw
from the very Berlin those early toils and pains had founded! It
was meet that I should be forced to disconnect myself from the
band of brothers, with whom I had stood shoulder-to-shoulder,
during the weary and uncertain months that had gone before—to
take myself out of their company, and plant myself down alone;
as if I belonged not to them, and they no longer belonged to me.
And it was meet that the pressure upon me should be so strong,
and all things should seem to me to have swelled to such a crisis,
that I was driven to take this step upon the very heels of our great
Convention; and even before the close of Convention-week, to call
another meeting of those same there assembled, to announce to
them, and the public, these news—that I had thus, so suddenly
and so strangely, cut loose from all that then was, of Berlin! It was
meet that the reaction with me should be such, that all the more
when it came it came! It was fitting I should thus—at such a
time, in such a way—expiate my long offense against my own Soul,
in being so bound up with those who were not of my faith, nor of
my life. It was the chalice of Justice to my lips; the sacrament of—
Retribution!

   And from the first, I had foreseen and expected all. From the
first, Nature—my nature—had urged me on to all. For from the
first, my Soul had forbid my ever uniting myself with those so

---

● Selection from *The Social Revolutionist*, IV (November 1857), 154–57.

unlike me. And thus it came, that from that earliest hour when I undertook this enterprise, I never did a single thing for Berlin, which was not done in my Soul's very despite—done under protest! I was not of that I worked for—and that I worked for was not of me—and still I had no home—most of all, I had no home with my Soul.

Purity was the rock on which I split with my brothers; and on Purity must I yet split with all—save the fewest few. I had *written* against Sensualism; and now I acted. For while I had written, I had still been in fellowship with those who wrote as strongly the other way; so that I was dividing myself, and tearing down faster than I builded. And I had also defended this Berlin (though thus not my own) against attack: boh here before a meetiing of citizens; and likewise afterward, in a card to the public, over my own name; as well as then, at several sessions of the Convention: so that by this time I was thoroughly merged in the rest; and made to stand sponsor for their life, and not mine. I had quieted myself till I could quiet no longer. But it was my own act had wrought all; and there was no escape but to meet its consequence. I paid the penalty in the separation.

Henceforth, I am an individual. I resolve into my original elements. In this great Universe, of such an infinite number and variety of folks, I will stand for one. I will be responsible for myself. I will live my own life. I will not be holden for the way of any other. I will not be mixed up with that which I can not approve. I will refuse the hand of fellowship to all who are not oned with me. I will flow only to those who can live my life; but they, shall be my home and my heaven. With them I will blend, to found another and a holier Berlin—a Home of Society, Freedom, Purity. I will not fear to give myself to these; for I know that I shall still have but one life to answer for; and that, my own!

I believe in Freedom; and am to the uttermost a Free Lover: and I will do what I can to redeem that glorious name from the dishonor of the sensual. I hate Marriage-Slavery: first, because I hate all Slavery; but most, because it compels millions of my sisters to lives of prostitution and ravishment. For myself, I put my heel on Marriage; and I will never bow my neck to its yoke. But I renounce and I denounce the perfect system; in my own name, and that of its victims. Were I to die to-morrow, I would execrate what gave up woman's chastity to somebody who owned her. The difference

between Man having *his* say-so in this matter, and Woman not having hers, is, that Might makes Right; and the stronger can have his
own way! And the difference between a public woman in the streets
of New York, and a compelled woman in the marriage-bed, is, that
the body of the one is sold for an hour, but the body of the other is
sold for life. And the difference between a woman subjected to
forcible violation, and a woman coerced in Marriage, is, that the one
suffers once; for she can cry, and be rescued; but the other may
suffer even nightly; for she dare not cry; but the laws are all on the
side of the rape. I am against all to the hilt! But I believe in men
and women flowing together in Pairs (but not in Isolation), and
thus two becoming One. I believe that Love (and not Law) makes
the twain One; and gives the right, as it creates the necessity, to live
together as One: and that this Love, so irresistible and free—
unchained, and even unclaimed—is instead of any and every
Marriage. I believe in Purity between the Sexes; and in a beautiful
and holy Innocence of their intercommunion—even a Vestalate of
everlasting Continence and Virginity: and this must exclude everything but the congress of Parentage; and all that is more, though I
should stand alone, I yet must forever excommunicate and anathe-
matize as Lust. I class all in one, be it least, or be it what—anything
but the naturalness of sexed but yet unsexed beings—the intrans-
fused oneness of incorporeal members. And I call it Lust, not
because I will; nor even because my nature will compel me to
(which could not possibly know how to go to work to grow into
conceit with it, nor to look upon it other than as repulsive, and a
perfect evil, to be afraid of, and saved from) ; but because, when I
would be good, and great, and noble, and worthy of my destiny—
when I would try to climb up, and become all angel and high—
then, it seems so low, degrading, sensual; so far down, down, down,
infinitely beneath a mortal or immortal Soul! To parent a child, is
clean, and chaste, and beautiful; and when men and women get to
be wise, it will be to save the world, for peopling it with infinite
Messiahs: but this other—this *profaning* Parentage, to satisfy the
clamor of ignoble desire, and glut a bodily appetite—what shall be
said of that? Ah! if my body could be pleased, yet my Soul could
never! But that, would scorn to be subjected to the lust of the flesh—
the greater enslaved to the less, the master to the servant—but would
instantly rebuke it, and compel it under: and then the harmonious,
self-poised *me*—my perfect, utter nature—would spurn, and hate,

and loathe, the base indulgence, that it could no longer possibly be any indulgence, but only a thing forevermore too vile and despicable, for me to stoop to have anything to do with it. The Soul will not barter its golden freight of loves, and hopes, and aspirations, and swellings to reach the eternal and infinite, and be all one with the perfect and ineffable Vast, for *less* than filthy lucre—filthy gratification—but it will still cling to the ark wherein its jewels lie hid, and hold on to its Virginity. Woman must be a Virgin, or the world is not safe, for she is its mother; and then man must be a Virgin, or woman can not be: but more, both yet *will* be Virgins; for they will grow to that, that their natures will not let them be any thing else. For I believe the future will bring an earth, wherein not one man nor woman will ever experience a temptation to prostitute this holy function of offspring, nor will even dream of any such thing; and then we can measure our own lack of goodness and perfection, by seeing how far we now fall short of this. And to me it is monstrous, that those who believe in an angel-world, and in angels standing thick around, and in communications from these immortal messengers, should yet lend their Souls to such low uses, as pandering to their base natures, in the gratification of this sensual and groveling commerce. And though my heart is kind, and it is an instinct in me to love all, yet I am revolted from those who lead this life, even if they should be the All, and there was not one left. I can not take delight in them; but I wish to get away by myself, and home with my own. I will not be at all bound up in their company, though I should have to be still more an exile than I ever was yet! I will not take home to my bosom and fellowship, one sheer jot of this, their life; which to me, is not worthy of a man who is so soon to cease; and therefore I will not live it—nor answer for it. I must prefer the risk of being called vain, weak, silly, or even of being so, to that of being "mixed up" with what my Soul so abhors, as Lust!

Yet not that I am as far from these in Berlin from whom I have come out, as from the rest of the world; for in coming out from them, I am far more coming out from the world, from which *they* have come out. In coming out from these, I am coming out from every body. Of a truth I know that the Berlin Socialists are purer than the world (though the world will not believe it), and that the world slanders them; and also their Freedom, is infinitely better than the world's Slavery; seeing it does not compel, but leaves all to live as purely as they will. But I must judge them, not by the

world's ideal of goodness, nor yet by their own, but only at last by
mine: and then I must bid them come up higher; and give them
my hand and my heart, as they shall grow to be still better and
purer yet. Most of them believe in the unending Life: and then will
they always live there, as they do now here? and then *will* they
live so, here? I have hope for these brothers.

And not that all this past of mine, in Berlin, has been a failure.
But indeed it has not been thrown away; but it shall all come
back to me, and to this *new* Berlin which shall yet be built. What I
have done, can never be turned aside from that true end for which
I did it; but the fates hold it in reversion, for those who will
further that first great end. It shall serve as a stepping-stone to a
nucleus, around which shall gather the selected elements, which
shall at length work out the destined though delayed realization—
a Home of Purity. What others have done, shall all be theirs; but
what I have done, shall yet inure to me and mine—this Home. And
then *that* will be—Retribution!

. . . So I wash my hands of Berlin (that is now—not that is soon
to be) ; and I wash my hands of all who live in Berlin; and I wash
my hands of the Race: and stand out—if there could be need—
alone, with that other world that is coming—that great world on-
and-on-and-on of the Ages—when the men and women shall be
good and noble, and very angels shall fill the places, of us who
walk on the earth to-day! I throw myself upon the stream of Time,
to be floated down to that great Awaiting, and drink in the just
judgment of the End. And I cast myself into the lap, and sink on
the bosom, of the perfect Universe of Infinite Existence! . . .

The Law of Progression in Harmony

James W. Towner, Thomas L. and
Mary S. Gove Nichols

This exchange took place in 1856, a few months before the Nichols took possession of their new premises in Yellow Springs, Ohio (Horace Mann, president of Antioch, delayed the occupancy by getting the sheriff to ban them from town). Some of their followers were disturbed by the new dispensation which seemed to be in the offing: not only did the Nichols announce that theirs would be a "despotic rule" at Memnonia, but they also proclaimed that free love no longer meant "free" in the sense of unbounded or unlimited; rather the limits of intercourse were now specified— for procreation only.

One free lover, James W. Towner of West Union, Iowa, wrote to complain that the "material" side of free love must not be abridged for the sake of the "spiritual." A frequent contributor to The Age of Freedom *and* The Social Revolutionist, *and later a member of both Berlin Heights and Oneida (see Introduction), Towner was clearly not among the "continent" school of free lovers.*

Berlin Heights, of course, was a rival to Memnonia, and the Nichols predicted its failure as soon as they heard of it. In the present state of society, they argued in the December 1856 issue of the Nichols Monthly, "the societies now to be established should be schools"—like Memnonia—not "social experiments," all of which were "failures," even Modern Times. This had brought replies from the Berlin Heights projectors, who went ahead with their plans and started in January.

By March 1857 Thomas and Mary Nichols had converted to Catholicism, and Towner, Francis Barry, and the Berlin Heights crowd jeered "I told you so." Only Joseph Treat, whose convictions on "intercourse for procreation only" matched those of the Nichols, mourned their passing: "They have done nobly to be true to their convictions. . . . I should have done as they, in their place."

James W. Towner
Thomas L. and Mary S. Gove Nichols
The Law of Progression in Harmony

In the second report of the Central Bureau of the Progressive Union, it was announced that the law of Progression, respecting the sexual relation, given to such as could accept it, and by its acceptance rise from the plane of natural life to that of spiritual life, is, that "material union is only to be had when the wisdom of the Harmony demands a child." Some have joyfully accepted this law as from the wisdom of the Heavens; others have rejected it for reasons which we have seen no more clearly stated than in the following letter, from an intelligent reformer in Iowa.

We publish this letter cheerfully as a clear, calm protest against the judgment of the spirits, who have announced the law to us, and intended to have made a suitable reply. In the meantime Mrs. Nichols wrote what was intended as a private note to Mr. Towner, but which we have requested to be allowed to publish with his, as the best answer, probably, that could be made, to some of his objections. Having given both letters we shall append a few remarks.

● Selection from *Nichols Monthly*, II (June 1856), 444–51.

Letter of Mr. Towner

To Mrs. Mary S. G. Nichols,
Dear Friend:—

Your letter in the April No. of the "Journal" was read with interest and pleasure. It is such an expression as I have been for some time anxious to see from you, as I felt that there was evidently a divergence about to take place between you and some of us who have been with you. Its kindly and hopeful tone pleases me very much, and in the same tone I desire to respond to it. I am free to say that I am one of those whom you describe as "parting company with you." But I do not say to you; "You are despots— you would rob us of our freedom." You recollect you yourselves said, of your proposed preparatory school at Yellow Springs; "Memnonia will be provisionally, and necessarily, a *despotism*," etc. I have only said, I deemed this to be inconsistent with the principles of the "Progressive Union." You addressed such as I am in kindness, and I hope you will allow me in the same spirit to speak through the "Journal" to you and yours.

To what you say in defining Love, I cordially respond. So, too, to what you say of the need of our being provident of our heart and soul wealth. Yes, we all, I hope, "ask for the balance or harmony of the faculties; that all have their rights; that no one or more of the passions, or faculties, be allowed to tyrannize over, and rob the remainder."

I think we do not differ respecting "Freedom." No one of us asks for liberty to do a wrong to himself. What we want is "liberty of the person from all ownership, bondage, restraint, or burthen; from all fraud or force; all despotisms of custom, law, or institutions. A holy freedom to follow the dictates of nature in her most sacred instincts." "True Freedom is the Right to do Right." "The right in each case to be settled by the individual conscience of the person interested, and not by any general or arbitrary law."

What we want, further, is to *find* the "law within us"; we call no one despotic who announces it to us with the clearness of demonstration, but hail the announcement with satisfaction and joy. But when you announce "the law of progression in harmony," as you call it, I doubt its being the law, or any part of it. Show me that it is, and I too will receive it and obey it. I could not receive it upon the "authority" of spirits out of, or in the form. And there is no need of "authority" to settle a question of this kind. If there be such a law respecting "material union", nature can reveal it to us; physiology can confirm it; it pertains to the province of science, and thither will we resort. But from all that I have yet learned from this source, I judge there is no such law. *You* do not assert it as a "finality, but as a law of growth and progress in harmony." But it seems curious that that which is not a law within us, can be a "law of growth and progress."

You speak of "material union" contrary to the "law or progression" as wasteful; and of garnering life, and maturing it by obeying said law. This is to me unmeaning. The ultimation of love in "material union" within the limits of the laws and functions of the sexual organs, I cannot see to be wasteful or destructive; nor refraining therefrom, saving or strengthening. Love's having an important influence in the development, and the tendency of love in healthy men and women being to thus ultimate itself, coupled with the fact that such ultimation tends to enhance the bliss and power of that sentiment, indicate that it does not waste or impoverish life, but, on the contrary, beautifies and ennobles. And, where there is a proper adaptation of constitution between lovers may not the sexual embrace result in an impartation from each to the other of their respective masculine and feminine attributes? So I believe and have experienced. Then it is a law of every organ and faculty that activity is necessary to its growth and maturity; necessary to preserve that tone and power which will enable it to perform its function in the best manner. Repression and inaction tend to debility and waste. Are the sexual organs and powers any exception? It seems to me that wisdom suggests that in any social state births should be few, with an interval of years between their occurrence. With this conviction, I can but think that the amative inaction prescribed by "the law of progression" would result in impairing the power of the sexual or procreative function, and so disqualify us for producing so "glorious children" as we might otherwise. I repeat, then, that your idea of *garnering* life through obedience to that law is to me unmeaning.

I doubt the assertion that "amativeness holds all the spiritual energy that feeds all the faculties." If it be so, I do not see how we can "give from all faculties to all faculties." I do not see how an individual can be developed, spiritually, before the age of puberty; nor how one who has lost the passion through age, disease, or otherwise, finds further food for the faculties. It is plain to me that there are many energizing passions beside amativeness; and we know that an extreme action of some others results in waste and destruction. Such is the case with destructiveness, cautiousness, adhesiveness and others.

It may seem curious that different persons or classes should call you "ascetics," "shakers" and "licentious and abominable Free Lovers." Nevertheless, in the course of our progress do we not often occupy positions relatively to others which are at once radical or conservative, "licentious" or rigid in opinion and action? Orthodox Protestants are "infidels" to Catholics, and "bigots" to Unitarians and Universalists. These are "infidels" to orthodoxy, and "bigots" and "sectarians" to Spiritualists, Rationalists, and Transcendentalists. The Republican Party is made up of "lawless abolitionists," in the estimation of the Slave Power, but of "conservatives" and timid, half-hearted anti-slavery men in the estimation of Garrisonians. All sects, parties, and classes contain those who are about midway between the foremost and hindmost, occupying an opposite position to the two extremes. I would not say, you occupy such a position; I only say such a one may be as real, as "curious." I would not, self-glorifyingly, say, that my position is in advance of yours; I should hardly be willing to admit that it is in the rear. I apprehend that our longitude may be about the same, though our latitude may differ.

But thinking that you are in the van, I am glad you can lovingly and patiently, like the All Good, *wait for us.* I trust we shall be able to reciprocate the kindly feelings and hopes which you express. Let us with fraternal and sisterly love admonish, exhort and help each other in being and doing, so that we may soon be able to inaugurate the reign of Freedom's Love and Love's Freedom.

James W. Towner

[Reply]

Cincinnati, O. 2nd May, 1856.

My Dear Friend:

You are very good, and I wish I might always differ from those as pure, honest, and philosophical, as I think you are.

We shall publish your statement. It is a good one from where you are, and if people can reach this standpoint, from them will come loving and seeing workers for the newness. The New Society is to me like a young tree, or an infant now. It needs its nonage, its growth, its vestalate. My dear Sir, you do not know woman as I know her. Every where women are diseased, or immature. We have no women for the new world, comparatively. We have to wait in a great rest, for health and maturity both to come.

What you say is true enough of man and woman as healthy beings;—but even then, a great purpose, like a battle, needs its own continence as a preparation. I know that persons must see from their own stand-point. I do not see much, but I love much. I take no "authority" in the sense which you understand the word, from the heavens or the earth. You doubt my postulates. I cannot argue or convince. Those who are in the same love and wisdom that we are, will fight this battle with us. You will do a good work wherever you are. There are plenty of people to be freed yet, so that they can garner, or use their amative life according to their best judgment. You will do the work that we have done, in freeing people from prejudice respecting the Love Life. This is to be done. It is as important to recruit soldiers for the battle of life, as to discipline them to stand shoulder to shoulder, and achieve in combination, what they can never do in an isolate warfare.

I trust such as you. If you go not my way to freedom and harmony, you still go. You cannot but find it in your heart of hearts to love and revere us, even *us*, as noble and true ones, who are coming, through fasting and prayer and a most sacred vestalate, to the harmony of all our faculties, and to the harmonic home. We claim not the merit that we are making a self-sacrifice, or an atonement in suffering, but we act in our highest freedom in living a most beautiful love life that has not the ultimate amative expression. It is our freedom to wait—to garner a life that civilization has crushed and worn away, and to help mature the same life in our younger brothers and sisters in temperance and purity.

Would the bird be wise, when weak from the frosts of winter, and amid the barren coldness of spring, to lay its eggs upon the bare ground? Destruction must be the result of such incontinence. We seek a home in the earth for freedom and right. Liberty to do right consists in some thing more than the conception of rights— as the warmth and foliage of May and June, and the downy nest, are needful to the bird-love and life, so the groups and series of the combined order are indispensible to the harmonic life.

We may see that it is our right to love, and to bear children more worthy of earth and heaven than any now living, but a very composite work is needful to secure this right to humanity. We must have freedom to secure these rights, and to make disastrous experiences in that direction, that we may be educated by our failures. If it is your freedom to work with us, and fail or succeed with us, you will do it. If you go a longer or shorter way to the glad result, you will still go—for you "are bound for the kingdom," and will reach it some time and some way.

I find no fault with your life, or your freedom. Do the best you can, I say to all—and all may be very sure that we shall do the best we can. Our past is the best guarantee for our future that we can give. I did not think to write so much to you when I began. It did not seem to me that you have need of me. I have a word to say, however, of the Law of Progression in Harmony. You say we do not announce it as a finality. Some who are with us believe it a finality. Some do not. For myself, I am as sure that it is *the* Law of Progression to the Harmony we seek, as I am that sunshine is a condition of vegetation. Farther than this I do not say, because I do not know. Of one thing I am sure, that when the balance of the faculties is reached, and the wealth of a harmonic life comes to us, such life will make its own laws. Law now is made by tyrant passions, and legislators who are dominated by tyrant passions. Laws and customs are made now mostly by two dominants—the lust of gain and the lust for women. Woman must come to be her own— and then her love will be a heavenly law giver. Now, the passion flower of her love is stained with blood. Everywhere our women are exhausted by oppression and repression, or they are immature. Dear friend, I claim to know more about this than you do. You may be a better logician than I am, but not a better physician, or a more ardent lover.

Women will come with me through the sacred vestalate to the new society. They feel their want of a holy freedom, if they do not know it. They feel the sensual clutch and claim of even the truest love they can find now—and they will give this tyrant sense the cure of hunger. "This kind goeth not out but by fasting."

I feel the Divine Prophecy within me, that woman will trust to love, and emancipate herself and man from the heavy bonds of the sensual life, that now forbid our progress in development and harmony, as absolutely as death. To-day a love is poured into many hearts, that if ultimated sensually would destroy men and women as surely as lightning kills.

If you cannot understand how this concentrated flame can be diffused, and become a genial and sustaining warmth, then I cannot teach you. I know my own freedom. I trust you will be just as wise for yourself. There is one eternal and immutable law for

us. It is that each must live to the highest love and freedom of
the spirit,—the law of life revealed within us. If we thus live true
to ourselves, we can be false to no one. If in this living, you and I
join hands in work, it will be very blessed. If we are severed and
joined to others, still it is our gain and good to be severed, and
so joined. I would sooner stand alone in the Universe and be
TRUE, than to have Kingdoms joined to me in falsehood. With
loving prayers for you and all who part company with us in our
effort to begin a true home in the earth.

I am, tenderly and truly, your friend,
Mary S. Gove Nichols.

We wish to add a few words. There seems to us no necessity
that those that do not with us accept the "Law of Progression," or
who cannot join us in the entire consecration of our lives to the
work of development and harmonization, by the means we believe
best adapted to that end, should therefore part company with us, or
withdraw from the Progressive Union, so long as they accept its
principles, and wish to make progress, they are with us.

Despotism is one of the necessities of discordant surroundings. At
Memnonia, for example, there would be enough of despotism to
protect the harmony, and prevent, exclude or expel discord. So
much would be surely needful.

Though there may be no need of authority to settle or enforce a
principle or law, there may be great need of high intelligences to
inform us of what we might otherwise remain in ignorance of. If
our advanced spirit friends can tell us nothing that we do not
know already, or which we could not have discovered just as well
for ourselves, there would seem to be very little use in their communications. Mr. Towner says, if there be such a law, nature can
reveal it. Our spirit friends are a part of nature. Physiology, I
believe, does confirm it. A law of progress, is not a finality, of
course; and the law of one stage of progress is not necessarily the
law of another stage.

It is a physiological mistake to suppose that the sexual organs
are among those which require constant exercise. This is not the
fact with animals or men. Before puberty, all know that any use
is injurious. The disuse, for many years after, is consistent with the
utmost vigor, not only of these, but of all the other faculties. With
other organs, continual, or daily use, is a means of strength—with
these of exhaustion and death. Intervals of months and years are

favorable, not only to general health, but to the perfection and vigor of this special faculty. This is proven by a multitude of observations. Men or women who abstain for months or years are in a better condition in consequence; and in a vast number of cases, this abstinence is needed for the health of the organism and a healthy procreation. The prevalent diseases of women, and their alarming mortality, would find a remedy in the general observance of this law. The question of "garnering life" by a wise chastity, may be left to the experience of those who have made the trial, rather than to those who have no such experience. The love life seems to us the central creative power, in man and the universe. Other passions are energising, or they use and diffuse energy. But in the love life is a fountain of power, and we are wise if we direct this power to all faculties, rather than waste it in the sensual action of a single faculty.

The law of progression finds a cheerful and loving acceptance from those who are ready to receive it. Probably there are not many now ready. Such as are will join with us, and the rest will come, when they see and feel as we do.

JAMES W. TOWNER.

Among the Free-Lovers

Artemus Ward

By 1860 Berlin Heights had become, in the public imagination, and in fact, the center of free love in America. As his vigilante informant complained to John B. Ellis, local citizens were "stared at" in Sandusky and Cleveland, and laughed at in New York and Boston. Humorist Artemus Ward published his contribution to the general amusement in Vanity Fair *for 1861. Although thoroughly fanciful, not to say malicious, Ward's sketch accurately reflects the popular notion of the rural spiritualists and free lovers at the time.*

Artemus Ward
Among the Free Lovers

Some years ago I pitched my tent and onfurled my banner to the breeze, in Berlin Hites, Ohio. I had hearn that Berlin Hites was ockepied by a extensive seck called Free Lovers, who beleeved in affinertys and sich, goin back on their domestic ties without no hesitation whatsomever. They was likewise spirit rappers and high presher reformers on gineral principles. If I can improve these 'ere misgided peple by showin them my onparalleld show at the usual low price of admitants, methunk, I shall not hav lived in vane! But bitterly did I cuss the day I ever sot foot in the retchid place. I sot up my tent in a field near the Love Cure, as they called it, and bimeby the free lovers begun for to congregate around the door. A ornereer set I have never sawn. The men's faces was all covered with hare and they lookt half-starved to deth. They didn't wear no weskuts for the purpuss (as they sed) of allowin the free air of hevun to blow onto their boozums. Their pockets was filled with tracks and pamplits and they was bare-footed. They sed the Postles didn't wear boots, & why should they? That was their stile of argyment. The wimin was wuss than the men. They wore trowsis, short gownds, straw hats with green ribbins, and all carried bloo cotton unbrellers.

Presently a perfeckly orful lookin female presented herself at the door. Her gownd was skanderlusly short and her trowsis was shameful to behold.

She eyed me over very sharp, and then startin back she sed, in a wild voice:

"Ah, can it be?"

"Which?" sed I.

"Yes, 'tis troo, O 'tis troo!"

"15 cents, marm," I anserd.

She bust out a cryin & sed:

"And so I hav found you at larst—at larst, O at larst!"

"Yes," I anserd, "you have found me at larst, and you would have found me at fust, if you had cum sooner."

● Selection from *Artemus Ward: His Book*, New York: Carleton, 1862, pp. 86–90.

She grabd me vilently by the coat collar, and brandishin her umbreller wildly round, exclaimed:

"Air you a man?"

Sez I, "I think I air, but if you doubt it, you can address Mrs. A. Ward, Baldinsville, Injianny, postage pade, & she will probly giv you the desired informashun."

"Then thou ist what the cold world calls marrid?"

"Madam, I istest!"

The exsentric female then clutched me franticly by the arm and hollerd:

"You air mine, O you air mine!"

"Scacely," I sed, endeverin to git loose from her. But she clung to me and sed:

"You air my Affinerty!"

"What upon arth is that?" I shouted.

"Dost thou not know?"

"No, I dostent!"

"Listin man, & I'll tell ye!" sed the strange female; "for years I hav yearned for thee. I knowd thou wast in the world, sumwhares, tho I didn't know whare. My hart sed he would cum and I took courage. He *has* cum—he's here—you air him—you air my Affinerty! O 'tis too mutch! too mutch!" and she sobbed agin.

"Yes," I anserd, "I think it is a darn site too mutch!"

"Hast thou not yearned for me?" she yelled, ringin her hands like a female play acter.

"Not a yearn!" I bellerd at the top of my voice, throwin her away from me.

The free lovers who was standin round obsarvin the scene commenst for to holler "shame!" "beast," etsettery, etsettery.

I was very mutch riled, and fortifyin myself with a spare tent stake, I addrest them as follers:

"You pussylanermus critters, go way from me and take this retchid woman with you. I'm a law-abidin man, and bleeve in good, old-fashioned institutions. I am marrid & my orfsprings resemble me, if I am a showman! I think your Affinerty bizness is cussed noncents, besides bein outrajusly wicked. Why don't you behave desunt like other folks? Go to work and earn an honist livin and not stay round here in this lazy, shiftless way, pizenin the moral atmosphere with your pestifrous idees! You wimin folks go back to your lawful husbands if you've got any, and take orf them skander-

lous gownds and trowsis, and dress respectful like other wimin. You
men folks, cut orf them pirattercal whiskers, burn up them infurnel
pamplits, put sum weskuts on, go to work choppin wood, splittin
fence rales, or tillin the sile." I pored 4th my indignashun in this
way till I got out of breth, when I stopt. I shant go to Berlin Hites
agin, not if I live to be as old as Methooseler.

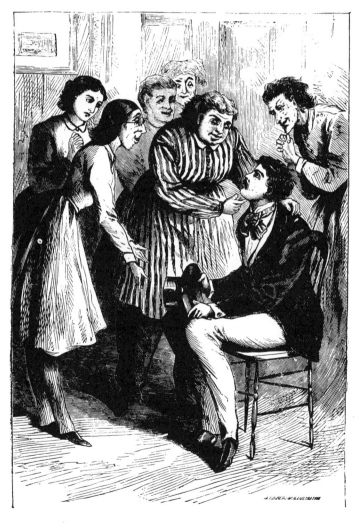

ARRIVAL OF A RECRUIT AT THE ONEIDA COMMUNITY.

VI

Complex Marriage at Oneida

The Bible on Marriage

John Humphrey Noyes

The following selection was part of a little book called Bible Communism, *which boldly presented the Oneida Community's extraordinary views of the proper relation between communal life and sexual intercourse—what they called "complex marriage."*

The author, John Humphrey Noyes, was the founder and spiritual leader of this group of antinomian Perfectionists. In 1834 he had been thrown out of the Congregationalist ministry for announcing his "salvation from sin"; in 1837 he had come to the conclusion that for those "saved" there was to be no more marriage—all were married to all, and sexual union with others who were saved was no sin; in 1846 he put the theory into practice among the small group of followers who lived with him in Putney, Vermont. Noyes was arrested for adultery in 1847, and the Putney group was broken up, but they soon resettled near Oneida, New York, where for the next thirty years they proved that "Bible communism" of persons as well as property actually worked, so long as their neighbors left them in peace.

485

The Perfectionist view of marriage was first publicly announced in 1849, after Noyes and his followers (now fifty-eight adults and twenty-nine children) had regrouped in Oneida. They wished to avoid another unpleasant situation like Putney, where they were accused of carrying on a clandestine free love society, and of secretly seducing local girls. So they explained their principles in their first Annual Report, *and Noyes sent it to the Governor and other public men of the state. This combination of prudence and bravado seems to have forestalled any immediate official action, but it provoked a good deal of vituperation in newspapers and pulpits.*

As always when dealing with this sort of crisis—threats of criminal prosecution or vigilante action—Noyes found a reason to leave the community temporarily. (In Putney his lawyer brother-in-law had advised him to flee—no doubt wisely; later, during the final days in 1879, he stole away one night and crossed the border into Canada, when it looked as if the local authorities were finally going to arrest him and close the community down after three decades of live-and-let-live.) Soon after the publication of the First Annual Report *Noyes left Oneida to open a Brooklyn branch of the community, where he lived for the next five years directing the propaganda operations of the* Oneida Circular, *along with a dozen other Perfectionists.*

It is too simple to judge this behavior as cowardly; before doing so, one ought to read his words—printed on the Brooklyn press—for it is not a timid spirit that could even think such things as Noyes thought. He was not iron-willed, inflexible; that was not the secret of Oneida's success. He was like a steel-spring, with give in him—full of expedients, a genius of social invention, quick to the touch of the moment and sure of his inspiration. That was part of what it meant to be "saved from sin."

Moreover, in the early 1850s leaving Oneida for Brooklyn was a little like jumping from the frying pan into the fire. At Oneida a group of members was questioned intimidatingly by the grand jury (of another county!) but their neighbors vouched for them and nothing further came of it. In Brooklyn Noyes was closer to the battleline of free love activity in America, what with the Nichols scandal at Port Chester, the colony at Modern Times, and the debate in the Tribune *between James, Greeley, and Andrews. In 1852 the tiny Brooklyn commune drew fire from the New York* Observer, *which had taken the lead in the crusade against free love. Noyes played it safe, with another temporary retraction of principle—a few months during which the community abandoned its most offensive practice, complex marriage—only to reaffirm it after things had cooled down.*

Then, perhaps to test public opinion again, Noyes published Bible Communism, *a compilation of the first three* Annual Reports *together with a few new statements, including "The Bible on Marriage" reprinted here. Again Noyes sent copies to the Governor, but by this time the community's neighbors had taken a strong stand for them, against prosecution in the courts or further harrassment in the form of vigilante threats. The period of hanging on by the fingernails was over at last, and the expensive and divisive dispersal of the community was no longer a necessary precaution. In December 1854 the Brooklyn branch was closed and Noyes came home.*

John Humphrey Noyes
The Bible on Marriage

We avow ourselves strictly and entirely Bible men—disciples of the New Testament, of Christ and of Paul, in relation to the subject of marriage. We do not on the one hand turn aside as some do, to independent philosophical speculation; nor do we appeal with others to the authority of a new revelation. We adhere only to the Bible, and feel bound in every respect to abide by the judgment of those who have gone before us in the gospel. We sincerely believe in the inspiration of the New Testament teachers, and that their views, sooner or later, will be found to be eternal truth, proceeding from God. All that we want is, to know precisely *what they did teach* in relation to marriage,—to have a thorough understanding of them, and not misrepresent their views to ourselves or others.

So much as this is perfectly clear: that they were not in favor of *freedom of divorce,* as a means of mitigating the difficulties connected with marriage. There cannot be any mistake about the fact that Christ, instead of being in favor of freedom of divorce, as it had existed under the Mosaic dispensation, restored the law to its simplicity and rigor, allowing no divorce except in cases of adultery. (Mark 10.) And Paul stood substantially on the same ground; that is, he forbade believers for any cause to sunder the external mar-

● Selection from *Bible Communism,* Brooklyn: Oneida Community, 1853, pp. 82–91.

riage tie. (1 Cor. 7.) It is true he supposed the case of separation
brought about by the departure of an unbelieving partner, and said
that the other was not in bondage in such cases. . . .—Whether this in
his mind amounted to the privilege of divorce and marrying again,
we cannot perhaps determine; but at all events, it was his will that
the whole movement and responsibility of separaion should be laid
on the unbeliever. He did not allow *the gospel* to introduce separation between husband and wife, or to relax at all the marriage code.

The Bible view of divorce may be illustrated thus: Suppose a
commercial system which brings people into a general condition of
debt, one to another. Now one way to mitigate this fact and release
people from such a state of things, would be by enacting a general
Bankrupt law, which would make an end of all obligations by legal
repudiation. The Bankrupt law operates to release a man from his
promises; and this is just the nature of any legal increase of freedom
of divorce.—Christ and Paul, however, were clearly opposed to any
Bankrupt law in relation to marriage, as being a mode of discharge
not contemplated in the original contract, and as dishonestly rescind-
ing unlimited obligations.

Sympathizing with them in this respect, we as Bible Communists
are on entirely different ground from that of the infidels and
Owenites of twenty years ago; and from that of James and
nearly all of those who are now seeking to bring about a revolution
in regard to marriage. We will loyally abide by the view of Christ
and of Paul on that subject. If there is to be any alleviation of the
miseries of marriage, it is not to come by freedom of divorce.

Again, we are clear that the teachings of the New Testament were
sufficiently distinct against *polygamy*. We do not recollect any thing
very positive and decisive on this point that can be quoted; but
there is a strong intimation of Paul's opinion in the passage where
he says, "a bishop must be the husband of one wife." (1 Tim. 3:2.)

We do not think it is fair at all to infer any thing against polygamy from the saying that "what God hath joined together men
must not put asunder"—the original doctrine of the inviolability
of contracts on which Christ insisted in regard to marriage—because
it is not a matter of course that a man shall abandon his first wife
by taking a second. No such thing did happen, under the polygamic
economy of the patriarchs; on the contrary it was well understood
that the contract with the first wife could be fulfilled consistently
with taking a second. Christ in that saying is pointing his artillery

against putting away. If polygamy were understood to be a nullification of any previous marriage, then that saying would operate
against it. But there is no intimation of any such thing in the New
Testament, and hence the objection to polygamy must be placed on
other grounds.

We have seen in the passage referring to bishops, an indication
of Paul's preference of monogamy over polygamy. —But it must likewise be noticed in this connection that he preferred agamy, or having no wives, to monogamy. His disapprobation of polygamy is not
necessarily to be taken as in favor of monogamy. On the contrary
his objection was against marriage altogether, as causing trouble in
the flesh, and as being a distraction to believers. (1 Cor. 7:28, &c.)
His objection to marriage in general is primarily an objection to
monogamy; and of course much more to polygamy, as being a still
worse distraction.

Here we may dwell for a moment on the identity in principle of
monogamy with polygamy. And it will then be seen, that in following Christ we are further from the position of polygamists than
ordinary society. It is plain that the fundamental principle of monogamy and polygamy is the same; to wit, the ownership of woman by
man. The monogamist claims one woman as his wife—the polygamists, two or a dozen; but the essential thing, the bond of relationship constituting marriage, in both cases is the same, namely, a
claim of ownership.

The similarity and the difference between monogamy and polygamy, may be illustrated thus: Suppose slavery to be introduced into
Pennsylvania, but limited by law, so that no man can own more
than *one* slave. That might be taken to represent monogamy, or the
single wife system. In another State suppose men are allowed to own
any number they please. That corresponds to polygamy. Now what
would be the difference between these two States, in respect to
slavery? There would be a difference in the details, and external
limitations of the system, but identity in principle. The State that
allowed a man to have but one slave, would be on the same general
basis of principle with the State that allowed him to have a hundred. Such, we conceive, is the relation between monogamy and
polygamy; and as we understand the New Testament, the state
which Jesus Christ and Paul were in favor of was neither, but a state
of entire freedom from both.

Monogamy allows a man but one wife; polygamy allows a plurality. In choosing between them Paul naturally prefers that which comes nearest to the resurrection-standard, and says virtually, "If you marry at all, it is best to have but one wife; but it is better still not have any." He set this example himself, and evidently intended to encourage the entire abolition of marriage, which is the furthest possible distance from polygamy—further from polygamy than monogamy.

We find ourselves, then, as followers of the New Testament, standing far apart from those who wish to ameliorate the miseries of marriage by a bankrupt law, i.e., a law for free divorce: and far apart from polygamists, who propose to give a liberty of multiplying wives; that is, to expand the principle of monogamy, which is ownership. The Bible position is entirely different from either of these.

And now we must try to ascertain more definitely the precise position of Paul and Christ on the subject of marriage. It is plain that the absolute constitutional principle in which they stood personally, toward which they were leading the church, and which they expected would expand itself, and occupy the field which is now occupied by monogamy, polygamy, &c., is declared in that saying of Christ, *"In the resurrection they neither marry nor are given in marriage."* They were pressing on the church the importance of living in heaven—becoming in reality citizens of heaven. "If ye then be risen with Christ, seek those things which are above." "Lay not up for yourselves treasures upon earth, where moth and rust do corrupt; but lay up for yourselves treasures in heaven," &c.; i.e., "Do not seek temporary fellowships, like marriage, &c., but lay up for yourselves eternal connections." And that we may be sure that they were bent on introducing the heavenly state of things into this world, Christ put that prayer into his disciples' mouths,—"Thy kingdom come, thy will be done ON EARTH AS IT IS DONE IN HEAVEN."

We have then their position defined, negatively at least, with perfect certainty—a position not in favor of divorce, not in favor of polygamy, and finally, not in favor of marriage itself; but tending to abolish it altogether. Such a view of their position, and such alone, will reconcile their various sayings and doings on the subject.

There is some seeming inconsistency in the idea of their being opposed to divorce and to marriage too. It may be said, "If marriage is to be abolished, that of course *is* divorce; and if they were in favor of the one, they must have been of the other." Inconsistency or not, we reply, these two things are there—on the one hand, prohibition of freedom of divorce, and on the other, a pressure against marriage altogether; and we must reconcile them as best we can.

In explanation of the difficulty we have to rise a little into what may be called a *spiritualizing* view of things: but to us it is none the less satisfactory, since it is surely the Christian view.

The doctrine that *death* is the legitimate end of the contract of marriage, is distinctly conceded by all. "A woman is bound by the law to her husband as long as he liveth; but if the husband be dead she is loosed from the law of her husband." Paul and Christ were certainly not in favor of divorce by any other power than that of death. They adhered to the principle of marriage *for life* without any essential exceptions. *But they found a way to introduce what may be called a posthumous state into this world, by the application of the death of Christ.* Their doctrine, as was shown fully in a previous article, was, that by believing in Christ we are crucified with him. "If one died for all, then all died." It may be said that the apostle did not intend to apply the death here spoken of to marriage. We reply, he certainly did apply it as a release from other worldly ordinances. The whole Jewish law was over the church, and it was like the law of marriage, in that it was over them *for life;* and the only outlet from its ordinances, to the conscientious Jew, was by death. —Yet Paul every where proclaimed release from them, by union with the death of Christ. Though he did not carry the principle out in reference to marriage, it is prefectly clear that the same logic that would make an end of any part of the Jewish law, would make an end of marriage. If that is a substantial principle of the gospel (and it seems to us to be the very *center* of it), then we can see how they could oppose divorce and yet favor the abolition of marriage, in view of the *posthumous* state that was to come in this world by virtue of the death and resurrection of Christ. They certainly contemplated that posthumous state as their landing place, and were pressing towards it; and in view of entering into it as fast as possible, they discouraged marriage; preferring not to encumber themselves with transitory ties, but seeking rather with their whole hearts the resurrection-state.

And here we will remark again, that this doctrine of the believer's death and resurrection by union with Christ, however foolish it may seem now, was in the Primitive church the very core of the gospel. They realized the fact that they were past death, and so were delivered from sin and legality, by the cross of Christ. This is the meaning of those frequent declarations of Paul, "I am crucified with Christ"—"I am determined not to glory, save in the cross of Christ, whereby I am crucified to the world, and the world to me," &c. This doctrine and belief had a tremendous practical bearing upon their character and position; and it is the grand apostasy of Christendom, that it has since lost sight of it. The cross of Christ, putting men through death and into a posthumous state, is certainly the spiritual truth which must be restored to the throne of Christianity.

This principle, as we have said, was not carried through into all its bearings on marriage; but Paul *did carry it out so far as to demand that the heart should assume the eternal, heavenly state;* for he says, "Let them that have wives be as though they had none." So that in fact he gave his word for abolishing marriage, in the heart, on the spot.

We have thus far traced, honestly and faithfully, the doctrine of Christ and Paul on the subject of marriage. The result is to us satisfactory. But we have yet developed only the negative view. We have found them not in favor of divorce, not polygamists, but pressing toward the cessation of marriage itself. But the question remains, as to what they expected would take the place of marriage in the posthumous, or if you please, the *angelic* state. It is distinctly said that there is no marriage there; but the question still remains as to *what* that state is; and in regard to it two theories may arise, and only two. The whole question lies between the Shaker doctrine, that there is no sexual relation or constitution in heaven; and the doctrine of what may be called *pantogamy,* which recognizes the continued existence of the sexual relation, but excludes ownership, and replaces human beings where they were as children—in friendship and freedom, without selfish possession. These two are the only theories that are possible as to the resurrection state; which state, be it remembered, Christ and his disciples adhered to as far as possible in this world, and contemplated introducing in its fullness.

We certainly have no disposition to wrest the scriptures, or misrepresent the principles of Christ and Paul in this matter. We can very readily consent to Shakerism, if that is their doctrine. All we want to know is what they really believed and taught about the resurrection state. If they saw there Shakerism, we wish to be Shakers; and if some other state of society, that form of society shall be ours. We are determined, for ourselves, *to follow hard after Paul and Christ,* and get at the soul of their intent in this thing.

But in the first place, we find no necessity whatever of a Shaker interpretation of the passage—"In the resurrection they neither marry nor are given in marriage." The question proposed by the Sadducces evidently referred to the matter of *ownership.* Seven men had been married to one woman, and dying successively, the question was, whose she should be in the resurrection. Suppose the question had been asked in reference to slavery instead of marriage, thus: A man owning a slave dies, and leaves him to his brother: he dying, bequeaths him to the next brother: and so seven of them in succession own this slave. Now whose slave shall he be in the resurrection? This, evidently, is the amount of the Sadducces' question; and Christ's answer is as though he had said, that in the resurrection there are neither slaves nor slaveholders. It is a nullification of the idea of marriage ownership. Can any thing more be made of it? To assume from this passage a nullification of the sexual relation, as the Shakers and others do, is as absurd as it would be to assume that, because there is no slavery, there is therefore no serving one another in the resurrection; whereas, the gospel teaches that there is more serving one another there than in the world. There is a very important distinction to be observed between the abolition of ownership and the abolition of love-relations.

While therefore, we are clear that marriage is to be abolished; it does not necessarily follow that agamy or antigamy is to take the place of it; but on the contrary the whole spirit of the gospel in regard to service and freedom, and the whole purport of the doctrine, "Except ye be converted and become as little children, ye shall in no wise enter the kingdom of heaven," go far the other way: indicating that in that posthumous state which we are taught to pray for and expect on earth, the relation of the sexes will be that described in Christ's prayer—that they "may all be one, even as I and my Father are one," which we call pantogamy.

Recurring to the illustration with which we begun, we may sum up and present in the shortest possible compass, the view to which the preceding examination of the Bible has led us, as follows:

Let a state of general debt, or in other words the credit-system, represent marriage. Then the divorce scheme of Owen, James and others, will be a bankrupt-law; the polygamic system of the Mormons and others, will be increased speculation, or an inflation of the credit-system; and the policy of the Shakers will be stoppage of business to avoid debt, speculation, &c.,—in other words, stagnation. Now it is conceivable that honest men should insist that all debts actually contracted shall be paid, and at the same time should be opposed to contracting debts. Such men would oppose a bankrupt-law on the one hand, and the entire credit-system on the other. It is also conceivable, that prudent men should oppose the entire credit-system, and of course dislike specially any increase of speculation, while still they might be in favor of FREE BUSINESS and opposed to stagnation. So we conceive Christ and Paul, as honest and prudent men, were opposed to divorce on the one hand, and to marriage on the other; and being opposed to marriage, of course specially disapproved of polygamy; and yet were not Shakers, but were in favor of free social relations, to be inaugurated as soon as existing obligations could be disposed of, and the old system of bondage removed safely and peaceably.

If we have made any mistake in regard to the subsequent state to be anticipated, or the interpretation of Christ's words concerning it, the error must be shown. We shall follow Christ and Paul, let the path lead where it will. It has unmistakably led us to the expectation that marriage is to be done away; and the only question is, What next? Shakerism, or something else? We call for discussion. If the conservative interpreters of the Bible, will convince us that the Shaker view is correct, relating to the posthumous state, which (bear in mind), we are to pray for and expect on earth, then let it be so. We shall thankfully accept anything that can be shown to be truth on this subject. In respect to their estimate of marriage, we think the Shakers nearer right than the popular churches. We agree with them in regard to the necessity of its abolishment, and the only question is as to subsequent institutions. This point, it is for the Christian world to discuss and settle. In the light which is now breaking, both from the Bible, and from reason, on the subject of marriage, all free-thinking believers will find themselves compelled to move; and it must be either toward our position, or that of the Shakers. We can see no other alternative. Then let there be a fair investigation of the whole subject—let us ascertain if possible, the social formation that belongs to the post-mortal, or heavenly and eternal state, and all agree to accommodate ourselves thereto.

History of the *Battle Axe* Letter

John Humphrey Noyes

It was this letter that cast the die for complex marriage, and as Noyes says, he felt pushed into his daring stance by Providence, for he had never intended to publish it. Why did he write it?

The woman whose love he "communized" in the letter was Abigail Merwin, with whom he had fallen in love. She had been his first convert to Perfectionism, and she figured centrally in his vision of the community of saints he was to establish—but she had fallen back into conventional Congregationalism, had married someone else and left town. Noyes followed her, hoping for a change of heart, and it was in this mixed state of fervor and frustration that he came to his "bible argument." At first this was merely a compensatory vision of the sexual dispensation in heaven, but then, in the light of his developing Perfectionist belief, it seemed a command to those who were "saved from sin" to establish the Kingdom here and now.

The Battle Axe *letter had repercussions outside Noyes' own circle too. There were people who carried it in their pockets, as*

495

*an example of the extremes to which "come-outerism" had arrived.
To William Lloyd Garrison, whose somewhat Perfectionist version
of abolitionism was just being put together, it was an embarrassment. Noyes had made a trip to Boston expressly to meet Garrison,
and afterwards had sent him one of his prophetic letters too, that
influenced Garrison's anti-government, non-resistant views at a
crucial moment: "I am writing," Noyes said, "that all men should
know that I have subscribed my name to an instrument similar to
the Declaration of '76, renouncing allegiance to the government of
the United States, and asserting the title of Jesus Christ to the
throne of the world." The letter contained Garrison's later abolitionist stance in embryo: "Every person who is, in the usual sense
of the expression, a citizen of the United States, i.e., a voter, poli-
tician, etc., is at once a slave and slaveholder—in other words a
subject and a ruler in a slaveholding government. . . . I have
renounced active cooperation with the oppressor on whose terri-
tories I live; now I would find a way to put an end to his
oppression."*

*A few weeks later Garrison wrote his friend Henry C. Wright,
"Human governments will remain in violent existence as long as
men are resolved not to bear the cross of Christ, and to be crucified
unto the world. But in the kingdom of God's dear Son, holiness
and love are the only magistracy. . . . And that kingdom is to be
established on the earth. . . . My own [religious views] are very
simple, but they make havoc of all sects, and rights. . . . Total
abstinence from sin, in this life, is not only commanded but necessarily obtainable. . . ."*

*The Perfectionism here is unmistakable. Noyes himself might
have written it—but he had already written the* Battle Axe *letter
too, and when it was published a few months later, the abolitionists
drew back instantly from their reckless compatriot. Government
was one thing, marriage was another. So Noyes methodically cut
himself off from potential allies over and over—not the least of
whom were the free lovers themselves—until he had pared down
his world to nothing but disciples, on whom he could rely no
matter what. This too was part of the secret of Oneida's remarkable
success.*

John Humphrey Noyes
History of the Battle Axe *Letter*

On the 15th of January 1837 (about three years after my confession of salvation from sin at New Haven) I wrote from Putney a long letter to David Harrison, a dear friend in Meriden, Conn., giving my ideas on various subjects that we had talked about in previous intercourse; and in conclusion I broached, for the first time, a theory which I had long been maturing, in respect to the social state in the resurrection world. That letter, though written solely for very private perusal, some few months afterwards was published surreptitiously and anonymously at Philadelphia in a periodical called the *Battle Axe,* and hence got the name of the *Battle Axe letter.* The terrible paragraph in that letter, which was the real *Battle Axe* that has been thundering and echoing in the doctrines and doings of all sorts of Free Lovers ever since, is the following:

"I will write all that is in my heart on one delicate subject, and you may judge for yourself whether it is expedient to show this letter to others. When the will of God is done on earth, as it is in heaven, *there will be no marriage.* The marriage supper of the Lamb, is a feast at which *every dish is free to every guest.* Exclusiveness, jealousy, quarreling, have no place there, for the same reason as that which forbids the guests of a thanksgiving dinner to claim each his separate dish, and quarrel with the rest for his rights. In a pure [the original reads *holy*] community, there is no more reason why sexual intercourse should be restrained by law, than why eating and drinking should be—and there is as little occasion for shame in the one case as in the other. God has placed a wall of partition between the male and female during the apostasy, for good reasons, which will be broken down in the resurrection, for equally good reasons. But woe to him who abolishes the law of the apostasy before he stands in the holiness of the resurrection. The guests of the marriage supper may have each his favorite dish, each a dish of his own procuring, and that without the jealousy of exclusiveness. I call a certain woman my wife—she is yours, she is Christ's, and in him she is the bride of all saints. She is dear in the hand of a stranger, and according to my promise to her I rejoice. My claim

_____
● Selection from *Oneida Circular,* XI (August 24, 1874), 276–77.

upon her cuts directly across the marriage covenant of this world, and God knows the end."

. . . It is important to observe that the theory broached in that letter is not Spiritual Wifehood but *Communism*. The usual landing-place of religious speculators, when they move out of marriage, is in spiritual coupling, or affinityism for two. This is Swedenborg's substitute for marriage, as it is that of the Spiritualists generally; and this was the hobby of the New York Perfectionists, with whom I was much mixed up during the three years when I was studying the social question. But I did not stop in this half-way system. Perhaps I would have done so if I had formed my theory and committed myself to it in the early part of that period of study, when my heart was most under the special attraction I have described. But I was kept quiet and searching till I could rise above personal passion, and see clearly the spirit of Pentecost presiding over the love of heaven. I well remember the spiritual *lift* by which I rose and reached the great idea of a universal marriage, and wrote the Battle Axe letter immediately after that lift.

It will be seen by a careful reading of that letter, that when I got this enlargement, I communised my claim on the woman, and gave her up to all.

I suppose that the theory of absolute communism in love was never before broached in this world. The Primitive Church only left on record the *negative* doctrine of *no marriage in the resurrection*, and this was very liable to be mistaken for Shakerism, as it has been by the Catholics and religionists generally, as well as by the Shakers. And all the *positive* theories of sexual relation in heaven that I know of, are, as I have said, theories of limited affinityism or spiritual wifery, which is really marriage and nothing better. The idea of Pentecostal love between the sexes was first developed, so far as I know, in the Battle Axe letter, dated Jan. 15th, 1837. . . .

It is difficult at the present time to conceive of the shock which the Battle Axe letter produced. I recognized the hand of God in its publication, but verily I felt as though he had taken a fearful advantage of me, and committed me to an awful step against my will. I am not sure that I should ever have broached our social theory deliberately and of my own free motion. I was caught in the snare of my own confidential whisper, and hung up as a gazing stock to the world. I felt in meeting my old letter as I presume Beecher has felt in meeting some of his. . . .

From the time of the publication of the Battle Axe letter, I felt that I was called, even under the heaviest penalties, to defend and ultimately carry out the doctrine of Communism in love; and I accepted the commission with a good heart.

GROUP PHOTO, ONEIDA COMMUNITY.

Beginnings of Complex Marriage

(Compiled by George W. Noyes)

After the Battle Axe *letter and its aftermath, Noyes settled down in Putney, Vermont, where he gathered about him a small group of followers, including his brother and two sisters, and a wife, Harriet A. Holton, whom he had converted and then wooed much as he had Abigail Merwin. By 1843 there were thirty-five members in the community, including twenty-eight adults. Among them were two new converts, George and Mary Cragin, who figured importantly in the next dramatic step, bringing complex marriage from theory to practice.*

George Cragin had been the editor of the Advocate of Moral Reform, *an anti-prostitution journal published by the Female Moral Reform Society of New York City. In 1837, not long after the publication of the* Battle Axe *letter, one of the most prominent ladies of the Society suddenly announced her conversion to Perfectionism. After the hubbub caused by Noyes's letter, being converted to Perfectionism—even if it wasn't the extremist group in Putney—was like abandoning oneself to precisely the life of sin that the Female*

Moral Reform Society existed to eradicate. Mrs. Green was expelled.

Cragin ran an article attacking Perfectionism in the Advocate, *and received a reply from Noyes, who, since the* Battle Axe *uproar, was taking all criticism of the sect as if directed personally at him. One thing led to another, until finally in the fall of 1840 the Cragins joined Noyes at Putney, where Mary Cragin slowly slipped into the symbolic role that Abigail Merwin had held before her, the living possibility of a sinless communal love among the saved. The selections reprinted here from George W. Noyes' collection of original Putney documents show how the* Battle Axe *letter bore fruit in complex marriage.*

George W. Noyes (Compiler)
Beginnings of Complex Marriage

Mary E. Cragin's Journal

January 1846.—At the request of Mr. Noyes I now commence a journal of what has taken place among us of late with regard to the increase of brotherly love.

This month Mr. Cragin left for Belchertown and Southampton, not intending to stay long. He did not go to Southampton as we expected, but went to visit the Prescott sisters. While absent he wrote a letter to Mrs. Harriet A. Noyes expressing his love for her as a sister in Christ. This letter, together with his visit to Prescott, gave rise to some remarks about his partiality for women. Mr. Noyes addressed a letter of friendly caution to him, in which he spoke approvingly of his love for the feminine character, but reminded him that such men as Dr. Gridley and Charles Mead were watching him with an evil eye. Mrs. Noyes was brought into tribulation by the remarks of some about Mr. Cragin's letter, and when Mr. Noyes talked with her upon the subject she made known to him her love for Mr. Cragin. Mr. Noyes approved of her feel-

●Selection from *John Humphrey Noyes: The Putney Community,* compiled and ed. George Wallingford Noyes, Oneida: By the Author, 1931, pp. 197–206.

ings, and appointed a meeting of the four, Mr. and Mrs. Noyes,
Mr. and Mrs. Cragin. We met one Saturday evening about the
middle of the month. Mr. Noyes requested Mr. Cragin to read the
letter of counsel referred to, and added words of caution which
Mr. Cragin confessed were needed. Mr. Noyes said this was the
negative side of the subject; we would now turn to the positive side.
He then called upon Mrs. Noyes to speak. She said that she was
pleased by Mr. Cragin's letter, and that her heart was drawn out
toward him by it. Mr. Cragin confessed a similar feeling toward
her, which prompted the letter. Mr. Noyes then asked Mr. Cragin's
leave to tell me that he loved me. Mr. Cragin heartily consented. I
said that I had loved Mr. Noyes so much that I feared he would
find it out; for I was not certain, my awe of him was such, that he
wanted me to love him so much. After these avowals we considered
ourselves engaged to each other, expecting to live in all conformity
to the laws of this world until the time arrives for the consummation of our union. The effect was most refreshing to our spirits.
We have formed a circle which it is not easy for the Devil to
break. We find this evidence that our love is of God; it is destitute
of exclusiveness, each one rejoicing in the happiness of the others.

A few days after this meeting Mr. Noyes said that he wanted to
extend the blessing to all as fast as they were able to receive it.
He talked with Harriet Skinner, and found her nearer ripe for a
community of hearts than he had supposed. Also at an incidental
interview Mr. Miller gave a satisfactory testimony.

Mr. Noyes gave a lecture upon the proper bounds of demonstrations of love between the sexes. He cut off kissing and everything
which would be considered as leaning toward licentiousness.

March 15.—Mr. and Mrs. Miller, Mr. and Mrs. Skinner, Mr. and
Mrs. Noyes, and Mr. and Mrs. Cragin met at Mr. Miller's. Mr.
Noyes spoke of Mr. Miller's testimony at the printing-office, and
remarked upon the increasing tendency to unity among us. He then
said that a nucleus must be formed in order to draw the others in;
and he asked whether, if he should find it necessary to commence,
there was sufficient confidence in him to prevent evil surmisings
and jealousies. An expression was obtained from each one, and the
conclusion was unanimous that Mr. Noyes as the head and pilot in
this matter had a claim on our confidence and an undoubted right
to do as he pleased.

Charlotte said at the meeting that her husband, she thought, did not love her so well as formerly. Mr. Noyes read to us the fourth chapter of First Thessalonians, dwelling with emphasis upon the sixth verse: "That no man go beyond and defraud his brother in any matter." I was brought into considerable tribulation by a spirit which accused me of being the occasion of Charlotte's difficulties. I will relate the particulars: Last June Mr. Smith of Rondout came to Putney to see Mr. Noyes. On hearing of his arrival I was plunged into distress. My husband was gone, and I felt desolate and wretched. Mr. Miller happened to call, and his sympathies were drawn out in my behalf. He acted the part of a brother toward me through all my tribulation, for which I felt very grateful. As I supposed that he still retained the exclusive affection for Charlotte which I knew he once had, I was not so much on my guard as I should have been. This winter some trifling familiarities took place, which gave me uneasiness. I feared that I had unconsciously attracted him, and I opened my heart to my husband for advice and rebuke if I needed it. I also told Mrs. Noyes from whom I have no secrets. Mr. Noyes called to give us advice. He had noticed how things were going. He did not condemn any one, but wished such intimacies put an end to before they went too far. I had the night before sent word to Mr. Miller by Mr. Cragin, requesting him to treat me with coolness and reserve for his own sake and Charlotte's and mine. Mr. Noyes said I must tell Mr. Miller myself, if it was necessary. In the afternoon Mr. Cragin went up to see Charlotte. While he was gone Mr. Miller, who had previously called to talk with us when Mr. Cragin was at home but had been interrupted, came in. He said that once he had felt disposed to see and talk about my faults, but that his feelings had changed; that he had a strong attachment for me, stronger than for any woman in the Community. I was surprised at this, and felt full of zeal to plead Charlotte's cause. I told him that I would not do anything that looked like defrauding her, and that I would seek her happiness before my own, because I considered her more worthy. He left, and I took the first opportunity of relating what had passed to my husband and Mr. and Mrs. Noyes. The next day in a conversation with Mr. Noyes at which Charlotte was present, Mr. Miller said that I misunderstood him. There the matter rests until all parties can be heard in their own defense.

March 22.—An interview took place between Messrs. Noyes, Miller, Skinner and Cragin with their wives at Mr. Noyes' house. Mr.

Noyes remarked that he hoped we had come together for peace and not for war. He then requested Mr. Miller to commence the conversation. This Mr. Miller declined to do, wishing me to bring forward my charges against him. It was finally settled that I should state the conversation which took place on the previous Wednesday, which I did. Mr. Miller said that I correctly stated it, but he insisted with much warmth that in his declaration of attachment to me he meant of course to except his wife. This seemed to be the point at issue between us. In reply to my defense of Charlotte that afternoon he had said nothing that looked like surprise at my having received the impression I did. Mr. Noyes labored to convince him that he had been imprudent in his course toward me, particularly in leaving that expression of attachment so unguarded. Mr. Miller again and again disclaimed all intention of doing wrong, of which no one accused him. Charlotte was much distressed that I should have received such an impression from what he said, and I was distressed that I could not conscientiously fully acquit him of having defrauded Charlotte for my sake. Finally Mr. Miller acknowledged that he might have been imprudent, and Charlotte said she thought her mind would become calm. So we parted. The next day Mr. Cragin tendered his sympathies to Mr. Miller, and begged him not to be so sensitive, assuring him that we all loved him and that what had taken place was an external affair.

March 24.—Mr. Miller wrote a letter to Mr. Noyes in which he fully and heartily sanctioned Mr. Noyes's course with him and acknowledged his imprudence in full. Charlotte remains distressed. Alas! That I should be an apple of discord in a family to whom I am under such untold obligation! But this seems to be my fate.

March 25.—Mr. Noyes called to state Mr. Miller's opinion of a remark which I made to him on the evening of our meeting, which was this: I said to Mr. Miller that I had not loved him, that I only felt grateful to him for his partiality to me. I felt as though I had not acknowledged enough as soon as I had said it, but did not know how then to alter it. I was irritated by what he had said just before about my having made an avowal of love to him, which I did not think I ever had. However the truth is that I did love him more than I was aware. I still love Mr. Miller as well as ever, but with a firm determination to infringe on no one's rights. "Love worketh no ill to his neighbor." I will just add that I think Charlotte has not been jealous of me without a cause.

J. H. Noyes

My First Act in Sexual Freedom

One evening in May 1846 Mrs. Cragin and I went for a stroll. Coming to a lonely place we sat on a rock by the roadside and talked. All the circumstances invited advance in freedom, and yielding to the impulse upon me I took some personal liberties. The temptation to go further was tremendous. But at this point came serious thoughts. I stopped and revolved in mind as before God what to do. I said to myself, "I will not steal." After a moment we arose and went toward home. On the way we lingered. But I said, "No, I am going home to report what we have done." On reaching Mr. Cragin's house I called a meeting of the four. A searching talk ensued. Mr. Cragin at first was tempted to think that I was following the course of Abram C. Smith, but he finally recognized the difference and gave judgment of approval. My wife promptly expressed her entire sanction. The last part of the interview was as amicable and happy as a wedding, and the consequence was that we gave each other full liberty.

Noyes to Harriet H. Skinner

[About] August 1, 1846.

"He that doubteth is damned if he eat." Mr. Miller doubteth. His last position with me was that he would not do again what he did on the road from Clarendon. He stands opposing my theory and withholding submission. Yet he is availing himself of the privileges of my theory. He embraced Mrs. Cragin last evening. What advances he is making to you I know not. But I wish you to be on your guard. You must tell him you will not allow him to do anything which he thinks is wrong and will be ashamed of afterwards, for to him such things are licentious. I cannot go along with him until he has decisively adopted our principles and has put himself wholly into my hands. He will need much discipline, and he has never yet shown that he knew the value of discipline. He will need to be instructed in regard to secretiveness and the law in relation to propagation before he can safely be trusted with liberty. But in his present spirit and position I cannot instruct him. I wish you therefore to hold yourself aloof from him, or at most to coquette with him, and not allow him to feel free with you until he openly avows our principles and submits to my instructions.

J. H. N.

John R. Miller to Noyes

Putney, August 18, 1846.

Dear Brother Noyes: . . .

I came into the store, and after praying earnestly that God would show me his will on the subject of our conversation I opened the Bible to these verses: "For we write none other things unto you than what ye read and acknowledge; and I trust ye shall acknowledge even to the end; as also ye have acknowledged us in part, that we are your rejoicing, even as ye also are ours in the day of the Lord Jesus." This seems to me to be plainly the manifestation of the will of God. As such I am willing to receive it, and follow the leading of his spirit through you without questioning or knowing why it is so. I believe that God is able and willing to show me the whole truth on this subject in due time, and I will wait patiently.

Your whole past life has been such as to inspire me with confidence. I can point to no one act which I do not think was right and directed by the spirit of God. In all my past difficulties I can plainly see the hand of God directing them for my good.

Yours in sincerity,
J. R. Miller

Mary E. Cragin to John R. Miller at Boston

Putney, September 17, 1846.

Dear Brother:

Don't, I pray, expect ready wit or anything else but commonplace sayings, written crookedly too, for I have little George on my lap assisting in his way, and John, who has just taken a fit of jealousy, pulling me to take him up too. However I am determined to write a little, if it is only to tell you that I love you some too, and I am confident that you will yet come out bright and happy and be able to say that you count your greatest trials as your greatest reasons for rejoicing, inasmuch as they will yield the most fruit. Doubtless you are enjoying yourself as well as you can considering you have left your heart behind you. I only hope that you want to see us as much as we want to see you. Georgy will not let me write any longer.

Yours affectionately,
M. E. Cragin

John R. Miller to Henry W. Burnham

                                        Putney, October 28, 1846.
Dear Brother Burnham:

. . . I never loved you, never felt so near to you as I do now. If you are going through the same sufferings that I have been through, I know how to sympathize. . . .

If God calls us to suffer, we must learn to rejoice in it. . . . We may not always see at the time why it is that God calls us thus to separate from things we hold dear. But I can now see that all the sufferings I have been through for the past summer have been for my everlasting good. I could never have gained such a victory over the world, the flesh and the Devil without it, and never should have had this experience if it had not been for Brother Noyes. I thought a good many times, "These are hard sayings: who can hear them?" And have been ready to go back into Egypt. But when I have come out from under the Devil's magnetism into the glorious sunlight of heaven, I have seen that it was not only the best thing that could be done, but the only thing to remedy the evil. I had an immense amount of worldly wisdom to be purged out before I could be brought into perfect fellowship with Christ. The great question was, what will the world think of this? But I have learned that to the children of God the question and the only question is, what will my Father think of this? And when we have once learned his will, the world is nothing more to us than if we were the inhabitants of some other planet.

It may seem to us that the course in which the spirit leads will bring us to ruin. But is not he, without whose notice a sparrow cannot fall to the ground, able to uphold us if we put our trust in him?

We should keep distinctly in mind that nothing is of any value to us that is not valuable to God. I say then, Away with everything else, the sooner the better. If I am going to buy goods, I do not want my pocket-book filled with good bills and counterfeit together. I want none but what are current in market. And I want nothing about me but what will pass in the market of heaven. . . .

When I have been led to doubt and hesitate about what we were doing, God has shown me his will as plainly as if I had heard a voice from heaven saying, "This is the way, walk ye in it." When I have looked back, all has been darkness and misery, but when I have gone forward in the course God has marked out, my heart has been filled with the peace and happiness of heaven. . . .

Yours affectionately,

J. R. Miller

Statement of Principles

About November 1, 1846.

We, the undersigned, hold the following principles as the basis of our social union:

1. All individual proprietorship either of persons or things is surrendered, and absolute community of interests takes the place of the laws and fashions which preside over property and family relations in the world.

2. God as the ultimate and absolute owner of our persons and possessions is installed as the director of our combinations and the distributor of property. His spirit is our supreme regulator.

3. John H. Noyes is the father and overseer whom the Holy Ghost has set over the family thus constituted. To John H. Noyes as such we submit ourselves in all things spiritual and temporal, appealing from his decisions only to the spirit of God, and that without disputing.

We pledge ourselves to these principles without reserve; and if we fall away from them, let God and our signatures be witnesses against us.

Geo. Cragin.

Harriet A. Noyes.

Charlotte A. Miller.

Harriet H. Skinner.

Mary E. Cragin.

John L. Skinner.

John R. Miller.

Decadence of Marriage

James W. Towner

This thumbnail history of free love in America could not have been written by a more knowledgeable observer. At the time he wrote it James W. Towner had only recently become a member of the Oneida Community. Before that he was in the Berlin Heights group, and had been actively involved in the movement, writing for The Social Revolutionist *and carrying on debates with Thomas and Mary Nichols since the early 1850s. He knew the free lovers inside and out.*

Of course all the Oneida members were interested in the progress of free love, for although they disapproved of every version of it but their own, it was only natural for them to want to know how others fared whom society identified with them. They liked the sturdy libertarianism of Ezra Heywood, and if Victoria Woodhull happened to say anything that made sense to them in one of her speeches, they were not stinting of praise, no matter what they might think of her general intentions. They admired her pluck, and liked seeing Henry Ward Beecher squirm.

The free lovers of the world likewise kept an eye on the success of Oneida, and often pointed to it as an example of the truth of their doctrines, though in fact Perfectionism was a far cry from any but the principles of Shaker celibacy—as Noyes kept reminding them, and as Towner affirms here. Free lovers like Stephen Pearl Andrews came to visit the community and see for themselves. The response of "the family," as Oneidans called themselves, varied according to cases, but was always cool. People like Andrews wanted to arrange some rapprochement that preserved their theories, expressing sympathy or affinity without giving up anything substantial.

Towner himself courted Noyes for years before he and his family made the fatal move to Oneida. Indeed his case shows how shrewd the community was in keeping its distance from these worldlings, for Towner could not conquer the spirit of contentiousness and pride in his own ideas, and it led ultimately to his being the leader of the anti-Noyes faction when the community broke up in 1879. The most important issue in that breakup was the future of complex marriage, and it was perfectly predictable that Towner should have been in favor of less supervision by the family patriarchs—in short, license—just what a Berlin Heights man would favor, whatever he might have said a few years earlier, in this article.

James W. Towner
Decadence of Marriage

The religious revivals which swept with such power over the country, beginning some fifty years ago, bred extensive social irregularities and inaugurated a revolution in marriage. Anti-revivalists aided that revolution in various ways. Fanny Wright and Robert Dale Owen greatly aided it by their attacks on religion, property and society, in 1828, which shook New-York city and even the nation, and indoctrinated its politics in various ways. Then came the elder Owen and Fourier with their writings upon Socialism largely contributing to the same end. Then came the writings of Swedenborg with his doctrines of mistress-keeping, concubinage, spiritual affinities and free and easy divorce; the last two of which doctrines obtaining a large acceptance and inoculating literature, have helped swell

● Selection from *Oneida Circular*, XIII (February 3, 1876), 36.

the tide against marriage. And lastly, those connected in one way or other with "Modern Spiritualism," now a host in this country, have rolled on the tide of marriage revolution, till, among the masses of the people, the decadence of marriage as a sacred and binding ordinance, has for some time been an established fact. Very many among the married discovered that they were mismated; a general hunt for affinities supervened; and to aid in getting them, great liberality and even laxity of divorce legislation has taken place; the courts have been crowded with a constantly increasing number of applicants, who, in a great majority of cases, are asking liberation only to unite with some already discovered affinity. Little but the form of marriage remains, the soul having long since well nigh departed.

The founder of our Community saw these things as they were transpiring, and realized the evils incident thereto. He saw a tendency to social anarchy in that revolution; that in the roaming about from mate to mate which took place, multitudes of people fell into hopeless licentiousness; that the blessings of the sexual relation and of the family were threatened with destruction; that, especially, was the natural desire for children dying out in general society; that the inconvenience of the burden of children in the race for affinities, and the natural dread of involuntary child-bearing in an age of growing intelligence, combined with other causes, had introduced the frightful practice of abortion, which forty years ago was of rare and secret occurrence but now became frequent and bold, and more common even in the older States and among people of respectability and high social standing than elsewhere. Seeing these things and many other evils which might be named, attending the natural revolt against the sexual bondage and affectional poverty of marriage, he set about devising some remedy for them, and saving what is valuable in the family, something to take the place of the "fashion of the world" that was passing away. An unwavering believer in the Bible and in Jesus Christ as a Savior from all sin, he naturally turned in that direction for such remedy and substitute. He found in Christianity the germs of a social as well as a religious system; that it was to introduce a reign of the heavens superseding all other kingdoms; and in the manifestation of the outpouring of the Holy Spirit on the day of Pentecost and in the Communism which followed, he found the key to understand Christianity as a social force and organization. Faithfully studying that and following its logical development through years of persecution and social outlawry, with great labor and unspeakable trial he brought forward our system of Christian Communism as a truly conservative method of averting social anarchy and the various evils above mentioned. And in this view is to be found its merit. It is not offered to the world in the interest of lawlessness and disorder. Our position may be one of non-conformity to lower laws in some respects, but we claim it to be in conformity to the higher law which should govern the truly humane, God-fearing and conscientious, the man who would love his neighbor as himself. We claim that in the social sphere our system is the natural complement of the improvements making in other departments of human knowledge and effort, whereby it is constantly demonstrated that any good can be better attained by coöperation and association, than by single persons or small partnerships. We have believed that candid, thinking people would study us in this aspect, and still believe they will do so. We are on trial, and we expect to be able to prove on the trial that we are in favor of good order, peace, industry and improvement. We expect, too, if we shall be allowed a fair trial, to prove that, as a practical fact, our system tends to promote in the intercourse of the sexes, delicacy, modesty, chastity and self-denial rather than indulgence; and that in fact there is less of the latter under our system than in any other society, except the Shakers or others who practice celibacy. We also expect to prove that we are able to produce in all the relations of the family, in the exercise of all the kindly charities of our nature—when regenerated—social blessings of the best quality and in the greatest quantity. If we can not, we expect to fail. We only ask lovers of truth and of our race to give us that trial, and we can not doubt that they will.

Woman's Mistake

"Stella"

Even today this argument of an Oneida woman who signed herself "Stella" will seem very radical to many readers, for it strikes at the very heart of woman's role in American society, as well as "woman's mistake." The "one-love system" has gone by other names—"union for life," "love at first sight," "romance," and "the double standard" —but essentially it still exists as described here, the basis of female dependence on some single man for economic and emotional support and social countenance.

At Oneida this traditional subjugation was undermined in every way possible, not only by complex marriage, but also by single sleeping apartments, communal nurseries, communism of both labor and its rewards, and so on. In a report on women in the community work force issued in 1867, they estimated twenty-eight or twenty-nine full-time in occupations ordinarily filled by men, including several superintendents of manufacturing departments. "From the 111 females that we now number . . . also deduct the 28 who are disqualified from the labor department by infancy, age and infirmity. Of the remaining 53, 6 are under 15 years of age, and 6 are over 65, so you have left 42 [sic] reliable women to attend to the household work. Cooking, washing, dairy, bringing up children, dress-making, hat-making and braiding; preparing bedding for the boarding-houses; and one woman to oversee them. To assist in the house-work, 6 men are appropriated and 4 hired girls." Although there is still an obvious division of labor on sexual lines, it must be clear that the women pulled their own weight economically, and this certainly reinforced their independence.

Complex marriage furnished the motive force for all the rest of these efforts at independence—and especially that aspect of complex marriage that absolutely forbade any "exclusive" attachments among members, even between mothers and their offspring. This rule was rigorously enforced, so that any pair who seemed "in love" in a romantic sense were quickly separated, if not by the first warning and criticism, then by literal banishment of one party to another branch of the community.

The practice of what they called "ascending fellowship"—initiation of young people into complex marriage by the older members— had the advantage of discouraging "first love" infatuations as well as more obvious uses. So did the go-between system, which involved the community in every sexual encounter, by making it a matter of at least one other person's knowledge, typically an older woman, who would be able to impede a pairing if not desired by both parties, or if the community frowned on it as tending toward exclusiveness or "descending fellowship."

Probably this need to enforce non-exclusiveness was both the essence of communal life and its downfall. In the end it was the young women in particular who resisted the rule of ascending fellowship and advocated a return to conventional marriage. Towner and his faction wanted to continue in the old way, without the burden of Noyes's authority weighing on it. But without that authority, and without the mechanism of complex marriage to give authority its access to the most intimate corners of every life, the rest of the intricate communal organization lost its vitality and cohesion. When complex marriage was abandoned, everything had to be abandoned.

"Stella"
Woman's Mistake

It seems to me that the one-love theory is the bane of woman. I admit that she *is prone* to this miserable theory, which casts all the treasure of her love upon a single throw, and accepts of happiness or misery as that wins or loses, but I think it must be one of the consequences of her fall from her first estate—a part of the punishment of her first transgression. And now to strengthen this proneness, society and education come in and train it into an immutable habit, and teach woman to prize it as her greatest virtue. She is taught to center all her hopes upon drawing one heart entirely to herself— and then make it a life-long study to keep it and her own in unchangeable devotion. But how few attain even a semblance of this. Does not disappointment almost invariably follow the unnatural attempt? Man is not by nature prone to the one-love theory as much as woman is—not at least so far as his own proclivities and inclinations are concerned, however much he may value it in her. And society, which after all is a reflex of masculine thought and opinion, does not require of him strict adhesion to the one-love theory—it on the whole rather admires the bold rover who has a string of hearts to show as trophies of his power. The woman then who stakes all her happiness on the unchanging fervor of one heart, often has everything against her—man's nature which demands novelty, and the secret toleration by society of his freedom. These forces always at work, make the one-love theory of woman almost an impossibility. What does she then do? Why, she goes on steadily pouring water into a sieve, or attempting to brush back the ocean with a broom. She lavishes at the feet of her thankless idol all the wealth of her affection. She goes on year after year fretting her heart out because she gets such small returns of that for which she has recklessly sacrificed her all.

Be the object of her love never so worthless, a mere parasite living on her greenness, and absorbing all the juices of her life, yet she delights in the sacrifice. Often the heart which she so jealously guards is lost through her very greediness. The more she frantically tries to keep it, the more it eludes her. She becomes repulsive where she wishes to charm. Then soured and chagrined

● Selection from *The Circular*, n.s. III (July 16, 1866), 139–40.

by the failure of her hopes, she becomes a fretful, frowning Mrs. Caudle. Softer and less aggressive natures succumb to disappointed affection, take to suicide, or pass away sadly and silently before their time. Why is all this true of woman? Why must her affections become a curse instead of a blessing to her? I would say first of all, because she does not know where to place them. Instead of centering them on *any man,* she should give them to God, wholly and unreservedly—not with the intention or expectation of *ever* withdrawing them from him, for he is unchangeable in faithfulness, and his fullness can make rich in love all who come to him. This will ensure her heart-comfort and strength if all else fails her. And then if she does fully yield herself to God, he will keep her from this slavish idolatry to any man, which is the bane of the one-love theory. She will learn to love in a way to nourish and strengthen her life. She will learn that a ruinous, suicidal abandonment in loving man is absurd, and no more noble or desirable than the same spendthrift spirit in any other undertaking. Men are sensible enough to withdraw from enterprises when it is all outgo and no returns. They do not generally throw themselves away. None but gamblers, drunkards, and the worst sort of men squander all their chances on one gratification. Women will some time learn to value themselves better than to throw away their hearts. Because women themselves set so little value on themselves, and rush upon heart-bankruptcy so recklessly, is probably one reason why men do not value them more. I believe you will find all down through history that those women who knew best their own value, were in a good sense the most independent of their lovers, had the most influence, and the best fortune. God will teach women who abandon themselves to Him alone, the secret of never being forsaken or heart-broken. It is thought a great gift to be able to grow old gracefully; it is a greater to know how to keep your heart—to love, and to withdraw from love gracefully at the right time.

The Loose Screw

Henry J. Seymour

Henry J. Seymour had been in Brooklyn with Noyes in the early 1850s, so he was an old member and spoke with some authority when he wrote this article for the Circular *in 1870. Known chiefly for his gardening ability—he once grew a strawberry nine inches in circumference!—he was also an intelligent observer of the world, and like other members who followed ordinary pursuits in field or factory, he sometimes wrote his thoughts down for the community. The Perfectionists really did achieve that combination of intellectual and manual labor that every utopia of the period strove for. "As a family we watch the current events of the world, and try to understand the lessons they teach."*

In the early 1870s there was a good deal to notice. It was in response to the Tilton-Beecher scandal that John Humphrey Noyes devoted an evening meeting to the history of the Battle Axe *letter, his own experience of public exposure of his sexual non-conformity. Seymour might have pointed out a similar connection between a current event and something out of the community's past, for it was during his period in Brooklyn that the first "love, marriage, and divorce" debate between James, Andrews, and Greeley filled the pages of the New York* Tribune. *Now, like an old volcano, James was rumbling again on the marriage question. Not only did he provoke a debate by his letter to the* Nation, *but in that same month he published an article in the* Atlantic Monthly *on "The Logic of Marriage and Murder," and not long after that he renewed his old argument with Stephen Pearl Andrews, now an editor of* Woodhull and Claflin's Weekly, *which printed every word of these deep-lunged patriarchs.*

James's position had not changed since the early 1850s, when he first reviewed Lazarus's Love vs. Marriage *and found himself vilified in the ultra-conservative New York* Observer. *Coincidentally, that episode had not only led to the* Tribune *debate, but also to James' first contact with Noyes and the Oneida Community, for the* Observer *was taking potshots at free love wherever it reared its head, and one place was the little group of Brooklyn Perfectionists putting out the* Circular. *James made a special trip to Brooklyn to meet them, and then wrote the* Observer *in their defense: "From a conversation or two which I have had with some of their leading men, I judge them to be persons of great sincerity, but of deplorable fanaticism. . . . Honest, upright souls they seemed at bottom, though sadly misguided by an insane sense of duty . . . ," and he condemned the* Observer *for its "descent on this starveling and harmless fieldmouse!" (See Section I for the rest of James's letter.)*

Noyes and Seymour cannot have appreciated being referred to as a "fieldmouse" or "fanatics" however grateful they may have been for supporters of their rights. By the time of Seymour's commentary on James, almost twenty years of the experiment had gone by, very successfully, and the community had earned the right to oppose its "mustard seed of truth" to James's Fourierist "winch" and the Observer's *or the* Nation's *"religionist despair of perfection and sinlessness in this world.*

It is worth mentioning too that Seymour's faith in the Perfectionist solution to the problem of "human nature" survived even the breakup of the community. He continued to live at Oneida, now called Kenwood, where from time to time he wrote articles or letters to the press (the Circular *being no longer published), arguing in the old vein: "please to observe that human nature which has made personal acquaintance with God, and which has the* Christ-

life developed in the heart, is not *the same as the human nature of those who are yet strangers to Him. It is only fair and reasonable to expect better things of the new kind of human nature."*

Henry J. Seymour
The Loose Screw

There has been a discussion between Mr. Henry James of Massachusetts and the editor of the *Nation,* from which we take a couple of extracts. They furnish an interesting text suggesting some reflections in respect to the condition of society in general, in its relation to the truth. These extracts certainly indicate a degree of candor that is not often found on either side in such discussions. The editor says in reply to a three-column letter of Mr. James:

"We have denied his premises—namely, that marriage as at present administered, is the cause of the 'hideous carnival of crime' from which society is suffering—as plainly as possible. We said nothing about final causes, because we knew nothing about them, and with the greatest respect for him—neither does he. He can no more tell why McFarland and his wife led such a shocking life for nine years, or why all marriages are not happy than we can. If he could he would have the secret of the universe, and there would be a rush to Cambridge from all parts of the globe. . . .

"We believe as Mr. James does, that 'there is a screw loose in man'; but we never said that marriage was 'the sovereign winch designed for tightening it.' Marriage is simply like education and other things, one of the means of reducing the amount of damage done by it. As Mr. James truly remarks, 'it is simply idle to expect crime to cease until the advent of a perfect society on earth'; in the meantime, however, it would be very foolish, he will admit, to dismiss the police, demolish the schools and jails, and shut up the courts."

Admitting that the editor in common with his opponent and the world at large know nothing of final causes, or of the divine purpose in permitting existing evils, do we not see in this ignorance a most deplorable state of things? Here is "a screw loose in man," in consequence of which the machinery of society is suffering frightfully from friction, and in danger of breaking to pieces. In this

---
● Selection from *The Circular,* n.s. VII (June 27, 1870), 113–14.

critical condition of things no one can discover how the screw
became loose, nor invent a method of tightening it. The most that
can be done is to institute schools, marriage, governments, courts,
police and jails, which barely serve the purpose of preventing
society from going to destruction, while they are incapable of preventing a "hideous carnival of crime."

Society being in this sad plight it would seem perfectly appropriate for any one who conceives that he has the remotest opportunity or capacity for discovering where the loose screw is, or of
contributing in the smallest degree to the work of tightening it,
to make the attempt. Fourier and his followers, to which school
Mr. James appears virtually to belong, claim that the loose screw
is not in human nature; but that the difficulty is to be found in
the governments, in marriage, in the schools, etc., which attempt
to regulate human nature. This class of philosophers have had a
fair field for advocating their views in this country for the last thirty
or forty years, as well as an opportunity for putting them in practice. But with all these advantages they have failed to establish their
theory. The Bible, and religionists generally, have maintained that
the loose screw is in human nature, but modern religionists hold
that the loose screw is situated so far within the vitals of human
nature that no one can ever find a way to get at it so as to correct
the evil, even in the case of a single individual, without destroying
his life. In short, they claim that it is only in another world where
people will not be troubled with bodies that the machinery can
be set right. They say that the most we can hope to do here and
now, is to make the best possible use of marriage, governments
etc., with a somewhat faint hope that in another world the
machinery will be perfectly adjusted, and will run with perfect
smoothness.

As we intend to mention all who in a general way have their
theories in regard to this matter, it seems proper that we should
speak of our own position as Bible Communists. We hold with the
Bible and religionists generally, that the loose screw is to be found
inside of human nature; but we believe, contrary to the opinion of
religionists, that the difficulty can be got at and remedied, in this
life, without putting off the body. Indeed we believe there is a
"sovereign winch designed for tightening" this loose screw, and that
it will tighten it effectually, here and now, which, all will admit,
marriage and all the world's institutions can not do. We believe

that a full and accurate description of this remedy can be found in the Bible, but that it has been sadly misunderstood and misrepresented. In assuming this somewhat bold position we are very far from complaining of our neighbors for not at once believing our declarations. Indeed we do not quite agree with the editor of the *Nation* when he says of Mr. James, that if he could tell why all marriages are not happy he would have the secret of the universe, and there would be a rush to Cambridge from all parts of the globe. We believe that it takes a comparatively long time for the mustard seed of truth to develop its true character so as to be popularly recognized as truth. In the meantime we thank the Providence that has put us in an age and country where we are permitted to work out our discovery, so that in due time its truth or falsity shall be manifest to all men.

Free Love Disclaimers

John Humphrey Noyes and Willam A. Hinds

In 1852, when Noyes reaffirmed the "social principles" of the
Oneida Community in the "Theocratic Platform," he spoke of the
"Cultivation of Free Love" (see headnote to preceding selection).
Only a few months later the phrase was changed to "Universal
Love," a revision designed to avoid the imputation of any similarity
between Oneida's complex marriage and the licentious pairing, on
the secular model, that went under the name of free love in Modern
Times, and also to make it clear that Perfectionists were not the
same as Spiritualists, theorists of affinities and soul-mating.

In 1865 Noyes deemed it expedient to compose an official disclaimer of any connection with the free lovers, and this statement
was frequently reprinted in the Circular, along with occasional
explanations and caveats by other members of the community. Here
is Noyes's original pronouncement, and one of the supplemental
articles, written by Circular editor William A. Hinds, himself an
important figure in the Oneida family, and a crony of James W.
Towner during the breakup.

John Humphrey Noyes
Free Love

This terrible combination of two very good ideas—freedom and love—was probably first used in our writings about sixteen years ago, and originated in the Oneida school of socialists. It was however soon taken up by a very different class of speculators scattered about the country, and has come to be the name of a form of socialism with which we have but little affinity. Still it is sometimes applied to our Communities; and as we are certainly responsible for starting it into circulation, it seems to be our duty to tell what meaning we attach to it, and in what sense we are willing to accept it as a designation of our social system.

The obvious and essential difference between marriage and whoredom may be stated thus:

Marriage is a permanent union. Whoredom is a temporary flirtation.

In marriage, communism of property goes with communism of persons. In whoredom, love is paid for by the job.

Marriage makes a man responsible for the *consequences* of his acts of love to a woman. In whoredom a man imposes on a woman the heavy burdens of maternity, ruining, perhaps, her reputation and her health, and then goes his way without responsibility .

Marriage provides for the maintenance and education of children. Whoredom ignores children as nuisances, and leaves them to chance.

Now in respect to every one of these points of difference between marriage and whoredom, *we stand with marriage.* Free love with us does *not* mean freedom to love to-day and leave to-morrow; or freedom to take a woman's person and keep our property to ourselves; or freedom to freight a woman with our offspring and send her down stream without care or help; or freedom to beget children and leave them to the street and the poor-house. Our Communities are *families,* as distinctly bounded and separted from promiscuous society as ordinary households. The tie that binds us together is as permanent and sacred, to say the least, as that of marriage, for it is our religion. We receive no members (except by deception or mis-

---

● Selections from *The Circular*, n.s. II (February 6, 1865); and *Oneida Circular*, VIII (August 21, 1871), 268.

take), who do not give heart and hand to the family interest for life and forever. Community of property extends just as far as freedom of love. Every man's care and every dollar of the common property is pledged for the maintenance and protection of the women and the education of the children of the Community. Bastardy, in any disastrous sense of the word, is simply impossible in such a social state. Whoever will take the trouble to follow our track from the beginning, will find no forsaken women or children by the way. In this respect we claim to be a little ahead of marriage and common civilization.

We are not sure how far the class of socialists called "free lovers" would claim for themselves anything like the above defence from the charge of *reckless* and *cruel* freedom; but our impression is that their position, scattered as they are, without organization or definite separation from surrounding society, makes it impossible for them to follow and care for the consequences of their freedom, and thus expose them to the just charge of licentiousness. At all events their platform is entirely different from ours, and they must answer for themselves. *We* are not "free lovers," in any sense that makes love less binding or responsible than it is in marriage.

William A. Hinds
The O.C. Record Concerning Modern Spiritualism and Anarchic Free-Love

The Community record is quite as clear and clean respecting godless and irresponsible free-lovers. There has been no fraternization during the past twenty years between us and the class mentioned. Ask those who were members of the old Berlin Heights School, ask the former members of the New York Free-Love League, ask any representative of the Pantarchy, or of the Woodhull and Claflin clique, ask any one on the old Nichols list of free-lovers, or on any other list, or any one favoring loose and irresponsible sexual relations, whether the Oneida Community or any member thereof has favored a departure from common rules of sexual morality in existing society; and you will obtain only a negative answer. No known free-lover has ever been received into the Community. We have time and again refused to entertain affinity hunters: indeed, it is customary for us to treat such folks with the kind of sincerity recommended by Paul in the eleventh verse of the fifth chapter of first Corinthians. The line of demarcation between the Oneida Communists and the free-lovers whose theories and practices tend anarchy-ward, is as plain and broad as that which separates the followers of the Pantarch from those of Pius IX. We have in fact given no countenance in our publications or otherwise even to the free-divorce doctrines so popular nowadays with a large class of reformers. The banner raised thirty years ago by our leader bore this inscription, "Holiness must go before free-love!" That is still our motto.

"But," says one, "you Communists believe in free love and practice it—why then object so strongly to being classed with others who also believe and practice the same principle?" We object for the same reason that you, friend, being heartily persuaded that republicanism is the best form of government for a people who have attained a certain degree of civilization, would object to being classed with such republicans as figured most conspicuously in the French Revolution of 1789, or such anarchic republicans as recently made Paris a pandemonium. You love liberty when combined with order, justice and religion: you detest it and consider it the worst form of despotism when separated from these elements. So we affirm that in a society which has attained a civilization that excludes selfishness, love may be legitimately free; and that then it will be found associated with every element favoring order and the best interests of individuals and of society. And this is not an affirmation based upon mere theory; it is sufficiently confirmed by experience.

Now in view of the facts above stated, we claim the right to insist that a distinction shall be clearly made in the public mind between the so-called "modern spiritualism" and the spiritualism of the Oneida Communists, and also between free-love as taught and practiced by the followers of Nichols, the Berlin Heights Company, Andrews, Woodhull and Claflin, and others, and free-love as taught and practiced by the Oneida Communists. We are willing to bear all the opprobrium that fairly belongs to us as radicals and innovators, but we shall steadily refuse to be made in any way responsible for the sayings and doings of those with whom we are in no way affiliated.

A Gynecological Study
of the Oneida Community

Ely Van de Warker

Ely Van de Warker was a prominent obstetrician and gynecologist who practised in Syracuse. The article which is reprinted here grew out of his examination of a number of Oneida women in the fall of 1877. Although it contains a number of interesting facts—including a concise sketch of the actual protocols of complex marriage—nothing in it is so interesting, perhaps, as its very existence—how it came to be written, or rather, researched.

These were difficult days for the community. One of the chief problems was leadership. John Humphrey Noyes was getting old, a bit deaf, and his voice was now chronically weak. He wanted to retire, but like King Lear, it was his hope to make his rule permanent by "dying" before his time, thus both to oversee the safe transfer of authority and to choose his successor, his own son Dr. Theodore Noyes, who had been born in the Putney period and was now a man in early middle age. The difficulty lay in Theodore Noyes's char-

acter, as might be expected. Although there is much to admire in his rather sweet, soft nature, he entirely lacked the faith of his father, either in himself or in Perfectionism. The first attempt to install him in office ended disastrously, with his father resuming the reins peremptorily after the elders complained that Theodore's method of reorganizing the community business enterprises consisted chiefly in putting the old guard "on the shelf." Theodore had a nervous breakdown immediately upon giving the leadership back to his father, and went off to James C. Jackson's sanitarium at Dansville to recover (see Section VII below on Jackson). This was in 1872. In 1875 a two-year "joint" leadership period began, with father and son sharing responsibilities, and in May 1877 Theodore was once more launched on his own. Again he began to busy himself getting things shipshape, though by now he had learned more tact with the central members. A medical doctor, trained at Yale in the latest science, and also something of a believer in Modern Spiritualism, which was the nineteenth century's materialistic substitute for religion, Theodore Noyes had an absolute mania for bureaucratic order and control, system, logic, method.

After his election to leadership, Theodore claimed that the community had been slowly drifting away from all the institutions that insured its health—evening meetings were "held lightly" by the younger members, people did not present themselves for criticism, a spirit of individualism infected the volunteering for work details, and most important of all, the old mechanisms for administering and surveying the operation of complex marriage had fallen into disuse. Instead of the system of using older women, central members of the community, as go-betweens, lovers were relying on personal friends to present invitations to sexual fellowship. The results in exclusiveness and violation of the rule of ascending fellowship could be seen in the general loose and light behavior of the young. As Theodore explained some years later, it was his view that complex marriage was the very bridle and bit of government at Oneida, and the power to discourage or otherwise regulate relations among the members—even if by no heavier touch than the mere holding of the reins—was the true secret of the patriarchal authority his father had always wielded. He was probably right about the importance of complex marriage, but wrong about how the power was vested in his father.

It is impossible to say whether Theodore had all this consciously in mind when he reinstituted the old system of go-betweens, and required a weekly report of all sexual encounters to be made to him, but surely it was the ultimate meaning of his decision. And the idea of bringing his colleague from Syracuse, Dr. Van de Warker, to make a complete survey of the sexual health and histories of all the Oneida women was clearly part of the whole "scientific" and bureaucratic surveillance that was Theodore's modern notion of filling his father's shoes.

It was a ruinous policy. The community could not cohere under the rule of science and reason, no matter how imitative of the previous rule of faith. Once again Theodore was asked to step aside for his father, who cancelled the weekly reports and cut short Van de Warker's examinations. But by this time the situation was out of hand; faith cannot survive such abdications and vacillations long. Already there was a large group among the young people dissatisfied with complex marriage, as is evident in the bitter revelations of a dissident member that Van de Warker printed at the beginning of his report. However biased that view, there can be no doubt that complex marriage was failing.

In its effort to erode the old go-between system with its authoritarian sanctions from on high, the Towner party had not realized that the only thing that stood between complex marriage as practised at Oneida and free love as practised at Berlin Heights was precisely the unquestioned spiritual authority of John Humphrey Noyes. When Noyes left the community again in 1879, in the midst of dissension and under fire in the local press and pulpit, that authority was completely withdrawn; there could be no result but that which did occur, on August 28, 1879—the abandonment of complex marriage and the return of the community, after over thirty years, to worldly matrimony.

Ely Van de Warker
A Gynecological Study of the Oneida Community

The Oneida Community was in some of its relations a great physiological experiment. As such it has a commanding interest to medical men, and especially to the gynecologist. Here were tried elaborate experiments in sexualism, and an act that is done crudely, passionately, or by reason of blind instinct elsewhere, was reduced to an art. With this strange people, the sexual relation was made to realize, in a certain sense, an artistic fulfilment, to conserve their general social relations, and to contribute to their most refined pleasure.

That sexualism formed the warp in the texture of their religion in nothing concerns us as scientific men; nor is it at all singular, for in all ages religions have existed in which this function entered as a rite.

And here, for the first time in the history of the race, was a deliberate attempt made to apply the rules that govern scientific breeding to an entire community of men and women. A new science was discovered, or rather created, that of "stirpiculture." Its laws were formulated upon those which govern the skilled breeder of short-horns, or the still more delicate art of the bird fancier who breeds to a feather; its practice consisted in combining known conditions of temperaments and mental aptitudes in the men and women who were "combined" in accordance with these traits, in order to produce given results in the children. The Community lived long enough to bring its fine art of coition to something like perfection; but, unfortunately for stirpiculture, it was too brief in existence to reach results. Here, under the rule of male continence and scientific propagation, was made the first attempt to apply the laws of Malthus to human increase. If, in the Community, the art of coition was sometimes a failure, it simply proved that all were not artists; and if scientific propagation resulted in unexpected and undesirable "combinations," it simply proved that human love and passion were eternal factors that mock alike at prison bars and scientific laws.

It is necessary to say something now about "male continence."

● Selection from *The American Journal of Obstetrics*, XVII (August 1884), 785–96, 803–04, 808–10.

The sexual practices of the Community were those usually understood under this term, plus male continence. Mr. J. H. Noyes, who invented, or discovered—it is difficult to decide which is the better word—this refinement of sexualism, has written of it without reserve. He says frankly that "the Oneida Community in an important sense owed its existence to the discovery of male continence, and has evidently been the Committee of Providence to test its value in actual life." As this gynecological study of the Community is made only with reference to the sexual practices which prevailed there, it is important that we understand just what is meant by the term. It is better to let Mr. Noyes describe it:

"We begin," he says, "by analyzing the act of sexual intercourse. It has a beginning, a middle, and an end. Its beginning and most elementary form is the simple presence of the male organ in the female. Then usually follows a series of reciprocal motions. Finally this exercise brings on a nervous action or ejaculatory crisis which expels the seed. Now we insist that this whole process, up to the very moment of emission, is voluntary, entirely under the control of the moral faculty, and can be stopped at any point. In other words, the presence and the motions can be continued or stopped at will, and it is only the final crisis of emission that is automatic or uncontrollable. Suppose, then, that a man, in lawful intercourse with a woman, choosing, for good reasons, not to beget a child or to disable himself, should stop at the primary stage, and content himself with simple presence continued as long as agreeable? Would there be any harm? It cannot be injurious to refrain from voluntary excitement. Would it do any good? I appeal to the memory of every man who has had good sexual experience to say whether, on the whole, the sweetest and noblest period of intercourse with woman is not that first moment of simple presence and spiritual effusion before the muscular exercise begins? But we may go further. Suppose the man chooses for good reasons, as before, to enjoy not only the simple presence, but also the reciprocal motion, and yet to stop short of the final crisis. Again, I ask, would there be any harm, or would it do no good? I suppose physiologists might say, and I would acknowledge, that excitement by motion might be carried so far that a voluntary suppression of the commencing crisis would be injurious. But what if a man, knowing his own power and limits, should not even approach the crisis, and yet be able to enjoy the presence and the motion *ad libitum?* If you say that this is impossible, I answer that I know it is possible, nay, that it is easy." Further on, Mr. Noyes gives the following illustration of male continence which is picturesque, to say the least, and deserves quotation: "The situation (male continence) may be compared to a stream in three conditions, viz., 1, a fall; 2, a course of rapids above the fall; and 3, still water above the rapids. The skilful boatman may choose whether he will remain in the still water, or venture more or less down the rapids, or run his boat over the fall. But there is a point on the verge of the fall where he has no control over his course; and just above that there is a point where he will have to struggle with the current in a way which will give his nerves a severe trial, even though he may escape the fall. If he is willing to learn, experience will teach him the wisdom of confining his excursions to the region of easy rowing, unless he has an object in view that is worth the cost of going over the fall." The reader has now both the theory of male continence and some practical instruction as well. There are some arguments in favor of the practice which the author calls Bible arguments, and we will remain just as wise if we omit them. One argument is so forcible, and gives the reader such a clear idea of the author's style and method, that I cannot resist the temptation to insert it. "It is seriously believed by many that nature requires a periodical and somewhat frequent discharge of the seed, and that the retention of it is liable to be injurious. Even if this were true, it would be no argument against male continence, but rather an argument in favor of masturbation; for it is obvious that before marriage men have no lawful method of discharge but masturbation, and after marriage it is as foolish and cruel to expend one's seed on a wife merely for the sake of getting rid of it as it would be to fire a gun at one's best friend merely for the sake of unloading it." As a scientific study of the subject, we have nothing to do with Mr. Noyes' arguments, and must concern ourselves only with results. For thirty years the Community existed under the rule of male continence. "Two hundred and fifty sober men and women have lived together in constant observation of its tendencies and effects."

Having said so much about the peculiar sexual habits of these people, it is necessary to say something upon the other side. The illumination must be direct and oblique to give us the lights and shadows—the good and evil that exist in it. There are no persons so well qualified to give the subject this oblique illumination as the women themselves. A lady of whom I asked some questions upon this matter requested me to write out those points upon which I wished information and she would answer them. I did so, and she returned home with the questions. The following is the result, and is just as I received it, except that some parts are omitted which contained repetitions.*

"1. The Community, or Mr. Noyes, who represented it, thought that girls usually had, as they termed it, 'amative desires,' when quite young, and that they would get bad habits unless these feelings were satisfied in the way of sexual intercourse, and so of course they were looked after and introduced into the social system *certainly* at the age of puberty and in quite a number of cases before.

"2. I am knowing particularly of at least four women of my own age who had sexual intercourse at ten years of age, and one case at nine years of age. One of these cases did not arrive at the age of puberty until five years after, another not until two years after, and the other two were unwell very soon after, before they were in the least developed. This was not confined to the girls; boys of thirteen and fourteen years old were put with old women who had passed the change of life, and instructed all about such things before they had begun to think of it at all.

"3. The sexual relations were encouraged very much. The young women were always instructed that the more unselfish they were in giving the men all the satisfaction they could in that respect, the nearer they were to God. They were encouraged so much that those in office would advise and urge it to both men and women if they thought they did not care much for it.

"4. In theory this relation was under a rule, and to a certain extent in practice. Still there was a *great* deal of rule-breaking in regard to it.

"5. There was a great deal of complaint by the young women and girls, a few years before the breaking up of the system, of too frequent demands upon them by the other sex. Ten years before, they *felt* just the same, but partly in bondage to their religious

---

* In order that no eye of suspicion should rest upon any lady at present resident of the Oneida Community Co., Limited, I will state that this paper has been in my possession several years, and was written by a lady who had left the O.C. never to return.

beliefs about it, and partly from fear of criticism and the knowledge the relation with a loved one would be broken up, they were quiet, and submitted. I have known of girls no older than sixteen or seventeen years of age being called upon to have intercourse as often as seven times in a week and oftener, perhaps with a feeling of repugnance to all of those whom she was with during the time. She would do this without complaint simply to gain the confidence of those in charge of such things so that she would be allowed to associate with some one she loved.

"6. Sexual relations did occur clandestinely, but were nearly always confessed and the parties criticised and separated; by this I mean the more common people. Those who held office did as they pleased, only they made some show of always having a 'third party.'

"7. A lady might refuse at one time without incurring criticism, and at another time be severely criticised, and, too, it made a difference who the person was that she refused. If it were one of the leading members she was just as likely to be taken out of any responsible position she held at the time, and not be allowed to do anything until it was thought she had a good spirit and was humble.

"8. Pregnancy was sometimes accidental. Ever since I remember anything about it there have been at least from six to eight pregnant woman during the year, and perhaps one or two of these by accident, and in some cases no possible way of telling who the father of the child was. This, of course, was in accidental pregnancy.

"9. Abortion was never practised while the social theory was in existence to my certain knowledge. What was done after people were married I will not attempt to say.

"10. Love affairs were frequent and caused a great amount of trouble, sometimes causing one or both of the parties to leave the Community (of their own accord). It was generally like this: If a young couple loved each other and were intimate, so much that they did not care for others, they were severely criticised and separated, one being sent to Wallingford, and all correspondence forbidden. It was frequently the case with those who had children that they were getting too 'special' to each other, and to the child. The consequence was that the child would be put into other hands, the father and mother separated, and one or both to have children by others.

11. I cannot say that there was any *special rule* governing the

ages of the parties to the sexual relations. It was very seldom that a young man under twenty years of age associated with a woman who had not passed the change of life, or who was not so near it that she would not be likely to become pregnant. Of course there were some exceptions to this. As to young women and girls—girls, after they were twenty or twenty-five years old, were allowed to associate with men who were not very much older than they were, but with the older ones, too. Girls under those ages did not, as a general thing, associate with men who were much under forty years, and then very seldom. They were considered better off, morally and physically, if they were sought after by men fifty and seventy years of age, and in fact were put under moral pressure about it."

If this investigation into the health of these people has any scientific value at all, it comes from the light thrown upon the physiology of the sexual relation. What they are physically must be understood in the light of what they do sexually.

It seems proper that I should say something about my connection with this investigation of the sexual health of the Oneida Community. In the autumn of 1877, Dr. Theo. R. Noyes, with whom I had been acquainted at that time nearly a year, spoke to me about the feeling of dissatisfaction, then growing in the institution, concerning the effect of their peculiar sexual practices upon the health. As the subject was one of great physiological interest, I expressed a willingness to undertake the necessary investigation. He returned to the Community, and in about a week after I received a letter inviting me to Oneida, to make a study of the subject upon the lady inmates. At that time, I have been since informed, there already existed the two factions, one in favor of, and one opposed to the sexual habits that were then practised, and which division finally resulted in breaking up the Community. Whether the examinations were allowed after consultations with one or both parties I do not know, but that visit was the only one I ever made for this purpose. About one-fourth of the lady inmates were examined when the investigation was stopped by, as I have since learned, the interference of the venerable head of the Community himself, Mr. John Humphrey Noyes, whom, by the way, I have never seen.

I commenced my work directly after breakfast, and continued until day-light began to fail. Each lady was brought into a small steam-heated room, the dormitory of Dr. Noyes, who was present and assisted at the examinations. From the order and manner in which they presented themselves, I am quite confident that there was no attempt to select cases by Dr. Noyes; but those, young or old, were brought in who were willing to submit to the examination. They were bright and intelligent women, and were modest and lady-like in their manner.

The lady, whose report I have included in this paper, says: "In theory this relation (the sexual) was under a rule, and to a certain extent in practice." It is but justice to the Community that I state what I know upon this subject, in contradiction to the extraordinary stories about drawing lots, and the ungoverned license which have been related by newspaper correspondents. I sought information upon this matter as a preliminary to my investigation. My informants were Dr. Noyes and Dr. Cragin, the then resident medical member. I have every confidence in the truth of these gentlemen. As the lady reporter says, these rules may have been violated, as all laws and rules are in sexual affairs, but such violations did not pass without criticism on the part of those in authority. In the Community, as in the world everywhere, the sexual approach came from the man. This was not made directly to the subject, but through a third party, and by whom the wishes of the gentleman were made known personally to the lady. She was at liberty to decline or accept, as she thought best. All reasonable grounds of objection were respected, but what those in authority did attempt to overcome were those objections which originated in too warm feeling toward any party other than the one making the advances. All those sexual solicitations made, as one may say, through the official channels were properly recorded so that the history of each individual was known to every one. Certain advances, such as known to the authorities, were discouraged if for any reason they were believed to be inexpedient. For instance, two individuals of very warm and impulsive temperament were not allowed relations for fear of the consequences; or when both were too young and inexperienced. There were probably other regulations governing the sexual affairs of the Community, but which were not confided to me. Many of them are incidentally referred to by the lady reporter. The sexes roomed separately.

. . . It will be observed that about one-half the women examined were originally from the rural population. This accords with what has been observed concerning heterodox religious movements. The morbid indwelling and religious inquiry necessary to those who depart in erratic religions seem to be fostered by the quiet and isolation of country life. Another point of interest to be noted is the early age at which a large proportion menstruated for the first time, namely, one at ten years, eleven at twelve years, and twelve at thirteen years. It follows that about fifty-seven per cent menstruated nearly two years in advance of the average age for girls in this latitude. Other causes may have operated to produce this, but the one most evident is the mental and physical stimulation due to the peculiar sexualism that surrounded them. Sixteen of these instances of early menstruation were exposed to communistic marriages from ten to thirteen years of age. . . . However repugnant it may be to our sense of manhood, we cannot resist the conclusion that sexual intercourse at this tender age does not arrest the steady tendency to a fine and robust womanhood. From what we all have observed of the stunted appearance of women who have borne children prematurely, it would seem that the extraordinary care with which impregnation was prevented in the Community was a redeeming feature of Mr. Noyes' system of sexual intercourse, in its humanitarian and physical relations. As a gynecologist, I think I may say further that in no other way than by male continence could impregnation be insured against.

In contrast to this phase of their sexual life, . . . we observe the comparatively advanced ages at which communistic marriages were first indulged in by several. Among five of these, we have an average age of forty-eight years, ranging from the extremes of forty-three to fifty-two years. These subjects all contracted regular marriages, before entering the community, rather later than is usually the case, the average being about twenty-seven years. One would suppose that these women joined the community and conformed to their practices when they were ill-prepared to change their sexual habits; yet if we examine their physical state . . . , we perceive that they enjoy a vigorous old age, and, upon a careful questioning concerning the symptoms at the change of life, they testified that they had passed this trying period without any unpleasant results. All, except [one], had an average of 3.5 years of menstrual life after joining.

Continuing our examination . . . , we observe an aggregate of fifty-eight children, forty of whom were born of mothers who con-

tracted regular marriages before entering the community, while
the remaining thirty women exhibit a fecundity of only eighteen
children. Those women who had contracted previous regular
marriages confess to two miscarriages, while the remaining four
miscarriages were distributed among the thirty communistic marriages. These figures prove conclusively, if any other proof were
needed, the thoroughness with which impregnation was interfered
with, and probably by the method peculiar to these people, namely,
male continence. . . .

Keeping before the reader's mind the fact that this is not a study
of a group of women having a promiscuous and regular sexual
intercourse, as the term is usually understood, but of a group having promiscuous sexual relations of the most artificial and extraordinary form known to us at the present time, we have . . . , upon
general physical conditions, a tabulation of great interest. . . .

In the [matters] relating to the nervous system, the number who
complain of pain in very many forms is the first point of interest.
Of the total, eighteen make complaints of symptoms that point
directly to the nervous system. Sacralgia and ovarialgia are the prevailing symptoms which indicate disturbance of the reproductive
nerve centres. They were not at all instances of habitual symptoms;
but pain, if any, was referred to the parts named. Mentally, low
spirits were complained of in a few instances, and if we examine
their ages, we perceive that, with the exception of one party, they
were at the time of life to suffer from disappointed affections. Hys-
teria was remarkably absent, in view of the other nervous symptoms. So far as I am able to judge, they appear to conform, in
degree of nervous health and vigor, to the condition of average
wives whose physical powers are severely taxed by the duties of life;
for it must not be overlooked that each of these women, unless
actually excused from duty by disability of disease or the infirmities
of age, had assigned her regular duties, either supervisory, clerical,
or manual. . . .

Women who had passed the period of menstrual life conformed to
communism in their sexual relation, but not as a rule under the
restriction of male continence. Boys who had not yet acquired the
art of male continence, and men who found it impossible to keep the
act of seminal emission under the control of the will, were obliged to
consort with women who had passed the change of life. Younger
women were not criticised for declining the company of men who

labored under this disability. Both by the law of stirpiculture and of male continence, one who did not possess this necessary credential was excluded from the peculiar sexual system of the Community. I may say here that I have been told by lady members that the practice of male continence was popular among the females, and was easily followed except by a few men. These exceptional men were relegated to the society of women with whom there was no danger of procreation. While continence was easy to conform to in the miscellaneous relations of the Community at large, it was difficult to practise between lovers, with whom the psychic influence of mutual passion rendered emission almost a necessity. This was one of the reasons why such constant vigilance was maintained over affairs of the heart.

• • •

There were no drones in the hive. To each was assigned the work best adapted to her mental or physical powers, and a debit and credit account kept, so that at the end of a week or a month it was known with rigid exactness how many hours of daily work, and with what result, each one had contributed to the industries of the Community. Such a tread-mill life as this must have required average health to its full extent. Further than this, the communistic theory of property under which they lived, deprived them of the stimulus of exertion for their private benefit, a motive that keeps many a weakly man or woman braced up throughout a lifetime. One other incentive to labor was wanting in the lives of these women, that of love and the instinctive longings of maternity. To the latter no woman's breast is a stranger that has once known man. These feelings were crushed out. The Community was a machine that kept its levers in operation to wring out of the heart of woman the emotions that make her all she is to man, love and its tender counterpart, the gentle instinct of maternity.

Now I ask any gynecologist if in the conditions I have tabulated he can trace one or more of them back to the peculiar sexual habits of these people as a primary cause? It is true that in the various tables I have not described well women; but are the habits of the Community, in matters aside from their sexualism, such as contribute to the physical well-being of women? If this is answered in the affirmative, then it is proper to assert that other factors than those which belong to male continence have helped to develop the local errors. I do not know as I am called upon to draw any conclusions, nor would I, if it were not for some tendencies which have entered into gynecology of late years to explain many of the uterine disabilities of women by evasions of the natural consequences of the sexual relation, and by irregularities in the act itself. It is within a recent period that this matter has been dignified with a place in literature, and from several authors it has received the importance due to a new discovery. But such irregularities are nearly as old as the human race, and whatever power they may possess now to produce disease has existed with equal force from the days of Onan down. It will be difficult to convince one who critically compares the physical and mental energies of the present generations of civilized men with those of the past that the race has deteriorated, as it most certainly would have done if such a prevalent and long-existing vice existed with the force lately assigned to it as a morbid factor.

The reader must clearly understand that I am not defending any possible evasions of the legitimate, physiological sexual relation. I am ready to grant that such evasions are physically and morally wrong; but what I am contending for is to give them no more than their just value, as disease-producing causes.

I have described in this paper one of the most artificial sexual mal-relations known to history, and in its most aggravated form, namely, a group of men and women under the laws of communism mingling promiscuously together. In the facts I have presented, without conscious bias, I can discover nothing but negative evidence relating to the effect of male continence upon the health of the Community. My conclusions are mainly based upon the summary already given, the minor character of the local lesions observed, and the unimpaired working capacity of the women.

Testimonies on Complex Marriage

In order to assess the workings of complex marriage, nothing could be more useful than the testimony of those who participated in it. Unfortunately, the diaries and journals that would have opened the matter most frankly to our understanding have all been destroyed. What remains are a few records like the defector's statement included in Van de Warker's report, above, or hints of other difficulties scattered here and there in Constance Noyes Robertson's admirable book on The Breakup *(Syracuse, 1972). On the positive side, there are various statements reprinted in the* Circular *over the years, and perhaps most interesting of all, the testimonials of individual members that were published in the first* Annual Report, *only a couple of years after the institution of complex marriage in the family.*

These testimonials, occurring so early in the history of Oneida, are necessarily colored by the fact that they were all written by recent converts—including the chief actors in initiating the community to free love: Mary Cragin, who was the first woman to join

Noyes outside the precincts of legal monogamy; Harriet Noyes, his wife; and Fanny Leonard, who was the Putney woman named in the indictment of Noyes for adultery. We must expect to hear a certain fervency in these voices, and ought to pay attention to the undertones.

Basically there are two kinds of discoveries to be made. On the one hand we can notice individual differences in the testimony, and try to interpret nuances of significance from those—Erastus Hamilton's sense of having been delivered from his "insubordinate amativeness," and his wife's discovery that amativeness was not "a low, sensual passion"; Mary Cragin's emphasis on how the "stronger passions" bring out "hidden" elements of character, suggesting her own release from repressed desire. On the other hand, it is obvious that much in these testimonies is identical, often phrased in the same formulas, as might be expected from the fact that the group met regularly to discuss the "social question," and especially to hear Noyes discourse upon it. Here we may see just which arguments and motives were becoming doctrinal in the earliest stages of the experiment. Certainly one of the most prominent themes is that of the tension between indulgence and discipline. The vocabulary of rigor—"purging," "refining," "abolishing," "annihilating," "destroying," "purifying"—is everywhere, to balance the language of liberty and access—"enlargement," "softening," "revivifying," and "invigorating." It is the see-saw of conversion experience, reinforced by its communal sanction in every heart.

Testimonies on Complex Marriage

What Has Been the Effect of the Social Theory of this Association, upon Your Character?

Sarah A. Bradley

If I had no evidence of the truth of the doctrines presented in the Bible Argument, but the change they have produced in my character, I should know they were of God. "A corrupt tree cannot bring forth good fruit." Previous to my knowledge of these doctrines, false modesty found a faithful representative in me; but I

● Selections from First Annual Report of the Oneida Association, Oneida Reserve, N.Y.: Leonard & Co., Printers, 1849, pp. 49–52.

have turned traitor and mean to do all in my power to annihilate it, and have true modesty take its place. I used to make a distinction between brotherly love and the love which I had for my husband; but I was brought to see that there was but one kind of love in the kingdom of God. I have found that true love is a great stimulus to improvement. Free love has brought to light defects in my spiritual character which nothing else could—idolatry, exclusiveness, and various other evils. Although the process of destroying selfishness has been an extremely painful one, I am very thankful for the experience I have had. It has brought me very near to God, and I now feel an interest in the happiness of all. I have learned that love is the gift of God.

Henry W. Burnham

The theory of sexual morality adopted by this Association, while it allows liberty which in the world would lead to licentiousness degrading to both soul and body, here produces the opposite effects; i.e. it invigorates with *life,* soul and body, and refines and exalts the character generally. It is calculated to abolish selfishness in its most subtle and deep-rooted forms, and practically adapted to fulfil the prayer of Christ in respect to the unity of the church, and thus introduce her gradually into the glories of the resurrection. My chief reason for believing this is because its development is invariably attended by the manifest judgment of God.

Abby S. Burnham

The effect that free love has had upon my character, has been to raise me from a state of exclusiveness and idolatry, to a greater enlargement of heart, and freedom of communication with God and this body. Selfishness is being purged out, and its place supplied with the pure love of God. I feel that I am not my own, but am bought with a price, therefore I am to glorify God with my body and spirit which are his. I see more clearly than ever before the beauty of Christ's prayer, that we all may be *one,* even as he and the Father are one.

Sarah A. Burnham

The social theory, as advocated by Mr. Noyes and this Association, and sustained by the Bible, has had a tendency to enlighten my understanding, and to try, enlarge and purify my heart.

George Cragin

The social theory of this community is, and has been from the first, associated in my mind with the end of this world, and the beginning of the kingdom of heaven upon earth. The evidence of its truth is as *firmly rooted* and *grounded* in my heart and mind as the gospel of salvation from sin; and my confidence therefore cannot be destroyed in one, without destroying it in the other. Of its effects upon my character I could say much. But in brief, I can say it has greatly enlarged my heart by purging it from exclusiveness—it has tamed and civilized my feelings, purified my thoughts, and elevated into the presence of God and heaven the strongest passion in the social department of my nature. I regard the "Bible Argument," so called, as the *social gospel,* second only to the gospel of salvation from sin, and destined to repair the second breach in the fall.

Mary E. Cragin

I think the development of the social theory most favorable to the formation of character. It brings out the hidden things of the heart as nothing else could, by exciting the stronger passions of our nature, and bringing them out where they can be purified. Love without law, yet under the control of the Spirit of God, is a great beautifier of character in every respect, and puts the gilding on life. It is the manifestation of the resurrection power—revivifying soul and body. The best result in my own experience has been, that it has brought me into fellowship and acquaintance with the Father and the Son, more than any thing else ever did—and thereby I know that the doctrine is of God.

Erastus H. Hamilton

The social theory brought out by Mr. Noyes investigates the strongest passion of humanity—one that by common consent is considered unapproachable—and disposes of the peculiar relations and restraints which surround this passion of amativeness, and which by the world are considered most sacred, in such a manner that the theory must of necessity stand or fall by its *results.* Its practical application to me, with the Spirit of truth which has accompanied it, has had an unmistakably healthy influence through my whole character. It has delivered me from the bondage of an insubordinate amativeness, which has been the torment of my life. It has brought me into a positive purity of feeling, that I am confident could come from no source but God. It has brought me near to God, increased life, been a most active means in causing me to hate my own life and in crucifying selfishness. The effect it has had upon the relation with my wife, has been directly opposite to what the world would expect to be its legitimate results; and for its fruits on this one relation alone, I should feel willing to give my decided testimony of approval.

Susan C. Hamilton

Since I have become acquainted with the social theory, it has had the effect of destroying selfishness, shame, and false modesty. It has also refined, strengthened, and increased my *respect* for love; and I look upon amativeness not as a low, sensual passion, but (under the influence of God's Spirit) as holy and noble. It has also taught me that there is no enjoyment in love, only when God takes the lead, and that the only way to perpetuate love is to walk in the spirit and learn to wait on him for it. Therefore I think our theory is the greatest safeguard against sensuality.

Stephen R. Leonard

The effect of our social theory upon me has been, to greatly quicken my energy for self-improvement and for every good work. It has brought me into more perfect sympathy with the designs of God, and has given force and direction to my whole character. It has opened the fountain of my heart, and increased its capabilities of loving a hundred-fold. It has tried and strengthened my faith, and given me a more vivid consciousness of God's approbation. The spiritual wisdom and skill displayed in the production of the document called the "Bible Argument," is conclusive evidence to me that the writer is in communication with the same God that dictated the Bible. I regard that document as the second volume of the New Testament.

Fanny M. Leonard

The effect of the social theory is like fire which purifies and refines. Its effect on my character has been an enlargement of the heart and softening of the spirit. It destroys envyings and jealousies, and draws us out from an isolated egotistical state, into the sunshine of God's free and eternal love—that love which envieth not and seeketh not its own.

Harriet A. Noyes

Our social theory has been like a fire to me bringing to light and destroying selfishness. It has enlarged my heart, and enveloped in it love that *thinketh no evil, envieth not,* and *seeketh not its own.* It has increased my happiness, my justification, and my acquaintance with God. It is the natural sequence of salvation from sin, and so intimately connected with it, that I have felt if I gave up one, I must give up the other; and God's providence has favored it so manifestly, that if I doubted its truth I must doubt the existence of God.

OUT OF THE FOLD.
"Oh dreadful! They dwell in peace and harmony and have no church scandals. They must be wiped out."

VII

Coitus Reservatus

Male Continence

John Humphrey Noyes

Noyes first began thinking about contraception in 1837, when he reviewed Robert Dale Owen's Moral Physiology *in his Perfectionist newspaper. Although he condemned Owen's withdrawal method as Onanism, he saw it as one possible solution to the problem of propagation, just as he viewed the Shaker expedient, complete celibacy, as the other, equally unacceptable solution. He was reading Shaker books in 1837 too, the year of the* Battle Axe *letter and the establishment of the Putney Community.*

Noyes married in 1838. During the next six years his wife bore five children, four of which were premature deliveries, stillborn. In 1844 Noyes told his wife that he could no longer subject her to this suffering, and had resolved on the Shaker solution. But then, probably under the influence of the new phrenological analysis of the sexual faculties—"amativeness" and "propagativeness"— popularized in a series of books by Orson and Lorenzo Fowler, Noyes "conceived the idea that the sexual organs have a social function which is distinct from the propagative function. . . . I experimented on the idea, and found that the self-control which it requires is not difficult; also that my enjoyment was increased; also that my wife's experience was very satisfactory, as it had never been before. . . ." He told George Cragin of the discovery, who also found it practicable, and two years later when the Perfectionists introduced complex marriage to their communal order, it was "male continence," a transcending of the polarity of Shaker celibacy and Owen's coitus interruptus, that made the new free love experiment possible.

Male continence had more virtues than one. First of all, it proved effectual in preventing pregnancies. In its first twenty years the community intentionally limited its children to an average of two a year, in a population of forty families. Some of these births were accidents, some by design. Among the "original Putney men" there were no unintentional children conceived. Furthermore, as Noyes's account just quoted suggests, male continence had the advantage of increasing the pleasure of intercourse, especially for the women, many of whom had perhaps not experienced orgasm before the men decided to forego it themselves. Even this is not the whole story of male continence at Oneida: the practice had its most far-reaching effect as an intimate incarnation of the chief principle of life in the community, the mystic amalgamation of indulgence or freedom with control and self-denial. This view is argued more fully in the Introduction; it is enough here to quote Noyes himself, from a family talk given July 10, 1870, on the extent to which male continence lay at the symbolic heart of the community: "the principle of Male Continence is carried through every enjoyment in heaven; self-control in all our passions, or the ability to leave one pleasure and go to another without gorging, makes heaven."

John Humphrey Noyes
Male Continence

New York, July 26, 1866.

Dear Sir:—Your letter addressed to the *Circular*, asking for information in regard to our method of controlling propagation, has been sent to me, and as it seems to come from a well-disposed

---

● Selection from *Male Continence*, Oneida, N.Y.: The Oneida Community, 1872, pp. 5–10.

person (though unknown to me), I will endeavor to give it a faithful answer—such, at least, as will be sufficient for scientific purposes. The first question, or rather, perhaps I should say, the *previous* question in regard to Male Continence is, whether it is desirable or proper that men and women should establish intelligent voluntary control over the propagative function. Is it not better (it may be asked), to leave "nature" to take its course (subject to the general rules of legal chastity), and let children come as chance or the unknown powers may direct, without putting any restraint on sexual intercourse after it is once licensed by marriage, or on the freedom of all to take out such license? If you assent to this latter view, or have any inclination toward it, I would recommend to you the study of *Malthus on Population*; not that I think he has pointed out anything like the true *method* of voluntary control over propagation, but because he has demonstrated beyond debate the absolute *necessity* of such control in some way, unless we consent and expect that the human race, like the lower animals, shall be forever kept down to its necessary limits, by the ghastly agencies of war, pestilence and famine.

For my part, I have no doubt that it is perfectly proper that we should endeavor to rise above "nature" and the destiny of the brutes in this matter. There is no reason why we should not seek and hope for discovery in this direction, as freely as in the development of steam power or the art of printing; and we may rationally expect that He who has promised the "good time" when vice and misery shall be abolished, will at last give us sure light on this darkest of all problems—how to subject human propagation to the control of science.

But whether study and invention in this direction are proper or not, they are actually at work in all quarters, reputable and disreputable. Let us see how many different ways have already been proposed for limiting human increase.

In the first place, the practice of child-killing, either by exposure or violence, is almost as old as the world, and as extensive as barbarism. Even Plato recommended something of this kind, as a waste-gate for vicious increase, in his scheme of a model republic.

Then we have the practice of abortion reduced in modern times to a science, and almost to a distinct profession. A large part of this business is carried on by means of medicines advertised in obscure but intelligible terms as embryo-destroyers or preventives of conception. Every large city has its professional abortionist. Many ordinary physicians destroy embryos to order; and the skill to do this terrible deed has even descended among the common people.

Then what a variety of artificial tricks there are for frustrating the natural effects of the propagative act. You allude to several of these contrivances, in terms of condemnation from which I should not dissent. The least objectionable of them (if there is any difference), seems to be that recommended many years ago by Robert Dale Owen, in a book entitled *Moral Physiology;* viz., the simple device of withdrawing immediately before emission.

Besides all these disreputable methods, we have several more respectable schemes for attaining the great object of limiting propagation. Malthus proposes and urges that all men, and especially the poor, shall be taught their responsibilities in the light of science, and so be put under inducements *not to marry.* This prudential check on population—the discouragement of marriage— undoubtedly operates to a considerable extent in all civilized society, and to the greatest extent on the classes most enlightened. It seems to have been favored by Saint Paul (see 1st Cor. 7); and probably would not be condemned generally by people who claim to be considerate. And yet its advocates have to confess that it increases the danger of licentiousness; and on the whole the teaching that is most popular, in spite of Malthus and Paul, is that marriage, with all its liabilities, is a moral and patriotic duty.

Finally, Shakerism, which actually prohibits marriage on religious grounds, is only the most stringent and imposing of human contrivances for avoiding the woes of undesired propagation.

All these experimenters in the art of controlling propagation may be reduced in principle to three classes, viz.:

1. Those that seek to prevent the intercourse of the sexes, such as Malthus and the Shakers.

2. Those that seek to prevent the natural effects of the propagative act, viz., the French inventors and Owen.

3. Those that seek to destroy the living results of the propagative act, viz., the abortionists and child-killers.

Now it may seem to you that any new scheme of control over propagation must inevitably fall to one of these three classes; but I assure you that we have a method that does not fairly belong to any of them. I will try to show you our fourth way.

We begin by *analyzing* the act of sexual intercourse. It has a beginning, a middle, and an end. Its beginning and most elementary form is the simple *presence* of the male organ in the female. Then usually follows a series of reciprocal *motions*. Finally this exercise brings on a nervous action or ejaculatory *crisis* which expels the seed. Now we insist that this whole process, up to the very moment of emission, is *voluntary*, entirely under the control of the moral faculty, and *can be stopped at any point*. In other words, the *presence* and the *motions* can be continued or stopped at will, and it is only the final *crisis* of emission that is automatic or uncontrollable.

Suppose, then, that a man, in lawful intercourse with woman, choosing for good reasons not to beget a child or to disable himself, should stop at the primary stage and content himself with simple *presence* continued as long as agreeable? Would there be any harm? It cannot be injurious to refrain from voluntary excitement. Would there be no *good*? I appeal to the memory of every man who has had good sexual experience to say whether, on the whole, the sweetest and noblest period of intercourse with woman is not that *first* moment of simple presence and spiritual effusion, before the muscular exercise begins.

But we may go farther. Suppose the man chooses for good reasons, as before, to enjoy not only the simple *presence,* but also the *reciprocal motion*, and yet to stop short of the final *crisis*. Again I ask, Would there be any harm? Or would it do no good? I suppose physiologists might say, and I would acknowledge, that the excitement by motion *might* be carried so far that a voluntary suppression of the commencing crisis would be injurious. But what if a man, knowing his own power and limits, should not even *approach* the crisis, and yet be able to enjoy the presence and the motion *ad libitum*? If you say that this is impossible, I answer that I *know* it is possible—nay, that it is easy.

I will admit, however, that it may be impossible to some, while it is possible to others. Paul intimates that some cannot "contain." Men of certain temperaments and conditions are afflicted with involuntary emissions on very trivial excitement and in their sleep. But I insist that these are exceptional morbid cases that should be disciplined and improved; and that, in the normal condition, men are entirely competent to choose in sexual intercourse whether they will stop at any point in the voluntary stages of it, and so make it simply an act of communion, or go through to the involuntary stage, and make it an act of propagation.

The situation may be compared to a stream in the three conditions of a fall, a course of rapids above the fall, and still water above the rapids. The skillful boatman may choose whether he will remain in the still water, or venture more or less down the rapids, or run his boat over the fall. But there is a point on the verge of the fall where he has no control over his course; and just above that there is a point where he will have to struggle with the current in a way which will give his nerves a severe trial, even though he may escape the fall. If he is willing to learn, experience will teach him the wisdom of confining his excursions to the region of easy rowing, unless he has an object in view that is worth the cost of going over the falls.

You have now our whole theory of "Male Continence." It consists in analyzing sexual intercourse, recognizing in it two distinct acts, the social and the propagative, which can be separated practically, and affirming that it is best, not only with reference to remote prudential considerations, but for immediate pleasure, that a man should content himself with the social act, except when he intends procreation.

Let us see now if this scheme belongs to any of the three classes I mentioned. 1. It does not seek to prevent the intercourse of the sexes, but rather gives them more freedom by removing danger of undesired consequences. 2. It does not seek to prevent the natural *effects* of the propagative act, but to prevent the propagative act itself, except when it is intended to be effectual. 3. Of course it does not seek to destroy the living *results* of the propagative act, but provides that impregnation and child-bearing shall be voluntary, and of course desired.

And now, to speak affirmatively, the exact thing that our theory does propose, is to take that same power of moral restraint and self-control, which Paul, Malthus, the Shakers, and all considerate men use in one way or another to limit propagation, and instead of applying it, as they do, to the prevention of the intercourse of the sexes, to introduce it at another stage of the proceedings, viz., *after* the sexes have come together in social effusion, and *before* they have reached the propagative crisis; thus allowing them all and more than all the ordinary freedom of love (since the crisis always interrupts the romance), and at the same time avoiding undesired procreation and all the other evils incident to male incontinence. This is our fourth way, and we think it the better way.

The wholesale and ever ready objection to this method is that it is *unnatural, and unauthorized by the example of other animals.*

I may answer in a wholesale way, that cooking, wearing clothes, living in houses, and almost everything else done by civilized man, is unnatural in the same sense, and that a close adherence to the example of the brutes would require us to forego speech and go on all fours"! But on the other hand, if it is natural in the best sense, as I believe it is, for rational beings to forsake the example of the brutes and improve nature by invention and discovery in all directions, then truly the argument turns the other way, and we shall have to confess that until men and women find a way to elevate their sexual performances above those of the natural brutes, by introducing into them moral culture, they are living in *unnatural* degradation.

But I will come closer to this objection. The real meaning of it is, that Male Continence in sexual intercourse is a difficult and injurious interruption of a natural act. But every instance of self-denial is an interruption of some natural act. The man who virtuously contents himself with a look at a beautiful woman is conscious of such an interruption. The lover who stops at a kiss denies himself a natural progression. It is an easy, descending grade through all the approaches of sexual love, from the first touch of respectful friendship, to the final complete amalgamation. Must there be no interruption of this natural slide? Brutes, animal or human, tolerate none. Shall their ideas of self-denial prevail? Nay, it is the glory of man to control himself, and the Kingdom of Heaven summons him to self-control in ALL THINGS. If it is noble and beautiful for the betrothed lover to respect the law of marriage in the midst of the glories of courtship, it may be even more noble and beautiful for the wedded lover to respect the laws of health and propagation in the midst of the ecstacies of sexual union. The same moral culture that ennobles the antecedents and approaches of marriage will some time surely glorify the consummation.

Of course, you will think of many other objections and questions, and I have many answers ready for you; but I will content myself for the present with this limited presentation.

Yours respectfully,

J. H. Noyes.

Marriage and Sexual Intercourse

James C. Jackson

Dr. James C. Jackson made a comfortable career, and even a kind of patrimony, out of health. The Jackson Health Resort (also called "The Hillside" and "Our Home") at Dansville, New York, was founded as a water-cure spa in 1858. Soon it had grown to country-club proportions, with a five-story main building, a dozen cottages, sixty acres including golf links. Fifty years after its founding, the resort was still in the hands of the Jackson family— father, mother, son, daughter, and other kin all doctoring wealthy invalids from Rochester and Buffalo. Dr. Jackson, like many water-cure physicians, was somewhat of a renegade in his practice; perhaps his most successful book was How to Treat the Sick Without Medicine *(1868). Abjuring the stock-in-trade of most doctors— calomel, opium, and other murderous concoctions—Jackson put his faith in pure diet, clean habits, exercise, rest, loving care, which he called his "psycho-hygienic philosophy." Given the state of medicine in the last half of the nineteenth century in America, it is not surprising that Jackson was successful.*

Part of Jackson's success was as an author as well as proprietor of a health resort. Although he wrote books on consumption and on the training of children, his specialty seems to have been sexuality and sexual disorders. In addition to the volume from which our selection is taken, The Sexual Organism and its Healthful Management, *Jackson also wrote* Hints on the Reproductive Organs *(published by Fowler and Wells, who first brought out so many of these sexual tracts), and* American Womanhood: Its Peculiarities and Necessities. *The house organ of "Our Home" was called* The Laws of Life and Woman's Health Journal.

In spite of his heterodoxy in matters of medicines and treatment of the sick, in his writings on sexuality Jackson shared many of the benighted opinions of the Victorian medical fraternity. He too believed that sexual intercourse, even in marriage, was likely to be harmful if indulged very frequently. Like William Alcott and others, he recommended that coitus be limited to occasions when pregnancy was desired. But Jackson was enough of an individualist to have developed his own special semantics of intercourse: "coition" was reserved for cases of love-making that eventuated in orgasm; whereas love-making that did not reach climax, no matter how close it came, was called "cohabitation." By this verbal sleight-of-hand he was able to have his cake and eat it too, allowing husband and wife to "cohabit" without seeming to condone "coitus." Borrowing the idea and even some of his terms from John Humphrey Noyes (see preceding selection), Jackson based his theory on a distinction between "amativeness" and "propagativeness," declaring that the former propensity might be safely enjoyed so long as no "paroxysm of feeling" occurred. Thus what Noyes had proposed primarily as a method of contraception (though he too developed other, "biological" justifications), Jackson adopted as a defense against the horrors of sexual debility painted so terrifyingly by Sylvester Graham. In the context of a widespread medical opinion that ordinary sexual pleasure was not only sinful but unhealthy, Jackson's compromise must be regarded as liberal, though he obviously was no believer in the innocence of sexuality—"The simple, unvarnished truth is," he wrote, "that human beings are born depraved." Although Jackson was far from the sexual radicalism of his fellow-hydropathists Thomas and Mary Nichols, still he was a more permissive counselor than most orthodox practitioners.

James C. Jackson
Marriage and Sexual Intercourse

To parties who enter into marriage, the question may be properly raised, at what times and under what circumstances cohabitation should follow. Of this I have to say, that most manifestly the law of sexual intercourse has a twofold bearing; that of propagation, and that of allowing a freer and more decided interchange of social feeling to take place, thus adding to the happiness of each and of both; and under these respective views should the intercourse proceed, either to what may be called a full or partial consummation. Now, when it is to be had complete on the part of the male and the female, the law obtains, absolutely, that it should only be had at such periods or times as may be followed by the female becoming pregnant: Nature never intending that a man should lose his semen for any other purpose than that of propagating his species; or that woman should ever exercise her sexual faculty so as to reach her highest paroxysm of feeling, unless with a view to conception. Artificial considerations come in, I am aware, to modify and qualify this statement: and I do not mean to be understood as affirming, that, where this rule does not obtain, great injury to health always ensues; but that this is the law, and that, abstractly considered, it is better to obey it than to violate it. I know that writers of decided ability combat this view, declaring that, while the rule obtains in regard to lower animals, it does not obtain in regard to man; and the distinction which is clear in their minds is to be drawn just at the point of separation between the lower animals and man, as indicated by his possessing an order of faculties higher than theirs. To them there is no liberty given, they argue, because they do not possess reason, and therefore must be governed by instinct, which is always exact and precise; but to man who is clothed in addition to instinct with reason, liberty of action has been given. In other words, that man is organized in this, as in every other direction, with discretionary power; and that this law cannot be said with propriety to operate with the same strictness of construction, with regard to him, as in the case of living organisms which are below him.

● Selection from *The Sexual Organism and its Healthful Management*, Boston: B. Leverett Emerson, 1862, pp. 255–61.

But I apprehend, that the fallacy of this reasoning is to be found in the extent to which it is carried. The reasoning faculties in man bear so close a natural relation to his moral sentiments, as that they are to be considered as constituting one, or nearly the same, group of organs or forces; and therefore are not to be separated. Now, man, as a human being of the male gender, in his individual and moral nature, cannot by any means receive the highest culture without daily association and intercourse with a human being of the opposite sex; and woman, as a human being of the female gender, is subjected to the same great necessity. This is true of both, from a period as early as the dawning of responsibility to the close of life. This view I have elaborated in a variety of ways in previous chapters, and endeavored to show that the sexes, in order to their highest individual development, should associate and be educated together; and that at adult age, other things not being in the way, marriage comes in as a consummation, and is therefore to be regarded as a sacrament as well as a civil transaction: carrying with it great force, imposing great duties; and, when properly lived out, affording the means of very great progression and happiness. But, because these two parties are thus necessitated to live together by an organic arrangement which is vital, it does not follow that they are to violate that law of their natures which has reference particularly, and I may say exclusively, to the propagation of the species; or, in other words, to the reproduction of themselves. Intercourse can be had, and, if people were properly educated and trained, would be had, short of all this. The man and his wife can be brought into sexual embrace without reaching the point of orgasmic action, and, in truth, inside of a full coition,—where the relation may be said to be cohabitation simply; and where the means of pleasurable enjoyment, as well as of such interchange of thought, sentiment, feeling, and impression, can be made much more permanent, and productive of much higher good, than possibly can result from the exercise of the act to its fullest extent. I urge this view because I am satisfied, from a thorough study of the organic relations of the sexes, that the faculty of amativeness has a twofold purpose, and should be always gratified by either sex from this point.

Where, then, the aim and intent are to have children, coition under sexual intercourse must take place. But, where only the gratification of the parties is to be had, cohabitation simply, and not coition, should take place.

The physical and moral results under this view are found to sustain it. Where coition takes places, the parties feel, subsequent to it, a decided lassitude. Evidently, the nervous system has been so taxed as to subject them to extraordinary expenditure of force; and this can only be justified under the necessities of the case: that is, it can only be justified when the parties intend to have children. So to relate themselves to each other as to be subject to this taxation twice a week, or once a week even, is surely to induce impairment of general vigor, and almost surely, at no distant day, to induce particular disease in some direction. Physicians know full well that a class of diseases arises from undue sexual gratification, such as congestion of the brain; pulmonary diseases; dyspepsia; liver complaint; irritation of the kidneys; irritation of the bladder; irritation of the urethra; stricture; impairment of the nutritive organs; wasting away of the flesh; premature decay, indicated by mothy conditions of the skin; corrugations and wrinkles on the face; exhibitions of posture, indicating debility. These, and many others, are the direct result of great taxation of the nervous system, by and through the inordinate exercise of the sexual function. Now, there is no justification for this in reason, certainly; nor is there in the moral sentiments: while, on the other hand, both protest against such use of this faculty as is legitimately productive of such results. And yet this is the only view that married people understand. They do not seem to know, or, if they do know, they do not educate themselves to act from any other view than this. Men do not know how to cohabit without they exercise the coitive function; and women do not know how to be cohabited with, unless they submit to the fullest completion of the sexual processes. And, for want of this knowledge, great evils flow out of the marriage relation,—so great, as in reality to be the cause of great unhappiness between the parties. I know that I but speak the truth when I declare, that, of married women, a large proportion live on terms of mere sufferance with their husbands: for the most part feeling toward them no high instinctive longings, but, contrariwise, feeling disgusted rather; and are very glad when, from any cause or circumstance, a temporary separation from their bed and their embraces is compelled.

And so, too, do men, when disassociated from their wives, often feel themselves wondering that while, notwithstanding they cherish toward them only the most decided conjugal fidelity, they have no particular desire to enter into any close or intimate exhibitions of husbandly love, outside of the spasmodic manifestations in actual embrace. Many are the husbands who, from week's end to week's end, show none of those exhibitions of attachment which they were so fond of bestowing during the period of courtship; and ignorantly and falsely attribute the lack of such feeling on their part to their discovery, subsequent to marriage, that their wives were lacking in the graces of character which they supposed them at that time to possess; when nothing is the cause of all this disrelish—I will not call it dislike—but a too frequent coition. No man can keep up in his own consciousness a desire for close and intimate high association with a woman, who plays the part toward her of husband chiefly or entirely from the animal point of view. He must, in all his relations to her, seek to stop short of this; and instead of depression will come exaltation; and instead of his loving her less after sexual embrace, will he love her all the more. For there is such a difference in the moral sentiment or emotion of husband and wife, when sexual intercourse has been merely co-habitative, from what it must be when coition has been performed as to make the distinction perfectly clear between the desire to remain in each other's presence, and the positive desire of getting away from each other. I do not believe that there is one case in a thousand where men and women so cohabit as to have coition, that they do not instinctively retire, feeling towards each other a state of indifference, and sometimes of disgust; whereas, were they to relate themselves to each other from points of strong spiritual assimilation, they would retire from such embrace with gentler and finer feeling than when they entered upon it: passing through, as it were, a group of desires, which relate the sexes to each other as animals, to a level of desire where the higher faculties come into play, and thus finding themselves by the process actually cultured and trained to a better order of growth and moral feeling.

Besides, the law of sexual intercourse, which has reference to the propagation of the species purely, and which therefore cul-minates in coition, cannot be violated without moral deterioration. This is to be seen in a great variety of manifestations, and might be enlarged upon extensively. I shall leave it to the reader's own good sense to carry out minutely the point already suggested: which is, that whenever such intercourse is had, from considerations that do not have reference to the propagation of the species, more likely than not the indifference or disgust which arises as a moral sentiment is to be found in close and intimate connection with the physical lassitude consequent upon such act. Take the view from this plane; and, carrying it into its radiations, see what must be the effect ultimately on the relations and happiness of the married pair who live thus fourteen, fifteen, twenty, twenty-five, or forty years. Instead of growing toward each other, they inevitably grow away from each other. Instead of becoming like, they become unlike; and instead of finding that marriage, though it has been productive of offspring, has been to them a source of comfort and increased enjoyment,—they find it to have been not only a tax upon their freedom, but also upon their moral virtue. The exercise of forbearance, and of all those qualities which teach us to be patient under afflictions, has steady and large drafts made upon it; and they live together rather by endurance than by mutual sympathy and affection.

If, therefore, married people will consent to be taught; and, being taught, will practise what they learn in this direction,—they may have all the pleasure arising from the use of their sexual forces, without the thousands of discomforts and the positive diseases which now rise up to curse them; while, at the same time, they may have an almost unlimited freedom of exhibition.

Dr. Foote's Replies to the Alphites

E. B. Foote and Caroline B. Winslow

In a letter read aloud to the first public meeting of the Institute of Heredity in 1881, Dr. E. B. Foote raised two problems he thought most pressing in the areas of the Institute's concern: first, the need for a solution to the Malthusian threat of overpopulation, and second, the censorship of all birth control information by the U. S. Post Office, in the person of Anthony Comstock.

He was soon answered, in a letter to his journal The Health Monthly, *that although the censorship was certainly deplorable, even more so was Foote's notion that "prevention" solved all the problems of human sexuality. What about "sexual excess" and its toll in sickly wives and debauched husbands? Would contraception do anything about the thousands of such cases? A better solution was Alpha, the doctrine that sexual intercourse should be indulged only for procreation, and absolute continence should otherwise be the rule. The debate which followed lasted some months, and was ultimately published in a little pamphlet, from which the selections here are taken.*

Dr. Foote's earliest brush with Comstock, when he was heavily fined for advertising contraceptive devices in his pamphlet Words in Pearl, *is recounted in the Introduction. Here in his debate with Dr. Winslow we can see that he was still being harrassed years later. Foote was a rather interesting character—along with Dio Lewis, James Jackson, and Nicholas Cooke, he helps us take the measure of the unorthodox Victorian physician, who was likely to belong to some particular school or camp, like homoeopathy or hydropathy, and therefore regarded professional polemics as part of his calling. This had its good and bad sides. One gets the impression that Foote was basically a "liberal"—fair-minded, prudent, progressive, not very brilliant but shrewd enough—who stumbled into a controversy he had no real stomach for, and was "radicalized" when he suddenly found himself, a thoroughly respectable citizen and a pillar of his profession, the victim of accusations and indictments for obscenity. He was a successful man—his book* Dr. Foote's Plain Home Talk *sold a quarter of a million copies—so he could afford the fines, stiff as they were, but he smarted from the affront to his dignity, and devoted himself all the more wholeheartedly to the problem he believed so important, the spread of accurate information and sensible advice about human sexuality.*

Why did Foote enter into this debate with Dr. Winslow and her extremist group of latterday Grahamites? Because it was around the issue of continence in marriage that serious discussion of sexual life centered in the last quarter of the nineteenth century. This was the result of a complex set of pressures—the Grahamite tradition which most medical men accepted unquestioningly, the free-love oscillation between indulgence and self-denial, Oneida's example of male continence, the absence of cheap and reliable methods of contraception, and Comstock's campaign of censorship and repression. These extraordinary factors combined to produce widespread popular delusions about the nature of sexual intercourse. To say a word of sense about sexual life, it was necessary to confront them boldly.

Moreover, Foote was himself tempted by some of these theories of sexual magnetism and potency. The stern admonitions of the Alphites did not convince him, but there were other varieties of sexology more intriguing—both Eliza Burns and Albert Chavannes (see other selections below) contributed their views to the debate in The Health Monthly, *arguing for a more radical interpretation of continence than Alpha. Foote was already in sympathy with the Oneida experiment in male continence, and these new theorists provided a pseudoscientific explanation of how it worked that appealed to his rather mechanistic imagination. As later editions of Dr. Foote's Plain Home Talk appeared, he gradually introduced more and more approval of Oneidan male continence as a means of contraception with possibly beneficial side effects like those the Alphites championed, but without the rigorous abstinence they insisted on.*

E. B. Foote
Caroline B. Winslow
Dr. Foote's Replies to the Alphites

Letter from the Editor of the *Alpha*
Washington, D.C., Sept. 15, 1881.
To the Editors of Dr. Foote's Health Monthly—*Dear Friends*: I have desired to write you since reading your July number of *Health Monthly*. But our national calamity, illness in my family and the intense heat, which has well nigh suspended the world's work, has prevented me up to this moment.

I wish to thank you for your report of the Institute of Heredity meeting in Boston and your criticism upon my paper from your standpoint. But will you for a moment look at the question from our standpoint and reply to a few interrogations? . . .

How many incurable cases have you met with that you have known to have come from the use of *checks* to population? They are *perversions of sexual uses*, and do they not cause derangement of the nervous system, congestions, sterility, impotency, prolapsus, tumors, and all the horrors that come from the perversion and desecration of the most sacred endowments of our person? It has been my experience that these unfortunate persons that have used these injurious devices have soon, one or both, come under medical treatment. I have two such cases under my care now, with shattered nerves, mental depression, almost despair, uterine induration and hypertrophy from repeated congestions, caused by using injections

---

● Selection from *Dr. Foote's Replies to the Alphites*, New York: Murray Hill Publishing Company, 1882, pp. 12–14, 19–21, 28–29, 31–32, 37–39.

after coition; and a third whose husband's nerves and digestive organs are wrecked, the result of habitual *incomplete* coition. All along my thirty years' labor in my profession do these cases present themselves.

I am fully persuaded that all these ingenious devices of men are *cheats* and *frauds* and fall under the double condemnation that follows the infringement of moral and physical law.

I believe in the wise use of the sexual organs, for the obvious purpose for which they were created, viz., procreation—the propagation and improvement of our species.

Children are blessings, and blessings *only*, when desired, loved and prepared for as they should be. *There will never be too many births under such circumstances*, and fifty per cent less premature deaths, and fifty per cent less suffering, mental depression or frenzy; and just so much more physical, moral and intellectual strength to perform the work of human regeneration. Every year I see more and more clearly the observance of the law of continence for the married and single is the door of salvation from disease and death, domestic infidelity and crime. It is the only cure for the social evil, the only means of effectually stamping out syphilis, scrofula, insanity and the innumerable causes of wretchedness that afflict mankind.

You think this impracticable—not to be attained. It is very possible and easy comparatively, with right thinking and hygienic living and dressing and the cultivation of a noble ambition for self-control and self-respect, with heart-love reaching out to bless those that by inheritance and untoward circumstances still grope in darkness.

These are subjects such philanthropists as you should consider. You teach physiological law as a means of salvation, and this is part of your work.

Let me entreat you to give the subject a dispassionate and careful investigation. Light will break upon your soul and you will be constrained to use your great influence for the spread of the *whole* truth, and thus becoming God's worker you will cease to prepare measures or give service that will encourage the desecration of God's temple for sensual purposes.

Very truly yours for purity and the best welfare of humanity.

Caroline B. Winslow

Dr. Foote's Reply to the Alphites

. . . To Question Four we answer that we have met with no incurable cases of that description; absolutely none. We have met those who had injured themselves from using objectionable devices and from following improper rules; but we feel sure that discussion on this subject if openly permitted in our medical societies and otherwise, would result in eliminating all the injurious methods. If the profession were to be encouraged, rather than threatened with fines and loss of personal liberty, for devising means to regulate human increase, discoveries would be made far superior to anything that has yet been presented, although there are means which are comparatively free from objection if the physician were at liberty to prescribe them. In consequence of having written freely upon this subject nearly twenty-five years ago, we have had exceptional opportunities of observing the effects of the best methods known under the name of "prudential checks," and we have certainly never met with one single instance where any one was known to have been injured by their use. We have been in consultation with thousands of people upon the subject; have prescribed them in thousands of cases. But when the Vice Society and its agent come in with $5,000 fine and five years' imprisonment for prescribing such humane devices we are quite willing to take a back-seat until the American people are awakened to the outrage perpetrated upon their liberties by a handful of pseudo-moralists.

It is our honest opinion that in the past one hundred years more women have been injured by excessive child-bearing than by injurious methods of prevention, omitting of course from this category the victims of foeticide, for preventionists have no sympathy with abortionists. Comstockism with its blear-eyed vision and canting morality makes no distinction, but we feel confident that Dr. Winslow and all other really intelligent people do. Scientists always do.

Much is written by the Alphites of the reckless waste of such vital material as that entering into the reproductive germ matter of the human family. But all through nature we find the same wastefulness, if it be proper to call it thus, in fructifying matter. It is certainly bountiful and is thrown broadcast by the flora in the spring of the year: it fills the air during the blossoming period of the fruit trees; it is strown by the acre along the stagnant ponds

which furnish the lower orders of aquatic life with homes; it covers
the beds of the ocean; it teems by the millions in the secretions
which are emitted by one orgasm of man or brute. Not one fructifying cell in a million, whether of vegetable or animal life, meets
with conditions suited to its development, and consequently to its
individual growth. It is true that in the higher orders of animal
life it cannot be thrown off from the parent body with impunity
except by the methods nature prescribes. Those natural methods
are compensative. But those natural methods can only utilize a small
percentage of them. With intelligent persons all may be sacrificed
as well as so large a part, without injury to health. In any single
instance the one-hundredth cell may be rendered unfruitful with
no more harm than is experienced in the sacrifice of the ninety
and nine. . . .

What is to be Done for our Young People

Social science has yet to meet and grapple with the problem of
what is to be done for our young people. With the growth of
civilization the chasm is continually widening between the period
of concupiscence and that which admits of marriage. Bishop Armi-
tage of Wisconsin is quoted as having advised young ministers not
to get married; "their pay," he urges, "is too small for the support
of a family." "Wait," says the Bishop, "for connubial felicities until
you are properly established." And this is really good advice if the
Alphite doctrine is true, or if the church is to uphold Comstock in
his warfare against physiologists who are seeking for means of
limiting the family to the ability of the husband and father to
support the same. But a different voice will come from the halls
of science and from the churchmen of broad and practical views.
Physiologists will by and by take hold of the question which our
friends of the Alpha school are pressing upon their attention, and
from our observations in practice for more than a quarter of a
century, and a correspondence upon this subject with thousands of
intelligent minds in both hemispheres, we have no doubt what
the final verdict will be. Meanwhile at this moment and every day
thousands of our children are ripening to puberty blindfolded
with ignorance and impelled by an impulse which is as strange as
it is irrepressible. Artificial bars of all descriptions surround them.
Custom is making it necessary for a young man to snatch a home

from the watchful and experienced old squatters, who have monopolized them, before he can be permitted to have a conjugal companion. More than that, he must have an established business or profession affording an income sufficient to enable him to keep up appearances. All these with growing expensive tastes on the part of every member of the family is making what is called a home a charmed spot which few can aspire to possess. Hence there are fifty old maids where there used to be one, and one of the main sources of revenue of the doctors arises from the cure of diseases resulting from vices which such a state of society fosters. Young men poisoned with disorders or wrecked by solitary vices; young women nervous and hysterical with ovarian and uterine diseases which result from suppressed desires or unnatural methods of relieving them. Few who at twenty-five or thirty are enabled to reach the gorgeous altar of marriage and pay the officiating minister a generous fee to start them on the road of life, as the Creator originally started them, with commands which have been echoing in their bosoms for ten or fifteen years unheeded, are in a fit condition to enter matrimony or at least to become parents! And, to think of it that this is *true*! . . .

Dr. Winslow must have cases of impotent young married women as well as we. We constantly have many of them. And the impotency has in many instances resulted from non-use of organs which were fitted by nature with every possible requirement, at the age of fifteen or earlier, and then hidden by their possessor like the talents spoken of in the Scriptures!

We confess that the problem presented is a difficult one; but when the ingenuity of man is earnestly turned upon it as it is directed to other questions which are considered more respectable to handle, the problem, with all its seeming difficulties, will be solved. Mrs. Dr. Winslow, Mrs. C. B. Whitehead, and our contributor who writes about "Holy Marriage," are helping to solve it. What they write will provoke discussion. The need of this article is caused by the people of the Alpha school, who have asked the questions we have felt bound to answer. In the present temper of the public mind we hesitated to enter upon the discussion. But a stern sense of duty impelled us. Our readers have both sides of the question presented —not all that can be said by any means—but some of the prominent points which may be urged by each. Let them judge between us. . . .

Dr. Winslow's Rejoinder

. . . Let us abandon this feverish desire for sex gratification and try the higher and truer life, whose joy never palls nor its sweets turn to ashes in the mouth. Seek for that diviner love that makes us forget self and raises us to our inheritance as the sons and daughters of God. It is not lawful or right to abuse any gift of the soul—music, art, eloquence, the love of the beautiful, or any avenue of enjoyment through the senses. When indulged to excess they become sensual in their abuse, the penalty is swift and sure, feebleness, shattered nerves, and a vacillating mind are the results. But a normal cultivation and exercise makes us happy and well, and they never bring a blush to the cheeks of the most sensitive. Neither should the proper exercise of the reproductive powers, and I am convinced it would not but for the shameful abuse to which they have been subjected.

I do not believe God made the sexes to victimize each other; nor the stronger to prey upon the weaker.

In replying to the second question you admit you know many human wrecks from self-abuse and vain imaginings, and acknowledge the deplorable ignorance of even the most enlightened nations on sexual physiology and heredity. And we concur.

You likewise admit the knowledge of numerous cases of ruined health and happiness from sexual excesses of married couples.

I do not deny the advantage to be derived by every human being from a true, harmonious, chaste marriage, where duty and disinterested affection displaces selfish lust or unlawful indulgence.

I know that the legitimate use of all the functions of the body or endowments of the soul tend to promote happiness, secure sound health and prolong life. But I fear business interests obscured your mental vision and influenced your rejoinder to my fourth query when you say you have met with absolutely no incurable cases from the use of "prudential checks to prevent conception," but have met cases that have injured themselves by using improper rules. As though it were possible for the sensitive and delicate organs of generation to be wrought up to the point of conception and expectancy and then fall back cheated and empty, without results strongly detrimental to health and nervous vigor. This is not possible. It is contrary to the law of life and the reward of good uses. The penalty of violated natural law is swift and sure. But there is no punishment so terrible as that which follows lascivious-

ness and the perversions of sexual life. No *human* law can divert
the misery of the retribution nor give a physician immunity from
the evil results to his or her patients by using any device, however
ingeniously or skillfully constructed. . . .

Dr. Foote's Surrejoinder

Our readers have not forgotten that our article in *The Health
Monthly* for October, 1881, in reply to a letter from Mrs. Dr.
Winslow, the editor of *The Washington Alpha*, brought out a
prompt response in her paper for November of the same year. We
know it has not been forgotten because we have received letters
quite frequently eagerly inquiring as to when we should publish
our rejoinder. Many have asked why our reply has been so tardy.
As briefly as possibly, we will first answer this question:

In consequence of our outspoken sentiments on the sex question,
we were, in the Spring of 1881, summarily excluded from the usual
mail privileges of publishers, and required to pay transient instead
of pound rates on the entire edition of this paper each month. We
were in the throes of this conflict with the U.S. Postal Department
when our discussion with Mrs. Winslow began. On removing our
publication office to Whitby, Canada, we thought to escape the
persecution with which we were pursued in our own country, and
in the October following we gave space to Mrs. Winslow's letter of
September accompanied with our reply. Much to our surprise we
were informed by our publisher that one of the inspectors of the
mails had dropped in at Whitby, and, in the course of conversation, warned him that if *The Health Monthly* continued to
publish such matter as the article in reply to Mrs. Winslow, it
was not impossible that the paper would be excluded from the
postal facilities of the Dominion of Canada! Finally, after being
driven into Canada and then out of it by our own postal authorities,
a change in the administration at Washington brought with it
changes of an auspicious character in the postal bureau, and in
April of this year we were partially restored to our rights by a
temporary permit, and on the 26th of last June we were regularly
admitted and registered. Not yet, however, did we feel sure of our
position until our present Postmaster-General, Judge Timothy O.
Howe—the first statesman who has occupied the office for years—
issued the recent welcome order that publications which were
acceptable to a large and intelligent class of citizens should not be

excluded from the mails on the charge of obscenity, unless they should have been condemned by the courts.

Let this, then, be our explanation in part for our delay, but we may further say that we really felt no impatience to reply to Dr. Winslow, because we did not think her answer to our October article refuted in the least degree our arguments. To this day they stand unanswered. To read Dr. Winslow's article in *The Washington Alpha* for November, 1881, copied into *The Health Monthly*, March, 1882, one would infer that Dr. Foote is in favor of sexual excesses, and that Mrs. Dr. Winslow, in opposition to his views, is an advocate of sexual moderation. This, be it distinctly understood, is not the issue. The discussion began because we took exceptions to Mrs. Winslow's avowed advocacy of no sexual intercourse except for the one purpose of reproduction. . . .

It is thought, perhaps, that we may be influenced by business interests in what we have said of "prudential checks." We have, for many years, had no business interests whatever in them, and were the Comstock laws to be repealed it is hardly likely that we should have, as our professional business requires more attention than we have the physical strength to give it. We believe in them, and when the American people throw off the impertinent yoke a handful of moralists has imposed upon them, we hope there will be those in the medical profession who will find time and profit in giving their attention to the supplying of prudential checks to the family. Dr. Winslow says it is not possible "for the sensitive organs of generation to be wrought up to the point of conception and expectancy and then fall back, cheated and empty, without results strongly detrimental to the health and nervous vigor." Now, what a haphazard statement this is to make in the face of the fact that there are thousands of couples in perfect health who do not, because they cannot, have children, and who, nevertheless, do not deny themselves sexual indulgence. We have such people come to our office for advice. Sometimes the weakness results from temperamental incompatibility; in some cases from inaction of the ovaries, and in not a few cases, from a want of viable sperm cells in the secretions of the male. Such people, it may be urged, are not perfectly healthy. In the cases of temperamental inadaptation they may be, and in the others there are no such fearful results to be discovered arising from "cheated and empty organs" as those which Dr. Winslow depicts. In no country are prudential checks to the family used so extensively as in France, and the French women will compare favorably with those of either England or America in regard to health. The French women indeed are less nervous than American women.

Dr. Winslow says that the waste of fructifying material is less apparent as the animal rises in the scale of life. Granted. It is nevertheless true that there are millions of spermatozoa in the secretions discharged in one orgasm in the natural and perfectly legitimate use of the reproductive organs, when only one zoosperm is actually needed or utilized in case conception takes place; and it is as evident that the sacrifice of this *one* will no more injure the health of either party than the inevitable waste of the millions which cannot be utilized. The only question which arises is, how it may be conveniently, harmlessly and effectually rendered inert. Encouraging progress was being made in this direction when a small band of bigots and fanatics, led on by mercenary detectives, hood-winked our lawmakers into the enacting of statutes which made all such discovery punishable with fine and imprisonment.

Having now touched upon all points which require our attention, we will take leave of the subject. All that we have passed over in Dr. Winslow's article is not relevant to the real question in controversy. Much might be added in support of our position, but this article is already longer than we intended to make it. If Mrs. Dr. Winslow should really attack the scientific grounds upon which we base the doctrine we advocate, we can bring further arguments to fortify them. As the lawyers say—we will here rest our case.

Diana

Henry Martyn Parkhurst

But for a chance reference in the posthumous manuscripts of
Ida Craddock, we would not know that the author of Diana: A
Psycho-fyziological Essay on Sexual Relations, for Married Men
and Women, was a scholarly professor of astronomy at the Brooklyn
Academy. Diana was published anonymously in 1882, and although
it went through several editions, Henry M. Parkhurst never publicly acknowledged it. The reason that Ida Craddock knew his secret
probably had less to do with her own advocacy of modified continence than with her belonging to the same circle of free-thinking
experts in phonography, the Victorian version of shorthand. Stephen
Pearl Andrews was the "father" of this curious clan, that also
included Parkhurst's publisher Eliza B. Burns, and Theron C.
Leland, another denizen of Modern Times. Why phonography, free-
thought, and sexual ideology made a syndrome is difficult to understand, but it was so.

Parkhurst was among the earliest and most successful phonographers—even Andrews worked for him once, during Parkhurst's

tenure as Chief Official Reporter of the U. S. Senate (1848-1854). He was also a tinkerer and inventor, like both Andrews and his mentor at Modern Times, Josiah Warren. For example, both Warren and Parkhurst set their own type, and printed their own newspapers, both devised new systems of musical notation, proposed alternative currencies, invented and constructed a variety of machines and instruments. Like Andrews, Parkhurst had also invented a "universal language" and advocated spelling reform. He was even a member of a utopian colony for a while in the 1840s— Brook Farm.

Perhaps Parkhurst first became interested in sexual reform through Andrews' influence, but his stance was much more conservative. It may be significant that his cousin, the Rev. Charles Parkhurst, made some name for himself as a rival of Anthony Comstock in the anti-vice crusades of the 1880s and 1890s. Rev. Parkhurst was particularly famous for demonstrating the links between prostitution and City Hall in New York City, but he was more interested in suppressing licentiousness than in reforming politics. It would be interesting to know what Henry Parkhurst thought of his cousin's activities, and those of his fellow phonographer Andrews. His own contribution to sexual purity was of another order altogether.

Diana obviously owes something to Noyes' idea of male continence, but even more to the dietary orientation of Graham and Alcott. The third ingredient in his recipe for sexual health is animal magnetism, a wilting pseudoscience that Parkhurst might have found in bloom at Brook Farm forty years earlier. It is surprising that a man who was so practical in most of his accomplishments, and so successful in a science that demanded both rationality and precision (he invented and constructed the first "star-mapper" ever devised, and in six years mapped 100,000 stars) should have had this secret life as a pseudoscientist of sex. The lesson for a modern reader may therefore be, not to dismiss Parkhurst's theories out of hand, but to try to see beyond his discredited physiology and nomenclature to the truths he may have glimpsed but then obscured in his attempt to codify them.

Henry Martyn Parkhurst
Diana

In order to secure proper and durabl relations between the sexes, it is essential to liv in harmony with the law of Alfism.

"Continence except for procreation"

But if that principl is adopted alone, no means being taken to provide for the due exercize of the sexual faculties, it wil be likely either to be abandoned or to lead to a life of asceticism. In order to make Alfism practicabl for ordinary men and women, another law must be obzervd:—

Sexual satisfaction from sexual contact

understanding by the term contact, not merely actual fyzical nude, external contact, but using the term in its more general sense, to include sexual companionship, or even corespondence, bringing the minds into mental contact.

The obzervance of this law wil lead to complete and enduring satisfaction in continence; and to the explanation of this, the reazons for it, and to considerations conected therewith theze pages wil be mainly devoted.

Theze fundamental principls cannot be overturnd by mere negativ testimony. If we hav positiv evidence that they ar true, as applicabl to a singl individual, and if it can be shown that their general adoption would put an end to acknowledgd evils, such evidence wil outweigh any number of failures.

•   •   •

Theory of Dual Functions

The ovaries in woman and the testicls in man, which may be calld the sexual batteries, hav two distinct functions; 1st, the production of ova, and of sperm to impregnate them; which may be calld their generativ function; 2d, the production of a fyzical force, giving masculinity to the man, femininity to the woman,

---

● Selection from *Diana: A Psycho-fyziological Essay on Sexual Relations, for Married Men and Women,* New York; Burnz & Co., 1882, pp. 7, 9–10, 14–20, 22–23, 26–27, 31–32, 38–40, 43–44, 49.

strength, helth and vitality to both; which may be calld their afectional function. It is the power which makes the perfect man, more noble than the eunuch. It is the source of sexual atraction. That this sexual atraction between man and woman, begining in erly childhood, before procreation becums posibl, and continuing after it has ceast to be posibl, is not merely mental, is shown by its continuing during sleep; that it is not merely the dezire for fyzical action, is shown by its being content without any action whatever, and its cuming to the condition of satisfaction in such mere contact, terminating in apathy, or even in a gentl repulsion.

Definition of Terms

Including all sexual emotions under the general term "amatory," I wud distinguish between the "amativ" dezires or feelings, which constitute the general atraction between male and female, arizing from the operation of the afectional function abuv stated, and the "amorus" dezires, which tend to generation, arizing from the operation of the generativ sexual function.

Direction of Force

Altho the two functions ar spoken of as distinct, perhaps the diference consists principaly, if not entirely, in the direction which the sexual force takes. If it is directed towards certain nervs of the genital organs, stimulating them, it produces amorus dezire; while if it is more difuzed in its action, extending thru the system and to the brain, it produces amativ afection, and cauzes littl or no perceptibl sexual secretion.

One indication of the truth of the theory of dual functions, is an obzervd fact which has been for years an unexplaind mystery; the tendency of an interuption of frendly sexual relations to lead to unuzual passional outbreaks. So long as the relations continue such as to call forth and satisfy the afectional function, calm and satisfied continence continues; but when that afectional function suddenly ceases to hav employment, there is a tendency for the sexual force to take the uther form, of its generativ function, cauzing an abnormal and unuzual tendency to passional feeling. If, at this juncture, the misunderstanding is explaind, or there is a reconciliation, there is an unuzualy strong fyzical temptation to intercommunication.

•　•　•

Independent Modes of Activity

When there is more than one mode of activity for the same organs, their use in performing one function, has no tendency to incite to activity or to satisfy the activity of anuther function. The use of the lips, teeth and tung, for instance, in talking, has no tendency to increase the dezire for food, or to satisfy the cravings of hunger. So the indulgence of amativ feelings has no natural tendency to create amorus dezires; altho the two classes of feelings hav been confounded in consequence of the limitation of the two manifestations to the same persons.

Choice of Functions

The fyzical question then is simply, which function shal be calld into exercize at any given time; and this is determind cheefly by anuther class of considerations.

Abnormal Conditions

Begining with the generativ function, both man and woman hav been for many generations in an unnatural state, perhaps hav never reacht a natural state. The production of the ova in woman is atended with an abnormal loss of blud in menstruation; and the sperm in man is uzualy secreted in such excessiv quantities, that he has rezorted to sexual abuses in order to dispoze of it. Masturbation, prostitution, and marital profligacy, alike rezult from this cauz. The iritability and discumfort which men often feel, aparently from a fulness of the seminal vessels, is not always a rezult even of excessiv secretion, but of the nervus derangement and stimulation produced by an inordinate demand upon the secretion. Experience proovs that the iritability is often greatest imediately after an excessiv drain, before there can hav been time for a new acumulation; and that if there is no disturbing cauz, the longer the period of continence, the less of this iritability and discumfort ar felt.

Medical testimony goes to proov that sensations of pain or discumfort do not always arize from disturbance in thoze parts of the body where the pain or discumfort is felt. It is sympathetic, depending upon nervus derangement of uther parts of the system. A burning sensation in the hands and feet is often dependent upon dyspeptic conditions, there being realy no increast heat in the hands and feet.

But if theze organs hav a dual function, theze dificulties disapear

just as soon as man and woman ar braut into normal conditions;
for it is not necesary that there shud be sperm expended in order
to derive from the genitals their full beneficial influence as the
source of sexual atraction, or to giv them activity in order to
prezerv their vigor. And the ovaries do not loze their vitality, or
their like beneficial influence, when woman reaches the turn of life.

The Efect of Sexual Contact

It is an obzervd fact that sexual contact incites to activity the
afectional action of the sexual organs, with their conected sensibilities extending over the whole frame, and by their exercize
satisfies them, without calling into action the special generativ
function of the sexual organs. And it is also an obzervd fact that
the repression of this afectional activity naturaly creates a dezire
for the exercize of the uther; so that the true remedy for sexual
intemperance is the full satisfaction of the afectional mode of
activity by frequent and free sexual contact.

Modes of Gratification

Sexual satisfaction may be derived from personal prezence, conversation, a clasp of the hands, kissing, caressing, embracing, personal contact with or without the intervention of dress, internal
contact, mutual friction, or the experiencing of the orgazm; in
greater intensity and with greater rapidity in the order here stated.

Complete Satisfaction

The degree of satisfaction necesary for the fyzical welfare of an
individual, depends cheefly upon his mental dispozition. When he
makes up his mind that he dezires sexual gratification of a certain
order, and that only, he wil be completely satisfied with that, for
the time, and it wil not be a temptation to a hiher order of
gratification. If he dezires gratification of a certain order, sexual
gratification of a lower order in the scale of intensity, may hav
either of two contrary efects. It may be accepted and understood
by him as tending towards that which he dezires; so that a kiss may
tend to an embrace, and that to a stil hiher order, for instance;
or it may be accepted and understood by him as a temporary substitute; in which case, the more kisses he takes the better satisfied
he wil be to postpone all hiher orders of sexual gratification. Let
the mind be convinced that the hihest satisfaction wil be found in

continence, and the lower orders of gratification wil asist in the obzervance of the law.

Afectional Exhaustion

The exercize of the afectional function of the generativ organs tends to satiety and exhaustion in the same way with all uther fyzical or mental exercize; but if it is not carried to excess it is a permanent benefit. There are three independent forms which the excess may take.

1. If the sexual contact or asociation is unuzual, there is danger, even in moderation; as the too closely garded child is eazily overcum by expozure to even mild wether. This is one great danger from ordinary customs, that a very sliht departure from the acustomd routine involvs injurius stimulation.

2. If the sexual asociation or contact is intimate and prolongd, it may lead to nervus depletion.

3. If the parties ar not mutualy and reciprocaly atractiv, the asociation wil soon becum exhausting. Especialy is this true of both parties, where either seeks from the uther a greater degree of reciprocation than is cheerfuly given; for the yerning of the one, and the rezistance of the uther, ar alike exhausting.

All theze cauzes of exhaustion can be avoided between parties who ar mutualy atractiv, and ar in a pozition to yeeld to the atraction, and the hihest benefits of mutual asociation can be secured, if their intimacy progresses with such moderation that neither wil feel dispozd to check it, yet with such manifest advance as continualy to furnish new exercize for the afectional function.

Male Continence

It is the common idea that sexual atraction leads from one step to anuther with accelerated velocity, so that at each step more and more self-denial is required to cum to a stop. The principl of "male continence" taut by Dr. Noyes, at Oneida, (which has no relation to the system of complex marriage formerly existing there,) is based upon the idea that the self-denial is so nearly the same at one stage as at anuther, that we may enjoy any amount of sexual gratification consistent with continence, and stil feel no irksum restraint from continence. But if the first principl abuv stated is true, there wil be no self-denial whatever involvd in continence if the relations of the sexes alow proper sexual companionship. Carrying out the same principl a littl further than Dr. Noyes has dun, but no further than experience has demonstrated, this full satisfaction may be reacht without even aproaching amorus excitement or stimulation. The theory herein set forth radicaly difers from the Oneida method of internal contact either with or without friction. One fatal defect of that method is that it necesarily stimulates into activity the generativ function of the sexual batteries; and this not only cauzes a wasteful use of sperm, but diverts the sexual batteries from their afectional function, diminishing amativ atraction.

The danger of impregnation from unexpected emission, against which the party most concerned has no protection, is anuther fatal defect.

Experience in each individual case can alone determin what degree and what form of external sexual contact wil aford the hihest satisfaction, and how long it requires to be continued to produce and to prezerv the feeling of fyzical content.

Influence of the Mind

Our fyzical wants depend upon two factors; 1st, the existence of certain faculties which require exercize, and nervs of sensation which perceive an injury to the system from want of use; and 2d, the action of the mind directing the atention to and stimulating thoze faculties and nervs of sensation. If we hav been without food until we need a new supply, we becum hungry; but the mind may be so diverted that the want may be overlookt until it becums overpowering; or it may be so directed to the subject of eating as to greatly stimulate the dezire for food; and may even so stimulate it that there may be a factitous hunger created before the system realy needs food. Or supoze, after a long walk, just as we think we ar about to reach our destination, we discuver that we hav mist our way and ar several miles distant, the general sense of weariness instantly becums very great; and yet we may not hav taken a singl step since making the discuvery. The fyzical weariness is no greater; but that which was a moment ago disregarded, suddenly becums, by the action of the mind, overwhelming. And so the form which the sexual wants may take, depends primarily upon the needs of the system, afected largely by the action of the mind.

The fact that the sexual wants ar stimulated by the mind, does not make them the less real fyzicaly; and after being calld into exercize by the action of the mind, it may not be easy for the mind to exorcize the spirits it has calld up. Under circumstances cauzing the mind to hav an abnormaly stimulating efect, there may be required a corespondingly abnormal degree of sexual gratification to produce fyzical satisfaction.

Abnormal Cravings

A dezire for the exercize of certain faculties, whether normal or utherwize, if not soon satisfied, may, thru sympathy, extend to uther faculties, which do not realy need exercize. Littl children, from want of sleep or rest, sumtimes get cross and fretful, wanting sumthing and not themselvs knowing what it is that they want. And children of a larger growth sumtimes find it dificult to discriminate between the natural dezire for sexual companionship, which perhaps wud be fully satisfied thru mental sympathy, with littl or no fyzical contact, and the unnatural craving which arizes from perverted habits. It is this, perhaps, more than anything else, which has led to free luv varietism; first the mistaken need, and hence the misinterpretation or misdirection of the craving which is felt; and then, atributing to ultimate sexual indulgence the releef, which actualy rezults largely, and in a normal condition wud rezult cheefly, from the mere companionship of mentaly and moraly, as well as fyzicaly sympathetic persons of oppozit sex.

• • •

Mode of Equilibration

The mode of sexual equilibration is not esential, whether it is by mere companionship, or by a greater or less degree of nude contact, provided it is efectual in producing a satisfied continence. So much depends upon habit, that it may be too erly to even conjecture whether the dezire for frequent and continued nude contact is an outgrowth of perverted passion, which wil diminish when sexual feeling prezervs habitualy its proper channel, or whether it is a normal and dezirable manifestion of vigorous sexual feeling.

Indeed, both fyzical and mental or spiritual contact ar required for complete satisfaction; and of the two, the spiritual contact is that which afords the greatest satisfaction. If a woman permits unrestricted fyzical contact as a matter of wifely obedience merely, while to her it is a matter of indiference or repugnance, it wil aford far less satisfaction than when the huzband feels that there is no mental aversion; even tho the state of her helth or uther unavoidabl circumstances, may make fyzical contact impracticabl. Between thoze who are truly mated, the fyzical contact wil be largely valued as a manifestation of the spiritual contact.

Sexual Polarity

The afectional action of the sexual batteries, produces a sexual polarity, which we may call pozitiv in the male, and negativ in the female. In sexual companionship or contact, there is a radiation or conduction which reduces the polarity, and restores the equilibrium, thus tending to prevent the action of the sexual batteries from taking the generativ form.

While polarity exists, there is atraction, or sympathy; when the polarity is satisfied, this is followed by equilibrium, or apathy. If the close contact is continued, there rezults an identity of polarization, which cauzes repulsion, or antipathy. The antipathy seems to be more forcibl than the atraction; as fyzical pain is generaly more violent than fyzical plezure. If peopl wil keep their distance, and avoid a forced identity of polarization, they can be on good terms, when the same peopl, thrown into closer relations, wil feel an unconqerable antipathy.

• • •

Objections Anserd

The principal objections to the law of Alfism take four forms:

1. The great majority giv way to their apetites, regardless of consequences. It is suficient for them that Alfism requires that the appetites be braut within the dominion of reason. Their objection is unanserabl, so long as they continue in that low stage of development. They must liv on wild fruit until they lern the art of cultivation.

2. The objection that man needs fyzical releef from a continuus secretion, is anserd by the theory, sustaind by many facts, that this secretion is normaly utilized in sexual afection; and by the admitted fact that men, not deficient in sexual vigor, liv for munths, and probably for years, in strict continence, without even nocturnal emission, and with no such fyzical inconvenience as is often complaind of by men who happen to be deprived of their acustomd indulgence for a week or two at a time.

3. The objection that Alfism deprives its followers of that luv manifestation which brings them into closest union, is anserd by the existence of prostitution, which demonstrates that merely fyzical sex dezire is not an evidence of real afection. It is only Alfism which enabls the parties to demonstrate to each uther pure and unselfish afection. The fyzical manifestations which do not invite ultimation, ar the best and surest evidence of sexual afection, and the hihest posibl manifestation of sexual luv.

4. The objection urged against the doctrin of Alfism that it rests upon a depreciation of sexual relations, aplies not to the doctrin itself, but only to the personal opinions of sum of its advocates. Ideas of shame or impurity conected with sex, cum only from the abuse of sex. Alfism knows no conceivable mode of reproduction, hiher or more pure than that which exists thruout the more develont classes of the vegetable and animal kingdoms, in diversified forms, culminating in the human race. But Alfism demands that so far as regards the fyzical functions of the sexual organism, they shal be restricted in the same manner as the functions of uther organisms ar restricted, to useful rezults. It is wel known that if the digestiv aparatus shud act when there is no food to digest, if the hart shud act beyond what is necesary to produce a normal circulation of the blud, if the organs of secretion wer to act when not required to serv a useful purpose, in either case it wud produce fyzical injury to the entire system. And since the sexual function is as much more important than any uther function of the body, as the prezervation of the race is more important and hiher than the prezervation of the individual, this fact givs everything conected with sex a sacred caracter, and makes sexual wrong a profanation.

• • •

Luv of Novelty

But the question wil arize whether a man and woman can be content, after having experienced the full plezure of a reciprocal and simultaneus orgazm, to liv on, year after year, with such posibilities within their reach, without repetition of them. Certainly not, if they beleeve that the repetition wil ad to their happiness. But it is not uncommon for peopl to enjoy to the utmost an experience which they wud not care to hav repeated. So the huzband and wife may apreciate to the utmost what they hav enjoyd together;

and yet, apreciating also the fact that every exhilarating experience tends to blunt the sensibility, and make them less enjoy the chaste plezure of sexual atraction, they may be wize enuf to chooz to prezerv undiminisht as long as posibl that which they can enjoy with mutual advantage as wel az plezure, rather than to sacrifice it for a momentary paroxysm.

•   •   •

Sleeping Together

In order to prezerv the sexual polarity from becuming excessiv, it is important that huzband and wife shud uzualy sleep together, with such degree of nude contact as may be adapted to each individual case. Fyziologists sumtimes asert that no two persons shud sleep together; and they asign two reazons; 1st, that the stronger wil absorb the magnetism of the weaker, so that while one wil sleep wel and be invigorated, the uther wil sleep restlessly and be debilitated; and 2d, that the weaker wil absorb the magnetism of the stronger, so that old peopl may keep up their vitality at the expense of the yung peopl sleeping with them. What is especialy remarkabl is that theze contradictory reazons ar uzualy advanced by the same individuals. I prezume the explanation is that they do not think it safe to asign the true reazon for their beleef, or els that the hindrances in the way of investigation of sexual facts hav prevented their lerning the actual cauzes of the facts they obzerv. When a man and a woman sleep together and one of them yeelds to the intemperate sexual demands of the uther, the helth of the weaker fails; and the fyzician prescribes change of climate, which separates them with a beneficial efect. And if the fyzician thinks that sleeping separately wil check their intemperance, he may venture to recomend that, when he wud not dare to giv the true reazon for his advice. The fact is also to be taken into consideration that with the exception of man and wife, whoze sleeping together is supozed to tend to sexual excess, it is persons of the same sex who sleep together, and in that case the magnetism being of the same polarity, and therefore repelant, the radiation of the magnetism of each is interfered with by the prezence of the other. On the uther hand, if persons of oppozit sex sleep together in satisfied continence, both wil be strengthend by the magnetic radiation. It is not unlikely that by habitualy sleeping together the huzband and wife may cease to feel a thril at every contact; but there wil be substituted for it a plezure giving more satisfaction and content. The thril is like the purling of the brook; but "stil waters run deep." The thril is like the flavor of an artificial drink; but there is nuthing that can quench thirst like pure cold water.

There are two efects of sleeping together, considerd by Dr. Foote and uthers as the principal objections to it, both of which apear to be reazons in favor of it. 1st. It is claimd that it tends to bring the parties into sexual equilibrium, and thus to diminish passional atraction. True; but continence being the hiher law, altho the huzband and wife sleeping together wil not hav so strong passional atraction, they wil hav a stronger and more enduring sexual atraction, from the exercize of the afectional function. 2d. It is claimd that it tends to bring the huzband and wife into a rezemblance to each uther, and thus to unfit them for passional atraction, founded upon the law of the oppozits. True, but the foundation of marriage being the law of the oppozits, in order that the excesses of the one may be balanced by the deficiencies of the uther, it is wel that when they hav dun bearing children, when there is no longer ocazion for passional atraction, the stimulation for it shud be diminisht, so that they shal be better adapted to each uther for sexual frendship, which does not depend upon that law of the oppozits, but rather upon similarity of disposition, and also better balanced as members of society at large.

There is a way in which separate beds for huzband and wife may be made useful in promoting Alfism. Let the wife's bed be sacred to the hiher law. It wil require no great self-denial to keep that rezolution; and yet the mere deliberation involvd in going to the uther bed, wil be likely to induce gradualy increasing temperance. The asociation wil be more free in the wife's bed, from the knowledge that it wil not be regarded as inviting ultimation; and after a time it wil be found that there wil be more satisfactory enjoyment there than anywhere else.

* * *

Advantages of Alfism

The principl of Alfism promises to be of special importance in two directions where reformers hav anxiusly saut for liht.

1st. It wil tend to diminish prostitution; not only by diminishing sexual intemperance, even if the principl is not at once accepted in practice to the full extent, thus diminishing the temptation of the prezent generation, and the hereditary temptation of future generations; but also by corecting the fyziological eror which has led astray so many, that entire continence is not conduciv to helth, or to the highest fyzical plezure, but that emission is an esential feature in male existence.

What wud a machine be good for, if sum of its parts wer frequently cauzd to be moovd oftener or faster than the wurk of the machine calld for? So Alfism is only the aplication to the sex question of a general principl cuvering all organic action, and all mecanical action.

2d. It furnishes a complete and satisfactory anser to the question of the best mode of preventing conception. There is no uther mode which is either reliabl or satisfactory. Even wer any reliable mode of preventing conception to be made known, it wud hardly be satisfactory to woman, for she cud no longer plead danger, to protect herself from unwelcum intruzion. Yet there ar few married wimen who wud not be benefited if they cud be saved from the burdens and the dangers of frequent pregnancy.

• • •

Recapitulation

The fundamental theory of Diana is that the sexual secretions hav two functions; their generativ function, and their afectional function; and that except when parentage is dezired, the sexual force shud be turnd into the afectional channel. The manifestation of the afectional function is by sexual contact, which may take such form, from mere companionship to fyzical nude contact, as mutual atraction may prompt; cauzing sexual equilibration and thus sexual satisfaction. The form of such manifestation wil be largely influenced by the mind, and largely by the force of habit; wherefore the gradual bringing of the mind into harmony with theze principls, and the gradual formation of habits consistent therewith, wil make more and more evident their beneficial operation.

Zugassent's Discovery

George Noyes Miller

George Noyes Miller was born in Putney, Vermont, during the early days of complex marriage, son of John R. Miller and Charlotte Noyes Miller, so that he was the nephew of the founder of the Oneida Community, and spent his life there until the breakup in 1879. He was of an age with John Humphrey Noyes's own son Theodore, a member of the first generation of children raised in the Perfectionist faith. Their place in the community was terribly important, for on them fell the responsibility to take over the leadership from their aging fathers and mothers. As it turned out, it was only in matters of business that they achieved this—it was Theodore, for example, who first suggested that the community should make spoons in its Wallingford Branch, and it was his cousin George who first proposed that they begin silver-plating their tableware, thus between them founding the business that was to be the chief source of income for the survivors of the breakup, Oneida Community Ltd. George Miller was the New York City sales representative of the business at the time he wrote his first book, The Strike of a Sex, *in 1890.*

*John Humphrey Noyes's nephew was devoted to him and his
ideas. Along with Alfred Barron he edited Noyes's Home-Talks
in 1875, and at the breakup, when the old patriarch retired to
Niagara Falls, Miller was part of the small Noyesite faction that
followed him and settled nearby, to aid in the silver-plating business
moved there from Wallingford, and to serve his uncle in the policy-
making role he still held,* in absentia, at Oneida. *The old man
probably remembered how George's father had been the mainstay
of the community in all practical matters during the early years of
poverty and hardship. He had relied on him especially while he
was busy in Brooklyn with the* Circular *in the 1850s.*

The Strike of a Sex *was one of the wave of utopian novels that
followed the huge success of Bellamy's* Looking Backward. *Conceiv-
ably it owed something to the 1882 anti-feminist novel,* The Revolt
of Man, *the anonymous work of Sir Walter Besant (who, ironically
enough in this context, was a disapproving kinsman of birth control
advocate Annie Besant).* The Revolt of Man *envisioned Great
Britain in the hands of the feminists, who oppressed the other sex
by throwing them into jail without evidence or trial on trumped-up
charges of wife-beating, etc. It is just barely possible that Miller
had this silly pot-boiler in mind when he invented his Lysistrata-
like plot, but much more important is the theme, or rather the
didactic purpose, of* The Strike of a Sex; *for unlike most utopian
fiction, it had a very specific practical aim, the adoption of Oneidan
male continence as a universal method of birth control. The "strike"
that the female sex has made in the novel is for "the perfect ownership of her own person" in respect to maternity. This is to be
accomplished by what is known as "Zugassent's Discovery," described in the selection reprinted below.*

*But the selection here is not from Miller's first book, for curiously
enough there is nothing in it to make clear just what Zugassent's
Discovery was! Evidently Miller was unwilling to risk any particulars
until quite sure of his audience, and thus readers had to wait until
the sequel,* After the Sex Struck, *to find out that Immanuel Zugassent, a benefactor of mankind obviously modeled after the author's
famous uncle, had invented coitus reservatus, the contraceptive
technique of the Oneida Community.*

None of this background is mentioned, and in The Strike of a Sex
*Miller hid his origins behind his middle initial "N." Yet he pro-
posed nothing very controversial, not a hint of complex marriage*

or any of the other Oneida institutions that John Humphrey Noyes regarded as the very raison d'être *of male continence. Indeed, it was well that Noyes was dead by this time, for he might have classed Zugassent's Discovery with the mere evasion of Robert Dale Owen's coitus interruptus, and perhaps even have preferred Alphite continence, just as he recommended Shaker celibacy as preferable to worldly monogamy when the community abandoned complex marriage. In* The Strike of a Sex *Miller spiced his propaganda with a thoroughly conventional romance between the hero and the heroine, a case of exclusive love that would have been squelched without mercy in Noyes' heyday at Oneida.*

George Noyes Miller
Zugassent's Discovery

Zugassent's Discovery! Zugassent's wonderful Discovery! beside which, in its enormous capacity for reducing the sum of human misery, the discoveries of Jenner, of Harvey, of Pasteur, and of Koch are but as the whirling wind-gusts of a summer's day! How can I approach this august subject in such a way as to impress the truth of this priceless discovery upon the young men and women of this illuminated age. In making the attempt, I am reminded of the agonizing prayer which Samson breathed when he blindly felt for the pillars which upheld the temple of his oppressors, "O Lord God, remember me, I pray thee, and strengthen me, I pray thee, only this once."

But is there any such bitter need of relief to woman from the primeval curse of "multiplied conception"? To answer this question I open my desk, and, thrusting my hand into a mass of letters, draw out one at random. Here it is:—

"My first rude awakening to the stern realities of married life came with the birth of my first child. The doctors said that my physical formation was not favorable to child-bearing, and my child was taken away from me dead. A year later I had gone through this same experience again, and was completely changed from a light-hearted, joyous girl to a sickly, nervous, irritable woman. Can you wonder that I shrank from my husband's embraces after this,

●Selection from *After the Sex Struck; or, Zugassent's Discovery*, Boston: Arena Publishing Company, 1895, pp. 49–81, 84–89.

and looked upon them as a cruel stab at my life? I determined to
have no more children, cost what it might. Nevertheless in the third
year of my marriage I found myself for the third time in the way
of becoming a mother. I was beside myself when I discovered it. I
left the house and almost ran through the streets to the office of a
physician, whom I had heard was not scrupulous in such matters. I
remember how people stared at me as I hurried along, and I am sure
that they must have thought me crazy. I begged the physician to
do anything to relieve me, even if it cost my life. After some attempts
to dissuade me, he consented and performed an operation. I
staggered home looking like a ghost. I have a dim remembrance
of putting a few things into a bag, of being helped by a stranger
on to a train, and of falling on the steps of my mother's house in
a dead faint. I could never return to my husband after that. His
own entreaties, the persuasions of friends, the dread of scandal
all fell upon an utterly deaf ear. I had escaped with my shattered
life from a destroying treadmill, and I could never return to it
again.

R. S. E."

There is no need of multiplying such painful recitals. The un-
written annals of every neighborhood contain them. They are as
obvious as a shadow to the student of human nature wherever he
may go. Even in a brief interim of this writing I strolled into the
Park, where nature was at her loveliest, and, seating myself on a
rustic bench, abandoned myself to the grateful influences of the
beauty around me. But my solitude was broken in upon by the
approach of a family consisting of a stout, robust young man, a
tall, handsome woman with a fine intellectual face, and three
children. One of these, a baby, was in its mother's arms, the other
two, aged three and four, caught at her skirts and ran along beside
her. Here was the typical, conventional picture of domestic bliss,
the sacred combination from which is believed to flow the perennial
stream of happiness, and I fell to studying the group with interest.
As they drew near, the woman sank wearily upon an adjacent seat,
and I looked into her face. There was no sparkle or smile there,
but only the hunted, hopeless look of an animal caught in a trap
from which there was no escape!

Noble St. Paul! He said "Love worketh no ill to his neighbor." A
man's wife is his nearest and dearest neighbor, but many a good

man is sadly perplexed to see that he is unintentionally working grievous ill to this "neighbor" whom he loves best. He is exposing her to bearing children faster than her health will permit, thus undermining her strength and depriving her of the beauty and sprightliness which charmed him so greatly in his days of courtship. He sees with unimagined disappointment that the beautiful flower whose bloom and perfume he so strongly coveted, and which he had plucked with so much ardor, is withering in his grasp. He sees also that the constant demands of maternity entailed upon his wife are depriving him, in great measure, of the society and help of a delightful companion. Thus, instead of a charming auxiliary to aid and encourage him in the battle of life, he finds that through marriage he has greatly multiplied his cares, and that he has become an attendant upon a chronic invalid.

How can all this be changed? How can husband and wife enjoy each other's life-renewing magnetism, "The life of life," and still limit their offspring and preserve their own health in a way that shall be scientific and innocent as with the innocent plans of childhood? Astonishingly simple as it is, Zugassent's Discovery offers such a way; and many married people have found that it is the one satisfactory solution of the darkest of all problems, how to subject human propagation to the control of reason.

And indeed, there is to-day among pure-minded people who believe that the sexual nature is sacred, holy, and glorious, a crying insistent demand for a pure and innocent method of limiting the size of their families and mitigating the woes of poverty and ill-health resulting from too frequent child-bearing. I have numerous letters from the most refined and religious people on this subject. These conscientious and God-fearing persons naturally recoil from the methods adopted by the irreligious. They cannot feel that such methods have the justifying and ennobling effect which should pertain to the associations of a sacrament. And shall such people as these be always left to misdirection, chance, and misery? Do not the infinite resources of Christianity contain an assured cure for this evil? Here is one that seems completely to supply this demand. It is not only intrinsically pure and innocent, but in teaching self-control and true temperance, without asceticism, it reacts powerfully for good on the whole character. It is not a merely nugatory device, but a splendid stimulus to spirituality.

Zugassent's Discovery offers itself to all pure-minded and scientific people who are seeking improvement in every department of life, but it addresses itself particularly and with tremendous appeal to the *young;* to progressive young men and women whose habits are unformed and to whom the things that were impossible to their forefathers are the commonplace facts of to-day. The young people who are now approaching marriageable age live in a world whose ideas, in nearly every department of life, have been largely modified, if not completely changed, by the advent of steam, electricity, the microscope, the telescope, the telephone, and other constantly multiplying agents of enlightenment. Is it not reasonable to suppose that there is the same opportunity for infinite improvement and revolutionizing discovery in such a vital department as that of the sex relation, and that the results of such discovery will be commensurate with the immense importance of the subject? The Discovery of Zugassent has been demonstrated to be such an improvement, and it alone provides a sure foundation for the perfect solution both of the sexual and population problems.

"Man's superiority to the brutes is read in his continual advance in the conquest of nature. The brutes stand still; men reflect, energize, and conquer. The seeds of the final supremacy over nature lie in the full subjection of man's own body to his intelligent will. There are already an abundance of familiar facts showing the influence of education and direct discipline in developing the powers of the body. We see men every day, who, by attention and painstaking investigation and practice in some mechanical art, have gained a power over their muscles, for certain purposes, which to the mere natural man would be impossible or miraculous.. In music the great violinists and pianists are examples. All the voluntary faculties are known to come under the power of education, and the human will is found able to express itself in the motions of the body, to an extent and perfection that is in proportion to the painstaking and discipline that are applied. So far as the department of voluntary outward habits is concerned, the influence of will and education to control the body is universally admitted. But there is a step further. Investigation and experience are now ready to demonstrate the power of the will over what have been considered and called the *involuntary* processes of the body. The mind can take control of them, certainly, to a great extent; and while it is not yet shown to what extent, neither is it apparent that there are

any limits whatever in this direction. All the later discoveries point
to the conclusion, that there are strictly no *involuntary* departments
in the human system, but that every part falls appropriately and
in fact within the dominion of mind, spirit, and will.

IMMANUEL ZUGASSENT."

The advance of civilization sometimes makes what appears to be
an indispensable and salutary safeguard to one generation a positively abhorrent practice to a closely following but more enlightened
one. For instance, the custom of *bleeding* was universal among
physicians a generation or two ago, and was resorted to for nearly
every physical ill that flesh is heir to. It is said that George Washington lost his life by it. To-day, the practice of bleeding, except
in rare and well-defined cases, is regarded with much the same
wonder and horror that we feel when we look back upon the
hanging of the witches at Salem—a compound of barbarism and
ignorance. An impressive monument, which stands in Euston Road,
London, notifies the passer that it was erected in 1855 as a
memorial to James Morison, because "HE WAS THE FIRST TO PROTEST
AGAINST BLEEDING." The physician who should now practice bleeding
indiscriminately would be looked upon as a stupid or criminal
blunderer, and his license would be practically taken away. Through
the enlightenment of Zugassent's Discovery a generation may be
expected to arise that will look back upon the present constant
and useless drain of the vital seminal principle with much the
same compassionate wonder with which we look back upon the
practice of bleeding.

Zugassent's Discovery consists then in making a clear, total, and
practical distinction between the sexual union of husband and
wife when propagation is desired and expressly intended, and when
it is not. That is, it makes two entirely distinct forms of sexual
union: one for propagation, which must be agreed upon and desired
by both parties; the other for innocent magnetic exchange as
innocuous in its results and as elevating in its effects as the most
refined conversation. In this latter interchange, in which procreation
is not intended, and which constitutes Zugassent's Discovery, the
husband is required only to exercise that self-control and effort of
will which would avoid procreation.

If this idea is new to the reader his mind will perhaps be immediately flooded with questions and objections, and it is not unlikely that he may exclaim without hesitation that such self-control

is *"impossible."* But the word "impossible" is one that it is growing harder and harder to find in the dictionary of *fin-de-siècle* progress. Had the reader been living fifty years ago and expressed the opinion then that in a few years men would be able to converse together in ordinary tones while standing one hundred miles apart, he would have been considered either a fool or a lunatic. Or if at a little earlier period he had questioned the wisdom of the practice of bleeding, he would have been deemed a presumptuous charlatan. The scores of married men who live in the hamlet where Zugassent passed his unselfish, august, and beneficient life will tell you that such self-control *is* possible, that to the young, who have not been perverted by sensual customs it is both *easy, natural,* and non-ascetic, and that it can be attained by almost any married man through suitable self-discipline.

It is true that sexual excitement could easily be carried so far that the restraint of the automatic part by the will would be injurious, but the conscientious practice of Zugassent's Discovery does not contemplate any such excitement. It chooses chastity, temperance, and an unselfish regard for the welfare of others.

(Testimony.)

"I am a young man, 24 years of age, enjoying the most vigorous health. For two years after becoming engaged I delayed marriage, simply because I did not think my income sufficient to support a wife and the children which I regarded as an inevitable consequence. Happily for me a friend, who knew my circumstances, wrote me about Zugassent's Discovery. The ideas contained in this discovery were so different from all my preconceived ideas of what constituted marital happiness, that I was inclined to reject them as utterly impracticable and absurd. But the more I thought of the matter the more clearly I saw that if there was a possibility of these new ideas being true, they were exactly adapted to a man in my circumstances, and that they made my marriage immediately practicable. The wholly new thought that retaining the vital force within himself would naturally make a man stronger, cleaner, and better also seemed to me not irrational. With some misgivings, therefore, I determined to venture upon marriage, and, thanks to Zugassent's Discovery, it has been found a complete success. I have had a continuous honeymoon for four years, besides having the daily benefit of my wife's invaluable services in my business. I have never been conscious of any irksome constraint or asceticism in my sexual experience; and my self-control and strength, mental and physical, have greatly increased since my marriage. In the light of my own experience I regard the idea that the seminal fluid is a secretion that must be got rid of as being the most pernicious and fatal one that can possibly be taught to young people.

J. G."

If the reader has further doubts as to the healthfulness of Zugassent's Discovery he cannot certainly question that it is healthy for his wife to be relieved of the physical curse and mental dread of excessive undesired child-bearing. The doubt moreover that a man can conserve his virile power, while he gives due exercise to his sexual and social affections, has been proved by long practice and scientific observation to be a veritable bogie, a hoary fallacy that has slain its tens of thousands, where the senseless practice of bleeding has slain its thousands. Learned physicians are beginning to see and to teach, and the followers of Zugassent have demonstrated with facts as inexorable and incontestable as the figures of Malthus, that it is eminently healthy to conserve the virile principle; that the seminal secretion has an immense *immanent* value, and if kept in the system is reabsorbed by the blood and adds enormously to a man's magnetic, mental, and spiritual force, a force which in ordinary married life is constantly being expended when it is not wished or expected that it shall produce anything. Other things being equal, the men who wisely conserve this force, as compared with those who waste it, will be in concentrated mental and spiritual power and effectiveness like a Daniel and his companions, as compared with the weaklings who ate of the King's meat.

As a promoter of domestic happiness and a preventer of the woes that lead to divorce, Zugassent's Discovery is entitled to the lasting gratitude of all good people, as is shown by a single one of the many testimonies on record.

(Testimony.)

"My age is seventy, and, thanks to Zugassent's Discovery, my health is good, and I am as vigorous as I ever was. My only regret is that I was not informed of it earlier in life. It is not only a splendid sanitary measure, but is the promoter of the greatest harmony in domestic life I know. It is my decided opinion that when Zugassent's Discovery is adhered to, except when reproduction is desired, that strife and contention, separation and divorce will seldom occur. It seems to me that no one who is seeking improvement would after experiencing the salutary effects of Zugassent's Discovery ever wish to go back to the crude sensual practice in whose wake follow satiety, exhaustion, disgust, and remorse. The waste of vital and nerve force attending the usual custom is, in my opinion, a leading cause of the craving for alcohol and tobacco. While in Zugassent's Discovery a new life is not developed, still both parties, where magnetism exists, experience a renewal of life force that is in the highest degree wholesome. If the young men of this generation would choose to abide by Zugassent's Discovery (as I have no doubt that a soon-coming one will), they would find that their self-control would be immensely enhanced in every department of life, and that they would retain their vigor to a much greater age than those under the present system.

W. S. F."

Perhaps if the reader is finally disposed to admit that the practice of Zugassent's Discovery may be (as it has been practically demonstrated to be) healthy, humane, and beneficial, a necessary protection to woman and an infinite blessing to the young, he may still say that it is ascetic and not in accord with his pleasure. Without stopping to argue the morality of a man's keeping his wife in constant dread and danger of the perils of childbirth in order that his passion may be "satisfied," may not the question be properly asked, "Is the passion of such a man conformed to the standard of advancing civilization?" But again we appeal to the sure testimony of the pure and conscientious people who have tested Zugassent's Discovery, and say that it is not ascetic, that it *is* satisfying, and that in thousands of cases it is the *beginning* of happiness to women.

LETTER FROM A WOMAN.

"Since my husband became acquainted with the philosophy of Zugassent, he has endeared himself to me a hundred-fold, and although our so-called "honeymoon' was passed five years ago, it was no more real, and far less lasting, than the ecstatic, the unspeakable happiness which is now continually mine. My prosaic and sometimes indifferent husband has changed by a heavenly magic into an ardent and entrancing lover, for whose coming I watch with all the tender raptures of a schoolgirl. His very step sends a thrill through me, for I know that my beloved will grasp me and clasp me and cover me with kisses such as only the most enthusiastic lover could give. And though the years lapse, I cannot see or feel any change in the way he cherishes me. To each other we are continually objects of the deepest reverence and the most sacred mystery. Our affection deepens, our romance seems as sure and enduring as the stars. My lover! my hero! my knight! my husband! I date my marriage from the time that he became a disciple of Zugassent, for that was the beginning of our assured happiness.

"But it is not alone as a cherishing lover that my husband has become my crown of happiness. He has grown perceptibly nobler in character, in purpose, in strength, in all the qualities that make a man God-like, so that besides a lover I have a strong friend and wise counsellor, and my happiness is complete.

L. S. T."

But while Zugassent's Discovery is far removed from a repelling asceticism and gives ample exercise to the affections, and opportunity for the exchange of sexual magnetism, its greatest crown of honor consists in its conducing to the highest and noblest *spiritual* development. It is the essence of the golden rule, the sweet aroma of charity. It considers the welfare and happiness of others in the most engrossing of human pleasures, and thus partakes of the divine. It lifts the interchange between the sexes from the purely sensual plane, tending toward death, into that of joyous social and religious fellowship tending toward life. It envelops those who really apprehend it in an atmosphere of purity and chastity sweeter and far more real than that possessed by nuns.

"How unfortunately taught are they who think of the sexual nature as unclean and debasing. Such persons despise that part of human nature which is noblest of all, except that which communicates with God. They profane the very sanctuary of the affections— the first and best channel of the life and love of God.

"True modesty is a sentiment which springs not from indifference or aversion to the sexual offices, but from a delicate and reverent appreciation of their value and sacredness. While the shrinking of shame is produced by the feeling that the sexual nature is vile and shameful, the shrinking of modesty is produced by the opposite feeling that the sexual nature is too holy and glorious to be meddled with lightly.

                                        IMMANUEL ZUGASSENT."

The transcendent spiritual value of this pure and salutary manner of life, as well as its immense economic importance, is referred to in the following letter from one of the most learned and far-seeing minds of this age. I take it from my unique files with feelings of deepest affection and reverence for the writer.

(Testimony)

"It gives me happiness to bear my testimony to the beneficial effects of Zugassent's Discovery, because I am earnestly convinced that no other discovery in physical science has ever been made which is of such importance to the welfare of the human race. As a statistical and financial adviser to the government of a growing colony, no less than as a student, I have had the problem of human poverty forced on my attention with terrible emphasis. I early realized that the Malthusian pressure of population was the one thing which dominated human destinies in this regard, but it was not until I became acquainted with Zugassent's Discovery that I could see any entirely satisfactory solution of the problem. Finding, however, that in proportion as I have followed Zugassent's ideas, life has become wholesome and happy, I have long reached the profound conviction that Zugassent's Discovery, in the sense intended by him, would be imperative for spiritual reasons, even if there were no population problem to solve. It avoids the opposite evils of asceticism and self-indulgence, and does more than any other single thing to make marriage a perpetual courtship. I am a husband of fifteen years standing, and therefore speak of matters that are not strange to me.

                                                          F."

To the young and to the teachers of the young Zugassent's Discovery appeals with the voice of a prophet. It concerns the happiness of millions yet to be. If it were taught to the young by enlightened and pure-minded teachers they would never be conscious of any sacrifice. On the contrary, they would prefer it, as has been demonstrated; and the tremendous compensations which such a wise conservation of force would bring would speedily make the earth astir with a new and prepotent race.

Extract from a letter from a wise physician:

"Those who perceive the crying need for a radical reformation in existing beliefs on sexual subjects, must look to the instruction of the *young* for the step in advance they earnestly hope to see.

"Let the young be taught that it was never nature's intention that man should take pride in his purely animal instincts and desires, and that the progress of the race depends more upon the absolute control of the sexual nature for the improvement of the species than upon any other one thing except the broadest idea of human brotherhood.

"Let them be taught that the organs for love's expression are entirely distinct from those of generation, and that it is an unworthy act to use the latter except for nature's purposes; that the *proper* use of the former raises the sexual act to a mental plane where it ceases to be the brutalizing and degrading animalism it often is, but becomes the next step toward soul development which is the appointed task of man."

•   •   •

The waters of Niagara, which are a concrete embodiment of the greatest physical force in the world, have for unnumbered ages been running to waste without rendering any other service to man than to please the eye. But now in this year of 1894 their tremendous energy has become subject to the skill and wisdom of man. Their mighty power has been conserved at last, to help forward the harmonious destiny of Earth's children. But the harnessing of the force of a thousand Niagaras would not bring a tithe of the illimitable blessings to the human race that will follow the final, predestined conservation of man's own distinctive, physical power. It will be a step of prodigious magnitude toward the conquest of death.

Do you love your wife? Do you want her to be a helper to you instead of a burden? Do you want to preserve her freshness like that of a sweet-scented flower to brighten and perfume your pathway through life? Learn self-control.

Do you wish to reduce the evils of poverty to a minimum, and avoid the anguish of seeing helpless objects of affection multiply around you to whom you can give neither adequate nourishment nor education? Learn self-control.

Do you wish to have healthy and well-balanced children? Let them be only those that are desired by both parents. Children who are not desired, and who live for nine months in their mother's womb under a kind of curse, can be neither happy nor well-balanced.

Do you wish to have your sons marry early enough to avoid a long and cruel suppression of a natural and innocent desire, and thus escape falling into ruinous habits which cloud their whole after life? Teach them self-control.

Do you value your own spiritual, mental, and physical power and magnetism, and wish to expend them where they will do the most good for all noble interests? Learn self-control.

All interests of heaven and earth summon you to the supreme importance of the study of self-control in a department of life in which it has never been taught, and which is therefore filled with the wrecks of an ungoverned force. Peace, order, and infinite happiness can be established there in this way, and this way only.

"And how," the reader may ask, "can so stupendous a reform be brought about?"

It *will* be brought about, sooner or later, simply by being discovered to be *feasible* and necessary by the scientific and by the religious. Neither the truly religious nor the truly scientific can always pursue a course which they believe to be disastrous and, therefore, morally wrong. With these two classes conjugal self-control will eventually become a matter of conscience, and a growing public opinion will thus be powerfully impressed upon the young from the earliest puberty.

With the right teaching of the young all difficulties of sexual self-control vanish into nothingness.

But even if the scientific and the religious among men were to fail (which cannot be expected), woman herself is advancing with a step as sure as that of destiny to an assured arbitration in the ethics of sex. For this function she is pre-eminently fitted. Her happiness, the happiness of her children, her health, even her very self-preservation depend upon her gaining this arbitration. The self-control of the male sex is to her a matter of life and death. She will not forever sacrifice herself to an ungoverned passion when she becomes aware that it can be tamed and refined. She will demand of the ardent lover, who is eager to accomplish impossibilities on her behalf, that he shall carry his self-denial and regard for her welfare into the closest intimacies of marriage.

Who can doubt that when woman becomes such an arbiter she will choose those things which are the most refined and refining; which tend to keep her in the estimation of men as the most desirable thing in the universe; and which insure to her, and to the world, the most perfect children?

Magnetation

Albert Chavannes

Albert Chavannes is a good example of the direction that the philosophy of free love took during the last quarter of the nineteenth century, after the great furor of Victoria Woodhull's campaign and the Beecher-Tilton scandal. Chavannes came to the United States as a boy. His family settled in Tennessee, but he left home early and spent a number of years in Berkshire, New York, where he learned woodworking and related trades. In 1870, after a religious crisis that led to his joining the free-thinkers, Chavannes moved back to Knoxville, where he lived with his wife Cecille until his death in 1903. He prospered in business—land, lumber, construction—was president of the local bank, and even ran for Congress in 1892. During the last twenty years of his life he devoted himself to "mental science," a huge intellectual project in which he wrote a dozen books and pamphlets trying to explain the evolution of future human beings and their institutions. Like J. William Lloyd, the anarchist and free love philosopher from whom he borrowed his key term "magnetation," Chavannes had theories of government, economics, and all the social sciences to offer, as well as his notions about marriage and the family. Also like Lloyd, and like George Miller, he wrote utopian novels illustrating how his theories might eventuate in actual societies.

Chavannes's view of marriage was "evolutionary": he thought polygamy and more promiscuous forms of mating belonged to the dawn of civilization, and that monogamy suited the present state of society; as an observer of Oneida he agreed with John Humphrey Noyes that sex and communism were "so intimately connected that their success or failure cannot be separated," and since he saw communism as the direction in which civilization was evolving, he assumed that some form of communal marriage would eventually prevail. For the time being, however, in competitive economic society, he believed in monogamy, tempered by divorce in cases of extreme hardship.

He argued that divorce was no "remedy for connubial unhappiness," however, and looked "for the improvement of the marriage relation" not in the relaxation of its bonds, "but in the increase of the knowledge of the laws which control the sexual relations, and my observation is that since the knowledge which is taught in such books as Diana, Karezza, After the Sex Struck, *and my own works on the subject has been somewhat disseminated, it has done more to draw married people together than all the laws which have been passed to regulate marriage." Thus the demands of the free lovers for a sexual order unconstrained by law and the state had come by the end of the century to this pseudoscientific asceticism within the sexual act itself, and all that was left of free love and communal marriage was its technique of contraception.*

Albert Chavannes
Magnetation
Self-Control

It has been said, correctly enough, that progress is due to the gradual control of the forces of nature by man, who seizes upon them and uses them for his benefit. But it is just as true that this control must be preceded by self-control, or the ability of man to control himself.

Self-control is the result of the development of vital force and its

● Selection from *Vital Force, Magnetic Exchange and Magnetism*, 2d ed., Knoxville, Tenn.: Albert Chavannes, 1897 (1st ed. 1888), pp. 81–93.

training in useful directions. As the brain increases in size and strength, it gains better control of the other faculties of the organism, and compels them to curb their propensities and to work harmoniously for the benefit of all the individuality.

In accord with that law of development, civilized man has attained a control of his faculties that can never be reached by the uncivilized man. As used in the arts and manufactures, his skill, which means the control of his hands and fingers, shows a steady increase, and to give no other example, the art of writing or playing on a musical instrument shows how far this control can be carried. But the brain of man has not only secured the control of the voluntary organs, he has also extended his power over the vegetative organs. The regular hours for eating and sleeping are due to an intelligent control of these faculties which are taught to adapt themselves to the needs of civilization. It is probably in the control of his digestive organs that man has made the most advance, teaching them to restrain their voracious desires and to conform themselves to rules calculated to increase his enjoyment. The difference between the gluttony displayed by the savage in possession of food and the rational enjoyment of the civilized man when partaking of his meals, is the difference between the blind surrender to impulses and an intelligent control of the organs of digestion.

But it seems as if the control of the organs of reproduction is the last in the line of development, and truly it can be said that it is only of late that man has tried to place them under his subjection. In the past their non-use has been taught and practised by ascetics, but the teachings of the Oneida community and of the author of *Diana,* who advocate self-control, are a late development. Such teachings would have been ahead of time and unheeded until the economic change of which I have spoken had progressed far enough to induce married people to limit the size of their family.

In the past, with whole continents uninhabited and war and pestilence running riot, population did not increase faster than was needed to promote civilization, and large families which is the natural result of uncontrolled sex force were in the line of progress. What was needed was the social regulation of this force, and that was provided by the institution of marriage, enforced by law and public opinion.

The history of the development of the use of the procreative force is a very interesting one, and but for the limited scope of this work, I would like to give it at length, but I will only briefly glance at it so as to make more clear the many reasons which are inducing the change from procreation to magnetation.

The law of the struggle for existence calls for unchecked procreation. All species of living organisms are surrounded by numerous enemies that threaten their existence, and it is only by excessive procreation that they escape utter destruction. This procreative process is then instinctive and not under any intelligent control, for no living organism except man has any idea of the object to be attained, and even in man, all observation goes to show that except in those who have reached the highest state of development, it is not the maintenance of the race, but the satisfaction of desire, that is the incentive to the act of procreation.

But as man slowly emerged victorious over all other animals, progress controlled by intelligence slowly replaced the instinctive progress of the struggle for existence, private property was established and in its train followed the marriage relation. To increase the incentive to the acquisition of property, inheritance was recognized, and as private property had led to the organization of the family, so inheritance followed the same line, and the integrity of the family had to be maintained.

But it was not an easy matter to maintain this integrity among individuals whose ancestry had, for untold ages, practised promiscuous intercourse. Thus new social virtues and new social views had to be recognized. Chastity, a thing unknown where private property does not exist, became a virtue, while wantonness, or the open manifestation of sexual desire, became a vice. Laws were enacted to further strengthen the sacredness of family life, and public opinion was invoked to restrain any association outside the marriage relation.

Even all these measures were found insufficient to accomplish the desired purpose, and new customs had to be adopted to strengthen the artificial relation. Among these customs were some prescribing different forms of garments for persons of different sexes, others formulating laws of etiquette for the conduct of individuals in society, others regulating the payment of visits among unmarried persons, as well as the elimination of certain subjects of conversation in respectable society. In a word, the highly artificial system under which we live was inaugurated to uphold marriage and inheritance, the twin offspring of personal property.

Under the present state of civilization such a system is a necessity. and if we consider the strength of inherited tendencies and the power of sexual desires its success is really wonderful and shows that sex force can be brought under the subjection of mankind. But at this time it is social control and not self-control. Just as prohibition is social control while temperance is self-control, so the sex control of to-day is social control, and in a very small measure only can it be ascribed to self-control. Society prevents the use of sex force outside of marriage, but within marriage all license is permitted without any restraint from self-control. Under cover of the shield furnished by the marriage relation, men and women have given full vent to their propensities; and within its sacred precincts procreation has run riot, regardless of the misery which followed in its train.

In the undeveloped stage which preceded the dawn of civilization, the propagation of the species required different manifestations of sex force in the male and in the female animals. The female manifested sexual desires only at such times as she could conceive, while the male was always under their influence, so as to be ready to beget its kind at the propitious moment. In the semi-civilized state in which we linger full license is given, within marriage, to both men and women to exercise these inherited propensities. The complete dominion of the husband over the wife enables him to satisfy his passions as often as he desires, and public opinion justifies a wife who brings children into the world to the full extent of her ability.

But we are slowly emerging out of this state of semi-barbarism to a condition where the true relation of married persons to each other is being recognized, and where marriage can no longer be used as a cloak for unbridled license and unchecked reproduction. The passive submission of the wife is being replaced by the recognition of her equal position in the family, and parents commence to see that they are responsible for the birth of their children.

This change in the views and beliefs of individuals is slowly leading them in the direction of self-control and teaching them how to pass from procreation to magnetation. For magnetation is sexual self-control and is in the line of progress if it is true that every advance in civilization is due to an advance by man in the control of his own organization.

And because magnetation is sexual self-control, no definite line of demarkation can be placed between procreation and magnetation, for the power of self-control of all persons is different, and the rule which would apply to one person might not to another.

What I can say is this: The persons who believe that their sex force can be turned back from its original function of reproducing the race to adding to their own physical powers, and wish to reap this benefit, must study themselves and find out the limit of their self-control, so as to avoid as far as possible that complete surrender to passionate desire which is always the precursor of procreation.

The effort is not nearly as difficult or hopeless as some persons suppose. We have all around us examples of the power of the brain to control the subordinate organisms, and there is no reason why the sex force should not be brought into proper subjection whenever men and women will have developed sufficiently to recognize how necessary it is to curb their inherited propensities, and how great will be the reward of this new advance in civilization.

Equilibrium and Waste

I have a thorough belief that all progress in civilization is due to man's desire for an increase of happiness, and do not believe that magnetation will supersede procreation unless experience shows that there is a sufficient reward offered to individuals for the exercise of the necessary self-control. I am no believer in asceticism, or in the innate depravity of our natural desires, and I hold that an increase of pleasant sensations is the incentive to all successful advancement. The control of sex force will follow the same line of progress, and men and women will only strive for its attainment when they become persuaded that their efforts will be properly rewarded.

And therein is found the difference between the old and the new philosophy. While the ascetics of old taught the non-use of sex force as pleasing to God and worthy of a reward after death, evolution philosophers teach self-control in the use of sex force as a means of increasing the sum total of happiness for those who exercise it.

What then is the incentive to magnetation? How will it increase personal happiness? Briefly told, it is claimed that it furnishes a more satisfactory and less wasteful method than procreation, for restoring the equilibrium of sex force.

The continual breaking of equilibrium and its restoration is one of the laws of motion and one of the conditions of progress. Just as man, when he walks, breaks his equilibrium when he moves his body forward and restores it by advancing one of his limbs, so all things in nature progress. The same law is true of the action of vital force. First comes an accumulation in the reservoirs provided for its storage, which becomes so large as to cause unpleasant feelings which only cease after actions that use the surplus until the equilibrium is restored. This is the case with the three different reservoirs of vital force, and unless we understand this fact, we can have no proper idea of the desires and motives which compel man to action.

But if forces stronger than our will compel us to restore this equilibrium, that is, induce us to increase the supply of vital force if it has decreased below the normal demands of the organism, or to decrease it if it is greater than the reservoirs can contain, there is a vast difference in the results upon our happiness according to the manner in which we use this excess of vital force.

Thus when used by the vegetative organs in the form of emotional magnetism, it more than returns to the individual the vital force consumed. The stomach and the lungs extract from the food and the air a much larger amount than they expend in doing their work. The conditions under which they work may be more or less favorable, depending upon their surroundings and upon the amount of intelligence possessed by the individual, but they are the providers of the whole organism, and upon them rests the task of securing from all available sources within their reach the needed supply of vital force which the individual will use intellectually, physically and sexually. On that account, intelligent persons will divert as large as possible an amount of vital force to the vegetative organs that it may be returned to them with a large interest.

The vital force used in intellectual or physical work makes no return in kind. The mission of the brain is to direct and of the limbs to act. Vital force in their department is rightfully employed or wasted according as the results are helpful or not to the vegetative organs, or conducive or not to personal enjoyment.

Sex force used for procreation is a pure waste so far as the physical welfare of the parents is concerned. It may be well used, either from the standpoint of personal happiness or of the benefit to society, when healthy and intelligent children are procreated, but the number of such is small compared to the amount of sex force used, and it is a fact that all physiologists have deplored that so much sex force should be wasted.

But the claim is now made that sex force used in magnetation, instead of being wasted, is returned to the whole organism, and that the equilibrium can be restored without the waste entailed by procreation.

Can such a claim be proven? I do not say that in the present state of our knowledge it can be done, but that strong arguments can be brought to its support.

Let us first examine the theoretical arguments, and then we will see if it is in accord with known facts.

These arguments are based on three assertions, two of which I have already discussed.

The first is that sexual force contains that peculiar condensation of vital force which has within itself all the elements of the living organism, that it is an epitome of the individual, and on that account is set aside for the work of reproduction.

The second is that this sexual force is in constant communication with the remainder of the vital force in the organism and is affected by all its changes.

The third is based up this second one, and it is that sex force can in its turn affect the vital force of the whole organism. As this third assertion is the foundation upon which rests the philosophy of magnetation, I must discuss it at some length.

The sympathetic influence of the different parts of the organism on each other is well recognized, and no one who accepts the theory of vital force explained in this book will doubt that this sympathetic influence is due to currents of vital force. Whenever any one influence is strong enough to permeate the whole organism, we recognize the fact in common speech, and say of a man that he is full of love, or affection, or of anger. In anger, the intellectual force stored in the brain is strongly stirred by some outward cause, and generates such a current as to permeate the whole individual and to control all his actions. In affection it is the sympathetic nerves that furnish the magnetism, while in love it comes from the sexual organs. In each case, the influx of one of these three kinds of magnetism is sufficiently strong to permeate the whole organism and control it for the time being.

As the sources of supply are different, so are its manifestations. Anger is evanescent, reaching great heights, but usually lasting but a short time. Affection is strong, steady, not very demonstrative, but causing an even and lasting influence. Love stands between the two, neither as evanescent as anger or permanent as affection, but its subtle influence is very penetrating and it is an important factor in our lives.

Not only does common speech—which is based upon common experience—recognize the fact of this control of individuals by the effusion of special portions of the vital force, but the difference is felt very clearly in the spiritual atmosphere of the persons thus influenced, and we can easily recognize the difference in the touch, especially of the lips or hands, of a person loving, affectionate or indifferent. Just as I have said that our vital force can recognize the difference between a message charged with one kind of knowledge and that charged with another, and yet we cannot explain how it is done, so we realize very soon that a person is under the influence of anger, love or affection, and yet cannot explain in what the difference consists.

If we admit that there is such a difference, it is evident that the sex force must first have been specialized. Before it can fill a person with love, the vital force must have been drawn to the sexual organs and there changed to sex force, and then, to do its perfect work and lead the individual to such actions as are necessary to procreation, it must return whence it came and take control of the organism.

To me it seems then plain that vital force, specialized so that it contains the reproducing power, must at times permeate the whole organism, which is the third assertion I have made, and in view of these facts I consider it as proven.

Then if we admit that vital force charged with all the necessary elements of life can return in the form of a current charged with these elements and course through the whole organism, the next question is what becomes of this sex force if not used in procreation.

When a man accomplishes a physical task, as walking a certain distance, he has used some of his vital force in exchange for physical results. His supply of vital force has diminished, but he has changed his relations to his surroundings.

But if two persons of different sexes, temperamentally adapted and in love with each other—that is permeated at the time by a current of self-generated sex force—hold each other by the hand, they will feel distinctly a current passing from one to the other, giving them a pleasant sensation due to the equilibration of their sex force. After a certain length of time the current will cease. Why should this current cease? Evidently because the supply is exhausted.

Each one has given off what he or she had to spare and the equilibrium has been restored.

But no such result has taken place as followed physical action. There has been no diminution in the supply of vital force, for what each has lost the other has received. Then what has become of this vital force, this substance which I claim each one has received? Evidently it has diffused itself all through the organism. There has been a blending of male and female sex force, and as it could not take place under such conditions as to create a new living organism, if its special life-giving powers came into play at all, they must be turned to the benefit of the persons themselves.

This is the principle of magnetation, and it differs from procreation in this, that while magnetation seeks to restore the equilibrium by the diffusion of the sex force all through the system and by blending the male and female elements while in that diffused state, procreation seeks to restore the equilibrium by localizing sex force and throwing it off while in that condition, resulting either in waste or in the creation of a new living organism.

But if what I claim should prove to be true, and if through magnetation the sex force can be re-absorbed by the organism, the man absorbing the sex force of the woman, and the woman that of the man, it does not absolutely follow that the process will be beneficent to them. In this investigation we must not depend only on arguments, but upon known results, for it is a practical question, and while it would be easy to prove that it ought to be beneficient, it might be disproved by experience.

If we turn to facts, we find that it has long been recognized that beneficient results follow the close companionship of persons of different sexes. As those results have been observed by persons who knew nothing of magnetism and magnetation, they have been ascribed to the stimulus of imagination, which excited the faculties to greater exertions. But no results due to excitement or imagination can be permanent unless there is an actual increase of vital force. Imagination can stir the faculties to greater activity, but it is at the expense of the supply of vital force, and in that case the evil effects of the reaction would equal the benefits received. For my part, I am more inclined to ascribe these beneficient results to the blending of sex force.

Co-education of the sexes is probably the best test of that question. It is well known that there is not a very large amount of love-making in co-educative institutions, so that only a mild form of magnetation can take place, yet such close companionship cannot exist between young men and young women without causing some exchange of sexual magnetism. I cannot see how any difference which may manifest itself in the results between separate and co-educative institutions can be ascribed to any other influence but the blending of sex force, and as the consensus of opinion among those best qualified to judge is that co-education results favorably for the scholars, the inference is clear that the exchange and blending of sexual magnetism has a good influence.

Much more marked are the results which follow the intimacy which usually takes place between lovers after they are engaged in marriage. The conditions are the most favorable that they can ever attain for complete magnetation. Their relations are then purely magnetative, without any of the waste entailed by procreation, and undisturbed by the cares of a home and family. Under these favorable circumstances young girls have recovered their health and spirits, and young men have found renewed strength to fight temptations or to overcome the difficulties which stood in their way.

But after all, while the presumption is all in favor of the good results of magnetation, it is like the question of self-control, one to be left for personal experience. Surroundings, temperaments, habits, inherited tendencies will have their influence. It may be very easy for some persons to diffuse their sex force, while for others the tendency to localization may be so strong that it cannot be overcome.

But what we may do is to teach that the practice of restoring the equilibrium of sex force by procreation is attended with more or less waste, and that it can be restored by magnetation with benefit to the health and happiness of the persons concerned.

Karezza

Alice B. Stockham

Alice B. Stockham was a Chicago physician specializing in obstetrics and gynecology. Her book on childbirth and motherhood, Tokology, was the most popular and influential treatment of the subject for many years, and is still to be found in second-hand bookstores. Its popularity encouraged Dr. Stockham to devote herself to a career in preventive medicine and "sex reform," chiefly through her own publishing company, which handled not only her tracts on pregnancy and related topics, but also much of the radical sexology of the day, including, for instance, George N. Miller's books on Zugassent's Discovery.

Dr. Stockham had her own version of Zugassent's Discovery, which she called "Karezza." Like its predecessors Diana and Alpha, it was rather mystical and pseudoscientific, and ultimately based on a view of continence as a good in itself rather than a technique of birth control. Although she was closer to Miller and Noyes in giving somewhat more emphasis to the pleasures of coition than Winslow or Parkhurst, she did not think of Karezza as a method of prolonging sexual stimulation for merely sensual reasons—as it later became among readers of J. William Lloyd's Karezza.

Dr. *Stockham had read all these early theorists, but in fact her own inspiration went back further still, all the way to Henry C. Wright, whose lecture on "Marriage" she had heard and whose book on* The Unwelcome Child *she had read in her youth. Wright's own position was in favor of continence except for purposes of procreation, the tradition of Graham taken to its extreme, as in Thomas and Mary Nichols' late phase. This influence may be seen in* Karezza, *modified by Noyes and Miller's ideas, but retaining enough of Wright's ascetic bias to make it seem even more ambivalent than these latterday arguments for coitus reservatus usually were.*

Alice B. Stockham
Karezza

Intelligent married people, possessing lofty aims in life and desiring best spiritual growth and development, have it in their power to so accord their marital relations as to give an untold impetus to all their faculties. It is given by and through a cultivated companionship and comradeship, in which the act of copulation is completely under the control of the will, and at the same time is an outgrowth and expression of love.

The ordinary hasty spasmodic method of cohabitation, for which there has been no previous preparation, and in which the wife is a passive party is alike unsatisfactory to husband and wife, and is at the same time deleterious to both the physical and spiritual man. It has in it no consistency as a demonstration of affection or as a reciprocity of mutual love.

Karezza consummates marriage in such a manner that through the power of will, and loving thoughts, the final crisis is not reached, but a complete control by both husband and wife is maintained throughout the entire relation.

The law of Karezza dictates thoughtful preparation, probably for days previous in which there should be a course of training that exalts the spiritual and subordinates the physical, and in which affection leads to increased loving attentions and kindly acts.

● Selection from *Karezza: Ethics of Marriage*, Chicago: Alice B. Stockham & Co., 1897, pp. 21–29.

Approaching the event, expressions of endearment and affection, accompanying general bodily contact, is followed by the complete but quiet union of the male and female organs. During a lengthy period of perfect control, the whole being of each is submerged in the other, and an exquisite exaltation experienced. This may be followed by a quiet motion, entirely under full subordination of the will, so that at no time the thrill of passion for either party will go beyond a pleasurable exchange. Unless procreation is desired, the final propagative orgasm is entirely avoided.

Given abundant time and mutual reciprocity, the interchange becomes satisfactory and complete without emission or crisis by either party. In the course of an hour the physical tension subsides, the spiritual exaltation increases, and not uncommonly visions of a transcendent life are seen and consciousness of new powers experienced.

Before and during the time some devotional exercises may be participated in, or there may be a formula of consecration of an uplifting character in which both unite. This will aid in concentration and in removing thoughts from merely physical sensations. The following has been helpful to many: "We are living spiritual beings; our bodies symbolize this union, and in closest contact each receives strength to be more to each other and more to all the world."

This method of consummating the marriage relation is erroneously called in *Tokology*, Sedular Absorption. Many scientists now believe there is no seed fluid secreted except through the demand of the final act of expulsion. If this is true, in Karezza there is no seed to be absorbed, as the act, under the direct control of the will, ceases short of the seed secreting period.

One writer called it Male Continence, but it is no more male than female continence; for to secure the greatest good, the husband and wife both equally conserve their forces under a wise control; besides, Continence has long been the accepted term for abstinence of the physical relation except for procreation.

The foreign word, Karezza, signifies "to express affection in both words and actions," and while it fittingly denotes the union that is the outcome of deepest human affection, it is used technically throughout this work to designate the relation just described.

Karezza is a symbol of the perfect union of two souls in marriage, it is the highest expression of mutual affection, and to those practicing it, gives revelations of strength and power. It must be experienced upon a higher plane than the merely physical, and can always be made a conservation of spiritual energy. Indeed, this should be called a spiritual companionship rather than a physical one, for union of soul and soul development rather than fleeting passional gratification is sought, with a due reverence for the deeper meanings of the association.

Karezza gives to the sexual relation an office entirely distinct from the propagative act—it is a union of the affectional plane, but at the same time, it is a preparation for best possible conditions for procreation.

Karezza should be devoid of lustful thoughts, that is, the mere gratification of physical sensations. It should always be the outcome, the emblem of the deeper emotions, and both husband and wife should hope and expect that the union will contribute to spiritual growth and development. The marriage bond has given the sex functions a special consecration, in and under spiritual law this consecration is renewed. There is no defilement or debasement in the natural and controlled expression of the sex nature.

Karezza is not the life of asceticism or repression; it is rather one of appropriation and expression. In acknowledging the life Source and conscientiously devoting the creative principle to achievement, to the activities and purposes of life, one is put in possession of new powers and possibilities.

Karezza as to time and frequency can be governed by no certain law. Yet experience has proven that it is far more satisfactory to have at least an interval of two to four weeks, and many find that even three or four months affords greater impetus to power and growth as well as greater personal satisfaction; in the interval the thousand and one lover-like attentions give reciprocal delight, and are an anticipating prophecy of the ultimate union.

At all events, *the demand for physical expression is less frequent,* for in Karezza there is a deep soul union that is replete with satisfaction and is more lasting. As a symbol it embodies all the manifestations of conjugal love. In all departments of life symbols become less necessary as one attains to the greatest spiritual development. So in this relation one may possibly outgrow the symbol. But both growth and satisfaction are attained through altruistic desires, and through the mutual recognition and response by husband and wife to the innermost natures of each—the higher selves.

Be patient and determined; the reward will come in happy united lives, in the finding of the kingdom of heaven in your own hearts through obedience to law.

Spencer truly said: "When any law works to the advantage of the human race, then human nature infallibly submits to it, since obedience to it becomes a pleasure to man." Yes, the pleasure is in obedience, for all our sufferings come from ignorance of the law of our being, and failure of adjustment to that law.

Men and women should be as willing to learn the law of sex expression as they are to study any other science of life, or any law of nature. It should not only be an intellectual study, but should be a study of experience and adjustment. In Karezza this expression and adjustment is so largely personal that special regulations cannot be given, but those seeking best development will soon establish conditions for that development. At all events, persons coming into knowledge of this theory or law of companionship should be willing to test it, and through their testimony add to the sum of knowledge.

Right Marital Living

Ida C. Craddock

In her suicide note (see Section III) Ida Craddock called upon the public to save her work from oblivion. The Wedding Night, *for which she had been arrested, was already interdicted, but another pamphlet,* Right Marital Living, *had not yet been banned. "I beg of you, for your own sakes, and for the future happiness of the young people who are dear to you, to protect my little book."*

Comstock succeeded well in his crusade against contraceptive and continence literature: E. B. Foote's Words in Pearl for the Married *is one of the rarest of books, and I have been unable to locate even a single copy of Craddock's* The Wedding Night *(the Library of Congress copy is "missing").*

Right Marital Living *has survived not because of any popular response to Craddock's last request, but rather as a result of public apathy. No one cared enough about it to try to distribute it, and so it was never suppressed. Craddock was right, however, in saying that it contained the "gist of my teachings," and it is reprinted here to give a sense of the remarkable scope of her work—not merely her mystical theories of continence, but also her frank and well-informed understanding of the nature of female sexuality, one of the most mythologized subjects of nineteenth-century medical science. In some of her views she was, as she knew, simply far ahead of her time; in others, like the "safe period" of the menstruation cycle, she merely passed the old myth along without questioning it. All in all, she is surprisingly modern.*

We ought to take care not to judge her more mystical doctrines too hastily. The notion that male orgasms may be experienced without ejaculation, for example, is not limited to Craddock and Chavannes, but may be found elsewhere too, from Andreas Capellanus to Tantric Yoga. When the New York Times reported her suicide, it called her the "high priestess of Yoga," but this was just their morbid quip. In fact Craddock was learned in the sexual history of world culture, and understood quite a bit of eastern religious mysticism, but the genealogy of her own Spiritualist and sexual beliefs is thoroughly local and American, coming from Oneida, from Parkhurst, Miller, Chavannes, Stockham, and so on—the continence tradition discussed at length in the Introduction and represented in the selections reprinted in this Section. Nonetheless, her views do have these more esoteric corroborations, and ought to be understood in that fuller context.

Ida C. Craddock
Right Marital Living

In the marital relation, there are two physiological functions—the love function and the parental function. These two functions are not always exercised conjointly. There are also two sets of organs for these two functions, respectively.

For the parental function, in the woman, the organs are the ovaries and the uterus (the womb); in the man, they are the testicles and the vesiculae seminales. The organs of the love function are those which contact—the erectile organ in man; the vulva (the external genitals) and the vagina in woman. The uterus, however, also seems to be with many women a love organ; for, during the final ecstasy, where the man's organ is not sufficiently long to touch

---

● Selection from *Right Marital Living*, Chicago: Published by the Author, 1899, pp. 2–9, 11–15, 17–21, 26–32, 34–38, 43–44, 46–48.

it, the uterus frequently descends into the vagina, as though seeking contact. It is probable that the uterus is intended by nature to always take part in the culmination of the act; but this, it will be observed, is merely as an organ of contact. When the uterus becomes a receptacle, it is then a parental organ.

The love function may and ought to be exercised periodically, in order that both husband and wife may have a healthy, well balanced physique and mentality.

The parental function may remain for years unexercised, without harm to either husband or wife.

It is popularly supposed that the love function should never be brought into play without at least an abortive attempt at exercising the parental function. That is, when the love organs of husband and wife have been brought into contact, it is supposed that the man's creative semen ought to be ejaculated, even though a child begotten at that time would be brought into the world under the worst possible circumstances—circumstances which would result in its being born a pauper or an idiot, or predisposed to drunkenness or insanity or criminality. To this mistaken belief (namely, that an attempt at parenthood should always terminate sexual intercourse)—a belief rooted in the popular mind by centuries of wrong living—the well-being of the future generation is daily sacrificed.

Of course, preventives to conception are always wrong. And there never yet was a preventive invented which is certain. Moreover, they are all forbidden by law; and to sell a preventive, or to lend it, or to give it away, or to have it in one's possession with intent to sell it or lend it or give it away, or to state where or how it can be procured, is to commit an offense which, if known to the authorities, renders the party liable to a heavy fine or imprisonment, or both. Most preventives are distinctly injurious to one or both parties at the time; many are said to injure the tissues of the woman later on. If used, they put no check upon passion; and they are, all of them, abominable and degrading. The condums, womb veils and pessaries, by interposing a foreign tissue between the genital organs of husband and wife during the act, render the relations masturbative for both parties. So do the various suppositories, which, by dissolving, cover the walls of the vagina with a coating of foreign substance. The syringe, by driving the spermatozoa nearer the mouth of the uterus, often helps along the very thing it is intended to prevent; and some physicians claim that, as it must be used while the tissues are still engorged, the shock is injurious to the woman. It likewise detracts from the delicacy of the conjugal act, for people of refinement. Withdrawal is an act of onanism; it is unhealthy and morally degrading. And men who habitually practice it are apt to carry the sign of their unclean habit marked on their faces and in their manner, for all knowing people to read. The popular fourteen day period (two weeks after the menses) is decidedly not a sure preventive, as a woman can become pregnant at any time in the month; and it is unnatural to have intercourse at the time in the month when the wife least desires it. Such coition tends to make her loathe the performance of her conjugal duty.

All these methods are degrading; they all coarsen what should be a pure and exquisite attraction; and at any moment they may fail to prevent conception, and will then, through the wife, stamp the child with unwholesome tendencies, mental perversions, or physical deformities.

Yet, to refrain from exercising the parental function (the ejaculation of creative semen) during coition, and to exercise only the love function (that is, the function of prolonged genital contact which mutually refreshes, stimulates and upbuilds the entire nervous system) is popularly supposed to be either unhealthy or impossible.

This is because, for many, many centuries, men have been perverting the natural functions of their sexual organism, until that which is really the best way has come to seem impossible to the many, and unwise to the few who have learned that it is not impossible. I refer to the suppression of the ejaculation of the semen upon all occasions, except at the time when the creation of a child has been prepared for by both husband and wife.

Let us remember that the seminal fluid is bestowed by Nature upon man for one purpose only—the creation of a child. It is quite true that Nature, in order to secure the propagation of the race, surrounds the act of creation with all sorts of allurements. If it were not so, people would seldom take the trouble to beget children. But the semen itself is given, not for mere sensual gratification, but for a creative purpose. To turn it aside from its natural purpose is to live wrongly as a husband. Also, to create children at random and by the wholesale, or in an environment unsuitable for either the mother or the child, is a degradation of the holy power of fatherhood.

If, then, the semen has been bestowed by Nature on man for the one purpose of creation, it is wrong to sow any seed in a woman after the child has begun to develop, for it is unnecessary, and is a waste of precious material. Now it is usually necessary to wait for over four months after the seed has been sown, in order to determine with certainty whether or not it has germinated. It is true that physicians do sometimes make fortunate guesses much earlier; but it is safer to wait until four or four and a half months shall have elapsed, by which time not only will the child have quickened, but also it will have become possible for a physician, by means of a stethoscope, to hear the child's heart beat. The latter is held to be the one sure sign by which to determine the existence of pregnancy; and if the educated ear of the physician distinguishes the quick beating of the child's heart then, separate from the slower beat of the mother's heart, of course there will be no further need for seed-sowing at that time. To persist in sowing seed during the remaining months of pregnancy is a violation of natural law.

It is true that a woman is sometimes more amorous during pregnancy than at other times, owing to the swollen condition of the uterus, which induces excitement at the genitals, so that she craves sexual satisfaction. Just as when a woman, during pregnancy, craves a peach or other wholesome food, she should be allowed to have it, so if she craves sexual intercourse during pregnancy, she ought to be allowed to have it; but only in moderation, and with care not to press upon the uterus, either from without or from within, in such a way as to injure the growing child. Of course this should not be made an occasion for seed-sowing. Genital contact should take place only for the purpose of interchanging sexual magnetism.

During the nursing period, it is unwise to unduly excite the mother sexually, as it is apt to render the milk feverish, and this will injuriously affect the infant. And to render the mother pregnant while nursing, as is sometimes done, is cruel to her and to both children.

And, surely, a little child is entitled to the care of its mother during the first two years of its life, is it not? Now, everyone knows that the care of a mother for a young child is likely to be interfered with, if she is undergoing the nervous fluctuations of pregnancy.

This brings the time for a man's abstaining from the ejaculation of semen up to two years and nine months—say, in round numbers, three years. But he may have sexual intercourse with his wife during that time, if he will refrain from ejaculating the semen.

It is popularly, but mistakenly, supposed that the semen is an excretion which a man needs to get rid of periodically. But the reverse is the truth. "The male semen," says Dr. W. Xavier Sudduth, a well-known nervous specialist of Chicago, "is an acknowledged tonic, ready prepared for absorption into the system." Every expenditure of semen means a loss of nerve energy. Instead of its being thrown forth upon the slightest emotional provocation, it should be reabsorbed through the lymphatic vessels which are so abundant in the walls of the vesiculae seminales and the vas deferens, in order that it may circulate in the blood throughout the entire body, nourishing the vocal organs which make a man's voice deep and masculine, nourishing the roots of the beard, building up brain and nerves, and intensifying his virility and manly bearing. . . .

Some years ago, Dr. Brown-Sequard discovered that the voluntary suppression of the ejaculation of the semen, just at the last moment, strengthens a man and conduces to long life. He wrongly inferred, however, that the strengthening effect of this suppression was due entirely to the semen, thus returned to the body; whereas it seems to be largely due to the mental act of self-control in accomplishing the suppression, which thus acts as a tonic for the nervous system.

An impression prevails among both physicians and the laity, that to exercise the organs of the love function without also at least an abortive attempt on the man's part at exercising the parental function, will be prejudicial to his nervous system, and, consequently to his health. That is, that it is dangerous to suppress the ejaculation of the semen during coition. This may be true, if the act of suppression be performed merely as a means for bodily, sensual enjoyment. It is *not* true, however, if the mentality (which, in its turn, as we all know, governs the nervous system) be kept in a state of serenity and exaltation, so that the inner spiritual forces may be brought into play.

It is a medical dictum that the nervous system regulates the bodily functions, and that these functions are perceptibly affected, for better or for worse, according as the nervous system itself is in good or in bad working order. Now, the nervous system is controlled by the mentality. And the mentality can be controlled by the inward self of the person—if he so desires.

Take the matter of blushing. A blush is caused by a mental state of embarrassment, of mortification, of exhilaration, or of passionate feeling. This mental state acts upon the nervous system; the nerves act upon the capillaries; the capillaries call the blood to the face and the face gets red. Children redden easily with very slight provocation; but, as they grow older and, with advancing years, more self-controlled, they tend less and less to crimson uncomfortably under trying circumstances. People sometimes explain this by saying that a grown person has become "less sensitive." What has really happened is, that the grown person, little by little, has learned to resist any suggestion on the part of his mentality that there is something to get red in the face about. That is, he has found out how to control his mentality in this particular, and, through the mentality, his nervous system, and through the nervous system, the capillaries, so that he need no longer blush, when to do so would render him annoyingly conspicuous.

The self-control which people usually learn to exercise in the matter of blushing, may be extended to other bodily functions, in many surprising ways. But, in order to do this intelligently, one needs to understand how important it is to have one's mentality well under control. It is important, because it is impossible for us to issue our commands directly to our bodies. All commands must be issued to the Mentality, and, through Mentality, be transmitted to the nervous system, which, in its turn, regulates the bodily functions. Thus, if we wish our hand to move, we may say, "Hand, move!" and we may keep on saying this to all eternity, but our hand will never move until we *think*, "I wish my hand to move!" That is, we practically say to our Mentality, "Mentality, I wish my hand to move!" Thereupon, Mentality transmits, with more or less accuracy (according as we have trained it well or ill), our command to the nervous system; the nerves act upon the muscles; the muscles contract and the hand moves.

If we wish the hand to perform a difficult piece of music on the piano, we must earnestly and resolutely give instructions to Mentality over and over again, until Mentality gets so well trained, that our slightest suggestion is sufficient to cause Mentality to attend to the muscular exercise of our hands with thoroughness and nicety, like a well drilled servant, leaving our inward and higher self meanwhile free to occupy itself with other thoughts, if we so desire.

What can be done (through Mentality) in enabling the hand to master a difficult piece of piano music, can be done similarly with other muscles of the body, especially with those which participate in the sexual embrace; but it must be by controlling Mentality.

The orgasm, according to Dr. Sudduth, "represents the height of nervous tension; it is a mental and physical act combined, which it is impossible to accomplish on a purely physical plane."

Control Mentality, therefore, from the plane of the higher, inward self, and you can control the orgasm (the ecstasy, or final thrill) which is set going by Mentality.

How can this be done?

There are three steps in the process:

(1) Total suppression of the orgasm itself when it is still afar off.

(2) Going gradually nearer and nearer to the verge, and stopping at the last moment, without the orgasm, and consequently, without ejaculation of semen.

(3) Going right through the orgasm, with the controlled and sustained thrill, but without any ejaculation of the semen; unless it be desired to create a child at that especial time, when the semen may be ejaculated at will.

The first step (total suppression of the orgasm) is accomplished thus: Just before the last thrill which precedes ejaculation, all motion on the part of both husband and wife should be promptly desisted from, and, on the man's part, the thoughts should be completely turned away from the bodily sensations, and fixed on something beyond and above the body.

If he believe in God, let him pray to God at that moment, not only consecrating his body to God and praying for strength, but also asking God to be the third partner.

If he be an Atheist and a Materialist, let him seek, in thought, to be in harmony at that moment with Nature, with the Ideal, the Beautiful, the True; with the Ultimate Force, the Unconscious Energy of the universe. . . .

I speak from the standpoint of a teacher of over six years' experience, when I insist to my pupils on the importance of aspiration to the highest during the marital embrace. Many a libertine stumbles upon this possibility of suppression of the orgasm, and, with it, the suppression of the ejaculation of semen, and practises it for awhile, only to find at last that he has wrought great harm to his nervous system, and has, possibly, also enlarged his prostate gland. But the libertine seeks mainly sensual gratification, and when he prolongs the act by suppression of the orgasm, it is with the thought of increased sensual, bodily pleasure distinctly in his mind. He would be the last person to think of praying to God at that moment, or seeking to enter into harmony with Nature, or trying to turn his thoughts, during sex union, resolutely toward the Ultimate Force or the Unconscious Energy of the universe. And so, being ignorant of the psychological law which works upon his body during sex union, he fails to establish healthy thought currents along his nerves. It is because the sexual orgasm is a mental, as well as a physical act, that it becomes so important at that time to have the mentality well under control of the inward, spiritual self—that inward self which all deeply religious people feel to be a part of God. I therefore most earnestly urge the masculine reader, when he takes his thoughts away from the bodily sensation just before the last thrill comes which precedes ejaculation, to fix them, not upon something on the bodily plane, but to lift his thoughts to that which he considers the very highest and grandest power in all the universe, call it by what name he will—First Cause, Unconscious Energy, Primordial Substance, Jehovah, Brahma, Allah, God, the Ultimate Force, the Divine.

This is not religious cant; it is not goody-goody talk; least of all is it idle sentiment. So far as my observations go, it appears to be a psychological *fact,* that only in aspiration to oneness with the impulsive power of the universe, whether phrased poetically as "Nature," or theologically as "God," or scientifically as "Ultimate Force," may the sexual orgasm be suppressed and finally controlled without harm to the health in the long run.

This first step—total suppression of the orgasm while it is still afar off—is quite easy, although it may seem difficult to the man who has never tried it. But he will speedily find, if he does take his thoughts away from the bodily sensation and aspire to the highest just before the last thrill comes which precedes ejaculation, that the tendency to ejaculate will subside. The erection will *not* subside immediately; and presently the movements may recommence.

The second step—going gradually nearer and nearer to the verge, and encouraging the orgasm, while he still suppresses the ejaculation of semen, and yet stopping at the last moment without an orgasm— is much more difficult. But the experience of mastery of the first step will help greatly in this. And let it be always borne in mind that the second step is merely a half-way house on the road to the controlled orgasm and the sustained thrill. It should never be considered as an ultimate act, but merely as a step in the training for self-mastery. Just in proportion as he masters this second step, will he be enabled to experience the controlled orgasm and the sustained thrill in a satisfactory manner. The second step is to be conquered in the same way as was the first step.

In the third step he should pass *through* the orgasm without ejaculating the semen, but with the full enjoyment of the final thrill, and in union with God, or Nature, or the Ultimate Force. It is to be mastered in the same way as were the first and second steps.

"The intense pleasure of the orgasm," says Albert Chavannes of Knoxville, Tennessee, a writer on psychological subjects, "is not, as is usually supposed, due to the ejection of semen. While they are coincident, it is quite possible for men to prevent, by the use of will force, the emission of semen at the time of the orgasim. . . . The enjoyment of sexual intercourse is due to the generating of a current of sexual magnetism, created by a certain degree of affinity between the parties, and increased by friction. When this current has become sufficiently strong, and a certain amount of magnetism has accumulated around the sexual organs, an overflow—orgasm—takes place, which, in obedience to inherited tendencies, sends a magnetic current to the testicles and causes a discharge of the seminal fluid. It is Nature's method to procure conception.

"Magnetation is the application of the power which man possesses of controlling this overflow, preventing it from taking its usual course and causing the usual discharge, and compelling it to take another direction. That direction is the dissemination of the magnetism through the system of both the man and woman, the woman assimilating the magnetism of the man and the man that of the woman. Magnetation requires for its successful practice self-control, affinity and union of purpose, but under right conditions it permits the full enjoyment of the overflow without the weakening influence of the emission . . . Magnetation is the art of regulating the course taken by the overflow of sexual magnetism. Uncontrolled, it goes to the testicles and causes an emission. Controlled, it diffuses itself through the organism."

The cleaner the thought and the more aspiring the impulse which prompts a man to seek the sex union which culminates in what I call the third step, the more satisfying to him physically, mentally and spiritually will this third step be. Those who seek only sensual pleasure therein are likely to be disappointed every time. But those who resolutely lift their thoughts to the spiritual plane at this time will experience thrills of physical rapture which they can experience in no other way. . . .

I have spoken of the duty of the husband to practise self-control and aspiration to the highest throughout the act. It is also the duty of the wife. She, also, has her own three steps to master:

(1) Total suppression of her orgasm, when it is still afar off. This is to be mastered in the same way as the man was directed to master his first step.

(2) To go gradually nearer and nearer the verge of her orgasm, and, just as her vagina is about to take its spasmodic hold upon the male organ, to stop resolutely, and refuse to allow that hold to be taken. This will doubtless seem cruel at the time; but it must be remembered that it is merely a step in the training for self-mastery. It is to be accomplished in the same way as was the first step.

(3) To go right through the orgasm, allowing the vagina to close upon the male organ. Keep self-controlled, serene, tranquil, and aspire to the highest. Pray to God, if you believe in God and in prayer; if not, think steadily and quietly what a beautiful thing it is to be at that moment in harmony with Nature in her inmost workings, and rejoice that you and your husband are part of Nature, pulsating with her, and according to her law. Rejoice that Nature at that moment feels through you also, and through your husband. Feel love, love, love, not only for your husband, but for the whole universe at that moment.

Remember that sex union between husband and wife is, according to the Bible, a divinely appointed ordinance ("the twain shall be one flesh"). And people who consider it impure are likely to reap little satisfaction in this third step.

"The pure in heart shall see God."

While the man's ejaculation of semen should be totally suppressed, yet there should be, throughout the act, an oozing of fluid from the male organ, which is probably intended as a lubricant, to assist it in effecting entrance easily, and also to render it more sensitive.

There should also be an emission from the woman, which acts as a lubricant, and which, mingling with the male fluid referred to, appears to form with it a sort of electro-chemical fluid which enables sexual magnetism to be interchanged with more intensity to both parties. Without this emission from the woman, she is likely to experience comparatively little pleasure.

For a wife to submit to genital union with her husband when she does not desire it, is to degrade herself so that she has no call to draw her garments aside from the harlot in the street. Indeed, the wife who allows her body to be used as a convenience for her husband has degraded herself below even the harlot. For the harlot leases her body for ten minutes or for two hours or for a night, and she is free to refuse embraces which displease her; but the wife leases *her* body for a lifetime, and she mistakenly imagines that she dare not refuse any embrace of her husband's, however repulsive to her finer sensibilities. And so, year by year, she coarsens and degrades the holy estate of matrimony, and paves the way for begetting children who shall be at least the children of a slave mother, if not also tainted with bestial propensities on the one hand, or, on the other hand, impressed during the nine months of pregnancy with an unnatural loathing for what was intended by Nature to be a pure and wholesome relation.

A great mistake is made by wives in consenting to genital union without previous lovemaking on the husband's part. A man is always ready for sex union; a woman is not, although she may frequently be aroused by lovemaking. This is Nature's indication that it is the woman, and not the man, who should indicate when union is desirable; and also that lovemaking should precede all attempts at coition. . . .

It usually requires from twenty minutes to a half hour of affectionate caresses upon any given night, to arouse a woman to the point of desiring genital contact. If, at the end of a half hour of tender and reverent lovemaking, she shows no signs of desiring genital union, her feelings should be respected.

Comparatively few men realize that, while a man is a sexual animal, a woman is not, but is a maternal animal. The normal woman desires to mother the man she loves—to hold him in her arms, close to her bosom, and to caress him thus, without genital contact. She likes, also, to be held by him, and to exchange sexual magnetism with him on the affectional plane, without genital contact. For there appears to be a secondary sexual centre somewhere in the breast, near the heart, so that husband and wife may, in one another's arms, without genital contact, interchange sexual magnetism which will refresh, soothe and uplift. Men usually imagine, when a woman evinces desire for affectionate caresses in her husband's arms, that she is ready for contact at the genitals. Never was there a greater mistake. The woman cares, at that moment, only for the interchange of innocent affection. And for a husband to display unequivocal evidence of a desire for genital contact then does not attract her; it simply repels, and often disgusts her. It is, however, quite possible that, if her husband behaved with consideration and self-control, and it were the right time in the month, she might eventually manifest a passion that same night which would amply satisfy him. What she needs is to be gradually aroused by the right sort of treatment. Husbands, like spoiled children, too often miss the pleasure which might otherwise be theirs, by clamoring for it at the wrong time.

The man who thinks this prolonged courtship previous to the act of sex union wearisome, *has never given it a trial.* It is the approaches to the marital embrace, as well as the embrace itself, which constitute the charm of the relation between the sexes.

One of these approaches—an approach too little practised between husbands and wives—is the chastity of relation possible in a close embrace, in one another's arms, night after night, with accompanying kisses and caresses, but with no genital contact. . . .

In right marital living, the nude embrace comes to be respected more and more, and finally reverenced, as a pure and beautiful approach to the sacred moment when husband and wife shall melt into one another's genital embrace, so that the twain shall be one flesh, and then, as of old, God will walk with the twain in the garden of bliss "in the cool of the day," when the heat of ill-regulated passion is no more.

One thing which men do not always realize is, that the average woman comes to the marriage bed far more ignorant of what is expected of her sexually than does the average man. For, even if a man has never had sexual experience with women previous to his wedding night, yet he usually knows, from the dreams of his boyhood, pretty well what the sensations of sex contact are. Very few women, however, have amorous dreams previous to having sexual experience. And so, with the first sensation of genital contact, whether it shock them so that their parts become rigid and difficult to enter, or whether it come naturally and healthfully after prolonged lovemaking, so that thrills of sexual magnetism will be interchanged immediately on contact, it is in any event a startling experience to a woman. Now, women in civilized, Christian lands are universally inoculated with the idea that it is immodest to show any liking for a man, and, very often, they carry this mistaken teaching into the intimacies of marriage. Too often, indeed, women think they have done their conjugal duty, if they submit passively to the conjugal embrace; and in some cases, they clinch their hands as they force themselves to lie still, resolutely trying to resist any answering throb of passion during sex union. Poor, mistaken creatures! And then they wonder why the husband, after awhile, goes out to a harlot, who, at least, will pretend to the rapture which the wife thinks it immodest to show that she really feels!

A wife who behaves as Nature intended her to behave, will instinctively perform pelvic movements during sex union. If she does not fall into the way naturally, she should consider it a solemn duty which she owes to herself and to her husband, to try to perform them. If she will bear in mind that her love organs (the organs which contact) are given to her for the purpose, not merely of receiving pleasure, but also of conferring pleasure upon her husband's love organ, she will be better able to study out the sort of pelvic movements which she should perform. And she will soon learn that these movements can be depended on to hasten her passion and to increase her lubricating emission, referred to above.

Let her also bear in mind that it is wrong for her to go through with these pelvic movements for sensual enjoyment alone. Every throb of passion must be brought under the control of the higher, inward self, and laid as an offering at the feet of Deity, or blended, in thought, with the Ultimate Force, if she would have the purest and sweetest satisfaction.

Nature has so made a woman that it takes her from a half an hour to an hour after the entrance of the male organ, to come to her orgasm. This is Nature's indication that the man ought to wait for the woman, and not to hasten through the act, as is too frequently the case. A man who gets through in from three to ten minutes after entrance, not only misses the most intense form of pleasure, but also fails to satisfy his wife properly. Her genitals being thus irritated, without being soothed by the discharge of her own sexual magnetism in exchange for his, a congested condition of the internal parts is frequently set up, which results at length in her having to be placed under a physician's care. Many a case of lifelong and hopeless invalidism in a wife is traceable to the husband's habit of hasty termination of the sexual act.

If a husband wishes to treat his wife considerately, let him not hasten, either the act itself or the approaches to the act. He should approach her gently, perhaps linger for awhile in contact with the outside only, enter slowly and with self-control, rest tranquilly after entrance, and let his first movements be gentle and slow. In all things, let him seek, not to get the most pleasure possible out of the relation for himself, but to give his wife the most pleasure. Let him study his own movements, in their possibilities of conferring pleasure, and remember that these should be in the nature of caresses of her love organs by his own love organ.

To approach the woman's genitals with the finger for the purpose of excitation, is distinctly masturbative, and therefore wrong. The only lawful finger of love at her genitals is his sexual love organ.

Also, an orgasm which is induced mainly at the woman's clitoris is unwise. The clitoris is a rudimentary male organ, with a similar power of erectility, though in a much lesser degree. To excite the woman at this organ chiefly, therefore, (as is sometimes mistakenly done by quite estimable men) renders it impossible for her to exchange with the man her natural feminine magnetism, and the act becomes more or less perverted, and destructive of her finer sensibilities. The clitoris should play a very secondary part indeed, and the orgasm should be induced within the vagina.

Every marital embrace should be the occasion for the exchange of intellectual ideas in conversation. Think and talk during the nude embrace, and also at intervals during the sexual embrace, of good books, pictures, statuary, music, sermons, plans for benefiting other people, noble deeds, spiritual aspirations. Do *not* speak of people against whom you cherish resentment, unless it be to throw out feelings of love toward them. Do not tell indelicate stories. Do not choose this time to worry over your household economies or business troubles. Shut out the world, with all its baseness, all its impurity, all its struggles for a livelihood, and let this be a time for the interchange of delicate, poetic sentiment, pure affection, playful, merry thought, and lofty religious sentiment. So strangely are human creatures constructed, that intellectual blending at this time is, by a psychological law, one of the most effective means of welding the natures of husband and wife into a beautiful and perfect oneness. . . .

While the natural position is for the woman to lie upon her back, and allow the man to be on top, yet, where the man is very heavy, or for other reasons, it is sometimes better for the woman to mount the man. Again, there are various side positions, which different couples can find out for themselves, by experimentation.

As to how frequently genital union should take place, no hard
and fast rule can be laid down. The one safe guide is the after result
to the husband and wife, mentally and physically. If the union take
place according to the method here set forth, and be not practised
intemperately, there should be no sense of depression at the close,
nor should there be any feeling of nervous irritation; but on the
contrary, both husband and wife should feel soothed and tran-
quilized. And the next day, they should feel serene and more than
usually clear-headed; they should feel as though they walked on air,
and as though the world were full of brightness and joy.

When either husband or wife is physically weary, or mentally
fagged out, all genital contact should be sedulously avoided. But
the quiet embrace in one another's arms at such a time, without
genital union, will be usually found to strengthen and refresh,
sometimes to such an extent, indeed, as to pave the way for genital
contact a little later. . . .

It is sometimes objected that it is unwise to spread among married
people the knowledge which is set forth in the foregoing pages, as
they would straightway cease to beget children, and so the human
race would die out. This objection shows how little the differences
in the mental attitude of men and of women toward the marriage
relation are understood. The average woman longs, with all the
intensity of her nature, to have a child or children by the man
whom she loves, at some time in her life; but it is for *her* to choose
the fitting time. A woman who is made pregnant against her will,
naturally resents the outrage.

I claim for this method of Right Marital Living, that the quality
of children born from people who have lived in this way will (other
things being equal) be superior to that of children who are the result
of accident or lust. . . .

Another objection which is sometimes raised to the spread of this
knowledge is, that if young unmarried people get to know of the
possibility of controlling the fecundating power, seductions, promiscuity and illicit unions of all sorts will increase. In reply, I would
say that I find that the average libertine is unwilling to try this
method, as he considers it "too high for his purpose." In fact, a
man who practises this method and who teaches it to the woman
(as he is apt to do, in order to increase his own pleasure) will not be
a libertine; for the habit of aspiring to union with God (or with
whatever else he recognizes as the Ultimate Force of the universe)

during the sexual act, and of encouraging the woman to do so like-wise, has the curious psychological effect of tending to make him too loyal to that one woman to want to break with her. For this method, while it always satisfies, never satiates a man; and it ren-ders the relation a perpetual honeymoon. On the other hand, should the man neglect to aspire to the highest throughout the act, but keep in thought upon the sensual plane, the result is likely to prove harmful to his nervous system, through the working of the psycho-logical law upon which I have spoken at length, several pages back. Also, the union will be far less satisfactory. There are, therefore, two inducements to any man who learns this method to rise above the merely sensual plane, and to aspire to the highest throughout the act: First, the increased satisfaction if he does, and, second, the dread of serious harm to his nervous system if he does not. And if he and his partner live this method, they will tend, with each suc-cessive union, to become more and more closely welded into a partnership which nothing could induce either of them to break. Thus the institution of marriage will be strengthened, not weak-ened, by the widespread knowledge of this method of Right Marital Living.

Index of Names

Index of Names